A Cultural History
OF THE
American Revolution

A Cultural History

OF THE

American Revolution

PAINTING, MUSIC, LITERATURE,
and the THEATRE
in the Colonies and the United States
from the *Treaty of Paris* to the
Inauguration of George Washington,
1763-1789

KENNETH SILVERMAN

THOMAS Y. CROWELL COMPANY
New York   Established 1834

Copyright © 1976 by Kenneth Silverman

All rights reserved. Except for use in a review, the reproduction or
utilization of this work in any form or by any electronic, mechanical, or
other means, now known or hereafter invented, including xerography,
photocopying, and recording, and in any information storage and
retrieval system is forbidden without the written permission of the
publisher. Published simultaneously in Canada by Fitzhenry & White-
side Limited, Toronto.

Designed by Ingrid Beckman

Manufactured in the United States of America

Library of Congress Cataloging in Publication Data

Silverman, Kenneth.
    A cultural history of the American Revolution.

    Includes bibliographical reference and index.
    1. Arts, American—History. 2. United States—History—Colonial
period, ca. 1600-1775—Miscellanea. 3. United States—History—Revolution, 1775-1783—Miscellanea. 4. United States—History—Confederation, 1783-1789—Miscellanea. I. Title.
NX503.5.S54   700'.973   75-35947
ISBN 0-690-01079-6

1   2   3   4   5   6   7   8   9   10

In Memory of My Grandmother, Bella Goldberg
Over the chained bay waters Liberty—
Hart Crane

Contents

BOOK TWO: *Arts and Arms*

BOOK THREE: *Virtue Against Luxury*

Illustrations

Musical Illustrations in the Text

Illustration Credits

The author and publisher would like to thank the following for permission to use illustrations: The American Antiquarian Society, Worcester, Mass., for Revere's *View of the Obelisk . . . Under Liberty-Tree* and *Bloody Massacre . . . in King Street*; frontispiece of Billings' *The New-England Psalm-Singer*. Amherst College, Amherst, Mass., for C. W. Peale's *James Peale*. The Baltimore Museum of Art, for Hesselius' *Charles Calvert and Colored Slave* (gift of Alfred R. and Henry G. Riggs). Brookline Historical Society, Brookline, Mass., for Chandler's *Rev. Ebenezer Devotion*. Colonial Williamsburg for C. W. Peale's *Nancy Hallam*. The Essex Institute, Salem, Mass., for Blyth's spinet. Harvard College Library, for American Company ticket. Harvard Theatre Collection, for Lewis Hallam, Jr., and John Henry. The Historical Society of Pennsylvania, Philadelphia, for Wollaston's *William Plumsted*, Wright's painting of Washington, and André's *Mischianza* cutout. The Historical Society of York County, York, Pa., for Durang's sketch. King's Chapel, Boston, for engraving of Selby concert. The Library Company of Philadelphia, for Copley's *The Deplorable State of America*. The Library of Congress, for frontispiece of Brownson's *Select Harmony*, and Reinagle's *Foederal March*; Music Division, for Billings' CHESTER, "When Jesus Wept," and JARGON and Law's "Bunker Hill" and Read's MORTALITY. The Metropolitan Museum of Art, New York City, for Pratt's *The American School* (gift of Samuel P. Avery, 1897); Copley's *Samuel Verplanck* and *Daniel Crommelin Verplanck* (gift of James Delancey Verplanck and Bayard Verplanck); C. W. Peale's *George Washington* (gift of Collis P. Huntington, 1896). Museum of Fine Arts, Boston, for Copley's *Boy with Squirrel*, *Samuel Adams*, *Paul Revere*, and *Brook Watson and the Shark* (the latter, gift of Mrs. George Von Lengerke Meyer). The Museum of the City of New York, Theatre and Music Collection, for 1785 playbill. National Art Gallery, Wellington, New Zealand, for Copley's *Mrs. Humphrey Devereux*. The National Gallery of Art, Washington, D.C., for Copley's *Epes Sargent, Sr.* and *The Copley Family*; W. Chandler's *Captain Samuel Chandler* (gift of

Edgar William and Bernice Chrysler Garbisch); Earl's *Major Daniel Boardman* (gift of Mrs. W. Murray Crane, 1948). The National Gallery of Canada, Ottawa, for West's *The Death of General Wolfe* (gift of the Duke of Westminster). The National Portrait Gallery, London, for Stuart's *John Singleton Copley*. The New-York Historical Society, New York City, for West's *Charles Willson Peale*; C. W. Peale's *The Peale Family Group*; Wilton's *William Pitt*; and pewterers' banner. The New York Public Library, New York City, for Doolittle's *The Engagement at the North Bridge in Concord*. John J. Snyder, Jr., for Tanneberger's organ. The Tate Gallery, London, for Copley's *The Death of Major Peirson*. The Toledo Museum of Art, for West's sketch of his home (gift of Edward Drummond Libbey). Virginia State Library, Richmond, for Houdon's statue of Washington. The Dean and Chapter of Westminster, London, for Wright's wax figure of Pitt. Yale University Art Gallery, New Haven, for West's *Agrippina Landing at Brundisium* (gift of Louis M. Rabinowitz); Trumbull's *The Battle of Bunker's Hill* and *Death of General Montgomery*.

Foreword

When the war began, the Americans were a mass of husbandmen, merchants, mechanics and fishermen; but the necessities of the country gave a spring to the active powers of the inhabitants, and set them on thinking, speaking and acting, in a line far beyond that to which they had been accustomed.

—David Ramsay, *History of the American Revolution* (1789)

Two extraordinary events occurred in America between 1763 and 1789, although only one is well known. The country established by war its independence from the British crown. At the same time it acquired the elements of a modern metropolitan cultural life. This history describes the swift rise of American culture during the American Revolution.

By the time the long series of French and Indian Wars ended in 1763, America had been planted for a century and a half. Yet it had produced few paintings or poems of consequence, perhaps a half dozen musical compositions, one or two unpublished plays, and no novels. No one who had ever been born in the country could be called in a traditional sense a painter or sculptor, a composer or instrumentalist, a poet or novelist, a playwright or actor. In the course of the political and military crises of the next twenty-five years, however, the number, scope, and skill of artistic works steadily grew; the audience for them greatly increased; dramatic experiences that called for representation in such works multiplied. By the time the country inaugurated its first president, in 1789, Americans could attend American plays, see dozens of good paintings by native artists, hear skillful performances of hundreds of tunes by native composers, read thousands of poems and stories written and printed in their cities and towns and grown out of their own experience. In a quarter-century of startling innovation, the country had produced its first novel, first epic poem, first composer, first professionally acted play, first actor and dancer, first museum, its first important painters, musical-instrument makers, magazines, engravers—indeed most of the defining features of traditional high culture.

The exact relation between the revolutionary war and the rapid progress of American culture cannot be reduced to a formula. It varied according to the personalities of individual artists, the intrinsic character of individual arts, and innumerable specific social conditions. It varied in time as well, for near the end of the period artistic and intellectual fashions pronouncedly changed. The convergence in this history of biographical, sociological, political, and esthetic matters makes for intricacy—an intricacy compounded by the many figures, works, and events.

The history is divided into three books, corresponding to the prewar, war, and postwar periods. Each book consists of two parts of rather different character. The first, broadly interpretive, surveys the state of individual arts at moments of high contrast and relative peace—1763, 1770, and 1784—glancing backward to measure change and development in art, music, literature, and the theatre. The second part of each book, broadly narrative, treats not individual arts but all the arts together as related responses to a succession of critical events—the Stamp Act, the Declaration of Independence, and so on. There is some overlapping. The interpretive part of each book does refer to events, and carries forward the careers of various artists; the narrative part pauses for interpretation. A political-cultural calendar appears before each of the three books, outlining the content and clarifying the chronology.

The courtesy of various institutions in supplying and allowing me to reproduce manuscript, typescript, and graphic material in their collections is acknowledged in the documentation and notes and the list of illustration credits. Research on the book was aided by an Arts and Sciences Fund Grant from New York University, and made possible in the first place by a generous Bicentennial Grant from the National Endowment for the Humanities. While writing, I have received encouragement, advice, assistance, or leads—and sometimes all four—from Sacvan Bercovitch of Columbia University; Pat Bonomi of New York University; Maud Cole of the New York Public Library Rare Book Room; Margaret C. Cook of the Earl Gregg Swem Library; Joan Dolmetsch of Colonial Williamsburg; Irma Jaffe of Fordham University; Lewis Leary of the University of North Carolina; and Peter Shaw of the State University of New York. Hugh Rawson of the Thomas Y. Crowell Company read the manuscript with equal sympathy for the reader and for the writer; his precise but tactful suggestions led to many improvements. Lynn Haims turned an arduous typing job into an act of criticism; between drafts the manuscript gained in clarity and exactness from her knowledge of early American literature. Richard Crawford of the University of Michigan reviewed the commentary on music with a thoroughness beyond what might be expected even from a brilliant musicologist, a lively friend, and a decent ballplayer, all of which he is. The luxury of thanking in print people one likes is matched by the satisfaction of acknowledging help given long ago but only made apparent by time. I am grateful to Caroline Gordon for having taught me that writing is a form of education, and to Quentin Anderson for having shown me that education is a form of pleasure.

Kenneth Silverman
New York City
July 1975

THE Muse, disgusted at an age and clime,
  Barren of every glorious theme,
In distant lands now waits a better time,
  Producing subjects worthy fame:

In happy climes, where from the genial sun
  And virgin earth such scenes ensue,
The force of art by nature seems outdone,
  And fancied beauties by the true:

In happy climes the seat of innocence,
  Where nature guides and virtue rules,
Where men shall not impose for truth and sense,
  The pedantry of courts and schools:

There shall be sung another golden age,
  The rise of empire and of arts,
The good and great inspiring epic rage,
  The wisest heads and noblest hearts.

Not such as Europe breeds in her decay;
  Such as she bred when fresh and young,
When heav'nly flame did animate her clay,
  By future poets shall be sung.

Westward the course of empire takes its way;
  The four first acts already past,
A fifth shall close the drama with the day;
  Time's noblest offspring is the last.

—GEORGE BERKELEY, "Verses on the Prospect of Planting
Arts and Learning in America" (written 1726, published 1752)

BOOK ONE

Peace and Learning

Calendar for February 1763– August 1770

[1763]

MAY 17 : Commencement exercises at the College of Philadelphia, and King's College in New York; students celebrate the recent Treaty of Paris

JUNE 20 : BENJAMIN WEST arrives in London; New York *Mercury* reprints John Wilkes' attack on the king in *North Briton* no. 45

AUGUST 3 : THOMAS GODFREY dies

DECEMBER 14 : Twenty Conestoga Indians killed near the towns of Lancaster and Paxton

[1764]

JOHANN SNETZLER sends organ to Trinity Church, New York
JOSIAH FLAGG, *A Collection of the Best Psalm Tunes* (Boston, engraved by Paul Revere)

[1765]

MARCH 22 : Parliament passes the Stamp Act

JULY 14 : CHARLES WILLSON PEALE arrives in Boston, in flight from creditors; soon he visits John Singleton Copley

AUGUST 14 : First Stamp Act demonstration, in Boston

[c. SEPTEMBER 1]: COPLEY submits his *Boy with Squirrel* for exhibition in London

OCTOBER 7: Intercolonial Stamp Act Congress meets in New York

2 5: DAVID DOUGLASS arrives in Charleston from London, bringing new actors and scenery, aboard a ship carrying stamped paper

3 1: *The Times* (perhaps by Benjamin Church) advertised in Boston

NOVEMBER 1: The Stamp Act becomes effective. "Liberty" buried in Newport and Portsmouth

1 1: *The Deplorable State of America* (probably by Copley) advertised

THOMAS GODFREY, *Juvenile Poems on Various Subjects* (Philadelphia)
MATTHEW PRATT, *The American School*

[*1766*]

MARCH 1 8: Parliament repeals the Stamp Act, and passes a Declaratory Act, ambiguously reasserting its authority

MAY 5: New York Sons of Liberty destroy the Chapel Street Theatre. Sometime in May, the first known "Concert of Musick" in Savannah, Georgia, is performed

JUNE 3 0: New York Assembly commissions statues of Pitt and the king

JULY 2 2: FRANCIS HOPKINSON arrives in London, and soon visits West

AUGUST 4: WEST writes to Copley, sending news of the reception of his *Boy with Squirrel* and inviting him to come abroad

NOVEMBER 1 2 or 1 4: DOUGLASS opens his new Southwark Theatre in Philadelphia, despite Quaker opposition

JOSIAH FLAGG, *Sixteen Anthems* (Boston)

[*1767*]

JANUARY 2 : SAMUEL GREVILLE, the first known American professional actor, makes his debut, in
Nicholas Rowe's *Tamerlane*

FEBRUARY 1 3 : PEALE arrives in London to study with West

APRIL 2 4 : DOUGLASS produces *The Prince of Parthia*, the
first American drama to be professionally
produced on the American stage

JUNE 2 9 : Parliament passes the Townshend Acts

AUGUST 2 6 : Five of Douglass' actors killed in a fire
aboard the brig *Dolphin*, from Jamaica

OCTOBER 2 9 : NATHANIEL EVANS dies in New Jersey

DECEMBER 7 : DOUGLASS opens his new John Street Theatre in New York *(The Beaux' Stratagem)*; first
American appearance of John Henry

First American edition of William Tans'ur's *The Royal Melody Complete*
BENJAMIN WEST, *Agrippina Landing at Brundisium with the Ashes of Germanicus*

[*1768*]

APRIL 4 : Verling's Virginia Company of Comedians
opens in Williamsburg *(Douglas)*

JUNE 3 0 : Massachusetts House votes against rescinding its Circular Letter declaring the
Townshend Acts unconstitutional

JULY 2 1 : *Virginia Gazette* prints John Dickinson's new
"Liberty Song"

OCTOBER 1 : 800 British troops enter Boston to protect
the customs officials

"Rusticus," *Liberty. A Poem* (Philadelphia)

[*1769*]

JANUARY : First issue of *The American Magazine* (Philadelphia)

FEBRUARY : HENRY BENBRIDGE arrives in London after
five years in Italy

MARCH : British troops riot at James Joan's concert in Boston

JUNE 29 : JOSIAH FLAGG performs at Concert Hall with "The First Band of Boston"

Sometime in June, Peale returns to Maryland from England

AUGUST 1 : The South Carolina *Gazette and Country Journal* publishes a long letter from John Henry, agreeing to abandon plans for a new theatre until the political turmoil subsides; in Boston, Governor Bernard sails for England, recalled from duty

Sometime in August, Douglass appears in Boston offering the *Lecture on Heads*

SEPTEMBER 18 : *Boston Gazette* advertises a "very curious Spinnet, being the first ever made in America. . . ."

NOVEMBER 16 : COPLEY marries Susannah Farnum Clarke, daughter of a prominent agent for the East India Company

[*1770*]

JANUARY 16 : WILLIAM TUCKEY gives the overture and sixteen numbers from *The Messiah*, in New York

MARCH 5 : British troops kill five civilians on King Street in Boston

26 : Boston newspapers advertise Revere's engraving of the Boston Massacre

APRIL 12 : Townshend duties repealed

JULY 10 : Pipe organ played for the first time in an American Congregational church, in Providence

AUGUST 23 : New Yorkers raise the equestrian statue of the king, commissioned in 1766, on the Bowling Green

Part One

Culture in British America between the Treaty of Paris and the Stamp Act, 1763–1765

1. Commencement: 1763

"Utrum status Naturae sit status Belli"—Whether the state of nature is a state of war.

For the distinguished audience gathered in St. George's Chapel on May 17, 1763, for the annual commencement exercises of King's College in New York, this famous maxim of Thomas Hobbes was the right, the inevitable, topic. Among those who listened to the students' orations and forensic disputes in Latin and English sat the governor of the colony and several members of His Majesty's Council, servants of a king to whom just three months ago had been ceded, by the Treaty of Paris, all French possessions in Canada. Preeminent among even these polite and notable men was the commander-in-chief of British forces in North America, Sir Jeffrey Amherst. Before his determination, if not exactly his military brilliance, had fallen Louisburg, Fort Duquesne, Ticonderoga, and ultimately Montreal. To the question of whether man was innately disordered and violent his career seemed to say yes.

Yet, inevitably, the young college orator said no. He refuted Hobbes's cynical maxim concisely and fully, as the occasion demanded. For the king's treaty in February had ended nearly three-quarters of a century of conflict in North America, bringing throughout the colonies a sense of relief that old enemies had no longer to be feared, and stirring desires for tranquility and the pursuit of happiness. In 1763, the great word was Peace.[1]

Peace also preoccupied the May 17 commencement of the College of Philadelphia, whose no less polite assembly included the college trustees and clergymen, the governor of Pennsylvania, and Benjamin Franklin. To climax the daylong program, students dressed as shepherds performed a verse dialogue-and-ode, surveying the current state and future prospects of their college and colony. Their call for the "piercing Fife" and the "Trump shrill-sounding" to retreat before the "deep-ton'd swelling Organ," and the college musicians' response, paid tribute to the new treaty, which had brought soothing harmony out of wearying cacophony; their pastoral names and rustic garb symbolized undisturbed content-ment.[2] And if the costumes and martial instruments failed to convey the message of Peace, a chorus of boys and girls repeated four times a salutation appropriate to the day:

> Blest *AEra* hail! with Thee shall cease
> Of War the wasting Train;
> On Thee attendant white-rob'd *Peace*
> In Triumph comes again.

But while they celebrated pastoral innocence, student shepherds expected from the "Blest *AEra*" something more. They foresaw, as the swain Philander said, a "Reign of LEARNING and of PEACE." The conjunc-tion was inseparable. The Peace of 1763 not only ended the fighting; it also renewed a vision which had existed as long as the fighting itself, the dream of an American Empire. A huge continent containing fewer than two million people could at last be populated, settled, and ultimately refined.

Refinement, for many of the students and their audience, was not the last consideration. Indeed, the chief blessing of the new era might be cultural development. As surely as Jeffrey Amherst drove forth the French, the swain Horatio said, the Muses might depose the powers of provinci-alism. America might become

> . . . a Land refin'd,
> Where once rude Ign'rance sway'd th' untutor'd Mind;
> Of uncouth Forms no more the dark Retreat,
> Transform'd to Virtue's and the Muse's Seat.

That at present the country was "rude," "untutor'd," "uncouth," and "dark" was a fact widely acknowledged, often in proof of the desire that it be overcome. Two months before the commencement, Benjamin Franklin, a trustee of the College, examined several graduating seniors. The next day he wrote to his friend Mary Stevenson in London, with indignant disbelief:

> Why should that petty Island, which compar'd to America is but like a stepping Stone in a Brook, scarce enough of it above Water to keep one's Shoes dry; why, I say, should that little Island, enjoy in almost every Neighbourhood, more sensible, virtuous and elegant Minds, than we can collect in ranging 100 Leagues of our vast Forests.[3]

Pained recognition of the vast inverse proportion of territory to accomplishment between England and her American colonies often served as a prelude to modest but firm claims of achievement. To Franklin it seemed that the unflattering balance might be righted by the Peace. For the conjunction of peace and learning rested on a larger principle. As Franklin went on to tell Mary, " 'tis said, the Arts delight to travel Westward."

The theory of the westward movement of the arts—*Translatio studii*—perhaps began in speculations during antiquity on mythical realms to the west. Interwoven with Christian ideas of the Millennium, it remained an important idea throughout the Middle Ages and the Reformation. During the eighteenth century, however, disciples of progress, especially those who glorified the expansion of England's empire, elaborated the theory into a virtual summary of contemporary thought. They divined in the history of civilization a super-pattern: the inexorable westward migration, the translation, of empire and next of arts from Greece to Rome to England.

In England's colonies the theory was so long and so often affirmed as to have become an assumption. Early in the nineteenth century, John Adams told Dr. Benjamin Rush: "There is nothing . . . more ancient in my memory than the observation that arts, sciences, and empire had travelled westward; and in conversation it was always added since I was a child, that their next leap would be over the Atlantic into America." [4] Invoked in newspapers, correspondence, and daily conversation, the notion of the irresistible translation of the arts westward had the reassuring familiarity of a motto or the ending of a fable. It promised Americans that if their vast territory lacked "sensible, virtuous and elegant Minds," it could not be for long.

Translatio studii was more than a future promise or a theory, however; it was also a factual explanation of the present. When a town widened its lanes, when a new college opened its doors, when an extra wharf suddenly became needed, British Americans understood the event as the result of

Translation. When they spoke of the 'light of Athens' or of the 'advent'rous Muse' reaching Philadelphia or Charleston they often had in mind the erection of a hospital or the publication abroad of some poems by a fellow citizen. Their language naturally magnified such events, since in their minds each improvement evidenced a larger process that at last would civilize and refine the continent. Each fresh accession of some major element of European culture brought confident visions of an American Empire.

Colonials scrutinized their surroundings for such signs of cultural progress. The founding of Yale College early in the eighteenth century, for instance, proved to Jeremiah Dummer that "religion & polite learning have bin travelling westward ever since their first appearance in the World." It led him to hope that the arts "won't rest 'till they have fixt their chief Residence in Our part of the World." [5] In 1744, Franklin himself hailed an American edition of Cicero's *Cato Major* as the "first Translation of a *Classic* in this *Western World*." Being the first, it portended the rest. Thus Franklin perceived the book as a "happy Omen, that Philadelphia shall become the Seat of the American Muses." [6] Throughout the century (and to this day), Americans prided themselves on firsts, since each unprecedented addition signified Translation.

The best-known statement of the theory of Translation was Bishop George Berkeley's "Verses on the Prospect of Planting Arts and Learning in America." The poem itself celebrates a feat of Translation, Berkeley's effort in 1725 to found a college in Bermuda. The poem appears in full as the epigraph to this history because after its first publication in 1752, virtually every large colonial newspaper and many books and magazines reprinted it in its entirety at some time during the third quarter of the eighteenth century. Berkeley's metaphors of Translation—a growing plant, a genial rising sun, the final act of a drama—seeped into colonial speech, so that diaries, orations, poems, and conversation everywhere in the period register a prophetic awareness of growth.

Colonials seized on other elements in the poem as well in trying to sense the direction of their society: on Berkeley's view of a Europe in "decay"; on his complementary belief that man's hope for regeneration lay in America, "Time's noblest offspring"; and, particularly, on his concept of the "rise of empire and of arts," in which the first makes possible the second. At a theatrical performance in Maryland in 1760, the speaker of the customary prologue called attention to the war being waged for the continent between France and England:

> Here, as we speak, each *heart-struck* Patriot glows
> With real Rage to crush *Britannia's* Foes! [7]

The next moment he called attention to what this epic struggle made possible—himself introducing a play in provincial Maryland. The Muse follows the course of empire,

> O'er takes his Sun, communicates his Fires,
> And rising Bards in Western Climes inspires!
> See! Genius wakes, dispels the former Gloom,
> And sheds Light's Blaze, deriv'd from *Greece* and *Rome*!

As Benjamin Franklin told Mary Stevenson, " 'tis said, the Arts delight to travel Westward. You have effectually defended us in this glorious War, and in time you will improve us."

Thus, to those who sat with Franklin or with Sir Jeffrey Amherst listening to the commencement speakers, the Peace of 1763 promised an era not only of contentment but of accelerated cultural progress. Britain had, after three-quarters of a century, claimed sole dominion in America, and in the train of empire came the arts.

But was the promised era likely to come? Despite the highflown young men reciting their verses in shepherds' weeds or disputing Hobbes, Franklin found few "sensible, virtuous and elegant Minds." What had America to show in painting, music, literature, and drama? What might it build upon now that England had established its empire and had created, after long war, Peace?

2. The Art World

Art, if not hurrying, was surely moving westward. In 1763, domestic demand for decorative and commemorative works supported a busy market in prints, modest collecting of European art works, and a prosperous group of itinerant portrait painters. Three painters in their mid-twenties showed promise. Charles Willson Peale, a Maryland saddler, had decided just a year before the Treaty that he might make a better living out of art. John Singleton Copley in Boston had been developing a strong talent for realistic portraiture. A young Pennsylvanian, Benjamin West, had settled in London, having already trained himself for two years in the latest European theory and technique.

A considerable market for prints and paintings existed in America in 1763. English prints were kept in constant supply by local printers and booksellers, who advertised the latest imports in local newspapers. At the

time of the Peace, public taste preferred prints of biblical subjects or
Roman antiquities, by Giambattista Piranesi and others, landscape and
scenic engravings of England and Scotland, portraits or "heads" of
English celebrities like Laurence Sterne and David Garrick, and depictions of royalty, particularly of the English royal family. Most popular
were the engravings of William Hogarth. His *The Idle and Industrious
Prentice*, depicting the idle apprentice at last hanged at Tyburn and the
industrious apprentice riding in a coach as Lord Mayor of London, was
advertised continuously in America from its publication in 1747 until
1771, after Hogarth's death.[1]

Pictures of Garrick or of the king brought a touch of London social life
to provincial homes or allowed for expressions of loyalty; but prints were
purchased mainly for decoration. Often displayed on the wall or stairs,
they were frequently advertised along with wallpaper, and sometimes
scarcely distinguished from it. The Philadelphia bookseller David Hall
asked his London agents to send brightly colored ornamental wallpaper
"fit [for] Pictures, for which Purpose the Country People do up a great
Deal." Colonials evidently amassed such pictures. The 1769 estate
inventory of Henry Vassal of Cambridge, Massachusetts, for instance, lists
eighty-four prints; other estate inventories of the period list prints by the
parcel or dozen.[2]

What Americans in 1763 chose to hang in their homes reflected the taste
and business sense of London dealers. Between 1764 and 1766, the
Williamsburg printer Joseph Royle ordered from the English publisher
Robert Sayers nearly £100 worth of prints, representing at least 700 items.
He did not ask for prints by Hogarth or Piranesi, but simply for £100
worth of prints. Colonial taste in prints was in this way circumscribed by
such overseas publishers as Sayers, who also supplied New York, Boston,
Philadelphia, and Charleston.[3]

With English prints plentiful and cheap, only a few American
printmakers had begun advertising native prints in 1763. Several of them
had been trained as silversmiths, since the technique chiefly used in prints
was line engraving, in which the design is cut in a metal plate (usually
copper) by a sharp steel tool, the incisions holding the ink when the rest of
the plate is wiped clean. Smiths could easily turn from engraving coats of
arms and inscriptions on silver plate to producing portraits and scenes on
copper. Thus in 1762, the silversmith-engraver Nathaniel Hurd advertised
for sale in Boston (a center of American printmaking) his pictures of the
popular young King George III, of the heroic General James Wolfe, and
of William Pitt. The next year, an obscure engraver named Michael De
Bruls tried to raise subscribers for a set of 12" × 21" views of New York,
including a street plan and a pamphlet describing the "wholesome

climate, pleasant situations, products, &c. of this province," at a price of twenty shillings per print. Bruls emphasized the novelty of his project, noting that "nothing of this Kind ever has been undertaken before by any body in this part of the world." Indeed, virtually no graphic works produced in America before 1763 had attempted to depict the local scene. An emergent interest in local views also appears in the advertisement in Charleston in 1765 of engravings of St. Michael's and St. Philip's Church in the city, and in the *General Map of the County on the Ohio and Muskingum*, whose cartouches depict an Indian camp and an Indian treaty in progress.[4]

Americans in 1763 collected paintings as well as prints. No public collections existed, but many individuals owned paintings worth seeing. Some European works hanging in colonial homes in 1763 had been brought to the country much earlier. What sketchy information remains about them is largely owing to the researches of Pierre-Eugène du Simitière, a Swiss artist who settled in Philadelphia in 1766 and became a passionate investigator of American antiquities. In 1768 he compiled a list of Dutch oils brought by early settlers of New York, which he found in garrets where they had been discarded as unfashionable or "looking old." Those "painted in holland by good masters" included an oil of Governor Peter Stuyvesant in military dress and oils of Stuyvesant's parents and of a woman in a large ruff. Tracking down European works in New England collections, Du Simitière discovered at John Smibert's house in Boston a "large collection of original Drawings of the best masters," Italian prints and pictures, "a good collection of casts in plaister of Paris from the best antiques, besides basso relievos seals & other curiosities."[5] Elsewhere in Boston and in Newport he found a portrait of Czar Peter I done, he thought, by Godfrey Kneller, a self-portrait by Anthony Van Dyck, and unidentified portraits of Oliver Cromwell, Charles II, James II, and George II, as well as European battle-pieces, still-lifes, and religious paintings.

Works by influential English and European artists arrived in the colonies also as public gifts, occasionally as merchandise, and often as keepsakes of travel. Governor Benedict Calvert had been painted amidst columns and statuary by the English painter Francis Brerewood; Queen Anne had had her portrait painted by Kneller, and had sent it in 1703 as a gift to the city of Annapolis, together with a portrait of Lord Baltimore by Van Dyck—a much respected painter in the colonies, perhaps partly because his aristocratic hauteur appealed to provincial yearnings for class.[6] Occasionally European and English works came up for direct sale. In 1763 the *New-York Gazette* advertised "PAINTINGS: Twenty-Four Fruit and Flower Pieces, very elegantly done by JONES, Just imported. . . ."

Immigrant itinerant painters sometimes brought along European works, as did a London painter named Warwell, who offered in South Carolina in 1766 a "Collection of Ancient Drawings. . . ." Perhaps the chief conveyors of European paintings to America, however, were the many colonials who made the Grand Tour. Becoming amateurs of the arts abroad, they often commissioned portraits from leading artists. Ralph Izard of South Carolina had himself or his wife painted four times in England, once by Thomas Gainsborough.[7]

In short, nothing prevented Americans with money and inclination from gathering sizable collections. Listing his property in 1794, the cultivated William Bentley of Salem counted "36 Pictures framed & Glassed of various sizes" (probably prints), a half dozen "small black framed pictures," "3 metal gilt framed pictures," and "Half dozen of elegant large Engravings with mahogany mouldings"—probably not an extraordinary collection.[8]

Whatever the demand for imported works, that for native painting gave steady employment to surprisingly many colonial artists. The nature of his work gave the colonial painter a crucial economic advantage over, say, the colonial engraver, musician, or writer. Prints, music, novels, or plays could be imported, and cheaply; personal portraits could not. Colonials who wanted portraits had to employ native talent, or go abroad. Because portrait painting also served the purpose of commemoration in a society without other visual means of preserving its ancestors, and because current ideals of interior design considered massively framed portraits as essential home furnishings, painting in 1763 was an active profession, giving employment behind it to painting shops, drawing masters, and framers.

Only the preeminent American painters, however, managed to establish themselves for long in one place. Once the painter completed his portrait his work was done, and not usually asked for again. Most painters belonged to the large band of musicians, actors, and other cultural itinerants who roamed the colonies. Even the better-known painters of the period appeared now in England, then in the West Indies, later in South Carolina, next in New York. Usually they announced their arrival and period of stay in the local newspaper, telling where specimens of their work could be seen—a coffeehouse, private residence, or often the printer's office. Universally they advertised two selling points: cheap rates and a good likeness. Most painters offered to accept no payment if the sitter found the likeness unpleasing.

For painters at least, this roving brought no social onus. Indeed, the relative costliness of the work and the demand for it made painting in colonial America a competitive and prestigious profession, a possible source of wealth and of social advancement. Far more than musicians or actors, painters profited from the economic abundance and fluidity of American society, by which, fairly easily, many poor men became economically independent and many men of modest property became rich. At his death in 1778, the Maryland painter John Hesselius, for instance, owned some 900 acres and property valued at £3,400, including scientific instruments, paintings, thirty-one slaves, and several musical instruments, among them an organ, a harpsichord, and three violins. At the other extreme, some painters obviously could not survive the considerable competition. The skillful Hudson Valley itinerant Thomas McIlworth ventured to Montreal in 1767 but managed to get only two commissions in two months. He disappears from the records cursing: "that blind Bitch Fortune still continues to haunt me like a Ghost, and I am really what you may call the picture of Ill luck." [9]

Most painters probably became neither rich nor destitute, but eked out a living between painting and related work. Laurence Kilburn in New York was one of several painters who also ran a color shop, advertising in 1764 at his Pearl Street establishment brushes, glass, turpentine, varnish, "Portrait Painter's Colours, Canvas, Hair and Fitch Pencils, Tools, and gilt carv'd Frames for Portraits. . . ." Other painters ran drawing schools. Returning from the West Indies to Philadelphia, the influential painter and writer William Williams opened a studio at "the Sign of Hogarths Head" (Williams looked like Hogarth), where he also gave evening drawing lessons and instruction in the oboe and flute.[10]

Success depended not only on the painter's skill but on the kind of painting he offered. Landscape painting, for instance, received "very little encouragement" (according to Charles Willson Peale), forcing a landscape painter named Beck to dispose of his works by lottery while his wife opened a girls' school to support the family. The situation would change; but landscape painting did not serve the purposes for which most Americans in 1763 bought paintings, namely to mark their social level and to record their achievements and person for posterity. Perhaps landscape painting languished also because a nation largely devoted to farming and pioneering lacked the "contemplative detachment" necessary for the esthetic enjoyment of nature.[11]

Landscapes had some limited popularity as decor, however, having become an integral part of room decoration in England. Itinerant house decorators who specialized in wallpaper, graining effects, and japanning also offered to paint landscapes over fireplaces or on boards used to close the fireplace during the summer. Many of these overmantels and fireboards, like much of colonial culture, were merely slight transformations of English works, copies of engravings with a few details changed to suggest the colonial locality. Few have survived, and those mostly from later in the period. An entire wall of the Wampatuck Club in Hingham, Massachusetts, is covered by seventeen painted panels, each with a different landscape.[12] Floors were sometimes painted as well, often to look like rugs, presumably for those who could not afford real rugs. Wallpaper, too, was often simulated, using trompe l'oeil architectural motifs. Few painters, however, specialized in decorative landscape painting. Warwell, the Londoner already mentioned, advertised in South Carolina in 1766 that in addition to building grottoes, topaz fountains, and other Gothic structures he "paints Altar-Pieces, Landscapes, Sea pieces, Scene painting, coaches, windows and coach Blinds, Deceptive Triumphal Arches" and so on. But such ads were rare. For provincials anxious to declare their taste, display their recent material gains, and record both for posterity, painting meant portrait painting.

Two major styles of portraiture existed in the 1760's, a period when styles were rapidly changing.[13] The first, more prevalent in New England than elsewhere, made little attempt to exalt the sitter's social position or graces. It stemmed from the first Puritan limners, whose lack of sensuous appeal filled the demand for a style expressive of the Congregationalist effort to strip Christian life of Catholic ornament. The distinctive qualities of the limner style are map-like outlines, local color, two-dimensionality, and symmetrical patterning. The subject seems a figure in a coloring book. The chief practitioner of the style in 1763 was Joseph Badger of Boston, born in 1708, a period close to the original inspiration of the limners. He began as a house painter and, like many limners, devoted much of his career to the allied trades of glaziering and sign painting. In his portraits dull colors and funereal solemnity prevail, without flattery.[14]

The second, more important style was practiced throughout the colonies. It descended from Van Dyck as interpreted by the English court painters Godfrey Kneller and Peter Lely. More naturalistic and three-dimensional than the limner style, it gave provincial high-bourgeois life an aristocratic look by emphasizing the subject's authority. This style had existed in the colonies since the beginning of the century, but by 1763 had often been altered by lighter rococo moods. While the sense of station remained, authority gave way to relaxed self-assurance, aristocratic magnificence to happily complacent fashionableness. Colonial portrait painters in 1763 supplied both the older stiffly aristocratic vision and its more recent, lighter derivative.

The most sought-after purveyors of the lightened Kneller-Lely style were John Wollaston, John Hesselius, and Jeremiah Theus. Around 1763 they were the painters of choice for the southern gentry and, often, for aristocratic families in New York and Pennsylvania. Wollaston, born in England around 1710, came to the colonies by 1749 and portrayed some of the most prominent families outside New England: Livingstons, Schuylers, Beekmans, Levys, Byrds, Custises, Randolphs. Like many provincial itinerants, he also worked in other British possessions, including India. The great appeal of his style is suggested not only by the number of important commissions among his 300 American portraits but also by the several poems that appeared in colonial newspapers praising him and by the influence his work had on other colonial painters, including Hesselius, whose success has been mentioned earlier. Born to a family of artists around 1728, probably in Philadelphia, Hesselius settled on a handsome estate near Annapolis in 1763, where he lived and painted until 1778. An artist-farmer, vestryman, and friend of the governor, he stood only a rung down the social ladder from the Calverts and Penns whom he painted in Maryland, Virginia, and Pennsylvania. The third leading purveyor of the style, Jeremiah Theus, was part of the large Swiss Protestant population that had emigrated to South Carolina because of religious persecutions in the Palatinate. His career centered in Charleston, where he first advertised in 1740. Rendering such prominent families as the Lowndes and Manigaults, he dominated art in South Carolina for thirty-four years and, like Hesselius, grew rich. His will included seven slaves and two hundred acres; his brick house sold for £8,000.[15]

Like the many lesser Knelleresque painters, this preeminent trio reproduced on one canvas after another a single ideal of personality. Typical of hundreds of their paintings is Wollaston's *William Plumsted* (c. 1755), depicting a Philadelphia merchant who was thrice mayor of the city (and who turned his warehouse into a theatre, where in 1749 was given perhaps the first American performance of Shakespeare). Like the Calverts, Levys, and Byrds, Plumsted represents a worldly success not incompatible with gentleness and good-natured domesticity (ill., p. 119). To create this vision of dignity without pomp, painters repeated ad infinitum the same few poses, expressions, and accoutrements, mostly derived from Kneller.[16] The male subjects set one hand on the hip or on a table or block, suggesting solidity, pointing the other hand downward to suggest command or, like Plumsted, thrusting it into an exposed waistcoat to suggest elegant self-possession. The women rest one hand on a pediment, the other lightly on their often-large bosoms. Kneller's emphasis on costume also helped his American followers to suggest their patrons' importance. Wollaston had been trained in London by a "drapery painter," a specialist who added clothes and background after the face painter completed the face—a legacy of the Van Dyck-Kneller tradition of workshop production. Again like Plumsted, Wollaston's men appear in large curled wigs, shirts with wrist ruffles, and expensive vests, his women in lustrous silks and satins.[17] The effect of prestige is softened by the gentleness of the faces. Wollaston gave all his sitters broad mouths slightly upturned in a simpering smile and large, almond-shaped (almost oriental) eyes, earning him the nickname of the "almond-eyed painter," a trademark which Hesselius took over from him.[18]

Working swiftly within lucrative commercial formulas and without great native ability, neither Wollaston, Hesselius, nor Theus gave much subtlety to the face or much vitality to the flesh. Only Hesselius grew as he aged, some of his later portraits depicting the sitter with uncustomary complexity, as in his slightly pained adolescent *Elizabeth Calvert* (1761) and his elderly Quakeress *Sophia Galloway* (1763). Occasionally he enlivened the portrait formulas with a dramatic element lacking in Theus and Wollaston. *Charles Calvert and Colored Slave* (1761) dramatizes black-white relations in the head of the slave boy tilted servilely upward at his Knelleresque boy master (ill., p. 119).

Still, the overwhelming effect in Wollaston, Hesselius, and Theus is of sameness. Formularism perhaps characterizes all of provincial culture as it tries mechanically to reproduce an inspiration sprung organically from a more sophisticated society. Yet the willingness of these painters to do and redo essentially the same picture suggests that they painted their clients—their "patients," Wollaston called them—as wealthy provincials wished to see themselves, look-alikes of the gracious beings in the imported Knelleresque mezzotints that often hung on their walls.[19] In painting after painting, the same well-bred, sickly-sweet smiles express the pleasant natures and provincial success of people who might have sat beside Sir Jeffrey Amherst in 1763, agreeing with the young orators who refuted Hobbes's cynical view of human nature and who foresaw an era of tranquility and progress.

The same people who commissioned Hesselius or Wollaston, and many less prosperous people, were likely to commission one other sort of portrait widely advertised in 1763. This was the "miniature" painted on a slice of ivory and usually cased in a pendant or ring. Traceable to the portrait-rings of antiquity, miniatures enjoyed a new vogue in mid-eighteenth-century England and instantly came west to the colonies. The miniaturist painted only the sitter's head and shoulders, the unbleached ivory itself serving for highlights on the flesh and giving a soft-silvery glow through the transparent color.[20] A visual record of the exacting technique survives, showing a miniaturist at work with the tools of the trade: a slender delicate brush, a small oval palette and color box, a small stretcher table, a glass of water, and a tilted drawing board to hold the miniature (ill., p. 124). One colonial versifier in the 1760's summed up the meaning of the miniature as a transportable reminder of some loved one, a

> . . . matchless art by Friendship first designed,
> To wear the looks of those we value most

Reflect the image which the faithful mind
Holds dearest, when the real form is lost.[21]

Unlike the portrait intended for public and family display, the miniature was private, personal, romantic, bestowed in affection on a lover, parent, or child—or soldier bound for the battlefield. Thousands, probably, were painted in America during this period.

By the time of the new Peace, Wollaston was already in his fifties, Badger had been painting in America for more than thirty years. What signs of possible progress in American art existed in 1763, existed in an emerging generation of younger colonial painters which had begun to compete with their longstanding success, to challenge their formulas, even to discard their assumptions about the career of painting.

One promising young man in 1763 was less busy painting portraits than fashioning saddles—twenty-two-year-old Charles Willson Peale. Later Peale wrote a Franklinian autobiography which remains, together with his voluminous letters and diaries, the chief source of information about his life.[22] His father, he recalled, had studied for a while at Cambridge University before becoming headmaster of a school in Chester, Maryland, where he taught Greek and Latin.[23] After the elder Peale's death the family moved to Annapolis, Mrs. Peale managing to survive by making "mantuas," probably silk dressing gowns and petticoats. Around the age of thirteen Peale was apprenticed to a saddler, and by 1763 he was advertising his wares in Annapolis, trying—as he always would be trying—to pay off heavy debts. To do so, he also undertook upholstering, chaise making, and some silversmithing of buckles, rings, and stirrups, hoping to expand into watch-and-clock repairing, in which he was self-taught.

Several events the year before contributed to his disquiet. Married in 1762, he had also received a letter from England notifying him that he was entitled to an Oxfordshire estate worth £2,000 and urging him to come abroad to claim it. At the same time, on a trip to Norfolk to buy material for his saddlery, he saw some landscapes and a portrait and was taken with a desire, he recalled, to paint. As a boy he had drawn patterns for his mother's mantuas, had once done a glass-painting of Eden based on *Paradise Lost*, and had portrayed a dead uncle, from the corpse. But it was after seeing the paintings in Norfolk, he wrote, that the idea of "making Pictures" took "possession" of him. He tried new landscapes, a self-portrait with a dismantled clock; when others asked him to do portraits for them, he realized that he "might do better by painting, than with his other Trades."

Peale's attraction to painting was, and would remain, less esthetic than philosophical and Franklinian. He shared the eighteenth-century deist's scientific curiosity about nature, whose operations he would later try to imitate mechanically, and whose plenitude he would try to preserve in his natural history museums. For many in this barely preindustrial age, when engravers also did silversmithing and composers experimented with mechanical improvements in the harpsichord, the line between the mechanical and the fine arts was thin.[24] For Peale, painting always remained allied with manual tinkering and inventions. At the same time, it offered prospects of advancement. Characteristically, he drew from his accumulated debts and from his chance encounter in Norfolk what he drew from all experience: the benevolist lesson that good in this best of all possible worlds grows from evil. Had he, he wrote,

> . . . not been perplexed with debts, perhaps he would not have made those exertions to acquire knowledge in more advantageous Professions than that in which he first set out with. And perhaps he might have been contented to have drudged on in an unnoticed manner through life.

Peale took up painting with the hope that by applying his dexterity, his curiosity about nature, and his interest in inventions to a more lucrative trade, he might no longer go "unnoticed."

Peale decided on his career having never seen a palette or easel, and knowing nothing about colors. To enlighten himself he journeyed to the one color shop in Philadelphia, whose owner, Christopher Marshall, gave him a list of paints and prices. Discovering that he did not know what to ask for, he went to James Rivington's Market Street bookshop to buy a book on painting. Rivington had only the popular *Handmaid to the Arts*, which Peale took back to his lodging and, he says, studied four days almost without stop, "in order to enable me to form some judgement on what colours I ought to purchase also the quantity." [25] Clearer about his needs, he returned to Marshall's and bought paint. Before returning to Annapolis he was driven by his interest in mechanical devices to St. Paul's Church, to hear the organ recently made by the Philadelphian Philip Fyring. He wrote a poem praising its maker and its "dulcet notes" that was published in a Philadelphia newspaper.

Once at home and eager to progress, he ventured across the Severn River—probably early in 1763—to Bellefield, the estate of the prosperous John Hesselius. He offered Hesselius one of his best saddles in return for lessons, and watched him paint two portraits. In one session Hesselius painted half a face and left him to finish the other half. On his 900 acres, Hesselius was hardly "unnoticed." Later Peale would name his German-town home Bellefield.

Peale was not the only young painter hopeful of the future. On

September 30, 1762, probably just a month or so before Peale journeyed to Marshall's paint shop, the twenty-four-year-old Bostonian John Singleton Copley wrote to the famous Swiss pastelist Étienne Liotard, asking him to send some of his best crayons. He anticipated Liotard's surprise in hearing from a painter in New England, where the arts were, he admitted, "feeble." Yet Americans were trying to improve: "it is not for want of inclination that they are not better," he said, "but the want of oppertunity to improve ourselves." And he reiterated the hopes of the commencement orators that, the war ending, American culture would ripen. "America which has been the seat of war and desolation, I would fain hope will one Day become the School of fine Arts. . . ." [26]

Copley's hopes and dissatisfactions had different sources than Peale's, for he was neither a neophyte nor "unnoticed." Since making his first mezzotints at the age of fifteen, he had worked hard. One sitter whom he painted in 1763 recalled that she had sat for him fifteen or sixteen times, six hours at a time; once, after posing many hours, she peeked at the canvas when Copley was out of the room, to find that he had rubbed it all out. Uncompromising effort brought steady technical improvement. Indeed, by the time Copley was twenty-four his reputation nearly matched that of Hesselius and of Theus. By 1765 he was receiving eight guineas for a portrait, his pictures hung in Scotland and Utrecht; he had received commissions from South Carolina and Halifax, offers to come to Quebec and Barbados.[27] For several reasons such offers did not tempt him. He had family obligations, he already had more commissions in Boston than he could handle, and, when he got free, he believed he would go to Europe.

Copley's success came not only from hard work and talent but in part from accidents of birth and place. His father, an Irish immigrant who owned a tobacco shop in Boston, died before he was ten. Fortunately for him, his mother married Peter Pelham, who not only taught a dancing school and carried on the tobacco business in Boston but was also a London-trained painter and engraver. It was Pelham, indeed, who had produced the first important American engraving, a 1727 mezzotint of Cotton Mather. Shortly after Pelham's death in 1751, Copley took over his stepfather's studio and produced his own first works.[28] Quite as important to Copley's development as his family life was the fact that Boston in the 1750's supported several artists, such as Robert Feke, John Greenwood, and Joseph Badger, whose influence appears in the limner-like effects of Copley's earliest works.

It was the influence of another painter, however, which also led Copley in the 1750's to do copies in oil of European mythological works—John Smibert (1688–1751). A Scot trained in Rome and London, Smibert had met Bishop George Berkeley, with whom he came west to Rhode Island in

1728 as intended professor of painting at Berkeley's projected college in Bermuda. Instead, Smibert established himself in Boston, the first professional artist of any reputation to settle in America. In Boston he painted his large *Berkeley and His Entourage*, the first important painting done in America. It remained in Boston until the early nineteenth century, and inspired the composition of several later American works.[29] In 1734, Smibert also set up the first color shop in Boston, where he sold paints, brushes, and prints. Among these were prints of his own paintings that had been made by Copley's stepfather, Peter Pelham, who had probably met Smibert in London.

Although many of Smibert's own works brought a refreshing realism to the Knelleresque formulas, they mattered less to Copley than did Smibert's studio, near Pelham's house. It was the closest thing in America to an art museum. Visited or lived in by a long succession of American painters, the studio remained well known as an art center throughout the period. For Smibert had brought with him from abroad copies, unique in America, of European old masters: two Raphael Madonnas, Titian's *Venus and Cupid*, Poussin's *Continence of Scipio*, Van Dyck's *Bentivoglio*, a cast of the *Venus de Medici*.[30] The collection inspired Copley while in his teens to attempt a *Return of Neptune*, a *Galatea*, and a *Mars, Venus, and Vulcan*, as well as anatomical drawings. These were not homely Badgeresque portraits, but large, ambitious, European treatments of mythological subjects, several of which contained nude figures, itself uncommon in Copley's Boston.[31]

Yet for Copley, as for any other American painter in 1763, painting meant portrait painting. As a working painter, he found his models not in Smibert's studio but in the works which had formed his sitters' tastes. His portraits of the early 1750's preserve the liney coloring-book quality of Badger (and traces of Smibert and Pelham), but are dominated by the formulas of Kneller: the glossy satin gowns, the overcoat parted over the rich vest, the forefinger pointing downward in command. Copley moved closer to the lightened Knelleresques of Hesselius and Wollaston in the mid-1750's, when his style felt the influence of Joseph Blackburn, then introducing rococo pleasantness to Boston in bright colors, informal poses, and such occasional pastoral touches as a shepherd's crook.[32]

While using the Knelleresque vocabulary, however, Copley used it fluently and freely. Even in adolescence he never merely repeated himself, and often expressively varied the position of fingers or the flicker of a smile in his mezzotint original. He worked more carefully than Wollaston or Hesselius, too, for instance painting his ruffles with such detail that they can be identified as a specific Flemish bobbin lace. Always changing, moreover, he began in the late 1750's to explore pastels, and to work with oil-on-copper miniatures in collaboration with the silversmith-engraver Paul Revere, who produced the gold and silver cases. At this time he seems also to have been led to depict his sitters even more informally by the example of Joshua Reynolds, who introduced into English portraiture a new intimacy, Italian in origin, which came to America through engravings of his work by James MacArdell.[33] With his new range of expression and his attention to esthetic effect, Copley soon eclipsed Badger as Boston's leading portraitist.

By the late 1750's, Copley could offer his sitters not only skill but also a unique vision that could be called Puritan. More often than not he preserved Badger's tight-lipped somberness, depicting his sitters in moods of melancholy and resignation. Indeed he was still painting Badger's world, names prominent in Massachusetts since the seventeenth century—Gerrishes, Princes, Hancocks, Cottons, Warrens—recording in paint the ministers, merchants, politicians, and Harvard pedagogues in whom still lived whatever remained of the original Puritan impulse. Even paintings that lack this somberness present startling contrasts between the sitters' lustrous finery and their porcine jowls, beady eyes, and hairy moles. In part, the physical ugliness of many of Copley's sitters reflects his passion for the visual likeness insistently stressed in the ads of the period. Likeness, he said, was "a main part of the exellency of a portrait, in the oppinion of our New England Conoseurs *[sic]*," many of whom, like their ancestors, were above flattery. The ideal of "likeness" included physical blemishes. John Dryden, in his preface to Dufresnoy's *Art of Painting* (a respected manual in the colonies), compared blemishes in portraits to tragic flaws in drama: "Such in *Painting* are the Warts and *Moles,* which adding a Likeness to the Face, are not therefore to be omitted." [34] Given the demand for visual likeness, even the Knelleresque itinerants often capped rich gowns with homely heads.

Copley's portraits of the early 1760's, however, intensify the conflict. His gowns are more beautiful than those of the itinerants, his minutely rendered warts are unrelieved by their simpering smiles and idealized eyes. The blunt realism raises the blemishes above "likeness" and makes them a Puritan *memento mori,* an intimation of mortality and corruption. His aging merchant *Epes Sargent, Sr.* (c. 1760) leans against a truncated column (ill., p. 119). The center of attention is his right hand, resting on his breast, gnarled, beefy, wrinkled as an iguana, old. "Prick that hand," Gilbert Stuart later said, "and blood will spurt out." An ambiguous mixture of strength and weakness particularly marks his many portraits, during the early 1760's, of old or aging women. The fattest or littlest of them are grotesques, such as old *Mrs. John Powell* (1764), seated in a huge armchair that seems, in her birdlike tininess, to swallow her up. The force of such works derives from an authentically Puritan esthetic, as defined by the photographer Walker Evans: a sense of the "deep beauty in things as they are." [35]

In his mid-twenties, Copley had arrived at a distinctive synthesis between the Knelleresque and the limner traditions. His works combined grace and severity, the airy elegance of Blackburn with the old New England harshness. The disharmonies would multiply as he progressed, the turn of a mouth or lift of an eyebrow repeatedly undercutting the main effect of the portrait, hinting at stupidity amidst stateliness or wit in drabness, as he stayed faithful to his ever more complex vision of personality. Thus Boston already supported a painter whose improving skill and maturing sensibility gave ground for the hope that "war and desolation" ending, America might become a "School of fine Arts."

Even so, Copley's early success reveals the limitations of colonial art in 1763 quite as much as its promise. Restricted to commercial portraits, not even the most gifted painter in America painted primarily for esthetic or intellectual ends. At the same time, many new subjects for painting and important new theories of art had opened up in Europe. Art circles abroad, in fact, placed portraiture near the nadir of painting. At the top stood the pictures of historical, biblical, mythological, or literary scenes generally called "history paintings." Only history painting, said Sir Joshua Reynolds later, ought to concern "any people desirous of gaining honours by the arts." [36] It was the lack of patronage for such works that, more than any other deficiency, made colonial culture seem to some young painters a shallow, unpromising backwater of Europe. Indeed, the young Pennsylvania painter Benjamin West had recently traveled eastward to the spring.

The scope of history painting gave the artist a large dignity and made painting one of the liberal arts. While the portrait painter usually had "no ideas of looking further than the likeness," wrote one professor at the Royal Academy, the history painter dealt with "the entire man, body and mind." [37] No mere artisan catering to his patron's ego, no rococo trifler daubing shepherds' crooks, the history painter addressed the public at large, at once a philosopher, historian, psychologist, and natural scientist —above all, a moralist forming standards of conduct by depicting noble behavior. What demanded such versatility were the related problems of narration and of decorum in history painting. An essentially narrative art, it conveyed its dramatic meaning through the figures' expressions and psychological relationships. The history painter needed to understand psychology and physiology in order to give each character the gestures, bearing, and facial expression appropriate to the situation. Each character must display not only the emotion proper to the event but the emotion proper to him. Moses must react as Moses, Nero as Nero. As a historian

intent upon producing an authentic historical scene, the history painter
was obliged to have a profound knowledge of the whole range of past
biography, social customs, geography, climate, costume, habits, and
architecture.[38]

These formidable demands were summed up by the English theorist
Jonathan Richardson, through whose works the philosophy of history
painting probably came to the colonies, where they were read by Copley
and others. According to Richardson, the painter must possess "all the
good qualities requisite to an historian" and know

> . . . the forms of the arms, the habits, customs, buildings, &c. of the age, and
> country, in which the thing was transacted. . . . he must yet go higher, and
> have the talents requisite to a good poet . . . the painter must imagine his
> figures to think, speak, and act, as a poet should do in a tragedy, or epic poem.
> . . . And as his business is not to compose one Iliad, or one Aeneid only, but
> perhaps many, he must be furnished with a vast stock of poetical, as well as
> historical learning.
>
> Besides all this, it is absolutely necessary to a history-painter that he
> understand anatomy, osteology, geometry, perspective, architecture, and
> many other sciences. . . .[39]

To gain such knowledge, Richardson stressed, the painter must study the
works of the ancients and of Raphael, and seek stimulating company
where he can hear refined sentiments.

Colonial life in 1763 could provide, of course, little of what the history
painter theoretically needed. In particular, it could not provide material
for the branch of history painting most valued abroad, that of classical
subjects. The 1760's was a period of rising neoclassical interest in England,
stirred by the excavations of ruins at Herculaneum and Pompeii. One
result was the publication of engravings of works from Herculaneum,
beginning with a series of folios issued in 1755 by the Accademia
Ercolanese and climaxed by the publication in 1764 of Johann Winckelmann's great *Geschichte der Kunst des Altertums*. Neoclassical history painting,
and the archeological investigation on which it was based, could flourish
only because of patrons wealthy enough to transport and publish the ruins
of Rome: The Herculaneum folios were initially not sold as books, but
given as gifts by the king of Naples, Charles of Bourbon. While cost alone
forbid the transmission of such works to the colonies, Quaker centers like
Philadelphia or Puritan centers like Boston would not have welcomed
their profusion of bare breasts and buttocks anyway.

Proclaiming history works the only worthwhile branch of painting,
requiring access to polished company, to the best classical models, to
extremely wealthy and sophisticated patrons, the theory of history

painting was for some colonials a siren call luring them to Europe. Painting was an itinerant business, often leading to the West Indies or Canada or England. At least one native painter had already expatriated. John Greenwood, born in Boston, went to Amsterdam in 1758, where he did history works and Rembrandtesque etchings as the pupil of a Dutch engraver, later working in Surinam and Paris.[40] Not surprisingly, then, Benjamin West had recently arrived in London, hoping to make himself a history painter.

West was born on a farm in Delaware county on October 10, 1738, the youngest of ten children in a family that arrived in America with William Penn. The available information about his early life appears in his later manuscript autobiography and in the semiofficial biography by John Galt, who allegedly had the details from West. The information in both accounts is suspicious in proportion to its charm, which is great. Nathaniel Hawthorne introduced his nineteenth-century children's biography of West—based upon Galt—with the innocently accurate remark that the "story of his life is almost as wonderful as a fairy tale. . . ."[41] The fairy-tale quality was in part supplied by West himself. Describing his youthful progress in his old age, after he had achieved perhaps the most celebrated career in the history of American art, he shaped the account according to the pattern of several powerful cultural myths: the myths of Franklinian success, of the romantic original (a sort of artistic noble savage taught by Nature alone), and, more than any other, the myth of America's cultural progress. West's deep identification with these myths led him to read rather many omens and moments of destiny back into his humble beginnings.

Thus, according to Galt, when West's mother was pregnant with him, an itinerant Quaker evangelist preached to her prophetically about the future glory of America. According to West, his "love for painting shewed itself at an early age"; when a child in Lancaster, he began spontaneously to paint, making brushes out of his cat's tail. Indians taught him how to make red and yellow paints out of roots, herbs, and bark. A Philadelphia Quaker named Pennington admired his childhood efforts, gave him real paints and canvas, and treated him to a visit to Philadelphia. There a Quaker friend of West's family introduced him to the fascinating painter, novelist, and rover William Williams, a Welshman by birth who as a boy had been bound to a captain in the Virginia trade. Without Williams, West later claimed, he would never have become a professional painter. Williams told him that he had "the sensibility proper for the study of painting" and asked whether he had studied the lives of the Masters. The Quaker West replied that he had read of no great men but those in Scripture. Williams then lent him the works of Richardson and of

Dufresnoy, which became, West said, "My companions by day, & under my pillow by night." [42]

Returned to Lancaster, West attempted the sort of subject favored by the history painters, a *Death of Socrates*. The painting was seen by the most energetic and selfless promoter of young talent in America, William Smith, provost of the College of Philadelphia.[43] Smith brought West to the College as a private, nonmatriculating student, encouraged him in his classical studies, and introduced him to other young men with literary, artistic, and musical aspirations at the school: Thomas Godfrey, Francis Hopkinson, and Jacob Duché. (On Smith and his pupils see "The Literary Scene" later in this section.) West listened to Godfrey recite his poems on the banks of the Schuylkill, sketched Hopkinson (who published a poem about him in 1758), and painted Smith, who publicly praised him in *The American Magazine*, which he had founded.

Although West had been drawn to history painting at least since his meeting with Williams, Galt implies that it was Smith who first suggested to him that portraits could be raised to "something greatly above the exhibition of a mere physical likeness . . . only inferior in dignity to that of history." Smith also imparted to the uneducated Quaker some of the substantial learning demanded by the art.

> He carried him immediately to those passages of antient history which make the most lasting impression on the imagination of the regular-bred scholar, and described the picturesque circumstances of the transactions with a minuteness of detail that would have been superfluous to a general student.[44]

With Smith's encouragement, West continued his experiments, drawing classical subjects, painting Smith in the attitude of St. Ignatius, and attempting a biblical scene, *The Trial of Susannah*. Still in his late teens, he also began to work as a commercial portraitist.

After two and a half years in Philadelphia, around 1758, West went to New York hoping to get high prices for his work. He disliked the city, Galt says, finding it wholly mercantile, and lacking the polish of Philadelphia. It was perhaps in New York that he saw works by the Knelleresque itinerants, whose poses and drapery appear in many of his early portraits, several of which, indeed, are uncertainly attributed either to West or to Wollaston or Hesselius.[45]

West's efforts brought him into conflict with his Quaker circle. The Quakers looked even more coldly than did the Puritans on figural arts like painting, which William Penn had specifically reproved. Galt tells of one monthly meeting at which the Quakers discussed West's standing in the sect. Affirming their doctrinal aversion to painting, they argued, however, that West clearly had been given extraordinary gifts by God, who clearly wanted him to succeed as a painter; they decided to encourage him. Their resistance was perhaps weakened by West's devotion to history painting, which in theory aided virtue. Certainly they could find nothing objectionable in Richardson, who emphasized that the good painter must be a good man:

> . . . as [the painter's] profession is honourable, he should render himself worthy of it by excelling in it; and by avoiding all low, and sordid actions, and conversation; all base, and criminal passions; his business is to express great, and noble sentiments; let him make them familiar to him. . . . The way to be an excellent painter, is to be an excellent man. . . .[46]

Looking back on his career, West himself stressed how his aim had been essentially moral:

> Mr. West [as he, like Peale, refers to himself] has ever considered, to instruct the rising generation in honourable and virtuous deeds, they are the good, and great points which the historical pencil has to effect—and that can only be done, by placing before them, those bright examples of their predecessors or contemporaries, and to transmit their virtues from generation to generation.[47]

All eighteenth-century esthetic theory, of course, defended the arts on moral grounds. But West's upbringing in a religion scornful of painting gives special point to his repeated claim of high moral purpose.

The place to launch this program of moral reform was Europe. Again it was Smith, Galt says, who urged Chief Justice William Allen of Pennsylvania to finance West's artistic education. Allen advanced him over £150, believing that "he is like to turn out a very extraordinary person in the Painting Way, and it is a pity such a Genius should be cramped for want of a little Cash." [48] With commissions from Allen and from Lieutenant Governor James Hamilton to copy European master-works, West embarked, sometime in 1760.

His destination was Rome. Only in Rome could be seen the antique and Renaissance works that had inspired the new classicism. West's arrival and early days in Rome, again, survive in accounts that are contradictory and suspiciously fateful. His first view of Roman grandeur, Galt says, reminded him of the translation of the arts to America:

> . . . his thoughts naturally adverted to the progress of civilization. The sun seemed, to his fancy, the image of truth and knowledge, arising in the East, continuing to illuminate and adorn the whole earth, and withdrawing from the eyes of the old world to enlighten the uncultivated regions of the new.

Dropped from the provinces into the very center of world art, no doubt West did indeed meet such important painters as Gavin Hamilton, Pompeo Batoni, and Anton Raphael Mengs, director of the Vatican school of painting, with whom he could spend all day seeing, talking, and painting. One is less inclined to believe Galt's story that, as they sat in a cafe in Rome, Hamilton translated for West the words of a blind Italian cafe singer who, like the Quaker evangelist, turned out to be prophesying the translation of the arts westward and the future glory of America. To Galt we also owe a more familiar anecdote. Some Roman nobles, wishing to see how antiquities might strike a child of nature, took West in a caravan of "thirty of the most magnificent equipages in the capital of Christendom" to see the Apollo Belvedere. West's famous reply was "My God, how like it is to a young Mohawk warrior!" [49]

West's Quakerism rebelled. Seeing vice and poverty everywhere, he felt that "everything in Italy was in a state of disease." French art he found affected, unable to help the reason "arrive at correct moral inferences, by furnishing a probable view of the effects of motives and of passions." In describing West's aversion, Galt has some support from West's son, who later wrote that his father disliked the religious and rococo art he saw in Italy because of "its employment to inflame bigotry, darken superstition, and stimulate the baser passions of our nature." Indeed, his son said, it was not Williams or Smith but the sight of these works that made West resolve "to struggle for a recovery of [painting's] true dignity, of its moral and pious uses," that is, to become a history painter.[50]

West himself, however, gives a different view of his life in Rome. Neither exhilarated by the possibilities of the artistic life nor repelled by rococo eroticism and Catholic bigotry, he was instead ill, he says in his autobiography, presumably of emotional upset:

> That sudden climax from the cities of America, where he saw no productions in painting but a few English Port[rait]s, and what his own pencil produced, to the city of Rome the seat of arts and taste, had so forceable an impression on his feeling, that he was under the necessity of leaving Rome in a few weeks, by the advice of his Physician and friends, or it would have put a period to his Life.

Anxious for his health, West returned to Leghorn for several months. When he resumed his studies in Rome, his health failed again after seven or eight months and he again returned to Leghorn. His friends advising him to go to Florence instead of Rome, he resumed his studies this time in the Pitti Palace. But again he became ill, even more seriously. Confined to bed for six months, apparently with rheumatism, he underwent surgery "in one of his ankels where the fevour had settled." He nearly lost his leg. English nobility in Florence nursed him, and he was able to paint and draw in bed on a specially constructed frame until, recovered, he took off once more for Bologna, Parma, Venice, and other cities, seeing and studying the Correggios, Titians, and, especially, the much-esteemed Carraccis, plus other Venetian and Lombard masters.[51]

Again West went to Rome to try out on canvas what he had learned during his two ill-fated years abroad. Although his precarious health limited his activity, he managed to send home some of the work his Philadelphia patrons had commissioned. He learned with pleasure that his copies of a Sybil and a St. Cecelia had arrived safely and were "judged deserving to be hung up in the Governor's House." Quite out of keeping with his later, legendary generosity, he asked that no one be allowed to copy them: "Not that I am jealous of any ones gathering Improvement from them if able, but because the paintings themselves might lose a part of their Merit of being the onely ones of the Kind in the Province. . . ." He received commissions for further copies to be sent to Philadelphia also, and attempted paintings of *Cimon and Iphigenia*, *Angelica and Madoro*, and other dramatic subjects. In Rome or shortly after in Florence, he completed a *Holy Family* depicting Mary feeding the Infant out of a saucepan, influenced by Correggio's sweetness and color. Joseph Shippen wrote to him that the painting was "excessively admired by everybody" in Philadelphia.[52] These works suggest not only a determined battle against ill health but a remarkable psychological break with Quaker iconophobia.

But again the heat of Rome aggravated West's rheumatism, swelling his ankle and driving him north to Florence. There a surgeon advised a second, deeper incision. The ankle was laid open to the bone, a piece of it coming away. West found himself, frustratingly, abed for four months in a house near the Pitti Palace "without being able to stir out to see anything there." [53] The duke of Grafton, too, had given him an important commission to copy the *Madonna della Sedia*. But he apparently had had enough of Italy. Stopping off first in Parma to finish a copy of Correggio's *Gerolimo*, he headed via Genoa, Lyons, and Paris for London. He arrived there on June 20, 1763,[54] just a month after the young commencement orators across the ocean announced the return of learning and of peace, and foretold that America would become "a Land refin'd."

3. Musical Life

In 1763 the North American colonies had no dominant or even well-known musicians, no one to compare in attainment or promise with Wollaston or Copley. Still, music figured prominently in both secular and sacred life.

The need for entertainment and the desire to learn social graces meant widespread playing of family music and employment for music teachers, music dealers, and instrument makers. Urban centers made available a modest number of modest concerts by itinerant professional musicians, often accompanied by local gentlemen-amateurs. The likeliest sign of westering progress in music was perhaps the recent response in the colonies to drastic changes in English church music. American churchgoers, particularly those who worshipped a rationalistic and benevolent God, were beginning to hear more instrumental music than before, and a different sort of vocal music. The innovations met resistance and debate. But they also created new prospects for organists, composers, and publishers of religious music.

The significant fact, however, is that in 1763 colonial musical life emphasized, overwhelmingly, the performance rather than the composition of music. As far as is known, only one American, James Lyon, had published any music of his own—a few short tunes that appeared in 1761.

Many Americans who in 1763 bought engravings at the Williamsburg Printer's Office or commissioned portraits from Wollaston or Copley were likely to play musical instruments. A society anxious to show refinement, containing many people with cultivated tastes, and lacking professional entertainment made do with at-home entertainment demanding some skill. Both sexes played the harpsichord and "spinet" (really a small harpsichord). Otherwise, women favored training in voice and guitar, while men favored the violin and, especially, the flute—a term which seems to have covered both the transverse flute and the recorder. In Philadelphia no less than three German music masters offered "flute" lessons, one of whom, the prominent John Stadler, opened in 1761 a *school* for teaching German flute. To the Virginia poet Robert Bolling, and perhaps to other tasteful southerners on remote plantations, flute playing offered a sense of 'keeping up' in the absence of the stage, concerts, and balls of London, as he wrote in a poem, "To my FLUTE," in 1763:

> WHILE exil'd in this solitude,
> Dull seat of boors and planters rude,
> With you, my Flute, in harmless play,
> I cheat the tedious hours away:[1]

Most colonials, however, no doubt chose the flute because it was relatively easy to learn, inexpensive to buy, and simple to make. Training in some instrument, at least on the higher rungs of society, often figured in eligibility and courtship. A versifying suitor in 1768 praised the divinity of *"Miss ANNE GEDDY singing, and playing on the SPINET"*:

> Corelli, Handel, Felton, Nares,
> With their concertos, solos, airs,
> Are far less sweet to me! [2]

The many surviving colonial portraits that depict young women with guitars and young men with recorders suggest that musical ability was considered a token of gentility.[3]

The ability came from a corps of itinerant music masters who, like the portrait painters, crisscrossed the colonies. They offered instruction at the pupil's home, in rented rooms, or on a plantation, occasionally at a private (and usually short-lived) music school. Information on fees is fragmentary. In 1767 Landon Carter of Virginia employed a teacher named John Gualdo to give his daughter Lucy guitar lessons. "His terms," Carter wrote, "are 2 days in every 3 weeks, that is, 34 times for the year, after the rate of 13 Pistoles. These times to be at my house. All lessons elsewhere, if she is in the way to take them, are to be gratis." Most teachers were probably lesser talents unable to compete in European and English music circles. Yet in the newspaper advertisements by which, from New Hampshire to Georgia, they announced their presence, they impressed upon their provincial clients their European training. The music master who advertised in New York in 1764 was not alone in asking potential clients to "signify their Intentions as soon as they conveniently can, because his Stay in Town at this Time will be but short." [4] In this hoary ruse—used by painters as well—another ad usually appeared the next week saying that the music master had decided to stretch his stay by a week, only.

Socially, the "Professor of Music" stood above the actor, level perhaps with the small tradesman, but beneath the leading portrait painters. Like the painter, he survived by offering related services—doubling as a church organist, sitting in with local music groups or the touring theatre orchestra, copying printed music by hand for his students' use. The least successful also advertised as barbers, netmakers, or chimney sweeps. As a jack-of-all-trades, the music master became a stock figure of fun in the period, prompting some music masters to make professionalism itself a selling-point. The New York teacher quoted above advertised that he had "applied himself to the Study, Practice, and Teaching of Musick, as his only Business." As the many advertisements directed to "young Gentlemen and Ladies" or "young Masters and Misses" suggest, he usually taught not only music but also the good manners and social graces that allowed the young to step out with assurance and finesse. At least one music master also taught Latin; several offered accounting, a female accomplishment that Benjamin Franklin and others considered essential if a young lady hoped to keep up her husband's business in widowhood. Many music masters were closely associated with dancing masters, or offered instruction in social dancing themselves.[5]

Little biographical information about these itinerants remains beyond notices of payment in their employers' account books and journals, and newspaper advertisements stating their names and' skills. Many seem to have been Germans; most concentrated in the South. In Charleston, Ferdinand Grundzweig taught string and keyboard instruments, and doubled as second organist of St. Michael's Church; in Virginia, John Schneider arranged concerts and balls in Fredericksburg, while the more prominent German master John Stadler (or Stadley, or Stedley) rode the Northern Neck to teach the Carter, Custis, and Washington families, appearing at least once a month from 1766 to 1771 at Mount Vernon. The tutor Philip Vickers Fithian, a knowledgeable judge, considered him "a man of great skill in music," adept at many instruments.[6] Beginning in 1763, Philadelphians could take lessons at the coffeehouse from James Bremner (kinsman of an important Scottish composer and music publisher), who also arranged and conducted concerts. Among the pupils he instructed in harpsichord, guitar, violin, or flute were Benjamin Franklin's daughter Sally and Francis Hopkinson. In New York, the organist Peter Pelham, a stepbrother of John Singleton Copley, advertised in 1764 to teach not only harpsichord and spinet but also—perhaps a unique case—composition, "the Rules and Practice of the THOROUGH BASS." [7] In all, perhaps a dozen or fifteen music masters are known to have been teaching around 1763.

Like engravings, imported sheet music and collections of songs could be purchased through the local bookseller and printer, who advertised his latest shipments in the newspaper. In larger urban centers, they were available at full-fledged music shops. Every colonial capital in 1763 offered for sale the works of such popular composers as Antonio Vivaldi, Francesco Geminiani, Arcangelo Corelli, and Thomas Arne. The most popular composer, and ever more popular, was George Frederick Handel. One Boston importer in 1766 offered for sale (besides "genteel Household Furniture"):

> Handle's *[sic]* Oratorio of Athalia, Messiah, Joseph, Jephtha, Joshua, Deborah, Belshazzar, Sampson, Solomon, Esther, Alexander; the occasional Oratorio, Time and Truth, Saul, Theodora, Susanna, Macchaboeus, Te Deum, the choice of Hercules, Alexander's Feasts, L'Allegro, Semele, Hercules, Acis and Galatea. . . .[8]

In addition to sophisticated instrumental and vocal music, a great deal of English theatre music was available through English magazines, such as the London *Gentleman's Magazine*. Several American collections of popular song-texts from the English stage also appeared in the early sixties, such as *The American Cock Robin; Or, a Choice Collection of English Songs . . . agreeable to the North-American Taste* (New York, 1764, known only through an ad) and

The Wood-Lark, or a Choice Collection of the Newest and most Favourite English Songs (Philadelphia, 1765). They contained pastoral songs in which Strephon lamented absent Delia, patriotic favorites like "The Roast Beef of Old England," hunting songs, anacreontics, Scots songs, but emphasized fashionable songs from recent English stage productions, giving together with the song the name of the actor associated with it. Thus *The Wood-Lark* contained within its nearly 200 pages "all the Songs and Ballads, sung last summer at *Vauxhall, Ranelagh,* the *Theatres, Marybone* and *Sadler's-Wells. . . .*" The subtitle, *agreeable to the North-American Taste,* suggests that the coarser English favorites were not included.

Imported instruments could be bought in several ways. Many colonists ordered directly from notable London manufacturers. Francis Hopkinson in 1765 sent for one of the famed Kirkman harpsichords (a double harpsichord with a swell and piano movement) and advised Franklin to import one for his daughter as well. Occasionally, good foreign instruments came up for private sale. A "Gentleman from London" offered in 1764 to sell Bostonians, for three dollars up, the flutes, hautboys (oboes), violins, and bass viols he had collected all over Europe. Another offered his English chamber organ—a fairly popular home instrument—"for the want of Money." [9] All of the larger colonial centers contained a music dealer who kept imported instruments in stock. In Philadelphia alone in 1763, Theodore Memminger advertised guitars, violins, and ivory flutes "made by the best Masters in High Germany"; Michael Hillegas (the largest dealer in the city) offered instruments, paper, and music; and Martin Fay sold "Cremona" violins. Many dealers also offered repair services, imported instruments being easily broken in transatlantic passage and notoriously sensitive to Massachusetts winters or Carolina summers. [10] For the same reasons, instruments in good working order were cherished. In the late 1760's, the devoted musical amateur Governor John Penn of Philadelphia listened to a British officer play upon the finest violin he had ever heard. Two years Penn labored to get the instrument, the transaction flowing from Penn in London, through Philadelphia, to the officer in Pensacola, Florida. He bought the violin even though the officer refused to sell it "without I took another too, which was of little value." [11]

Although most large instruments in 1763 were imported, some locally made instruments could be purchased, usually from immigrant instrument makers. In Philadelphia, Gottlieb Klemm had been making spinets since at least 1739. In New York in 1767 a German named Jacob Trippel, trained in London, advertised to make "all sorts of Violins, Base and Tenor Viols, English and Spanish Guitters, Loutens, Mentelines, Mandores, and Welsh Harps" reasonably and "as neat as in Europe." [12] In Williamsburg Benjamin Bucktrout (also in 1767) made and repaired spinets, harpsichords, and instrument cases, as well as cabinets and coffins. (An excavation of his store site also turned up an oboe.)[13]

One untraditional instrument created a sensation in America in 1763, and was admired although not widely played throughout the later century—the armonica, Benjamin Franklin's improved version of the musical glasses. Franklin skewered a set of graduated glass bowls on a horizontal spindle, which rotated them through a trough of water; when the wet rims were touched, the glasses produced a soft, warbling sound. He built his first model around 1761; the final version, with exactingly blown glass hemispheres, arrived in Philadelphia late in 1763. Following Franklin's improvements, descriptions and engravings of the armonica appeared in Europe, Christoph Gluck performed on it in London, Mozart and Beethoven wrote for it. The poet Nathaniel Evans heard Franklin himself play the instrument in Philadelphia (where it was also played in concert) around 1764, and described its effect:

> Hark! the soft warblings, sounding smooth and clear,
> Strike with celestial ravishment the ear,
> Conveying inward, as they sweetly roll,
> A tide of melting music to the soul. . . .

The sweetly ethereal sound of the armonica, resembling the human voice, appealed to an age of sentiment which equated soft feelings with virtue, to which "celestial ravishment" meant aroused feelings of benevolence and domestic affection.[14]

The family music catered to by the music masters and instrument makers was played throughout the American colonies in 1763, at least by the fairly affluent. Its level of aspiration and achievement, however, was perhaps highest in the South. Sophisticated musical amateurs existed elsewhere, surely, usually among colonial officialdom: Governor Benning Wentworth, an avid musician, held musical soirees in New Hampshire; Governor John Penn and Francis Hopkinson of Philadelphia appeared in concerts in 1764 with such professionals as John Stadler and James Bremner, performing works by Handel, Scarlatti, and others. Benjamin Franklin not only built an armonica but also corresponded at length with Lord Kames about harmonic theory, and later may have written a string quartet in F major for three violins and cello, using *scordatura* for ease in playing.[15] Yet music was pursued most intensively in the South, because the scattered and isolated nature of southern plantations forced cultivated planters to build miniature private civilizations. Several planters re-created for their own use the music shops and concert life of the distant cities, providing for their entertainment in the same self-sufficient spirit by which they built bakehouses and foundries.

Many prominent southerners seem to have been unusually well trained in music. Patrick Henry played the violin, the lute, the flute, the harpsichord, and the pianoforte. Thomas Jefferson was a lavish and finicky collector of instruments and music (most of his purchases coming after 1765) and a lover of ensemble playing. Even as a young man he performed in amateur musicals at the Governor's Palace in Williamsburg. (The palace itself, according to a survey in 1775, contained "3 organs, a Harpsichord, a Piano-Forte, and other Musical Instruments.") [16] The most imposing southern musical amateur was Robert Carter of Nomini Hall, owner of 60,000 acres. Philip Vickers Fithian, the tutor at Nomini, described him as "indefatigable in the Practice," possessed of "a good ear for Music, a vastly delicate Taste and . . . good instruments." Carter's instruments included a harpsichord, pianoforte, guitar, violin, and several German flutes, as well as an armonica and a two-stop chamber organ built in part according to his own design. He could play them all. With several instruments at hand, and plenty of music in the library, concerts were part of the routine of family life at Nomini Hall, Carter often playing the harpsichord, his son Ben and tutor Fithian playing flutes, the children's music teacher, John Stadler, listening to their renditions of William Felton's popular gavotte or Handel's flute works—or to Carter, solo, playing Handel's "Water parted from the Sea" on his armonica.[17]

Much other music on plantations was supplied by slaves and servants. Some of the many black musicians in the southern colonies were products of a Virginia statute of 1738 which required free mulattos, Negros, and Indians to serve in the militia as unarmed drummers or trumpeters, a practice which spread to other colonies.[18] Most, however, filled a demand for domestics who could also play the fiddle at dances or play the part of a gentleman's gentleman. Many ads in the 1760's and later state the slave's musical skills. The *Virginia Gazette* in 1767 offered a young slave who "has every qualification of a genteel and sensible servant. . . . He shaves, dresses hair, and plays on the *French* horn . . . which the purchaser may have with him"; one planter needing a groom noted that if "he can play upon the FRENCH HORN, it will be more agreeable." The same skills served to identify runaway slaves and servants, black and white. Typical is the 1768 ad for a North Carolina black named Ned who "can play on the violin, and will endeavor to impose upon the publick and pass for a freeman." [19] Some slaves brought native techniques and instruments with them from Africa. A traveler in 1775 described a Virginia schoolmaster who made "a Niger come & play on an Instrument call'd a Barrafou," a sort of xylophone, found in Africa, consisting of loose sticks laid across an open box; another reported slaves dancing to "a banjor (a large hollow instrument with three strings), and a quaqua (somewhat resembling a drum)." A few black musicians achieved at least local celebrity. The courtly Sy Gilliat, a servant to Lord Botetourt, was the official fiddler at state balls in Williamsburg, where he played music and gavottes with his black assistant London Brigs.[20] In all, evidence of dedicated proficients like Carter and of many black horn and fiddle players suggests that in 1763 amateur musical performances were on the whole more skillful and more common in the South than elsewhere in America.

Professional performances in the early 1760's offered the prophets of cultural progress not much encouragement. Many were no more than social gatherings for the eligible followed by dancing, like the concert advertised in the *Boston Evening-Post* in 1768:

> Of Music there will be a Concert,
> Perform'd on next Monday, the Day after Sunday,
> By various Masters of some sort;
> When Concert is over, each Lass with her Lover,
> May dance till the Clock strikes Eleven.

Socializing at concerts irritated at least one New Yorker, who complained in 1764 that "nothing is heard during the whole performance, but laughing and talking very loud, squawling, overturning the benches"—the result, he said, of women trying to make themselves noticeable to men. Colonial professionals were not unique in having to please an inattentive audience. Eighteenth-century concerts in Europe were notoriously noisy, and distinguished musicians abroad routinely performed dance and dinner music. Yet, like the itinerant portrait painters and the instrument makers, few colonial 'professionals' were full-time musicians. The John Stevens who offered a "Concert of Musick" in Savannah, Georgia, in 1766 was also deputy postmaster general.[21] For musicians of such uncertain standing, a useful sort of performance was the popular subscription concert, a semiprivate affair often sponsored by some society for its own benefit. One or more musicians proposed the concert in a newspaper, usually inviting amateurs to join in; enough subscriptions being raised, the program was announced, the ad running until the day of performance in hopes of filling the remaining seats.

Concerts could be found in all of the larger cities. Boston had subscription concerts at least by 1766, probably earlier. Much of the city's musical life centered in Concert Hall, a brick Corinthian-style building on Queen and Hanover streets containing a mirror-lined room some sixty by thirty feet. From 1754 to 1769 the hall was run by the organist Stephen Deblois, who operated a music store on the ground floor.[22] In New York, subscription concerts had been organized since about 1760 by the enterprising and extremely popular dancing master William Hulett, who was to his profession what Wollaston and Hesselius were to theirs. In 1765, Hulett and a partner established the first of the city's summer gardens, Ranelagh Garden, where two shillings' admission bought an outdoor concert of vocal music, accompanied, if one wished, by "gammon, tongues, alamode beef, tarts, cakes" and capped by fireworks.[23] Hulett also sold tickets for vocal and instrumental concerts given in the city by itinerant dancing and music teachers, like the obscure "Mr. Jackson" who featured in his 1763 program a timely "ODE on the Restoration of Peace . . . with proper Choruses." Philadelphia began subscription concerts not long after the Peace, with a mixed group of amateurs and professionals, although they ceased after about a year. Like almost all cultural activity in Philadelphia, musical life centered around the College of Philadelphia, where in 1765 Bremner gave a concert to aid a local charity school. Assisted by local amateurs, singers from the College, and a church organist, he performed overtures by Johann Stamitz, Arne, and Martini; a harpsichord sonata; Geminiani's Sixth Concerto; and other works.[24]

In the South, concert life centered around the "Public Times," ceremonial occasions when outlying planters and their families came to town, transforming county seats like Williamsburg from villages into thronged villages. Musicians and actors carefully arranged their itineraries around such occasions. The climate of Charleston, however, created special conditions which made that city the capital of southern musical life. From July to October, planters around Charleston moved into the seacoast city to escape the heat of the lowland areas. For four or five months they became urbanites, maintaining expensive townhouses and patronizing local artists. In this period, concerts and plays thrived. Just a year before the declaration of peace, Charlestonians had founded the St. Coecilia Society, the oldest musical society in America, devoted to music and elegant socializing. The society engaged musicians by the season for its fortnightly concerts, advertising for them as far away as New York, Philadelphia, and Boston. It thus provided a stable home for professional musicians that was unique in America. It also drew on local amateurs and church organists, and on singers and musicians from the itinerant theatre troupe. Other concerts in Charleston were offered by local dancing and music masters, such as Thomas Pike, who performed on the French horn and bassoon for "all lovers of harmony." In 1767, Charleston also had an outdoor Vauxhall where an evening of vocal and instrumental music ended with a ball or, sometimes, a magician who taught card tricks.[25]

These music dealers, instrument makers, and semiprofessional musicians served an audience interested, overwhelmingly, in the performance of music. Willingly, it remained dependent for original works upon England, whence music like Handel's flowed cheaply and abundantly west. So far as is known, by 1763 no American had published a piece of secular music. Sophisticated amateurs like Carter probably tried composition, but little has survived and perhaps not much was written. One of the few memorable attempts was made by Francis Hopkinson, who around 1759 composed an art-song entitled "My Days Have Been so Wondrous Free," a setting for a poem by Thomas Parnell. It is perhaps the first known composition by a native American. When Sally Franklin in 1763 tried to collect some native compositions to send abroad and found only "a few Airs," her father explained accurately, "Music is a new Art with us." [26]

By "Music" Franklin of course meant secular music, since in the colonial churches music had been sung, and in places played, for over a century. In that time its strict denominational character and its repertoire had changed little. Instrumental music, that is organ music, had been confined to the few Anglican churches; Congregationalists had continued singing from the same repertoire of English and continental psalm tunes.

Roughly coincident with the Peace, however, instrumental music began to gain tolerance among denominations that had shunned it, and more and different kinds of tunes began to appear, a few by native composers. These changes were only a byproduct of the long, complex development of eighteenth-century rationalism. Its merciful God, ruler of a benign universe, seriously challenged—if He never utterly dethroned—the vengeful Calvinist God dangling man by a thread over the molten abyss. To a God who loved him, man signified his obedience by being happy. "An inward chearfulness is an implicit praise and thanksgiving to Providence," Joseph Addison had said, "a kind of acquiescence in the state wherein we are placed, and a secret approbation of the divine will." [27] Happiness, Alexander Pope declared, is "our being's end and aim." The message that a benevolent God had designed content and commanded happiness for man reverberated in the smiling colonials painted by Wollaston and Theus, in the concise refutation of Hobbes's cynicism given by the King's College orator, and in the recent Peace itself.

To many in the non-Congregational churches it seemed that such a Ruler desired praise that was cheerful and harmonious. Cheerfulness in worship, wrote one Philadelphian in 1763, would allay factional and church controversy. Addressing himself to "All (Particularly the Presbyterians and Baptists) Who Have Hitherto been taught to Look Upon the Use of Instrumental Musick in the Worship of God as Unlawful," he argued that organ music would help to regularize the singing of psalms, would beautify the churches, and might prove a means of grace, allowing God to "move us by ways suited to our Nature." In Boston in 1764, the Anglican head of the mission for the Society for the Propagation of the Gospel argued similarly that music in worship could calm the agitated mind, compose the spirit, and lift up the heart "in an holy chearfulness and serenity." The very word *psallo*, he noted—"psalm"—means to sing to an instrument, making the use of instruments in worship "a matter of *right* and lawfulness." Indeed, he said, all of the "fine arts, not only of Music and Poetry, but those of Architecture, Sculpture, and Painting, the powers of Eloquence, and every true expression of taste and genius, are all undoubtedly derived from GOD." [28]

The same vision of a harmonious and benign universe, which thus turned ministers into estheticians, gave specific encouragement to the importation, manufacture, and playing of organs. God desired, the Philadelphia writer said, not fiddles or the other instruments of backwoods worship which "excite carnal Mirth and Wantonness"; He had revealed His desire in Scripture, Psalms, chapter 4: "Praise Him with Organs." Such praise had existed in the colonies for at least fifty years, providing a fading and hostile Puritan leadership audible signs of Anglican inroads.[29] Cotton Mather gloated in 1714 over the failure of the organs newly introduced into the Boston Anglican Church to win it converts. In the 1760's, however, influenced by new arguments for instrumental music in worship, the volume of organ importation and building swelled dramatically.

Several organs, the best so far to have arrived in America, came from Johann Snetzler, the most admired organ builder in eighteenth-century England. He sent at least two organs to America in the early 1760's: to Christ Church (Cambridge) in 1761 and to Trinity Church (New York) in 1764.[30] The Cambridge organ took two years to build. Snetzler built the quite fully documented New York organ in consultation with the Trinity Church organist at a price of £650. The church considered, but abandoned, the addition of an open diapason stop of sixteen feet, which would have cost an additional £150. The surviving contract for the organ itemizes the stops to be used, specifies the material and the number of pipes, and concludes that the instrument is "to be putt into a neat Wainscott Case with proper carving, to consist of three setts of keys, with sound boards, Bellows, Rolerboards and all the proper movements, & other requisites, the front pipes to be gilt with the best gold, the compass to be from Double Gamut long Eights up to E in alt." The frontispiece would be "ornamented & finished" by Snetzler's brother, a carver to Oxford University.[31]

The call for more instrumental music encouraged native organ makers too. Indeed, as the Philadelphia writer quoted earlier noted, organs could be "made here in *as great Perfection* as in *England,* and near *one Half cheaper.*" Several organs had been built in America, largely by German-born makers. Most were of the small chamber or bureau type with a single keyboard, the pipes on the front being usually dummies. A large organ had been built by the Philadelphia craftsman Johann Klemm, consisting of twenty-six stops and at least two mixtures. Others were made by John Spiceacre (or Speissegger) of Charleston, who had been associated with Snetzler, and by Moravian craftsmen in the frontier settlement at Wachovia, North Carolina.[32] The most prominent organ maker in America in 1763 was Philip Fyring of Philadelphia, who built instruments for three Philadelphia churches: St. Paul's (1762; the instrument praised by Peale on his visit to buy paints), St. Peter's (1763), and Christ Church (1766). The very size of the 1763 organ created difficulties; it took up nearly half the gallery, shrinking the seating accommodations and making the seats under the gallery tremble. The vestry later tried to replace it with a smaller organ.[33]

The wider encouragement given to instrumental church music also gave new opportunities to organists. Some remain mere names, such as John Rice, organist of Trinity Church, New York, from 1765 to 1795. Others shifted, quite like music masters and itinerant portraitists, to make a living. Samuel Blyth, organist at St. Peter's in Salem from 1760 to 1773, also made spinets and did house, ship, and "fancy" painting (ill., p. 348). (His brother Benjamin, also of Salem, was a painter and prolific pastel portraitist.) Both James Bremner and Francis Hopkinson served as organists at St. Peter's Church in Philadelphia; Frederick Hoff, organist for a time at St. Michael's in Charleston, also tuned and repaired organs and other keyboard instruments in the city.[34] Even the more prestigious organists (for that matter, even Johann Sebastian Bach in Leipzig) were required to perform at funerals, or to instruct children in psalmody, and were closely supervised by the clergy.

The most prominent organists were those in the South, probably because the Anglicanism of the region had never provided the barrier against instrumental church music that Congregationalism had erected in the North. Indeed, in 1763 the southern organists were probably the best trained and most skilled musicians in America. Among them was Benjamin Yarnold, who arrived from London in 1753 to become organist at St. Philip's Church in Charleston, where he composed and tried to publish an anthem and ode. When he left St. Philip's in 1764 he was succeeded by the organist Peter Valton (d. 1784), who played there until 1781. Valton had been a student and assistant of William Boyce and James Nares, composers and professors of music at the King's Chapel in Westminster Abbey. During his tenure at St. Philip's, he sold instruments, taught music, and gave concerts with singers from traveling theatre companies. Bruton Parish Church in Williamsburg had enjoyed the services, since 1759, of John Singleton Copley's stepbrother, Peter Pelham.

Pelham's importance rests in the probability that he had studied in Boston with Carl Theodor Pachelbel, the son of Johann Pachelbel, a great German organist who taught J. S. Bach's elder brother. With his training in baroque organ music, Pelham may have introduced Bach into Williamsburg. He supplemented his annual salary of £60–75 by playing with the theatre orchestra, by offering evening religious concerts, and by accepting civil appointments from the House of Burgesses, including the supervision of the printing of treasury notes. Like the other leading southern organists, he also composed music.[35]

At the same time that instrumental music was spreading outside of the Anglican churches, the vocal music long used by the Presbyterians and Congregationalists was coming to seem worn out. Indeed, vocal music had reached a point of stylistic transformation. The molting stage is vividly represented by the coexistence in 1763 of two works: Thomas Walter's *Grounds and Rules of Musick Explained* (5th ed., Boston, 1760, first published by James Franklin in 1721) and James Lyon's *Urania* (Philadelphia, 1761). Although both collections of vocal music were used in 1763, a glance conveys their unlikeness. Walter's book contains 36 pages of music, Lyon's 198; Walter's title page looks stolid beside the engraved rococo curlicues introducing *Urania*, whose very title announces neoclassic elegance. Yet both books clearly exist as stages on a continuum of Protestant church music winding back through the first settlers of New England to the Reformation itself.[36]

The 1760 edition of Walter's *Grounds and Rules* was only the latest issue of a work from which the singers in the Congregational churches of New England had sung for forty years. It embodied the hope of Boston Congregationalism in the early eighteenth century to align American Puritanism with new elegancies of European culture, to offer some recreation in worship for the young (thus to encourage a faltering piety), and to "regularize" singing in the Massachusetts churches, that is to reduce it to rule, to teach the church singers how to read music. Since the late seventeenth century, church luminaries like Cotton Mather (Walter's uncle) had protested the decay of church singing, largely attributable to the practice by which the congregation imitated the intonation of a church deacon or elder as he 'lined out,' line by line, the psalm to be sung. The result, Walter wrote, was "like *Five Hundred* different Tunes roared out at the same time," and an unscriptural rendering of the texts, "left to the Mercy of every unskilful Throat to chop and alter, twist and change. . . ." His book appeared with a commendatory preface by Increase and Cotton Mather, and other prominent ministers, encouraging "all, more particularly our *Young People*, to accomplish themselves with Skill to *Sing the Songs of the Lord*, according to the *Good Rules* of Psalmody."

Directing his collection at *"the meanest Capacities,"* Walter provided brief instructions for singing by note, an essay by the rationalistic Isaac Watts, "Thoughts on Poetry and Musick," and a group of short psalm tunes, printed in diamond notes and without text. His book went through several editions and remained in use until 1764, and even later. It increased the repertoire of church songs from the dozen or so known to congregations in Mather's time to perhaps thirty-five—all drawn from the British repertoire, all harmonized in block chords—which were printed over and over again in tunebooks before 1760.

Lyon's *Urania* represented the first change in colonial psalmody in forty years, and the first real departure in more than a century. As its frontispiece hinted, it introduced into America a style of elaborate, modern British music unlike anything in Walter. The full title sums up the differences: *Urania, or a Choice Collection of Psalm-Tunes, Anthems, and Hymns.* The inclusion of hymns and anthems was a key step in a process that subtly separated Presbyterian and Congregational vocal music from its scriptural subject matter and gave the music an independent esthetic existence.

Lyon, of course, did not invent hymns and anthems. By publishing them in *Urania* he simply recognized them as now-standard parts of the repertoire of church vocal music. Hymns had been gaining such recognition for several decades. The older Puritan psalmody found both its justification and its material in Scripture. Puritans justified singing in worship on the precedent of David's musicianship and his songs of praise to God. But here the precedent ended. Only David's songs—the Psalms— were to be sung. The singing of hymns—i.e., of non-biblical texts or of texts drawn from portions of the Bible other than Psalms—grew up in new, rationalistic sects to which the Puritans accommodated themselves in alarm over the possible subversion of Christianity itself. Its spread in America was largely owing to the popularity among Puritans of the English divine and hymn writer Isaac Watts (whose rationalistic tendencies they also feared) and to the voyages to America in the 1730's of the Methodist Wesleys, who spread evangelical hymnody during the Great Awakening. (John Wesley's first hymnbook was printed in South Carolina in 1737.) The Wesleys introduced not only new texts for singing but also a vocal style embellished with trills and turns that brought an element of performance to the earlier plain singing. Their efforts were furthered by the Reverend Samuel Davies of Princeton (where Lyon had trained for the ministry), who continued to popularize hymns.

By the time of *Urania*, many colonial poets were publishing hymns in colonial newspapers, although some Presbyterians and Congregationalists still felt uneasy about them. In 1762, for instance, a Presbyterian minister in Virginia named John Todd preached a sermon defending "*The Propriety, Necessity and Use, of Evangelical Psalms* [i.e., hymns], *in Christian Worship.*" [37] Like the earlier Puritans, Todd argued his case on scriptural grounds. But he turned around the instruction of Paul which the Puritans had constantly invoked to discourage a merely musical performance oblivious to the meaning of its text: to "sing with the spirit, and with the understanding also." In Todd's version, this indicated that the singers should make their own songs in their own language. David's psalms were "suited exactly to the *jewish [sic]* day, and this is one of their great excellencies; and a very plain reason why they do not suit us under the gospel. . . ." Since Presbyterians, he said, "are blest with these spiritual privileges in *Christ Jesus,* let us not be covered with a *jewish vail,* nor force ourselves or others, to sing in IGNORANCE, *the dark sayings of David upon the harp.*" His arguments resound with battles over the relation between the Old and New Testaments that had been fought since the Middle Ages, and cannot be explored here. More important than the grounds of his arguments is the need for argument itself, suggesting how in the early 1760's the singing of hymns was still not unopposed.

Urania thus sanctioned a kind of sacred vocal music which in some quarters still needed to be defended, especially against charges of unscriptural innovation. Together with old, favorite plain-tunes like MEAR and WINDSOR, Lyon included a selection of hymns, usually a page long. Even more significant, however, was his inclusion of more than a dozen anthems, often seven or eight pages long.

Anthems were the chief expression of a new style of English Protestant church music. The style first appeared around 1730 in the works of such British psalmodists as William Knapp, John Arnold, and William Tans'ur. Most were Anglicans who, unlike William Boyce and the great eighteenth-century cathedral composers, specialized in music for smaller, usually rural, congregations. Abandoning the simple syllabic settings of the older psalmody, they introduced more elaborate psalm and hymn tunes in a more exuberant style, marked by trills, graces, lively tempos, textural changes, and brief sections of imitation. Their collections, intended for Anglican congregations and choirs, influenced dissenting musicians as well. In the 1750's, their works began to circulate in the colonies, helping to create dissatisfaction with the limited tonal range and rhythmic patterns of the Puritan psalmody typified by Walter.[38]

The most important work in popularizing the new English music in the colonies was William Tans'ur's *Royal Melody Complete* (1755). It went through eleven American editions. The first apparently appeared in 1767, although some of the several English editions of the work must have circulated earlier. Tans'ur's preface declared a new attitude toward sacred vocal music. Whereas Walter had quoted on his title page Psalms 150:6, "Let everything that hath Breath praise the Lord," Tans'ur quoted Psalms 100:1, "O be Joyful in the LORD, All ye Lands: Serve the LORD with Gladness. . . ." [39] Like the defenders of instrumental music, he explained that God gave man a sense of harmony "both for his *Service,* and our own *Recreation.* . . ." That the singing might be "decently" performed, he included a section of instructions unthinkable in, and quite unnecessary to, Walter's collection—explanations of the gamut, of clefs, rests, keys, time, transition, pricked notes, characters, graces, concords, and discords, plus a glossary of about a hundred technical terms like "Eptachord" ("A Seventh"), "Diatessaron" ("A perfect Fourth"), and *"Musico-Theorico"* ("A Person who studies *Musick,* writes *Treatises,* and *explains* dark Passages therein; and publickly gives *Instructions* by *Practice,*" i.e., a music teacher). Nor were Tans'ur's instructions overly ambitious considering the music that followed them: psalms and hymns with trills, shakes, melismas, and "Choro Grandos" and anthems.

The anthems particularly represented a much more ambitious kind of music than New England congregations sang. Most were four- or five-minute pieces for unaccompanied, mixed, four-part chorus, with short parts for any or all of the voices, often ending with a Hallelujah section. The music was set to some freely handled (often merely paraphrased), unversified passage of Scripture, not usually from Psalms. Whereas the psalm and hymn tunes kept close to their devotional purpose, the anthems gave play to an esthetic impulse by increasing and varying the singers' musical resources, offering dotted rhythms, reductions of the four-part chorus to two or three parts or to a solo line, melisma on descriptive words like "rejoice" and "glory." No doubt the new anthems met an already existing demand for more sophisticated music to test the abilities of singers who, since Walter's time, had been trained to read music. More important, they provided a profound challenge to a new generation of colonial composers growing up in the 1760's.[40]

Lyon's *Urania* incorporated into the older American psalmody the changes that had been accumulating in English and colonial church music for fifty years and more. It introduced "Entirely New" tunes of some difficulty, in one to four parts, featuring dotted rhythms and imitating scriptural words like "fly" or "harps" with shakes and runs. It also included an instructional preface, which, while not as elaborate as Tans'ur's, offered a detailed guide to note reading, explanations of time (Semibreve, Minim, Crochet, Quaver, Semiquaver; i.e., half, quarter, eighth, sixteenth, thirty-second notes), and sections on the graces, which, except for the trill, were "seldom used in plain Church Tunes" but were "very proper in Hymns & Anthems." *Urania* is entitled to several firsts: the first American tunebook in which ornaments appear, the first to include English anthems and fuging-tunes (of which more later); the first to have four-part choruses, detailed explanations of tempo and rhythm, and words printed under the notes. Since Lyon printed several of his own compositions, it was also the first to include sacred music by a native American.[41]

Although published in Philadelphia, *Urania* attracted attention in New England, where the new psalmody was being established at virtually the same time. Between 1764 and 1766 the printer and compiler Daniel Bayley issued in Boston and Newburyport no less than three editions of a work entitled *A New and Compleat Introduction to the Grounds and Rules of Musick*. After the first six words, the title is simply that of Thomas Walter's *Grounds and Rules* of 1721. Bayley took Walter's prefatory essays by Cotton Mather and Isaac Watts, and Walter's tunes and essay on singing, but added to them a long essay on music from Tans'ur's *Royal Melody Complete*—a hybrid of old and new that epitomizes the stylistic transformation occurring in psalmody at the time of the Peace. In 1764 the Boston concert manager Josiah Flagg published *A Collection of the Best Psalm Tunes* (engraved by Paul Revere), including some hymns by Tans'ur and citing Lyon as a source. Two years later Flagg issued *Sixteen Anthems* containing fairly ambitious pieces by Williams, Tans'ur, Knapp, and other English anthem writers, plus a song from Handel's *Saul*.

Collections like *Sixteen Anthems* and *Urania* were bound to perpetuate the spiral that brought them into being. From the time of Thomas Walter onward, as Congregational and Presbyterian singers became more accomplished they called for more demanding music, which called for more sophisticated training, which produced even more accomplished singers. As early as 1762, the congregation of the town of Rowley voted to allow those skilled in "the art of singing" to sit together in the front gallery of the church, in effect forming a choir—a departure from the communal singing traditional to the New England churches.[42] The interplay of more difficult music and more skillful singers begged for well-trained teachers, perhaps for singing schools, and for local composers, more familiar with local church life than overseas Anglicans could be, to provide their own instructional manuals and their own music.

4. The Literary Scene

In his search for "sensible, virtuous and elegant Minds" Benjamin Franklin must have found the literary scene discouraging. The muses of poetry and drama seemed little inclined to migrate to the west. In 1763 England, that "petty Island," produced roughly ninety issues of poetry and plays and about twenty-five of prose fiction. In the same year, England's "vast" North American colonies produced no fiction, no plays, and about seven issues of poetry, of which the longest was twenty-seven pages.[1] *The vast country supported not a single magazine. In a professional sense, there were no American writers in 1763. No one earned a living by writing. No one on the American continent in 1763 had published a play or a novel. Indeed, no one who could be called an American had ever published any work in any of the longer, major European literary forms.*

If the British colonies lacked writers, however, they did not lack readers, and if Americans did not write for wealth or fame, they did write. The weekly "Poet's Corner" of newspapers in Boston or Charleston never lacked locally written pastorals, drinking songs, and satires. Verse being a popular medium of public discourse, Americans filled broadsides and pamphlets with anonymous poems on issues of the day, while their colleges nurtured a generation of young men with literary ambitions.

The absence of professional literary life, paradoxically, resulted from the abundance of literary works available. Colonials could not take music lessons or buy portraits of themselves without employing painters and musicians in the flesh. But they could import all the novels, poems, and plays they wished and never see a writer. They read avidly, too, providing steady business for the book importers who existed in all of the larger urban centers. Between 1748 and 1772, the Philadelphia bookseller David Hall imported from the famous London dealer William Strahan, alone, about £30,000 worth of books, stationery, and miscellaneous items. Colonial taste in books, as in prints, was often determined abroad; Strahan's policy was simply to send Hall two or three copies of current London best sellers. The policy was probably satisfactory to colonial readers, who wanted to stay *au courant*. In Charleston the bookseller Robert Wells (who claimed to have the largest stock of books in America) emphasized in his ads that he could obtain from abroad any title not in stock quickly; he advertised Samuel Johnson's *Dictionary* for sale only a few months after its publication. Some dealers made their books available even to non-buyers by circulating part of their stock. At his "London Book-Store" on King (now State) Street, John Mein of Boston operated such a circulating library—with 1,200 volumes—from ten o'clock to one and three to six daily, at a cost to members of £1 8s. a year.[2]

Booksellers did more than supply imported reading matter. Most published books and pamphlets themselves; several also published newspapers. The most prominent provided the organization and materials that made colonial cultural life possible at all. Such a cultural entrepreneur was the New York printer and bookseller James Rivington (1724–1802).

He had learned the book business in the mother country, where his father—a friend of Samuel Richardson and other famous English writers—had taken over a noted English publishing house among whose overseas customers was Cotton Mather. Largely by underselling his competitors, the younger Rivington himself became a leading exporter of books to America. In 1760, some London dealers brought suit against him for piracy, bankrupting the firm, a result hastened by his weakness for betting on horses. Emigrating to New York the same year, he opened a shop on Hanover Square, but quickly left it in care of a partner and opened a second store in Philadelphia—the store at which the saddler Charles Willson Peale bought a *Handmaid to the Arts*. Rivington created enmity by underselling the Philadelphia book dealers too, and by cutting into the monopoly of local music and instrument dealers. Although he opened a third store in Boston in 1762 (and perhaps a fourth in Bermuda), he concentrated after 1765 on his shop in New York. He had married well in the city and befriended such influential citizens as Sir William Johnson.[3]

In ways typical of the bookseller-printer-editor in other colonial cities, Rivington became indispensable to New York's cultural life. In his shop he sold books, prints, sheet music, strings, reeds, and music paper. He also sold tickets to the concerts and plays which he advertised and often reviewed in his newspaper (begun in 1773). He exhibited paintings by the same itinerant portraitists who announced their arrival in his columns, and served as a middleman for patrons who desired sittings. He arranged lessons with itinerant music masters and collected subscriptions for proposed volumes of poetry. His newspaper gave the city an outlet for its literary aspirations and shaped its image of the literary life. He printed verse by New Yorkers and glimpses of overseas culture—anecdotes about Handel or Hogarth, theatrical gossip from Paris and Edinburgh. A theatrical dabbler himself, who entertained guests at his boarding house with performances from *Othello*, he worked in virtual partnership with traveling theatre companies, as did other printers. Theatre companies gave the printer substantial business, advertising in his newspaper, ordering programs from his press, and selling tickets at his shop. In return, the printer often espoused the actors' cause in his newspaper against local anti-theatre groups, favorably reviewed their performances, and, it seems certain, allowed the managers to insert anonymous plugs. Without printers like Rivington, musicians, actors, and itinerant painters could hardly have existed.

Nor, since Rivington and the others were also publishers, could any literary life have been possible. Little that they issued in 1763, however, was intended for entertainment. Centered in New England and the

Middle Colonies, the American printers mostly produced public documents (laws, charters, assembly records), almanacs and newspapers, and religious writings (especially sermons), works that met local needs without duplicating the books they imported and sold. A smaller but particularly important category of locally published books was reprints of older American works, such as Cotton Mather's *Malachi* (1717; rpt. Philadelphia, 1767), William Wood's *New England's Prospect* (1635; rpt. Boston, 1764), or the many works of Jonathan Edwards, whose religious writings stayed in print throughout the century. The continuing availability of such works made possible a living sense of the leaders and events of the colonial past, a feeling of continuity with the first settlers.

No comparable sense of the colonial literary past was possible, however. Little earlier American poetry remained in print, and some had never reached print at all. Two classics of American Puritan poetry were reprinted: Anne Bradstreet's *The Tenth Muse* (1650; rpt. Boston, 1758) and Michael Wigglesworth's *Day of Doom* (1662?; rpt. Boston, 1751). But few, if any, colonists in 1763 knew of Benjamin Tompson's *New-Englands Crisis* (1676) or Ebenezer Cooke's *Maryland Muse* (1731). The best poetry yet written in America, that of the Puritan minister Edward Taylor, remained in manuscripts known only to their caretaker, the Rhode Island minister Ezra Stiles, and to those who heard of them from Stiles, as did Thomas Jefferson. (Perhaps the best belletristic prose of the earlier period also remained in manuscript, William Byrd's *Histories of the Dividing Line*.)

Not many volumes by contemporary American poets were available either. In the quarter-century before the Peace, probably fewer than ten had been published. The Horatian ideal of rural retirement inspired some popular poems stemming from John Pomfret's *The Choice*, such as William Livingston's *Philosophic Solitude* (1747) and Benjamin Church's *The Choice* (1757), stressing the contemplative pleasures of country gentlemen of taste and means. Slender volumes appeared in the 1740's and 50's by Mather Byles and Joseph Green of Boston, and by the Irish clergyman James Sterling of Maryland. One or two volumes by Americans were published abroad. In 1764, the Long Islander Benjamin Young Prime published his volume of poems, *The Patriot Muse*, in London, where he was studying medicine.

The paucity of volumes of American poetry, however, deceptively suggests a greater dearth of native talent and demand than actually existed in 1763. Some volumes were advertised but never appeared. As happened with Taylor's poems, other volumes remained in manuscript, such as the still-unpublished "Hilarodia" of the cultivated Virginia poet Robert Bolling, a London-educated descendant of Pocahontas. Written mostly during the early 1760's, his collection of biting, learned satirical and amatory verse (and bawdy drawings) contains some of the freshest poetry written in America up to its time. The scarcity of published volumes of native poetry no doubt represented, in part, difficulties of distribution and prohibitive competition from easily imported volumes of Pope or James Thomson. Much of the verse that never made its way into volumes went into the anonymous "Poet's Corner" featured by Rivington and other newspaper editors, or into the poetry columns of the London literary magazines. Between the two, Bolling managed to publish at least thirty-five of his poems, and probably more that have not been identified. Thus, despite the paucity of American volumes of poetry, between 1763 and 1765 approximately 200 poems by colonials appeared in American newspapers and English magazines.[4]

These poems differ little from ephemeral verse written in England, or from each other. Like the Knelleresque portraits, they suffer from formularism in their provincial reaching after a metropolitan manner. They most often managed to escape stylish clichés when animated by some local issue, the subject matter itself differentiating the poem from others written in England at the same time. In fact, colonials used verse widely as a medium of public discussion and debate. The more deeply felt local and imperial issues produced sudden outbursts of verse in newspapers, broadsides, and pamphlets by writers of every degree of skill and every social class. The result was a large body of anonymous verse on colonial affairs, ranging from learned satire and political philosophizing in blank verse to invective screed and semiliterate testaments of personal conviction in ballad meter. Broadside verses, printed on one side of single sheets, were particularly popular. Closely related in origin and purpose to the newspaper, broadsides were a street literature used to report disasters, crimes, and other urgent events. They were particularly suited to radical and inflammatory politics, having no identifying marks of printer or writer and being easily tacked up at night around town, or left on doorsteps, or read to gathered groups.

Whatever the degree of sophistication in these local newspaper and broadside verses, their language is almost always densely allusive, saturated with references to local personalities and issues and thereby opaque to modern understanding and, indeed, to the understanding of colonists who lived outside their range of reference. A typical occasion for verse occurred when the Virginia General Court in 1766 freed on bail a burgess named John Chiswell, who had been charged with murder. Several poems on the case appeared in the *Virginia Gazette*, one by Robert Bolling, who charged the court with favoritism and attacked the other local poets in a witty "Satire on the Times." Readers outside the Williamsburg vicinity were not likely to have appreciated his barbs:

WHEN Judas lavish'd laud on honest WAYLES,
Men, laughing, thought they heard VERMILIO's tales;
To him should grateful W——— like praise return,
Mankind would swear all language was forsworn—
. . . .
  Yon interlauding couple raving find
Their fancied talents scatter'd in the wind,
The BUCKSKIN's *flowers* but *thistles* to display
And METRIOT's READY PEN turn READY BRAY.[5]

Any local issue of moment was likely to produce a spate of verses on some locally known "BUCKSKIN" or "W———."

Weightier imperial issues also engendered poems, although in language more widely understood, and usually addressed to all of the British colonies as to a single audience. Indeed, the recent Peace itself had provoked controversy and discussion in verse. On the very day that Benjamin West arrived in London, the New York *Mercury* reprinted a remarkable essay that had been published in that city by the English radical John Wilkes, number 45 of his series *The North Briton.* Wilkes attacked a recent speech before Parliament in which the king had defended the Peace. He also attacked the king's speechwriters and the foreign policy of Lord Bute. The young Princeton graduate Benjamin Young Prime sided with Wilkes (and with William Pitt), in believing that the Peace terms humiliated and despoiled England and risked war again with France in Canada. In ceding Guadeloupe, Martinique, and St. Lucia to France, and Cuba and the Philippines to Spain, England had been tricked out of hard-won territory:

> *Britannia,* MISTRESS OF THE WORLD NO MORE!
> By foes deluded, by false friends betray'd,
> And rifled of the spoils her conquests made;
> Curs'd with a treaty, whose unequal terms
> Check in mid-progress her victorious arms,
> And, at th' expence of a defrauded state,
> Rescue deceivers from impending fate. . . .

Other versifiers in the colonies found Wilkes's criticism disturbing and disloyal. Over three issues, the *Newport Mercury* ran a lengthy, anonymous verse skit entitled "PATRIOTISM! A Farce." In one scene Wilkes appears reading from Satan on rebellion in *Paradise Lost*—a popular literary image of sedition—implying that, like Satan's attack on God, Wilkes's attack on the king is motivated by envy. Peeved that he was not awarded the administration of Canada and must live on a pension, Wilkes soliloquizes:

> At present the word is LIBERTY
> [*Pensive* and *silent again;* then aloud.]

> O Canada! what a fine thing wou'd it have been
> with a thousand or fifteen hundred a year,
> besides perquisites!—O Bute! how
> shall I forgive thee!
> To be reveng'd on thee, I could commit—
> even sodomy of soul. . . .

By discrediting the Peace, Wilkes hopes to topple the ministry, and ultimately to overthrow the king and turn America into a commonwealth.[6] Constant concern over imperial affairs insured a steady flow of political verse throughout the colonies, in this case a dark undercurrent in the more prevalent hopes for a new era of Learning and Peace.

The most clangorous verse controversies erupted where local politics was most complex and shrill—in Philadelphia. Here verse was not only an established medium of political expression but a particularly important means of public debate, rivalling the literary wars of London itself. One series of events just after the Peace fomented dozens of scurrilous broadsides and pamphlets that were hawked about in taverns, barbershops, and throughout the city. The occasion was the so-called Paxton affair and the subsequent Philadelphia elections of 1763–64. In December 1763, some Scotch-Irish Presbyterians murdered six Indians who were living under the protection of the government near the frontier town of Paxton, and fourteen more Indians harbored in the workhouse at Lancaster. On February 4, 1764, rumors reached Philadelphia that between 700 and 1,500 "Paxton Boys" were marching on the city to kill the Indians in the barracks. When news arrived the next morning that the pack had reached Germantown, alarm bells rang and the militia collected. But the presumed marauders turned out to be a company of German butchers and bakers. A second alarm arrived on the seventh, and also proved false. Benjamin Franklin and others met with the actual Paxton men in a tavern near Germantown and persuaded them to return home, after promising to consider their grievances.[7]

The Paxton affair had something of the impact of the My Lai massacre. Reflecting longstanding conflict between the militancy of the Pennsylvania western frontier and the pacifism of Quaker Philadelphia, it kindled many smoldering issues. The December raids were mounted in retaliation for earlier Indian raids on white frontier settlements. But the Paxton settlers had killed friendly Indians, suspecting that they were shielding hostile Indians. Many Philadelphians considered the justification a shallow excuse for a religious crusade by Presbyterians bent on exterminating heathens. In Philadelphia, many Quakers took up arms, to the distress of many other Quakers, and to the satisfaction of those who considered Quaker pacifism hypocritical. Each issue became the subject of ballads, broadsides, skits, and newspaper poems, only a few of which can be noticed here, in a wide variety of literary forms. Evidently they were widely read, for some went into two editions. Virtually all of the many prose pamphlets in the controversy quoted Pope, Thomson, Swift, Shakespeare, and classical poets, while in his "Narrative of the Late Massacre" (1764) Benjamin Franklin quoted at length from *The Odyssey* to illustrate the laws of hospitality and proper treatment of strangers. The fact that an event which aroused such passion could be treated in such terms demonstrates both the highly literary approach to politics in the period and the value which the major English poets and playwrights had as political thinkers.

Versifiers condemned or defended the behavior of the Paxton Boys and the Quakers. The pseudonymous author of *The Paxtoniade* reviled the Presbyterians out of their own mouths as religious fanatics "fill'd up to the Brim with internal Lights" who regard the Indians as *"Cananites"* and hope to:

> Destroy them quite frae out the Land;—
> And for it we have God's Command.
> We should do him a muckle Pleasure,
> As ye in your Books may read at leisure.

In defense of the frontiersmen the author of *"A New* and Mild METHOD *totally to* extirpate the INDIANS" depicted the Indians as "greasy Sons of Murder" and recommended

> A scheme to please the tender-hearted,
> Who cannot be from *Indians* parted.
> No shooting then through Head or Liver,
> We'd serve 'em as they do the Beaver,
> For while some lusty Fellows held 'em,
> Some others should not *scalp,* but *g–ld* 'em.
> Then would our Offspring ne'er by Scoundrils
> Be vilely hack'd and murder'd round Hills.

A more elaborate work, a sixteen-page skit entitled *The Paxton Boys* (Philadelphia, 1764), included engravings of some Indians burning cottages, butchering children, and scalping, with engraved verses beneath the vignettes stressing the need to take up arms. Other verses charged the Quakers with indifference to the actual suffering of the frontiersmen, whose annihilation increased their political power in the city, or with hypocrisy for refusing to fight the Indians but taking up arms against the Paxtons, according to a special rule "By which 'tis plain, they may be right/ Whether they do, or do not fight." [8]

The Paxton controversy remained alive in the Pennsylvania elections of

1764, whose main issue was whether to retain the proprietary government in Pennsylvania or, as Franklin hoped, bring the colony directly under the Crown. In the voluminous accompanying literary war, the pro-proprietary party dug out of one of Franklin's essays a presumed ethnic slur against "Palatine Boors," i.e., Germans, for establishing their language and manners in Pennsylvania. Franklin's supporters claimed that by "Boors" he had meant "peasants." Yet, with a libelous scurrility distinctive to the political-literary combat of Philadelphia, the tag was used to solidify German resentment against Franklin. He appears in one satirical engraving pointing at a group of distant Germans and remarking, "See how those Palatine Boors herd together." The Germans reply, "None call us Boors but Sons for Whores." An engraved verse beneath the vignette proposes a toast:

> Drink a Health to the Boors
> Who turn'd BEN out of Doors
> And like Heroes erected their Banners
> For he said they were Swine
> Who did *Herd* and combine
> To spread both their Language and Manners.

Other versifiers abused Franklin's mother or charged him with fathering an illegitimate child by his maidservant, whom he then released to beg in the streets. Tit for tat, Franklin's chief defender, Isaac Hunt (the father of the essayist and poet Leigh Hunt) besmirched the faculty of the College of Philadelphia, including Provost William Smith, who had brought Benjamin West to the school. In eight distinct pamphlets he accused them of drawing the anti-Franklin engravings, and balanced the paternity charge against Franklin by charging "Black SMITH" with lusting after black women. Among the other faculty members he found instances of pederasty, wifebeating, spreading venereal disease, teaching scatology at the College, and secret wishes to *"Fling up your Mother's Duds."* [9]

If not often written in the language of the "elegant Minds" Franklin sought, the voluminous topical verse at the time of the Peace contained its own sort of literary promise. Quickly written to meet evolving and escalating crises, journalistic in intent and usually meant to sting, it was for the most part crude. Yet it drew literary men of varying gifts into politics, encouraged people of all social classes and degrees of literacy to express their views, and both stimulated and fulfilled a public demand for poetry. However limited and local, too, events like a preferential bailment or Quaker traffic in arms aroused well-understood passions. They gave writers twin advantages that colonial culture as a whole lacked: the sense of a subject and the sense of an audience. They granted importance to the local scene in the uniqueness of its "Buckskins" and squaws, affecting people's lives in a way that inspired concrete utterance, as the attempt to merely imitate the pastorals and odes in vogue overseas did not. The willingness to treat the local scene and the awareness that other citizens desired to hear about it promised that public events of greater moment and wider impact, should they occur, might inspire something finer and less parochial, verse perhaps of eloquent feeling and continental thrust.

In one place outside of local politics, too, literature was pursued with an intentness that the few volumes of poems published in America fails to suggest: the colonial colleges. Indeed, most of the volumes were the works of college students. In April 1763 the *Massachusetts Gazette* reported that a collection of poems from Harvard on the recent accession had been presented to the new king and "most graciously received by him." On its front page, the newspaper printed remarks on the volume from the London *Monthly Review*, allowing that "what we could not endure from an illustrious University, we can easily pardon in an infant Seminary." Although the Harvard poems lacked the "classical elegance and correctness, which distinguish the productions of Oxford and Cambridge," the reviewers felt pleased as Englishmen "to see science and literature extending themselves with our conquests." [10] Colonials probably read no condescension into such remarks, and gladly accepted invidious comparison as praise.

Another "infant Seminary" provided less qualified evidence that literature was following the route of English conquest. The College of Philadelphia had been chartered to grant degrees in 1755, under its twenty-eight-year-old provost, William Smith. The son of a physician in Aberdeen, Scotland, Smith had tutored for a while in London before emigrating to New York in 1751. Two years later he published an important pamphlet on education, *General Idea of the College of Mirania*. It led to his being chosen to head the Academy of Philadelphia, which he transformed into the College. While serving as provost, he became prominent in local politics and, although damned as "Black Smith" in the recent election, remained a busy, liberal Anglican clergyman more interested in the rewards of virtue than in punishment for sin.[11]

By profession a politician, preacher, and educator, Smith was by disposition a literary man. He had attended the University of Aberdeen during a period of basic reorganization in the Scottish school system, when the study of scholastic logic and metaphysics gave up its primacy in the curriculum to such modern subjects as natural history, mathematics, and, particularly, rhetoric and belles-lettres. In the early 1750's Smith published his poetry in newspapers in the Middle Colonies, and issued a volume of his prose and verse in New York. In his *General Idea* he invoked

Lord Kames's popular argument that taste resembles the moral sense, and proposed that by encouraging the arts, the colleges could contribute to the solidity and tranquility of the state. "Mirania," his utopian school, would offer comprehensive instruction in rhetoric, composition, and literary criticism. Under his guidance, "Mirania" became the College of Philadelphia.[12]

An important product of Smith's views was the public commencements held at the College, such as the one celebrating the Peace in 1763. Although other colonial colleges held lengthy commencements, those at Philadelphia were particularly elaborate and literary. Smith advocated recitals to build character, to prepare students for the bar or the pulpit, and to elevate the country's oratorical standard. Declamation "corrects unbecoming bashfulness," he wrote, "gives the youth presence of mind, habituates them to speak in public, and has been the means of producing many young orators, that have occasionally entertained large audiences; and it is hoped will soon become an honour and an ornament to their country." Smith had support for his views from his political enemy Benjamin Franklin, who in his own "Idea of the English School" urged that "Speeches and Scenes in our best Tragedies and Comedies (avoiding every Thing that could injure the Morals of Youth) . . . be got by Rote, and the Boys exercis'd in delivering or acting them. . . ." The local *Gazette* added that training in correct speech was the more necessary in Pennsylvania, "where the true Pronounciation of the *English* Language might soon be lost, without proper Care to preserve it in the rising Generation, as we are a Mixture of People from almost all Corners of the World; speaking a Variety of Languages and Dialects." [13] Emphasizing training in public speaking in his curriculum, Smith built a rostrum for classroom use and a stage for public exhibitions.

Although the exercises were justified as a socially useful branch of forensics, they took on a life of their own. Carefully composed beforehand by the students and often distributed as printed pamphlets to commencement-goers entering the College Hall, the exercises were in effect plays, smuggled into Philadelphia in full view of Quaker maledictions against the stage.

The theatrical character of 'public speaking' at the College is illustrated by a performance during the Christmas holidays of 1756–57 of *Alfred*, a masque by Thomas Arne adapted from James Thomson. The *Pennsylvania Gazette* devoted a good part of four issues to reprinting the work with explanation and comment.[14] Smith's choice was significant, for Thomson was a highly regarded poet in the colonies, not only for *The Seasons* but also for his politics. The Anglo-Saxon government of Alfred was itself in many minds the original of English free institutions, so that Thomson's work, according to the *Gazette*, celebrated "a Love of Liberty and a Concern for the Commerce and Glory of Great Britain." Smith and his students altered the masque to include a hymn with words by Milton and music by Handel—perhaps the first public performance of Handel in the colonies. They also added a Berkelian prophecy of artistic progress in America, extending Thomson's "Prophecy of the future Greatness of *England*," the *Gazette* said, "so far as to include these Colonies."

Smith's alteration may have established what became a convention for later college exercises, particularly commencements. Not only in 1757 and in 1763, but again in 1765, one student during the commencement period dedicated verses to the trustees of the College, prophesying that like England, which had once been a wasteland, its sparsely settled colonies would also increase in population and urbanity, begetting poets to hallow American rivers and estates:

> Just so, in time (if right the Muse descries)
> Shall this wide realm with tow'ry cities rise;
> The spacious Delaware, thro' future song,
> Shall roll in deathless majesty along;
> Each grove and mountain shall be sacred made,
> As now is Cooper's hill and Windsor's shade.[15]

Quite naturally, since the young graduates themselves embodied the future, commencements became ritualistic occasions for public expression of the theme of cultural progress.

Not only through his curriculum did Smith try to create "future song." He was also a vigorous projector and fund-raiser and, most important of all, a responsive and inspiring teacher. In 1757 he and a "Society of Gentlemen" in Philadelphia created the *American Magazine*, the most distinguished literary periodical yet to appear in the country. Although it survived only a year, it featured poems by many of his students, and articles by him praising their work. At the time of the Peace, newspapers as far away as Savannah, Georgia, were reporting his efforts abroad to raise money for the College. He managed not only to have the 1763 commencement poem inserted in the *Liverpool Advertiser* but also to meet the great English actor David Garrick, who, he wrote home to the trustees, was "exceedingly kind in the matter [of fund raising], gave his House at first asking, and was sorry that the Season was so far advanced & that he had no night disengaged sooner." The result of Garrick's willingness to donate a night's receipts was a performance at the Theatre Royal in Drury Lane on April 27, 1763, for the benefit of the College of Philadelphia and King's College in New York. Under the direction of Felice di Giardini (a popular composer in the colonies), vocal and instrumental performers and boys from the Chapel Royal presented *The Cure of Saul* and airs by Handel, and songs.[16]

By the time of the benefit, Smith had already educated a group of students who were unique in the colonies, an elite literary, musical, and artistic coterie. The main figures in the group, all in their mid-twenties at the time of the Peace, were the painter Benjamin West, now in London; the poets Thomas Godfrey and Nathaniel Evans; and the Franklinian poet-musician Francis Hopkinson. Peripheral figures included Jacob Duché, who not long after playing the title role in *Alfred* entered the church; the Philadelphia socialite and poet Elizabeth Graeme; and the musician James Bremner, who gave a concert of "SOLEMN MUSIC, vocal and instrumental" at the College, with singing by the students.[17] Omnipresent, too, despite Smith's enmity, was Franklin, to whom the young poets addressed several poems.

Quite unlike the vitriolic topical verse of the period, the poetry of Smith's students has an academic gentility or pastoral blandness that is the literary counterpart of the amiable faces painted by Wollaston and Theus. Thomas Godfrey, perhaps the most promising student, was the son of a member of Franklin's self-improvement club, the Junto. A sensitive boy who had wanted to be a painter, he wrote in a variety of moods and forms: pastoral songs and verse epistles depicting his youthful artistic idylls with West, Hopkinson, and Evans along the Schuylkill; dialogues in the manner of the college commencement exercises; poems of incipient romantic melancholy portraying the "pleasing terrors" of Imagination.[18] Smith published several of his poems in the *American Magazine* and helped to have them reprinted in an English periodical. Godfrey undertook his chief work, however, after graduation, while working as a factor in North Carolina in 1759. It was *The Prince of Parthia*, a heroic tragedy in blank verse that deserves to be called the first play written by an American (see the later discussion). Godfrey's friend, Nathaniel Evans, born in Philadelphia in 1742, took an M.A. at the College, and carried letters of recommendation from Smith when he went abroad seeking a missionary post. Admitted to holy orders by the bishop of London, he returned to America in 1765, intending to establish a mission in New Jersey.

Anyone numbering the signs of promise in the colonial literary scene in 1763 might have begun with Godfrey and Evans as the most ambitious and gifted young poets in America. But both died young. The corpulent Godfrey, riding out into the Carolina country, was overcome by heat in August 1763. In 1765, Smith and Evans published his work in Philadelphia as *Juvenile Poems on Various Subjects*, while Evans mourned his friend in verse:

> Stranger, who e'er thou art, by fortune's hand
> Tost on the baleful *Carolinian* strand,

Oh! if thou seest perchance the POET'S grave,
The sacred spot with tears of sorrow lave;
Oh! shade it, shade it with ne'er-fading bays.
Hallowd's the place where gentle GODFREY lays.[19]

Evans, however, was no luckier. He had just entered his mission in New
Jersey when he died on October 29, 1767. Smith later edited and
published his poems.

The member of Smith's original group who possessed both talent and
staying power was Francis Hopkinson. Born in 1737, he was the first
student to enter the College of Philadelphia, where he displayed a
versatility that would make him poet, musician, artist, politician, a sort of
lesser Franklin. His early verse records American culture in the later stages
of the French and Indian War: the college commencements, the inspiring
presence of Smith, his friends Godfrey and Evans, Philadelphia belles, the
paintings of Wollaston and West, the visiting theatre company. As a
student, he may have composed the music for Smith's production of *Alfred*.
He also took up the harpsichord, exploring a repertoire of Italianate music
fashionable in European salons that lastingly shaped his taste. In touch
with the new English psalmody, he also wrote some anthems, one of which
James Lyon included in *Urania*. After taking an M.A. under Smith in 1760
he studied law in Philadelphia but stayed in close touch with the College
and with local cultural activities, writing odes for the College commencements, playing chamber works with other local amateurs, composing, and
serving as organist at St. Peter's Church in Philadelphia. Here, said one
listener, he "had a gallery of Ladies all dressed in white to sing to him &
made fine Musick." [20]

5. The Theatre

*Of the four major kinds of artistic activity in the North American colonies, the
professional theatre was the least developed and the least desired. No play by a native
American had ever been published or produced; only* The Prince of Parthia *and one
or two other plays had been written by Americans. No American had ever acted, danced,
or sung professionally on the stage. Since the first third of the eighteenth century, small
English theatrical troupes had found largely friendly audiences in the southern colonies
and in New York. Elsewhere, many colonists who otherwise hoped for or else cared
nothing about cultural progress signed petitions and called town meetings trying to repel
actors from the shores of America. In Quaker Philadelphia the theatre survived in a
climate of scorn; north of New York it was outlawed.*

Theatre in British America meant one troupe, although in 1763 it had two names. The London Company of Comedians, eternally sensitive to the moods of a ticklish public on whom its survival depended, changed its name at around the time of the Peace to The American Company of Comedians. The change was more than nominal, since the troupe had appeared in the colonies for more than a decade. They had been preceded by several smaller, short-lived troupes who since the early eighteenth century had performed in the principal rooms of colonial taverns, in private houses, in warehouses, or in primitive theatres. But sustained seasons, trained if not skilled acting, presentable costumes and scenery—a semblance of the London stage—came to the colonies only in the 1750's, one branch of an exfoliation of provincial theatres in England that brought English actors to Jamaica and Halifax and sent to America the London, now the American, Company of Comedians.[1]

The managers of the Company were David Douglass and the numerous Hallam family. The Hallams had played in London at fairs and at unlicensed theatres in the provinces since at least the 1730's. Around 1750, as managers of the New Wells Theatre in London, they found themselves harassed by new restrictions on theatrical performance. The theatre closed, but Lewis Hallam, Sr., gathered some of the family and undertook, his daughter said, to "try his fortune in America."[2] They arrived in Yorktown in 1752, and opened in Williamsburg. Here Lewis Hallam, Jr., twelve years old, made his debut as Portia's servant in *The Merchant of Venice* (and, in one account, froze and ran off the stage in tears). Upon the death of Hallam, Sr., in Jamaica around 1756, his widow married a printer-turned-actor named David Douglass. Together with the ex–Mrs. Hallam, Douglass reorganized and managed the Company. By 1763 they in effect monopolized the theatre in the North American colonies.

Like portraitists and music masters, actors were itinerants. They shuttled among urban centers like Newport, New York, Philadelphia, Annapolis, Charleston, Jamaica, and Barbados, playing en route in smaller places like Hobb's Hole, Fredericksburg, or Dumfries, and occasionally returning to England.[3] They timed their schedule to public events like the Annapolis racing season or the April session of the Virginia burgesses in Williamsburg, when the town filled with people from remote districts who had seen nothing recently and who eagerly took on the holiday mood.

The Company's flimsy buildings and crude properties did not give the audiences of 1763 much to look at. Theatres had been built for the Hallams in Williamsburg in 1752 and in New York in 1753. Around 1760, Douglass began to build a chain of new theatres. Lieutenant Governor Cadwallader Colden of New York gave him permission in 1761 to erect a theatre on Chapel (later Beekman) Street, a building some ninety feet long and forty wide. Costing about £650 to build, it seated about 350 spectators. The pit was probably sloped and flanked by two tiers of boxes, which probably could be reached only by passing over the stage. The gallery was probably reached by a narrow winding staircase from the small lobby. A nineteenth-century newspaper account described it as a "wooden building, in poor condition, with paper scenery, and a wretched wardrobe." In 1763, Douglass also contracted for a new theatre on Queen Street in Charleston, some seventy-five by thirty feet. The old theatre, long unused, had been vandalized by "evil disposed persons," one newspaper reported, who "cut and destroyed the scenes and furniture of the house." [4]

Divided into boxes, pit, and gallery, the theatres were lighted by candles made of tallow mixed with spermaceti, which dripped less than ordinary tallow. Footlights were probably metal boxes filled with oil, in which floated corks pierced with wicks. As happened in England, the Company often employed local decorative and portrait painters to paint scenery. William Williams—the Welsh sailor who inspired Benjamin West to his career—did scenery for Douglass in Philadelphia, although the Company's chief painter was Jacob Snyder (or Shnydore), whom Douglass hired in Providence in 1759. The Company used contemporary dress for contemporary plays, and for the most part in productions of Shakespeare; Hallam—like Thomas Betterton or David Garrick in London—apparently played Hamlet in frock coat, knee breeches, and tie wig. For other plays they seem to have used stage costumes standardized on the London stage. The Company employed a tailor named Weston, who also acted, as well as local barbers, hairdressers, play copyists, and related personnel. The nineteenth-century actor John Bernard—an important source of firsthand information about the Hallam-Douglass company—estimated that the theatres were fitted up to take in £150 nightly at a cost of about three times that sum. The cost of scenery and wardrobe was about the same, "so that the entire outlay, at starting, came under £1200. . . ." [5]

The Company usually performed on Monday, Wednesday, and Friday nights, with an occasional Saturday. The program was announced through ads in the local newspaper and by handbills sown throughout the city (ill., p. 120). Prices remained fairly steady throughout the century and everywhere in the colonies, typically four, six, and eight shillings for gallery, pit, or box. Curtain time was usually at six o'clock, although after the mid-1760's it became customary for spectators to send servants earlier to hold their seats. Another valuable witness, William Dunlap, recalled how between four and six o'clock "the front seats of the boxes were occupied by blacks of every age, waiting until their masters and mistresses made their appearance." In the lobby, one might buy the music for the evening's performance and, between acts, apples, raisins, peanuts, oranges, mince pies, and brandy and gin.[6]

An evening at the theatre in 1763 meant an entire evening. Performances lasted four or five hours. A typical program consisted of a long play (tragedy, comedy, or long ballad opera), an afterpiece (a short ballad opera, farce, or masque), and interludes of vocal and instrumental music—plus frequent encores of favorite songs and bits of business. The Company gave substantially the same offerings wherever they played, repeating anything that for one reason or another proved particularly appealing to a local audience, but often changing the program so that people could go week after week. Occasionally, plays or afterpieces were 'bespoken,' that is, performed at the request of some wealthy patron or civic group, insuring a good house. Benefit nights were frequently held for the profit of individual actors, the actor paying the expenses of the house and collecting the rest of the proceeds for himself.

In 1763 no play by an American had ever been produced; the Company featured what was most popular in London. Gossip about the London stage often appeared in local newspapers, and seems to have made an important fund of chitchat among colonials, to whom it epitomized metropolitan life. A versifier in the *Virginia Gazette* described some rather longing theatre gossip at a Williamsburg card party in 1769:

> This new scene of Garrick's I long much to see:—
> The cards are with you, Ma'am, but pray drink your tea—
> The dances so sprightly, the dresses so fine—
> I hope to be married; we only are nine:
> For taste and for elegance Drury Lane house—
> But mum—on this subject be still as a mouse;
> Some judges have told me, at fam'd Covent Garden,
> The masquerade scene is not there worth a farthing.

By far the most popular playwright on the colonial stage—reflecting the great midcentury revival of his plays in London—was Shakespeare. From the incomplete record that has survived, Hugh Rankin has computed that before 1776, fourteen of Shakespeare's plays were performed in the colonies at least 180 times, perhaps as many as 500 times. The single most popular play in the colonial theatre from 1763 to 1774 was *Romeo and Juliet*, the same play most frequently performed from 1747 to 1776 at both Covent Garden and Drury Lane theatres in London.[7] The American Company of Comedians used the same versions of Shakespeare that appeared on the English stage, heavily altered by David Garrick, Nahum Tate, and others.

The most popular comedy in the Company's repertoire was probably

George Farquhar's *The Beaux' Stratagem*. Another very popular play, although perhaps more often discussed than performed, was George Lillo's *George Barnwell*, a didactic sentimental drama sometimes said to be the first play that directly attempts to correct vice from the stage. It shows the temptation of a young man to steal and murder because of an unscrupulous woman. A Charleston newspaper commended it as "well adapted to the holidays when youth generally forms a considerable part of the audiences," its lesson being salutary for young men "who are trained up to the branches of mercantile business and who often have large trusts confided to their care." *George Barnwell* was one of a class of moralistic, middle-class works which the Company found it useful to mount in the several places where plays were unwelcome, hoping that it might, Douglass said, "have some influence with those who are otherwise no friends to the theatre."[8]

Another perennial favorite in London that became extremely popular in the British colonies was the ballad opera. The term applies to plays with songs in which the texts are set to old and familiar tunes, as in John Gay's prototypical *Beggar's Opera*. Ballad operas were long-lived. They had been performed in America at least since 1735, the date of a Charleston production of *Flora, or Hob in the Well*, which held the stage until late in the eighteenth century. In an abbreviated form, the ballad afterpiece, they were often used to conclude an evening at the theatre and to send the audience home lighthearted. One such afterpiece, *The Devil to Pay*, was first produced at Drury Lane in 1731 but remained popular in the colonies, being performed at least sixteen times between 1763 and 1774. Typical of the whole genre, the work features knockabout action and a reversal of social ranks. At one end of the social scale, Nell is beaten and abused by her husband Jobson, a cobbler. At the other end, Lady Loverule tyrannizes over her husband, servants, and tenants. An astrologer who has been ill-treated by high and low alike tries to get revenge by transposing them. Nell is exalted to the luxury of the manor and Lady Loverule is properly beaten and tamed by Jobson.[9]

The evening might also end with a short masque or farce. Masques consisted of songs, dances, poetry, and often of allegorical spectacle, based on some classical story. The masque of *Neptune and Amphitrite* was particularly popular as an afterpiece to performances of *The Tempest*, with music by Henry Purcell. "Farce" originally meant any short piece in one or two acts, heavily dependent on intrigue and usually bawdy, but came to mean any short afterpiece, such as *The Devil to Pay*. Very many works performed by The American Company of Comedians demanded music, and gave employment to local musicians, professional and amateur, half a dozen of whom were needed for the theatre orchestra, sometimes more.

Many contemporary accounts of the Company's actors have survived, around 1763 and later. The last third of the eighteenth century was itself a rather histrionic era, not only a great period for the stage but much devoted also to amateur theatricals, impersonation, masquerades, and the like. The many reviews of plays in colonial newspapers are largely reviews of performance, making it possible to reconstruct the styles of the Company in considerable detail. The number of actors in the 1763 company is uncertain, perhaps a dozen or fifteen. Most, even by provincial standards, were distinctly minor talents. None was a native American (no American had ever acted professionally). The Morrises were popular actors, known mostly, however, through accounts in the 1780's. Mrs. Morris was a "tall imposing, well-formed person" with a "very mysterious manner," one spectator recalled, although she often relied on the prompter. Her husband became celebrated for comic roles, in which "he seldom fails to excite ROARS OF bravo, bravo, bravissimo, encore. . . ." Douglass played important parts, but served more as manager of the Company. One contemporary described his wife, the ex–Mrs. Hallam, as a "respectable, matron-like dame, stately or querulous as occasion required." In order to applaud her it was "absolutely necessary to forget, that to touch the heart of the spectator had any relation to her function." [10]

Her son Lewis Hallam, Jr., was a youthful star who became for about twenty years the leading actor in America (ill., p. 121). Of medium height, thin and straight, an accomplished pantomimist, dancer, and fencer, he appeared in virtually all of the Company's productions, handling low rustic comedy roles as well as Hamlet and harlequin. A fencing accident gave one of his eyes a slight cast, at times imparting to his face an odd expression, which some reviewers criticized. He also had a reputation for being irascible and stingy when dealing with other actors, and for constantly "interlarding the text with small oaths." [11]

As the colonial standard of excellence in contemporary art, music, and poetry is summed up in the names Reynolds, Handel, and Pope, its theatrical standard is summed up in the name David Garrick. To judge from their diaries and essays, quite a few colonists had seen Garrick perform in London. Inevitably, he was the model against which Hallam and other leading actors were judged. Hallam invited the comparison by specializing in roles which Garrick had made famous in London. Some reviewers tasked him with slurring his speech, one advising him to "take copy from the inimitable *Garrick*, and speak plain English, whenever he assumes a Character that may be supposed to understand the Language." Others charged that his acting style was "stiff and prim," and inclined to rant. "His manner," said one witness, was of "that peculiar kind . . .

called 'the Old School,' and which Garrick effectually exploded. In tragedy he 'spouted,' by which I mean declaimed without passion." [12]

Many of Hallam's shortcomings, as his contemporaries considered them, belonged as much to colonial life as to him. Provincial culture is always conservative. It retains styles long after they have become unfashionable in the metropolis. In this case, Hallam's formalized style lagged behind the more natural style which Garrick had introduced to the London stage. It drew upon a vocabulary of gestures that had been standardized by the actor Aaron Hill and in older manuals like *The Thespian Precepter*. They prescribed gesture and voice for states like Vexation, Admiration, or for example, Wonder: "The eyes should be open, fixed upon the object of wonder, if visible, with the look of fear. If the hands hold anything, immediately allow it to drop. The whole body should be fixed in a contracted stooping posture, with the mouth open and the open hands held up." By London standards, Hallam was probably wanting, and indeed when he later returned briefly to Covent Garden in *Hamlet* he was considered inadequate for the role. Yet to provincials who had not seen Garrick he was good enough. Perhaps the most just appraisal of Hallam's abilities came from Alexander Graydon, who saw the Company perform when he was a law student in Philadelphia. He recalled that all the dramatic leads were "*his* without a competitor" and found Hallam "always a pleasing performer," inclined to tear a passion to tatters but the embodiment of a ripe theatrical tradition matured through generations of his family:

> No one could tread the stage with more ease: Upon it, indeed, he might be said to have been cradled, and wheeled in his go-cart. In tragedy, it cannot be denied, that his declamation was either mouthing or ranting; yet a thorough master of all the tricks and finesses of his trade, his manner was both graceful and impressive.

To a colonial Philadelphian, Graydon said, the versatile Hallam was "as much the soul" of the theatre "as ever Garrick was of Drury Lane." [13]

Unlike itinerant painters and music teachers, actors stayed within the pale of respectable society only barely. Even people connected with the theatre were often suspect. When advertising for local musicians to fill the theatre orchestra, Douglass felt bound to assure them of "protection from any manner of insult." That actors were widely and deeply suspected of being scoundrels is suggested by how insistently their sympathizers identified them as gentlefolk. The adjective routinely applied to actors in friendly reviews and letters (and which they routinely applied to themselves) was "genteel." Reporting the funeral of one actress in the Company, Mrs. Harman (a granddaughter of Colley Cibber), a sympathetic New York newspaper observed that her corpse was "attended by a very genteel procession to the cemetery." [14]

The degree of mistrust varied distinctly by regions, becoming more intense and outspoken as the Company advanced northward. In South Carolina and Virginia, Douglass could usually count on a large and friendly house. Philadelphia, however, contained several religious and social groups hostile to the theatre. Beginning with William Penn's "Frame of Government," the Quakers had consistently and expressly discouraged the stage, arguing that it lured people from their work, induced them to squander their money, deluded young women, and gave a false picture of life. In 1682 the Pennsylvania Assembly passed a law providing public condemnation, fines, and ten days' imprisonment with hard labor (or twenty shillings) to "whosoever shall introduce into this Province, or frequent such rude and riotous sports and practices as prizes [probably for fencing, wrestling, or boxing matches], stage-plays, masques, revels, bull-baitings, cock-fightings. . . ." A similar proposal was made for the Jerseys, of which Penn was also the proprietor, but was never enacted into law. When the elder Hallam first tried to play in Philadelphia, in 1754, he touched off a flurry of petitions and newspaper attacks. When the Company, reorganized under Douglass, tried to erect a theatre on Society Hill, Quakers and Presbyterians forced an act through the Assembly forbidding the building, even though Douglass had permission from the governor and although an equally large number of Philadelphians enjoyed the theatre.[15]

In New England, contempt for the theatre was even more intense and ingrained. Opposition went back to Increase Mather's *A Testimony Against several Profane and Superstitious Customs* (1687) and beyond that to William Prynne's violently anti-theatre *Histriomastix* (1633) and, behind that, to a large patristic literature condemning plays. Mather flatly pronounced the theatre "dangerous to the souls of Men." By a 1750 law, theatre was simply banned from Boston. Apparently as part of a larger strategy to reinvigorate the Company by changing its name and building new theatres, the younger Hallam and Douglass had tried shortly after the Peace to extend their itinerary, and to open at least some territory in New England. Skirting impregnable Boston, they ventured into Rhode Island, and attempted a trial run in Newport in August 1761. To rally support and evade their opponents, they used several familiar gambits. They printed in the *Newport Mercury* a testimonial signed by the governor, Council, and a hundred citizens of Virginia testifying to the "discretion in their private character" and recommending them as "capable of entertaining a sensible and polite audience." They advertised the performances as "Moral Dialogues," touting *Othello*, for instance, as a "Moral Dialogue in Five Parts." They promised to end the evening by 10:30 so that the spectator might "go home at a sober hour, and reflect upon what he has seen, before he retires to rest." Finally, a favorite ploy, they opened with a benefit performance, to buy corn for the poor.

The campaign of ingratiation worked, at least for several weeks. The Company managed to play until the end of October, after which the *Mercury* commended them for being everything the Virginians had promised, skilled actors and "irreproachable" persons. The newspaper thanked them for giving a second charity performance, a deed that "can not without an uncommon degree of malevolence be ascribed to an interested or selfish view." [16] Very likely a friendly printer or even Douglass himself wrote this blurb, since another of his tactics was to befriend journalist-printers, who, we have seen, reaped business from the Company in printing handbills, tickets, and advertisements, and perhaps in commissions, the printer often serving as ticket agent.

This surprising success encouraged Douglass and Hallam in July 1762 to attempt a run at an improvised theatre in Providence. This time they did not succeed. A town meeting resolved to prohibit plays and applied to the Assembly for a formal act suppressing theatre in the colony. With characteristic cheek, Hallam and Douglass played on. Enraged, the town meeting met again, insisted that the current drought and its scarcities made expensive diversions unseemly, and presented a petition with four hundred signatories. A counter-petition was circulated, asking that the players be allowed to perform a while longer, as many people in theatreless Boston wished to see them. The Assembly, however, clamped down. It enacted a formal anti-theatre law, modeled on that of Massachusetts but more severe. Whereas Massachusetts had imposed a £20 fine for each day's leasing of a building to actors plus a £5 penalty on each of the actors, the Rhode Island law imposed £50 each day and £100 on the actor.[17] The act was to be publicly declared by beat of drums through the streets of Providence. The sheriff took it with him to the theatre and read it after the performance. Some opponents of the act, by one account, tried to storm the temporary theatre, which was defended from the nearby gun-house by cannon.

Rhode Island thus joined the rest of New England, and half of Philadelphia, in treating The American Company of Comedians as moral criminals. Lewis Hallam, David Douglass, and their actors, Garricks or not and under whatever name, were not the sensible and virtuous minds they wanted or needed.

The distinguished audiences gathered in New York and Philadelphia for the commencement exercises of 1763 expected a new era of tranquility and of quickening translation. The cultural life they knew as colonial Englishmen in some ways made their expectations seem extravagant, and in other ways sustained them.

America maintained a nursling of English culture that drew its tastes and ideas from the mother country and from Europe, that gave back little if anything, and that remained virtually unknown to its splendid parent. The tone of professional concert life was sociable and frivolous. The theatre meant a mediocre troupe of English actors given to shabby ruses performing in theatres thrown up for a month, a crude standard which half of British America, moreover, found so offensive to decency that it repulsed it with fines, petitions, insults, and in one case cannons. By the form of cultural accounting most colonists used, America in 1763 had still to acquire for the first time most of the features of metropolitan cultural life. No American paintings hung in any important European collections. Only one native American, James Lyon, had published any music, and in his case only a few tunes. The colonies had no magazines and no professional writers, indeed no one who had published a very long poem or a novel. No play by an American had ever been published or produced, nor had any American ever acted professionally on the stage. No body of American criticism existed to recognize talent and to mediate between artist and public. There were no dominant artistic personalities; hardly a name conjured up a style, a temperament, a vision. Except, perhaps, for young Benjamin West, no one aimed very high or created with much urgency. At its core, American culture lacked ambition and focus, the sense of a subject.

More encouragingly, a large and enthusiastic audience existed for the arts, and supported them in their homes and through their churches and colleges. Colonial Englishmen demanded prints, as well as portraits and miniatures, to record their dignified ease and benevolent prosperity. Three painters in their mid-twenties promised that the country would not lack for portraitists as Wollaston, Hesselius, and Theus retired. If few colonials cared about history painting, there were enough to send Benjamin West abroad to learn its theory and technique, his health and genius permitting. Music dealers and instrument makers in the larger urban centers supplied the needs of young ladies and gentlemen preparing to step into the world with polish. Anglican churches gave employment to several skilled organ makers and organists. The long-established Congregational and Presbyterian vocal music had recently been invigorated by new English fashions, establishing the new repertoire and new style of Lyon's *Urania*. Young men with sophisticated literary aspirations might find public figures like

William Smith eager to promote them, and educational ideals designed to practice and display their talent. Limited as was its appeal, too, the topical verse on the Paxton affair or the Virginia General Court issued from a reservoir of anonymous literary ability that might be enlarged by issues of larger moment, and addressed itself to a public that enjoyed and respected poetry as a medium of debate. If scorned by one half of British America, David Douglass had an enthusiastic audience in the other half, and a long theatrical tradition behind him. Like the founder of the new-named American Company he had decided to "try his fortune in America," and he was not easily discouraged.

The question was whether, as many believed, this lively but distinctly provincial culture would rapidly progress now that England had established its empire in North America and brought Peace.

Part Two

Demonstrations—American Culture 1765–1770

The Peace welcomed by the young commencement orators, Americans soon learned, had its price and was hard to keep.

To maintain the large army it needed in North America to secure its recently established empire against France and Spain, the British government initiated a program of taxing the colonies. The Stamp Act of 1765 incensed many colonists, who burned effigies in the streets, refused to buy or use English goods, and indited vehement verses accusing England of devouring those she was obliged to safeguard. Their emotional protests, and sympathy for their plight in London, led to a repeal of the act in 1766. Americans rejoiced again in the return of peace, composing poems of loyalty and commissioning statues of the king and of Pitt. But in 1767 Parliament passed another tax program, the Townshend Revenue Act. Renewed protest led to the occupation of Boston by British troops and the killing of several civilians. This act, too, was repealed. In 1770, statues of the king and of Pitt were set in place, as peace resumed once more.

Cultural activities continued amid the alternating defiance and gratitude, in some ways hampered, in others not. The tax programs provoked scores of poems and skits. The aspiring painters of 1763 began to fulfill their promise. In London, West devoted himself to history painting and took on his own first pupils, among them the Maryland ex-saddler Charles Willson Peale. (Not much is known about their careers during the Stamp Act crisis, making the first few sections on West and Peale that follow quite fragmentary.) In Boston, Copley grew in skill and wealth but considered going to

London, where an exhibition of his Boy with Squirrel *brought emphatic praise and invitations to study. The depressed economy and calls for stringency fed existing displeasure with* The American Company, *although the managers introduced an impressive new repertoire and new personnel, and found a part for the first professional American actor in the first professionally produced American play.*

6. Stamp Act Protests: August–December 1765

In April 1764—only a year after the long French and Indian wars had been ended by treaty—Parliament passed a Sugar Act, placing a three-penny tax on molasses. The act produced not mere grumbling, but shock. Several colonists published pamphlets contesting it, buttressing their commercial arguments by broad philosophical and political principles, and assertions of their rights as Englishmen. Governor Francis Bernard of Massachusetts reported home that the act caused greater alarm in the colonies than had the fall of Fort William Henry to the French in 1757.

Also in 1764, Lord Grenville prepared a Stamp Act, passed by Parliament on March 22, 1765. Some twenty-five pages long, the printed act described taxes for pamphlets, newspapers, almanacs, and such documents as college diplomas. These would have to be printed on paper embossed with a stamp and available from a stamp distributor. Newspapers were taxed a penny a single sheet; a tax of a shilling per sheet was laid on pamphlets or papers totaling more than one and fewer than six sheets in octavo, twelve in quarto, or twenty in folio. These taxes produced not mere shock, but outrage. The outrage subsided and peace returned, but for nearly a year the colonists assailed these penny taxes in angry pamphlets, verses, cartoons, and demonstrations.[1]

The anger had several sources. Coming only months after the Peace, the taxes grated on expectations of renewed contentment. The Sugar Act, too, hit hard at large overseas traders: "the Merchants say," Governor Bernard reported, "There is an end of the trade in this Province." The method of collecting customs also proved irritating, the Navy interrupting commerce to inspect ships. Both acts came amidst a depression that had already caused several notable bankruptcies. Expecting economic ruin, one versifier called upon the world to:

> Come, see our Poor, and bring a Bit of Bread!
> Come, see our Liberties without a Head!

> Come, see our Trade declining more and more,
> And ragged Want approaching ev'ry Door!

Moreover, in taxing legal documents and the press, the Stamp Act disturbed basic social arrangements. In a verse "DREAM," the bond, the summons, the diploma, the newspaper, each type of stamped paper spoke a verse paragraph, revealing with "grievous moan" or "heart-felt anguish and distress" how, without itself, property rights would be insecure, debts unpaid, widows and orphans undefended, learning neglected:

> The *Probate Papers* next, with many a sigh,
> 'Must we be st—pt' with tender accent cry:
> 'We who our life and breath, so freely spend,
> 'The fatherless and widow to defend.
> 'And dare their needy and defenceless state,
> 'So boldly plead against the rich and great.
> 'Let not that cruel st—p destroy our pow'r,
> 'To help the helpless, in the needy hour.'

Lamenting that their grievances had so far been ignored, the papers called on king and Parliament to repeal an act destructive to the fabric of society.[2]

The colonists' anger arose not only from such immediate economic and social woes but also from their way of perceiving the mother country's intent. In many minds the new taxes carried sinister political implications charged with powerful emotional overtones (see the next section, "Excursus: Whig Sentimentalism"). Colonials made sense of the Stamp Act in terms of a familiar ideology drawn from classical authorities, Enlightenment rationalists, common law, and Puritan Covenant theology, and made coherent by the ideas of English country and coffeehouse politicians at the turn of the century. Perhaps the best known and most quoted of these Whig radicals were John Trenchard and Thomas Gordon, authors of *Cato's Letters* (1720) and *The Independent Whig* (1721). Opponents of the government of Prime Minister Robert Walpole, they created an image of the mother country which many Americans retained throughout the century: England awash and sinking in corruption. What enabled them to see this was their respect for the individual and their neo-Puritan mistrust of government. They described liberty as an "unalienable Right," and defined it as the "Power which every Man has over his own Actions, and his Right to enjoy the Fruit of his Labour, Art, and Industry, as far as by it he hurts not the Society, or any Members of it, by taking from any Member, or by hindering him from enjoying what he himself enjoys."[3]

Trenchard and Gordon saw liberty threatened by man's lust for domination. Lust for domination accounted for the success of despotism in

Turkey, Germany, and Denmark, and the rise, they felt, of despotism in England. Despotism began not in Providence or in nebulous historical forces, but in the ambitions of particular, ruthless men (thus the constant analysis of motives following the Stamp Act and in later protests, the many 'confessions,' soliloquies, and parodies of speeches). Most Americans saw the Stamp Act arising from court favorites around the king, usurpers who were blocking the king from his people, ultimately hoping to seize power for themselves. The most reviled of them was the Earl of Bute, a Scotsman who had been the tutor of the young king, and from 1761 to 1763 his chief minister of state. Many in England and America believed that Bute was the actual author of the Stamp Act, as well as the lover of the king's mother.[4]

To Whigs who had seen despotism unfold in Denmark or Turkey, each new English measure thus seemed the next step in a long-range plan to enslave England and America. The proliferation of stamp distributors and other office-seekers sending money and taxes back to the ministry was part of a tried and proven scenario, preliminary to the destruction of parliamentary liberties and the introduction of standing armies. As Bernard Bailyn summarizes the radical Whig understanding of official English policy, "the fear of a comprehensive conspiracy against liberty throughout the English-speaking world—a conspiracy believed to have been nourished in corruption, and of which, it was felt, oppression in America was only the most immediately visible part—lay at the heart of the Revolutionary movement." [5]

The conspiratorial Whig view of the Stamp Act appeared with answerable complexity in a 1765 cartoon entitled *The Deplorable State of America* (ill., p. 126). Offered for sale by the Boston engraver Nathaniel Hurd, it was very likely the creation of his friend the Boston painter John Singleton Copley.[6] Such prints, popular in England since midcentury, were known as "caricaturas," differing from modern political cartoons in being crowded with figures and balloons instead of grossly exaggerating a few essential features. Copley traced the Stamp Act to a French plot to win back America through Lord Bute. The figure flying at top right represents France, which extends a money-filled purse to a comet marked with a boot—a visual pun on Bute—which sheds rays of influence on Britannia, flying below. France says in a balloon, "What a surprising virtue there is in Gold. With it I make the very Stars shed their influence as I please." Britannia in turn holds out a box to a toga-clad figure representing America, saying, "Take it Daughter its only ye S____p A__t." Minerva —Wisdom—cautions America that it represents Pandora's Box, packed with irrepressible calamities. Some of these have already sprung. To the left, a figure of Mercury, signifying Commerce, flies away. In the background stand several ships drydocked for sale and a group of unemployed sailors, as well as a group of well-dressed men who lament declining trade. (A gravedigger nearby shovels dirt on stamp distributors, asking, "Will you resign?"; they reply, "Yes, yes, I will!") The larger effect of the act appears in the central image of the Liberty Tree, against which leans Loyalty. As a blast of wind shakes the tree from above, Loyalty cries, "O tis a horrid blast I fear I shall lose my support." Beneath the tree lies the stricken and expiring figure of Liberty itself. Out of some Scottish thistles in the foreground—another hit at Bute—a viper emerges and stings the stricken figure. The only hope held out in this representation of the deplorable state of America is a dog inscribed "W. P - - t's Dog." It urinates on the thistle—illustrating the hope that the new ministry which had replaced Grenville's would repeal the act.

This conspiracy against liberty would actively begin its work on November 1, the date appointed for the Stamp Act to become operative. As it approached, the colonies tried to unite in opposition. In June, the Massachusetts House of Representatives called an intercolonial Congress to discuss the tax measures. The *Constitutional Courant* of Burlington, New Jersey, repeated the call, adopting on its masthead a device based upon the famous "Join or Die" device created in 1754 by Benjamin Franklin, a snake severed into eight parts representing colonies.[7] Meeting on October 7 in New York, the Congress adopted a *Declaration of Rights and Grievances*, written by John Dickinson, stating the colonial constitutional position on the Stamp Act.

Many individual communities met in the streets. The first large public demonstration, staged in Boston on August 14, was apparently organized by some artisans and shopkeepers who called themselves The Loyal Nine, the core of a group that soon became known as The Sons of Liberty. They probably enlisted leaders of the traditional November Fifth—Pope's Day—ceremonies. Contingents from the South and North ends of Boston that traditionally fought for an effigy of the Pope now joined in hanging an effigy of the stamp distributor for Massachusetts, Andrew Oliver.

The purpose of such effigies, as John Drayton of Pennsylvania explained, was to "speak to the sight and sense of the multitude," that is, the presumably excitable and illiterate lower classes. To arouse "the multitude" and intimidate the stamp distributors, such effigies seem to have been fashioned realistically, perhaps to a likeness. Charles Willson Peale described an effigy that he saw the same August: "The face was a well made mask which was generally believed to resemble the Chief Judge which gave him such a Pannick that he Left the Town Secretly." As if at a real execution, too, Oliver's effigy was hanged next to his house from a large elm, to which a plaque was soon affixed designating it The Tree of

Liberty.[8] Alongside the effigy hung some verse and pictures, especially a large boot (i.e., Bute) with a devil crawling out of it.

Oliver's effigy swung until cut down by demonstrators later in the day, as described by an anonymous Boston versifier:

> With rapid haste some to the tree repair,
> And on their shoulders bear a ladder there.
> One draws his knife, and running to their aid,
> Ascends the limbs, that bear each lifeless shade.
> Then cuts the ropes in presence of them all,
> And as he cuts the ghastly *objects* fall.
> Down on the earth in horrid form they lie;
> A frightful sight to each beholding eye. . . .

After marching the dismounted effigy to the Town House as a threat to the Council, the demonstrators returned to Oliver's home, to behead it. Grown by evening, said the *Gazette*, into "some Thousands," they paraded to the docks, setting fires, tearing down fences, pilfering liquor and silverware, and demolishing a new building intended for a stamp office. They took the effigy to Fort Hill, symbolically stamped on it, and burned it, using wood from a building owned by Oliver, returning to Oliver's home to destroy his furniture. Although he had never received an official commission as stamp distributor, Oliver promised nevertheless to submit a letter of resignation.[9]

His promised resignation, and the widely reported Boston demonstrations that forced it, inspired effigies, verses, and liberty trees elsewhere. A week later the townspeople of Norwich, Connecticut, emulated the "noble patriotic fire," one of them said, which "shone so conspicuous at Boston. . . ." A procession bore through town the effigies of a local stamp man and of the Devil, "attended by such invectives, huzza's and disdainful music as are the pure emanations of injured freedom. . . ." The Devil held the Stamp Act and wore a cautionary motto, quoted from Joseph Addison's play *Cato*:

> When vice prevails and impious men bear sway,
> The post of honour is a private station.

The effigies were burned on a hill, followed by toasts. Citizens of Newport hanged and burned an effigy labeled The Stamp Man which held the Stamp Act in one hand and a letter from Bute in the other. A song posted at the Town House praised liberty and explained:

> He who for a Post or Base Sordid Pelf
>   His Country Betrays, Makes a Rope for himself
> Of this an Example Before you we Bring
> Of these Infamous Rogues, Who in Effigy swing.[10]

Inhabitants of Lebanon, Connecticut, treated the stampman Jared Ingersoll to a mock trial. After being 'virtually represented' his effigy was put in a cart, a rope on its neck, and drawn through the streets for public "ignominy and contempt" before undergoing a mock execution.

The cart contained a sort of animated cartoon. On one side was an effigy of America, Ingersoll's "injured country, represented by a lady dressed in sable, with chains rattling at her feet." America begged Ingersoll not to enchain her, to which "her ungrateful, degenerate son replied, in a label proceeding from his mouth, *Perish my country, so that I get that reward.*" America's reaction was spelled out "glowing in capital letters upon her breast":

> "————*Heaven crush those Vipers,*
> *Who, singled out by a Community,*
> *To guard her Rights, shall for a grasp of Ore,*
> *Or paltry Office, sell them to the Foe.*"

The cart also contained effigies of Lord Grenville and of the Devil, who offered Ingersoll a purse to enslave America. At one point the Devil "turned up his breech and discharged fire, brimstone, and tar, in Ingersoll's face, setting him all in a blaze; which, however, Mr. Grenville generously extinguished with a squirt." At last the effigy was hanged and, at the bidding of the Devil, plunged amidst huzzas into a pyramid of fire.[11]

The demonstrations did little to halt the arrival of stamped paper, however, much less the approach of the day appointed for the Stamp Act to take effect, "the fatal first of November."[12] October 31 brought several last-minute instructions, vows, and efforts at decisive action. Some two hundred New York merchants agreed to import nothing more from Great Britain until the Stamp Act was repealed. On the same date, a versifier in an "extraordinary issue" of the *Massachusetts Gazette* issued some "Advice from the COUNTRY" in which he urged Americans generally to subsist on their own produce, however unrefined:

> Their Cates, and their Gear,
>   We want not, to chear,
>   The Apples and Ox are our own:
> Our Palates to please,
> Beef, Butter, and Cheese,
>   And Cyder in plenty to crown.
>
> With Us of the Woods
> Lay aside your fine Goods,
>   Contentment depends not on cloaths;
> We hear, smell, and see,
> Taste and feel with high Glee,
>   And in Winter have Huts for Repose.

If Parliament laid new taxes that "Might and not Right must sustain,"

> Let us hive with the Bee,
> Eat the Crust of the Tree,
> And away to the Fig-Leaf again.

Such advice made the symbolic shepherds' weeds of the 1763 commencement exercises a form of real political action.

Also on October 31, Boston newspapers announced publication of a lengthy poem called *The Times.* The author (perhaps Benjamin Church), presented himself as a swain of rude integrity:

> This humble cot conceals a tyrant's foe;
> By nature artless, unimprov'd by pains,
> No favour courts me, and no fear restrains,
> Wild as the soil, and as the heav'ns severe,
> All rudely rough, and wretchedly sincere. . . .

The vehement swain recalled the volume of college panegyric poems presented to the king in 1763 and praised by English reviewers as evidence of "science and literature extending themselves with our conquests" (see section 4). Having been misled into contributing to the volume himself, he warned his readers against official doublethink, which might beguile them into surrendering liberties hard-earned and long-guaranteed:

> That what we won by hardy war, was *given,*
> That non-resistance is secure of heaven;
> That persecution in our infant state,
> Was nursing kind compassion in the GREAT;
> That emigration was not to secure
> Our liberties, but to enslave the more;
> That charters, privileges, patents, powers,
> Were our's till now, and now no longer our's;
> To claim exemption by the charter-seal,
> Will rashly violate the common-weal;
> *Juries* are nusances and *Traffick* worse,
> And to be blind, sagacity of course;
> The STAMP and LAND-TAX are as blessings meant,
> And opposition is our free consent. . . .

For all his snarling, the writer mustered up only "modest boldness" when deciding what to do on this Day Before. He urged a cutback on imports and asked his countrymen to make "a chaste sufficiency suffice." Indeed, he ended the poem with an oblique reminder that the adoration expressed in the earlier college verses still existed for the man whom Bute and Grenville had led an "injur'd people" to distrust—a plea for the reawakened guardianship of "GEORGE! Parent! King!"

Next day, Liberty died. As seen by a Rhode Island newspaper, November 1 resembled "a description in Addison's Cato—'The dawn was over cast, and heavily in clouds brought on the day'—the great, the important day! . . . The sons of freedom sunk beneath the horrid gloom, and every one was struck with melancholy at the approaching funeral of their departed, beloved friend, LIBERTY!" The mock trials and mock executions of stampmen gave way throughout the colonies to mock funerals. In Newport a "prodigious" crowd marched at noon from the Crown Coffee House to the burial ground: "persons of all ranks, from the highest even down to the blacks, who seem'd from a sense of their masters sufferings to join the mourning course." When, with funereal tread, they reached the resting place of "their old friend LIBERTY," a Son of Liberty stepped out of the crowd and addressed the corpse: "Oh! *Liberty!* the darling of my soul!—glorious *Liberty!* admir'd, ador'd, by all true Britons!—*Liberty* dead! it cannot be!" On the same day, in Portsmouth, citizens bore through the streets a coffin marked "LIBERTY, aged 145"—alluding to the date of the Plymouth landing and suggesting that the Stamp Act betrayed the country's very essence and inception. With drums and firing of guns the procession wound half a mile out of town to the burial ground. The funeral orations, in the words of the *Boston Gazette*, were "greatly in favor of the Deceas'd." [13]

Indeed, these skits undertook not really to bury Liberty but to assert its ability to survive November 1. From the coffin at Newport rose a groan,

> . . . for old *Freedom* was not dead—The goddess Britannia had order'd a guardian angel to snatch old *Freedom* from the jaws of frozen death, to the orb of the reviving sun, to remain invulnerable from the attacks of lawless tyranny and oppression. . . . The moment he ascended, the God of day appear'd in his greatest beauty, the clouds dispersed, and once more clear'd the face of heaven.

At Portsmouth too, those at the graveside detected life in the corpse, after which "the Inscription was immediately altered, and then appeared to be *Liberty Revived*—and the *Stamp Act* thrown into the Grave and buried—at which the Bells immediately altered their melancholy to a more joyful sound. . . ." Newporters ended the day decorating the courthouse, ringing bells, and singing an "evening song":

> *The birthright of Britons is Freedom,*
> *The contrary is worse than Death's pangs.*

CHORUS
> *⎡ HUZZA for George the Third.*
> *⎨ Britannia's Sons despise Slavery,*
> *⎣ And dare to be nobly free!*

Bostonians reserved their rites of renewal for November 5—Pope's

Day—although on November 1 they hanged effigies of Grenville and others on Liberty Tree and rehanged them on a gallows before dismembering them. The traditionally hostile leaders of the North and South ends and their contingents joined on King Street "having Musick in Front and Flank." At noon, carts were hauled from both ends of town containing the Pope, the Devil, and effigies of Tyranny, Oppression, and Slavery. (To preserve order, blacks were forbidden to approach the carts.) The two groups joined up again at Liberty Tree for refreshment, before marching to Copps Hill burial ground, where they committed the effigies to a bonfire.[14]

As November 1 receded, poets continued to lash out at stamp distributors and royal officials, encouraging disobedience toward the tribe of "pension'd blockheads." Governor Bernard, a favorite target, explained to the Massachusetts House on November 8 that he did not like the Stamp Act but was powerless as governor to oppose it. Several Bostonians, employing a long-popular colonial form, travestied his speech point by point, closely following its language. One writer took off Bernard's argument that he had acted from duty, not desire, committing only the "Offence of my Office":

> But when the Tax was laid it became my Duty
> To act such a Part as I knew would not suit you.
> This is all the Offence I have committed:
> But it was my Office, and not I that did it.
> You should have quarrel'd with the King for putting me into Commission;
> And not with me, ye Sowers of Sedition!

Bernard also urged compliance with the act on the ground that if the colonists showed obedience the king would lift the tax:

> I have thought if I could perswade you into a quiet Submission
> It would be the readiest Means to secure my Commission.
> If you should appear to be willing and able to pay,
> The Parliament would then pity you, and take the Burthen away—
> But if you appear to be Poor and much discontented,
> It's the likeliest Way to have the Burthen augmented.[15]

In pleas for cooperation, colonists now detected the transparent self-serving of a placeman.

The end of the year brought more direct efforts to insure the survival of liberty. In December, Boston merchants reached a non-importation agreement. Many courts which had adjourned rather than use stamped legal documents prepared to reopen, using unstamped documents in defiance of the act. At the source, in London, Benjamin Franklin prepared to testify on the need for repeal. Sometime before his appearance at the

House of Commons on February 13, 1766, he produced a cartoon entitled *Magna Britannia her Colonies Reduc'd*, which he printed on cards and, it is said, hired someone to hand to M.P.'s as they entered the House to vote. The cartoon grimly parodies the familiar symbol of British power—Britannia seated on a globe, a spear in one hand, a shield with Union Jack in the other. Franklin reduced this to an anguished-looking, stringy-haired, armless and legless torso. He placed it not atop the globe, but propped against it for support, amidst its own dismembered and scattered limbs, labeled "Virg.," "New Eng," "New York," and "Pennsyl." In the distance of the desolate landscape appear several ships with brooms on their masts as for-sale signs. Across Britannia's truncated lap lies a banner reading *Date Obolum Belisario*—"Give a dime to Belisarius"—alluding to the Byzantine general who conquered Italy, only to be dismissed and reduced to beggary. The gist, Franklin said, was "that the Colonies may be ruined, but that Britain would thereby be maimed." [16]

Some colonists doubted, however, that the message would reach home. The *Boston Gazette* closed out 1765 on a note of tired pleading. On the front page of its end-of-year issue it printed a poem entitled "Cato's Soliloquy Imitated," in which America pondered the soul's natural love of liberty and dread of slavery, closely following the speech of Cato in Act V of Addison's play:

> 'Tis the Divinity that stirs within him,
> 'Tis Heav'n itself points out his Birth-right to him
> And intimates fair *Liberty* to Man.

Still echoing Cato's language, America pointed at the Stamp Act on the table before it:

> . . . If there's a GEORGE in Britain,
> (And that there is his thund'ring Fleets proclaim
> Thro' every Clime) he must delight in FREEDOM,
> And that which he delights in must prevail.
> (But why *this* land was made for B[ut]e or G[renvill]e
> I'm weary of Conjectures—here I'll end them.)

Like Cato weary of trying to discern God's goodness in the creation, America was weary of puzzling out a king who loved freedom but did not keep his scheming ministers from murdering liberty.

7. Excursus: Whig Sentimentalism

Whether verse, cartoons, or public demonstrations, all the forms of Stamp Act protest share two related features: a distinct literary quality—a habit of alluding to *Cato* or Shakespeare while excoriating Bernard or Bute; and a peculiarly vehement emotionalism—a pervasive idiom of groaning, mutilation, and rape that might be called Whig Sentimentalism.

Whig theory reached the colonies through a literary as well as a political tradition. English poets and playwrights contemporary with Trenchard and Gordon adapted Whig ideas to current literary conventions, using the ancient poetic commonplace of rural contentment, for instance, as a counter-image to the rampant bribery and despotic ambition of current city politics. One monument of the Whig poetic tradition was James Thomson's long poem *Liberty*, published in five parts in 1735-36. The meaning Thomson ascribed to liberty is complex, but in its full extent represents progress itself, the means by which civilizations mature and by which mankind as a whole advances to higher levels of consciousness. English drama of the period was also highly politicized. Eighteenth-century theatregoers often saw resemblances to current political events in Shakespeare's history plays and laid political interpretations upon them. Works like *The Beggar's Opera* and *The Clandestine Marriage* portrayed all classes and professions of English society as wallowing in dissoluteness, falsehood, and chicanery, confirming what Trenchard and Gordon charged, while overtly Whiggish plays such as *Gustavus Vasa*, *Douglas*, and *The Roman Father*—all of them popular in the colonies—celebrated freedom and patriotism. George Lillo's play *The Christian Hero* contains the phrase "unalienable right," applied to freedom, as well as the phrase "sons of liberty."

By far the most quoted Whig literary work, omnipresent in the Stamp Act protests, was Joseph Addison's *Cato*. The edition of *Cato* which appeared in Boston in 1767 also marked the first publication in America of an English play. Because of his many activities, Cato was portrayed throughout classical and later literature according to ideological vagaries: Both Whigs and Tories claimed him. Addison, however, emphasized the disinterested republican martyr who opposed Roman corruption and committed suicide rather than accept the tyrannical rule of Julius Caesar.[1] First produced in England in 1713 and for the first time in America in 1735, the play applied in virtually every line to the colonial situation in 1765, and later. Its language directly inspired some ringing colonial declarations of purpose, as a few quotations suggest:

Gods, can a Roman senate long debate
Which of the two to choose, slavery or death! (II, i)

The gen'rous plan of power delivered down,
From age to age, by your renowned forefathers,
(So dearly bought, the price of so much blood)
O let it never perish in your hands! (III, v)

. . . What pity is it
That we can die but once to serve our country! (IV, iv)[2]

Being what Dr. Johnson called "rather a poem in dialogue than a drama," *Cato* was ideally suited for production by amateurs, who needed only to strike an attitude and declaim; it had a long career in the colonies as a school play.[3] Its politics, too, gave a sanctity to performances that made foes of the theatre cautious. Magistrates in anti-theatre Cambridge were anxious to avoid prosecuting a student production in the early 1770's because, according to one witness, "the prosecution might be misconstrued as if levelled against the sentiments. . . ." The American Company often used the play when under attack by moralists. The play also suggested to the Whig theorists Trenchard and Gordon the title for their essays, *Cato's Letters*. To eighteenth-century readers and theatregoers, the name "Cato" was thus packed with ideological meaning. The career of the historical Roman, the events of Addison's play, and the ideas of the English radicals merged, as Bailyn says, in a powerfully resonant "Catonic" image.[4]

The Stamp Act protests could be described as literary, then, only from a modern perspective. Colonial Whigs could have seen nothing peripheral to politics or merely decorative in comparing November 1, as one newspaper did, "to a description in Addison's Cato," or in publishing on the front page, as another did, a poem entitled "Cato's Soliloquy Imitated." The contributor to the *Boston Gazette* who presented his views on taxation in the form of a version of a scene from *Henry VIII* was doing something which his age understood as politics quite as much as literature.[5] Such pieces should be read not with a mind to the officialese of modern political discourse, but recalling that Benjamin Franklin quoted Homer against the massacre of Indians on the Pennsylvania frontier, that Jefferson wrote on English versification, that James Otis produced not only *The Rights of the British Colonies Asserted and Proved* but also a *Rudiments of Latin Prosody*.

Thus verse and drama of the period are rife with Whig ideas, just as political pamphlets are rife with verse and drama. The Whig literary tradition, fully established after the Glorious Revolution of 1688, became nearly as important a source of political ideas in the colonies as the works of Trenchard and Gordon. Colonists quoted Addison, Thomson, Pope, Milton, and Shakespeare as political authorities hardly less often than they quoted Locke or Montesquieu. Even in nakedly political pamphlets it is often impossible to tell which is the nearer source of ideology.

English poets and playwrights were drawn to Whig theory because they found its moralistic politics congenial to popular moral ideas about benevolence, charity, and the importance of feeling. The connection of commerce with economic relief for the lower classes, for instance, made trade a matter of sentiment and a natural subject for poetry. This fusion of political theory with popular moral sentiment in the Whig literary tradition charged discussions of taxes with powerful emotional associations. The tearful lament of the probate papers,

> . . . with many a sigh,
> 'Must we be st - - pt,' with tender accent cry:
> 'We who our life and breath, so freely spend,
> 'The fatherless and widow to defend. . . .

is not very different in feeling from the poem published in the *Virginia Gazette* in 1767 on the death of an infant:

> WHO, that beheld the lovely boy expire,
> But must have join'd his tears to see
> The weeping mother, and the sobbing sire,
> Involv'd in so much misery? [6]

Whig Sentimentalism made new taxes seem not merely a burden, nor even ministerial extortion, but ultimately a brutalization of those who sigh and are tender, producing the anguished cries at mock funerals, the doleful face of wretched Britannia in Franklin's cartoon, the groaning woe throughout the Stamp Act protests. Similarly, the rural swains who narrated Stamp Act poems or urged a return to the fig leaf or celebrated at Liberty Tree made the tax seem a barbaric affront to the integrity, innocence, and good nature symbolized by pastoral life.

Whig Sentimentalism, then, invested the Stamp Act with emotions belonging to the violation of the most general and highly cherished ideals. None of these ideals was more often invoked by the protestors than that of loving domestic relationships. The verses and demonstrations insistently depict the Stamp Act as primal disloyalty, inflicting pain so unexpected, unwarranted, and unnatural that it can be compared only to a loved parent disowning its child, or a loved child betraying its parent. The comparison underlies pleas to "GEORGE! Parent! King!" as well as William Pitt's famous reminder to the House of Commons, in 1766, that "The Americans are the sons, not the bastards, of England." It mingles and blends with pervasive images of rupture and mutilation—severed snakes, stab wounds, torn limbs, and hacked effigies—that similarly convey a sense of anguish at the cutting of deep bonds. At the August 16 demonstration in Lebanon, a female effigy with chained feet, representing America, howled against colonial stamp distributors as prodigal sons:

> . . . thus pleading with her base, unnatural child.—*My Son! remember that I have treated you with the utmost tenderness, and bestow'd on you my highest honours, pity your country, and put not on me these chains;* to which her ungrateful, degenerate son replied, in a label proceeding from his mouth, *Perish my country, so that I get that reward:* upon the utterance of which, such indignant wrath swell'd the bosom of this venerable matron, that her power of speech fail'd. . . .

In another version of disinheritance, England appeared as an aging, increasingly odd parent, jealous that her colonies have developed a distinct personality:

> We have an old Mother that peevish is grown,
> She snubs us like Children that scarce walk alone;
> She forgets we're grown up and have Sense of our own. . . .[7]

Complementing such images of family strain the protests contain many images of new lineage, of better parentage. Many demonstrators claimed a transcendent loyalty, calling themselves sons and daughters of Liberty rather than of England. As mourners drew through Portsmouth the coffin of Liberty marked with the date of the Plymouth landing, the author of *The Times* asked whether the colonists were not obliged primarily to the ideals of the first settlers, and to their own future progeny:

> Is it for you their honour to betray?
> And give the harvest of their blood away?
> Look back with rev'rence, aw'd to just esteem,
> Preserve the blessings handed down from them;
> If not, look forwards, look with deep despair,
> And dread the curses of your beggar'd heir. . . .

As people began identifying themselves more closely with the colonial than with the English past, there emerged the notion of a single origin common to Bostonians and Charlestonians alike, the legend of the forefathers.

The colonists invested their protests with emotions belonging to one other kind of relationship, more subtle and powerful in its appeal than the rest. Feminizing the concept of liberty, they saw themselves as defenders of virtue against an act of rape. "Fair Liberty"—the master symbol of the protests—was a commonplace of Whig literary tradition, although it had an older and continuous history. About 135 B.C. the Roman statesman Graccus created a temple of Liberty in Rome, where he represented Liberty as a Roman matron—*Libertas*—holding a pike topped with a cap. The Romans gave such a cap—a *pileus*—to freed slaves as the sign of their emancipation. The liberty pole and liberty cap became standard accoutrements of Libertas. A coin of Nerva, A.D. 97, shows a female liberty figure and staff, as does a fifth-century coin minted in the reign of Brutus, the executioner of Caesar. Libertas with cap and staff appears widely in Dutch and French prints of the sixteenth century; Addison in *Tatler* no. 161 (1710) gave an allegorical sketch of the Goddess of Liberty, depicting her with a liberty cap, aided by Plenty and Commerce; during the Seven Years' War, Libertas with cap and pike became a very popular image in English prints.[8]

In America, the Libertas image had had wide currency since the 1750's, when the English Whig Thomas Hollis, a benefactor of Harvard College, commissioned a representation for Jonathan Mayhew's *Discourse Concerning Unlimited Submission*, a classic of the American Whig tradition. He first had a gem made depicting a seated Britannia holding pole and cap, beneath which was the date January 30, 1648, marking the execution of Charles I. Hollis then employed the Italian artist Giovanni Battista Cipriani to make a print of the gem, which he sent to Harvard, together with some books on which he had the image stamped.[9] In the last quarter of the eighteenth century, Libertas was an omnipresent image in America, enabling a Son of Liberty to step forward at one mock funeral and groan with the passionate bereavement of a lover, "Oh! *Liberty!* the darling of my soul! glorious *Liberty!* admir'd, ador'd, by all true Britons!—*Liberty* dead!" In defending Libertas, Americans attached to their cause the full force of the sentimental love tradition that defended the guileless purity of daughters and wives against scheming seducers bent on befouling them.

How Whig Sentimentalism affected direct political action is difficult to say. Urgent times reach deep; sensibility becomes ideology. It is by no means clear that sentimentalism was less important than political theory in causing people to feel outraged over the implications of taxing probate papers. Sentimentalism itself contained a subversive impulse, as Leslie Stephen observed, a "vague feeling of discontent with the existing order of thought and society." [10] Yet to address outrage to some abandoning mother was to divert the outrage from what produced it. The Liberty Tree ceremonies and mock funerals provided a caricature of the political situation which absorbed hostility. The actors paraded through town yelling "Stamp him" and beating "him" with sticks, purging their anger through an effigy.[11]

The prevalence of metaphor, the air of theatricalism throughout the Stamp Act protests, suggests a tentative state of mind, emotion raised rather to the point of intimidation than of retaliation, a state of becoming. Posturing and attitudinizing as angry swains, bereaved lovers, disinherited children, Sons and Daughters of Liberty, the colonists were testing out new possibilities of conduct, acting toward an ideal of behavior as yet diffuse. At the end of 1765, John Adams drew on another extremely popular and descriptive metaphor to sum up the meaning of the "Magnanimity and Spirit" which the colonists displayed during the year. "America," he felt it had been shown, "was designed by Providence for the Theatre, on which Man was to make his true figure. . . ." [12]

8. Benjamin West's American School in London: June 1763–Early 1766

Fluctuatingly but seriously ill, Benjamin West had arrived in London in June 1763, by way of Parma-Genoa-Turin-Lyons-Paris, intending to return to Philadelphia in the spring of 1764. Sir Joshua Reynolds and Richard Wilson, however, had urged him to contribute some works painted in Rome to a show in April 1764. The paintings got a favorable reception, including the publication of several adulatory poems addressed to the painter. Applause and the advice of his friends persuaded West to stay on in London. The Society of Artists, incorporated in 1765, invited him to become a member. [1]

As a boy, West had seen copies of works by the old masters, and had tried to imitate them. But in the few years since leaving America, he had taken over their ways of seeing, renouncing the world of the Knelleresque portrait for the worlds of Raphael, Titian, Correggio, and classical sculpture, worlds that he made more and more personal as his technique and self-confidence grew. Precisely as he had set out to do when he left Philadelphia, he began to devote himself to history paintings. Mostly he depicted domestic situations from the Old Testament, often young children and infants seen in ideal relations with their parents, as in his *Jacob Blessing Ephraim and Manasseh* (1766) or the later *Tobias Healing his Father's Blindness*, and *The Return of the Prodigal Son*. Though painted an ocean away from the bonfires and groans, and gotten up in Rembrandtesque turbans and Roman togas, these scenes of family tenderness and joy spring from the same vein of feeling in the period which experienced the Stamp Act as a disinheritance.

In 1764, West took on his first pupil, Matthew Pratt. Born in Philadelphia in 1734, Pratt worked as a portraitist in the city, managing,

he said, to make "money fast, with the approbation of every employer."
Nevertheless, in June 1764 he shipped to London together with West's
father, and with West's fiancée, Betsy Shewell. West had become engaged
to her before going abroad, but according to one account, the prominent
Shewell family opposed her marriage to a struggling young artist and
rejoiced when West left the country. To their chagrin, West sent for her as
he gained recognition in Rome and London. Her brother, however, locked
her in her room until the ship on which she intended passage had sailed.
At this crisis, some of West's friends, including Francis Hopkinson,
engineered her escape. They sent a rope ladder by which she exited from
the room and took her by carriage to Chester, sixteen miles from
Philadelphia. There she joined West's father aboard ship, accompanying
him and Matthew Pratt to London.[2]

Pratt himself moved in with West after touring England and stayed with
him for two and a half years. West, he said, "rendered me every good &
kind office he could bestow on me, as if I was his Father, friend and
brother." Probably at this time he copied West's copies of Correggio's
Madonna with St. Jerome and Guido Reni's *Europa and Zeus*, which he later
advertised for sale in Williamsburg. More important, he painted *The
American School*, leaving a nicely detailed visual record of West in his
London studio (ill., p. 122). West appears in green knee-breeches holding
several brushes and a small palette, pointing at and discussing a drawing
held by the thirty-one-year-old Pratt, seated and wearing a violet suit.
Several other students look on, probably including Abraham Delanoy, Jr.,
of New York, the latest member of a family of American limners stretching
back to 1681.[3]

In the same year that Pratt and Betsy Shewell joined West, another
Philadelphian emigrated to the European art capitals who, as it happened, was Betsy Shewell's cousin, twenty-one-year-old Henry Benbridge.
His career began around 1758, when his stepfather commissioned a
portrait from John Wollaston; during the sittings Benbridge received his
first instruction. Not two years later he was filling the walls of his family's
house with life-sized copies of Raphael prints. Much was expected of him.
Receiving his inheritance in 1764, he went to Italy, where he perhaps
studied with West's own teachers, Pompeo Batoni and Anton Raphael
Mengs, and roomed with the Irish sculptor Christopher Hewetson, who
may be one of the seated figures in Pratt's *American School*.[4]

9. Charles Willson Peale Flees to New England: Summer 1765

Though barely launched on a painting career after receiving a little instruction from John Hesselius, Charles Willson Peale was forced to leave his pregnant wife in Annapolis and flee to Virginia, vomiting, suffering toothache, nearly £900 in debt and pursued by the sheriff. If his financial problems were caused by the economic dislocations of the Stamp Act, he was not alone, for in 1765 even the wealthy portraitist Jeremiah Theus joined some South Carolina merchants in addressing a petition for relief to the Commons House of Assembly. Peale himself believed his troubles were political, the result of his conservative creditors serving writs to punish him for joining "the sons of Freedom. . . ." [1]

His flight, however, proved instructive. From Virginia he took a schooner to Boston, where he arrived on July 14. Sightseeing, he noted the irregular, pebble-paved streets and the many Presbyterian churches, attended the Harvard commencement, and bought some paints at the color shop run by John Smibert's uncle, who showed him some of Smibert's works. As he later recalled the event,

> . . . hunting for colours I found a colour shop which had some figures with ornamental signs about it; these I suspect was painted by a Mr. Smibert, becoming a little acquainted with the owner of the shop, he told me that a relation of his had been a painter and he said he would give a feast; leading me up stairs introduced me into a painters room where there were a number of Pictures unfinished . . . several heads painted of the antient Philosophers, and some groups of figures, these were the last works of Smibert.

Peale had seen and been impressed by the most important collection of paintings in America, "in a style," he said, "vastly superior" to any he had seen before. Armed with his paints, he took a schooner to Newburyport, where late in July he did six paintings "at Small Price" and the next month observed a Stamp Act demonstration with effigies. [2]

Hoping to improve himself, as always, Peale returned to Boston. He lodged at the Exchange Tavern at a reduced rate, in return for teaching the owner's son to draw. At his earlier visit to the color shop he had heard of John Singleton Copley. Now he "went and introduced myself to him, as a person just [beginning?] to paint portraits." Copley, he said, "was then in great business" but received him "very politely." In Copley's picture room he found a "great feast," a large number of portraits, "many of them highly finished." Copley lent him a portrait done by another painter and a painting of a candlelit scene to copy.[3]

Few other details of Peale's stay in New England have survived. He began doing small portraits and miniatures. To keep afloat, he attempted to get work as a saddler, and sold his watch. But down literally to his last shilling and sixpence, he returned by ship to Virginia. On board he painted and displayed a portrait which captivated a passenger, who commissioned him to render his family. Peale stayed with this family in Accomac, Virginia, for the next six months, exploring shared interests in mechanics, the arts, and music and doing some silversmithing, watch repairing, and painting.[4]

10. Copley's *Boy with Squirrel:* Fall 1765

From the vantage point of Peale, a penniless fugitive with artistic aspirations and no training, Copley's situation understandably seemed a "great feast." But Copley viewed it with misgiving, conscious of his limitations, aware of the greater art world he had glimpsed afar through the imitations of imitations in Smibert's collection, slightly uneasy over the political climate. From outward signs, artistic and financial, Copley prospered. Mastering the use of pastels, from 1765 on he was producing crayon portraits perhaps unmatched in the history of American art, such as his *Mrs. Edward Green.* He continued to work in his style of unapologetic realism, depicting Puritanism grown prosperous, couched on velvet but staring out with the old crabbed intensity. A stunning example in 1765 is his painting of Nathaniel Hurd, the engraver who sold and advertised his Stamp Act *caricatura.* Copley depicted his brawny friend in a plunging, open shirt, a brown velvet cap on his closely shaven head, five o'clock shadow on his heavy cheeks, his hard look and careless dress suggesting the out-of-doors, insouciant toughness of the Stamp Act protests.[1]

What implies that despite his outward success Copley remained dissatisfied is his decision to submit something for exhibition at the next showing of the Society of Artists in London. What he sent was a major work in his development, a painting of his half-brother, Henry Pelham, at the age of sixteen (ill., p. 125). It shows the boy seated at a table holding a delicate chain, at the end of which a small tethered squirrel nibbles nuts. The polished table surface reflects the nutshells and a half-full tumbler of water. Copley painted the squirrel—a common accessory in portraits of children in the period—with the curiosity of a naturalist. Its appearance in the painting is comparable to the allusions to whippoorwills, rattlesnakes, and other unique and indigenous creatures in a long succession of colonial poems, bespeaking an avid, international interest in American flora and fauna. The main effect of the painting, however, is of frail evanescence. The elfin mincing animal, the dreamy adolescent with faun-like ears and silken hair, his lips parted, compose a moment of still abstractedness. The dreaminess marks something emergent in Copley's vision, intimations of which can be detected in his earlier pastoral works. Although the clothing, table, and draperies remain intensely seen, intensely physical, the far-off look of the sitter records an insurgence of escapism, a desire to abandon the present practical world for a world of delicate fancy.

That Copley could have painted his *Boy with Squirrel* at the same time that he engraved a Stamp Act caricatura in which a dog urinates on the British viper suggests that he was trying to accommodate two different worlds, which in different ways made him uneasy. In September 1765, he wrote to the captain of the merchant vessel aboard which his painting was headed for exhibition in London. The first stamped papers, he wrote, had arrived in Boston; several people connected with the Stamp Act had been victimized or had fled the city; currently there was "a strong Military watch kept every night which keeps the Town in quietness." The fate of his painting, however, made him equally tense. Some of his pastels had been lost once en route to Quebec; a change in colors resulting from the voyage might unfit the work for exhibition; and, he confessed, "I am under some apprehension of its not being so much esteem'd as I could wish." [2]

11. Douglass' New Troupe in Charleston: October 25–November 4, 1765

On October 25, 1765, a ship from London arrived in Charleston carrying stamped paper to be distributed the next week. In response, the muffled bells of St. Michael's Church tolled all day; effigies labeled "Liberty and No Stamp Act" were hanged and burned.[1] Quite certainly this same ship brought to Charleston from London David Douglass and several members of his American Company. After playing at his newly built Charleston theatre during the 1763–64 season, Douglass had gone abroad to continue his program of refurbishing the Company. Bent on making an impressive new start in the provincial theatre business, he recruited new players, bought new scenery, and built a new repertoire.

A week later, the day before the "fatal first of November," Douglass placed an optimistic notice in the *South-Carolina Gazette*. He had brought back with him, he said,

> at a great expence, a most excellent set of scenes done by Mr. Doll, principal scene painter to Covent Garden house, and collected some very eminent performers from both the theatres in London, particularly in the *Singing Way*, so that English COMIC OPERA, a species of entertainment that has never yet appeared properly on this side the water, is likely to be performed here this winter to advantage.

In effect, Douglass had returned with a whole new theatre. He had acquired sets by Nicholas Doll (or Dall), an outstanding English stage designer, and a new repertoire of 'comic operas' which he advertised as "Never acted in America." [2] These differed from the ballad operas and ballad afterpieces familiar to colonial audiences. The ballad operas fitted out popular tunes with new lyrics; in the comic opera, lyrics and music were composed fresh. The ballad opera was an actor's medium that required some singing skill; the comic opera was essentially for singers who could act. In the form in which Douglass introduced it in Charleston— Thomas Arne's and Isaac Bickerstaffe's *Love in a Village* (1762)—this sort of musical theatre is more accurately called *pasticcio*. It used music by well-known composers throughout, but not all of it was composed for the play. *Love in a Village* used music by Arne (the composer of "Rule Britannia"), but also by Handel, William Boyce, Geminiani, and others. After Douglass introduced *Love in a Village* in 1766, comic operas became immensely popular in the colonies, being printed in American editions, sold at the theatre, sung at home, and used as settings for patriotic songs.[3]

Like the earlier ballad operas, the *pasticcios* and comic operas reinforced Whig sentiment. They often glorified the integrity of rural life, showed English society awash, by contrast, in dissolution, and depicted inter-class marriages which were in effect fantasies of extreme social change. In *Love in a Village*, the scion of an upper-class family takes on the disguise of a lower-class villager for the sake of love. Given the close connection between love and democratization, the language is often indistinguishable from Whig rhetoric. Lucinda, protesting against her despotic, profligate father, sings:

> Justly those we tyrants call,
> Who the body would enthral;

Tyrants of more cruel kind,
Those who would enslave the mind.

The robust outdoorsman and hunter "Hawthorn" (whose song "The Jolly Miller" became a vehicle for many patriotic songs) makes a case for the democracy of love and stresses that "an hale cobler is a better man than a sick king." [4] In offering an entertaining version of Whiggish ideas, such works perhaps shaped the political perceptions of Americans who did not read Locke or *Cato's Letters* but who did frequent the theatre.

The comic operas made virtually operatic demands on the actors, and to perform them Douglass had, as he announced, "collected some very eminent performers from both the theatres in London, particularly in the *Singing Way.* . . ." Among the six new singer-actors were Miss Wainwright and Stephen Woolls, pupils of Thomas Arne himself. They gave the performances authenticity and perhaps a caliber not very different from that of London. For many years Woolls remained the first singer in the Company, featured in such singing leads as Macheath in *The Beggar's Opera* and Hawthorn in *Love in a Village*. The new group also contained the tenor Thomas Wall, who had worked as a musician at Drury Lane and Haymarket theatres. He specialized in comic singing roles, sometimes accompanied Miss Wainwright on his guitar in entr'acte musical numbers, and gave guitar lessons wherever the company played. Two other newcomers were Henrietta Osborne, apparently from Jamaica, who had played in Drury Lane in 1759; and William Verling, a Mason who advantageously drew brother Masons to the theatre. Finally, Douglass brought Lewis Hallam's cousin, Nancy Hallam, who played various parts and could accompany herself on the guitar, harpsichord, and spinet. Her arrival in the fall of 1765 marked her return to the colonial stage, for she had appeared with the company in 1759 in Philadelphia, acting children's parts.[5]

Despite his new players, new scenery, and new productions, Douglass' hope of an impressive fresh start failed. The cause was not the Stamp Act, but the delay of the rest of his troupe in Barbados. Two weeks after advertising his triumphant arrival, he announced his contemplated departure. He told readers of the *South-Carolina Gazette* that his full troupe would have made possible "a superior degree of excellence to any that have hitherto appeared in America"; but, he just learned, they were unable to leave Barbados until March. Embarrassed, he had planned to depart for Barbados himself, avoiding "the contemptible light I might stand in with many, for presuming to treat the publick with plain dishes after having given them so sumptuous a bill of fare." But some loyal patrons pressed him to open the theatre "with the little strength I have brought from London with me," urging that a run in whatever form would help him to cover his expenses. To compensate for the thin performance, he reduced ticket prices by five shillings.[6] He opened with a company of nine, of whom six were the promising newcomers gathered in London.

One work which Douglass found suited to his diminished troupe was George Alexander Stevens' *Lecture on Heads*, which he performed several times toward the end of the Charleston season. Stemming from the general eighteenth-century fondness for mimicry, and from a phrenological craze involving J. C. Lavater's *Essays on Physiognomy*, this quasi-play was given as a five-act lecture. According to the stage directions for Act I, "The Lecturer stands behind a long Table, covered with a green cloth resembling a counter. Two screens placed behind obliquely form his ambuscade, from whence he conveniently draughts his forces." The lecturer uses different props—wigs, shirt fronts, hats—in presenting a series of impersonations, satirizing such London types as the blood, the prostitute, the young master, the connoisseur, the "Jew conjuror" (with Yiddish dialect), the Italian opera singer, lawyers, politicians, and physicians. The work provided a flexible format which could be combined with musical interludes or freshened and repeated by adding timely impersonations. A favorite of colonial audiences, it was published in several American editions, performed in variants like the "Critical Dissertation on NOSES" and the "Lecture on HEARTS." Mostly, however, Douglass used the *Lecture* as still another dodge, a way of offering plays in disguise. As a compromise with standard theatrical fare, the *Lecture* got by, usually, in places with vigilant anti-theatre groups.[7]

12. Repeal of the Stamp Act: January–May 1766

The non-importation agreements concluded in the fall, especially in the northern cities, led to a decline in the consumption of British imports. Early in 1766, apprehensive British merchants themselves petitioned the new ministry of Charles Rockingham to repeal the act, which was debated in January in the House of Commons. William Pitt, advocating repeal— "I rejoice," he said, "that America has resisted"—was opposed in debate by George Grenville, who predicted a revolution if Parliament knuckled under. Meanwhile, George III had become affronted by Grenville, whom he never liked. The king having recently recovered from an illness, Grenville drew up a bill forbidding him to appoint his mother—widely believed to be Bute's mistress—as regent should he become incapacitated. In February, with the merchants, the king, and Pitt already aligned against Grenville, the Rockingham ministry called for repeal, but simultaneously with a bill declaring the authority of Parliament to legislate for the colonies. On March 18, a bill repealing the Stamp Act was passed.[1]

The colonies greeted it with a rash of poems, cartoons, paintings, and demonstrations which illustrated an unlooked-for result of the Stamp Act. As Joseph Warren pointed out, with the act had come congresses and agreements which "the most zealous Colonist never could have expected! The Colonies until now were ever at variance and foolishly jealous of each other, they are now . . . united . . . nor will they soon forget the weight which this close union gives them." [2] Although geographically scattered, the celebrations were much the same. When Bostonions learned about Repeal on May 16, they rang the city bells, displayed ships' colors, discharged cannon, and released debtors from jail. A few days later the Sons of Liberty erected on the common a large, four-sided obelisk on a doric base (ill., p. 127). As described in the *Gazette*, the upper panels on each side contained paintings of the king, the queen, Wilkes, Pitt—to whom many credited Repeal—and other patriots. Verses on the middle panels asserted the colonists' devotion to liberty, abhorrence of slavery, and detestation of Bute and Grenville, using the ardent language of Whig sentimentalism:

> O thou whom next to Heav'n we most revere,
> Fair LIBERTY! thou lovely Goddess hear!
> Have we not woo'd thee, won thee, held thee long,
> Lain in thy Lap and melted on thy Tongue. . . .

As later engraved by Paul Revere, who may have helped build it, the obelisk also contained several caricaturas. America, represented by a female Indian, leans dejectedly against a tree, while to her right a winged Libertas with pole and cap flies away, representing "America in distress apprehending the total loss of LIBERTY." In the second panel, America on bended knee implores some colonists, pointing at a Scotchman and priest who hold another colonist in chains; in the fourth panel, the king, in Roman garb, introduces Libertas to the Indian America. On the following night, 108 lanterns were hung on Liberty Tree to honor "the glorious Majority" who voted for Repeal. Nearby houses displayed life-sized paintings of the king and Pitt, and of a Libertas who addressed herself to these heroes in an inscription:

> *Hail,* PITT! *Hail, Patrons! Pride* of GEORGE'S *Days.*
> *How round the Globe expand your Patriot Rays!*
> *And the* NEW WORLD *is brighten'd with the Blaze.*

Illuminated at night, fireworks exploding everywhere, Boston "shone like Day." [3]

(The panels on the obelisk, it should be explained, glowed by means of 280 lamps within. These so-called transparencies, used more and more for public celebrations, were usually painted on canvas or thin paper, pasted over a framework. One method, described in an early nineteenth century manual, involved India ink, colored washes, and varnish for the transparent portions, applied on both sides of the canvas or paper. On nights when the town was to be illuminated for celebration, transparencies were often applied to window shades by priming the shade cloth with white wax and turpentine, mixed together hot.[4] Highly combustible, the transparencies occasionally caught fire. Indeed, the large Boston obelisk was to have been removed to Liberty Tree, but it ignited and burned up.)

Elsewhere, celebrators in Newport hung before the courthouse a four-part painting, eight by fourteen feet, showing the harbor, the king with Pitt, a landscape with produce, and Rockingham, Isaac Barré, and other friends of America surrounding Libertas. In Portsmouth, the harbor was decorated, and, said the *New-Hampshire Gazette*, "the Bells rang an incessant Peal, Drums and Music contributed to make the Harmony of Sounds concordant to the apparent Tempor *[sic]* and Disposition of the People." In Philadelphia, *A New Song, on the Repeal of the Stamp Act*, told gaily how the Devil initiated the ministerial plot, tempting his old friend Grenville, who invited his friend Bute to share the proffered wealth:

> Quoth the Devil to Gr-nv-ll I've drawn up a plan,
> And think in my conscience that thou art the MAN,
> When e'er I intend any evil to do,
> You may always be sure I will pitch upon you.
> *Taral Laddry*, &c.
> O'er-joy'd at the news like a courtier polite,
> He thanked the Devil, and thought all was right;
> Expecting large share, of the profits in fact,
> Arising by virtue of the *Noble Stamp Act*—
> *Taral Laddry*, &c.

A broadside in German, dated May 19, depicted a sun radiating through dark clouds on a tree, on a globe marked "AMERICA," and on a figure of "FREIHEIT" rising from a grave. Verses underneath conceived Repeal as a pastoral return of spring and light:

> Die Sonne dringet durch, das Land wird fruchbarlich,
> Ihr Licht bestrahet den Sarg, die Freiheit richt sich auf. . . .[5]

Many of these events, like the earlier Stamp Act protests, were directed by the Sons of Liberty. They remained politically active and now destroyed Douglass' New York theatre. Two members of The American Company, an actor named Tomlinson and his wife, put together a makeshift troupe to perform in the city in February and March 1766, at the theatre built by Douglass five years before on Chapel Street. Why they did so is unknown, conceivably to while away the absence of the Barbados contingent. Permission for them to perform in New York had been granted by General Thomas Gage, commander-in-chief of the British armies in America (succeeding Jeffrey Amherst). Gage oversaw the troops who might have to be used should the home government decide to enforce the Stamp Act. Perhaps because of Tomlinson's link with Gage, the Sons of Liberty put the theatre under surveillance. In April, while burning a stack of tax-stamps at the Coffee House, they also burned some of Tomlinson's playbills. On the date that Repeal became effective—May 1—Tomlinson announced that in addition to *The Twin Rivals* he would offer a "Song in Praise of Liberty," adding: "As the Packet is arrived, and has been the Message of Good News, relative to the Repeal, it is hoped the Public has no Objection to the above Performance." [6]

But they did. Tomlinson's ads offended many New Yorkers who, according to the *Gazette*, "thought it highly improper that such Entertainments should be exhibited at this Time of public Distress, when great Numbers of poor People can scarce find Means of subsistence. . . ." A rumor went around town: If the play was performed, the audience would "meet with some Disturbance from the Multitude." The threat kept many home. Those who attended witnessed a blurring of the line between acting and action. At the signal of a candle being lighted and a huzza, one spectator said, "the Rivals began in earnest." A British officer named John Montresor described the riot that ensued:

> This Evening a Play was acted by permission of our Government, to be performed by a company of Comedians or Strollers, notwithstanding the Sons of Liberty without any Reason given pulled down the play house the beginning of the 2nd act, put out all the lights, then began picking of pockets, stealing watches, throwing Brick Bats, sticks and Bottles and Glasses, crying out Liberty, Liberty then proceeded to the Fields or Common and burnt the materials.

By other accounts, once the lights went out in the theatre, people jumped out of windows; many "lost their Caps, Hats, Wigs, Cardinals, and Cloak Tails of Smocks torn off (thro' mistake) in the Hurry." An actor, dressed for a female part, "being caught in the She-Dress was soon turned topsy turvey and whipped for a considerable Distance." The "Multitude who burst open the Doors, and entered with Noise and Tumult," as the *New-York Gazette* put it, left several people "dangerously Hurt." A boy had his skull fractured. He was trepanned, but died. The theatre building seems to have been annihilated: "both Inside and Outside was torn to Pieces, and burnt . . . to the Satisfaction of Many at this distressed time. . . ." [7]

Gratitude, on the other hand, toward Pitt and the king created a new, but also controversial, public demand and support for commemorative works of art. Public commissions for such works began with the Stamp Act itself, when a Boston town meeting voted in 1765 to place a picture of Isaac Barré in Faneuil Hall. With Repeal, a portrait of Pitt was ordered for New York's City Hall, and, apparently as the result of pressure applied to the Common Council, a portrait of the king was also ordered, as balance.[8] More unexpected was the sudden support given to sculpture, a virtually nonexistent art in British America, except for tombstone carvings. The Sons of Liberty in Dedham, Massachusetts, commissioned the native woodcarver Simeon Skillin, Sr., to carve a bust of Pitt, which was placed on a Pillar of Liberty on March 18, 1767, across the road from the almanac writer and tavern keeper Nathaniel Ames, who brought it from Boston. Apparently goaded by the New York Sons of Liberty, the mayor of New York, John Cruger, proposed that the Assembly also commission a statue of Pitt. Warned, however, that favoritism to Pitt might make the king jealous, the Assembly voted a statue of George at the same time. One New Yorker believed that if the Assembly "had not voted a statue for Pitt, the King would have had none, for in truth they were disposed to give none. . . ." In a similar quandary, the South Carolina House voted £1,000 for a marble statue of Pitt; a motion to substitute a statue of the king failed to obtain a second. The New York and Carolina commissions went to the English sculptor Joseph Wilton.[9]

Not everyone harbored resentment against the king for the recent penny taxes. On June 4, some Philadelphians celebrated his birthday with an entertainment on the banks of the Schuylkill, at which they sang "A Grand Chorus":

> Happy! happy! happy we,
>   To GEORGE our Father and our King,
>   True-born Sons of Loyalty. . . .[10]

At least some lately disinherited sons of Liberty thus took pleasure in reverting to their original lineage, peace having, again, returned.

13. Hopkinson and Peale in London: July 1766–Spring 1767

On July 22, Francis Hopkinson, another sojourner from the College of Philadelphia, reached London, hoping to secure a government post through his kinsman the bishop of Worcester. Entree to the bishop had been smoothed for him by some letters from Benjamin Franklin, who, having remained in London since being examined as a witness on the Stamp Act, was friendly with Hogarth and West, a part of the scene himself. While seeking a government post, Hopkinson spent the time agreeably. Perhaps he played Franklin's armonica at a public concert, and he attended a performance of *The Messiah* at Gloucester, so enthralled that he felt nothing when his large boil burst.[1] In London he stayed with West and his bride, who, he wrote, received him "with the utmost cordiality." He boated with them down the Thames to Greenwich, and probably took lessons from West, whose neoclassical *Pylades and Orestes* had been acclaimed at the 1766 exhibit of the Society of Artists. In one of the several poems he wrote while abroad, Hopkinson praised the boldness of his countryman's talent:

> . . . West, whose Genius Nature made to rise,
> And claim Attention from uplifted Eyes;
> Which, like an Eagle, meets the Blaze of Day,
> While little Birds but hop from Spray to Spray
> Whose quick Conception forms the great Design,
> Whose skilful Hand runs o'er the flowing Line;
> Soft on the Canvas spreads the glowing Thought,
> And views the Wonder which his Hand has wrought.

Like his verses, Hopkinson's jaunt abroad was pleasant enough but not successful, for he failed despite his connections to obtain a post.[2]

Charles Willson Peale, still pestered by creditors, managed to return sometime in 1766 from Accomac to Annapolis. There, luckily, one of his works was shown to John Beale Bordley, a provincial judge, a member of the governor's Council, and afterward a lifelong and benevolent friend. Bordley offered to relieve Peale's debts and to give him a trip abroad "to get improvement." He also provided a letter of recommendation from Justice William Allen of Pennsylvania—one of Benjamin West's patrons. In December, after making a violin for the voyage, Peale sailed for London, where he arrived on February 13, 1767. He bought himself a "half dress suit" and went to see West.[3]

Peale, too, found him "truly affectionate." Later he recalled West saying "that if he had not brought any recommendation, as an American he would have given him all the assistance in his power, but that the recommendation from Mr. Allen, was the most powerful he could have brought. . . ." Desiring Peale to lodge nearby, West took him to a house recently occupied by Abraham Delanoy, Jr., another of the young expatriate painters beginning to form an American School in London around West. Delanoy had not vacated the house, as West thought, but was only readying himself to return to New York. In what Peale took as added evidence of "goodness of heart," West invited Delanoy to come to his house and copy one or two pictures to take back to America, since "his friends would expect to see some of his work and it would be an advantage to him." The house occupied, Peale settled instead in Silver Street, at Golden Square.[4]

One of Peale's self-appointed tasks was to investigate the estate left to him, he had been told, in Oxfordshire—possibly his salvation from chronic debt. Aided by Beale Bordley's half-brother, the London lawyer Edmund Jenings, he spent much time discovering that the estate did not exist. But most of his time he spent in "close study." Not satisfied to know one way of painting, and an inveterate tinkerer, he explored "the whole circle of arts," including plaster-casting and mezzotinting. Throughout—as he wrote home to several correspondents—he found West unfailingly willing to instruct and encourage, so that "I have great Hopes of Returning Home a tolerable proficient and give Some Satisfaction to my Bene-factors." [5]

Although only three years older, West, at twenty-nine, was distinctly the teacher, Peale the student. James Northcote, the apprentice and biographer of Reynolds, believed that West offered the best teaching in England. In addition to his sincere interest in his pupils' welfare, West taught them traditional rules of art, reciting chapter and verse for any problem. He believed that his students should, like the old masters, early and at once surmount the mechanical difficulties of painting, "that is the Handling of the Pencil and the Management of Colours, that their Hand might keep pace with their Ideas, so as to receive Pleasure from their Performances." He started his students off by having them copy biblical and classical scenes. Peale's first assignment was to make a small watercolor copy of West's own *Elisha Restoring to Life the Shunammite's Son.*[6] Soon Peale was doing a Venus and Adonis, copying miniatures, painting a work for exhibition, and even selling a few portraits at a reduced rate. In return for West's help, he mended a small palette which his teacher had broken and discarded. West thereafter used it all of his life, even for his largest paintings.

A homebody, Peale badly missed his family and "always felt himself alone." He took at least enough advantage of London, however, to attend a few plays and pleasure gardens, to buy some books (including Leonardo da Vinci's treatise on painting), and to call, too abruptly, on Franklin. He sketched in his diary the scene he barged in on: Franklin with a woman on his knee. Just the same, Franklin received him cordially and reviewed for him, a fellow inventor, his experiments with electricity.

14. Success of *Boy with Squirrel*: August 1766

The news from London was a long time coming. On August 4, 1766, Captain R. G. Bruce wrote to John Singleton Copley concerning the painting which his ship had conveyed to London for exhibition a full year ago. Considering Copley's apprehensions at the time, the news perhaps made up for the wait. Everyone agreed, Bruce said, that it was "the best Picture of its kind" at the exhibition. At first it was mistaken for the work of an English artist. Reynolds thought it excellent in itself and, considering its provincial origins, *"very wonderfull."* Bruce enclosed a letter from Benjamin West, who desired Copley's friendship.[1]

The news came with sympathetic criticism as well, some of it useful, some perhaps dangerous. West reported that some viewers found the work too "liney." He considered the objection just, adding that "endevouring at great Correctness in ones out line . . . is apt to Produce a Poverty in the look of ones work." Reynolds, Bruce said, also criticized "a little Hardness in the Drawing, Coldness in the Shades, An over minuteness, all which Example would correct." Such "over minuteness," Reynolds and others pointed out, led to compositional weaknesses, the inclusion of peripheral detail that distracted attention from the dramatic center of the picture.[2] West and Reynolds both urged Copley to amend these faults by studying abroad. West advised three or four years' viewing of the great masters; Reynolds believed that sophisticated instruction would make him "one of the first Painters in the World." But the instruction must come soon, Reynolds said, "before your Manner and Taste were corrupted or fixed by working in your little way at Boston." Next month the Society of Artists made Copley a Fellow and called on him to attend the next meeting in London to be formally admitted.

Copley was perplexed what to do. His success in London both delighted him and inflamed him with a sense of the deficiencies of his situation in Boston. Pleasurably he wrote to his half-brother Henry Pelham—the subject of *Boy with Squirrel*—to say that the painting had been ranked with "none but the Works of the first Masters" and that he wished now to flee "this frosen region" in order to be "heated with the sight of the enchanting Works of a Raphael, a Rubens, a Corregio and a Veronese." He wrote to West as well, saying he was flattered to hear from a fellow artist he much respected, "my Country man, from whom America receives the Same Luster that Italy does from her Titiano and Divine Raphael." He agreed with West that his picture was too liney, the result of "two great presition in the out line." A trip to Europe would give him "inexpressable pleasure" because, as West knew, America provided nothing to learn from: "I think myself peculiarly unlucky in Liveing in a place into which there has not been one portrait brought that is worthy to be call'd a Picture within my memory, which leaves me at a great loss to gess the stile that You, Mr. Renolds, and the other Artists pracktice." [3]

Yet, to West's and Reynold's insistent suggestions that he come abroad Copley did not reply. He had many qualms, some of which he confessed to Captain Bruce. It would hardly matter if he went to England, he felt, only to return to America "and Bury all my improvements among people intirely destitute of all just Ideas of the Arts." His success in England had enabled him to get higher prices in Boston; he might not do as well in London, and, should he be unsuccessful there, his reputation at home might suffer. He had obligations, too, to his mother and brother, whom he felt compelled "not to Desert as Long as I can live." [4] In this tossing state of mind, feeling responsible for his family, contemptuous of the opportunities at home but fearful that the effort to expand them might expose his own inadequacies, Copley submitted, at West's request, a picture for the 1767 exhibit, a portrait of a young girl with a bird and dog.

Again Bruce and West wrote to Copley after the exhibition. Bruce said that it was thought the best-executed portrait in the room. But everyone condemned the subject, "which is so disagreable a character, as to have made the Picture disliked by every one but the best Judges who could discern the excellence of the Painting." This was also the opinion of Reynolds and West, who found the overall effect less agreeable than in *Boy with Squirrel*. West again commented on Copley's failure to subordinate his parts correctly. The brightness of the girl's gown, the black and white spaniel with its meticulously rendered hair, the intricate design in the Turkish carpet, were all distracting. The "over minuteness" which led to improper 'subordination of parts,' however, was part of Copley's vision, perhaps better left alone, a flaw only from the point of view of a particular camp. The accessories of even his teen-age Badgeresque paintings were not only bits of incidental social symbolism but objects intensely seen and preciously valued for themselves. The exquisitely rendered glasses of water, engraver's tools, bits of thread, quills, represented a fascination with the mere weight of the world that would be weakened by subordinating the existence of one thing to that of another. Behind Copley's fidelity to what his eye saw—a fidelity animating much later American art, including the haphazard visual catalogues of Walt Whitman and the minutely drawn nuts and bolts of Charles Sheeler—behind this fidelity lay a Puritan determination to see the world as God created it, untransformed, without metaphor or imaginative reshaping. The repeated advice of West and Reynolds pointed Copley in a new, not entirely authentic direction.

Again Bruce, West, and, through them, Reynolds emphasized that these criticisms came from very high regard for Copley's talent. Again West urged him to come to Europe, offering his own house, "whare you will have an oppertunity of Contemplateing the great Productions of art, and feel from them what words Cannot Express. For this is a Scorce the want of which (I am senseble of) Cannot be had in Ameria." These latest encouragements and criticisms only exacerbated Copley's sense of his situation in Boston and of the limitations of provincial life. "The people generally," he now realized, regard painting as "no more than any other usefull trade . . . like that of a Carpenter tailor or shew maker, not as one of the most noble Arts in the World." [5]

15. Opening of the Southwark Theatre: November 1766; the First American Actor; the First American Play, *The Prince of Parthia*: April 24, 1767

Continuing his program of building new theatres in the colonial urban centers, David Douglass and his still-incomplete company arrived in Philadelphia in the summer of 1766, while the new Southwark Theatre was rising. Their arrival was denounced by the Quakers, who prepared an address to Governor John Penn, beginning:

> . . . we have with Real Concern heard that a Company of Stage Players are lately arrd in this City with Intention to Exhibit Plays, which we Conceive if Permitted will tend to subvert the Good order, morals, & Prosperity we desire may be preserved among us.

Governor Penn, a well-known lover of music and the theatre, simply scoffed. The address was "very ridiculous," he said, "drawn up in great form, in which they had neither considered Sense or grammer [sic]." In July, Douglass and Hallam went to visit the governor at Black Point. They wanted him to confirm his promise that he would allow them to perform in the city; otherwise local tradesmen would be "scrupulous of trusting them." Penn said their journey was unnecessary. He had no intention of retracting his promise.[1]

On November 12 or 14, 1766, although the second branch of the Company still had not arrived from the West Indies, Douglass opened his new Philadelphia theatre. Despite the favor of Governor Penn, he had had the theatre built in the Southwark district outside city limits, presumably to stay clear of the Quakers. Some fifty feet wide and ninety-five feet long, it was two and a half stories high, the foundation and first story of brick, the second of wood, topped by a cupola that may have served for ventilation. Although the theatre stayed in use until 1821, in its own time it was criticized as ugly and ill-made—very hot in summer, very cold in winter, leaky, a firetrap. The view from the boxes was obstructed by large, square wooden pillars that supported the upper tier and roof. In wet weather, the outside became so muddy that a boardwalk had to be laid, and carriages might take an hour pulling up to the door.[2]

Still, Douglass opened the Southwark with probably the most varied and innovative season yet brought to the American stage. He offered at least forty different full-length plays for about a hundred nights, including twenty-six Philadelphia premieres. He apparently managed to fill out his troupe by recruiting several other actors, including Tomlinson, from the wrecked Chapel Street theatre, and the aristocratic Margaret Cheer, who had played with the Company earlier.[3] Perhaps not only to supply a cast but also to enlist local support, Douglass hired Samuel Greville—the first known native American to become a professional actor. Greville made his debut on January 2, 1767, in Nicholas Rowe's *Tamerlane* and later appeared as Horatio in *Hamlet*. Little is known about him. Described as a good-looking young man with a clear voice, he came from a respectable South Carolina family, attended Princeton and the College of Philadelphia, and studied law with Joseph Galloway. One of his friends speculated that he joined the Company either because he needed money or had been smitten by an actress. Apparently a high liver pitied by his friends for his plight, he disappeared from the Company in 1768.[4]

It may also have been the hope of currying local favor in the face of Quaker disdain that decided Douglass upon presenting—for the first time—works by native American playwrights. For April 20, 1767, he advertised a performance of *The Disappointment*—the first American comic opera. It was probably written by a local merchant named Andrew Barton, a native Philadelphian who had been educated at the College.[5] He based the play on a local incident. Rumor got around Philadelphia that the pirate Blackbeard had cached some of his treasure on the banks of the Delaware; several Philadelphians began hunting for it. In the play, the sparks Hum, Parchment, Quadrant, and Rattletrap invent a tale of buried treasure in order to dupe the socially ambitious Washball and Raccoon. Barton's comic treatment of Scotchmen, Irishmen, and other national types shows the influence of the *pasticcios,* in whose titles quite often appears the word "Disappointment." But he reversed the socially radical action of the *pasticcios,* depicting the lower-class characters as fools who fight among and gull themselves, and deserve the place in society which they occupy.

The more striking features of *The Disappointment* are its punning bawdiness and the character Raccoon. One scene takes place in the bordello of Moll Placket, a prostitute who "rais'd and laid 500 in my time" and whose slang surname means vagina. Her "cock-a-dandy" lover is Raccoon, an aging, courtly black man. He hopes by discovering the rumored treasure to make Moll "fine as de queen of Shebe" and to make himself "cut de figure in life, and appear in de world wid de proper impotance. . . ." In his gullibility, timorousness, and speech patterns, Raccoon represents the first instance of the "Northern Dandy" type of stage Negro and the beginnings of lasting literary conventions in the characterizations of blacks.[6] Raccoon also sings an equally portentous, somewhat risqué song:

AIR IV. YANKEE DOODLE.

O! how joyful shall I be,
When I get de money,
I will bring it all to dee;
O! my diddling honey.

Although the first datable words to "Yankee Doodle" had been written about twenty years earlier, after the capture of Louisburg, the song evidently was becoming popular in the mid-1760's.

Douglass no sooner announced *The Disappointment* for performance than he canceled it. Some local businessmen apparently saw themselves satirized in the play and became incensed.[7] Probably loath to withstand their indignation on top of the Quakers', Douglass withdrew the April 20 performance. Instead, four days later, he produced a work which a local playwright had shown to him in 1759.

Thomas Godfrey's *The Prince of Parthia* thus became the first American drama to be professionally produced on the American stage. It was also the first American play published in America, having appeared in 1765 in the author's posthumous *Juvenile Poems* (Philadelphia). Douglass presented it on April 24 with a cast including himself, Lewis Hallam, Jr., Morris, Misses Wainwright and Cheer, and Samuel Greville.

The Prince of Parthia is a blank-verse tragedy in five acts with a relatively straightforward plot. Vardanes, son of King Artabanus, is overcome with envy of his brother Arsaces' fortune: Arsaces, as the first-born son, is Prince of Parthia; Arsaces is a successful warrior, adulated; Arsaces is loved by Evanthe, who disdains Vardanes. With the aid of Lysias, an officer at court, Vardanes leads the king to believe that Arsaces desires his overthrow—both from overweening ambition and because the lustful king also loves Evanthe. Lysias kills the king and is able to shift the blame to Arsaces. First imprisoned then freed, Arsaces joins the citizenry in an attack on the usurping Vardanes. Vardanes is killed along with Lysias. But Evanthe mistakenly believes that the victim is her beloved Arsaces. She takes poison and dies; on learning of her death, Arsaces commits suicide.

Godfrey put together this highly literary play by rearranging *King Lear*, *Macbeth*, and *Othello*; adding bits of seduction from Richardson, overprotective fathers from sentimental dramas, and paeans to spring from college commencement exercises; and giving the whole a frenzied consistency derived from revenge tragedy and suited to the many shown and described acts of parricide, suicide, incest, rape, insanity, and sadism, including the king's wife beating out her brains against a tree. The action is loosely based on actual events in Parthian history reported in Tacitus' *Annals*. Although the author's friend Nathaniel Evans considered the play "very unfinished," Godfrey shows considerable technical skill, particularly in his Shakespearean use of dramatic images.[8] Characterization and narrative both progress through recurrences and transformations of conflicting, complex images of light and dark, calm and storm, harmony and chaos.

The remoteness of ancient Parthia, moreover, is only apparent, for the characters' perceptions of events are no different from many colonists' perceptions of the Stamp Act. Godfrey used Parthian history to give dramatic form to Whiggish ideas. Vardanes is a haughty anti-democrat who hates and dies cursing the "common rubbish"; Arsaces is the ideal Whig leader, unambitious, a prince who would rather be a swain, "My throne some hillock, and my flock my subjects." The political main plot and the romantic subplot use the identical Whiggish language of "slaves," "chains," and "tyrants." In one place, referring to the king, Evanthe calls upon "the sons of men/ To join, and crush the tyrant!" In another place the "Tyrant" is love, which "Despotic rules, and fetters all our thoughts." Like the demonstrators beweeping "fair Liberty," the play's political action draws in larger moral ideas of the period and its language comprehends domestic, political, and other relationships. On one level or another, *The Prince of Parthia* keeps probing questions of power, slavery, ambition, and rebellion—often hysterically, but often too with remarkable prescience.

In attempting to mount two plays by Philadelphians, Douglass probably hoped to ingratiate his company to a populous, potentially lucrative city where opposition to the theatre also happened to be intense.[9] He tried in other ways also. He lowered prices from seven, five, and three shillings— boxes, pit, and gallery—to five, three, and two shillings. Ads for *The Mourning Bride* and *Love for Love* came with considerate announcements that because William Congreve had in some places *"given the Rein to his wanton Muse"* Hallam had *"taken the Freedom to crop such Luxuriances and expunge every Passage that might be offensive either to Decency or good Manners."* Woolls and Miss Wainwright gave a charity vocal concert for relief of the local poor.[10] But none of this worked. Only about a week after the Company gave the Philadelphia premiere of *Love in a Village*, a writer in the *Gazette*, probably alluding to the destruction of the Chapel Street Theatre, applauded the citizens of New York for having driven the actors out with "righteous Indignation." The same actors, he said, who "pretend to improve the Manners of others" themselves live in "shameless Violation of Laws human and divine." Another columnist quoted Tertullian, Clement, Chrysostom, and a long list of other church fathers to prove that great Christians have deemed plays *"Impediments in the Way of Salvation."* [11]

On the same pages with these blasts, however, appeared The American Company's own ads for its productions, "By Authority," of *High Life Below Stairs* and other plays. The authority—Governor Penn—was a powerful ally. In February 1767, he received an allegedly interdenominational "Remonstrance" urging him to repulse the actors because they hurt trade by encouraging idleness and diverting apprentices, and because of "their direct repugnance to the spirit, temper and precepts of the Gospel." Penn did nothing of the sort. As the Philadelphian Thomas Wharton wrote to Benjamin Franklin in London, " 'Tis said that, he constantly attends them [plays], and that, he has had the Players to dine, or sup with him. To such a State is Pennsylvania reduced, that when N York, and the other Colonies had refused those Wretches an Assylium; they found this their only Sanctuary!" [12]

Begun by the Quakers in the summer of 1766, the battle over The American Company continued in the Philadelphia press through the spring and summer of 1767. One decisive question batted around the twenty or so essays that appeared in the *Journal*, the *Chronicle*, and the *Gazette* was whether the stage inspires virtue. The view that it could, rested on the eighteenth-century connection between ethics and feeling. The stage does not simply teach moral lessons; rather, by helping us to feel deeply for another's plight, it stirs up the intrinsic goodness of the heart, arousing pity, benevolence, and humanitarianism. Thus "Z" argued in the *Journal* that the stage is the "best school of *practical morality*," for the artful combination of playwright and actor can excite the "passions which fix the basis of society, and render man . . . sociable. . . ." Because the stage works more on the affections than on the intellect, it is particularly useful in promoting virtue among those untouched by history and art, the "inattentive multitude," the "unfeeling crowd." [13]

Against this, opponents argued that the feelings aroused by the stage were not those of benevolence but of lust. In the guise of teaching virtue, actors offered

> love-intrigues, blasphemous passions, profane discourses, lewd descriptions, filthy jests, and all the most extravagant rant of wanton, profligate persons of both sexes, heating and enflaming one another with all the wantonness of address, immodesty of motion, and lewdness of thought, that wit can invent.

Instead of sending their children to Europe to be educated, draining the country of money, American parents could send them to the theatre, where they would learn the same things:

> . . . our youth may hear and view, at a trifling expence, every refinement of politeness, every sentiment of honour, and every scene of debauchery and villainy represented in their most striking colours. Here the fine gentleman may be taught the genuine airs, manners, and insincerity of a court; the rake all the lasciviousness and ribaldry of a stew; and the man whose native genius leads him to prey on his fellow-creatures, may here find ready invented to his hand, every species of fraud and iniquity, that the heart of man can conceive.

"Theatricus" illustrated the notion that the stage is a "School of Virtue and Knowledge" by giving a long extract from the popular afterpiece *The Lying Valet*, which was rich in words like "bawd" and "pimp" and in instances of pickpocketing and hard drinking. Another writer mocked even *Cato* as an example not of heroic self-sacrifice but as "a most shining Pattern of the laudable Action of Self-murder. . . ." [14]

The question of whether the stage teaches virtue raised wider questions about clerical authority and the current health of Christianity. On these questions, proponents of the theatre ranged from freethinkers, who accused their antagonists of superstition, ignorance, and inquisitorial tyranny, to rationalistic Christians, who accused them of teaching a God of gloom and vengeance. The freethinking "A.B." challenged the writer who quoted the church fathers against the stage. It surprised him, he said, that anyone could think the "mere *ipse dixit* of any of the fathers would pass for sound reasoning." He appealed instead to the "bar of reason," which proved that "for a few bigotted people to usurp a prerogative of the Deity . . . and erect a tyranny over the wills of others, is most impious and impudent." [15] Among the rationalistic Christians was the author of a twenty-two-page pamphlet published in Philadelphia in 1767, entitled *True Pleasure, Chearfulness, and Happiness, The immediate Consequence of Religion . . . With some Remarks on the Theatre,* very likely the work of the Anglican clergyman William Smith, provost of the College. He addressed himself to a young woman who recently rejected her suitor, a clergyman, because he delighted in dancing and plays as *"innocent amusements."* The writer bolstered the clergyman's case with some doctrine: Over the universe presides a triune God who has reconciled Himself to sinning man through His goodness. He brings, in the words of the Gospel, "inestimable tidings of Joy, Peace and Harmony." Unlike the fanatics who crucified Christ, God does not hate, but loves man. This "amiable doctrine" of an "affectionate" Redeemer of boundless mercy—the certainty of salvation—makes it impossible for a Christian to be "gloomy, melancholy, or discontented:—on the contrary he must of consequence be chearful." The stage helps humanity to be what God wishes it to be: happy.

Implications that opponents of the theatre were irrational fanatics or false gospellers begot counter-implications that its defenders were disguised atheists hoping to destroy Christianity in the name of free inquiry or universal salvation. "A Free Thinker," with heavy irony, trusted that Philadelphians were too "sensible and intelligent" to be "blindly led by their pastors, or the dull stoicks of the age." Dropping his mask, he made clear, not illogically, where the doctrine of all-forgiving cheerfulness led: *"if there is no* GOD, *no future rewards and punishments, Theatrical Entertainments may be allowed and encouraged in the world."* [16] Rationalistic Christians made theatre permissible by denying sin and dispensing with God.

Douglass himself entered the print controversy in March. He published in each of the Philadelphia newspapers an essay which he had written five years earlier in New York, a many-sided defense of himself, of actors, of freedom of thought, and of the ability of the stage to teach virtue. "I should look forward with terror," he said, "if I thought myself engaged in a business that could be productive of the horrid consequences imputed to it." To the charge that the theatre undermined religion he replied that St. Paul quotes Euripides and that if the stage had been abused so had the pulpit. To the charge that actors, being depraved, could not teach virtue, he answered that Cicero befriended Roscius and that because of "their modest and genteel deportment" actors had been "caress'd by the best families in America." He repeated the libertarian argument that people themselves, not their legislatures, should decide whether they go to the theatre, and the pedagogical theory that the stage provides models of elocution for budding ministers and lawyers. Strategically, and emphatically, he argued for a theatre "under proper regulations," in effect for institutionalized censorship. Probably he trusted that friendly governors like Penn would go through the motions, cramping the Company a little but appeasing its enemies. For himself, he said, he was persuaded "that theatrical entertainments, under due regulations, are not only innocent amusements, but may be rendered extremely profitable. . . ." [17]

Douglass played on through the hubbub, having a new theatre, an American actor, and an American play to show for the large promises he had made but seen evaporate in Charleston. In midsummer, he moved on to New York.

16. The Townshend Acts: June 1767; Liberty Songs and Poems 1768–69

The verses sung to the king by "Sons of Loyalty" on the banks of the Schuylkill did not echo long. Gratitude toward England for ending the Stamp Act cooled in the gradual, chilling recognition that the Declaratory Act, passed the same day as Repeal, contained an ambiguity concerning Parliament's power to tax. Any doubts that this ambiguity was intended to affirm the right of taxation were resolved by the passage of the Townshend Revenue Acts in June 1767. The acts set duties on glass, painters' colors, paper, tea, and other goods much consumed in the colonies.

Behind these taxes was not the need of raising money to support British troops but a concern for restoring the effectiveness of British government. Grenville and many members of Parliament believed that Repeal had been a mistake, a confession of weakness to Americans who in fact wished to be independent. The new duties, devised by Charles Townshend, chancellor of the exchequer, could be used to pay the salaries of royal officials in the colonies, freeing them from the control of colonial legislatures. Two other laws were passed at the same time, one establishing a separate Board of Customs in Boston to collect the duties, the other suspending the New York Assembly until it complied with the Quartering Act, which required colonial authorities to supply food, lodging, and supplies for British troops. [1]

Opposition to the new measures developed slowly, beginning with a

low-keyed revival of the tactic of non-importation. In the fall of 1767, a
Boston town meeting called for voluntary non-consumption of such
luxuries as ribbon, lace, tea, and imported clothing; by winter, other
colonies adopted similar resolutions. In an "Address to the Ladies" at the
end of the year, a Virginian asked women to forsake fancy headdresses for
homespun:

> And as one all agree that you'll not married be
> To such as will wear London factory,
> But at first sight refuse, tell them such you do choose
> As encourage our own manufactory.
> No more ribands wear, nor in rich dress appear,
> Love your country much better than fine things,
> Begin without passion, 'twill soon be the fashion
> To grace your smooth locks with a twine string.

Good-humored counsel, however, gave way to stern warning as many
colonists began to see Repeal as only an intermission in the long-range
scenario of enslavement. In November, newspapers throughout the
colonies published the first of John Dickinson's *Letters from a Farmer in
Pennsylvania*. Dickinson cautioned the colonists to stay alert; even slight
encroachments, such as taxes on paper, could signal the mobilization of
the design. "A free people," he said, "can never be too quick in observing,
nor too firm in opposing the beginnings of alteration either in form or
reality, respecting institutions formed for their security." Obfuscating
terms like 'regulations of trade'—a euphemism for 'revenues,' Dickinson
said—demanded "the most watchful attention," else "servitude may be
slipped upon us, under the sanction of usual and respectable terms." [2] One
other fact heightened the feeling of watchful disillusionment: The
Townshend Acts had been passed under the ministry of the man to whom
most colonists effusively credited Repeal, of whom they had only recently
commissioned statues and paintings—William Pitt. He was now physically
and mentally ill, his popularity waning, his ministry all but disintegrated.

With the new year, anger and disaffection mounted. In January, the
newly created Colonial Department was given over to Lord Hillsborough,
who could be brusque. In February, the Massachusetts House of Representatives approved a letter drafted by James Otis and Samuel Adams,
and ordered copies sent to the legislatures of the other colonies. This
so-called Massachusetts Circular Letter declared the Townshend Acts
unconstitutional, denounced them for trying to make royal officials
"independent of the people," and called on the other colonies to unite in
protesting them to the king. The letter reached London amidst new
elections, riots, and the return of the outlawed radical John Wilkes. In no

indulgent mood, Hillsborough sent orders to Governor Bernard of Massachusetts. He must require the House to formally disapprove and to rescind the letter. If the House refused, Bernard must dissolve it.[3]

June brought two jolting events. On June 10, British officials seized the significantly named *Liberty*, a sloop belonging to John Hancock, for landing some Madeira wine without paying duties. In turn the officials were physically attacked by a mob. They wrote home asking for British troops to protect them in carrying out their function in the future. On June 30, the Massachusetts House voted against rescinding its Circular Letter, as Hillsborough demanded, by ninety-two to seventeen. The numbers, part of a burgeoning symbolic lexicon of trees and jackboots, became talismanic. Paul Revere, for one, engraved a caricatura, called *A Warm Place—Hell*, in which a devil pitchforked the seventeen rescinders, listed below, into a fire-breathing monster's jaws; later Revere made a punch bowl, honoring Wilkes and the anti-rescinders, weighing forty-five ounces and holding forty-five gills, from which forty-five toasts were drunk, to honor Wilkes's famed *North Briton* no. 45. Conservatives spoofed the whole business. In 1770, a New York Son of Liberty named Alexander McDougall—regarded as a local Wilkes—was visited in jail by a group of radical women. As a conservative wit reported the incident, the group sang to him the forty-fifth psalm, and consisted of forty-five virgins who were all forty-five years old.[4]

One day after the vote in the House, Governor Bernard dissolved the General Court. Three days later, John Dickinson sent to James Otis a "song for American freedom" which encouraged the swelling mood of determined unity and made it conscious of itself. The "Liberty Song," as it quickly became known, was probably the first set of verses by an American to be learned by heart by a large, intercolonial audience. Dickinson sent the song with a letter noting that eight lines had been written by Arthur Lee, and that for himself he had "long since renounced poetry." What led him to "invoke the deserted muses" was the realization that "indifferent songs are frequently very powerful on certain occasions." The propaganda value of songs had long been recognized and was well understood by the patriot leaders. Samuel Adams used his good voice as a political instrument. A "Master in vocal Musick," he was later accused of "instituting singing Societys of Mechanicks, where he preesided; & embraced such Opportunities to ye inculcating Sedition, 'till it had ripened into Rebellion." Dickinson himself observed that Cardinal de Retz, the archbishop of Paris, "always inforced his political operations by songs. I wish our attempt may be useful. . . ." [5]

Dickinson's song became not so much useful as indispensable. Actually, Dickinson wrote again to Otis two days later calling his first version "rather too bold" and enclosing a revised copy. The first version has become lost, but the second appeared swiftly in several newspaper and broadside editions. Its first printed appearance was probably in the July 21, 1768, issue of the *Virginia Gazette*, under the heading "Philadelphia, July 7" and near news from London about Garrick and Arne; in Philadelphia it appeared in a broadside version entitled *A New Song, to the tune of Hearts of oak*; in Boston it was advertised in a musical version adapted to the German flute and violin, and in a version for voice entitled *The New and Favourite Liberty Song*.[6]

The song became a favorite in little more than a month. On August 14 the Boston Sons of Liberty celebrated the anniversary of their first Stamp Act demonstration, the one at which an effigy of Andrew Oliver had been hanged from what became Liberty Tree. As reported in the *Evening-Post*, "The Musick began at high Noon, performed on various Instruments, joined with Voices; and concluding with the universally admired *American* Song of Liberty, the Grandeur of its Sentiment, and the easy Flow of its Numbers, together with an exquisite Harmony of Sound, afforded Sublime Entertainments to a numerous Audience, fraught with a noble Ardour in the cause of Freedom." Afterward the Daughters of Liberty appeared in windows around town, French horns blew, and cannon resounded ninety-two times before the drinking of forty-five toasts at Roxbury—a potent combination of numerology, singing, and wine. In October, Charleston mechanics sang Dickinson's verses to consecrate a liberty tree, from which they dangled forty-five lights, after which they toasted the ninety-two.[7] The same month, patriots in Halifax erected a liberty pole and employed "some boys to sing the Liberty Song through the streets." At the August 14 celebration in Dorchester the next year, 350 Sons of Liberty were said to have sung the chorus in an open field. "This," John Adams said of the singing, "is cultivating the Sensations of Freedom." [8]

Adams' remark identifies one of two main reasons for the immense success of Dickinson's song: It cultivated sensations. It enabled people to experience directly the idea of strength in unity, by enacting it in boisterous choral singing. The sensation of oneness, no doubt, gained from the new musical training being offered throughout New England by a score of church-related singing schools. This training equipped the singers not simply to bawl but to produce what the *Evening-Post* described as "exquisite Harmony of Sound"—a harmony in this case both ideological and musical. Dickinson set his words to the tune "Hearts of Oak" by the English organist William Boyce, whose anthems and arrangements were widely advertised in British America. By wedding the current political arguments to music, Dickinson knew, he drew on emotional resources that the words alone could not muster.

Another reason for the success of the song is that Dickinson summarized the ideology of 1768 in memorable form, retaining the emotional appeals of Whig Sentimentalism. He couched his appeal for unity in the Richardsonian language of "fair Liberty," associating the patriots with the bold who will not allow America, like a virgin, to be 'stain'd with dishonor':

> COME join Hand in Hand, brave AMERICANS all,
> And rouse your bold Hearts at fair LIBERTY's Call;
> No *tyrannous Acts* shall suppress your *just Claim*,
> Or stain with *Dishonor* AMERICA's Name————

As the work of "the Farmer"—often referred to as the "Song of the Farmer"—the text also claimed for its views the guileless integrity of pastoral life. Dickinson likewise invoked the powerful forefathers theme, noting the heritage of Liberty descended from the first settlers, who "dying bequeath'd us their *Freedom* and *Fame*————" He also provided a graphically compact but comprehensive explanation of the Townshend Acts as a ministerial scheme to consume the labor of hard-working Americans:

> Swarms of PLACEMEN and PENSIONERS soon will appear,
> Like Locusts deforming the Charms of the Year;
> Suns vainly will rise, Showers vainly descend,
> If *we* are to *drudge for* what *others* shall *spend.*

(In a footnote to this stanza, Dickinson wrote: "The *Ministry* have already begun to give away in PENSIONS *the Money* THEY have *lately* taken out of our Pockets WITHOUT OUR CONSENT.") Finally, Dickinson treated liberty as a birthright whose loss diminishes life in an essential aspect. The chorus, repeated after each of the eight stanzas, reiterates the idea:

> In FREEDOM we're BORN, and in FREEDOM we'll LIVE,
> Our Purses are ready,
> Steady, Friends, Steady,
> Not as SLAVES, but as FREEMEN our Money we'll give.

Generally, the metronomically regular rhythm of Boyce's tune is not well adapted to the verse rhythm of this chorus; but it nicely emphasizes the 'steadiness' that Dickinson counsels. The main theme of the song, however, is unity, the need to "join Hand in Hand" in a manner and spirit suggested by the mass singing itself.

Reprinted in newspaper after newspaper and sung everywhere, the "Liberty Song" became a symbol of colonial resistance to the Townsend programs. In September the *Boston Gazette* published "A Parody upon a

Well-Known Liberty Song" denouncing the patriots as screechers, plun-
derers, and sots fit for the gallows, and charging, not without some truth,
that they were hypnotized by the concept of "fair Liberty":

> Come shake your dull noddles, ye pumpkins, and bawl,
> And own that you're mad at fair Liberty's call;
> No scandalous conduct can add to your shame,
> Condemn'd to dishonor, inherit the fame.
>> In folly you're born, and in folly you'll live,
>>> To madness still ready,
>>> And stupidly steady,
>> Not as men, but as monkeys, the tokens you give.

In November "The Parody Parodized"—probably by Benjamin Church—
attacked the parody:

> COME swallow your bumpers, ye tories, and roar,
> That the sons of fair Freedom are hamper'd once more;
> But know that no cut-throats our spirits can tame,
> Nor a host of oppressors shall smother the flame.

Quickly the "liberty song" became not a title but a type, the model for
broadsides like *An Excellent New Song, for the Sons of Liberty* and *A Song, to the
Tune of Hearts of Oak* and *A New SONG address'd to the SONS of LIBERTY, on
the Continent of AMERICA; particularly to the illustrious, Glorious and never to be
Forgotten NINETY-TWO of BOSTON.* The last, to the tune of "Come jolly
Bacchus," commends the farmer, blasts the seventeen, and calls on the
audience to claim their "NAT'RAL RIGHTS":

> Obey, my *Brothers, Nature's* call,
>> Your *Country* too demands it!
> Let LIBERTY ne'er have a *Fall!*
> 'Tis Freedom that commands it.[9]

With the defiance of the ninety-two and other events of the summer, the
relatively mild, voluntary non-importation movement begun in 1767 gave
way to stringent formal agreements. On August 1, 1768, Boston merchants
entered into an explicit non-importation pact, calling for a one-year
boycott of all British goods, beginning in January 1769. By the end of
1769, every colony except New Hampshire had such an agreement. While
short poems and songs on liberty continued to appear, the seriousness of
the measures and the growing complexity of political debate occasioned
several lengthy poems published in pamphlet form: *Liberty. A Poem*
(Philadelphia, 1768), by "Rusticus"; *Liberty, A Poem, Lately Found in a
Bundle of Papers, Said to be Written by a Hermit in New-Jersey* (Philadelphia,
1769), by Thomas Hopkinson; and *America. A Poem* (Philadelphia; 1769?),

by Alexander Martin. A shorter but impressive poem, "On LIBERTY-
TREE," by "Philo Patriae," was published in the *South-Carolina Gazette* on
Sept. 21, 1769. This group of liberty poems contains most of the ideological
elements of the earlier Stamp Act poems, the same ones condensed in
Dickinson's popular song: the feminizing of liberty; the theme of
disinheritance ("*We are thy offspring*—Heav'ns! how have we lov'd/ Our
mother's name. . . ."); the groaning grief of Whig Sentimentalism ("One
gen'ral deluge of unnumbred woes"); and the influence of Whig pastoral-
ism in the attribution of the works to "Rusticus" or to a New Jersey
hermit, men whose lack of ambition makes their political values trustwor-
thy and correct. Like the Stamp Act poems, they interpret events as the
outcome of ministerial conspiracy—" 'When Mi--st-rs to feed insatiate
Pride,/ 'Their *Truth*, their *Country* and their K--G misguid" *[sic];* stress the
need to repulse even slight encroachments, "latent poison"; and in general
call for prudent resistance: "With modest Boldness make your Troubles
known."

The new elements in the liberty poems are their lengthy passages of
historical and philosophical exposition. Alexander Martin traced the
rights claimed by the colonists back to the Anglo-Saxons. This view,
sometimes called the doctrine of "Northern Liberty" or the "German
Translatio," developed through a long tradition beginning with Samuel von
Pufendorff and Hugo Grotius and including Thomson's *Liberty* and
William Paterson's play *Arminius* (1740). It derived British freedom from
the people depicted by Tacitus in his *Germania*, the Saxons who by curbing
royal power and devising parliamentary representation gave birth to the
British form of mixed government. Liberty was thus translated from the
Saxons to England and, by implication, to the English colonists. Martin
prodded Americans to recover their heritage of "*Freedom* from *Alfred*—
handed down to GEORGE!":

> Say! whence this fatal inconsistence rose?
> That *Britons*, freeborn *Britons* should enslave
> Equal in fame, as gen'rous great and brave,
> To whom, those ancient glorious *Rights* belong,
> Which those great *Chieftains* claim'd from whom they sprung.

The German Translation allowed the colonists to maintain strict loyalty
while changing their lineage, by claiming joint descent with England from
an older, common Saxon stock.[10]

The search for historical sanctions accounts for the introduction of
another non-British forebear. The liberty poems contain what seems to be
the first appearance in American literature, as more than a name, of
Christopher Columbus. In *Liberty* by "Rusticus," Columbus tells the

colonists that Grenville has been preparing to "invade" their freedom, counsels them that "On *Care* and *Union* your *Success* depends," and addresses Jove (King George) in their behalf. Columbus also appears in Martin's *America*, the first in a line of explorers including Hudson and Cabot; he juxtaposes their discoveries with the Townshend Acts and asks, "Was it for this?"

Other liberty poems found legitimacy for the colonial position not in history but in God and Nature. "Philo Patriae" explained that kings hold their power in trust from God, and hold it rightfully only so long as they preserve the laws to which their subjects have consented; when they substitute their own laws, they must be resisted:

> Those RIGHTS, which God and Nature mean.
> RIGHTS! which, when truly understood,
> Are Cause of universal Good.
> RIGHTS! which declare, "That all are free,
> "In Person and in Property.
> "That Pow'r supreme, when giv'n in Trust,
> "Belongs but to the Wise and Just.
> "That Kings are Kings for this sole Cause,
> "To be the Guardians of the Laws,
> "That Subjects only should obey,
> "Only submit to sov'reign Sway,
> "When Sov'reigns make those Laws their Choice,
> "To which the People give their Voice.
> "That in free States, 'tis ever meant,
> "No Laws should bind, without *Consent:*
> "And that, when other Laws take Place,
> "Not to *resist,* wou'd be Disgrace. . . .

To Thomas Hopkinson, however, the doctrine of the divine origin of rights suggested not resistance but, except in despair, quietism. The God who gives liberty must be trusted to punish its usurpers:

> Let man be active, rational, and free,
> The GOD OF NATURE said.—If then we see
> *That* liberty destroy'd, which NATURE gave,
> The weaker by the Stronger made a Slave,
> A haughty Tyrant's will become a law,
> And *man* approaching *man* with trembling awe;
> That vengeance *will* o'ertake the villain's crime
> We know;—but of the *manner and the time,*
> Let HIM alone be Judge. . . .

These and the other long poems of 1768–69 elaborated the earlier technical discussions of taxation and the hits at Bute into a broader, though often rather general, historical and philosophical examination of the concept of liberty. In doing so they of course reflect a public sense of the growing seriousness of the issues involved, and something more. The style of the liberty poems—the plethora of capitals, italics, exclamation marks, and dashes—conveys impatience. Amid the lofty explanations of natural law and Saxon precedent, the many shorthand references—allusions, initials, numbers, allegorical figures, and other symbolic bits—imply an accumulation of matters too well understood to need explaining.

17. West's *Agrippina*, Peale's *Pitt:* c. Spring 1767–Spring 1769

Abroad, Benjamin West had produced and profited from a canvas some five feet high and eight feet wide entitled *Agrippina Landing at Brundisium with the Ashes of Germanicus* (ill., p. 123). The history of its composition remains vague. By one account, the archbishop of York read to West a passage about Agrippina from the *Annals* of Tacitus and asked him to paint it. West drew a sketch before going to sleep that night. The next morning he showed it to the archbishop, who proposed (but finally failed) to raise £3,000 so that West might wholly give up portraits for history painting. West probably completed the work shortly before the arrival in London of Charles Willson Peale. Not long after, perhaps two months or so before passage of the Townshend Acts, the archbishop praised the painting to King George, who asked to meet the painter.

The work which brought about this meeting was West's first major achievement. Germanicus, a great but merciful general, had died near Antioch in A.D. 19, probably poisoned. His wife Agrippina, the daughter of Augustus, had accompanied him on his campaign, and returned to Rome bearing his ashes. West chose for his subject the moment of her landing, as described by Tacitus,

> when the fleet slowly approached, its crew, not joyous as is usual, but wearing all a studied expression of grief. When Agrippina descended from the vessel with her two children, clasping the funeral urn, with eyes rivetted to the earth, there was one universal groan. You could not distinguish kinsfolk from strangers, or the laments of men from those of women. . . .[1]

West showed Agrippina on a stone pier, as on a stage, her two cherubic children tugging at her cloak, hooded women in her train. Staring, her

The Van Dyck–Kneller–Lely tradition dominated colonial portraiture in the 1760's. TOP: John Wollaston, *William Plumsted* (oil on canvas, 50 × 40). John Hesselius, *Charles Calvert and Colored Slave* (oil on canvas, 50¼ × 40¼). BOTTOM: John Singleton Copley, *Epes Sargent, Sr.* (oil on canvas, 49⅞ × 40).

THEATRE.

By the Old American Company.

On *Wednefday Evening*, the 30th of *November*, will be performed,

A COMEDY, of *Shakefpear's*,

CALLED, THE

Merchant of Venice.

Shylock,	Mr. HENRY,
Baffanio,	Mr. HARPER,
Gratiano,	Mr. BIDDLE,
Lorenzo, *(with Songs)*	Mr. WOOLLS,
Launcellot,	Mr. MORRIS,
Salanio,	Mr. LAKE,
And, Anthonio,	Mr. WIGNELL.
Neriffa,	Mrs. HARPER,
Jeffica,	Mifs TUKE,
And, Portia,	Mrs. MORRIS.

End of Act 3d, a *Hornpipe*.

To which will be Added,

An ENTERTAINMENT, *Called,* The

Miller of Mansfield.

King Henry,	Mr. HENRY,
Dick,	Mr. HARPER,
Joe, *(with a Song)*	Mr. WOOLLS,
Lord Lurewell,	Mr. BIDDLE,
And, The Miller,	Mr. MORRIS.
Peggy,	Mifs TUKE,
Margery,	Mifs DURANG,
And, Kate,	Mrs. MORRIS.

The Doors will be open in future at *Five,* and the Curtain drawn up precifely at, *A Quarter after Six o'Clock.*

Places in the Boxes may be taken of Mr. *Delamater,* at the Box Lobby, every Day, from *Ten* to *Twelve* in the Forenoon, and from *Four* to *Five* in the Evening; where alfo TICKETS may be had, and at Mr. GAINE's Book-Store, in *Hanover-Square.*

Ladies and Gentlemen are requefted to defire their Servants to take up and fet down with their Horfes Heads towards the *Eaft-River,* to avoid Confufion; alfo as foon as they are feated, to order their Servants out of the *Boxes.*

BOX 8s. PIT 6s. and GALLERY 4s.

⁎⁎ *No Perfon to be admitted behind the Scenes, on any Account whatever.*

The Public are refpectfully informed, the Days of Performance will be, *Mondays, Wednefdays* and *Fridays.*

Vivat Refpublica.

Playbill for a New York performance, November 30, 1785. The ingredients for an evening at the American theatre remained the same throughout the revolutionary period: a long play, a musical interlude (in this case John Durang's hornpipe), and a short afterpiece. Hallam's actors performed as the "Old" American Company after the war.

ABOVE: Postwar ticket for The American Company, with an oval of thirteen stars.

BELOW: Leading actors and later co-managers of The American Company. LEFT: Lewis Hallam, Jr., "as much the soul" of the American stage "as ever Garrick was of Drury Lane." RIGHT: John Henry, a fine singer and shrewd businessman, dressed as Ephraim in *Wild Oats*.

Matthew Pratt, *The American School* (oil on canvas, 36 × 50¼). Benjamin West stands at the far left, pointing at a sketch held by Pratt,

West's first major history painting was *Agrippina Landing at Brundisium with the Ashes of Germanicus* (oil on canvas, 64½ × 94½), a historicist lesson in patriotic forbearance and domestic fidelity.

TOP: Charles Willson Peale, *James Peale* (oil on canvas, 30 × 25). Both Peales were prolific miniaturists. BOTTOM: Benjamin West, *Charles Willson Peale* (oil on canvas, 28½ × 23). Peale studied with West in London for two years.

John Singleton Copley sent his *Boy with Squirrel* (oil on canvas, 30¼ × 25) for exhibition to the Society of Artists in London, where it was highly praised.

The Deplorable State of America, probably by John Singleton Copley. Used by permission of The Print Room, Boston.

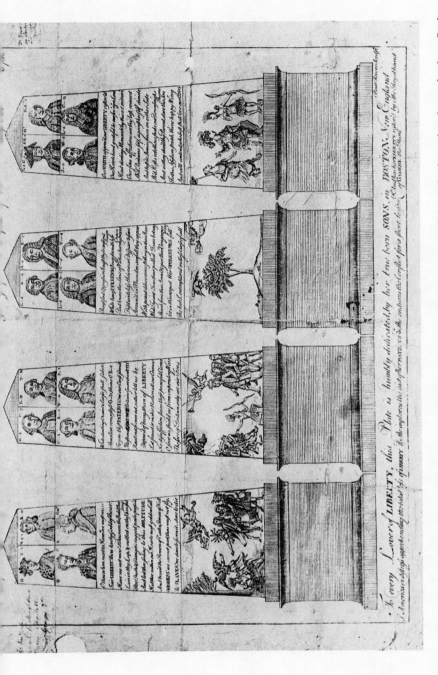

Paul Revere, *A View of the Obelisk erected under Liberty-Tree.* Lamps housed within the obelisk made the painted panels glow. Such "transparencies" were a standard feature of public celebrations in eighteenth-century America.

Paul Revere, *The Bloody Massacre perpetrated in King Street.* By one written account, the massacre occurred just before 10:00 P.M.; Revere has set the hands of the First Church clock at 10:20.

mouth slightly agape, she presses to herself the cinerary urn. To the left, mourning men and women await her progress, heads bowed. To the right, muscular young sailors ply the oars of a just-landing ship in whose prow a captain gives commands. The background is filled with figures wailing.

History painting, West wrote to Copley in June 1767, "demands the greates Cear [i.e., care] and intelegance . . . amaginable." In *Agrippina* West applied all his acquired theory and knowledge to these demands: to expressing emotions through gesture, bearing, and narrative relationships; to giving the historically correct social, geographical, architectural, and climatological details; above all, to teaching virtue. The work impressively displays West's knowledge of Roman history, costume, architecture, and shipbuilding, and his ability as a psychohistorian to extrapolate the emotions that Agrippina, Nero (her infant son), and other important figures might have felt on the occasion. Without violating the requirements of history painting, he managed to subordinate them to a dramatically compelling form, to supply the focus which, he had warned Copley, *Boy with Squirrel* lacked. He set Agrippina and her cortege in the center of the painting, picking them out from the other, shadowed groups by a strong light and arranging the docking prow of the ship and the hand of the captain to point to them for double emphasis. He gave the central group the pallid, frieze-like appearance called for by the ideal of noble, anti-sensual beauty which his age, led by Johann Winckelmann, ascribed to classical art. Clearly outlined, precisely drawn, and thinly painted, the statue-like figures make a moral comment, affirming the other extreme from the wanton prettiness of Jean Antoine Watteau or François Boucher. No doubt West's easy control of the chaste neoclassical style was largely due to his Quaker upbringing, which allowed him to bring to the style a temperament already shaped to its demands.[2]

West's didactic intent appears more directly, however, than in his style. *Agrippina* is a textbook case of the *exemplum virtutis*, the work which seeks to produce moral reform by illustrating virtuous conduct. Tacitus himself saw Agrippina as an emblem of Rome before its corruption and decline, "the solitary example of the old times." He praised Germanicus less for being a great general than for being "temperate in his pleasures, the husband of one wife, with only legitimate children." Such private rectitude, for Tacitus no less than for Trenchard and Gordon, was the foundation of a just state. Tacitus suggested that Germanicus was poisoned because he "had the idea of comprehending in a restored era of freedom the Roman people under equal laws." [3] West made the same juncture of morals and politics. He depicted Agrippina as simultaneously and inseparably a devoted mother with two clinging infants, a devoted wife holding her husband's ashes, and a national symbol of virtuous forbear-

ance surrounded by sympathetically grieving citizens. It is as if the heroic
moments in history depended on monogamy—as for Tacitus, for West,
and for many Whigs they did.

In spirit and even in appearance, *Agrippina* thus renders a scene little
different from that being enacted across the ocean as hundreds or
thousands bewept the lowering of "fair Liberty" into her grave. The
disguised contemporaneity of West's work illustrates an older phenomenon
which pervades poems, plays, paintings, and even music of the period:
historicism. Historicism is the use of historical epochs as a metaphor of the
present. Ancient Greece, ancient Parthia, Palestine, Anglo-Saxon England
become pictorial or narrative settings for what concerns modern Philadelphia. Indeed, West's earlier scriptural paintings project the same Quaker-
Whig asceticism as his Roman works. What necessitated this remote
treatment of current interests or made it appealing can only be suggested
here. The eighteenth-century theory of general human nature encouraged
historicism, for by proposing that human nature was always and
everywhere the same it implied that a John Dickinson, say, was much like
a Cato or a Germanicus. The related cyclical view of history also
encouraged historicism, since it implied that the forces which brought
down Greece or Rome, if allowed to develop, would again bring down
England or America. For the democratic middle class, historicism was an
ideal artistic language, imparting grandeur to its domestic ideals; the
politics of historicist works like *Cato*, *The Prince of Parthia*, and *Agrippina* is
only a heroic version of bourgeois domesticity—sobriety, considerateness,
and fidelity raised to patriotism.

Historicism also served naturally to justify radical changes in values and
goals by fixing their origins. Imposing the present on the past, it gave new
beliefs an ancestry, therefore the legitimacy of descent. The historicist past
is always what Georg Lukacs calls "the pre-history of the present." [4]
Agrippina with the ashes of her poisoned, monogamous husband is the
immediate ancestor of those who resisted ministerial placemen, since the
values which historicism finds in the past are the very values that provide a
new vision of the past. In historicism, the past is the present camouflaged.

Whatever its larger significance, *Agrippina* lifted West's career. It
brought him to the attention, as the colonists imploringly said, of
"GEORGE! Parent! King!" The documents, again, leave the date of
West's first interview with the king uncertain. Perhaps two months before
passage of the Townshend Acts, Peale saw his teacher depart for the
palace wearing court dress and, against his custom, sporting a sword. The
king helped West to set *Agrippina* in a favorable light, called in the queen,
and praised to her the simplicity of West's design and the beauty of his

coloring. He asked West to paint for him a scene from Livy, the Departure of Regulus.[5]

Peale continued to miss his wife badly. Had he taken her with him he would have felt happier and more settled, and the "encouragement of Arts being so much greater in England than in America," he wrote later, he "would have been induced to continue . . . and with diligence in his profession he must have advanced his fortune more considerably than he could in America." But homesickness spoiled this Franklinian formula for parlaying diligence into success. After a year in London he decided to return home. West offered him free board and urged him to stay another six months, to be "more fully benefitted by the advantages he had then before him." But West himself seems to have been a source of Peale's dissatisfaction. Peale was no less unstinting in praise for West's work than in thanks for West's generosity. He wrote to Bordley that he had seen the work of Reynolds and others but that West "Exceeds them all by far." Yet his constant remark in letters home that West was interested only in history painting intimates some dissatisfaction with West's teaching; Peale's domestic nature inclined him to family groups and portraits. At West's urging Peale did linger, however, taking on a few portrait commissions and some miniatures for a London jeweler.[6] Somewhere around this time, West did his portrait, a serious sensitive-looking young man somewhat abstracted from his surroundings (ill., p. 124). Through West too, Peale came to exhibit at the Society of Artists, in the fall of 1768, a painting of a young girl with a toy horse.

Peale's first publicized work, however, came about through Beale Bordley's half-brother, the lawyer Edmund Jenings. He was the London agent for the Westmoreland planters who had raised money for a large portrait of Pitt, following repeal of the Stamp Act. Most of the planters wanted Reynolds for the work, although Richard Henry Lee preferred West, as an American. It was probably Jenings' relation to Bordley and his work for Peale on the nonexistent estate that led him to choose Peale, who so far had shown slight capacity, or even desire, for important commissions. Pitt proved difficult: In faltering health and reputation, he repeatedly broke engagements for sittings. Peale was forced to make the painting from the statue of Pitt then being sculpted by Joseph Wilton for the New York General Assembly. Wilton historicized Pitt in the attitude of a Roman orator, wearing a consular habit, feet sandaled. Peale turned this into a canvas as large as *Agrippina*, from which he made a mezzotint entitled *Worthy of Liberty, Mr. Pitt Scorns to Invade the Liberties of Other People.*

Like the painting, the broadside print shows Pitt speaking in defense of the colonists, Magna Carta in hand. He points to a figure of Britannia who

holds a liberty pole and cap but perversely tramples upon the petition
from the New York Congress. On the pedestal beneath this figure appears
an erect Indian, bow in hand, listening to Pitt. This figure, according to an
advertisement for the print, represents America, "watching, as AMERICA
has done for Five Years past, the extraordinary Motions of the BRITISH
Senate." The dog at the Indian's side represents "the natural *Faithfulness
and Firmness of* AMERICA." The prominent background of the print—a
view of Whitehall—bluntly recalls the beheading of King Charles and
suggests "the results of attempting to invade the Rights of the BRITISH
Kingdoms." [7] Except for the view of Whitehall and the perverse Britannia,
however, the print seems weak as propaganda—lacking in visual impact,
and in places fanciful rather than political. The dog seems emblematic less
of American firmness than of Peale's fondness for painting dogs. As a
commemorative work, it is too awkwardly drawn and composed to do the
subject much honor.

Peale had not greatly profited from his stay abroad; at least he
underwent nothing like the metamorphosis by which almost overnight
Benjamin West became an interesting history painter. After two years and
two months in London, he was clearly anxious to return home. Before he
left, West made him a gift of a painter's adjustable "throne chair" to place
his sitters at the proper height. He left London around March 1769; by
June he had arrived back in Maryland.

Peale returned with something he had not had before he left:
reputation. His painting of Pitt, preceding him, had been praised for its
"glow of fire & expression." He found himself the subject of a biographical
sketch in the *Virginia Gazette*: "a native of Maryland, who was formerly
apprentice to a sadler . . . his natural talent for, and great inclination to
the pencil being made known, he was sent home by a number of
Gentlemen, at their own expence, to perfect himself in the art he
discovered so great a genius for." [8]

Fresh American arrivals in London balanced Peale's departure. Young
Benjamin Rush of Philadelphia had come in 1768. West painted him and
introduced him to Reynolds, through whom Rush found himself spending
an evening with Dr. Johnson and Oliver Goldsmith. During dinner,
Goldsmith read the company part of the manuscript that became *The
Deserted Village*. At the end of 1769, after Peale had returned to Maryland,
Henry Benbridge (the cousin of West's wife) arrived. Having made the
grand tour and come to know James Boswell, he settled into a house on
Panton Square, a few doors from West, who received him, he said, with "a
sort of brotherly Affection." A caricature of Benbridge at about this time
shows a potbellied, rather sloppy man of twenty-six, in need of shaving his

several chins. Yet he was a very skillful painter who had learned much in Italy and was esteemed by London connoisseurs. Anxious for his country-men to see his improvement, he planned to do a portrait of Benjamin Franklin, as a gift for Franklin to take back with him to Philadelphia. "I hope he will meet with due encouragement in his own country," Franklin wrote to his wife, "and that we shall not lose him as we have lost Mr. West." [9]

18. Arrival of John Henry: August 1767; The Virginia Company of Comedians; The American Company Thwarted Again in Charleston: August 1769

The American Company's 1767–68 season began disastrously. En route to New York, one of Douglass' wagons overturned in a river, drowning the actress Mrs. Morris. On August 26, 1767, the brig *Dolphin* from Jamaica, carrying rum, sugar, and, at last, the rest of Douglass' troupe, caught fire off Block Island, in sight of shore. Aboard were nine or ten actors; five were killed. From Jamaica had come an acting family named the Storers, consisting of Mrs. Storer—a well-known singer in Ireland—and her daughters Ann, Maria, Fannie, and Helen. Helen perished trying to rescue from the cabin her two children, who also perished. Her husband, the Irish actor John Henry, and the other survivors landed at Newport, where they received the aid of the Sunday contribution at church. From Newport, what was left of the troupe for which Douglass had apparently waited two years joined him in New York.[1]

Still, John Henry and, among her family, Maria Storer were important additions to the cast. Henry had made his debut in 1762 at Drury Lane, where he appeared under the patronage of Thomas Sheridan, father of the playwright Richard Brinsley Sheridan, but was poorly received (ill., p. 121). He fared better in the West Indies and in the thirteen colonies, where he was highly praised as a fine singer and in dramatic parts ranging from pathetic fathers to high-toned Irishmen to Othello. William Dunlap considered him "one of the best performers in the colonies." A gigantic, handsome, and engaging man, he was said to be the only actor in America who kept a carriage, in which he rode to the theatre. Wary of arousing envy in his fellow actors, he emblazoned on the carriage doors as a coat of arms—in reference to his gout—two crutches, with the motto "*This* or *these*." He advertised in 1769 that as Harlequin in the pantomime he would "run up a perpendicular scene twenty feet high." Given the American Company's dependence on personal influence, Henry's charm was a business asset.[2] The soprano Maria Storer, according to one contemporary, became a "prodigious favorite" in America. She sang such leading roles as Lucy in *The Beggar's Opera*, often gave independent concerts, and was honored by a volume of music published in Virginia in 1772, called *The Storer, or the American Syren*.[3] Dunlap thought her beautiful and talented, the best singer in America before the end of the century. She was also known to be jealous of other actresses and sometimes capricious and temperamental. Henry and the Storer family swelled the cast; in 1769 Douglass mounted *King John* in New York with nineteen actors, of whom two or three were probably children.

While awaiting the Jamaica part of his company, Douglass had been building still another new theatre, to replace the one destroyed on Chapel Street in New York. Located on John Street, between Broadway and Nassau streets, it closely resembled the Southwark, except that it had a covered walkway, presumably as a shelter against rain and mud. It also seems to have held a slightly larger audience than the Southwark. A full house probably meant around 900 spectators, the boxes accommodating around 200, the pit around 400, the gallery around 300. Boxes seem to have seated eight people in a space about eight feet wide and seven deep. On the doors of the boxes, later if not at first, were painted the names of season boxholders.[4] At eight shillings, box seats were also slightly higher than at the Southwark.

Douglass opened his new theatre on December 7, 1767, with *The Beaux' Stratagem*, starring John Henry as Aimwell. The time, however, was riper for Agrippina. On the opening day, an indignant writer in Hugh Gaines's *Mercury* snipped: "The Pomp and Parade of the Theatre, the Decorations of the Scenes, the Novelty and Splendour of the Dress, the Sprightly and animating Music, and the Exhibition of a Variety of Characters, conspire in one general Assault upon the Passions." This was only an opening salvo. On January 14, a writer in the *Journal* attacked actors as creatures of "dissipation, extravagance, and debauchery"; next week another New Yorker attacked plays because they "enervate the mind, sap the foundation of virtue, and weaken the force of moral and religious sentiment"; the week after, another attacked the new theatre as a place where the "modest ear is familarized [sic] to obscene discourse"; the following week's attack scored the audience, who because they "mix often in scenes of amusement . . . find themselves growing habitually indisposed to meditation and retirement." [5]

The opening of the John Street Theatre aroused even more rancorous opposition than Douglass had experienced the previous season in Philadelphia, lasting until the end of the season in June. It lacked the concerted, sectarian protest by the Quakers and revolved less around religious than around economic issues. Although New York as a whole opposed the Massachusetts Circular Letter, it, too, frequently appealed for frugality and non-importation to combat the Townshend programs. By January 1768 an economic crisis existed in New York which many blamed on the rapid disappearance of paper money. Like Governor Penn in Philadelphia, Governor Sir Henry Moore of New York enjoyed the theatre and gave the Company official permission to perform. But by May 1768 he reported that money had grown so scarce that "many of the poorer inhabitants have been ruined and all ranks greatly impoverished." All of New York's money, he said, would be gone by November.[6] One result, in New York and elsewhere, was a widespread demand that time and money be put to better use than amusement. In February 1768 the Massachusetts legislature resolved to urge the suppression of extravagance and idleness. Economic arguments against the theatre went back at least to Calvin, who insisted that money should be used only to forward God's purposes. But the self-denying atmosphere of the Townshend period and the economic emergency in New York gave such arguments forceful new life and made Douglass seem a bloodsucker.

The victims of the American Company, many believed, were the poor. One New Yorker listed the several ways theatregoers squandered money—on tickets, on suitable dress, on drinks afterward at a tavern: "The mind, with all these accumulated expences, is turned from charitable purposes." The £300 taken in weekly by Douglass was food from peoples' mouths and clothes off their backs. "The money thrown away in one night at a play," said "Philander," "would purchase wood, provisions and other necessaries, sufficient for a number of poor." Not only did the theatre divert what little money existed from those who needed it most. The pittance given to the poor bought no warmth and nourishment, but was squandered at the theatre by the poor themselves. "Thrifty" complained that many of the unemployed to whom their townsmen had extended jobs or charity—even those who stood on the verge of debtors' prison—turned up with their families at the theatre. "Is this properly requiting the generosity of their benefactors?" he asked. "Will this be a future recommendation for the like beneficence?" Furthermore, the attendance of the poor at the theatre sapped their ability and desire to struggle: "the love of pleasure naturally tends to cut the sinews of industry," a writer in the *Journal* explained, "and therefore if this passion [playgoing] spreads among the lower sort of people, where industry is their only means of subsistence, it must have a fatal effect upon them." Much as political leaders asked the colonists to boycott British goods, he and several other writers called upon prominent families, fashionable young men and women, and "fellow-citizens who must work hard to support your families" to stay away from the theatre, setting an example for the down-at-heels.[7]

The publication of these attacks in newspapers beside John Dickinson's *Farmer's Letters* and denunciations of standing armies amounted to sizable discouragement for Douglass—not to mention the financial crisis in the city, the memory of his destroyed theatre and of his recent troubles in Philadelphia, and the deaths of several of his actors, now including Allyn, who died during the New York season and was buried in Trinity churchyard.[8] Yet the same newspapers that attacked Douglass printed his ads, and the Company persevered. The high point of the season came on December 14, 1767, just a week after the John Street Theatre opened. What drew a crowded house was not the new building or the play, but the audience. Ten Cherokee chieftains, including the famous Attakullakulla (the Little Carpenter), had come to New York on a state visit from South Carolina, to ask General Gage to mediate a peace with the six nations. Douglass offered them *Richard III* (with the American actor Samuel Greville) and a pantomime ballet requested by Governor Moore. The chiefs received the play "with seriousness and attention," the *Journal* noted, but owing to the language barrier "their countenances and behaviour were rather expressive of surprise and curiosity than any other passions." They came again on April 8 and saw a comedy by Mrs. Centlivre, after which they gave a war dance on stage.[9] On the anniversary of the repeal of the Stamp Act, to unbalance his critics Douglass produced *Cato*.

Despite such inducements, Douglass barely scraped by. On March 3, the *Journal* reported that he had submitted a proposal to the city on which hung, he said, the Company's survival. He asked permission to sell tickets for next season now. For his part of the bargain he would offer thirty box tickets at a reduced rate of ten pounds for the season. "Democritus" in turn submitted a "Proposal for advancing OEconomy in the City of New-York," based on Douglass' scheme. "Methinks," he gloated, "the CITY groans under the Prospect of so distressing a Bereavement! Should the *Actors* no longer exist as a *Company*, how is it possible that *we* can exist with any tolerable Degree of Happiness?" He offered counter-proposals. He would personally buy thirty tickets if the actors agreed to run away; or the city might raise £3,000 on the condition that Douglass and his actors "shall sink into *immediate non-Existence as a Company*." [10]

The scorched-earth mentality of some New Yorkers may have driven off some of Douglass' actors. That seems the likeliest explanation for the arrival in Norfolk, early in 1768, of a new group of players calling themselves The Virginia Company. (They may also, of course, have been simply dissatisfied for some reason with Douglass' management, or anxious to strike out on their own.) The Douglass personnel in the Virginia Company included its manager, William Verling; Henrietta Osborne, whom Douglass had brought from London to Charleston in 1765; Sarah Hallam, the now-divorced ex-wife of Lewis Hallam, Jr.; and the dancer James Godwin. The troupe seems also to have included actors from an obscure troupe in North Carolina, which disbanded when one of its members applied to the bishop of London to take holy orders.[11] The Company used substantially Douglass' repertoire. During its three-month season in Williamsburg it offered *The Beggar's Opera* (with music conducted by Peter Pelham, organist of Bruton Parish Church and town jailer) and Home's Catonic *Douglas* (attended by Thomas Jefferson, who spent four shillings on refreshments).[12]

Douglass may have been well rid of Verling and the others, who seem to have been archetypal Rascally Strollers. An epilogue delivered in Norfolk by Henrietta Osborne conveys something of the Company's crass effort to make and milk new friends:

> . . . though thus doom'd perpetually to roam,
> Still when at *Norfolk* [I] thought myself at home,
> And wish'd, *yes* often *wish'd,* but oh! in vain,
> With such dear friends I ever might remain.

The note of elegant pathos perhaps served as facade for the risqué performances. "Clarinda," who saw Verling's Company in Annapolis, objected to "the barefaced, illiberal, and very often indecent Insertions of some of his Actors . . . which is generally substituted for what they have either forgot, or perhaps, which is more likely, never perused." Henrietta Osborne specialized in being seen in tight breeches, making her the nearest thing to a colonial burlesque queen. Other actors apparently contracted debts and slipped away at night. The *Virginia Gazette* advertised for a thirty-five-year-old slave named Nanny, who allegedly fled from Williamsburg "with some of the comedians who have just left this town, with some of whom . . . she had connections, and was seen very busy talking privately with some of them." [13] One of the actors, Christopher Bromadge, was forced to stay behind to clear his debts. Local amateurs played a benefit for him, in which Bromadge spoke the prologue, telling of his hard lot, appealing for charity, and explaining that he wanted to give the whole thing up:

> Pester'd with warrants, writs, and fieri facias,
> With dire petitions—and your cursed casas:
> Yet,—thanks to *Friends*—their friendship has been *warm!*

By their kind aid—I yet may brave the *Storm;*
In happier scenes may pass my future days,
And bid adieu—to *Epilogues* and *Plays.*

What Bromadge hoped, Sarah Hallam did; she settled down in Williams-burg to run a boarding house. Of the actors who fled Williamsburg, a few may have gone to Savannah, where in June 1768 was announced a 'reading' of the farce *Lethe* plus vocal and instrumental music, "By His Excellency's Permission"—the first professional dramatic performance to be given in that growing town.[14]

The rest (and perhaps all) of the Williamsburg fugitives moved on to Annapolis. Hoping to lure an audience, they changed their name to The New American Company. For the same reason, they made use of local amateurs in *Hamlet* and *Othello*—as Hamlet and Othello. But even these heroic concessions failed. Several actors again ran up debts and were threatened with suits—Godwin for property damage, Verling for rent and salaries—including a suit by the now-retired Sarah Hallam. Verling came out unscathed because most of the plaintiffs failed to appear.[15] With the close of the 1769 season, however, The New American Company apparently ceased to exist.

To maintain his own existence, Douglass meanwhile adopted some new stratagems. Perhaps hoping to avoid publicity during the 1768–69 season, he drastically curtailed the number and the length of his ads in Philadelphia newspapers. On opening night at the Southwark, Lewis Hallam spoke a prologue written by Francis Hopkinson, appealing for toleration of the theatre because the players inspire genius and offer moral clarification. In December, obviously straining for an audience, Douglass added an exhibition of fireworks, "the first upon any stage in America," by "two Italian Brothers."[16] When he moved to New York in January, he offered an unusually large number of non-plays including the *Lecture on Heads* and *Lecture on Hearts*, given by John Henry. Between acts Maria Storer delivered such right-thinking songs as "Come, Ever-Smiling Liberty" from Handel's *Judas Maccabeus*. To encourage attendance, the box and pit seats were "laid together" at a single price of eight shillings. Like Verling, Douglass starred local amateurs, presumably to lure in their friends and relatives, a local officer of engineers appearing as Othello.[17]

The quasi-season in New York contained an important premiere, however, that of a comic afterpiece entitled *The Padlock*. First performed at Drury Lane in 1768, and then a phenomenal 142 times in eight seasons, it became without equal the favorite afterpiece of the colonial stage, with approximately forty known performances before 1774.[18] The story, based by Isaac Bickerstaffe upon Cervantes, concerns a young lady whose house is locked and double-locked to preserve her virtue. But the work owed its success to the go-between who unites the young lady and her lover—a low-burlesque black servant named Mungo. Comparing his harried life to a dog's, this "poor Neger man" complains:

> Night and day 'tis de same
> My pain is dere game;
> Me wish to de Lord me was dead. . . .

Although his appearance as a comic type is antedated by the figure of Raccoon in *The Disappointment*, Mungo was the Ur-source for many later comic treatments of the irascible, muttering black. The name "Mungo" also became a popular derisive epithet, like "Jemmy." At Drury Lane the part owed its great success to David Garrick; often emulating Garrick, Lewis Hallam, Jr., made it his first starring role in the colonies. Indeed some spectators considered Hallam a better Mungo than Garrick himself. He brought to the role first-hand knowledge of Jamaican dialect, "a truth," Dunlap felt, "derived from study of the Negro slave character." [19] *The Padlock*, it could be said, marks the beginning of American black minstrelsy.

But the atmosphere of New York had changed little, and the 1769 season was a financial failure. In February, ominously, Douglass advertised the John Street Theatre for let.[20] When he ended his New York season in June, he did not return to the city until 1773. Apparently he had decided to seek out new audiences. He obtained permission from Governor Moore to play in Albany, a town of fewer than three thousand people, where he managed to fit out the hospital as a makeshift theatre and to perform for a month. At the same time he sent John Henry to Charleston to open there a new and perhaps permanent theatre. Henry took with him Ann Storer, the sister of his deceased wife, now probably his mistress. His arrival in Charleston, however, was ill-timed. In May, George Washington had introduced into the Virginia House of Burgesses a resolution asserting that the right to lay taxes in Virginia belonged only to the burgesses. Next day the governor dissolved the House; the day after that the burgesses met informally at the Raleigh Tavern and adopted a specific non-importation agreement.

Henry arrived in Charleston as the southern colonies were forming other non-importation alliances on the defiant model of Virginia's. The result appears in a long letter Henry sent to the South Carolina *Gazette and Country Journal*, published on August 1, 1769.[21] Tactfully shirking responsibility for his presence, he explained that Douglass had sent him from New York. Finding South Carolinians "involved in the present disagreeable (though glorious) Struggle," he had asked his former patrons whether it would be wise to build a theatre at this time. They answered that "till those unhappy Differences were subsided, it would be disagreeable to the Majority of the Inhabitants." Henry thanked them all, noting ruefully that the Company had spent some one thousand pounds "in every Decoration." Able to do little else, he lay in a store of good will for the future, when "every political affair that Concerns the Welfare of this valuable Colony is settled to general Satisfaction. . . ." Then, he hoped, "under such generous and respectable Patrons, like every other of the Polite Arts, the British may not exceed, if equal the *American Stage.*"

19. British Troops in Boston: October 1768–March 1770

At least since the Stamp Act Bostonians had warned each other that Britain might enforce its policies, if necessary, by arms. When news came that troops were being sent from Halifax and Ireland to protect the customs officials in the performance of their duties, Boston patriots asked Governor Bernard to call the legislature into session. When he refused, a town meeting was called for September 12. It declared the British action illegal and proposed a convention of towns. Ten days later the towns met, without Bernard's approval, and considered armed resistance.

But their considering did not change the news. On September 28 an artillery company and the larger part of two regiments arrived from Halifax in Boston harbor. One poet dramatized fair America's reaction to the sight of the troop ships:

> Down sinks th' angelic fair, oppress'd with woe,
> With head reclin'd her copious sorrows flow,—
> Her swelling Bosom heaves with deep-fetch'd sighs,
> The full round drops run streaming from her eyes. . . .

Oblivious to or eager to prick such tender sentiments, a military band aboard one of the anchored ships struck up an increasingly popular, faintly razzing march tune, "the Yankey Doodle song." [1] On October 1 some 800 troops came ashore under the guns of the fleet, unopposed. Paul Revere suggested the potential of the situation in an allegorical frontispiece which he engraved for the *North-American Almanack*, announced for publication on October 31.[2] He drew female figures of Britannia and

America conversing, each with a liberty pike and cap. The liberty cap had fallen from the pike of Britain and was falling from the pike of America. In the distance two storm-tossed ships dashed against the rocks, illustrating the terse dialogue. Britannia said "Collidimur"; America said "Frangimur." We collide, we break.

Over the next eighteen months, the new British garrison and the citizens of Boston did collide. Varying in severity from public drunkenness and fife-playing on the Sabbath to robberies and rapes, the collisions often involved Boston's cultural activities. In November 1768, the commissioners of the customs established residence and offices in Concert Hall, the brick building on Queen and Hanover streets which contained a Corinthian-style concert room adorned with mirrors. As winter came on, some troops tried to establish a series of weekly concerts at the hall, followed by dancing.

The allegory of Fair Liberty Seduced came to life in the prospect of Boston girls mingling with customs officials and British troops, who in fact threatened both their politics and their virtue. In a feminine version of the forefathers legend, one writer asked the "Young Ladies of Boston" to honor "that cause for which their Great-grand-mothers left a land flowing with milk and honey to encounter the dangers of a savage people and the horrors of a desolate wilderness." Modesty as well as matriotism required them to shun the proposed diversions:

> Plays, Balls, and Concerts, are agreable and amusing entertainments; but will you gratify yourselves at the expence of your reputation? For such certainly will be the case when you are conducted to them by persons who are not only strangers to you but whose principal character is the love of gallantry and intrigue. Nay, some of whom are profest enemies to the country which gave you birth, and who are even now endeavoring to rob you, your friends, relations and country, of the invaluable blessings of the best constituted government upon earth.

The advice was heeded, for the radical *Journal of the Times* reported that a recent concert had been attended by only "ten or twelve unmarried ladies." Otherwise, the daughters of liberty proved unwilling to "dance in their fetters." [3]

In the spring, the concerts turned violent. Some of them were supervised by a musician named James Joan (or Juhan). Unknown in Boston before the arrival of the troops, he probably came in their wake from Halifax along with many other civilian camp followers. He stayed in Boston a year or so, teaching French, dancing, and music, and making musical instruments, before moving on to Charleston. In March, the *Evening-Post* recorded that "*Joan the Italian's*" concert had ended in a riot. So had what it sneeringly called the *"court concert"* the following week. After this concert, some army officers demanded the customary dancing. They were told that Governor Bernard—perhaps as a gesture to public sentiment—did not approve. At this, said the *Post*, the officers "called out to the band to play the *Yankee Doodle* tune, or the *Wild Irishman*, and not being gratified they grew noisy and clamorous." They snuffed out the candles "to the no small terror of those of the *weaker sex*." They assaulted the "old honest music master" Stephen Deblois (owner of Concert Hall), who was "actually in danger of being *throatled*." Sword fights erupted. The elderly Deblois returned the subscription money and decided to stop the concerts "until he should again have it in his power to preserve order and decency in such an assembly." [4]

On top of their offensive pursuit of local dancing partners and demands for "Yankee Doodle," British troops gave one particularly wounding affront. On March 13, citizens reported to the town meeting that the soldiers were making preparations, in Boston, for a play. The town selectmen informed the officers that a Boston law of 1750 prohibited theatrical performances. The officers informed them that an act of King William III of 1690 permitted theatrical performances. Pitting a provincial law against a law of the realm, the local confrontation resembled the broader political debate.[5] Whether British troops managed to defy the 1750 law is uncertain; they probably did. In December 1768, a soldier in the twenty-ninth British regiment advertised to print by subscription *The Miser: or the Soldier's [HU?] MO [R?]*, "As it is acted by his Majesty's Servants." (This may, of course, have meant 'acted in Halifax' or elsewhere.) Whether or not the troops succeeded, their effort made way for some quasi-theatrical activity unthinkable in Boston under normal circumstances. In March 1770, James Joan gave a 'reading' of *The Beggar's Opera* at Concert Hall, singing the songs himself. Another, unnamed actor or actors gave readings of *Love in a Village* at a room on Brattle Street, and of *The Provok'd Husband*, with songs between acts. The cheekiest offering was of three performances, in August 1769, of the "Moral, Satirical, and Entertaining Lecture on HEADS." The lecturer was the enterprising David Douglass. While John Henry was discovering the reluctance of Charlestonians to patronize a new theatre, Douglass brazenly ventured to Boston, probably counting on the troops to shield him from otherwise certain abuse and prompt expulsion.[6]

If the *court concerts* and theatrical lectures offended Bostonians, Bostonians offended in turn. They vilified the long-hated and now loathed Governor Bernard. Just a week after the landing of the troops, someone mutilated John Singleton Copley's portrait of the governor, hanging in the Harvard College hall. A note explained that the heart-shaped piece had been cut from Bernard's breast to spare him the guilt he must feel when considering his administration. Copley himself restored the piece six months later, probably as much in artistic pride as political sympathy. "Our American limner, Mr. Copely *[sic]*," said the New York *Journal*, "by the surprising art of his pencil, has actually restored as *good a heart* as had been taken from it; tho' upon a near and accurate inspection, it will be found to be no other than a *false one*. There may it long remain *hanging*. . . ." A "Son of Liberty," probably Benjamin Church, contributed to the anathematizing of Bernard in *An Address to a Provincial Bashaw*, asking that the "Parricide" and his progeny never be forgiven:

> Th' infectious Follies of a tainted Sire,
>   Entail Contagion on his wretched Race.
> Not all the Wealth that Rapine can acquire,
>   Shall screen his Offspring from deserv'd Disgrace.

In shouting capitals and exclamation points, the author of a forty-five-stanza *Elegy to the Infamous Memory of Sr. F—— B——* accused Bernard of lust, greed, and low birth, and treated him as already dead.[7]

After some of Bernard's letters home appeared in the press, opposition to him became so great that the Assembly was able to have him recalled. In June 1769 the governor disingenuously informed the House that he had been summoned to London by the king, "to lay before him the State of this Province." His face-saving explanation begot one of the delicious speech parodies in which colonials had grown accustomed to puncturing official puffs. The *au courant* parodist compared Bernard with Mungo, the irascible black pander of the recently produced *Padlock*:

> A MESSAGE, sir!
> NOW Gentlemen I think it proper,
> To make you stare, and tell a Whopper;
> My noble Master, Sirs! I tell you,
> Conceives me such a clever Fellow,
> As to command me to repair
> To Court—and bring my Budget there:
> Where I sir Mungo Nettle'em, Bart,
> By Lying, Pimping, Fraud and Art
> Am now advanc'd to such great Credit,
> "It must be true if Mungo said it."[8]

Upon Bernard's actual departure on August 1—with ringing of bells and hoisting of a flag on Liberty Tree—treatment of him returned from ridicule to abomination. A broadside entitled *The Tom Cod-Catcher* (Boston, 1769) saw the governor off with a fine hatred:

> GO B——d, thou minion!—to thy country go.
> For BOSTON, loud proclaims you, Freedom's foe;

Why will you stay, where mankind scorns your name
Where ev'ry year adds blackness to your fame,
Where if you die, few friends your deeds will bawl,
In British cries, or ditties of Fingall?
Haste, haste O B____d, and betake your way,
Where snows eternal chill the face of Day. . . .

Virtually every month in 1769 brought some addition to the politiciza-
tion of cultural activity and with it, often, some increase of tension. In
February, a British lieutenant appeared at Edes and Gill's printing office
demanding the name of the author of some anonymous satirical verses.
The printer said "he should not comply with his demand, as it would be
an infringement of the liberty of the press. . . ." The soldier threatened to
come after him with his sword, but did not. In May, British troops
overthrew the bust of Pitt by Simeon Skillin, placed two years ago on a
liberty pillar in Dedham. In June, some provincials gathered on a Sabbath
to hear the band play during a changing of the guard. Among them was
Governor Bernard's son. The wardens dispersed the crowd, asking young
Bernard to move along as well lest they be accused of partiality. As he
began leaving, however, a captain of the guard called him over to stay, in
defiance of the wardens. The officer then called on the musicians, said the
Journal of the Times, "to play up the Yankee Doodle tune, which compleated
the conquest of the military, and afforded them a temporary triumph." [9]
The non-importation agreements gave special significance to the announcement, in September, of what the *Gazette* proudly called "a very
curious Spinnet, being the first ever made in America. . . ." This
instrument was the work of John Harris, a well-known London spinet
maker who settled on King Street after arriving in Boston in May 1768.
The *Gazette*'s claim was imprecise, since the first American spinet had been
built twenty-five years earlier in Philadelphia by Gustavus Hesselius,
father of the portrait painter.[10] Yet given the resistance to the Townshend
Acts and the calls for native manufactures, Harris' instrument with its
mahogany herringbone inlay had roughly the meaning of Communist
China's first automobile.

In November, at the annual Pope's Day celebration, Bostonians
paraded through town an effigy of the bookseller John Mein. It was Mein
who published the first American edition of an English play *(Cato)*; his
detailed ads for new works like *The Vicar of Wakefield* amounted to small
critical essays; his "London Book-Store" on King Street carried a serious
and discriminating list of literary works, psalm and hymn tunes, and
prints. But Mein's newspaper, the *Boston Chronicle*, now supported the home
government, opposed non-importation, and attacked Samuel Adams,
"alias the Psalm singer." Dressed as the Pope, Mein's effigy was hauled

through town in a cart labeled "WILKES AND LIBERTY, No. 45" and adorned with intimidating verses:

> Now shake, ye Torries! *[sic]* see the Rogue behind,
> Hung up a Scarecrow, to correct Mankind.
> Oh had the Villain but receiv'd his Due,
> Himself in Person would here swing in View. . . .

Threatened, Mein fled to a British warship, disguised as a soldier. The *Boston Gazette* began the new year by introducing onto its masthead a new image, cut by Paul Revere, that suggested the trapped and restless mood of a garrisoned city and warned obliquely of the consequences. Atop the January 1, 1770, issue appeared a seated Minerva with pike and liberty cap releasing a bird from its cage.[11]

Yet Bostonians found prolonged daily contact with the British army, however oppressive, also stimulating. The eighteenth-century army served, among other things, as a school for politeness. The urbane officers who delighted in dances, plays, and concerts were to many provincials at once repulsive and charming. First denouncing then imitating, many Bostonians felt challenged to best the officers at their own, however worthless, game. They countered the military dancing assembly by setting up their own "Liberty Assembly." They countered the military bands—in reality small chamber orchestras—by organizing their own bands. Josiah Flagg— who in 1764 had published a collection of psalm tunes engraved by Revere—brought together and drilled musicians from the militia who became known as The First Band of Boston. For the next few years the band played works by J.C. Bach, Handel, and others in Boston, beginning with a concert at Concert Hall on June 29, 1769.[12]

Bostonians similarly countered the derisive playing of tunes like "Yankee Doodle" by creating their own songs of derision. One anonymous writer took the tune of "The British Grenadiers"—a famous song identified with the British army—and set to it the words of a liberty song. Thus inverted, it was sung by Josiah Flagg at Concert Hall on February 13, 1770, and published the same year in Boston as *The New* Massachusetts *LIBERTY SONG*, composed by "a Son of Liberty." Like the speech parodists, the writer closely copied the language in which the British military glorified themselves, in order to taunt them with the hollowness of their boasts. "The British Grenadiers" celebrates British soldiers as superior to those of Greece and Rome:

> Some talk of Alexander, and some of Hercules,
> Of Hector and Lysander, and such great names as these;
> But of all the world's brave heroes there's none that can compare,
> With a tow, row, row, row, row, row, to the British Grenadiers.

Extending the comparison until it condemned itself, the parodist retorted that Greece and Rome were vanished empires such, he implied, as Britain might soon become:

> THAT Seat of Science ATHENS, and Earth's great Mistress ROME,
> Where now are all their Glories, we scarce can find their Tomb:
> Then Guard your Rights, AMERICANS! nor stoop to lawless Sway,
> Oppose, oppose, oppose, oppose,——my brave AMERICA.

Having begun by denying to the army in Boston the qualities alleged in "The British Grenadiers," the writer ended by claiming those qualities for Americans instead:

> Some future Day shall crown us, the Masters of the Main,
> And giving Laws and Freedom, to subject FRANCE and SPAIN:
> When all the ISLES o'er Ocean spread, shall tremble and obey,
> Their Lords, their Lords, their Lords, their Lords of brave AMERICA.

With its calls to "Oppose, oppose, oppose, oppose," and to "shout, and shout, and shout," the song made for an effective "sensation" of determined unity and seems to have rivaled Dickinson's original "Liberty Song" in popularity.

Whenever the colonists came into contact with the cultivated officer corps of English and European armies, we shall see, there prevailed the same spirit of retaliatory emulation. Yet if the British presence goaded Bostonians into organizing bands and writing songs, the goading was no less irritating. Sporadically—at Joan's concert, at the Dedham liberty pillar—troops and civilians collided. Beginning in February 1770, as Revere had predicted eighteen months earlier, they collided and broke. On February 22 a worker in the Boston Customs House named Ebenezer Richardson tried to remove an effigy which had been placed before the shop of a Boston importer. In the scuffle that followed, Richardson fired a shot, killing an eleven-year-old boy named Christopher Seider. The boy received a martyr's funeral with patriotic demonstrations. Richardson was jailed. The author of some broadside verses, drawing on the genre of execution speeches, presented the guilt-tormented Richardson confessing to

> . . . sending SEIDER out of time!
> This cuts my heart, this frights me most;
> O help me, LORD, I see his ghost.[13]

Although Richardson was found guilty of murder, Lieutenant Governor Thomas Hutchinson refused to sign a writ for his execution.

On March 5, soldiers and civilians scuffled on King Street. The guard opened fire, killing five people. Their deaths produced a burst of broadsides whose crude woodcuts and awkward, naive verses—close to folk poetry—suggest that the pain and shock of the event were intense enough to stir even in nonliterary persons a need to express their feelings. Typical is a broadside poem set beneath five black coffins, entitled *On the Death of Five young Men who was Murthered* March 5th 1770. *By the 29th Regiment.* With "streaming eyes," the author told haltingly how:

> Tall in their Bodies log'd the fatal Lead,
> Beat low the Force of Life, and left them dead;
> They have made their Dress with scarlet Flame:
> Like the deep red which speaks a modest Shame.

A Poem, In Memory of the (never to be forgotten) Fifth of March, 1770, printed within black mortuary borders, called lurid attention to the scene:

> Look into king street! *[sic]* there with weeping eyes
> Repair O Boston's sons, there hear the cries!
> There see the men lie in their wallow'd gore!
> There see their bodies, which fierce bullets tore! [14]

The writer asked for vengeance, including the death of Richardson.

On March 26, Boston newspapers advertised a graphic rendition of the event by Paul Revere, $7\frac{7}{8}$ inches high by $8\frac{11}{16}$ inches wide (ill., p. 128). The print remains controversial because Henry Pelham (Copley's half-brother, the subject of *Boy with Squirrel*) accused Revere of plagiarism, charging in a letter to him that "you was not capable of doing it unless you coppied it from mine." [15] Pelham's print was not advertised until a week after Revere's, by which time Revere's had flooded the market. Entitled *The Fruits of Arbitrary Power, or the Bloody Massacre*, it shows the troops firing at close range on a small crowd; blood spurts from visible holes in the several dead and wounded. At the bottom appears a quote from Psalms and, reinforcing its warning of vengeance, a small emblem: lightning breaking from a dark cloud to destroy a sword.

In fact, Revere's scene is nearly identical with Pelham's and his propagandistic message is the same: The perpetrators must not, like Richardson, go unpunished. Yet Revere's print is far more striking. He emphasized the presence in the crowd of a helpless woman, the billowing turbulence of the rifle smoke, especially the red blood spreading on the street, pouring from the rent waistcoat of one victim, staining the broken forehead of another. He seems to have hired an artist named Christian Remick (come to Boston from Spain) to color the engraving, so that the blood appears bright red, linking it with the also-red uniforms.[16] On a building behind the British troops and next to the Customs House he included a telling sign, omitted by Pelham, which reads "BUTCHER'S

HALL." Whereas Pelham rendered the faces of the troops vaguely, Revere showed them grimacing in brutish rage. A verse beneath interprets their expression:

> . . . fierce Barbarians grinning o'er their Prey,
> Approve the Carnage and enjoy the Day.

Revere depicted not a bloody altercation, like Pelham, but lustful sadism, a massacre.

In the wake of the climactic shootings on King Street, Lieutenant Governor Hutchinson did give in to demands that British troops be withdrawn from Boston. In April, the twenty-ninth regiment was ordered to New Jersey.

20. Repeal of the Townshend Acts: April 1770; Statue of King George Raised in New York: August 23, 1770

April brought a more widely appreciated event as well. Early in 1770, Frederick North, the earl of Guildford, became prime minister of England. As a gesture of reconciliation with the colonies—whose non-importation measures had reduced English exports to America by more than a third—he saw through Parliament a bill which repealed the Townshend duties, effective April 12. As a token of Parliament's authority over taxation, a three-penny tax was retained on tea. Throughout the summer the colonists debated whether to continue non-importation. Some argued that a continued boycott would force repeal of the tea duty; the more radical urged that resistance continue until all grievances were redressed. One by one, however, the cities gave in, dissolving their agreements and alliances until, by mid-October, the protest movement against the Townshend Acts had effectually ended.

The resumption of trade and the vivid easing of tensions arrived, coincidentally, together with suitable means of symbolizing them—the statues of the king and of William Pitt commissioned, as an ideologically balanced pair, shortly after repeal of the Stamp Act. They had been wrought by the English sculptor Joseph Wilton for the Assemblies of New York and Charleston. Charlestonians met the Pitt in the harbor and carried it to the center of town; on July 5, 1770, it was placed at the intersection of Broad and Meeting streets.[1] When the New York statues arrived in June, a local wag published a *Speech of the Statue, of the Right Hon. William Pitt, Earl of Chatham. To the Virtueous and Patriotick Citizens of New-York*. Few citizens of conservative New York could have mistaken his intent as he had Pitt address the "Sons of Liberty, foes to Tyranny, glorious Non-Importers, disinterested Merchants, Guardians of the Liberties of America!" The writer was taking off, obviously, the radical slogans that for the last five years had been heard or seen wherever the colonists thwacked effigies, sang liberty songs, or ran in mobs to cries of 'Stamp him Stamp him.' The marble statue told New Yorkers that his "guts are wore to fiddle-strings" in the American cause. He expected to be well paid for his effort, and supposed he would share in the respect accorded his "mettle companion" (ill., p. 526).

Of gilt metal, the equestrian statue of the king was raised August 23 upon a fifteen-foot-high marble pedestal on the Bowling Green, at a ceremony attended by members of His Majesty's Council and accompanied by band music, the discharge of thirty-two cannon, and the drinking of loyal toasts.

BOOK TWO

Arts and Arms

Calendar for September 1770— December 1783

[1770]

SEPTEMBER 12: Commencement exercises at Yale College; John Trumbull, the poet, delivers his "Essay on the Use and Advantages of the Fine Arts"

DECEMBER 10: *Boston Gazette* advertises William Billings' *The New-England Psalm-Singer: or, American Chorister*

WINTHROP CHANDLER, *Reverend Ebenezer Devotion* (c. 1770)

[1771]

MARCH 7: DAVID PROPERT advertises the first known American concert performance of the pianoforte

11: WILLIAM TUCKEY of New York proposes the first intercolonial subscription for a volume of music

SEPTEMBER 9: DAVID DOUGLASS opens his new Annapolis brick theatre, the first permanent theatre in America *(The Roman Father)*

25: PHILIP FRENEAU and HUGH HENRY BRACKENRIDGE'S "A Poem, on the Rising Glory of America" read at the Princeton commencement exercises

NOVEMBER: JOHN SINGLETON COPLEY paints several

members of the Verplanck family during his
seven-month stay in New York

BENJAMIN WEST'S *Death of General Wolfe* exhibited at the Society of Artists
CHARLES WILLSON PEALE, *Nancy Hallam as Imogen*

[*1772*]

JANUARY: JOHN TRUMBULL, the painter, visits Copley
in Boston

MAY 18: PEALE arrives at Mount Vernon to paint
George Washington

PATIENCE WRIGHT settles in London
JOHN TRUMBULL, the poet, *The Progress of Dulness* (Part One; New Haven)
FRENEAU, *The American Village* (New York)

[*1773*]

APRIL: JAMES RIVINGTON begins his *New-York Gazet-*
teer

MAY 10: Parliament passes the Tea Act
SEPTEMBER 2: PHILLIS WHEATLEY returns from London
NOVEMBER 30: COPLEY speaks on behalf of his in-laws at a
Boston town meeting
DECEMBER 16: Boston Tea Party
22: DOUGLASS opens his new theatre in Charles-
ton *(A Word to the Wise)*

WHEATLEY, *Poems on Various Subjects, Religious and Moral* (London)

[*1774*]

FEBRUARY 28: Presentment against Douglass made to a
South Carolina grand jury

MARCH 14: Boston Port Bill passed
MAY 13: GENERAL THOMAS GAGE arrives in Boston
with fresh troops
JUNE 10: COPLEY sails for Europe
JULY 15: COPLEY visits Benjamin West in London

SEPTEMBER 5 : First Continental Congress convenes at Carpenter's Hall

OCTOBER 18 : Congress adopts the Continental Association, discouraging plays and other entertainments

Rules of the St. Cecilia Society (Charleston)
JOHN STICKNEY, *The Gentleman and Ladies Musical Companion* (Newburyport)

[*1775*]

JANUARY : MERCY WARREN'S *The Group* published
COPLEY visits Naples and Pompeii on an excursion from Rome

FEBRUARY 2 : DOUGLASS and several actors leave America, for Jamaica

APRIL 19 : Battles at Concord and Lexington

MAY 15 : Second Continental Congress, meeting in Philadelphia, votes to put the colonies in a state of defense

JUNE 17 : Battle of Bunker's Hill

JULY 3 : GEORGE WASHINGTON takes command of the armies around Boston

6 : FRENEAU'S *American Liberty* advertised

(c. OCTOBER) : NATHANIEL NILES, *The American Hero*

NOVEMBER 13 : Expedition under General Richard Montgomery takes Montreal

27 : PEALE arrives in Charleston

DECEMBER 2 : *Zara* performed at Faneuil Hall, now a playhouse

23 : Colonies closed to all trade by royal proclamation

Yankee Doodle, or (as now Christened by the Saints of New England) The Lexington March (London)
JOHN BEHRENT of Philadelphia announces the manufacture of the first American-made piano

[*1776*]

JANUARY 8 : A performance by British troops of *The*

Blockade of Boston is interrupted by news of an American raid on Charlestown. Trumbull's *M'Fingal* (Philadelphia) is published the same month

FEBRUARY [?] : *The Farmer and his Son's return from a visit to the CAMP,* classic text for "Yankee Doodle"

MARCH 1 7 : British evacuate Boston; sometime in the spring Freneau sails to the Caribbean for the next two years

MAY 1 9 : Congress commissions Peale to paint Washington, who sits for him in Philadelphia on May 30 and 31. In Philadelphia the same month appears John Leacock's *The Fall of British Tyranny*

JULY 4 : As it approves the Declaration of Independence, Congress appoints Jefferson, Adams, and Franklin to design an official Seal of the United States

9 : Citizens of New York topple the gilt equestrian statue of the king

OCTOBER : BRACKENRIDGE, *The Battle of Bunkers-Hill* (Philadelphia)

DECEMBER 2 5 – 3 1 : PEALE and his militia company join in Washington's attacks on British outposts in New Jersey. The same month, Gilbert Stuart writes for aid to Benjamin West, who takes him in as a pupil and assistant for nearly five years

[*1777*]

JANUARY : British military theatre opens in occupied New York, continuing in operation until 1783

OCTOBER 1 7 : GENERAL JOHN BURGOYNE's troops march off to "Yankee Doodle" during surrender ceremonies at Saratoga

DECEMBER 1 7 : France recognizes American independence

[*1778*]

J A N U A R Y 1 9 :   GENERAL WILLIAM HOWE'S actors open their season at the Southwark Theatre in occupied Philadelphia

A P R I L 1 5 :   FRENEAU, returned from Santa Cruz, joins the New Jersey militia

M A Y 1 1 :   American troops at Valley Forge produce *Cato*

1 8 :   British troops hold a *Mischianza* for General Howe, one week before his return to England

J U N E 1 8 :   The last British troops evacuate Philadelphia; next day, Benedict Arnold enters as military governor. Also in June, William Billings applies to the Massachusetts legislature for a copyright, probably for his *New-England Psalm-Singer*

J U L Y 2 3 :   At the Yale graduation exercises, Joel Barlow delivers his long poem on *The Prospect of Peace*

A U G U S T 1 9 :   JOHN HIWELL appointed inspector and superintendent of music for the Continental Army

O C T O B E R 1 6 :   Recent attempts by American troops to produce plays in Philadelphia prompt Congress to pass a new anti-theatre law

D E C E M B E R :   ANDREW LAW, *Select Harmony* (New Haven)

WILLIAM BILLINGS, *The Singing Master's Assistant* (Boston)

[*1779*]

J A N U A R Y :   First issue of the *United States Magazine* (Philadelphia), edited by Freneau and Brackenridge. The same month, the Supreme Council of Pennsylvania commissions Peale to paint Washington; in February Peale visits Trenton and Princeton to take views for the background

MARCH 6 :   WILLIAM WILLIAMS advertises in occupied
                New York to paint portraits

AUGUST :   While serving as an usher at Timothy
                Dwight's Northampton school, Barlow out-
                lines his *Vision of Columbus*

OCTOBER 3 0 : PHILLIS WHEATLEY calls for subscriptions
                toward the publication of a new volume of
                poems and letters

[*1780*]

MAY 1 2 :   Fall of Charleston. In this month, a second
                congressional committee attempts to design
                an official seal

JULY 1 2 :   FRENEAU, emaciated, released after six
                weeks as a British prisoner. The same
                month, the Charleston *Gazette* rumors the
                return of The American Company

OCTOBER 2 :   JOHN ANDRÉ hanged for his part in a plot to
                deliver West Point to the British

NOVEMBER 2 0 : TRUMBULL, a pupil of West's, is charged
                with treason and jailed for the next eight
                months—in reprisal, he believes, for André's
                execution

DAVID HUMPHREYS, *A Poem, Addressed to the Armies of the United States of
America* (New Haven)
WINTHROP CHANDLER, *Captain Samuel Chandler*

[*1781*]

JUNE :   FRENEAU, *The British Prison-Ship* (Philadel-
                phia)

SEPTEMBER 2 0 : The band of the count de Chaleur, en route
                to Yorktown, supplies an orchestra for The
                Maryland Company of Comedians, man-
                aged by Thomas Wall and Adam Lindsay

OCTOBER 2 0 : MAJOR GENERAL CHARLES CORNWALLIS sur-
                renders at Yorktown

DECEMBER 1 1 : FRANCIS HOPKINSON'S *The Temple of Minerva*

is performed in Philadelphia, George Washington attending

[*1782*]

JANUARY 2 : WASHINGTON attends a performance in Philadelphia of Pierre de Beaumarchais' *Eugénie*,
with a prologue by Freneau

APRIL 2 7 : First known public performance of Haydn
in America, in New York

MAY 2 2 : PIERRE DU SIMITIÈRE announces the opening
of his private collections, the foundation of
the first American museum. The same
month, Copley exhibits his *Brook Watson and
the Shark* and becomes a full member of the
Royal Academy

JUNE 2 0 : Congress adopts an official Seal of the
United States, designed by William Barton
and Charles Thomson

JULY 1 5 : *Dauphinade* held in Philadelphia, attended
by Washington

NOVEMBER 3 0 : Preliminary articles of peace signed in Paris.
In this month Peale opens his portrait
gallery of distinguished Americans; Barlow
and Law arrive in Philadelphia at around
the same time

[*1783*]

JUNE–AUGUST : The Maryland Company of Comedians,
now managed by Dennis Ryan, performs in
New York on the eve of the British evacuation

AUGUST : First public concerts in New Hampshire.
Around August, William Dunlap and Jo-
seph Wright paint Washington at Rocky
Hill, New Jersey, where he awaits a conclu-
sive sign of peace while consulting with
Congress

SEPTEMBER 3 : Treaty of Paris signed

2 6 : Charleston passes ordinance restraining plays

N O V E M B E R 2 5 : WASHINGTON reoccupies New York

D E C E M B E R 8 : WASHINGTON arrives in Philadelphia; during his week's stay he is painted by Peale and by Wright

2 4 : WASHINGTON returns to Mount Vernon, accompanied by David Humphreys

OLIVER BROWNSON, *Select Harmony* [New Haven?]

Part One

Culture in British America during the "Quiet Period," 1770—1773

21. Commencement: 1770

The North American colonists, a people expectant about their rising generation and eager for diversion, loved commencements. But the audiences that had gathered in Philadelphia and New York for the college exercises of 1763 might have thought the verses at the Yale commencement of 1770 deeply ironic and a little startling.

The speaker—a twenty-year-old M.A. graduate named John Trumbull —chose for his subject the "Use and Advantages of the Fine Arts." Like the college orators who had addressed Sir Jeffrey Amherst and Benjamin Franklin in the afterglow of the Treaty of Paris, he speculated on the prospect of refining British America. Belonging, however, to a new generation, one which had grown up as Sons of Liberty destroyed the Chapel Street Theatre and as Paul Revere engraved the King Street Massacre, he made no attempt to refute Hobbes's cynical maxim that 'the state of nature is a state of war,' nor did he echo the shepherds of 1763 who prophesied a "Reign of LEARNING and of PEACE."

On the contrary, in conjuring up a vision of American artistic possibilities, Trumbull asked the assembly at Yale to consider gore:

See where her Heroes mark their glorious way,
Arm'd for the fight and blazing on the day:
Blood stains their steps; and o'er the conquering plain,
'Mid fighting thousands and 'mid thousands slain.[1]

Not only did Trumbull link learning and the arts with war rather than peace. Besides the swains' modest expectation that America would become "a Land refin'd,/Where once rude Ign'rance sway'd th' untutor'd Mind," his vision of the arts was dazzling. He declared that America would rival England and Italy in commerce, architecture, music, and painting, producing poets who would "with lofty Milton vie." England, he said, was narrow, dull, and dying; America was bold, inquiring, and growing, certain to become

The first in letters, as the first in arms.
See bolder Genius quit the narrow shore,
And unknown realms of science dare t'explore;
Hiding in brightness of superior day
The fainting gleam of Britain's setting ray.

That was hardly what Benjamin Franklin meant when he wrote his friend Mary Stevenson in London in 1763, "You have effectually defended us in this glorious War, and in time you will improve us." For Trumbull it was not a question of looking to England with fear and admiration for improvement. On that "narrow shore" the sun was about to set. England must now look to America, "the first in letters, as the first in arms."

The years which divide the Townshend Acts from the Tea Act, 1770–1773, provide a period of relative quiet in which to assess the cultural progress that emboldened Trumbull to speak as he did. The same years provided, too, the first widely influential American painting, a whole new group of American poets, and the first American composer—signs of further progress to back his boldness up.

22. The Art World

By the early 1770's, and in advance of the other arts, painting in British America had already realized much of its promise. Even in 1763 it had been evident that painting was slowly moving westward: A large band of itinerants headed by Wollaston and Hesselius supplied a busy market in portraits; Peale showed determination; Copley already painted well; West had begun to study history painting. A decade later, the demand for portraits and the interest in art had, if anything, grown: Peale and the young native-born painters of 1763 had replaced the older foreign-born itinerants and matched their prestige; Copley's matured intelligence gave him more business than he could handle and made him more conscious than before of his provincial limitations; West, already the creator of a celebrated neoclassical painting, was preparing to startle the European art world by depicting modern history in modern dress. And as the painters of 1763 flourished, a still younger, second generation of American painters appeared.

By 1770, literally dozens of painters seem to have been working in the British colonies. Most of their increased number represents simply a rapid growth in the populations of major colonial cities. Between 1760 and 1775, New York grew from 18,000 to 25,000 inhabitants, Philadelphia from about 23,000 to 40,000, Newport from 7,500 to 11,000, Charleston from 8,000 to 12,000; by 1771, a small town like New Haven contained over 8,000 people.[1] With the steady growth in population came a steady influx of obscure but new artists from abroad, bringing new European fashions and stressing their English and continental training. Between 1772 and 1774 alone arrived the French, or perhaps Swiss, miniaturist "Mr. Fournier" who advertised in Georgia and South Carolina; the seemingly English "Henry Purcell" who appeared as an engraver in New York; the pastelist "Miss Reid," a "niece of her Majesty's Portrait Painter"; the portraitist William Birchall Tetley, arrived in New York "From LONDON"; the John Grafton claiming to be a "Late pupil to Sir Joshua Reynolds." [2] Their works have disappeared into the scores of unidentified paintings left from the period, testimony of a swelling population with increasingly urbane tastes. One émigré of more than statistical importance was John Norman, "Architect and Landscape-Engraver, from London," who in 1774 opened a shop opposite Pewter-Platter Alley in Philadelphia. Specializing at first in architectural engravings (while vending general merchandise, including "Coffin Furniture"), he later emerged as one of the most active engravers and book illustrators of the period.[3]

The larger demand for paintings suggested to at least a few artists that patronage might exist for modest art schools. Since the early eighteenth century, lessons in drawing had been available from portraitists eager to supplement their commissions or from itinerant dancing and music masters offering an extra social grace, or as part of the curricula of colonial private schools. Now, however, at least two new schools came into being devoted solely to drawing and painting. The first was advertised in Philadelphia in 1769 by James Smither, engraver for the new *American Magazine*, at twenty shillings a quarter and ten shillings' entrance fee. The uses of drawing, he emphasized, are "so extensive, that there are few arts or professions in which it is not serviceable":

> A young gentleman possessed of an accomplishment so exceedingly desirable, both for amusement and use, is qualified to take the sketch of a fine building—a beautiful prospect of any curious production of art, or of any uncommon and striking appearance in nature . . . to persons of leisure and fortune, it affords a most pleasing entertainment, and enables them to construct and improve [architectural] plans to their own taste, and judge of designs, &c. with Propriety. . . .

Five years later the Charleston artists John and Hamilton Stevenson announced a more imposing "Drawing and Painting Academy." Fulfilling expectations of westward progress, they offered training in all branches of art "after the Manner they are taught in the Roman Schools." Appealing, too, to the rising aspirations of less wealthy classes—which must have contributed to the increased market for paintings—they recommended the school to both "Ladies and Gentlemen, as a Branch of polite Education, and to Mechanics as an Assistant in their respective Employments." [4]

As in 1763, painting in the British colonies meant, overwhelmingly, portrait painting. Faint signs, however, appeared around 1770 of support for other kinds of native art. In the spring of 1768, just two months after the drafting of the Massachusetts Circular letter denouncing the Townshend Acts, John Durand placed what seems to be the first offer in the colonies to paint history works on commission. His lengthy ad in the *New-York Gazette* amounts to a brief treatise on the philosophy of history painting, the branch of art whose attainment seemed to West and others impossible in an America lacking antique models and polished society. To potential patrons who might regard such works as "superfluous Ornament," he observed that history painting "besides being extremely ornamental, has many important uses." It presents "some of the most interesting Scenes recorded in ancient or modern History"; it recalls "a long Train of Events, with which those Representations were connected"; it sets before us, as "Silent Lessons," images of those "who have distinguished themselves for the good of their Country and Mankind." (Although Durand thus attempted to educate his own public, and offered to work cheaply, he seems to have found no encouragement.) A few other artists began to advertise landscapes, including the vagabond painter-sailor William Williams, in New York on one of his periodic returns to the colonies. Early in 1773 a New York newspaper advertised an engraving of Niagara Falls, "one of the most wonderful aspects of Nature," as the first in a series of engravings depicting "many other great and stupendous Scenes throughout America." [5]

These hints of interest in landscapes and history works, however, are only the blurred finer dimension of a plainer, larger transformation of American art since 1763. By the early 1770's the older generation of prominent Knelleresque painters had been replaced. Badger and Wollaston had died by 1770; Theus lived until 1774, Hesselius until 1778. Their reputations and clientele had been assumed by men in their twenties and thirties—Pratt, Benbridge, Peale, and others—native Americans who had studied abroad, several of them with West. They not only replaced the dying older generation, but supplanted its gently elegant Knelleresque formulas with a more informal style.

Matthew Pratt had studied in London for two and a half years with West, "whose rising Reputation," he wrote, "has already done great Honour to *America.*" In the Middle Colonies and the South he found a distinguished clientele of urban officialdom and other self-confident, privileged people. Typical is his full-length painting of Cadwallader Colden, some six and a half feet by four feet, commissioned, significantly, by New York's Chamber of Commerce—Colden in a red velvet suit, with sword, masts in the harbor visible over a balustrade behind him, an exponent of merchant princes with a sneering, rugged face. Pratt gave his women sitters soft features and sunny lighting reminiscent of Thomas Gainsborough and indicative of first-hand acquaintance with much good painting in London. Although one unfeeling wit later wrote beneath one of his canvases "Pratt is no Titian," Pratt was a cosmopolitan painter who preserved the intelligence, success, and worldliness of the American aristocracy for half a century, without the hackneyed Knelleresque poses and accoutrements of 1763.[6]

The steady, lucrative market for portraits in Charleston—which during a career of more than thirty years allowed Jeremiah Theus to remain at home and grow very rich—passed to the Philadelphian Henry Benbridge. He returned to America around 1770, at the age of twenty-seven, having studied with Mengs and Batoni in Italy and having lodged for six months near his cousin, Elizabeth Shewell, and her husband, Benjamin West. West sent him back to Philadelphia with a letter of introduction to Francis Hopkinson, promising that Benbridge was "an Ingenous Artist and an agreable Companion—his Merit in the art must procure him great incouragement and much asteem." Perhaps because of West's endorsement, Benbridge was elected in 1771 to the American Philosophical Society; the next year he married the Philadelphia miniature-painter Hetty Sage, a pupil of Peale's. His asthma, however, led him and his wife in 1773 to the warmer climate of Charleston, where he painted for the next twenty years, succeeding Theus as artist-in-residence. He rendered local celebrities such as Charles Cotesworth Pinckney in a luminous style with glazed, jewel-like colors and dark backgrounds, more like the enameled look of miniatures than like the typically dullish palette of most colonial itinerants. Although, like Theus, he had many commissions, he seems to have tolerated the city only because of his health, finding it otherwise, he wrote, "very dull, the only thing attended to is dress and disapation." He comforted himself with reaping his clients' "superfluous Cash." [7]

The painter most aware of and most anxious to profit from new opportunities in the colonial art world was Charles Willson Peale. Barely started on a painting career in 1763, when he had offered one of his best saddles to the prosperous John Hesselius in exchange for painting lessons, Peale returned to Maryland in 1769 after more than two years of study with West in London. Twenty-eight years old, he settled in Annapolis, where he quickly found success of the kind he hoped for. "The people here have a growing taste for the arts," he wrote, "and are becoming more and more fond of encouraging their progress amongst them." Delighting in his pupil's prospects, West wrote in the summer of 1770 that he nevertheless hoped the lack of competition "will not let you loose that great desier for improvement you carry'd from hear." [8]

West's hope perhaps betrays a suspicion of shallowness that, if it indeed existed, was deserved. Peale's dedication to painting succumbed to his distracting interests in technology, politics, and natural science, while his affectionate concern for the financial well-being of his large family led to much haste and compromise. To a large degree he only wished to excel as a painter in order to succeed as a father and husband. He forthrightly told one benefactor that he hoped "to improve for now according to the age of man I must be going down the Hill of Life and have a fond Wife a child and more coming, which my success in the Art I hope will enable me to provide for." His model for his career was not so much West, the self-taught painter, as Franklin, the self-made man. In a letter thanking Franklin for favors in London, he remarked on his admiration for him, "occasioned perhaps from my particular Circumstance early in life, being deprived of a Father born to an affluent fortune, nor connected by family relation to the great." Unperturbed that he aspired below the standard of West, Peale did not delude himself about his talents either. He told his patron Beale Bordley in 1772 that he lacked skill and dedication for first-rate history or portrait painting: ". . . I have not the Execution, have not the abilitys, or am I a Master of Drawing. . . . and not half the application that I now think is necessary." His fate was to "improve myself as well as I can while I am providing for my support," content if the westering Muse brought him a comfortable living.[9]

Understandably, then, despite his success in Annapolis, Peale longed to establish himself permanently in Philadelphia as the chief portraitist in the chief colonial city. By the fall of 1771 several prominent Philadelphians—particularly John Dickinson, the "Farmer"—had urged him to move, as he hoped to do after clearing his debts. His strategy was first to gain favor with the Quakers, a "principal part of the Money'd People there": "If I can get a few of the Heads to have their familys portray'd, I need not fear having all the encouragement I can desire." [10] But when he ventured to Philadelphia he found more encouragement than business. The harsh winter, too, made it difficult for his family in Annapolis to do without him. Having completed a drawing of "the great Mr [David] Rittenhouse" and a few portraits, he returned to Maryland after about two months, still intent, however, on setting up in Philadelphia eventually. [11]

Back home, Peale found steady work, and a commission that affected his entire career. Early in 1772 he joined the Hominy Club, a convivial group that met at the Annapolis Coffee House for supper, drinking, social verse, and cards. Its atmosphere can perhaps be gathered from the record of one meeting in 1773, describing the president's toast:

> With look benign, & Joyous front
> He fill'd his glass, & toasted Cu_t.

Smut could not have drawn the uxorious and sentimental Peale to the Hominy Club, but patronage could. The club contained such prominent people as Jonathan Boucher, William Eddis, and William Paca; Peale hoped to portray all of the members, and joined up much as other painters, actors, and musicians joined local Masonic groups. (Peale also belonged to the Annapolis Independent Club, and probably to the Masons.) In 1772 he went to Mount Vernon to paint, for ten guineas, John Parke Custis—a pupil at Jonathan Boucher's Annapolis boarding school and the stepson of George Washington. He spent several sociable days with the Washington family, who sent him home with a souvenir teacup and saucer. Next year the family called him back to do an oil portrait of Washington himself as a colonel of the Alexandria militia. Peale depicted him in uniform, a silver gorget on his chest—a heavy-set, rather swarthy man of forty. It was the first of many portraits of Washington by Peale, and the beginning of a lifelong, and to Peale fateful, friendship. [12]

Still hoping to establish himself permanently in Philadelphia, Peale again tried in the summer of 1772 to see "how far the Arts will be favoured in this City." This time he brought for display significant samples of his work, including portraits of Mrs. John Dickinson, of Rittenhouse, and of a Quakeress; he also printed up a broadside advertisement and distributed five hundred copies. The exhibition of his wares perhaps helped. He found that "none of the Painters heretofore have pleased in Likenesses"; visiting New Yorkers who saw his work gave him, he said, "the character of being the best painter of America—that I paint [more certain?] and handsome likenesses than Copley—." Although business during this visit seemingly flourished, Peale found it difficult to settle in Philadelphia. Oddly, he confessed to Bordley that he did not want to leave Annapolis permanently until he became "a little before hand in the world first." [13] Even while painting in Philadelphia he returned home several times, once because of the death of his infant from smallpox, another time partly because of the homesickness of his wife, Rachel, who accompanied him on one business trip.[14] Clearly he found the move difficult psychologically as well as financially, and over the next few years he virtually commuted between Annapolis and Philadelphia.

While painting, Peale managed to do much else. He began to train painters himself—early patrons to whom he felt lasting gratitude, conventional apprentices, members of his family who might increase his income and carry on his business. Beginning with his twenty-five-year-old brother James, whom he instructed in copying and pastels, he raised and taught a prodigious family of Peale painters named after famous or admired artists—Raphaelle, Angelica Kauffmann, Rembrandt, Titian, Rubens, Sophonisba Angusciola, Rosalba Carriera. He also indulged his Franklinian fondness for technology and natural science, building a surveying machine, sending sassafras blossoms and descriptions of the effects of Jimson weeds to London. Now and throughout his life, he wrote voluminously, maintaining a large correspondence with friends and family as well as extensive diaries, journals, and notebooks. However busy, he never failed to keep West posted on his progress, to send "kind compliments to my fellow Students" abroad, nor to ask West's candid opinion of works he sent to England: "from you, who I have the Honor to be a Pupil of, it will be kind to tell me how I might have done better." [15] More than any other documents of the period, these writings record the commercial and technical aspects as well as the practical difficulties of being a painter in eighteenth-century America: Peale's taking to Williamsburg in 1773 his unsold prints of Pitt to sell personally, together with "holster Pistolls as they may be usefull to me on this long journey"; his thoughts on the "charge and danger" of transporting paintings in tobacco ships where "the heat of Tobaco causes a sweat to hang on all the . . . inner part of the ship which might destroy the Gilding. . . ." [16]

Peale's painting in the first years after his return from Europe reflects this energetic and amiable life, and a temperament devoted to family and friends, eager for rather conventional success, and easily distracted. Copley detected a westering Muse in his engraving of Pitt and sent congratulations on "the fair prospect it affoards of America rivaling the continant of

Europe in those refined Arts that have been justly esteemed the Greatest Glory of ancient Greece and Rome." Yet Peale virtually abandoned whatever European fashions he brought back. Aside from some classical urns or statues, he could have picked up the vocabulary of his portraits by visiting Smibert's painting room, or seeing the works of Copley and of the prominent earlier itinerants. More than his other contemporaries, he retained the "long downward curve of command," the hand-on-hip formulas of the Kneller–Van Dyck school, although almost always with a more relaxed contrapposto or jauntily crossed legs.[17] Except for perhaps a dozen fine canvases, too, his work often betrays haste and boredom, the weave of the canvas showing through the paint here and there, a grotesquely awkward arm or leg, a child literally indistinguishable from a large doll. His soft sensibility, too, permitted none of Copley's psychological acuteness. Most of Peale's subjects have the same slightly almond-eyed, slightly Mongoloid expression of benign affability, projecting Peale's own trust in a benevolent universe.

Yet when painting his own family, Peale invested a degree of care, a degree of thought in understanding human relationships, and an affection lacking in much of his other work.[18] In 1771 he began his large *Family Group*, which he worked on and exhibited in his studio throughout his career. The completed painting shows ten members of the Peale family around the table, in every generation from infants to grandmother, plus sketches, incomplete canvases, sculpture, the family dog—an anthology of the things and people Peale loved best (ill., p. 343). At the left is James Peale, next to him St. George, who sketches the Peale grandmother facing him across the green tablecloth. The orange rinds on the cloth are carved in the Hogarthian serpentine curve whose shape appears throughout Peale's work, giving some of his figures a curiously sinuous appearance. The shape appears also in the ear of Peale's dog, itself an oddly lifeless creature, a stuffed exhibit from Peale's later museum. The main effect of the scene, however, is its fond consanguinity. The members of the family, all lookalikes, touch one another in a variety of affectionate gestures, Peale himself bending over to see the sketch in progress—a world without glamour, yet radiating the sunny compassion and content of the sentimental tradition. Like the Vicar of Wakefield in Goldsmith's novel (published in Philadelphia, it happens, in 1772), Peale was "by nature an admirer of happy human faces," faces which "never felt the deforming hand of ambition or distress." Indeed, with their remarkable resemblance to each other, Peale's family might serve as a book illustration of the Vicar's own, in which "a family likeness prevailed through all, and properly speaking they had but one character, that of being all equally generous, credulous, simple, and inoffensive."

Peale painted his family often in this period, inspiring several complimentary verses, and producing at least one powerful picture, his 1772 *Rachel Weeping*. Arranged like a Pietà, it shows his tearful wife, face uplifted, standing behind a table on which rest medicines and the Peales' dead infant, prepared for burial. The strap of a nightcap binds its chin, white satin ribbons tie down its arms, the unmoving head rests on a large pillow. Peale exhibited the work in his painting room but kept it covered in deference to parents who had lost children, undraping it only on request. Some verses printed in 1782 explained his reticence:

> Draw not the curtain, if a Tear,
> Just trembling in a Parent's eye,
> Can fill your awful soul with fear,
> or cause your tender Breast to sigh.
>
> A Child lies dead before your eyes
> and seems no more than moulded clay,
> while the affected mother cries
> and constant mourns from day to day.[19]

Rachel Weeping, it could be said, was Peale's domestic answer to West's *Death of General Wolfe*, whose enormous success in London he had been hearing about.

If so, *Rachel* is one of several expressions by Peale of muted regret over his failure to achieve the larger fame he had once desired. As the paintings he shipped for exhibition in London failed to get hung, he could scarcely conceal his disappointment. "Amongst the several pieces I have sent," he wrote in March 1773, "[I] did expect some would have been at the Exhibition . . . if any of them were tolerably well done, as coming from America. . . ." Yet he consoled himself with the view, expressed repeatedly in his letters and diaries, that he had no need for the cosmopolitan art world. Nature, he told Bordley, "is the best Picture to Coppy, and I do not regrett the Loss of the Anticks, or the works of a Raphael and Corregea, since I am obliged dayly to portray the finest forms. . . ." [20] Only later in life, in his autobiography, did he wistfully concede that the mind could be compared to a fine soil, for which "cultivation is *absolutely necessary*"; hard work alone might "overcome the greatest difficulties, but there must be stimulus to to [sic] produce a continued exertion."

Despite occasional regrets over the quality of his career, and occasional self-deception, Peale had attained much of what he desired when, as a young saddler in 1763, he took his first lessons from the rich John Hesselius on his estate across the Severn River. He now traveled in a sulky himself, and owned two slaves.[21] Together with other young Americans like Benbridge and Pratt he had taken over the clientele of a disappearing older generation of painters; poems about his work appeared in the press; he knew intimately prominent persons in Maryland and Philadelphia, and at Mount Vernon.

No other painter, however, makes more evident the reality of cultural progress than does John Singleton Copley. Even in 1763, his prestige and prices matched those of Hesselius and Theus. Since then, he had been elected a Fellow of the Society of Artists. Reynolds had called his *Boy with Squirrel* "*a very wonderfull Performance*"; others considered it superior to anything any English painter could do. By 1770 his prosperity and fame outstripped not only Hesselius and Theus but every other painter who had ever worked in America. Thirty-two years old, he had become a celebrity, his name appearing in the journals and letters of people at home and abroad who did not know him personally. The great Wilkes himself described him as a product of "the generous sons of Freedom in America, who remain undebauch'd by the wickedness of European Courts, and Parliamentary Prostitution." "One Mr. Copley of this Town," a Bostonian wrote a friend in 1773, "has, by Genius & Application made himself a great Master in that business, & acquired a large Fortune in a few Years." Indeed, offered more commissions than he could handle, busily crating his paintings for Scotland, Utrecht, Portsmouth, Quebec, New York, and London, Copley was able to make 300 guineas a year without stirring from Boston.[22]

On November 16, 1769—weeks after the mobbing of the bookseller John Mein—Copley had married Susannah Farnum Clarke, the daughter of Elizabeth Winslow and Richard Clarke. On her mother's side, "Sukey" derived from the Winslows of the *Mayflower*; her father headed the firm of Richard Clarke and Sons, a leading agent for the far-flung East India Company. Copley, the son of a small tobacco dealer on the Boston wharf, marked his new status by purchasing a twenty-acre estate on Beacon Hill, adjacent to wealthy John Hancock, containing three houses, a barn, and an orchard, and known as Mount Pleasant. Depicting himself in a self-portrait, he donned the silk damask banyan with satin lapels in which he customarily dressed successful young merchants.[23]

Copley's progress, unlike Peale's, was not only commercial but also esthetic. In the fecundity of his invention, in patient skill, in psychological penetration, he took American painting immeasurably far from the formulaic sameness and simpering insipidity of the portraitists of 1763. In his works of the late 1760's and early 1770's he continued to perfect his ambivalent visual realism. The smooth, fleshy cheeks of *Mrs. Humphrey Devereux*—the mother of Copley's artist friend John Greenwood—contrast startlingly with her wrinkled mouth and eyes, youth and age intertwined in a stunning emblem of mutability (ill., p. 345). (Greenwood, abroad, had asked Copley to show "the good Lady's Face as she now appears, with old age creeping upon her.") [24] *Samuel Adams* stands tensely erect, lips clenched, glaring fiercely—the moment, perhaps, when he confronted Governor Hutchinson the day after the Boston Massacre and noticed the governor's knees tremble (ill., p. 338). In one hand Adams grips a paper inscribed "Instructions of Town Boston"; his other hand points to the table before him on which rests the Massachusetts charter, the barely controlled passion of the scene dramatized in his slightly disheveled hair and clothing. *Paul Revere* appears in shirtsleeves and jerkin, a silver teapot in one hand, his own chin in the other, staring at the viewer with a slight sneer, a slightly cocked eyebrow, none too friendly (ill., p. 345). The glassy table top at which he sits mirrors his minutely painted silversmithing tools, suggesting Copley's kinship with Dutch masters of domestic detail like Vermeer and De Hooch.[25]

The quality of such works brought Copley repeated invitations to paint in other cities. Those from New York came with particular insistence, from people like Myles Cooper of King's College and from several British army officers. One officer promised that twelve half-length portraits were already subscribed; another vowed that Copley's presence was wished "by some of the finest women in the *World.*" Copley accepted. Placing a large order to London for glass, white lead (200 pounds), putty, oil, and other supplies to be sent on by his half-brother Henry Pelham, he arrived in New York in the summer of 1771 and set up in a large, north-lighted room, nine feet high, twenty feet long, and the same broad. His regime was to rise by six, breakfast at eight, and work until three, when he and Sukey dined, followed by riding at six. He enjoyed New York. It had more grand buildings and cleaner, broader streets than Boston, he felt, plus the admirable statues of the king and of Pitt. He also discovered that "painting much engages the attention of people in this City." His customers were demanding and sophisticated, able to "distinguish very well, so I must slight nothing." Always very careful, he worked harder than ever. He thought his New York portrait of General Gage's wife the best female portrait he ever did, a feeling shared by Matthew Pratt, present in New York at the same time as Copley, who predicted that "It will be flesh and Blood these 200 years to come, that every Part and line in it is Butifull. . . ." As he expected, he did well: "vas[t] numbers of People of the first Rank" visited him, he told Pelham, people "who have seen Europe and are admirers of the Art." Forced to turn down many commissions, he did one or two portraits a week, and in barely two months had earned some 300 pounds sterling.[26]

The thirty-seven portraits which Copley completed in the city from June to December 1771 form a distinctive phase of his career, for in depicting his homogeneous clientele, the "Gentry of this place," he altered his style. He often worked with a more muted palette than before, dramatizing his sitters in a flood of light against dark backgrounds. He drastically simplified the settings (perhaps to save time), eliminating most of the beautifully observed but unbalanced accessories in his earlier works. The lack of accessories, the chiaroscuro, the very subdued and serious, often sad, quality, unmistakably identify Copley's New York portraits. Typical are his several portraits of the wealthy and cultivated Verplanck family, owners of Dutch and English paintings, some presented to them by Sir William Howe. Daniel Crommelin Verplanck, about eight years old, sits beside a column, a delicate little boy in a plum-colored suit, black tie, and black shoes with gold buckles. By a chain he holds a squirrel with a huge, raised, bushy tail, its tiny claws nipping his slender calf (ill., p. 346). Gulian Verplanck was twenty when Copley painted him, just returned from an apprenticeship in the banking business in Amsterdam. His brother Samuel, aged thirty-two, had been a member of the first graduating class of King's College and was a founder of the New York Chamber of Commerce (ill., p. 346). Copley painted these two men of affairs on three-quarter-length canvases with great virtuosity, showing buttons on Gulian's waistcoat, for instance, in several odd perspective angles—flat, on edge, or tilted—as determined by the contours of the seated figure's stomach. The solidly dark backgrounds refer the viewer back to the faces, on which Copley concentrated all his gifts. The expressions combine great self-assurance with great guilelessness, worldliness with sensitivity, as if his dreamy *Boy with Squirrel* had grown into a colonial merchant prince.

In painting the world he aspired to himself, Copley saw no contradiction between tenderness and wealth. Despite John Wilkes's identification of him with the "generous sons of Freedom," such works reflect Copley's wish to keep art apart from politics. Tolerant of complexities, and anything but Manichean, he was slow to take sides, "desireous of avoiding every imputation of party spir[it]," he wrote West from New York, "Political Contests being neighther pleasing to an artist or advantageous to the Art itself. . . ." [27] The impartial viewpoint of Copley's New York paintings explains his ability to paint equally well the indignation of Sam Adams and the beauty of General Gage's wife. His allegiance was to his eye.

After a brief visit to Philadelphia, Copley returned to Boston in January 1772. In his absence, Pelham had looked after his intricate affairs, collecting rent from wandering tenants, tending his and Copley's mother, carrying out Copley's instructions for the building of the new Chinese piazza and twenty-four-foot-long painting room at Mount Pleasant.

Copley no sooner moved into his new house than, the same January, he received a call from John Trumbull, a cousin of the Yale commencement poet. This Trumbull longed to be a painter. Instead, argued down by his father (the governor of Connecticut), he was on his way to Harvard. He found Copley about to dine with guests, an "elegant looking man, dressed in a fine maroon cloth, with gilt buttons." Better, Copley's paintings were "the first I had ever seen deserving the name"; they "riveted, absorbed my attention, and renewed all my desire to enter upon such a pursuit." [28] Nearly a decade earlier, Peale had gazed on Copley no less admiringly, unaware of Copley's pained sense of limitation. Trumbull could not have guessed either that despite his fine maroon clothing and splendid home, so "dazzling" a personage was deciding, perhaps had decided, to leave for Europe.

Just when Copley decided is uncertain. Reports of his growing reputation abroad perhaps attracted him to Europe, as political agitation at home perhaps repulsed him from Boston. Even after repeal of the Townshend programs, many Bostonians campaigned to keep the non-importation agreements in effect until the repeal of all duties. By the end of 1770 Copley found party spirit still "so high, that what ever compliments the Leaders of either party is lookd on as a tassit disapproba-tion of those of the other." He feared displaying a portrait of a young man who had been named after Wilkes, lest it be taken for a political gesture. While distressed over the political climate, he kept receiving, and kept agonizing over, invitations from West. In January 1768, after two drafts and many corrections, he had sent a carefully composed reply admitting that his work suffered from a lack of criticism, but explaining that with an ill mother and a younger brother to support, he could not go to Europe without assurances of earning as much there as in Boston. Again West urged him to come "while young and befor you determin to Settle"; he could not stress enough the importance of seeing masterworks to attain "Possesions of Powers [sic] . . . that Cannot be Communicated by words." Privately, West confided to Gulian Verplanck in London that Copley "only wanted the advantage of studying proper masters to be one of the first painters of the age." [29]

Sometime in 1772, Copley decided to make the trip. Like West, he would begin his tour in Italy, "the Sorce," West said, "from whance true tast in the arts have flow'd." Following West's curriculum, he could view classical sculpture and study Raphael for expression, Michelangelo for anatomy, Correggio for chiaroscuro, Titian for solidity. At first West bluntly advised him to leave Sukey in Boston, else he would have to cultivate friends for her, retarding his "pursuit of the grand object." Later he relented a little and advised him to send for Sukey after his Italian tour, when he settled in London. Intending to leave in the spring of 1773, Copley delayed going. He remained in Boston throughout the summer, talking, one townsman noted, "of going to Europe to make himself more perfect" but being "so full of business that he finds it difficult to get away." [30] It turned out that he was not able to leave until after the large shipments of tea sent from the East India Company arrived for his father-in-law, Richard Clarke.

While Copley's continuing growth provided colonial patrons with native works of sophisticated vision, West gave America its first artist of international influence. Only five years after arriving in London in June 1763, a barely literate Pennsylvania Quaker laboring under a serious rheumatic ailment, he had been named by King George III as one of four artists charged with planning a new Royal Academy of Arts and painting a *Departure of Regulus* for its opening. With his *Agrippina* in 1768 he had become an established figure in the English art world. And with the display of his innovative *Death of General Wolfe* at the 1771 exhibition of the Society of Artists, he became a figure in the history of modern art (ill., p. 341).[31]

Wolfe created more interest than any other American work that had ever been shown. David Garrick, who tried to imitate Wolfe's attitude and countenance as West depicted them, went to the exhibition in the early morning, hoping for an uncrowded view, but found a crowd already there. On a canvas some five feet by seven feet, West presented, in his own words, "a British Hero on the heights of Abraham in North America expiring in the midst of Heros, and in victory. . . ." [32] He placed his heroes against a deep perspective of contending armies and anchored men-of-war, under sky dramatically split into white gunsmoke and dark clouds. In the foreground, he surrounded the supine Wolfe, gasping and mortally bleeding, with thirteen comrades-at-arms. A worried-looking surgeon stanches Wolfe's wounds with a towel. A squatting Cherokee Indian watches as a scout arrives with news, ironically, of victory, which he delivers to Sir William Howe.

West used the scene to fully develop the psychological, documentary, and dramatic possibilities of history painting. The painting abounds in relationships. One kneeling comrade holds the arm of the fallen general, gazing not at him, however, but, apprehensively, at the kneeling surgeon. In contrast to the prayerful young grenadier with tousled hair, the stoical Indian looks upon the scene dispassionately, as if contemplating mortality. The painting also abounds in carefully detailed uniforms and flags. West placed prominently in the foreground, and elaborately painted, a grenadier's cap, a flintlock, an Indian tomahawk, and assorted military gear. Following the advice of the art theorist Charles Dufresnoy, who urged placing the main figure "fair in front in all the blaze of light," he floodlighted the dying Wolfe. Following his own advice to Copley, to subordinate lesser elements to the dramatic center, he reused the "bridge formula" of his *Agrippina*, placing minor figures to the sides of the canvas while using their attitudes to direct the viewer's eye to the central group.[33] He transfigured the pointing sea-captain and docking prow of *Agrippina* into the knees of the squatting Indian and the craning-forward heads of the distressed onlookers, converging like poles of a tent on fallen Wolfe.

The huge success of the painting was partly owing to the contemporary interest in the subject and, more than that, to West's novel treatment of it. His celebration of Wolfe on an ambitious canvas reflects a wider effort some half-dozen years after the Treaty of Paris to digest the meaning of the French and Indian Wars and to estimate their significance. As a hero, Wolfe was mentioned in all of the colonial commencement poems of the 1770's; in January 1773, the *Virginia Gazette* published two whole columns of verse and prose epitaphs on him. To those who viewed the painting in London, however, what commanded attention was less this distanced, esthetic contemplation of recent events than West's use of contemporary dress. Although several earlier painters had done as much, it was West who in his own time and later received credit for the innovation, whose implications for history painting and for art were profound. Earlier theory held that since history painting teaches ideal behavior, it must depict ideal universal types, Nature as it should be. Painters should not make their heroes look too much like themselves or their neighbors, who were properly subjects for portraiture. As West himself summarized the theory of costume, "modern dresses could not be admitted into pictures where Heroism, and dignity were the caractoristicks. . . ." Joshua Reynolds tried to dissuade West from doing Wolfe in modern dress. West's patron, the archbishop of York, feared that West would lose his reputation.

West justified his use of modern dress on several grounds. He invoked the doctrine of decorum, a keystone of neoclassical theory, by which all elements in a painting must be appropriate to the time and place depicted. He reminded the archbishop and Reynolds that the event took place in Canada, "in a region of the world unknown to the Greeks and Romans." He also considered the history painter a genuine historian, responsible to facts: "I want to mark the date, the place, and the parties engaged in the event." [34] More important, he believed that Roman costumes did nothing in themselves to teach ideal behavior. This he considered his key argument and his real innovation. Since *The Death of General Wolfe*, he proudly observed in his autobiography, "It is now universally admitted, that the dress in a picture has no influence over the passions of the mind; it may add to the picturesque, and be made ornimental but cannot give any movement to the energies of the soul. . . ."

West's arguments for decorum and for documentary realism are deceptive, however. He found other means of influencing "the passions of the mind" which, if less direct than Roman garb, were no less dignifying and no less remote. His chief device was to load the painting with allusions to Christian iconography. While he denied Wolfe the sacrificial patriotism of a dying Roman, he gave him the pathos of the crucified Jesus. Drawing for his composition upon the scheme of the Lamentation, West produced what one critic calls "the first *pieta* of nationalism." Wolfe's posture recalls several depictions of the descent from the cross, while the hand-wringing and swooning comrades who support him recall figures in traditional lamentations over the body of Christ. No doubt West's own pious upbringing helped him to solve the problem of how to elevate and moralize the depiction of modern history. Yet for all its tasteful mere allusiveness, the comparison of Wolfe to Christ also harbors a romantic impulse to see blessedness in the democratic average.[35]

West's use of modern dress betrays another sort of romantic inclination as well. It heralds a slow, general shedding of historicism in art, literature, and politics, a forsaking of historical impersonation in favor of realism. Behind this change lies a new emphasis on personal experience, on being not some generalized self but oneself in particular. The greater subjectivity of *Wolfe* quite as much as the costuming distinguishes it from the earlier *Agrippina*. William Pitt—who had placed Wolfe in command in Canada— decided after seeing the painting that it expressed too much dejection. The historical Wolfe, he felt, would have faced death without self-pity, having grandly conquered for his country.[36] West's Wolfe dies in exquisite languor. His expiration climaxes a long evolution in the historicist depiction of noble deaths. The earlier treatments implicitly denounced the gentle eroticism of rococo art in the name of stoic fortitude and heroic sorrow. But as deathbed scenes proliferated in biblical, classical, and medieval settings, they became vehicles for the new sensibility of deep feeling and tears.[37] In West's sacred-secular *Wolfe*, the historicist setting has receded, its ghostly remnant serving less to reprove sensuality than to legitimate the subversive romantic undercurrent. West only accentuated and brought to the surface an idealized morbidity which had begun penetrating politics and literature as well, in the moaning over the death of "Fair Liberty," or in the dying speech of the queen in Godfrey's Whiggish *Prince of Parthia*:

> How sweet the eloquence of dying men!
> Hence Poets feign'd the music of the Swan,

When death upon her lays his icy hand,
She melts away in melancholy strains.

Events in America over the next decade would provide occasions for many more such expressions of Sadean pleasure-in-pain.

Equally significant as its exploration of new romantic currents, West's *Wolfe* made daring, indeed unprecedented, use of the American past. Although West continued to paint such standard 'history' subjects as *Venus and Europa* and *Cupid Stung by a Bee*, he quickly followed *Wolfe* with the even more popular *Penn's Treaty* (1771), painted at the request of Thomas Penn and exhibited at the Royal Academy. Again he turned to modern history in modern dress, including detailed ethnographic documentation of Indian life. Painted and repainted, engraved, lithographed, embossed on stove plates, linens, and tureens, "that detestable picture," as the English critic Roger Fry called it, became one of the great public images of the nineteenth century.

In *Wolfe* and *Penn's Treaty*, West was depicting not only contemporary history but, specifically, two epic moments in the civilizing of the American continent, moments such as the young commencement poets of 1770 had begun celebrating as they traced the Rising Glory of America (see the discussion in section 24, "The Literary Scene"). One of West's later pupils, William Dunlap, perhaps came closest to identifying West's own intention. The death of Wolfe during the conquest of Canada represented, he wrote, "one of the most influential causes of mighty effects which the world has known. The victory gained by Wolfe, annihilated the power of France on this continent, and established reformed religion, English language arts and literature, and more than English liberty from Mexico to the North pole, and from the Atlantic to the Pacific." [38]

West was depicting, that is, his own prehistory, the history that made it possible for him to break with the standards of the grand style and introduce the contemporary into history painting. His injection of mere mortals like Wolfe or Penn into the space previously occupied by mythological, scriptural, or classical figures mirrored his own experience of being lifted from nonentity beside the Schuylkill River to the center of the London art world. As he heroicised middle-class figures like Penn on canvas, his country was producing middle-class heroes like Franklin in fact, who as surely as Penn and Wolfe were becoming secular saints. In creating what he called "a revolution in the dressing of figures in historical pictures," West had changed not only the subject of history painting but also its message. He no longer provided instances of ideal virtues for the refinement of the refined. Now he painted memories of a significant recent past, for men of no very exalted rank or birth, a past created by men like themselves but ennobled by devotion and suffering: "to instruct the rising generation in honourable and virtuous deeds," he wrote, "they are the good and great points which the historical pencil has to effect—and that can only be done, by placing before them, those bright examples of their predecessors or contemporaries, and to transmit their virtues from generation to generation." [39] West's attempt to ennoble American history confirmed and forwarded progress in colonial art. It gave the colonies claim to a now-illustrious artist, encouraged later painters in the use of native material, and granted reality to the nobility it perceived.

Transatlantic respect for colonial achievement was heightened by the appearance in London, soon after the exhibition of *Wolfe*, of a woman who could be called the first American sculptor—Patience Wright, of Bordentown, New Jersey. She arrived together with her son and two daughters in 1772, at around the age of fifty. A Quaker, like West, she had sculpted faces in fresh bread and putty as a child; later she sculpted in wax as a hobby, a popular diversion in the colonies, especially for women.[40] Exhibitions and even lessons in the art were advertised in America, filling what small market existed for native sculpture. While stone was prohibitively costly and difficult to work, wax was cheap, pliable, plentiful, and easily reproduced for friends and relatives by plaster casts. Although wax models were done as early as the fourth century B.C., and by major artists like Michelangelo throughout the Renaissance, in England they became newly popular in the early eighteenth century, apparently stimulated by the liking for portraiture.[41]

Even as a hobbyist, Mrs. Wright had gained some reputation. In May 1767, William Shippen sent to the Royal Society, via Benjamin Franklin, her wax model of Siamese twins. After her husband's death in 1769, she began to sculpt professionally to support herself and her children, exhibiting in Charleston, Philadelphia, and New York with her sister and fellow waxworker Rachel Wells. In May 1771, Rachel displayed eighteen figures in Philadelphia, including George Whitefield and John Dickinson, "executed in such a masterly manner," according to a local newspaper, "as would do honour to an *Italian* painter." A measure of Patience Wright's own prominence are the several newspaper accounts in June 1771 describing a ruinous fire in her New York home that destroyed most of her figures, and her sister's models of Whitefield and Dickinson.[42] Undiscourageable, she promised to make up the loss by molding and exhibiting new figures; instead, she went to London, where she undertook wax sculptures of English celebrities. Her son, Joseph, meanwhile, began studying painting with West and with the fashionable portrait painter John Hoppner, who began courting her daughter Phoebe.

Patience Wright's success in London was electrifying, in part because of her intense appearance and manner. Elkanah Watson later described her as "a tall and athletic figure . . . with a firm, bold step, as erect as an Indian," with piercing eyes that had "almost the wildness of a maniac's." Her glance, said the *London Magazine*, was "of that quick and brilliant water, that it penetrates and darts through the person it looks on." (Less entranced by her boldness, Abigail Adams considered Patience Wright the "Queen of Sluts.") Watson left a vivid picture of her at work:

> . . . with a head of wax upon her lap, she would mould the most accurate likenesses, by the mere force of a retentive recollection of the traits and lines of the countenance; she would form her likenesses, by manipulating the wax with her thumb and finger. Whilst thus engaged, her strong mind poured forth an uninterrupted torrent of wild thought, and anecdotes and reminiscences of men and events.

Patience Wright's sculptures made an equally strong impression, largely because of their trompe-l'oeil effect: "in likeness to their originals," said the *London Magazine*, they "surpass paint or any other method of delineation." The *New-York Gazette* relayed to Americans the news of her acclaim in London. In November 1772, it reported that she had begun a figure of Garrick, and finished figures of Franklin and of the Whig historian Catharine Macaulay, which she was sending home for exhibition, in order to "oblige her Friends in America, with a View of the most remarkable Persons of the present Age." King George III, the newspaper boasted, had recently sat for a likeness himself.[43]

While the prosperity of the native-born itinerants, the maturity of Copley, the reputation of West all evidenced the progress of colonial art since 1763, the early 1770's provided omens of future progress as well. John Trumbull—the aspiring but temporarily chastened young painter who visited Copley at Mount Pleasant—was only one member of an entire new generation of painters, musicians, and poets, a second wave of creative energy unfurling atop the crest of the first. A technically limited but forceful new painter was Winthrop Chandler of Woodstock, Connecticut, just twenty-three years old in 1770. Descended from a family that arrived in Massachusetts in 1637, he may have studied painting in Boston in his teens, before settling with his wife and, eventually, seven children on Chandler Hill in Woodstock. By profession a house painter, he avoided the itinerancy of colonial portraitists. Mostly he painted his family and neighbors: rural ministers, educators, lawyers, and physicians, people in whom the combined vigor, simplicity, and intellect of the older Puritan piety lived on undisguised by the velvet gowns and lacy fichus of Copley's Bostonians. Between them, Chandler and Copley depict all of eighteenth-century New England Puritanism, both the survival of the older Puritanism in the Connecticut Valley and its transformation in urban Boston.[44]

The original, tougher Puritan note in Chandler's works derives not only from the intense faces of his sitters but equally from his way of seeing them, his intense symmetry and literalism. His Puritan love of pattern maps out his paintings in rows of matching buttons, zigzagged or striped fabrics, lines of tacks on chairs, rosettes and bows, shapes that recall the chiseled gravestones and domestic carving of early New England. The eyes of *Mrs. Levi Willard* nest in concentric black cusps—eyebrow, eyelid, eyelash, and bags beneath—like targets. Chandler's Puritan literalness forbade him to rearrange the accidents of existence. In its fidelity to God's universe, his eye duly recorded the loose button, the missing carpet tack. A viewer accustomed to the formulaic character of much early American painting must look closely at Chandler, whose vision is always startlingly fresh. He is at his most literal when painting the books which appear, clearly titled, in virtually all of his paintings, symbols of the literacy, the reverence for The Book, on which the rural Puritans he painted based their lives.

At around the same time that West produced his *Wolfe*, Chandler produced one of the most memorable American paintings of the eighteenth century, *Reverend Ebenezer Devotion* (ill., p. 339). About sixty-five years old when Chandler painted him, Devotion was pastor of the Third Church in Windham, Connecticut.[45] A Yale graduate, an eminent clergyman, and an ardent politican who represented his town in the General Assembly, he was a living relic of the Puritan ideal of ministerial accomplishment. Chandler depicted him in a white wig and black suit with clerical neckbands, seated on a mahogany chair, a squat, monumental figure silhouetted against the library behind him. His right hand holds a book, one finger inserted inside; on the duck-foot table beside him lie two quill pens and notes for a sermon. He stares at the viewer with pursed mouth, small, pouched hazel eyes, age-lines gouged into his massive jaws, his face blazing with piety. The forthrightness of his expression is emphasized by a general clarity and lack of rhetoric. The chair he sits on conspicuously is missing one of a row of brass tacks. The Puritan divine's library behind him, on molded shelves with a scalloped partition, is painted as if seen by Devotion's own consuming eyes, the titles of works by Owen, Henry, Locke, and others rendered clearly. The books are as lovingly painted as faces: The torn binding of one reveals peeling patches of inside-paper which reveal the sewn fascicles; three titles appear upside-down; other books are thrust into the shelves binding first, their pages facing the viewer; another shelf holds a stack of pamphlet sermons, cantilevered to suggest use. In both form and subject the painting epitomizes Puritan life, while its liney intensity represents a revival and perfection of the earlier limner style.

Another young artist had begun painting by 1770, although barely in his teens: Gilbert Stuart. Very little is known about Stuart's early life, and, like the information about his later life, much of it is fanciful, the invention either of Stuart or of those who detested him. He was born in Narragansett on December 3, 1755. His father was a Scotch Presbyterian minister from Perth who became the partner of another refugee, Dr. Thomas Moffatt, in a tobacco and snuff manufactory. The partnership probably influenced Gilbert Stuart; Moffatt collected paintings and prints, and was the nephew of John Smibert.

Stuart showed early promise and a keen eye. If the rather idolatrously protective account later written by his daughter can be believed, he had been able as a young child to tell the identity of a hooded hangman by observing his shoes. While still very young, he composed music and learned several musical instruments, and probably took some lessons in oil painting from Samuel King, a Newport portraitist, house painter, and instrument maker only seven years older. (One story has it that Stuart got his first drawing lessons from a slave who sketched on the heads of casks.) [46]

A more sophisticated teacher appeared during the Townshend Acts crisis, when the Scottish portraitist Cosmo Alexander settled in Newport. Alexander had been in the colonies since 1764, painting fashionable rococo portraits in Philadelphia and New York. Imprisoned for debt in 1769, he was rescued by one of his creditors, a Jewish physician named Gratz. His politics seem in part to have prompted his jailing, but Alexander decided to stay in America: "though one interfers never so little in politicks," he wrote, "the living at London [cannot] be agreeable at present, & these commotions & differences betwixt us must affect Trade in General; so that its full as well to be at present a Painter as a Merchant. . . ." Instead of abandoning his trade, he opened a painting studio in Newport. He found business among the Scotch residents of the city, one of whom, Dr. William Hunter, got him to train Stuart. Hunter had called professionally at the Stuarts' house and after seeing Gilbert's drawings on a fence commissioned the child to draw his dogs (the picture is extant). Stuart watched Alexander in his studio, fortunate in having a teacher whose standard of technique and inspiration was superior to that of most itinerant portraitists. It seems likely that Alexander's unstereotyped and penetrating portraits influenced Stuart's later decision to concentrate on face painting.[47]

As the political situation worsened, Alexander decided to return to Scotland, and invited Stuart to go with him. Little, again, is known of Stuart's life there. When Alexander died in Edinburgh in the fall of 1772,

Stuart for a while worked as a portrait painter in the city but found few commissions, perhaps because of his youth. He found more work when he returned to Newport the next year: He portrayed several wealthy Newport Jews, such as the Sephardic Lopez family; a portrait of his grandmother led to a commission from Philadelphia. A great fabulist in adulthood, Stuart said that after his return from Scotland he "took part with the revolutionists" so that his conservative father sent him to England "to get him out of the way. . . ." [48] Whether for political reasons or, more likely, because he simply had saved enough money to go, Stuart departed again, sometime before 1775, for London.

23. Musical Life

The progress of musical life in the American colonies since 1763 can be measured in several slight changes and in one absolute difference. A continued demand for family music continued to support many music teachers and music shops, but with slightly less reliance on the mother country for printed music. Concerts, distinctly sociable and semiprofessional before, gained in sophistication and variety from the arrival of several immigrant musicians who often performed their own works, although their careers remained chancey. Good organs continued to be imported, but somewhat wider acceptance of church instrumental music stimulated the manufacture of excellent American organs, and attracted well-trained organists from London who joined in the concert life of the larger urban centers.

In contrast to these tangible but slight evidences of westward progress, one fact absolutely distinguishes American musical life in 1763 and in 1770. The invigoration of long-established Congregational and Presbyterian vocal music by new English fashions, already apparent in 1763, had resulted over the Stamp Act and Townshend Acts period in the growth of a large movement of vocal instruction in New England. It brought into being a flock of singing schools and singing masters. And in 1770 it produced a great divide—the first volume of American-composed music.

As far as one can tell, the playing of family music remained widespread, little changed since 1763. Landon Carter of Sabine Hall recorded in 1771 that "from every house a constant tuting may be listened to, from one instrument or another." While many of the earlier itinerant music-masters had moved on, a corps of new ones, similarly obscure, took their place—the German violinist Francis Christian at Mount Vernon and Nomini Hall; the Italian master Francis Alberti, who taught Thomas Jefferson and Benjamin Taliaferro; the Williamsburg teacher Francis

Russworm, whose death by drowning brought an extravagant verse tribute in the *Gazette*: ("Oh Handel! Handel! could'st thou now but hear/ Thy second self. . . ."); the more ambitious John Stevens, who opened a school in Savannah, Georgia, teaching "Theory as well as *Practical Parts* of Musick," the school lasting only six months.[1]

As in 1763, dedicated amateurs on remote plantations filled leisure hours with diligent practice and study. Landon Carter conducted experiments with pitch, sent to London for the latest books on music, added to his collection of instruments, and, the tutor Fithian recorded, "made great advances in the Theory, and Practice of music." As in 1763 too, black musicians in the South provided musical entertainment. A London merchant named Nicholas Cresswell, traveling in Virginia in 1774, witnessed a "Negro Ball" featuring a banjo "made of a Gourd something in the imitation of a Guitar, with only four strings and played with the fingers in the same manner," to which the slaves sang songs relating "the usage they have received from their Masters or Mistresses in a very satirical stile and manner." [2]

The fondness for family music continued to support colonial music dealers. James Rivington in New York, who sold sheet music and printed up concert tickets and programs, advised the Boston bookseller Henry Knox that "If you were to deal in the Music Branch it would be a profitable addition to your others." Music shops continued to keep on hand a large variety of imported music. In 1771, the Williamsburg printers Purdie and Dixon offered for sale at their shop, in addition to violins, flutes, and books of music instruction:

> Instructions for the Harpsichord, Violin, and German Flute, Pasquali's Thorough Bass for the Harpsichord, Boccherini and Burgess Senior's Lessons for the Harpsichord, Voice, German Flute, Violin, or Guitar; The Maid of the Mill, and Cunning Man, for the Harpsichord, Violin, German Flute and Hautboy; Periodical Overtures for the Harpsichord, Piano Forte &c. eight Italian Sonatas for two Violins or Flutes, with a Thorough Bass for the Harpsichord, by several eminent Composers; Fisher's Minuets, with Variations for the Harpsichord; Arnold, Galuppi, and Mazzinghi's Sonatas for the Harpsichord, Pasquali, Campioni, Schobert, Just, Pugnani, Florio, Lates, and Richter's Sonatas; Stamitz's Concertos, Duets, and grand Orchestra Trios; Gasparint's Trios; Corelli's Solos; Vivaldi's Cuckoo Concertos; Barbella and Reinard's Duets.[3]

Perhaps influenced by the non-importation agreements, however, colonials had begun to print their own editions of secular music. In Boston in 1769 appeared an *Abstract of Geminiani's Art of playing on the Violin* (by Francesco Geminiani, 1680–1762), covering hand position, fingering, and bowing, and stressing directness and plainness of performance—the first book of violin instruction printed in America. The April 1774 issue of the Boston *Royal American Magazine* contained the words and music to "The Hill Tops"—the first music, apparently, to appear in an American periodical. If the fondness for family music had stayed constant, the means of satisfying it had, slightly, changed.

Compared with the concert life of 1763—largely improvised affairs at which local amateurs joined touring professionals, usually followed by a ball—that of 1770 seems less thin and less frivolous, if not exactly robust and sophisticated. All of the major urban centers gained from the emigration to America of perhaps a dozen professional instrumentalists. To Boston in 1771 came David Propert, a self-styled "Professor of Musick" who advertised a joint concert with the Italian James Joan in which he would perform on a pianoforte—the first performance on that instrument, as far as is known, in America. The pianoforte was itself a recent instrument, apparently introduced in public when Charles Dibdin accompanied a singer on it at Covent Garden in 1767, and given respectability when Johann Christian Bach played it in concert a year later. Propert soon offered to also teach the new instrument, which caught on in America rapidly: Thomas Jefferson wrote to Europe in June 1771, canceling a recent order for a clavichord and requesting a pianoforte instead; in 1773 William Hulett, the durable New York dancing master, advertised a concert on the instrument; by 1774 piano lessons were being offered in Baltimore and Philadelphia as well as in Boston.[4] Propert also began a new series of subscription concerts at the Coffee House in Boston, in conjunction with Flagg's band and a boy choir. The concerts featured harpsichord works by "the most celebrated Masters of *Italy* and *London*," and parts of "Mr. *Handel's* Oratorios." At least one listener remarked on the "very fine Musick & Good Performers." [5]

At some concerts, Propert was joined by another immigrant musician, W. S. Morgan, who also arrived from London in 1770. Advertising himself as a pupil of Giardini, he appeared several times in Boston, Newport, and Portsmouth in 1770–71. Something of a tippler and a rascal, he ran into trouble when with a small entourage he offered a disguised theatre performance in Portsmouth in 1772—"An Oration on the Origin, Progress, and Utility of the Stage"—hoping for success where Douglass had failed. The response was a petition with sixty-one signatories protesting his performance as a waste of time and encouragement to lust, whose success would draw "others of like Character" to Portsmouth, "to the no Small Detriment of the Town. . . ." Morgan returned to Boston, quarreled with other musicians there, and joined David Propert in competing with still a third recently arrived immigrant musician, William

Turner. Apparently the increased competition forced Morgan to return to Portsmouth, modestly, to teach music and dancing.[6]

Philadelphia had had small subscription concerts, really chamber music soirees for a dozen or so musicians directed by Francis Hopkinson and the organist James Bremner. These seem to have ended when Hopkinson went abroad but were revived in 1769 by John (anglicized from Giovanni) Gualdo. He first appears in 1767 giving guitar lessons to Landon Carter's daughter. In Philadelphia he apparently opened a wineshop, whose failure bankrupted him; hoping to recoup, he opened a music store on Front Street, with a staff of repairmen, a servant boy who copied music so that patrons need not buy an entire collection, and himself to compose or adapt music for occasions. In November 1769, he proposed a series of biweekly concerts at Davenport's Hall. He issued a broadside addressed *To the* Philharmonical *Merchants,* inviting local performers to participate in the vocal and instrumental music and stressing that no drunkards would be admitted: "He flatters himself to be capable of conducting a Concert to the general Satisfaction. Decency, good Manners, and Silence shall, at all Times, be regarded." Those who did not wish to attend the post-concert ball received a refund of half a crown. Although the concerts ran from November 1769 through February 1771, and included works by Handel, Arne, and Bach, Gualdo was no more fortunate in his musical career than in his wine business. Francis Hopkinson (returned to Philadelphia after ordination in London) noted in October 1771 that *"Sig^n Gualdo* lies in Chains in one of the Cells of the Pennsylva Hospital." Gualdo died a few months later, insane. His death left music in Philadelphia, Hopkinson said, "in a very deplorable Condition." [7]

Concert life in New York was expanded by the arrival of other musicians, German and Italian, whose immigration dramatized the reality behind theories of the westward movement of the arts. In 1773, a violinist named Herman Zedtwitz, claiming to have studied with eminent violinists in London and Germany, performed at Hull's Assembly Room with the recently organized Harmonic Society in the city, and later with members of Douglass' Company (including Maria Storer).[8] More significantly, early in 1774 he performed with a group of recently arrived Italian musicians: Signora Mazzanti, Nicholas Biferi of Naples and Paris (who taught voice and harpsichord), Pietro Sodi (a dancing master), and Joseph Cozani, a language teacher who changed his name to Caze. The last three jointly advertised in May 1774 the opening of "A NEW ACADEMY FOR TEACHING MUSICK, DANCING AND THE Italian and French Languages," the price for instruction being twenty-four guineas a year and three guineas' entrance fee. They concertized not only with Zedtwitz but also with members of the Harmonic Society, and with William Hulett, Sodi's nine-year-old daughter appearing in a rigadoon with Hulett's ten-year-old son. Tickets for these concerts, available from Rivington, cost a dollar. The academy never got going, however, and the musicians split up. Well received in Philadelphia after dancing "a new Philadelphia cotillon *[sic]* of his own composition," Sodi opened a dancing school on Chestnut Street. Biferi settled on Peck's Slip in New York to teach harpsichord, composition, and "singing after the Italian way." [9]

In Charleston, musicians might find steadier employment at what were perhaps the best-supported concerts in America. The St. Coecilia Society, begun just at the time of the Peace, had become an established and thriving institution. Its bylaws—printed in an eleven-page pamphlet in 1774—called for an admission fee of £35, candidates having to await a vacancy in the 120 allowable memberships. The Society hired musicians on long-term contracts, apparently a unique situation in the colonies. Several times in 1771, it advertised for professional violinists, oboists, and a bassoon player to play under contracts of one to three years. The musicians must have been well trained. When Josiah Quincy visited Charleston in 1772, he was treated after dinner with a concert of six French horns—"most surpassing music"—including a solo by a performer salaried at fifty guineas a season by the Society and "said to blow the finest horn in the world." In the early seventies, Charleston also had an Orphaeus Society, as well as open-air concerts at the Orange Gardens by the flamboyant Morgan of Portsmouth and Boston. [10]

Sacred musical life had changed even more dramatically. Over the Stamp Act and Townshend period, more organs had been installed in colonial Anglican churches, and new organists arrived from abroad to play them. The non-importation agreements did not prevent St. Michael's Church in Charleston from installing in 1768 a two-manual organ costing £528, built by the great London manufacturer Johann Snetzler, in consultation with William Boyce, organist and composer to the Chapel Royal. Second in size in the British colonies only to Snetzler's Trinity Church organ in New York, it contained about 900 pipes. By 1774, every Philadelphia church except the Quaker used an organ in its services. [11] Cities which had not had organs acquired them. One came to Christ Church in Savannah as a gift in 1765. Another was installed in 1771 at King's Church in Providence, at a concert of organ and vocal music by Josiah Flagg and local gentlemen, followed by a sermon on the "Lawfulness, Excellency and Advantages of INSTRUMENTAL MUSIC in Public Worship." This organ came to Providence from Boston, a former fixture of the Deblois' Concert Hall where British troops had recently rioted at Joan's concert. Ezra Stiles of Newport applauded that instead of "promoting Festivity, Merriment, Effeminacy, Luxury & Midnight Revellings" the organ was now "to be used in the Worship of God." [12]

Stiles himself had overseen a far more significant transition. In his Providence First Church a tradition of nearly a century and a half of Congregational opposition to organ music ended. An organ consisting of about 200 pipes was played there on July 10, 1770—the first pipe organ to be heard in an American Congregational church.[13]

The growing acceptance of organs stimulated native organ building. In 1763 the leading American organ builder was Philip Fyring of Philadelphia, whose instruments Charles Willson Peale had seen and praised on his early visit to the city to buy paints. In the late 1760's new organs appeared around Philadelphia which the *Pennsylvania Gazette* judged "much superior in workmanship and sweetness of sound to any made by the late celebrated Mr. Feyering *[sic]*, who is so generally taken notice of for his ingenuity." They were made by the greatest colonial instrument maker, David Tanneberger, a joiner from Saxony who had come to Philadelphia in 1749, at the age of twenty-one, and learned organ building from the Philadelphian Johann Klemm. In 1765, Tanneberger moved to Lititz, where he began to produce a series of impressive organs for churches in New York and Pennsylvania. The English traveler Thomas Anburey heard the organ which Tanneberger built for the Lutheran church in Lancaster. Completed by 1774, it was a labor of at least three years, during which he made every part with his own hands, at a cost of £2,500 (ill., p. 348). Anburey marveled at the "amazing circumference" of the pipes and at the many pedals, such as he had seen only at the Savoy Chapel and at St. Paul's in London, "but then they had only four or five of these wooden keys, whereas this organ has a dozen." The sound, Anburey said, was "astonishing, it absolutely made the very building shake. It is the largest, and I think the finest [organ] I ever saw, without exception; and when you examine it, you wonder it did not take up the man's whole life in constructing. . . ." [14]

With more organs being used and produced, organists in 1770 enjoyed a more prosperous and professional existence than in 1763. When St. Michael's Church in Charleston, for instance, sought an organist for its new Snetzler organ, the vestry wrote to a native South Carolinian named George Hartley, currently playing at King's Chapel in Boston. They assured him that his future "from the present Taste for Musick here, is very favorable. . . ." Hartley took the post, and from performance at church, playing the harpsichord at the Charleston musical society, and teaching, he managed an income of about £500 annually.[15] Such "very favorable" prospects attracted skilled organists from abroad. In 1774 Peter

Albrecht van Hagen advertised in Charleston as "organist and director of
the City's Concert in Rotterdam." His father had been principal organist
of Rotterdam, and a pupil of the Geminiani whose treatise on the violin
had recently been published in Boston.[16] A more influential newcomer was
William Selby (1738–98), organist at London's Holy Sepulcher Church,
which had a distinguished musical history. In 1771 Selby emigrated to
Boston, where he remained most of the rest of his life as organist at King's
Chapel. Beginning in 1770, New York newspapers advertised—probably
for the first time in America—instruction on the organ.[17]

The organists' growing prosperity came not only from the spreading
tolerance for sacred instrumental music but also from the expansion of
secular concert life and from Douglass' more musical repertoire and cast.
Organists increasingly concertized on their own, or with other musical
groups, or with leading singers from the now semioperatic American
Company. Selby offered six recorded concerts in Boston before 1775, one
of them with Josiah Flagg's band. The Charleston organist Peter Valton
gave several local harpsichord concerts and performed with Sarah
Hallam; the Williamsburg organist Peter Pelham, Copley's stepbrother,
gave concerts of Felton, Handel, and Vivaldi, and joined Stephen Woolls
in performing the "Solemn Dirge" from *Romeo and Juliet* at the 1770 funeral
of Governor Botetourt.[18] William Tuckey, the organist at Trinity Church
in New York, appeared as Peachum in a Douglass production of *The
Beggar's Opera* and formed a sort of oratorio society to bring church music
before the general public.[19] From this society came a New York
performance of the overture and sixteen numbers of Handel's *The
Messiah*—the first full, or nearly full, performance of the work in America.
The date, January 16, 1770, was a year before its first performance in
Germany. Significantly, Tuckey gave the concert not in Trinity Church,
but in a private concert room, together with instrumental pieces and a
French horn concerto.

The overlapping of sacred and secular musical life, and the growing
number of musicians in both, had another important result. Far more
original instrumental music was being written and played in America in
1770 than in 1763, and with a geographically wider audience in mind.
The programs of most of the Italian immigrants included one or two of
their own works: Cozani (Caze) played his Spanish guitar sonata; Gualdo
offered his own flute concerto, symphony, minuet, and trio for two
mandolins or violins with harpsichord or violoncello (which has survived
in manuscript). Church musicians did the same. Selby played his organ
and harpsichord concertos in Boston; in Charleston, Valton featured a
harpsichord concerto by one of his own pupils.[20] Equally important, some
of these works were proposed for publication, although unsuccessfully, by

intercolonial subscription. In 1768, Valton advertised in Charleston and New York for subscribers to his *Six Sonatas for Harpsichord or Organ.*[21] He was quickly outreached by Tuckey, the New York organist, who in 1771 offered his *Two Select Pieces of Church Music* to subscribers in New York, Philadelphia, and Boston. Two years later Tuckey proposed a complete church service, consisting of a *Te Deum, Jubilate Deo,* burial service, and *Hosanna,* to be published "in score" of sixty folio pages at a dollar and a half. Orders for the service could be placed with Gaine, Rivington, or Holt in New York, Hillegas in Philadelphia, Draper in Boston, Purdie and Dixon in Williamsburg, and with agents in Charleston, Annapolis, Baltimore, and Providence.[22]

By birth Englishmen or Europeans, these performer-composers evidenced the Muse's westward progress since 1763. Evidence that, once transplanted, the Muse flourished came from the Congregational churches of New England, where in a few years had risen innovative singing schools, singing masters, and the first native American composer.

This "late revival of singing," as the *Connecticut Courant* called it in 1771, had begun "perhaps about ten years ago," at around the time of James Lyon's *Urania.*[23] Then, as mentioned in an earlier section, the new English church music had just begun to transform long-established Congregational and Presbyterian traditions of psalm singing. During the 1760's Congregational churches argued the propriety of the new church music and the wisdom of training church members up to the level of proficiency which it demanded. This "revival of singing" is treated here because in 1770 it produced its first decisive and lasting expression. Yet to treat it under any one chronological division is in some ways to misrepresent it. Of all forms of colonial artistic expression, it was the least affected by political developments—partly because it involved great numbers of nonpolitical adolescents, partly because it was bound up with older worshippers' memories of their early training, partly because of its nonliteral content, since music, of all the arts, unfolds most completely at the behest of inner dynamics. By and large it developed as if no fourpenny tax had been levied on newspapers or as if Fair Liberty had not been buried in a dozen different graves. Its development was also uniquely affected by the nature of Congregationalism, which demanded that each church fix its own polity. Congregational singing developed at a different rate and in a different direction from church to church also. Nor can its development be separated from a continuing history, back to the call for "regular singing" (or singing by note) at the time of Cotton Mather, and ahead to the early nineteenth century, in which many of the new church composers worked—even into the present, when the works remain popular and are still sung, especially in rural areas.

The growing acceptance of the new church music gave rise during the 1760's to three inseparably related phenomena: the singing school, the Congregational church choir, and the itinerant singing master–composer. The first was not new, since private schools for teaching psalm singing had existed in New England since the early eighteenth century. The "revival of singing," however, swelled their number, and changed their character in ways that suggest the sacred-secular nature of the music itself.

Two types of singing schools can be distinguished: the independently sponsored school and the congregation school. The first was taught by an itinerant singing master who advertised in a local newspaper to teach all denominations. The congregation school was sponsored by a particular church desiring to train singers for its service. The itinerant school generally met at a local schoolhouse or tavern for two or three nights a week over perhaps three months. At the congregation-sponsored school, church members hired a room for the singers to train in, or offered their own homes for the instruction; at least that was the arrangement in Salem in 1766 when the members agreed "for the better Incouragement of our Singers" to "hire a Chamber for them, and to entertain them at our Houses once a Month . . . ," each member accepting the singers for a specified time period.[24] The course of instruction ended with a "singing assembly" (a public choral concert) or a "singing lecture" (concert plus sermon) to demonstrate for parents and friends—usually by virtuoso choral works—the singers' new prowess. A representative "lecture"—from Westborough, Massachusetts, in 1779—consisted of an anthem ushering the audience into the meeting house, followed by a prayer, the reading of a psalm which was then sung, another prayer, another psalm tune, a sermon, a prayer, a hymn, and a blessing, climaxed by a program of tunes and anthems.[25]

The fullest remaining records of these schools unfortunately begin in the 1780's, although considering that the rural schools changed little in the period they probably represent the operation of similar schools in 1770 as well. An itinerant rural school has been described by Moses Cheney, a singing master himself, who, with the other boys in town, attended a rural singing school every year but two between the ages of twelve and twenty-one, beginning in 1788. The desks were boards across kitchen chairs, at which the students stood. The singing books contained only one part, being either bass, tenor, counter, or treble books. The singing master read off the rules of solmization, for example:

FLATS

The natural place for mi is in B
But if B be flat, mi is in E.

If B and E be flat, mi is in A.
If B, E, and A be flat, mi is in D.
If B, E, A, and D be flat, mi is in G.

The pupils then tried to 'rise and fall the notes,' following the master in singing up and down the scale. The effort, especially of "the large boys, full twenty years old," often touched off "Great fits of laughing, both with boys and girls. . . ." The rudiments acquired, the master proceeded to the singing of tunes. At least in Cheney's school, the master sang over each of the parts several times, those who owned tunebooks reading along, those without them listening. "In this way, the school went on through the winter." At the close of the school term the scholars settled with the master: a shilling and sixpence per night, paid in Indian corn at three shillings a bushel.[26]

The workings of a congregation school can be reconstructed from the ledger of William Bentley, pastor of the East Church in Salem. The Salem school was taught by a singing master named Buffington. Each scholar paid a dollar per quarter for instruction, the rest of Buffington's salary being supplied from a public fund. Classes met at the houses of local citizens, who were paid two shillings per night for use. Gifted or specially punctual or cheerful students received tunebooks as prizes. The congregation schools demanded active participation from the minister himself. Bentley collected money for the master, purchased and sold singing books for the pupils, bought pitch pipes and candles, fixed the singing school stove, and saw to the repair of seats.[27]

In addition to the private, itinerant schools and the congregation schools, some demand had begun by 1774, in Boston at least, for public singing schools, although town-supported schools did not appear in Massachusetts until the late 1780's. Singing schools also were held at some colleges by 1772, when one opened at the College of Rhode Island. The number of singing schools held between 1760 and 1800 cannot be determined but must have been great, each new generation in each town requiring instruction. Before the end of his career, a singing master named Redfield had taught seventy-one schools with close to 4,000 pupils.[28]

Most students in the singing schools were adolescents. Among William Bentley's fifty-eight singers in 1792, the youngest was five, none was over thirty, and the median age was seventeen. The schools served an important recreational function and allowed a degree of social control over the town youth. As Cotton Mather was aware earlier, and modern ministers who employ rock groups have been aware since, the music also kept the young attached to the church, if only nominally, by bringing the sexes together. Half the singles in Bentley's group were male, half female.

"I am almost sick of the World," wrote a Yale undergraduate in 1782, "& were it not for the Hopes of going to singing-meeting tonight & indulging myself a little in some of the carnal Delights of the Flesh, such as kissing, squeezing &c. &c. I should willingly leave it now." [29]

While these social and recreational possibilities drew youths into the schools, they also created trouble for the singing masters. In 1771 the *Connecticut Courant* published several letters, allegedly by boys, testifying to the folly of misbehavior. One presumably repentant youth confessed how he would throw chips at the school windows, yell, rap his cane, make fun of the singing master, whisper in girls' ears, and make the singers laugh. Outraged, the master hit him with a "quarter staff"—a warning to prank-minded young readers—bringing him to his senses, although first to near death. Obedient now to the singing master and proficient in singing, he realized that singing disposes the young to "civility, harmony and good agreement." A fourteen-year-old singer also testified that the instruction led students

> . . . to industry that we might gain time to improve in said art, to a dutiful obedience to our parents, that we might gain their good will and concurrence to the thing. We naturally learn good manners, as our skill often introduces us into the company of gentlemen of polite education.[30]

Such letters, very likely, were written by singing masters themselves, showing mothers and fathers of prospective students the benefits of training and demonstrating the teacher's watchfulness over "kissing, squeezing &c. &c."

These singing masters formed a band of itinerants who moved from town to town, at first in New England but after 1780 throughout the country, together with the mass of peddlers, portraitists, actors, and artisans. The singing masters differed in several ways from the secular music masters of the 1760's. Most were self-taught, or educated by other singing masters. Unlike the Ferdinand Grundzweigs and Francis Albertis on southern plantations, they represented an *a capella* tradition and were not instrumentalists; nor were they immigrants, but almost always native New Englanders of distinctly proletarian origin. Few made their livings entirely out of music. Some taught both singing and common school (i.e., the three R's), as did Noah Webster, and Ichabod Crane in "The Legend of Sleepy Hollow." Many only made forays into other towns to teach, but basically stayed at home working at some trade. Among the important singing masters and tunesmiths of the period, Daniel Read was a New Haven merchant and combmaker, Timothy Swan a hatter, Supply Belcher a tavern keeper, and Justin Morgan a horsebreeder. Although neither amateurs nor professionals, the singing masters had grown enough in numbers and importance by 1769 to warrant a convention of singing masters. It was held at the South Meeting House in Hartford in order "to encourage Psalmody." [31]

The justification of the singing schools was the improvement of devotional singing, but the students used their skills on a variety of other occasions—funerals, dedication ceremonies, ordinations, spinning-bees, Election Days. Much part-singing also went on at home, sometimes to accompany family religious observances but also as entertainment. In terms of recreation, the singing schools were what New England had instead of a theatre. They served larger social and political purposes as well. Singing was a useful lure in converting the Indians, and a test of their integration into Protestant life. At the ordination of an Indian missionary in 1773, some sixty Indians performed "the Psalmody Both at the Beginning & Close of the Work in three parts with Great Exactness" and sang "an Anthem in Indian." No doubt the wide training offered by the schools also enhanced the effectiveness of works like John Dickinson's "Liberty Song." During the non-importation crisis, some girls in Bridgewater met at their minister's house to make homespun, then marched to the church, where they heard a sermon and several anthems and sang about "the virtuous Woman's price":

> How frugal in oeconomy!
> To save her sinking Land.
> Foreign productions she rejects
> With nobeleness of Mind,
> For Home commodities, to which
> She's prudently inclin'd.[32]

The training in the singing schools must have given such patriotic performances a particular spiritedness and bravado that strengthened feelings of political solidarity.

The growth of the New England singing schools was only one of several related consequences of the new music. The schools created a group of trained singers, mostly young, able to perform music that was too ornate and too difficult for the congregation at large. Church by church, in the 1760's and 70's, the best singers were separated from the congregation and seated together in the gallery, where they were led by a "chorister," elected by the group. By 1770, at least ten such choirs existed in Massachusetts churches. The typical gallery was shaped like a truncated pyramid so that, for those seated below, the music seemed to come from three directions, an effect enhanced by the imitative writing in some tunes, a motif being tossed back and forth in an effect that one composer called "striving for mastery" [33] (ill., p. 347).

By 1770 the quality of singing in the choirs had become worthy of remark. John Adams (who confessed that he had spent too much time in his youth singing tunes) described a choir in Middletown, Connecticut, in 1771:

> Went to Meeting . . . in the Afternoon, and heard the finest Singing, that ever I heard in my Life, the front and side Galleries were crowded with Rows of Lads and Lasses, who performed all the Parts in the Utmost Perfection. I thought I was wrapped up. A Row of Women all standing up, and playing their Parts with perfect Skill and Judgment, added a Sweetness and Sprightliness to the whole which absolutely charmed me.

The establishment of the choirs also disturbed and in many places ended the practice of lining-out which had been used in Congregational churches in America since the seventeenth century. Gradually, it also introduced instruments previously forbidden: first pitch pipes as an aid to singing; then a "bass viol," or primitive cello, for support; and finally, around 1790, a full ensemble of winds and strings called the "gallery orchestra." [34]

Not all of New England, of course, shared John Adams' rapture over the young singing lighthearted sacred music in four-part harmony. The removal of the better singers to the gallery, begun around 1762, meant the displacement of those who ordinarily sat there—in fact, their displacement from a traditional part of the service. The idea of an isolated choir violated the Congregational idea which, apart from Communion, demanded full participation of everyone in all aspects of church life. In many cases it placed at odds the two groups involved, namely the old and the young. One New Hampshire writer in 1764 publicly attacked the "new Method" of psalmody that had been proposed by the "young and gay," who wanted to monopolize the singing for themselves "by singing such Tunes, as it is impossible for the Congregation to join in." Instead of those "plain and easy Compositions which are essential to the Awful Solemnity of Church Music, away they get off, one after another, in a light, airy, jiggish Tune, better adapted to a Country Dance, than the awful Business of Chanting forth the Praises of the King of Kings." One attempt to raise public subscriptions for a singing school brought a refusal from a man who said he had "no inclination to encourage a parcel of giddy young folks to sit in the gallery to show off their skill, which is apparently all they care for." Even the more pious among the young, it seems, found the levity disturbing. A "Clarissa," writing in the *Boston Gazette* in 1766, praised the advances in singing but denounced a "singing party" at which "a large company, in all the spirit of gaiety" mixed wine and jokes with "the most solemn addresses to the Deity," so that "Conscience whispered is not this a solemn mockery of JEHOVAH?" [35] In fact, the new psalmody justified such objections, since to keep adolescents within the church in an increasingly secular age and an increasingly urban environment it mixed devotion with recreation.

The attempt to introduce first pitch pipes, then instruments, also generated dissent. With the introduction of the bass viol around 1776 for accompaniment, churches divided into "catgut churches" and "anti-catgut churches," opponents calling the instrument the "Devil's fiddle." When a bass viol was first played at Roxbury Church in 1788, one old church member stood at the door and mocked it by caterwauling. Controversy also arose over the earlier practice of lining-out, in which line-by-line the psalm was first read by a church deacon, then sung by the congregation. The abandonment of the practice ended one of the deacon's most cherished privileges. In 1773 the Worcester, Massachusetts, church voted to end lining-out; the Saturday after the vote, an aged deacon in the congregation arose and started lining-out the psalm. The singers sang on, the deacon kept lining-out. The choral singing at last overpowering his voice, he left in tears, and was censured and deprived of Communion in the church.[36] Undoubtedly, because of such opposition, the older way of singing and the older repertoire continued in use in some churches throughout the period, probably side by side with the new.

On the other hand, the need to counter such charges and justify the innovations in Congregational singing gave rise to some new musical-religious theory. It came in sermons, often delivered at singing-school graduation ceremonies, works such as Zabdiel Adams' *The Nature, Pleasure and Advantages of Church-Musick* (Boston, 1771; significantly "Published at the Request of the Choir") and Lemuel Hedge's *The Duty and Manner of Singing in Christian Churches* (Boston, 1772), preached at a singing lecture in Warwick. Revealingly, both ministers were young—Adams thirty-two, Hedge thirty. Many of their arguments go back to Thomas Walter's 1721 *Grounds and Rules* (which remained in print in New England throughout the 1760's) and to the introduction to Tans'ur's popular *Royal Melody Complete*, a chief conduit of the new English music to the colonies. No less than Walter and Tans'ur, each minister explained the scriptural basis for psalmody, tracing it to the Hebrews or to the singing of a hymn following the first Communion, and defending the lightness of the new English church music by citing such texts as "Serve the Lord with Gladness."

The sermons differ from the earlier works, however, in their awareness of new problems created by the increased skill in singing. Adams observed that his choir had "in the compass of a few years past, carried vocal musick to a degree of perfection unknown in this part of the world till now." To objections that its "noble ambition to excel" had little to do with the "awful Business of chanting forth the Praises of the King of Kings," he replied that if trained singing did not regenerate the singers, it at least produced a civility akin to virtue. If "frequent hearing of church musick, well performed" will not "infallibly make a person religious, it will do much towards polishing his manners; and if to delight therein does not demonstrate a man to be devout, yet it is for the most part an evidence that there is nothing in his nature that inclines him to be flagrantly wicked." Turning the pious complaints of the musically ungifted back upon them, Adams urged those unseated by the gallery choir to be content "to make melody in their hearts."

Both ministers tried to place the innovations in worship on solid doctrinal and scriptural ground. Adams assured those who viewed the introduction of pitch pipes and of the "motion of the hand" (i.e., conducting) as *"ceremonies"*—devotional practices not found in Scripture— that attempts in the early eighteenth century to introduce regular singing had created the same commotion, and that "no person of common sense can see the least connexion between popery and the late improvements in our church-musick." As for the abandonment of lining-out, Lemuel Hedge told his Warwick congregation that Scripture failed to mention the practice altogether. The Jewish psalm-books contained musical notes "which directed their voices as they pronounced the words in singing. Christ and his Apostles were trained up in this manner. . . ." Lining-out, he speculated, came in with the Reformation, when the Pope's campaign of destroying Protestant psalm-books created a scarcity of them, so that lining-out became necessary. As to the belief that lining-out was sanctioned by its use in the early New England churches, he noted that Cotton Mather, in his *Ratio Disciplinae,* reported that some churches did not use it.

Of the several results of the new music, however, none showed more dramatically the progress in colonial musical life than did the publication of new collections and new compositions designed to meet and to raise the new level of performance. During the 1760's, the initial demand created by the combined influence of *Urania* and the new singing schools was met by reprints of English works or by modest collections drawn from English composers. Tans'ur's *Royal Melody Complete,* first published in London in 1755, went through seven American editions between 1767 and 1774. A further edition of *Urania* seems to have been published in 1767 as well. Throughout the decade, Daniel Bayley of Newburyport published collections of sixteen to twenty-four pages combining materials from Walter and Tans'ur, such as the *New and Complete Introduction to the Grounds and Rules of Musick* (Newburyport, 1768) and *The Essex Harmony* (Newburyport, 1770). The metamorphosis in the ambition of Congregational singing that seems to have jelled around 1770 is dramatized by Bayley's 1773 *New Universal Harmony* (Newburyport). It contains some 104 pages of "Anthems, Hymn-Tunes, and Carols." (The carols—"O Sight of Anguish" and "The Counsel of Grace"—are the first to appear in a New England tunebook.) More significant than the length was Bayley's aside, that since all the tunes were by English composers, he hoped in a later collection to include "some curious Pieces that are the Productions of *America*, by some masterly Hands. . . ." Such "Productions" now existed.

In Boston in 1770 appeared *The New-England Psalm-Singer: or, American Chorister. Containing A Number of Psalm-Tunes, Anthems and Canons. In Four and Five Parts. Never before Published.* It was the work of William Billings, barely twenty-four years old, of the same generation as the older members of the new singing schools. The lack of detailed biographical information about Billings makes one of the sorriest gaps in the history of the arts in America, for he was not only the first important American musician but of permanent importance in the history of American music.[37] His career tests the power of American life to nurture the arts as clearly as do those of Poe or Whitman or Henry James. They faced the same lack of a native tradition, the same problem of using folk material for high artistic purposes, and similar material conditions affecting development and success.

What we know of Billings' early life can be stated in a paragraph. Born in Boston on October 7, 1746 (four years after Handel produced *The Messiah* in Dublin), the son of a shopkeeper, Billings as a youth was apprenticed to a tanner, a profession he practiced during much of his career. As a boy he probably had some instruction in music from a French émigré named John Barry, who at one time led the singing at New South Church, and with whom Billings advertised a singing school in October 1769. One member of the New South was his lifelong friend and neighbor Samuel Adams. (Together they made and sang a paraphrase of the One Hundred and Thirty-seventh Psalm.)

Much else of what is known about Billings comes from people stricken mostly by his grotesqueness. Nathaniel Gould, a nineteenth-century writer who had known several of the early singing masters, remembered him as "somewhat deformed in person, blind with one eye, one leg shorter than the other, one arm somewhat withered, with a mind as eccentric as his person was deformed. . . ." Lucy Swan (daughter of the tunesmith Timothy Swan) described him as having a broken shoulder and a missing eye. Reverend William Bentley of Salem saw him as "a singular man, of moderate size, short of one leg, with one eye, without any address, & with an uncommon negligence of person."[38] A passion for snuff made him still unseemlier. "He used to carry it in his coat-pocket, which was made of leather," Gould recalled, "and every few minutes, instead of taking it in the usual manner, with thumb and finger, would take out a handful and snuff it from between his thumb and clenched hand. We might infer, from this circumstance, that his voice could not have been very pleasant and delicate." Indeed, Billings' voice seems to have resembled the bass he favored in his compositions. His friend Dr. Pierce described it as "stentorian," so powerful that when Pierce stood by him to sing he could not hear his own voice.[39]

But Billings was not only a gargoyle. Those fascinated by his single eye and "almost incredible" liking for snuff remained aware of his talents and achievement. This "self taught man," Bentley wrote, "had the direction of all the music of our Churches . . . he spake & sung & thought as a man above the common abilities." Billings, it was said, had first introduced the violoncello into the Congregational churches, had first used a pitch pipe to set the tune. More than that, he imaginatively repossessed the new English church music and, analogously to his fellow Bostonian Copley, turned it into musical forms and a musical style distinctive to provincial America.

The publication of Billings' *New-England Psalm-Singer* in 1770 makes it difficult to find, as Richard Crawford and David McKay remark, "another single publication in the history of American music—in the history of western music, for that matter—whose priority in its tradition is more conspicuous." It was the first published collection of entirely American music as well as the first tunebook produced by a single American composer. It began a cascade of American tunebooks which by 1800 would number some 111 collections, 26 consisting of music written entirely by American composers, mostly New England singing masters, men composing for friends and neighbors in a society where music became as integral a part of daily life as it had been in Elizabethan England. In November 1770, Billings also applied to the Massachusetts General Court for a copyright on his collection. So far in American history, nothing protected publications from piracy, although few if any native works had enough buyers to make pirating them worthwhile. The court let the petition drop, but Billings reapplied some eighteen months later. On July 14, 1772, the Massachusetts legislature approved the "William Billings Copyright Act," forbidding persons unauthorized by Billings from printing, selling, or bartering his works in whole or part for seven years. Only the refusal of Governor Hutchinson to grant the act final assent prevented Billings from setting another precedent of profound consequence to American culture.[40]

The New-England Psalm-Singer consists of instruction and tunes combined in an oblong volume 6½ inches high by 8½ inches wide, costing eight shillings. Designed specifically for singing schools rather than for use in church, it is to be distinguished from the book-shaped "tune supplement," a briefer and simpler collection meant to be bound in with a hymnal. Just six months or so after his Boston Massacre print, Paul Revere engraved a frontispiece for the book, depicting six men and a singing master seated at a circular table, perhaps representing a home musicale or an itinerant urban singing school (ill., p. 347). The scene is contained within an oval musical staff on which is written a six-part canon. The circular canon and the singing scholars, each of whom places one finger on the tunebook of his neighbor, express a theme of union appropriate to the book's celebration of musical and political harmony.

From its frontispiece on, then, the collection has very much the atmosphere of Boston and of 1770. Written by Billings, engraved at least in part by Revere, sold by Flagg, it also contains three pieces by Cotton Mather's nephew, Mather Byles (whom Billings must have known well), three tunes to texts by the recently deceased and much mourned George Whitefield, and a poem on music dated from Harvard. Identifying himself on the title page as "William Billings, A Native of Boston, in *New-England*," the composer gave his tunes the names of such local places as Westfield, Harvard, Lynn, Medford, Marshfield, and Brookfield. In other ways, the book records the effects of the Stamp and Townshend acts. The title page announces that copies can be had from "Deacon Elliot, under Liberty-Tree." Billings notes that he delayed publication for eighteen months in order to print on American paper, and, as countless verse and broadside writers had done, he calls upon American women to supply linen for native paper mills.

At first glance, Billings' politics seem conciliatory. On the title page he printed the text for the tune EUROPE, asking for a political harmony with the mother country matching the harmony of the singers:

> *O Praise the Lord with one Consent; and in this grand Design,*
> *Let Britain and the Colonies, unanimously join.*

In the collection itself, however, EUROPE appears facing CHESTER, a tune destined to rival "Yankee Doodle" in patriotic appeal and to become a permanent part of American musical tradition. Its text makes a powerful symbolic contrast to the facing text of EUROPE:

> Let tyrants shake their Iron rod
> And slav'ry Clank her galling Chains
> we fear them not we trust in god
> New englands god for ever reigns.

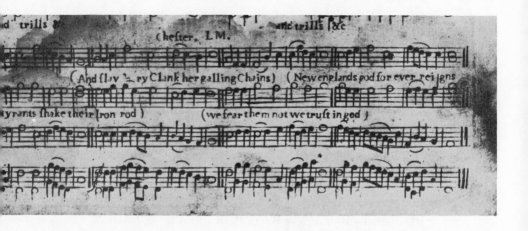

Billings also set Mather Byles's "New-England Hymn" to a tune titled AMERICA, the text recalling the forefathers' flight from persecution in England to where "Liberty erects her Throne." The initial appeal for Anglo-American harmony fades beside the more numerous assertions of New England's principled dauntlessness, an independence of spirit whose reality the very existence of the book confirms.

In format, the *New-England Psalm-Singer* typifies the score of tunebooks which followed. To describe its parts amounts to describing the generic New England tunebook. It opens with several sections of instruction and theorizing, indebted to Tans'ur but much enlivened by Billings' witty prose. Just the same, the reliance on Tans'ur indicates the considerable borrowing among later tunebook compilers, many of whose prefaces sound, and are, alike. Billings' prefatory material begins with a seven-page essay (by Dr. Charles Stockbridge of Scituate) on the "Nature and Properties of Sound"—part of a broader eighteenth-century interest in the physics and physiology of music—discussing the ear, the aural nerves, vibrations, echoes, intervals, and music as a cure for tarantula bite. Such knowledge apparently began to seem irrelevant to the singing masters, who soon dropped it from their tunebooks, as did Billings himself. More useful was the next section, an "Introduction to the Rules of Musick." Since Billings and the later tunesmiths aimed at musical literacy, this includes a "gamut" (a table of the complete normal range of voices); description of clefs, scales, and pitch pipes; and a discussion of time, particularly important because of the rhythmic and metrical complexity of the new music. Singers needed to understand how to beat correctly in accordance with the so-called moods of time, of which most tunebooks distinguished nine: four in duple or common time, three in triple time, and two in compound time (e.g., $\frac{2}{4}$, $\frac{3}{2}$, $\frac{3}{8}$—called "two from four" or "three to two," depending on whether the upper or lower number was larger).[41] The tunebooks disagree considerably on correct tempi; aware of the ambiguity of some of their time signatures (which had specific tempo connotation), compilers advised performers to consult the character of the music.

The introduction also contains vocal exercises and directions on singing, but not in great detail. Billings and many other tunesmiths caution against nasality, urge singers to choose parts appropriate to their voices, and provide "Rules for Tuning the Voice" designed to associate the printed with the aural sound. But all the tunebook compilers agree on the importance of consulting a singing master in order to get the right sound. Since most compilers also taught singing, their insistence that such matters cannot be learned properly from a book probably reflects some wariness lest they publish themselves out of business as teachers. Because they similarly agree on the need for consultation in learning trills and graces, instruction on these "ornaments of expression" in the tunebooks is rather unclear and sketchy. (Dynamic nuances and expression marks—accent, staccato, and swells—were also considered "ornaments of expression.") The "tr." sign designated a variety of trills. Billings prescribes a short three-note and five-note trill; other compilers substituted a simpler turn. The "grace of transition," second in popularity to the trill, was an improvised ornament not annotated in the music, in effect a short passing note between long melody notes a third apart. Billings gives skimpy practical description of it, although he extolls its virtues and uses it extensively for melodic ornamentation.[42]

After instruction in trills and graces comes a section of "Thoughts on Music," describing the sound to be sought in choral performance—a bottom-heavy sound featuring a strong bass foundation for the other parts. Billings recommends a proportion of three to one: Of forty singers, twenty should sing bass; of the other twenty, six or seven should sing ground bass—the effect, he says, being "so exceeding Grand as to cause the Floor to tremble." All the tunewriters agreed that half or more of the choir singers should sing bass, although given the singers' youthfulness, the desired bottom-heaviness was probably impossible to attain. Solo parts should be sung softly, Billings urges, like an echo, "in order to keep the Hearers in an agreeable Suspense till all the Parts join together in a full Chorus, as smart and strong as possible." A widespread practice was to 'double' soprano and tenor voices, a few treble voices singing the tenor part an octave higher than the men, a few tenors singing the treble part an octave lower than the women. Billings recommends this conjunction as "beyond expression sweet and ravishing." The result of the doubling,

Irving Lowens remarks, is "the odd organum-like six-strand texture [that] is a hallmark of the style." [43]

Billings follows this discussion of the choral sound-ideal with a philosophical essay on the relation of music to states of feeling. He and his contemporaries assigned distinct emotive qualities to modes, the "flat key" (i.e., the minor mode) arousing sadness, the "sharp key" (the major mode) arousing happiness; one serving for cheerful texts, the other for melancholy texts, men finding them equally pleasing, women preferring the minor. In setting his texts, Billings also distinguishes between specific keys, G minor, for example, being "more pensive and melancholy" than A minor. Although this happy-sad dichotomy has a musical history going back at least to the Renaissance, it also reflects elements of eighteenth-century sentimentalism to which we shall return in discussing Billings' own compositions.

As is not typical of the later tunebooks, Billings concludes his instructional material with funny, impudent advice on composition, addressed to "all musical Practitioners." He announces that little can be learned by example. As grammar does not make poets, "all the hard dry studied Rules that ever was prescribed, will not enable any Person to form an Air. . . ." In his own writing, "I don't think myself confin'd to any Rules for Composition laid down by any that went before me." Nor should others imitate him, the best rule being "for every *Composer* to be his own *Carver.*" *"Nature,"* he says, *"is the best Dictator."*

The sauciness as well as the uncertain sweep of Billings' remarks make them worth pausing over. Some musicologists interpret them as the declaration of a musical rebel; others take them for a narrow rejection of specific harmonic prescriptions. They do echo both the larger attack on 'the rules' belonging to an emergent romantic esthetic and the great neoclassical injunction to Follow Nature. On the other hand, Billings clearly has in mind that in devising singable melodies for four voices, melodic fancy must be given free play, and that it is better to violate rules of harmony than to "cross the Strain that Fancy dictated. . . ."

What complicate the question of Billings' allegiance to traditional harmony are the colonial situation in 1770 and larger questions about the relation between metropolitan and provincial art. Billings' statements recall such Stamp Act poems as *The Times*, whose author portrays himself as "rudely rough," "wild as the soil," "A wild exotic neighbour to the bear":

> No Muse I court, an alien to the Nine,
> Thou chaste instructress, NATURE! thou art mine. . . .

Within months of the appearance of *The New-England Psalm-Singer*, Peale and West also stressed their allegiance to nature. "One rude line from Nature," Peale wrote (and would often repeat), "is worth an hundred from coppys." It "enlarges the Ideas and [makes?] one see and feel with such sencesations *[sic]* as are worthy of the author." His teacher Benjamin West wrote that growing up in America was "the most fortunate Circumstance that could have happen'd to me: My having no other Assistance but what I drew from Nature (the Early Part of my Life being quite obscured from Art) this grounded me in the Knowledge of Nature, while had I come to Europe sooner in Life, I should have known nothing but the Receipts of Masters." [44] Such claims for "Nature" around 1770 partake of changed estimates of colonial life, in which the conspiratorial place-seeking and court-fawning of London life made the traditional provincial limitations of rusticity and simplicity seem positive virtues.

In another sense, too, the recent emphasis on nature differed from neoclassical and preromantic demands to follow nature. It was one thing for a London poet who could see Garrick, hear Handel, or quip with Dr. Johnson to talk about 'following Nature'; it was quite another thing for a twenty-four-year-old tanner in Boston who had little else to follow. As Kenneth Clark comments, nature plays a unique role in provincial art, since the artist, cut off from metropolitan centers of theory and experiment, perforce falls back on his own inspiration, his own eye, ear, and pen. "Truth to nature and individual judgment," Clark says, are "the recurrent catchwords of provincial art. . . ." [45] In painting, provincialism produces "sharpness of vision, acceptance of fact." Copley paints what his eye sees, disregarding the formal and dramatic demands of the canvas. Billings, one might speculate, emphasizes the melodic lines, disregarding the need to harmonize the different voices for the sake of a larger design. Billings' regard for "Nature," like that of Peale and West, reflects a provincial process, enhanced by radical ideology, of turning provincial liabilities into assets, a way of justifying the artist's practice, not despite, but in the absence of tradition and of first-rate models for emulation.

The longer part of Billings' collection, to return to *The New-England Psalm-Singer*, consists of 116 pages of music and text containing 126 tunes, mostly in four-part settings. Lyon's *Urania* being the only measure, the collection multiplied by ten times the number of native compositions in print, since all of the tunes are by Billings himself. Some appear in the block-chord style of the older psalm tunes, others in a more florid style suitable to the "modern Air and Manner of Singing." Five of the tunes—AMHERST, BROOKFIELD, CHESTER, HINGHAM, LEBANON—entered the list of the most frequently reprinted tunes of the eighteenth century, forming part of what Richard Crawford calls the "core repertory" of Congregational psalmody.[46]

The forms of the tunes are as significant as their number and popularity.

Billings included five anthems, compositions based on some scriptural text other than Psalms and longer than psalm tunes, works that epitomized the new English church music and often served as *pièces de résistance* in singing-school commencement exercises.[47] He also included a form that had come into fashion at the same time as the anthems and among the same English composers—the so-called fuging-tune. As described by Irving Lowens, the typical fuging-tune begins

> with a homophonic section in the course of which a definite cadence is reached, frequently but not always on the tonic of the key. A fresh start is then made, in which each individual voice makes its entrance in succession, the order varying according to the inclination of the composer. In this second section—which was customarily referred to as the "fuge"—some form of imitation, in most cases quite free, was utilized for a measure or two. Normally, the fuge was repeated, thus making the whole a small, rather tightly organized ABB form.[48]

In his preface, Billings himself defines *"Fuge"* as a composition "where the Parts come in after each other, with the same Notes. . . ." Few American composers would have agreed on a definition of the fuging-tune, but all understood by it a tune containing passages in which two or more different voices sing different words at the same time.

The three fuging-tunes in *The New-England Psalm-Singer* are the first in the form by an American. Their appearance seems to have quickened the spread of the form; in his own next collection in 1778, Billings included ten fuging-tunes. By 1810 some one thousand different fuging-tunes had appeared in American tunebooks, the best of them coming in the 1780's, most of them from Connecticut tunesmiths.[49] Religious revivalists later spread them into the Middle Colonies and the South, where they continued to be sung well into the nineteenth century from shape-note collections. Their immense popularity is probably owing to their ideal fitness for the new singing schools: They abandoned simple harmonization and gave every voice a good tune to sing; their impetuous, careering effect probably appealed to the young singers; they sound more difficult to sing than they are, satisfying a provincial weakness for easy virtuoso effects. Like Copley's magically real satin dresses, they create an effect of difficulty unwarranted by their actual technical demands. Perhaps their popularity also gained from the emerging spirit of resistance, something of whose assertiveness they shared. In one of her short stories, Harriet Beecher Stowe recalled hearing the fuging-tunes as a girl: "there was a grand, wild freedom, an energy of motion in the old 'fuging tunes' of that day," she said, "that well expressed the heart of the people courageous in combat and unshaken in endurance." [50]

The distinctive facts about Billings' tunes, however, are neither their number nor their forms but their peculiarly dissonant sound and their literary, rather secular texts. Many of the tunes use marked, dancelike rhythms only occasionally heard in earlier English music that remained characteristic of popular music in America. The rhythmic pattern of the carol BOSTON is that of an Irish jig. Many of the melodies echo such traditional Anglo-Celtic folksongs as "Greensleeves" and "Lord Randal." In itself this tradition may account for the many parallel fifths and octaves, the clashes of natural and sharpened versions of a tone, which give the music its distinctive dissonance.

The dissonance may have other sources, however. It may be a legacy of earlier Scottish Protestant music, which often omitted the third of the chord; it may be a relic of the Renaissance modal progressions, in which parallel fifths and octaves often occur;[51] it may derive from Tans'ur, who allowed for fifths and octaves when the alternative was to ruin the melody: "two *Fifths*, or two *Eighths* (and no more) may be taken together in *Three*, or more *Parts* (when it cannot be well avoided) rather than spoil the Air" [52]; or it may derive from a combination of the contrapuntal method of the fuging-tunes and the tunesmiths' ignorance of European harmony, their inability to handle simultaneous melodies.

Whatever the source, few of Billings' tunes—or those of the later tunesmiths—lack parallel octaves and fifths. The result is an archaic, dissonant sound that resembles European music three centuries earlier and a century and a half later than itself, which an ear tuned to Arnold Schönberg finds natural and congenial. Continuing into the late eighteenth century an earlier Puritan aversion to pretty and sensuous effects—like the liney style and warty faces of Copley and Chandler—it represents a high point of Protestant culture in America, later sustained and transcended in the harsh cacophony of Charles Ives.

Billings set his music to texts notable for their literary quality. Himself one of the liveliest prose writers in eighteenth-century America, he considered literature "the Spring and Security of human Happiness." "Poetry and Music are in close Connection," he wrote, and "like true friends often hide each others failings." He chose texts carefully, so that with its several selections from Isaac Watts, Addison, and Byles, *The New-England Psalm-Singer* makes a good anthology of eighteenth-century religious poetry. Billings wrote several of the texts himself, certainly CHESTER and probably SHILOH ("Methinks I see a heav'nly host"). His literary imagination drew him to texts which invited musical word-painting. Words like "shake" and "roll" are regularly text-painted, while in the anthem "The Lord Descended" twenty-seven half notes convey "flying." In the beautiful canon "When Jesus Wept," graces of transition, dotted eighths, and similar stuttering devices musically evoke the weeping described in the text.

Given their enthusiasm for such effects, Billings' compositions must be called sacred-secular. They reflect the demands of the new singing schools, where devotion had become submerged in esthetic play and sociable virtuosity. Although written for 'psalm-singers,' they often remind one less of scriptural traditions than of esthetic and political currents of the moment. The sobbing melismas of "When Jesus Wept" recall the sentimental abandonment to grief which the song shares with the burial-of-Liberty ceremonies and the downcast visage of West's Agrippina:

In CHESTER, already quoted, the psalm tune has become indistinguishable from purely secular performances like propaganda verse, royal birthday poems, and even plays:

> Let tyrants shake their Iron rod
> And slav'ry Clank her galling Chains. . . .

The word "shake" has a long history in the tunebook tradition (one of the ornaments is itself called a shake), but otherwise the text derives from entirely secular sources, largely the rustling and clanking noises popular with Thomas Warton and the other English poets of melancholy. Although meant to be sung by a Congregational church choir in Boston, the imagery can be found full-blown in works for the stage. In Thomas Godfrey's *The Prince of Parthia*, for instance, the King says, "Now shake your chains, shake and delight your ears/ With the soft music of your golden fetters." In a Princeton commencement poem of 1763, a senior also declaimed how slavery "its tyrant Weapon shakes,/ And drags its Iron

Chains. . . ." [53] Several of Billings' texts seem closer to literary than to scriptural traditions, including a Sapphic ode taken from Isaac Watts's *Lyric Poems*, in which, "Vigoroso," the singers mimic how "the fierce North wind with his Airy forces/ Rears up the Baltick to a foaming fury."

The number of purely secular works in the New England tunebooks, including Billings' own, would grow the longer the tunebooks were produced. For the sacred-secular quality is one measure of the waning of orthodox Congregationalism. Understandably, one of Billings' greatest admirers, Reverend William Bentley of Salem, was an early Unitarian minister. The good-naturedness of much of Billings' music must have appealed precisely to Congregational churches passing through a rationalistic phase on their way to adopting the benign Unitarianism of the early nineteenth century. In later collections Billings often chose his texts from the poems of the universalist preacher James Relly. Even in *The New-England Psalm-Singer* he included three texts by the notorious punster Mather Byles, the same Mather Byles who explained that he galloped his horse because "It is Fast day"; who asked a Boston distiller to still his wife; who told his corpulent bookseller friend Henry Knox that "I never saw an ox fatter in my life"; who, asked by a friend where to have a tooth drawn, sent the man to John Singleton Copley; who, to the cry of some Bostonians that they wanted their grievances redressed, pointed to troops on the Common and said that now people could no longer complain "that our *grievances* are not *red-dressed*"; and who, when told that he had "two d's," replied that he got them—his D.D.—from Aberdeen.[54] While Billings included nothing outrageous, he did set psalms to jigs and call upon the singers (in QUEEN STREET) to "Clap your hands & shout for joy/ With triumph & with mirth." Cheerfully emphasizing the resurrection more than the crucifixion, Billings' music was the kind that conservative ministers feared would come into the church if the older restrictions on psalmody were relaxed.

The ungainly Billings and his joyfully harsh music could not have been what Benjamin Franklin hoped for when in 1763 he reflected that "the Arts delight to travel Westward." The new Tanneberger organs and the new composer-organists like William Selby, the first American performance on a pianoforte, the two- and three-year contracts offered by the St. Coecilia Society in Charleston to professional musicians, the new immigrant musicians performing and trying to publish their own works—these were probably better evidence of the "elegant Minds" Franklin found lacking in America. By the largest standards, he was right. The year 1770, in which *The New-England Psalm-Singer* appeared, was also the year of the birth of Beethoven. Yet Billings provided a fresh impulse. Neither folk music nor art music, neither sacred nor secular, his compositions were, in

Hans David's apt phrase, a "low-brow cultivated music" expressive of a democratic standard toward which much later American culture has striven. His influence was immediate. In December 1772, the first parish of Plymouth closed its exercises with his AMERICA, sung with "uncommon melody." At rehearsals, Nathaniel Gould recalled, "his room was crowded, inside and out, with listeners, like the hearers of Jenny Lind . . . he could not possibly make them desist, except by promises to sing publicly, in some church, and give them a chance to hear." [55] His idiom, we shall see, was immediately taken up and practiced by an ever-expanding group of New England tunesmiths.

Billings' appearance in 1770, at the age of twenty-four, marks not only new promise. With their dancelike enthusiasm and exuberantly pious spontaneity, their greatly gifted naiveté, his compositions mark the achievement of a new grade of maturity and invention in American musical life.

24. The Literary Scene

Although no one in the colonies had written a work as talented or daring as The Death of General Wolfe *or* The New-England Psalm-Singer, *the literary scene, too, had visibly improved. In 1763, the country lacked most features of metropolitan literary life: It supported no magazines, it had no prominent literary personalities to inspire emulation, its presses turned out few volumes of belles-lettres. Public appreciation of poetry as a medium of debate on local issues, however, and encouragement for aspiring talent in the colleges both hinted that the country might be receptive to a transplantation of the literary Muses. By 1770, the hints were more numerous and more sharply defined. A few magazines had appeared for brief runs, the Stamp and Townshend acts had provoked scores of indignant poems and skits, urgent and complex issues had demanded ambitious treatment. Together with young painters like Stuart and young composers like Billings, young poets appeared who had grown up during the political crises of the 1760's. Most were graduates of colonial colleges which over the last half-dozen years had increasingly emphasized literary study. Their considerable talents gave ground for the hope that was the major theme of their poetry, the hope of larger progress, of the Rising Glory of America.*

While the country still lacked an established literary magazine in 1770, more poems, more plays, and more essays were being written, printed, and read, by more people, in more places, than ever before.[1] In 1763, colonial presses issued, roughly, seven items of belles-lettres; in 1773 they issued forty-five items. When Henry Knox opened his "London Book-Store" in Boston in 1771, the city already contained ten printers, eight booksellers, and six printer-booksellers. Rivington of New York, alone, in one year, ordered from Knox 140 copies of 24 different plays.[2]

Much of this growth was a direct result of increased population, but it also fed on events of the 1760's. The success of the non-importation agreements suggested that, like other manufactures, literary works could be printed at home and priced cheaper than imported editions, keeping currency within the country. English works that had been imported began being printed. In 1771, the printer Robert Bell proposed "To the AMERICAN WORLD" a five-volume edition of Blackstone's *Commentaries*. He calculated that the importation of a thousand sets sent nearly ten thousand pounds overseas; the printing of a thousand sets in America, for a third the imported price, would save "seven thousand pounds to the purchasers, and the identical three thousand pounds which is laid out for our own manufactures is still retained in the country, being distributed among manufacturers and traders." A Philadelphia printer offered his 1772 edition of Oliver Goldsmith's *The Vicar of Wakefield* to "Encouragers of American Manufactures" on Pennsylvania-made paper, for half the price of the English edition. The result of this literary non-importation movement was the publication, between 1771 and 1773, of single American editions of Robert Blair's *The Grave*, Thomas Gray's *Elegy Written in a Country Churchyard*, Goldsmith's *The Deserted Village*, and Laurence Sterne's *Sentimental Journey* (two volumes), as well as two American editions of Goldsmith's *She Stoops to Conquer* and four separate editions of Garrick's *The Irish Widow*.[3]

More important, the Stamp and Townshend acts provided urgent issues that made native literary activity highly visible. Poems were everywhere— in political pamphlets, in newspapers, nailed to trees, slipped under doors, read at the burial of Liberty, painted on transparencies. They continued appearing between 1770 and 1773 as rumbles of unresolved strain with England disturbed the "quiet period." Conflict between local officials and the South Carolina Assembly over using local funds to help John Wilkes pay his debts; the continued stationing of British regulars at Castle William in Boston Harbor; the burning of one of the king's custom ships, the *Gaspee*, in Rhode Island—wherever tension accumulated, verse sprang out.

Thus Philadelphians were reminded that despite the repeal of the Townshend Acts, a tax on liquor remained:

> Ye Ladies so modest, who drink no small Beer,
> But keep in your Closets a little good Cheer;

The *Inquisitor* comes, and so carefully pries,
That you never can jockey that Fiend of Ex-se.

Bostonians were reminded that Ebenezer Richardson, who had killed young Christopher Seider shortly before the Boston Massacre, remained unsentenced, although convicted two years ago:

. . . You Laws defy,
But Heaven's laws shall stand when KINGS shall die.
Oh! Wretched man! the monster of the times,
You were not hung "by reason of *old* Lines,"
Old Lines thrown by, 'twas then we were in hopes,
That you would soon be hung with *new made* Ropes. . . .

Beginning in 1771, the anniversary of the Massacre itself was marked by tolling bells, mottos ("FOUL PLAY"), orations, and gory transparencies. Verses were read, reminding citizens of the "Theatre of Blood," of their violent disinheritance, and of their continuity with the past:

From realms of bondage and a Tyrant's reign,
Our Godlike Fathers bore no slavish chain,
To *Pharoah's* face th'inspired *Patriarchs* stood,
To seal their virtue, with a Martyr's blood:
. . . .
In Vain shall B____n lift her suppliant eye,
An alien'd offspring feels no filial tie,
Her tears in vain shall bathe the soldiers feet,
Remember, *Ingrate, B_st_n's* crimson'd street.[4]

The literally dozens of such poems written between 1770 and 1773 kept alive the emotions aroused by recent events while reminding British officials that new depredations were not likely to be tolerated. They also increased an ever-swelling body of colonial verse.

As the numbers of topical works continued growing, the works also changed in kind. The very weight and complexity of the issues made the earlier brief skits and verse dialogues inadequate. By the early 1770's— perhaps with encouragement from a new vogue of college and home theatricals and from the production of *The Prince of Parthia*—closet dramas and even full-fledged plays began being written on political subjects. Ephemeral examples, both published in 1771, are "Hodge Podge improved," in which John Dickinson delivers a long soliloquy denouncing "the inhabitants of this stupid country, where there is not one MAN OF GENIUS EXCEPT MYSELF," confirming the author's contention that Dickinson is insane; and the *Trial of Atticus Before Justice Beau, for a Rape* (Boston, 1771), where the patriotically named Atticus exposes quack physicians, merchants who sell diluted rum, and venal local officials.[5]

More sophisticated were the "dramatic sketches," as she called them, of Mercy Warren (1728–1814), a descendant of a *Mayflower* family whose house in Braintree, near John and Abigail Adams, was a rendezvous for popular leaders. Copley painted her in a rather Knelleresque portrait of the early 1760's, enigmatically sad-smiling, with concentrating eyes that suggest a piercing intelligence. Although she wrote political verses for her coterie, verses animated by her outrage at the beating of her brother, the unstable James Otis, by a British tax commissioner, Mercy Warren had never seen a play. What moved her to write two closet plays was an episode which itself threatened to end the "quiet period." In June 1773, hoping to oust Governor Thomas Hutchinson, Samuel Adams read in a secret session of the Massachusetts legislature some private, highly inflammatory letters written by Hutchinson and by his brother-in-law, Lieutenant Governor Andrew Oliver. Sent by them to friends in England in 1767–69, the letters urged that the Crown declare martial law, make the judges independent of provincial control, and suppress the Rhode Island charter. The eventual publication of the letters in newspapers and a pamphlet led to a petition to the king for their removal. In writing her plays Mercy Warren hoped to aid Adams and, by undeceiving Americans about Hutchinson and Oliver, to "strip the Vizard from the Crafty." [6]

The Adulateur. A Tragedy, As it is now Acted in Upper Servia (1773), recounts events in Boston between the Stamp Act and the Massacre in order to expose Hutchinson and to enlist support for popular efforts against him. It uses a neoclassical setting as the vehicle for its Whig-Puritan analysis of Hutchinson's psychology. After a quote from *Cato* urging Roman defense of liberty, it opens with a historicized scene in Mercy Warren's parlor, in which Brutus and Cassius (James Otis and John Adams) lament the death of liberty in "Servia" and determine to rouse their countrymen in the name of their forefathers. Rapatio—Hutchinson—is introduced brooding on the Stamp Act mob that ransacked his house, willing to destroy the state that nurtured him in reprisal:

> O'er fields of death, with hastning step I'll speed,
> And smile at length to see my country bleed:
> From my tame heart the pang of virtue fling,
> And mid the general flame, like Nero sing.—

Hutchinson's Neronian lust for revenge results in the killing of young Seider. Brutus, enraged but prudent, realizes that retaliation will only confirm the image of Servians which Rapatio wants to create, of a people "Headstrong—rebellious—factious—uncontroul'd"; he urges redress through the courts. The wisdom of restraint is challenged, however, by Portius (John Hancock), who points out that the judges themselves are

Rapatio's mere tools, and, more so, by the next event (the Boston Massacre), when the "streets of Servia sweat with human gore." As the bleeding corpses are borne in, Brutus addresses a crowd of enraged citizens who demand recall of the troops. Rapatio at first protests that he only serves higher authority; but when his councilors insist that the people mean to fight, he orders the troops withdrawn. The play ends with the revelation that having recalled the troops, Rapatio continues to plot: "Dispotic *[sic]* rule my first, my sov'reign wish."

The Adulateur was written before the disclosure of the Hutchinson-Oliver letters, to which Mercy Warren had probably been given access by Samuel Adams. She returned to the same cast and the same setting after the reading of the correspondence before the Massachusetts House. *The Defeat* opens with Rapatio sitting before a pile of money, again bemoaning his ransacked property, a despot unstrung like Milton's Satan by inner uncertainty and conscience: "The wooden latchet of my door ne'r clicks,/ But that I start. . . ." His anxiety turns to alarm when the letters explore his effort to use "pretended Fear" to establish that "Bane of Freedom, and the Badge of Slavery . . . A Standing Army." Unmasked, Rapatio and Limpit (Oliver) discuss the likelihood of being hanged—and, despite everything, plot new deceptions to whitewash the Hutchinson-Rapatio administration. The play offers no program for action: The courts cannot be trusted for redress, yet popular uprisings will confirm Rapatio's picture of Servian rebelliousness. Its argument rather consists of the Miltonic, psychohistorical characterizations of the "corrupt junto" and its adversary, the "band of patriotic writers." The author explains the satanic Hutchinson's present behavior in terms of his inborn avarice, his lust for rule, and his unquenchable resentment, while portraying patriot leaders like the Adamses as shrewdly sober and deserving of trust. Nor does the play offer a catharsis. It ends on a moment of dramatic suspension, with the disclosure that Hutchinson, however stripped of pretense, is busy inventing fresh pretenses and must never be believed.[7]

Other events of the early 1770's inspired what is probably the first actual play on a native political theme, *The Candidates or The Humours of a Virginia Election*, by the Virginia burgess Robert Munford. Educated in England, Munford found time while growing tobacco and practicing law to become, as he styled himself, "Virginia's first and only comic son."[8] His play concerns an election for delegates to the Virginia House of Burgesses. His hero is the seignoral Woud'be, pained to serve an unthinking electorate, but compelled to by a sense of communal responsibility—a prototype of the Virginia ideal of un-selfseeking public service:

> Must I again be subject to the humours of a fickle crowd?
> Must I again resign my reason, and be nought but what each voter

pleases? Must I cajole, fawn, and wheedle, for a place
that brings so little profit?

Woud'be's sacrifice is the more necessary given the other candidates,
drunks like Sir John Toddy and uneducated, lower-class types like
Smallhopes and Strutabout. They bet on the election, and offer to fight
Woud'be by fists. The electorate is not much better: As Munford reveals
during a lively hog-barbecue scene, they choose the candidates who tell
the best jokes or pour the most liquor. The play is also noteworthy for its
characterization of Ralpho, Woud'be's slave, a prototype of the Plantation
Darky of later southern romances:

> RALPHO: God bless your honour! what a good master! who would not do
> every thing to give such a one pleasure? But e'gad it's time to think of my new
> clothes: I'll go and try them on. Gadso! this figure of mine is not
> reconsiderable in its delurements, and when I'm dressed out like a gentleman,
> the girls, I'm a thinking, will find me desistible.

Given this childlike egotism, Woud'be's slaveowning seems an act of
kindness not unlike his disinterested public service.[9] In the end, Woud'be
defeats his inebriated lower-class rivals and proclaims in the courthouse
yard that the electorate has shown a "judgment, and a spirit of
independence becoming Virginians." Yet the play shows the electorate to
be credulous, bribable, and stupid, and Munford seems not so much
confident that southern noblesse oblige will supply leaders as uneasy over
democratic tendencies.

The American editions of English classics, the poems, sketches, and
plays on political affairs were not the most vital evidence of literary
growth, however, nor the most promising. Of features of urban culture
thus far absent from the colonies perhaps the most germinative were
literary celebrities, names that like Pope's or Dr. Johnson's evoked a style,
a subject, an image of the literary life. But between 1770 and 1773, four
talented young poets made attention-getting and nearly simultaneous
debuts.

One of them, unexpectedly, was a black slave girl. She had been taken
from Africa in 1761, and bought by John Wheatley, a liberal Boston
merchant interested in the Methodist missionary movement. Phillis
Wheatley (c. 1753–1784) thus became one in a long line of blacks and
Indians since the seventeenth century who were Christianized, or more
accurately, Puritanized, in New England. Her first known poem appeared
in the *Newport Mercury* in 1767, when she was about thirteen. An
accompanying note explained that two mariners dining at the Wheatley
home had told of being shipwrecked, when *"this Negro Girl at the same Time,
'tending Table, heard the Relation"* and wrote some verses attributing their

salvation to "the Great Supreme, the Wise." [10] Her interest in poetry was not unusual. Often the test of missionary work was the converts' ability to perform feats that their genteel, pious foster-families cherished as ultimate marks of civilization, like addressing the "Great Supreme" in verse.

Unlike most other black converts, however, Phillis Wheatley kept writing. During the occupation of Boston she wrote a poem "On the Death of Mr Snider *[sic]* Murder'd by Richardson," memorializing "the first martyr for the common good." She first attracted wide public notice with a broadside elegy on George Whitefield in 1770, advertised as the work of "PHILLIS, *a Servant Girl of* 17 *Years of Age* . . . *but* 9 *Years in this Country from Africa.*" She praised Whitefield's eloquent preaching to the Africans—even though he defended slavery—and the comforting knowledge of his love for America at the time of the Massacre, only months before his death:

> When his AMERICANS were burden'd sore,
> When streets were crimson'd with their guiltless gore!
> Unrival'd friendship in his breast now strove:
> The fruit thereof was charity and love
> Towards *America*. . . .

Although Phillis Wheatley's was only one of literally dozens of elegies praising Whitefield as the greatest preacher since the Apostles and a special friend to America, other versifiers singled out the "young Afric damsels virgin tongue" for particular praise.[11] The poem was republished in Newport, New York, Philadelphia, London, and four more times in Boston.

As a Christian convert, eventually a communicant of Old South Church, Phillis Wheatley concerned herself far more with salvation than with taxation. Yet directly and indirectly her success grew out of the political situation. The killing of young Seider and the Boston Massacre afforded subjects of recognized public importance, hence a willing audience. Indirectly, a receptive climate for her works was created by awareness of a vulnerable inconsistency, or at worst outright hypocrisy, in the colonial position. "The Negroes in America are slaves, the whites enjoy liberty," wrote John Wesley in England. "Is not then all this outcry about Liberty and Slavery mere rant, and playing upon words?" [12]

The painful fact that many who cried for liberty practiced slavery received much public discussion. Several tracts of the early 1770's reassessed slavery in the light of the evolving political argument; students at the 1773 Harvard commencement debated the legality of slavery; at the death in 1773 of John Jack, "A Native of Africa," a Massachusetts stonecutter chiseled onto a bitter tombstone:

> Though born in a land of Slavery,
>   He was born free;

> Though he lived in a land of Liberty,
>   He lived a Slave.

When Phillis Wheatley herself pondered the situation of colonial blacks, she found it not ironically deprived but ironically privileged. Imploring the earl of Dartmouth to lift oppression in America, she explained that her own enslavement gave her a special appreciation of freedom:

> I, young in life, by seeming cruel fate
> Was snatch'd from *Afric's* fancy'd happy seat:
> What pangs excruciating must molest,
> What sorrows labour in my parent's breast?
> Steel'd was that soul and by no misery mov'd
> That from a father seiz'd his babe belov'd:
> Such, such my case. And can I then but pray
> Others may never feel tyrannic sway?[13]

The startling ambivalence of the passage—oppression appears both as a "seeming cruel fate" and as "tyrannic sway"—indicates that Phillis Wheatley adopted her owners' missionary viewpoint. The process that "seiz'd" and "snatch'd" her from her parents was only a "seeming cruel fate," a fortunate fall that brought her out of the darkness of pagan Africa to the redeeming light of Puritan Boston. However intricate its ironies, public discussion of slavery and liberty made a responsive setting for Phillis Wheatley's debut.

In the fall of 1772, ill, Phillis joined the Wheatleys' son in a health-seeking voyage to England. Like West and others whose attainments could be seen to mark the spread of English empire and civilization, she was met by self-congratulating enthusiasm. Even before she arrived, the *London Magazine* published her poem "Recollection" as the work of "a compleat sempstress, an accomplished mistress of her pen, and . . . a most surprising genius." The Lord Mayor of London, Brook Watson, presented her a folio edition of *Paradise Lost*, while the nobility and gentry, she wrote, treated her with "unexpected and unmerited civility and complaisance. . . ."[14] Most important, some of her poems were read to the pious countess of Huntingdon, whose private chaplain had been George Whitefield.

Probably it was the countess who subsidized the publication in London in 1773 of Phillis Wheatley's *Poems on Various Subjects, Religious and Moral*. The volume included an engraving of the poet and a thumbnail biography by John Wheatley, reporting that she had learned English in sixteen months on her own, soon could read the most difficult parts of the Bible, and was making progress in Latin. An attestation signed by John Hancock and other prominent Bostonians affirmed that she wrote the poems herself, despite repeated suggestions of a hoax. The collection opened with an Augustan address to Maecenas (a type of the patron of the arts), alluding familiarly to Homer, Vergil, and Terence, and dropping words like "circumfus'd." The rest, more than three dozen poems, consisted of family poems on the Wheatleys; biblical poems on David and Goliath; philosophical verses on Providence, Recollection, and Imagination; elegies on departed ministers; and temperate and loyal political addresses to the earl of Dartmouth and the king. Models of correct taste, genteel learning, and sound doctrine, they express the world of the Boston literary clergy of the day and might have been written by one of the lesser eighteenth-century descendants of illustrious Puritans, such as Mather Byles.

Despite their tameness and self-conscious elegance, Wheatley's poems seemed to her contemporaries, and still seem, incredible performances for a teen-aged slave girl. Voltaire himself praised her *"très-bon vers anglais."* Several English magazines reviewed the volume, agreed that the poems were remarkable considering their origins, and pecked at the sore-point: "We are much concerned to find that this ingenious young woman is yet a slave. The people of Boston boast themselves chiefly on their principles of liberty. One such act as the purchase of her freedom, would . . . have done them more honor than hanging a thousand trees with ribbons and emblems." Phillis herself unexpectedly left England in the summer of 1773, before she was to be introduced at court, to attend her dangerously ill mistress in Boston. Early the next year her volume was advertised in Boston, New York, and elsewhere for three shillings, four pence. In public and in private, colonials spoke of her as "the extraordinary poetical Genius" or as "the famous Phillis Wheatley, the African Poetess." [15] Except that she was taken less as a poet than as a proof of the hypocrisy of Whigs or the mental ability of blacks, Phillis Wheatley came near to supplying the literary celebrity which the colonial literary scene lacked in 1763.

Three other young poets, less celebrated than Phillis Wheatley at first and more celebrated later, emerged at the same time and commanded a similarly expectant attention: John Trumbull (a cousin of the painter), Timothy Dwight, and Philip Freneau. They were not slaves, but students, products of a diffusion and transformation of collegiate education in the colonies over the last half-dozen years. This change needs to be described in some detail, not only as a formative milieu but also as a measure of cultural progress itself, and a stimulus to further progress.

William Smith, to recall, had brought with him to America educational ideals derived from the reorganization of the Scottish university system, where the study of scholastic logic and metaphysics gave way to the study of rhetoric, belles-lettres, and other modern, secular subjects. By 1763,

Smith's emphasis on the writing of poetry and the performance of odes and dialogues had nurtured several promising young poets at the College of Philadelphia. Their potential was aborted, however, as the less gifted entered the ministry and the most gifted, Thomas Godfrey and Nathaniel Evans, died young. Smith's own influence, moreover, waned as his political conservatism became more pronounced. Yet he was a prophetic forerunner.

Around 1770, older colleges independently adopted the kind of literary curriculum Smith had introduced a decade earlier at Philadelphia. Between 1765 and 1772 Yale underwent a revolution. "About this time," recalled Samuel Miller at the end of the century, "the study of the Mathematics, and of the Ancient Languages, began to decline, and that of Belles Lettres to be an object of more attention than before"; the tutors "encouraged among the students, both by precept and example, a new degree of attention to the best writers in their own language, and to the graces of composition." [16] A similarly profound change took place at William and Mary College in 1770, when an examination in classical languages was no longer required for entrance, and where William Small offered systematic lectures in belles-lettres. Harvard in 1767 listed composition, elocution, and belles-lettres as part of the curriculum. In 1772 the Harvard Overseers voted to have tutors read portions from some celebrated English writer each Saturday morning to improve the students in elocution; the same year, the merchant Nicholas Boylston left in his will £1,500 for founding a since-distinguished professorship of rhetoric and oratory.[17] A high degree of proficiency in English became particularly required at schools with Scottish presidents, probably owing to chronic Scottish anxiety about writing correct English. Thus when John Wither-spoon (a classmate of Hugh Blair's at the University of Edinburgh) became president of Princeton in 1768, he made the study of belles-lettres, languages, and history almost as important for ministerial candidates as conversion, setting out the principles of spoken and written English in sixteen lengthy "Lectures on Eloquence." What Ezra Stiles called the "College Enthusiasm" increased the cultural impact of these changes. The number of colonial colleges rose from three in 1745 to ten in 1776.[18]

The spread and deepening of literary study gained momentum and added justification from the political crisis as well. A corollary of the Whig theory of liberty was the close bond between liberty, the arts, and learning. The commencement orator at the College of Rhode Island who spoke in 1769 on "The Advantages of Liberty and Learning, and their mutual Dependence upon each other" only repeated what had been formulated fifty years earlier by Trenchard and Gordon in several of *Cato's Letters*, such as *"Polite Arts and Learning naturally produced in Free States, and marred by such as are not free,"* ideas reiterated and expanded by James Thomson in his long poem *Liberty* and by David Hume in his essay "Of the Rise and Progress of the Arts and Sciences." Whig theorists, caught up in the larger Enlightenment effort to overthrow superstition, virtually identified liberty with free inquiry. "Servitude mars all Genius," said Trenchard and Gordon; oppressed people "want Vigour as well as Leisure to cultivate Arts." "The high spirit of poetry," as Lord Shaftesbury put it, "can ill subsist where the spirit of liberty is wanting." [19]

As the Stamp and Townshend acts focused attention on liberty they recalled the axiomatic bond between liberty, learning, and the arts. After singing Dickinson's "Liberty Song" during a 1768 ceremony, some Sons of Liberty drank forty-five toasts including "42. *The* Republic *of* Letters." Inevitably, John Adams saw the college literary exercises as an appropriate forum for Whig sentiment: "Let every declamation turn upon the beauty of liberty and virtue and the deformity, turpitude, and malignity of slavery and vice," he asked in 1765. "Let the dialogues and all the exercises become the instruments of impressing on the tender mind, and of spreading and distributing far and wide, the ideas of right and the sensations of freedom." [20]

The support for college literary studies which many found in Whig theory, however reverenced, was perhaps superfluous. In theory, William Smith, too, had justified the writing of poetry and acting of verse dialogues as training for the pulpit and the bar. Yet in practice such activities became self-justifying, no less so at Philadelphia in 1757 than at Yale, Harvard, and Princeton in 1770. The changes introduced into the curriculum went further than intended and took on a life of their own. At Yale, Samuel Miller recalled, what began as an effort "only to raise the study of polite literature to its proper station . . . soon began to usurp the place of the more abstruse sciences, and of the ancient languages. . . ." By 1770, over half a dozen college literary societies had come into being. Princeton had two, an American Whig Society and a royalist Cliosophic Society, which did battle in political verse salvos. The King's College "Literary Society" offered books or engraved medals as prizes in Greek, Latin, and English poetry.[21] Students at the College of Philadelphia gave public readings of Pope and Thomson and advertised proposals for a reading, by subscription, of *Paradise Lost!* In place of or in addition to the forensic debates on religious and moral questions, students addressed themselves to topics of more immediate interest. Whereas in 1763 they had debated *Utrum status Naturae sit status Belli*—whether the state of nature is a state of war—a speaker at the Dartmouth commencement of 1774, John Wheelock, discoursed on the "Beauties and Excellencies of Painting, Music, & Poetry." Students at Princeton in 1771 proved the superiority of ancient poets to modern,[22] while those at the new Brown College in 1774 debated "whether Stage Plays do not corrupt the morals of men and are inimical to a State?" [23]

This question—decided by the president in the affirmative—was particularly significant. Nothing better illustrates how college literary studies trespassed their theoretical justification than does the growing popularity of college theatricals, usually in defiance of academic authorities. Between 1771 and 1773, the Yale literary society (the Linonian) defied the College *Laws* of 1755 and mounted Richard Steele's *The Conscious Lovers* plus a farce (one of the actors being Nathan Hale), George Farquhar's *The Beaux' Stratagem*, and Richard Cumberland's *The West Indian*. Some performances were held at a tavern, across the street from the home of Chauncey Whittelsey, pastor of the First Church. One student present for *The West Indian* wrote that "the scenery & Action were on all hands allowed to be superior to any thing of the kind heretofore exhibited on the like occasion. The whole received peculiar Beauty from the Officers appearing dress'd in Regimentals, & the Actresses [probably local girls] in full & elegant suits of the Lady's Apparel." Several times in 1769, students at the College of Philadelphia, in the absence of The American Company from the city, gave productions of *Love in a Village*, *The Beggar's Opera*, and other works, even adopting Douglass' dodge of advertising them for *"Lovers of Elocution."* [24]

The college theatricals brought on quarreling, which divided along the same generational lines dividing the older singers from the new choir singers in the singing schools. At Harvard, students had gathered together at least since the 1750's to read tragedies aloud, as preparation for the law and ministry. In the summer of 1766, however, they not only performed a play, but a play satirizing the idea of Judgment Day. Next year a law was passed penalizing student actors:

> If any Undergraduate shall presume to be an Actor in, a Spectator at, or any Ways concerned in any Stage Plays, Interludes or Theatrical Entertainments in the Town of Cambridge or elsewhere, he shall for the first Offence be degraded—& for any repeated Offence shall be rusticated or expelled—and if any Graduate residing at the College, shall offend against this Law, he shall have his Chamber taken away from him. . . .

The law specified that it did "not prevent any Exhibitions of this kind from being performed as Academical Exercises under the Direction of the President and Tutors." Yet a short play presented at the 1771 commencement satirizing a local minister begot a heated exchange of correspondence in the Boston newspapers. Many complained that theatricals had usurped education: "what an exalted idea must people in general have of a College Education, when those take Degrees of Bachellors of Arts who discover no skill in any art, but the art of *Buffoonery,* & a *meer Antick* receives power from the President to preach the Everlasting Gospel!" Another writer felt for parents at the ceremony who discovered that "their Children have gained little else than a lively turn of mimickry, a knack to take One off, (as it is called) to repeat a Comedy, rehearse a Farce, or act a Pantomime," in defiance not only of the laws of Harvard, he added, but of the "good and wholsome" anti-theatre laws of Massachusetts.[25]

The transformed college curriculum, with its runaway enthusiasm for modern literature, gave birth around 1770 to John Trumbull and Timothy Dwight of Yale, and Philip Freneau of Princeton. They represented the literary quotient of a new generation that included Gilbert Stuart and William Billings, a generation that grew up seeing "fair Liberty" revive in her grave, younger countrymen of two artists with international reputations.

Born two years apart, Trumbull (1750) and Dwight (1752) came from the same place as well as time, a Connecticut beginning to rival but not outdo the more urban colonies in cultural promise. They also shared a revered Puritan ancestry: Trumbull's mother was a cousin of the great Jonathan Edwards; Dwight's mother was one of Edwards' own daughters. Their precocity did credit to their ancestor's genius. Trumbull, according to Ezra Stiles, read the Bible through before he was four and "catched" Latin at six. A year and a half later, familiar with Vergil's *Eclogues* and the Greek Gospels, he passed the entrance exam for Yale, but delayed entering until he was thirteen, in the meantime reading Milton, Thomson, Fénelon, and *The Spectator.* At nine he could say the Pater Noster in Hungarian. Easily Trumbull's match, Dwight learned the whole alphabet in one lesson and was teaching the catechism to Indians at four. By eight he, too, was ready to enter Yale, but also delayed doing so until thirteen, meanwhile reading Josephus. An inexhaustible student when he did enter, he parsed a hundred lines of Homer each morning by candlelight before chapel—contributing to the eventual ruin of his eyes—and as the reward of fourteen hours of daily study shared valedictory honors at graduation in 1769. Dumbfounding as these prodigies seem, they fell within the New England tradition of learning, even lagging in brilliance behind the extraordinary essay on insects which Jonathan Edwards had written at the age of twelve.[26]

Trumbull and Dwight differed from their progenitor, however, in having more purely belletristic interests. Indeed it was largely they, rather than the administration or the older faculty, who introduced the study of belles-lettres into the Yale curriculum. Unlike William Smith at the College of Philadelphia, presidents Thomas Clap and Naphtali Daggett at

Yale did nothing to encourage literary pursuits. Trumbull said that in his undergraduate days "English poetry and the belles-lettres were called folly, nonsense and an idle waste of time." Authentic literary reformers, he and Dwight challenged the administration when they became tutors at Yale in 1771. Dwight lectured on style and composition after school hours; the class petitioned the Yale Corporation to hire him to teach rhetoric and belles-lettres in addition to his usual assignments. Both tutors, although barely twenty years old, could draw on long experience in writing. Trumbull started writing poetry at the age of four, and before the age of nine had versified half the psalms. While at Yale he wrote a graveyard elegy on a drowned Yale tutor ("Dark Melancholy spreads her airy train,/ And Friendship calls and Grief inspires the song") and published a group of nearly fifty satirical essays. At the 1770 commencement he delivered an important address and poem on the "Use and Advantages of the Fine Arts." Dwight also wrote poems at Yale, collected church music and songs, and acted in the Linonian production of *The Conscious Lovers*.[27] At the 1772 commencement he delivered an equally important address on the "History, Eloquence, and Poetry of the Bible."

In their commencement addresses, Dwight and Trumbull justified their efforts to introduce literary study and championed the literary ideals of their generation. Trumbull defended esthetic experience on essentially religious grounds. Experience of the arts gives rise to noble feelings akin to feelings of charity and benevolence. The "Divine Being," he said, "hath implanted in our minds a taste for more pure and intellectual pleasures." This esthetic "taste" resembles the spirit of Christianity itself: "I appeal to all persons of judgment," he told the Yale undergraduates, "whether they can rise from reading a fine Poem, viewing any masterly work of Genius, or hearing an harmonious concert of Music, without feeling an openness of heart, and an elevation of mind, without being more sensible of the dignity of human nature, and despising whatever tends to debase and degrade it?" Trumbull of course derived his equation of taste with the moral sense from English and Scottish theorists like Lord Kames. Yet the equation was uniquely useful in his specific situation, averting the kind of charges against literary study likely to be raised at strongly Congregationalist Yale College.

Dwight, too, couched his defense of new literary fashions in terms likely to disarm his audience. On the authority of Scripture, he exalted nature and attacked the concept of fixed literary genres. To the critic "who doubts whether he may eat, or breathe, unless by *Aristotle's* rules," he opposed the writers of the Old Testament, poets free of "Critical manacles" who "gave their imaginations an unlimited range" and spoke in the "natural, unstudied language of affection." Although the question of the 'rules' had been fought for half a century in England—where many Tories associated esthetic irregularity with Whig cries for Liberty—the colonies were quite unused to hearing literary manifestoes. Aside from its rhetorical value in suggesting the propriety of literary study, Dwight's treatment of the Bible as poetry reveals how Scripture had come to be viewed as imaginative material for literature, as for music and painting. Like Dwight, Tans'ur in his *Royal Melody* praised the book of Psalms as poetry because of "the beautiful Variety of its *Stile* . . . even from the *Majestick, Sublime, Magnificent, Triumphant,* and *Exultory:* down to the *Mournful, Condoling, Commiserating, Pathetical,* and *Expostulatory*. . . ." [28] The use of Scripture became an alibi that allowed artists reared or working in the more radical Protestant traditions to safely indulge a purely esthetic interest in protoromantic moods, scenery, and states of feeling. For the Quaker West, the Congregationalist Billings, the Puritan Dwight, Scripture became another aspect of historicism not unlike Roman or Anglo-Saxon history, a sacred-secular vehicle for the cultivation of new sensibility.

Trumbull's interest in reforming the Yale curriculum went beyond belles-lettres. Out of his intimate experience at Yale as a student and tutor he published a poem of 1,800 lines, the longest and best verse satire written in America up to its time, *The Progress of Dulness.* The first part was published in New Haven late in 1772, the second and third parts in 1773, when Trumbull also issued a revised version of Part One. Although many of its criticisms of college life strike the modern reader as pungent, they were blander than Trumbull wished. While writing the poem, he told a friend that "the subject affords opportunity for a great deal of Satire; but there are many things which I am a little afraid to speak my mind freely on. The method of education at College, the proceedings of the Clergy . . . I have passed over slightly." The published version would thus be "as wellmeaning & harmless a piece, as a halfway-cov'nant Dialogue." But even his tiptoeing wakened resentment. He added a preface to Part Two explaining that he had been called a Separatist or Sandemanian and denounced for wanting "to ridicule religion, disgrace morality, sneer at the present methods of education, and in short, write a satire upon *Yale-College* and the ten commandments." Not everyone was offended, however. He learned that "the first Classical Scholar in Boston" remarked, *"His Prose is equal to Swift's & his Poetry to Butler's."* [29] The comparison was undeserved but not unmeaning, since Trumbull drew on the satiric tradition of Jonathan Swift, Charles Churchill, and Samuel Butler, and on other popular sources: the scenes of progressive moral deterioration in Hogarth's *Rake's Progress,* the controversy over education stirred by Jean Jacques Rousseau and by works like Fénelon's *De l'Éducation des filles.*

Trumbull concentrated his varied criticisms of Yale and of American society in three representative social types of the period: the dull clergyman Tom Brainless, the nouveau-riche farmer's son Dick Hairbrain, and the coquette Harriet Simper. He devoted one part of the poem to each of these three young people. Tom's dullness, however, is largely the creation of the college, while Dick's vulgarity and Harriet's vanity are much more the creation of their parents. Perhaps the offense taken at Part One—as if it disgraced *"Yale-College* and the ten commandments"—led Trumbull to redirect his satiric thrusts from the college itself to the social pretensions of the newly rich. In Tom Brainless, Trumbull did put down colleges and the ministry, the two chief intellectual institutions of New England. He followed Tom's career from the time when, to avoid manual labor on the farm, he mislearns Latin and Greek from a dozing parson; through college, where feigned and psychosomatic ailments provide some relief from metaphysical disputation and rote classical scholarship; to Tom's licensing as a minister, when he pilfers sermons and disguises his stupidity as orthodoxy; until he finds an unsettled town which hires him for life despite his dull and awkward but arrogant preaching. Dick Hairbrain undergoes the Hogarthian progress of a "Country-fop." The son of a wealthy, dishonest farmer who has risen to local office, he is sent to college to dignify his parents' new money. He manages to indulge his vices, flaunt a fashionable deism, and prolong his childhood before going abroad on his inheritance, there to perfect his coxcombery and sink into lonely old age, a "superannuated Beau." Harriet Simper, her education mistakenly assigned by her father to her mother, is groomed to be a coquette and sent to the city, where she devotes herself to fashion, gossip, and the novels of Richardson, only to find that as she ages the beau monde slights, then despises her; she retreats to a country parish, where she becomes the embittered and slatternly wife of Tom Brainless.

Throughout the poem, just as Billings allied himself with the "modern Air and manner of Singing," Trumbull attacked the antiquated "fopperies of learning" that restrain America's "rising worth." The present approach to classical literature, he said, prevents the development of intellectual independence and a spirit of critical inquiry. Students

> Read antient authors o'er in vain,
> Nor taste one beauty they contain;
> Humbly on trust accept the sense,
> But deal for words at vast expence. . . .

At the same time, a heavy diet of scholastic logic and Dissenting rhetoric keeps alive a stagnant provincialism, producing seventeenth-century minds that

> Draw motives, uses, inferences,
> And torture words in thousand senses;
> Learn the grave style and goodly phrase,
> Safe-handed down from *Cromwell's* days,
> And shun with anxious care, the while
> Th' infection of a modern style. . . .

The "fopperies of learning" serve the fashionable, however, as well as the stodgy.

Trumbull shared the uneasiness of those Americans who viewed the trebling of the number of colonial colleges over the last thirty years as a sign of democratic tendencies. One newspaper writer complained that the sons of "our lowest Mechanics" go to college and acquire "with their Learning, the laudable Ambition of becoming Gentle-Folks," until Americans have "no such Thing as common People among us." [30] Accordingly, Trumbull also attacked the socially nondescript who use learning and the arts to make themselves respectable. At college, Dick Hairbrain tries to riot, whore, and drink away the very rusticity which the extravagance of his transformation proclaims:

> The suit right gay, tho' much belated,
> Whose fashion's superannuated;
> The watch, depending far in state,
> Whose iron chain might form a grate;
> The silver buckle, dread to view,
> O'ershad'wing all the clumsy shoe
> The white-glov'd hand, that tries to peep
> From ruffle, full five inches deep;
> With fifty odd affairs beside,
> The foppishness of country-pride.

Dick Hairbrain goes abroad to complete his metamorphosis into a "clockwork-Gentleman." Effete, pomaded, having conquered his native simplicity and directness, he hires a dancing master, quotes Voltaire with fashionable raillery, and achieves a show of taste with none of the substance.

Finally, Trumbull attacked the neglect of female education:

> But why should girls be learn'd or wise?
> Books only serve to spoil their eyes.
> The studious eye but faintly twinkles,
> And reading paves the way for wrinkles.
> In vain may learning fill the head full:
> 'Tis Beauty that's the one thing needful. . . .

Denied even the "fopperies of learning," Harriet Simper becomes addicted to fashion and gossip, "A judge of modes, in silks and sattens,/ From tassels down to clogs and pattens." She is attracted to men not of merit but, predictably, of lace, coaches, and money. Limited to the intellectual pursuits of the nouveaux riches, she reads sentimental novels in close identification with the seduced. *The Progress of Dulness*, in sum, pleads for the serious study of modern subjects, modern English literature particularly, in the colleges. If its self-assurance and air of challenge bespeak Trumbull's youth, its wit and intelligence mark the achievement of some of the very maturity which the poem demands.

Born the same year as Timothy Dwight, 1752, Philip Freneau of Princeton did not share the precocity of his Yale counterparts nor their distinguished Puritan ancestry. His father—one of several impoverished children left in New York by a French Huguenot émigré—married the daughter of a prosperous Scotch farmer from Monmouth County, New Jersey. Freneau grew up comfortably on Mount Pleasant in the Monmouth countryside, as his prospering father amassed real estate and a lumber mill. By his teens he was studying classics, preparing, as his father hoped, for a ministerial career. By the time he was admitted to the sophomore class at Princeton in 1768, however, his father had died, his wealth much depleted.

Stimulated by such literary classmates as the Virginian James Madison and the Pennsylvanian Hugh Henry Brackenridge, Freneau started to write poetry of several kinds himself, on themes that would preoccupy and trouble him all of his life. Like others in his generation he began with Scripture, writing a biblical paraphrase in four cantos on "The History of the Prophet Jonah" at the age of sixteen. The poem anticipates Freneau's lifelong interest in the sea, his torment as a sensitive man in a violent world, and, like Jonah, his unwillingness to serve as a prophet of doom. Two years later he explored ancient history in "The Pyramids of Egypt" and "The Monument of Phaon," poems related to the English school of graveyard melancholy that likewise announce a lifelong, and later highly personal, brooding over the destructiveness of time. Egyptian scenery appealed to many in Freneau's generation who were fascinated with the Progress of Empire theme (see the end of this section). Many regarded Egypt as the first civilization and parent of the others, thus a prime mover of the historical process. Yet Freneau regarded the pyramids as symbols less of the dynamics of history than of the futility of human effort:

> How many generations have decay'd,
> How many monarchies to ruin pass'd!
> How many empires had their rise and fall! [31]

The Egyptian or Greek or biblical or pastoral settings of Freneau's early verse are simply different vehicles for projecting the same mood of rather stereotyped disconsolateness, a mood which he would recreate more authentically later out of bitter experience.

These early verses on Egyptian monuments already betray another of Freneau's enduring traits, his escapism. Political activity was lively at Princeton, where students appeared in homespun dress to protest the British tax programs. Yet, the year of the Boston Massacre, Freneau and his classmate Brackenridge wrote a fragment of a novel entitled "Father Bombo's Pilgrimage," whose hero leaves New Jersey for Mecca. In the same year, Freneau also wrote "The Power of Fancy," celebrating the mind's ability to transcend history. Through his Fancy, the "Wakeful, vagrant, restless thing,/ Ever wandering on the wing," the poet escapes space and time, traveling in imagination from dungeon to Arcadia, frigid Norway to scorching Bermuda—anywhere away from a harsh present which his New England peers, in their descent from Jonathan Edwards, could tolerate better, even enjoy.

Vagrant as Fancy itself, Freneau found it difficult to settle down. Immediately after graduating from Princeton he taught school on Long Island, employed by "some bullies, some merchants, and other scoundrels" who sent him eight children under ten years of age and when he left—as he did after thirteen days—threatened to maim him if he returned. He went to Somerset Academy in Maryland as an assistant to his classmate Hugh Henry Brackenridge, intending to remain a year but confessing to Madison that teaching "by no means suits my 'giddy wandring brain.' " He continued to write poetry that like his collegiate verse revealed troublesome conflicts. His very interesting "Discovery" (1772)—much indebted to Charles Churchill's *Gotham* (1764)—celebrates Columbus as a New World Faust, questing for experience and vital knowledge, "New seas to vanquish, and new worlds to find." But Freneau's approval of the quest and his commitment to progress alternate with primitivist longings for pastoral ease, blasts at ambition, and suspicions that human nature, "Fond of exerting power," will discover then destroy:

> Alas! how few of all that daring train
> That seek new worlds embosomed in the main,
> How few have sailed on virtue's nobler plan,
> How few with motives worthy of a man!—[32]

("Discovery" also instances growing interest in Columbus, whose name was beginning to be used to designate the colonies. A poem in the *Boston Gazette* on September 7, 1772, described Grenville and Townshend as wanting to "seize *Columba's [sic]* Money," and France and Spain as trying to divide "*Britain* and *Columba* fair.")

Uncertain whether to settle down in the ministry or the law or whether to escape to sea—and vacillating in his religious beliefs but leaning to deism—Freneau managed in 1772 to publish a volume of poems in New York, *The American Village*. The title-poem, he told Madison, was "damned by all good and judicious judges." Despite this typical self-denigration, the balanced and varied volume gave added evidence, with Wheatley's *Poems* and Trumbull's *Progress*, of literary growth. The America of the title is not the militant place which Trumbull hoped would produce Addisons and Popes, however; indeed it is not a place but a Great Good Place, the domain of "harmless people, born to small command,/ Lost in the bosom of this western land," removed from "rav'nous nations" and "dread commerce," a haven from reality. "The Farmer's Winter Evening" is spent not joining hands with John Dickinson but delighting in rural melancholy, like some graveyard Horace, imploring the winter night to "clasp me in thy sable arms." By contrast, in "The Miserable Life of a Pedagogue," Freneau scorned the teacher's life as arduous, unremunerative, trifling, and, most important, open to contempt. A brief dramatic episode in the poem expresses a Villon-like rage at being slighted by pretentious inferiors to which Freneau would return obsessively. A "city dame" with her "horsemen, chairs and coaches," having hired the narrator to teach languages to her son, imperiously drives away—while he is in the middle of a sentence. The poet is left standing on the street, a "laughing stock to half the crowd." Abashment—a smoldering resentment over unprovoked disregard—is perhaps the distinguishing, most personal mood of Freneau's poetry, the sour distillate of his life as an American and as a poet.

While differences of temperament, family, belief, and education distinguish the satirical Trumbull, the pious Dwight, and the anxious Freneau, their enlarged ambitions, reformist tendencies, and romantic leaning stamp them as members of a single generation, beside which the poets of the 1760's like Godfrey and Evans seem genteel and timid. What separates them even more dramatically from the older generation and links them even more dramatically together are their awareness of new elements in American culture and their complex attempts to divine America's destiny.

The hopes of Translation which had existed in America since the first third of the eighteenth century continued to exist. In 1763, the *Virginia Gazette* published in its entirety, still once more, Bishop Berkeley's poem on the westward movement of the arts. The preceding decade, however, had offered some proof of the theory. The large numbers of poems, songs, and engravings called forth by resistance to the Stamp Act and the Townshend programs; the literary activities in the colonial colleges; the eminence of West in England; the singing schools and the spread of musical literacy—all were felt to be evidence of the imminent accomplishment of Berkeley's prophecy. The arts had traveled from Rome to England and, observably, were hastening to America. "An American" addressing "the LITERATI of AMERICA" in the *Royal American Magazine* in 1774 claimed that "AMERICA will soon be the seat of science, and the grand theatre where human glory will be displayed in its brightest colours. . . ." Even in England, Horace Walpole believed he saw literary genius declining abroad and reviving in America, so that he predicted in the same year: "The next Augustan age will dawn on the other side of the Atlantic. There will, perhaps, be a Thucydides at Boston, a Xenophon at New York, and, in time, a Virgil at Mexico. . . ." [33]

The theme of the westward movement of the arts, long in the background of colonial thinking, became a prominent issue. The theory of progress, like everything else, progressed. It is the elaboration and more insistent proclamation of the theory that most dramatically distinguishes the poets of 1770 from those of 1763. In contrast to the light satiric verse and pastoral love poetry of Evans and Godfrey, Trumbull, Dwight, and Freneau each wrote an orotund Augustan progress poem on American empire, grandiose in sentiment and climaxed by a boastful vision of the future. These speech-like poems reflect the tie between oratory and poetry in the college curriculum, and could be called verse orations. Indeed, Trumbull's poem appeared as a long appendage to his 1770 commencement address on the fine arts. Timothy Dwight's *America*—which Trumbull felt resembled his own poem in "sentiments & descriptions"—circulated in manuscript at Yale in 1771 and was published later in New Haven. Philip Freneau's *A Poem, on the Rising Glory of America*, written in collaboration with Hugh Henry Brackenridge, was read at the Princeton commencement on September 25, 1771, and greeted, according to James Madison, with "great applause by the audience." [34]

These works differ from the earlier, brief prophecies of Translation in not merely forecasting America's cultural progress but in attempting to explain it. Behind them lies a tradition of neoclassical 'progress pieces' in England and of Scottish 'theoretical histories' like Adam Ferguson's *Essay on the History of Civil Society*, culminating in Gibbon's *Decline and Fall of the Roman Empire*. Such works treated the arts as a branch of social science, and social science as a branch of moral philosophy. In studying the evolution of society, they understood institutions as outgrowths of human nature, and the arts as an institution similar to commerce or agriculture.[35] History, as in West's *Agrippina*, became ethics.

John Trumbull drew on this body of thought to justify his belief that "America hath a fair prospect in a few centuries of ruling both in arts and arms." In his commencement address and poem he considered the arts in

America in terms of ineluctable facts of human nature that had stimulated or thwarted the arts in the past, and necessarily would do so in the future. Describing the successive rise and decline of arts in Greece, Augustan Rome, and eighteenth-century England, he showed how in each case a virile desire for national glory had nurtured the arts, while passivity and self-indulgence had led to their decline. The same impulse gave birth to poets and to warriors: "The same ardour of ambition, the same greatness of thought, which inspires the Warrior to brave danger in the conquering field, when diffused among a people will call forth Genius in every station of life, fire the imagination of the Artist, and raise to sublimity the aspiring Muse." By the same reasoning, when national ambition languishes it gives rise to political corruption and likewise to "false taste in writing" at once. That was happening at the moment, Trumbull believed, in England, whose literature bore traces of organically related tyranny in politics and dissipation in manners. English writers "sacrifice ease and elegance to the affectation of classic correctness, fetter the fancy with the rules of method, and damp all the ardour of aspiring invention."

Since cultural institutions, according to this quasi-scientific analysis, develop with the certainty of laws, Trumbull could predict a new Augustan age for America. Political turmoil had aroused a manly spirit of resistance that simultaneously vanquished corruption and false taste, that produced a greatness of thought identical with the artistic impulse. "Happy, in this respect," Trumbull said, "have been our late struggles for liberty!" From them must inevitably follow the painters, architects, musicians, and poets who would make America

> The first in letters, as the first in Arms.
> See bolder Genius quit the narrow shore,
> And unknown realms of science dare t'explore;
> Hiding in brightness of superior day
> The fainting gleam of Britain's setting ray.
>
> . . . .
>
> This Land her Steele and Addison shall view,
> The former glories equal'd by the new;
> Some future Shakespeare charm the rising age,
> And hold in magic chains the listning stage. . . .

Trumbull's exuberant forecast was not, however, a call to cultural nationalism. Trumbull shared with other eighteenth-century writers a belief in the Republic of Letters, in a transnational community existing apart from place and time, embracing in one ecumenical present the writers of Athens, Rome, London, and shortly, he implied, New Haven and Philadelphia. To break with this community in the name of some 'distinctively American' literature, as Emerson and Whitman demanded later, would be not a cultural necessity but an admission of defeat. America was about to join the Republic of Letters, not to start its own. The moral-historical conditions operating in Greece, Rome, and England, based as they were on the same facts of human nature, had produced like results, and would do so again in America, which would soon take its place beside the great cultures of the past, but not in distinction from them. What will be, was. Enough that America have "her Steele and Addison."

Trumbull's friend Timothy Dwight foresaw a similar Augustan age in his *America; or, a Poem on the Settlement of the British Colonies; Addressed To the Friends of Freedom, and their Country.* Tracing the progress of mankind outward from Asia, through Columbus, the Elizabethan voyagers, the Puritans, and the French and Indian Wars, he glimpsed "more glorious ROMES" arising in America and the arts gloriously arising with them: "See all the powers of Poetry unite/ To paint Religion's charms divinely bright"; "See Sculpture mould the rude unpolish'd stone,/ Give it new forms and beauties not its own"; "Behold the canvas glow with living dies,/ Tall groves shoot up, streams wind and mountains rise!" Dwight's poem, however, lacks Trumbull's reasoned attempt to prove by the laws of human nature and social development that the present moment bears uniquely the conditions for American grandeur. To Dwight, the grandson of Jonathan Edwards and, later, the leader of American Calvinism, history was not ethics but providence. Events unfold, institutions develop, according to God's disposition:

> At thy command, war glitters o'er the plain;
> Thou speak'st—and peace revives the fields again,
> Vast empires rise, and cities gild the day:
> Thou frown'st—and kings and kingdoms melt away.

Theoretically, since the fate of nations depends on God's frown, one cannot say what the present situation in America portends. Just the same, Dwight invented a "Spirit of Freedom" who foretells a vast imperial America, mighty in commerce and dominion, whose

> . . . power shall grow
> Far as the seas, which round thy regions flow;
> Through earth's wide realms thy glory shall extend,
> And savage nations at thy scepter bend.
> Around the frozen shores thy sons shall sail,
> Or stretch their canvas to the ASIAN gale. . . .

If inconsistent with his own providential view of history, Dwight's prophecy of extended glory was faithful to his and his friends' sense of impending cultural maturity.

In the longest and most complex of the Rising Glory works, Freneau and Brackenridge's *A Poem, on the Rising Glory of America*, the swains Leander, Eugenio, and Acasto attempt to explain in blank verse how

> . . . this recent happy world arose,
> To this fair eminence of high renown
> This height of wealth, of liberty and fame.

The view of history that accounts for the cultural progress evident in the colonies and that makes the future predictable is neither cyclic like Trumbull's nor providential like Dwight's, but linear. The swains "reason from the course of things,/ And downward trace the vestiges of time." As they chart the progress of civilization through Columbus, the English and Spanish explorers, and the great migrations of 1630, they see that America in 1770 is the frontier of an ancient, worldwide process of unification and refinement rooted in man's instinct for exploration. The agents of evolution have been a succession of hero-navigators whose enterprise opened new territories for the expansion of humankind. The progressive peopling of the globe united distant lands, increased trade, commerce, and population, and provided the material and spiritual conditions in which the arts flourish.[36] In Freneau and Brackenridge's version, the progress the colonies had achieved by 1770 thus resulted not from a resurgent cycle of Augustan arts and arms called forth by the luxury-denying stringencies of the Townshend period, but from a cumulative growth and improvement of mankind.

America is not only the latest frontier of human questing, but also the last. As the last continent to be discovered and the last that can be populated, it represents the "final stage" of history, "the last, the best/ Of countries. . . ." The view that America stands at the end of the historical process derived from popular millennial theories and from Bishop Berkeley's much-published poem. Berkeley also used the stage—a widespread metaphor for progress—to suggest that the discovery and settlement of America completed the civilizing of the planet:

> Westward the course of empire takes its way;
> The four first acts already past,
> A fifth shall close the drama with the day;
> Time's noblest offspring is the last.

For Freneau and Brackenridge, America's destiny is to be the receptacle of all earlier human achievements, the synthesis of a long process of exploration, international commerce, and cultural interbreeding, a summary of history, a sort of historiopolis:

> . . . far in the West appears
> A new Palmyra or an Ecbatan

And sees the slow pac'd caravan return
O'er many a realm from the Pacific shore,
Where fleets shall then convey rich Persia's silks,
Arabia's perfumes, and spices rare
Of Philippine, Coelebe and Marian isles,
Or from the Acapulco coast our India then,
Laden with pearl and burning gems and gold.
Far in the South I see a Babylon,
As once by Tigris or Euphrates stream. . . .

Freneau and Brackenridge's vision of American possibilities is a spiraling version of the *Translatio studii,* in which civilization and arts are not merely carried westward but gain in transit the achievements of their carriers. America will be what great empires have existed that it might become.

As its title suggests, the poem concentrates its theory of cultural progress into a single, current image. Like Libertas, the Rising Glory was an older icon that had been revived and redefined to give shape to an inchoate, emerging ideology. In graphic arts, the image appears as a full sun with prominent rays, or a nimbus (technically a "glory"), or as a three-quarter sun rising behind a mountain. Earlier, the image had been used in conjunction with Libertas or with the New World. A medal of Louis XIV (1679) depicts Gallia (Gaul) with a liberty pole and cap beside a glory containing an open eye, like the image above the truncated pyramid in the current dollar bill.[37] A large Rising Glory enclosing Hebrew letters inside appears beside an Indian emblem of the New World on the frontispiece of the English clergyman Peter Heylyn's *Cosmographie* (1652). Repopularized in the colonies in 1770, the image symbolized the theory of *Translatio studii.* A writer in 1774 proposing an American Society of Language noted that America's "rising posterity" would soon "light up the world with new ideas bright as the sun." "EVER since I was capable of reflecting on the Course of Things in this World," William Smith remarked in 1773, "it hath been one of the most delightful Employments of my contemplative Hours, to anticipate the rising Grandeur of America; to trace the Progress of the Arts, like that of the Sun, from East to West. . . . THAT *Day* hath even now more than dawned upon us."[38]

Skillfully used by Freneau and Brackenridge, the Rising Glory radiates still subtler meanings that make it a vibrantly condensed, affecting symbol of still wider colonial ideals and aspirations. The rising sun in their poem expresses both America's infancy—" 'Tis but the morning of the world with us"—and the accumulating enlightenment, the "dawning light" of science and arts, which the infant will inherit. "Rising" also suggests how despite their infancy the colonies have already attained prominence, a "fair eminence of high renown," a "height of wealth, of liberty and fame."

Repeated verbal play on height and light draw into the image other
qualities associated with future progress: the towering aspirations of
American poets, "New Theban bards high soaring reach the skies"; the
ennoblement of character among citizens of the New World, where "virtue
rais'd them to the rank of Gods"; demographic and commercial growth, as
"turrets rise" or "Unnumber'd towns and villages arise," or the masts of
New York harbor seem "shady forests rising on the waves." The warmth of
the rising sun nurtures what Bishop Berkeley called the "Planting of Arts
and Learning" so that whatever is "Transplanted from the eastern climes
dost bloom/ In these fair regions." Older human achievements swept by
the course of history to virgin America will be nourished: "the arts shall
rise and grow/ Luxuriant, graceful. . . ." The irresistible, luxuriant
growth symbolized by the rising sun is illustrated throughout the poem in
visions of swarming numbers and rapid increase, of future "mighty
nations," "hundred towns," "thousand navies," "Unnumber'd towns and
villages," "Unnumbr'd [sic] boats and merchandize and men."

Seemingly hyperbolical, such visions did come to life in America. In the
image of the "rising glory of this western world" Freneau and Brackenridge concentrated their and their contemporaries' exuberant hopes, yet
stayed faithful to an observable growth and diffusion of culture. The
heliotropic theory of progress merely raised to the level of generalization
the fact that the British colonies in 1770 were becoming cosmopolitan. The
theory, it bears repeating, should not be confused with the calls for cultural
independence by nineteenth-century nationalists. While affirming the
bond between the arts and Liberty—"sweet liberty!/ Without whose aid
the noblest genius fails"—and while championing Bostonians as the "firm
supporters of our injur'd rights," the poets declare themselves "we the sons
of Britain."

Nor, certainly, should the hopes of the college poets be confused with
their accomplishments. Exuberant but often vague and trite, the poems of
1770 are less important for their substance than for their manner. Their
boldly prophetic tone signifies a raised level of aspiration, a feeling of
imminence, an awareness that some of the best of European culture had
come to America and was being transformed and expanded, that a new
world had risen and was still rising.

Indeed, the literary scene remained provincial. The presses of the vast
country still issued no literary magazines and relatively few volumes of
belles-lettres, although more than in 1763 and often in direct competition
with England. The country still lacked professional writers, although in
Phillis Wheatley, John Trumbull, Timothy Dwight, and Philip Freneau it
had a generation of new poets—young and of yet-uncertain staying
power—some of whom commanded notice at home and abroad, whose

names registered. The literary curriculum at the colleges and the pressure of weighty events had produced some volumes longer and less local than those of 1763, often notable for their wit and skill, and addressed to a larger audience brought together in political crisis, works like *The Candidates*, *The Progress of Dulness*, *The American Village*. The curriculum also brought a vogue for school theatricals that was bound to create tolerance for the professional theatre. Most important, the country itself had become aware of these evidences of change and growth. It quite consciously tried to understand them, crystalizing its knowledge and its hopes in the image of the Rising Glory of America.

25. The Theatre

Whether the theatre would rise in glory along with the other arts remained uncertain. In 1763, theatre in the North American colonies meant The American Company of Comedians, a mediocre English troupe performing in flimsy theatres, as often insulted as applauded. No play by an American had ever been published or produced, nor had any American acted professionally on the stage. But like his father, Lewis Hallam, Jr., was determined "to try his fortune in America." He and David Douglass were dogged businessmen bent on refurbishing the company and making it succeed. A decade later, they retained a virtual monopoly on the American theatre and had improved the quality of their performances. Despite personal disasters, disharmony in the troupe, postponements, physical assaults, and denunciation by political, social, and religious groups, the 1770 Company featured talented singer-actors like John Henry performing a new repertoire of demanding comic operas. Its new theatres in New York and Philadelphia contained handsome scenery built by prominent London designers. The first American play had been produced and the first professional American actor had acted. During the 1770–1773 lull, Douglass and Hallam erected the first brick theatre in America, changed their repertoire and itinerary, and brought forth the first star of the American stage. Still, they often played to thin or truculent houses, and although they improved the Company they were unable to improve its prospects. Their main activity, calling for only brief description, was perseverance.

Some fourteen years' experience in British America had apparently led Douglass to a new strategy for survival. He would turn the American Company into something like a regional repertory theatre. Instead of the customary annual circuit which brought him from Charleston to New York, he decided in 1770 to spend two years in the South, followed by about a year in the Middle Colonies.

Perhaps Douglass had simply tired of packing every few months aboard coastal schooners, ferries, and overland coaches. Or his decision may have been made in financial desperation. In June 1770, he lamented to the printer Thomas Bradford that "very bad success this Season" had left him "much straitn'd for money." He may have hoped that the cycle of two years south and a year north would place him longer before friendlier audiences. A two years' absence, also, would starve audiences into hungering for his return, while the awareness of another famine to ensue when he left would encourage them to see him while they could. That seems a probable explanation of the fact that the Company played from summer 1770 to fall 1772 in Maryland and Virginia, after which Douglass announced that he would go north and probably "not return for several Years." [1] He in fact spent the entire 1772–1773 season, October to August, in Philadelphia and New York.

In deciding to appear for a long time before the same regional audience, Douglass ran the risk of being taken for granted. To excite interest and to keep audiences coming he introduced novelties. He sent to London for new scenery and seems to have dispatched John Henry abroad to recruit new actors. In Philadelphia, he hired some extra attractions in 1772, offering "a COMIC DANCE by Monsieur FRANCIS, from the THEATRE in AMSTERDAM" and singing by a Mrs. Stampfer, "from the Theatre-Royal in Edinburgh." Hoping, one assumes, to snare an audience that could or would not attend in the evening—his exclusive time of performance—he gave several matinees. The planter George Washington attended five performances during his nine-day stay in Williamsburg in 1771, noting several times in his diary that he "went to the Play in the Afternoon." [2] (An avid theatregoer, he also attended in Annapolis and Dumfries.)

Douglass also tried to offer his audiences more new plays. During his long Maryland-Virginia season he introduced some of the sentimental comedies which had become popular in London in the late 1760's and early 1770's, including Cumberland's *The West Indian* (1771) and *The Fashionable Lover* (1772) and Hugh Kelly's *False Delicacy* (1768) and *A Word to the Wise* (1770). Anxious to cash in on the publicity that surrounded the enormous success of these plays, he rushed them onto his stage at their peak of popularity and with little rehearsal. The result was probably a slipshod performance, but his determination to please was applauded. One writer expressed gratitude for the Company's 1772 production of *The Fashionable Lover*: "Such is the industry of the American Company that although the piece has not been above ten days in the country it has been rehearsed more than once and is already, we hear, fit for representation." During his 1773 New York season, Douglass whipped up a production of

She Stoops to Conquer only months after its London premiere—a coup. In this "unexampled" success, said a New Yorker, the actors seemed "thrice themselves" and provoked "excessive mirth." [3] Although the performance of such recent plays may have been opportunistic, part of an attempt to keep a friendly but limited audience interested, it also meant a narrowing gap between London and colonial fashions, an acceleration of the process of Translation.

The new plays suited Douglass' purposes not only because of their London success. Their content ideally suited colonial audiences. The so-called weeping comedies of Kelly and Cumberland turned the stage into an entertaining pulpit, providing amusement but giving moralists nothing to hoot. They did so by assigning to characters traditionally treated as comic types, such as Irishmen, virtuous opinions that suggested the essential goodness of human nature. Cumberland's formula for creating Irish dialect, for instance, was to combine "expressions that excite laughter" together with "sentiments that deserve applause." Douglass' audiences were perhaps surfeited with *George Barnwell* and other heavies, with programs designed less to amuse them than to appease the foes of the theatre. They welcomed the new sophisticated moralism as a departure. A correspondent to the *Virginia Gazette* in 1772 praised Kelly's *A Word to the Wise* for making the stage "(what it ought to be) a School of Politeness and Virtue." How much the combination of entertainment and rectitude appealed to colonial audiences appears in the fact that *The West Indian* and *The Fashionable Lover* were published in several editions in Philadelphia in the early seventies; from 1770 to 1774 Douglass mounted *The West Indian* alone twelve times. The plays suited colonial audiences in another way also. The comic types to whom they gave superior sentiments were often English provincials, Irishmen, Scotchmen, West Indians, characters who stood in much the same relation to England as did the American colonists. The *Virginia Gazette* reprinted a lengthy letter by Kelly addressed to the Lord Mayor of London, who had attacked him both as a poet and as an Irishman. Kelly defended the freedom of the press and advised the mayor to "avoid the meanness of national reflections." [4] The virtuous provincial types in the plays must have appealed to colonials who had been claiming a moral and political superiority beneath their provincial drabness.

The plays held such implications, of course, only for those who cared to find them. At the moment any depiction of English life could be taken politically. But Douglass, desperate to avoid controversy, could not have had a political intent. Indeed, in a further effort to afford novelty, he produced a play which could have been taken as a rebuff to provincial radicalism: George Cockings' *The Conquest of Canada; Or, the Siege of Quebec*, a five-act historical tragedy written in Boston by a British civil servant, part of a small repertoire of works produced in the colonies but not in London. First published in London in 1766, it was reprinted in Baltimore (the second book printed there), Philadelphia, and Albany in 1772 and 1773. Douglass staged the play in Philadelphia on February 17, 1773, continuing either intentionally or coincidentally to introduce plays that had been written in America in that city. Like West's *Wolfe*, the play reflects recent detachment from the French and Indian War, whose meaning it attempts to digest. In the context of the early 1770's, its fanatic nationalism could only have reminded the colonists that in the mother country they faced a courageous, clever, proud adversary unaccustomed to losing. The play depicts the defeat of 12,000 firmly entrenched Frenchmen, Canadians, and Indians by 8,000 English troops who, it is emphasized, rival those of Greece and Rome. With frequent barrages of offstage thunder, artillery, drums, and shouts, it shows the departure of General Wolfe (played by Hallam) from his mother, conversations between Wolfe and other generals in Quebec, and the fatal wounding of Wolfe on the Plains of Abraham. Douglass gave the play for three nights, using military and naval personnel from local garrisons as well as authentic artillery and boats, an unusually rich production. The stage was so heaped with machinery that he had to omit the customary afterpiece.[5]

Douglass decided to spend half of his two years in the South in Annapolis. His reasons for settling there remain unknown, but he could expect an enthusiastic audience. Annapolis was a rising provincial center with a distinct older literary tradition, the residence of Peale, of the sophisticated Tuesday Club, and of Governor Horatio Sharpe (a friend of the theatre), a place, according to one witness, where "it was customary for the people of any fashion in the country to come and see the plays." For his extended seasons, Douglass erected in 1771 an impressive theatre on West Street, with seats for about 600 people—the first brick (that is, permanent) theatre in British America.[6]

Douglass tried to raise money for the building by subscription, participants receiving up to two seasons' worth of tickets. Although Governor Sharpe headed the list, the money only trickled in, forcing Douglass to announce that he could not meet the bills he soon expected from workmen and suppliers, and to ask his subscribers to pay up. He hurried to open the theatre by race week in September, and did so at the cost of playing in an unfinished building. The theatre opened on September 9 with *The Roman Father*, Douglass himself speaking the prologue. In the heliotropic language of the young commencement poets, he traced the progress of the stage from Athens to Annapolis:

> Thus has true taste, like the revolving sun,
> From East to West, in even tenor run.

Now on these shores the goddess stands confest
And reigns supreme in every generous breast. . . .[7]

Douglass was not, to say the least, speaking for himself. If his new brick
theatre in Annapolis did "confess" the migration of the theatrical Muses,
the course that brought it into existence had surely been no "even tenor"
but all along uphill and bumpy.

Still, Douglass found for his pains an appreciative audience that was
quick to commend. William Eddis, an English customs surveyor in
Annapolis, described the new theatre for those at home: The building was
too narrow for its length, but "the boxes are commodious and neatly
decorated; the pit and gallery are calculated to hold a number of people
without incommoding each other; the stage is well adapted for dramatic
and pantomimical exhibitions; and several of the scenes reflect great credit
on the ability of the painter." Although the theatre stood on land
belonging to the church, Douglass received the blessing of even the rector
of Annapolis, Jonathan Boucher. Thinking the building "very handsome,"
Boucher wrote a poem entitled "Church and Theatre" in which the
personified Church asks the citizens of Annapolis to grant it an "equal
portion" of concern but treats the American Company rather as the
partner than the foe of Maryland Anglicanism:

> I've seen, I own, with some surprise
> A novel structure sudden rise.
> There let the stranger stay, for me,
> If virtue's friend, indeed, she be;
> I would not if I could restrain
> A moral stage. . . .[8]

After years of placating or battling off his northern audiences, Douglass
might well have been comforted to read, in several issues of the *Maryland
Gazette*, that "every man of sense in America" considered the Company
superior to most English companies; to hear that his costumes were
"remarkably elegant"; to learn that one of his new imported sets—"a
View of a superb Apartment, at the end of a fine Colonade of Pilars [sic] of
the Ionic Order"—had "a most pleasing Effect." Perhaps to show
gratitude, Douglass put up a purse of £50 for a special four-mile race
during the 1772 race week.[9] There was little doubt, William Eddis
concluded, of the Company's "preserving the public favor and reaping a
plenteous harvest" in Annapolis.

During this high point of the Company's career in the colonies emerged
the first American dramatic star. She was Nancy Hallam, whose
performances in Annapolis and Williamsburg brought rhapsodic praise.
Apparently Lewis Hallam, Jr.'s cousin, she had appeared as a child actress

with the group in 1759, returned to England, then returned to America
with Douglass during the Stamp Act period. Although she had attracted
good notices in the 1760's, her stardom came in the long 1770–1772
southern season, particularly after she appeared as Imogen in *Cymbeline*.
The Company seems to have given Nancy special treatment. The account
book of the Williamsburg wigmaker Edward Charlton records that in
August 1770 he charged the Company twenty-five shillings for dressing
Mrs. Douglass but forty shillings for dressing Nancy Hallam. The *Maryland
Gazette* printed an unprecedented succession of rapt testimonials to her soft
elocution, her understanding of Shakespeare, her skill in acting tender,
then pitiable, then comic. One admirer stressed that her talent overcame
even the deficiencies of the new theatre:

> Such delicacy of Manner! Such classical Strictures of Expression! The Musick
> of her Tongue! The *vox liquida,* how melting! Notwithstanding the Injuries it
> received from the horrid Ruggedness of the Roof, and the untoward
> Construction of the whole House. . . . How true and thorough her
> Knowledge of the Character she personated! Her whole Form and Dimen-
> sions how happily convertible, and universally adapted to the Variety of her
> Part.

Another Annapolitan confessed that he had read Shakespeare since
boyhood but had never conceived his power until seeing Nancy Hallam
act. He wrote some verses in which Shakespeare himself thanked the
actress for translating and expanding his fame:

> "Long have my scenes each British heart
>   With warmest transports filled;
> Now equal praise, by Hallam's art,
>   America shall yield."

A young man named Hudson Muse, after attending the Williamsburg
theatre every night for eleven nights, summed up local feeling in two
words: Nancy Hallam was "super fine." [10]

Reverend Jonathan Boucher urged that Nancy Hallam be painted by
his fellow Hominy Club member "self-tutored PEALE." A sometime
Annapolitan actually struggling to get out, Peale did paint her, the result
being a more than usually careful work, which he displayed in his painting
room (ill., p. 349). He chose a theatregoer's point-of-view, from the right
and slightly from above, as if Nancy Hallam were seen from a righthand
box. She has brown hair and eyes; for her role—Imogen disguised as a
boy—she wears a cap and coat of pale blue and silver, pink trousers, and a
scabbard. The tip of her upraised sword points to the forest cave from
which she emerges in distress. Generically, Peale's painting derives from
the so-called theatrical conversation piece popular in England in the

1760's and exploited by Garrick, showing well-known actors in parts they had made famous.[11] Although Peale endowed the actress with his standard idealized eyes and symmetrical eyebrows, his painting is a precious document, the only surviving depiction of a colonial stage and of Douglass' costuming and scenery.

For all the local verse bouquets to Nancy Hallam and the new brick theatre, Annapolis contained, by 1775, only about 3,700 inhabitants. To fill the playhouse during the Company's six-month stay, every man, woman, and child in Annapolis would have had to see a performance roughly every other week. The town simply could not support a repertory theatre. Indeed, the same writer who lauded Nancy Hallam's *"vox liquida"* added that, surprisingly, the house was thin. And even with crowded houses in Williamsburg, a local account book records Douglass accepting country pay for tickets: "David Douglas *[sic]* to tickets for 12 l[oa]ds wood £3." [12]

And when he again left the South after his two-year sojourn, in the fall of 1772, Douglass found himself again in a war zone. His opening performance in Philadelphia was interrupted by "ruffians in the gallery." In December other "ruffians" assaulted two doorkeepers at the Southwark Theatre, tore off the gallery door, and carried away the iron spikes dividing the gallery from the upper boxes. Several perpetrators were brought to the workhouse; Douglass offered a ten-pound reward for the others. By May he was asking "the more regular and better dispos'd People" to either eject nuisance makers themselves or point them out to the constables he had hired to patrol the theatre.[13]

These constables, on one hand, and Nancy Hallam, on the other, represent an uneasy balance that kept the American Company suspended as America's cultural glory arose. For Douglass and Hallam the problem remained not progress but survival.

The commencement poets of 1763 had expected a "Reign of LEARNING and of PEACE," an era of rapid Translation in which British culture would follow the course of British empire westward to North America. A decade later their expectations had, in part, come about—not with Peace, as it happened, but amidst tirades, pacts, assaults, demonstrations, and shooting. Had culture progressed, as John Trumbull believed, because of strife?

Asked in this form, of course, the question precludes an answer, since it raises the wider, virtually theological question of historical causation. In fact, the relation between the arts and politics varied according to the personalities of individual artists, the state and nature of individual arts, the social and political conditions of individual places. Such a psychological, esthetic, and historical maze can itself be penetrated only by drawing continual distinctions, not in the straightforward generalizations of a summary. And even here there is no escaping ambiguities of language that threaten to soar again into an empyrean of first causes.

Warily, then, and rather crudely, it can be said that some kinds of cultural growth occurred in spite of the strife. The mounting influx of musicians and painters reflected an older, steady process of urbanization by which Philadelphia, for instance, nearly doubled its population between 1760 and 1775; more artists turned up in such urban centers simply because they contained more people. Older forms of cultural activity continued quite as if no effigies flamed in the streets. Alongside the Farmer's letters and diatribes against Governor Bernard, newspapers published a large amount of love poetry, nature verse, elegies, drinking songs, and Addisonian essays; less than three weeks after the Boston Massacre, James Joan gave a reading of *The Beggar's Opera* at Concert Hall to an audience of over a hundred people. In other cases, political events advanced cultural progress. Verse being a popular medium of public discourse, the number of poems published after 1765 rose in direct proportion with crisis and tension. Calls for non-importation spurred the production not only of native woolens and tea substitutes but of native paper for native tunebooks, and native violins and spinets. The emergence of political celebrities created a new demand for statues, portraits, and prints. In still other cases, political strife impeded progress. The American Company suffered most. The relevance of much of its repertoire to divisive issues divided Douglass' audience, the actors were considered Englishmen, and the relative extravagance of the performances outraged many people who cultivated austerity. Finally, where politics did not advance progress it very often channeled its character. The appearance of CHESTER, of Phillis Wheatley's *Poems on Various Subjects*, and of the Rising Glory poems can all be traced to the early 1760's, when Lyon published *Urania*, when a pious Boston family undertook to civilize a teen-age slave, when American colleges began to absorb the new Scottish curriculum. Yet none could have taken the form it took had not the Stamp Act and Townshend crises created a new self-awareness in colonial life, a common focus, the sense of a subject. Cultural growth seemed to occur irresistibly, both in spite of and because of the political turmoil, with it or without.

Indeed, at the level of causation it makes as much sense to ask the question the other way around. Had political strife arisen because of cultural progress? The first volume of American music, the new singing schools, the first permanent theatre, the success of West, the long commencement poems formed a single climate of creative exuberance that not only fed on itself but also exerted its own influence, giving rise to claims that the American colonies were not to be taken for granted. The burning effigies and the new tunebooks seem twin products of one underlying maturation in American society, of a new thoughtfulness and cohesion—signs of adolescence, perhaps, which of all stages of growth least tolerates scolding, bullying, and condescension.

Part Two

Battles—American
Culture 1773–1783

Like the brief interlude of peace following repeal of the Stamp Act in 1766, the longer lull which followed repeal of the Townshend Acts in 1770 turned out to be a resting place between bad and worse. After passage of the Tea Act in 1773, relations between England and her American colonies deteriorated without pause.

The colonists' defiance of the new tea prices provoked Parliament in 1774 to close Boston as a port, which provoked other colonies sympathetic with Boston's plight to convene a Continental Congress, the first since the Stamp Act. In April 1775, British troops attempted to destroy stores at Concord and Lexington; armed colonials mauled them as they returned to Boston, and afterward fanned out around the city, joined by volunteers from nearby towns, to form the nucleus of a Continental Army. In June, Congress appointed George Washington their commander-in-chief. He walled in Boston until March 1776, when the British army sailed away to Halifax—the prelude to an invasion of New York. After the formal Declaration of Independence, several armies and fleets began battling at Morristown and Saratoga, occupying or reoccupying cities like Philadelphia and Charleston, launching offensives and counteroffensives across half the continent. The fighting was climaxed by a week of shelling at Yorktown in 1781 and the surrender of some 8,000 British military personnel. With Washington, and not many others, staying wary, the war petered out in desultory combat and prolonged treaty-making that lasted into 1784.

The eruption of armed conflict left some cultural activities unaffected. The singing schools continued, West kept receiving students. Yet the war brought with it many new conditions that did affect the rate and character of cultural progress. Painters found themselves as often carrying a gun as a brush and profiting from new government commissions for commemorative works. Concert life virtually ceased in some cities and boomed in others, while the Continental Army offered training in musical instruments in order to supply its own drums, fifes, and bands. The volume of print fell off, but virtually every skirmish produced some poems. Young poets enlisted, and found time at camp to work at epic-length poems which they might publish when the war ended. Among other austerity measures, Congress officially discouraged plays, driving professional actors into exile but stimulating theatre at the colleges and in the army. Many gifted people of conservative or wavering sympathies left the country, even as foreign officers brought into it a higher cultural standard than Americans had ever known before, inspiring them to emulation.

The fortunes of war made the relation between the arts and significant events not only more intricate than before but also more haphazard. Important poets and painters chanced to turn up at minor battles; decisive battles happened to lack combatants who might turn them into a play or engraving; important cultural activities, too, occurred off the battlefield altogether. After describing the events that led up to the Declaration of Independence, the account in Part Two traces the line of greatest cultural activity, following wherever the arts happened to be, a path which winds in and out of the more familiar contours of political and military history.

26. The Tea Act and the Boston Port Bill: May 1773–September 1774

On May 10, 1773, Parliament passed a Tea Act intended to help the East India Company avoid bankruptcy. By allowing the company to sell large quantities of surplus tea directly to retail merchants, skipping the London wholesalers, the act enabled the company to lower its prices sharply. The cheap tea was the sign for which many colonists had remained vigilant during the 'quiet period,' proof that the design of enslavement, twice repulsed, had not been abandoned.

Here was a new, but subtle, encroachment. The price of the company's tea, however cheap, included a threepenny duty still in effect according to an unrepealed provision of the Townshend Acts. To flout this duty, many colonists had abstained from tea, drunk smuggled tea, or brewed tea from a bush growing along the banks of New England rivers. Many regarded the low price as a bait for innocents, luring them into an admission of

Parliament's right of taxation. A lady poet in the *Virginia Gazette*, receiving a china tea service, saw through the bargain to the trap:

> . . . thou migh'st *[sic]* have been
> Chiefest Favourite of the Fair;
> Now thou art with Horrour seen
> As a ministerial Snare.

Perceiving the Tea Act in terms of this long-familiar scenario, the colonists responded by reviving the kinds of protest and propaganda which they had more recently invented to halt its unfolding. In October, Josiah Flagg, founder of the Boston militia band, gave a concert at Faneuil Hall. He featured fifty performers singing a chorus from *The Messiah*, but concluded with a singing of John Dickinson's "Liberty Song." [1] Farmer-ideologues, severed snakes, disconsolate orphans again appeared as again "fair Liberty" came to life, threatened more seriously than before by her seducers.

Resistance to the new encroachment gathered in the late fall and early winter as the first shipments of tea approached Boston. On November 5, Henry Pelham, lately an engraver of the King Street massacre, recorded hearing outside his house the "passing of Carts and a constant throng of People, the shouting of an indisiplined Rabble the ringing of bells and sounding of Horns in the night . . . the ratlings of Carriages, the noises of Pope Drums [beaten because it was Pope Day]. . . ." [2] Boston Sons of Liberty called on the tea consignees—the merchants named by the East India Company to receive the shipment—to resign publicly at Liberty Tree.

As the *Dartmouth*, the first of three tea ships, arrived in Boston harbor on November 27, citizens were alerted by a notice posted around town, beginning "Friends! brethren! countrymen!" [3] A town meeting was held on the thirtieth, moved to Old South Church from Faneuil Hall because of the overflow crowd. The meeting hissed a letter from Governor Hutchinson and voted to ignore his order to disperse. The meeting also considered a letter from the tea consignees, who explained that they had no power to return the tea but agreed to store it and await further instructions from the East India Company.

On this point, the meeting heard from John Singleton Copley. Preparing to leave for Europe at any time—after eight years of invitations from West and others—he spoke at Old South in behalf of his family. His father-in-law, Richard Clarke, was not only a nephew of Governor Hutchinson but also a large tea consignee and the principal Boston agent for the East India Company. Ten days before the *Dartmouth* arrived, a mob showered Clarke's house with stones, then broke in through the lower windows and damaged his furniture. Recently Clarke and his sons had fled for safety to Castle William in the harbor, a fortress guarded by British troops. Copley proposed bringing the Clarkes to Old South. He asked the audience for a vote insuring that his in-laws would "be treated with Civility while in the Meeting, though they might be of different Sentiments with this Body." The meeting complied, and adjourned for two hours while Copley fetched the Clarkes.

The mission took longer than expected. Copley did not return until late afternoon, when he informed the meeting that he had spoken to the Clarkes, guaranteed their safety, and "used his utmost Endeavours to prevail upon them to give Satisfaction to the Body. . . ." They replied that since nothing could be done but return the tea, which they lacked the power to do, they thought it best not to appear. They offered once again to store the tea under the inspection of a committee. Further, they said, they could not go, "without incurring their own Ruin; but as they had not been active in introducing the Tea, they should do nothing to obstruct the People in their Procedure with the same." The question was put to the meeting whether Copley's report was "in the least Degree satisfactory to this Body." Unanimously the body declared no.[4]

The day after his appearance, Copley wrote to Clarke's sons, describing his effort to convince the radicals that the Clarkes were only fulfilling a trust, the failure of which would ruin them financially. He had argued, he told his brothers-in-law, that "you had shewn no disposition to bring the Teas into the Town, nor would you; But only must be excused from being the Active instruments in sending it back." He had assured the meeting that the Clarkes were not, as some charged, operating for the now-unmasked Governor Hutchinson. He believed, too, that he had a little pacified the hostility against the Clarkes. If the elder Clarke stayed put and avoided contact with Hutchinson, Copley felt, he could return honorably to Boston.

Whatever Copley's intervention did for the Clarkes, it did nothing to ease the situation. Alongside Griffin's Wharf lay the ships *Dartmouth* and *Eleanor*, each with 114 chests of tea, and nearby the brig *Beaver*, with 112 chests—some forty-five tons of dutied tea worth about 9,000 pounds. The meeting resolved to return the ships to London without payment of the duty. To protect the cargo, it also appointed a watch of twenty-five men, probably armed. On December 16 the *Dartmouth* became subject to seizure for nonpayment of duty, and possible landing and sale of its tea. To prevent this, some 200 Bostonians forced customs officials ashore. Then in about three hours they chopped open the chests and dumped the tea into the harbor. Most were vaguely disguised with bits of paint, old blankets, and soot, to look like Indians. The author of "A New Song" saw the event as a sort of first warpath, under the auspices of the Whig gods:

III.

Arm'd with hammer, ax and chissels *[sic]*,
  Weapons new for warlike deed,
Towards the herbage-freighted vessels,
  They approach'd with dreadful speed.

IV.

O'er their heads aloft in mid-sky
  Three bright Angel forms were seen;
This was HAMPDEN, *that* was SIDNEY,
  With fair LIBERTY between.[5]

The use of Indian costumes did not constitute a premiere: Colonists in the South dressed up as Indians during Saint Tammany Day festivities; the ship *Gaspee* had been burned in 1772 by Rhode Islanders in Indian dress, such costumes serving at once as disguises and as assertive revelations of new identities.[6]

As dutied tea arrived elsewhere in the colonies it brought similarly theatrical responses. A New York writer asked to know "the author of the curious East-Indian farce, lately prepared in England to be played in America for the entertainment of the British Colonies":

It is generally ascribed to Lord North; at least the finishing and preparing of it for exhibition on the American stage. It was intended only as a kind of an overture, prelude or introduction to a grand performance (I don't know whether to call it Comedy or Tragedy) in which the whole British nation were intended to be actors.

To give New Yorkers "suitable musical decorations" for their parts, the writer offered an "Ode Sung at the Opening of the Grand Indian Opera, Performed at Boston, 16th of December, 1773. By Signiora Boheti [i.e., Bohea tea]." With the refrain "Sweep all!" the "Signiora" sang everyone to the harbor to fight oppression:

Away then, away!
To harbor repair;
Plunge all in the sea
Their Green and Bohea.
Sweep all! Sweep all!
'Tis America's Call. . . .

In the final New York version of the "Grand Indian Opera," Sons of Liberty threw consigned tea into the harbor while a sassing band played "God Save the King." [7]

As the political 'theatre' reopened, the real theatre suffered. Passage of the Tea Act coincided with Douglass' second effort to erect a new playhouse in Charleston. John Henry had failed to negotiate a new theatre there in 1769, when he found the city, he said, "involved in the present disagreeable (though glorious) Struggle" against the Townshend Acts. In mid-1773, Douglass tried again. Probably encouraged by his recent success in Annapolis, he began raising in Charleston a second permanent, brick theatre, on a plot 50 feet wide and 130 feet deep on, of all places, Church Street.[8]

Hardly had Douglass announced the engagement of builders for the theatre than he was indicted in the local press, on more counts than usual. "Philo Patriae" accused him of fooling with a theatre at a time when

> . . . it is universally acknowledged, that there is neither a Sufficiency of Currency or Specie in Circulation, to transact common Business—When the *increasing* Poor are ready to starve, from the *scarcity* and Dearness of common Necessaries—when the Rich can scarce find Ready-Money to pay for what they drink and eat, and wear—when the Public Treasury itself is represented as nearly in a State of Bankruptcy—when none of our principal Staple Commodities, viz. Rice and Indico, sell to the same Advantage in Europe as formerly—when, under these Circumstances (not to mention many others, equally disadvantageous) in less than Six Months, this Province has become indebted to Great Britain, in a Sum little short of 300,000 l. Sterling, for Negroes only—when our Country swarms with Objects of visible Distress, and many respectable Families (ashamed to reveal their real Situations) are silently feeding on the Bread of Affliction. . . .

Those who subscribed to Douglass' theatre, he concluded, "wish to see us effeminized or tamed into vassals, fit for Despotism. . . ."[9]

As many Charlestonians came to feel that the evolving tea struggle called for resolute action, the debate over Douglass' building focused on the charge that the stage produces effeminacy of spirit. Douglass' defenders argued that his new theatre, and the other signs of cultural growth, made passive acquiescence to 'slavery' an ignoble disgrace. One Charlestonian called attention to the *"elegant Theatre"* as well as to the new schools and the new wharf, the

> great Attention [that] is also paid the *fine Arts,*—the St. Caecilia Society having warmly patronized *Music;* while many Gentlemen of Taste and Fortune, are giving the utmost Encouragement to *Architecture, Portrait-Painting,* and the ingenious Performances of the *first* capital *Landscape-Painter* that has visited America, whose Works will do him Honour.—And shall it be said that *such a People, will suffer themselves to sink into Slavery?*

"Atticus" defended Douglass by recalling that in ancient Greece, "the brave Hero, who had toiled in the Field of Honour and lavished his Blood in his Country's Cause, came to enjoy Amusements, which, far from unmaning, elevated his Soul, and re animated him in his glorious Career." On the other side, "Cleopatra" inadvertently revealed what sort of people "Atticus" spoke for. She had championed his views, she reported, while drinking tea with some acquaintances, even when the "saucy Jade in Waiting," apparently a radical, spilled hot tea on her foot.[10]

On December 2, a shipment of dutied tea arrived in Charleston. A town meeting voted to have the East India Company return the cargo, but an internally divided group of planters, merchants, and mechanics failed to prevent it from being landed and stored, drawing a stiff reprimand from Samuel Adams. On December 13, amidst much alarmed writing about tea and calls for united resistance, Douglass announced the opening of his new theatre. The first performance (*A Word to the Wise* on December 22) was noticed in James Rivington's conservative New York *Gazetteer*, which applauded the elegant house, the "well designed" new scenery, the "pleasing" music, and the "extraordinary theatrical talents" of Lewis Hallam, Jr. But Douglass could not escape the consequences of opening in a politically confused city, within a few weeks of the arrival of ships bearing the tainted tea. In February, a presentment drawn up for the grand jurors of the district court included an article against the American Company:

> IX. We present as a GRIEVANCE, the Company of Players: A Play-House in Charles-Town being unfit for the present low Estate of the Province; for, although there is a great Want of Money to procure the Conveniencies, and even the Necessaries of Life, yet large Sums are weekly laid out for Amusements there, by Persons who cannot afford it; and is a Means of promoting the frequent Robberies that are committed, and of Vice and Obscenity. We recommend that the Legislature may suppress the same. . . .[11]

Although the presentment was quashed, and although the Company managed to play in Charleston until May, the tea crisis put the country in no mood to be amused; Douglass was in trouble.

The home government countered colonial resistance to its Tea Act by new measures which escalated the conflict. Even supporters of the colonies like Burke and Pitt believed that the time had come for firmness. On March 14, Parliament passed the Boston Port Bill, effective June 1, the first of the so-called Intolerable Acts. It forbade shipping in and out of Boston, except for food and firewood, until the inhabitants paid for the destroyed tea. In effect, the act abolished Boston as a port. Parliament enacted other severe measures as well: an Administration of Justice Act, allowing for trial in England of an official or soldier accused of a capital crime in the colonies; a Quartering Act, allowing the colonial government to quarter troops; and an especially ominous Quebec Act, providing among other things for toleration in Quebec of Roman Catholics. Finally, Thomas Hutchinson was replaced as governor of Massachusetts by General Thomas Gage.[12]

Gage arrived with fresh troops on May 7, making Boston once more an occupied city. In their reentry one "Daughter of Liberty" saw trade strangled and social life devoured:

> See! how the Locusts in huge Swarms ascend,
> New England's Fall and Ruin they intend.
> Thy Passages are stopt,—this murd'rous Brood,
> Thirst for our Lives to wash their Hands in Blood!

As the city filled with soldiers, thousands of Bostonians left for the country or for other towns; stores closed, property values fell; citizens protested episodes of drunkenness, brawling, or insult. To the troops he brought with him, Gage added others from Quebec, New York, and England, the number reaching some 4,500 by the start of 1775. Again these included polite officers, for whose entertainment W. S. Morgan, one of the many new musical immigrants of 1770, joined William Selby and some army and navy personnel in a concert of vocal and instrumental music that boasted "Clarinets, Hautboys, Bassoons, French Horns, Trumpets, Kettle Drums, &c." Like similar events during the previous occupation, the concert was deeply resented. A Newburyport citizen complained that "most thinking people" believed that concerts and other entertainments should be suspended "now at a time of general distress and anxiety throughout the whole continent of America." [13]

Rakish as well as polite, the troops revived fears for the virtue of Boston girls and, more intensely than before, for the inviolateness of "fair Liberty." "How will you feel," asked "Cato" in the *Newport Mercury* in August, "to see a ruffian's blade reaking from a daughter's heart, for nobly preserving her virtue." With its threat of actual rape, the entry of troops made the image of violated rights not metaphorical but literal. For many Bostonians, the political situation was only the social situation writ large. "A Liberty Song" in October pointed feelingly at Lady Boston:

> Hark! hark! my country-men, what is the dismal groaning,
> Sure 'tis some ravish'd lady sits desparately moaning:
> Hear the sigh——fly——fly
> 'Tis the voice—'tis the voice of fair liberty.[14]

In an engraving of *The able Doctor, or America Swallowing the Bitter Draught,*

Revere showed a female, bare-breasted America lying on the ground, struggling, while a pot of tea is being poured into her throat, her ankles held by a lascivious figure who, as she regurgitates the tea, peers under her dress.

By punishing an entire city, Parliament had wielded an authority more menacing than any right to tax. Moderate Whigs who had disapproved the Tea Party began to see its legitimacy. Overnight, one historian remarks, "mobbish Boston became martyred Boston." In New York, the printer John Holt placed on the masthead of his *New-York Journal*, in June, a snake severed in nine parts, with the motto "Unite or Die." The device had been used by Franklin in 1754 and had appeared on a single issue of the short-lived *Constitutional Courant* during the Stamp Act crisis. Now, however, as the Boston popular leaders asked support for their cause, other newspapers printed the device as an emblem of intercolonial resistance. In July 1774, Isaiah Thomas introduced a snake with the motto "Join or Die" on the masthead of his *Massachusetts Spy*, where it opposed a dragon, representing Great Britain, bent on consuming it. In Philadelphia, the Bradfords copied Holt's device on the masthead of their *Pennsylvania Journal*. James Rivington ridiculed the devices, suggesting that the snake more properly connoted perfidy than union:

> Ye sons of Sedition, how comes it to pass
> That America's typed by a snake—in the grass?
> Don't you think 't is a scandalous, saucy reflection
> That merits the soundest, severest correction?
> New England's the head, too—New England's abused—
> For the Head of the Serpent we know should be bruised.

The Bradfords, a little illogically, answered

> . . . "How comes it to pass?"
> Because she is pester'd with snakes in the grass;
> Who by lying and cringing, and such like pretensions,
> Get places *once* honoured, disgraced with pensions.[15]

Far more than during the 1769 occupation, other colonists identified themselves with the plight of Bostonians, sending food and supplies into the embargoed city. Disregarding Douglass' fate, a Charlestonian proposed that since the "elder Gentlemen of Property" had contributed to the relief of Boston, the younger people might help to alleviate *"the Distresses of their suffering Countrymen"* by producing a play, provided "the Elder and better-judging Members of the Community approve." He suggested Edward Young's *Busiris, King of Egypt*, which shows "an injured gallant People struggling against Oppression." Rice or money would be accepted for tickets, the proceeds going to victims of the Port Bill. Although donations of rice did get sent to Boston, another Charlestonian felt that the city suffered less from poverty than from English vengefulness. He considered the meaning of "the POOR of BOSTON being employed *in paving the Streets*":

> IN spite of *Rice,* in spite of *Wheat,*
> Sent for the Boston-Poor—to eat,
> In spite of *Brandy,* one would think,
> Sent for the Boston-Poor—to drink;
> Poor are the Boston-Poor indeed,
> And needy, tho' there is no Need:
> They cry for Bread; the mighty Ones,
> Instead of *Bread,* give only *Stones.*

In Williamsburg, the *Gazette* printed for its readers, in August, the text of John Dickinson's "Liberty Song." Philip Fithian recorded that at Nomini Hall, as perhaps at other southern plantations, sympathetic Virginians entertained themselves by "singing 'Liberty Songs' as they call'd them, in which six, eight, ten or more would put their Heads near together and roar. . . ." [16]

Much other roaring over the Port Bill vented itself on Thomas Gage, commanding General of the British army in North America, and now governor of Massachusetts. As "Cato," "Junius Americanus," "Lucius Publicola," and others slashed him in letters to the press, verse parodists took off his many proclamations and speeches. In New York, Gage had given the permission to Tomlinson's actors which seemingly inspired the Sons of Liberty to wreck the Chapel Street Theatre. In Massachusetts, rather surprisingly, he issued a proclamation on July 21 calling for "the Encouragement of Piety and Virtue, and for preventing and punishing of Vice, Profanity, and Immorality." [17] He professed to speak in imitation of the moralistic King George, who had issued a similar proclamation in the first year of his reign. His proclamation, however, connected sin, which New England was notorious for condemning, with popular dissent. It exhorted Bostonians against "Sedition, Licentiousness, and all other immoralities," indirectly accusing the radicals of hypocrisy and in effect playing another form of "Yankee Doodle" at them.

Parodists did not let Gage's rhetorical strategy go unrecognized. According to one, Gage under cover of preaching morality was demanding passive obedience.

> [I, Gage] Do *issue,* after mature Deliberation
> In *our first Year,* a like *Proclamation,*
> Exhorting our Subjects to avoid and fly
> Licentiousness, Sedition, and Hypocrisy,

> Thankfully to God and Man expressing,
> Of our wise, mild Government the Blessing. . . .

A New York parodist saw Gage as wanting to be a little king himself, treating Americans like good little children *"Obedient* to *my Will:*

> To all the pretty Girls and Boys,
>   That live in our Town,
> This Proclamation I address,
>   In Hopes of great Renown.

But the doting parent was merely a mask of the crude bully:

> You shall have Cakes and Sugar Plumbs,
>   And many Things beside;
> You shall be dress'd in Tunicks fine,
>   On Cock horse for to ride.
> But if you should *rebellious* prove,
>   For all that do amiss,
> I keep at *Home* a monstrous *Rod,*
>   A *Rod,* well soak'd in P---.[18]

One of the Intolerable Acts made it Gage's duty, beginning in August, to appoint members of the Massachusetts Council, who were no longer to be elected by the House. These so-called mandamus councillors represented a loss of self-government of the sort which Bostonians since Puritan times had intensely feared, so intensely that they usually spoke of it in terms of the Apocalypse. Mercy Warren attacked Gage and his appointees in a dramatic sketch, published anonymously in the *Boston Gazette* in January 1775, entitled *The Group.* Recalling the political graphics and even the painting of the period, the work is a sort of verbal caricatura. One scene features "a swarm of court sycophants, hungry harpies, and unprincipled danglers, collected from the neighboring villages, hovering over the stage in the shape of locusts"; another scene occurs in the dining room of a councillor's house, where a case of books, catalogued in the text, suggests the intellectual backgrounds of conservative treachery: Hobbes, Bernard Mandeville, Edmond Hoyle on whist, and the history of Massachusetts by the now-departed Governor Hutchinson.

In explaining how a group of native-born Massachusetts men turned against their province—nine of the characters graduated Harvard—Mrs. Warren refused to paint all her villains with the same brush. Several officials reveal through soliloquies their state of mind. Privately, they are disheartened by the colonists' resistance, tormented at having betrayed their friends and countrymen, and aware that they have been duped by

Thomas Hutchinson, who promised them place, wealth, and polish, escape from provincial rusticity. Hazelrod (Peter Oliver) and Hateall (the councillor Timothy Ruggles, the one unmitigated villain in the piece) rebuke their guilt as cowardice, each revealing his own motive: gain for Oliver, sadism for Ruggles. Gage himself (Sylla) appears as purely a servant of the Crown eager to bring it more glory and worried about a possible revolt from the colonists, whom he fears as countrymen of Wolfe, Marlborough, and Locke:

> . . . shall I rashly draw my guilty sword,
> And dip its hungry hilt in the rich blood
> Of the best subjects that a Brunswick boasts,
> And for no cause, but that they nobly scorn
> To wear the fetters of his venal slaves!

Sylla's attitude dismays the others, who go off determining to urge him to put down the rebels. As they leave, a curtain rises on the back stage disclosing one councillor's wife, who prophesies that "conq'ring Hero's must enrich the Grave."

Not many other Massachusetts radicals following the Tea Act and the Boston Port Bill were able to grant Gage and the councillors such mixed motives. Sharing the sentimentalist view of the basic goodness of human nature, and perhaps writing more in sorrow than in anger, Mercy Warren provided interesting psychological and political explanations of their behavior, and wittingly or not created some sympathy for their position. "Copeley's [sic] Pencil could not have touched off with more exquisite Finishings," John Adams told her, "the Faces of those Gentlemen." [19]

27. Copley in Europe:
July 1774–March 1775

Adams' remark, a questionable esthetic judgment, was true literally, for less than a month after Gage entered Boston, Copley sailed, at last, for Europe. The prospect had agitated him since 1766, when he learned that his *Boy with Squirrel* had been highly praised at its London exhibition. His inclination to go abroad, however, was balanced by contentment with his prosperity at home, doubts about his abilities, and feelings of family obligation.

The political turmoil, probably, gave inclination the edge. Animus against his in-laws, the Clarkes, spread to Copley himself. In April 1774, knocking at the door awakened him and Sukey around midnight. Outside was a crowd. They demanded to know whether Colonel George Watson of Plymouth, a mandamus councillor, was in the house. Copley said no; the crowd asked for his word, which he gave. Then, he wrote, they "desired to know how I came to entertain such a Rogue and Villin." He explained that Watson had been visiting John Hancock nearby, and had stopped over to see him. Satisfied, the crowd left, but soon returned with Indian yells, promising that "my blood would be on my own head if I had deceived them." As it happened, Copley had pressed Watson to spend the night, but Watson refused. Copley had been lucky. "I must either have given up a friend to the insult of a Mob," it occurred to him, "or had my house pulled down and perhaps my family murthered." He sailed hastily on June 10, leaving Sukey in Boston and without a farewell to his mother, arriving on July 9 in London.[1]

His first impression of England—as a wealthy man of property who recently outfaced a mob—was of law and order. In traversing seventy-two miles of English road en route from Dover to London, he saw garden after garden without a fence or hedge, "yet not a spire of Grass Grain or Beans trampled no more than if such a trespass would be instant Distruction to the offender." In America, even good fences failed to prevent trespass on private property "in the most shameful manner." Writing to Sukey two days after his arrival, he reflected that a friend "was greatly mistaken when he said we were Saints & Angels in America compared to those that inhabit this Country. . . ." Indeed, by contrast with the English, "we Americans seem not halfway remov'd from a state of Nature. . . ."[2]

Copley's initial impression of contrast between orderly England and lawless America gave way to simple absorption in London life as he passed the next six weeks in the city. The politeness and sophistication of London society, and the painting he saw, greatly impressed him. But unlike the young West he did not find them overwhelming. Copley was, after all, an infinitely better painter than West had been when he arrived. He had come to a city where he was already being compared to Van Dyck and Rubens. After four days in London he visited West and, like everyone else, found in him "those qualitys that makes his friendship boath desireable as an artist and as a Gentleman." As for the now-famous *Wolfe*, he wrote Sukey, it was "sufficient of itself to Immortalize the Author of it." West introduced him to Reynolds and took him to the Royal Academy, "where the Students had a naked model," probably the first Copley had seen. Just ten days in town, he accompanied West to the palace. They visited the queen and went aboard the queen's yacht.[3]

Copley settled into a house a few doors from West, where he planned the Italian tour which West had recommended. He saw many paintings—too many, he wrote, to talk about, although he promised to send home to Henry Pelham the recent lectures of Reynolds, with whom he breakfasted. He found himself constantly invited to dine and, indeed, dining with the most hated people in America: with Governor Thomas Hutchinson, whom Boston had tried to impeach; with Lord North, who had brought before Parliament the Boston Port Bill. Lord Dartmouth, considered a friend to America until he took witnesses from Boston before the Privy Council to be interviewed about the Tea Party, had promised to ask the king and queen to sit for him. Copley postponed this commission until after his Italian journey, although he considered it exciting and flattering, "an Honour and an Introduction that seldom falls to the share of great Artists, In so short a time to be so imployd." It promised, moreover, to generate other commissions at court. As he once agonized over whether to leave Boston, he now considered whether to return. He hoped, he told Sukey, "soon to be with you either here or in America, which ever Providence orders." [4]

His near-future secured, Copley set out on tour. At Paris the first week in September, he enjoyed the countryside, the churches, the opera, finding the wines not as strong as New England cider. He saw works by Raphael, Correggio, Veronese, Poussin, Titian, and Rubens. The cornucopia of masterpieces, however, again did not overwhelm him. Writing from Paris, he told Pelham that he had gone about as far as he could in Boston, and that his earlier training, not any new knowledge, counted most. "I have got through the Dificultys of the Art, I trust, and shall," he said, "reap a continual Source of pleasure from my past Industry. . . ." He never considered what he saw without asking whether it could help to make him a better breadwinner, able, he wrote his mother, "to provide for my Dear Children in such a way as to bring them into the great World with reputation." [5]

The impression of Philistinism conveyed by these letters came not from insensitivity or crassness but from indecision and conflict. Copley's avowal that Europe had left him unmoved and unchanged seems in part an attempt to tell those back home the reassuring things he believed they wanted to hear, one which also served, as his later letters and actions indicate, to fend off the tremendous allure of Europe and the insistently arising idea of permanent expatriation. If his first letters to Pelham lack the young West's provincial rapture, they are filled with detached, technical analyses of Rubens; and if he often did not report what he saw, it was often because he had seen too much to report. Arriving by October in Genoa, he told Sukey that as his sense of things cleared he would decide whether she should come abroad, or he return to America. If he felt able to earn in three or four years abroad "as much as will make the rest of my Life easy," it would be best for her to stay in Boston and await his return. Meanwhile he had purchased some lace ruffles and silk stockings and looked, he thought, "a little tinctured." [6]

On his way to Rome, Copley traveled with an English artist named George Carter, who kept a journal of the trip, leaving a lively picture of Copley at the time. To Carter he looked "very thin, pale, a little pock-marked, prominent eyebrows, small eyes, which, after fatigue, seemed a day's march in his head." For the journey he wore a white French bonnet that could be pulled over the ears, atop a yellow-and-red silk kerchief "such as may be seen upon the necks of those delicate ladies who cry Malton oysters. . . ." The kerchief, Carter noticed, "flowed half way down his back." Copley also wore a cinnamon-colored greatcoat and a friar's cape hanging down to his heels, "out of which peeped his boots." Under his arm, seemingly for protection, he carried a sword he had bought in Paris and an ivory-headed hickory stick.

Carter found the American's personality no less odd than his dress. Copley seemed "happy at taking things at the wrong end." Suspecting that he had caught a "cold upon his lungs," he sat near the fire, one handkerchief around his head, another around his neck, fueling the blaze although the heat made Carter feel faint. The anxious hypochondriac, Carter felt, was also a know-it-all, highly defensive about America. Copley "laboured near an hour" to prove that a "huckaback towel" was softer than a Barcelona silk handkerchief and delivered a "long-winded discourse upon the merits of an American wood-fire, in preference to one of our coal." Copley also lectured him on Rising Glory, forecasting that if the Americans continued for the next hundred years as they had the past hundred and fifty, "they shall have an independent government: the woods will be cleared, and, lying in the same latitude, they shall have the same air as in the south of France; art would then be encouraged there, and great artists would arise." [7]

Like many other gifted Americans abroad, Copley could be harshly critical of the country himself but touchy and argumentative when foreigners criticized it. In fact, his resistance to Europe was already weakening. Only a month after writing his first, bland letters from Paris he was writing to Sukey, from Genoa, that he had seen so many large buildings adorned with so much sculpture and painting that "if I could be suddenly transported to Boston . . . I should think it only a collection of wren boxes." [8]

It seems likely that around mid-October Copley received the dispiriting letter which Pelham had sent him in late July from Boston. Food and supplies unthinkingly donated to the city by other colonies, Pelham said, were prolonging the political struggle. The "once happy but now too fatally deluded and distressed People" continued bewitched by subversive ideas and planned a Continental Congress for September. Although four regiments and artillery were encamped on the Common, which "glows with the warlike Red," Pelham found the din of cannons, drums, and fifes "incomparably to be preferred to the infernal Wistle and shout of a lawless and outragious rabble." Friendly with the British troops, he also sent word from an army captain, who told him that Reynolds had said, "I would give 100£ Str. that I could paint white equal to Mr. Coply." The news from home made Copley fear that the soldiers would damage his Beacon Hill estate and leave it valueless; he wished he had sold it. He learned, also, that his tenants were refusing to pay their rent. Boston now held for him "not one Charm one attraction left seperate from my very Dear friends; and I fear it will not be better. . . ." At the end of October he informed Sukey, from Rome, that he would stay in England, "where I have no doubt I shall meet with as much to do & on better terms than in Boston." He sent through her his regards to General, now Governor, and Mrs. Gage.[9]

But it was not all that easy. Copley spent November and December in Rome, where, finding it sometimes too cold to sit in the museums, he talked much with friendly Englishmen at the English Coffee House. Additional incoming news left him "fearful that Boston will soon become a place of bloodshed and confusion." Worried about his family, he continued to argue his situation up and down. The air was better in America than anywhere else. Indeed he had found "no place so calculated to make people happy as far as nature is concerned." If Americans could not be happy with the lives they had known, it was their own fault: "A great deal depends on mens own conduct & I wish they were more enlarged in their sentiments in this England has the advantage (by many degrees) of America." He wished, too, that it would all go away. "I avoid engaging in politics," he wrote in December, "as I wish to preserve an undisturbed mind and a tranquillity inconsistent with political disputes." Yet he believed that England would not again back down. Were he to return home "I should have nothing to do, and cannot think of going back to starve with my family." [10]

In January, at the urging of Gulian Verplanck (whom he had painted brilliantly in New York in 1770), Copley took an excursion to Naples. His feelings about Europe, as about America, remained ambivalent. Naples, he told Sukey, was "very large, very Dirty & very pleasantly situated." Much of what he saw repulsed him:

> . . . as I pass the streets they stink often to that Degree as to make me quite sick; and the People are as Dirty as the Streets; every step you take you will

see People picking the Lice from one another, I have even seen a well Dressed
Shop Keeper leaning over his Shop Window with a Man Picking the Lice
from his Head. . . .

Nearby Pompeii, however, thrilled him. He sent home lengthy descriptions of the buildings and roads, and of the ongoing excavation. He found
it hard to express his feelings upon seeing "these wonderful scenes, so
complete, so fresh, and yet built by those that lived in so remote an age." [11]
The month he spent in Naples visiting Pompeii and Herculaneum and
studying the collection of the king of Naples (especially Raphael's *Holy
Family*) made him more willing to acknowledge and to express the depth of
his feelings about the riches of European art. Later he was able to
formulate the process by which he had passed from interest to passion.
There is, he observed to the painter John Greenwood, "a kind of luxury in
seeing, as in eating and drinking, and the more we indulge our senses in
either the less are they to be restrained." [12] Even during his winter in
Rome he sent home long, adoring descriptions of Raphael. Now, having
seen the Pompeiian antiquities and painting of the Roman school, he
wanted badly to see Venetian and Flemish works.

Returning to Rome from Naples, Copley seems to have brought back
some new ideas. He painted Mr. and Mrs. Ralph Izard of Charleston,
whom he had accompanied to Paestum. He depicted them against the
distant coliseum, surrounded by classical statuary and other objects. The
clutter suggests that Copley had seen so much as to paralyze his ability to
discriminate; or perhaps he wished to flatter the industrious collecting of
the Izards. He included on the canvas every sort of texture and color
imaginable—pallid flesh, glossy black marble, a white veil, green satin,
majolica, a gold wedding band, lace, black velvet, white marble, candy
pinks, roses, and light greens. What a viewer of Copley's earlier painting
misses most is some hint of acerbity to neutralize the confectionary flavor.
Depending on one's taste, this *tour de force* shows the beginning of a drastic
alteration, or of a deterioration, in the provincial realism Copley had
perfected in Boston.

Breaking still more sharply with his earlier career, Copley began doing
history paintings. Until now he had been content to paint portraits,
probably because of his success in obtaining through them the luxuries and
prestige he desired. He bought up plaster casts of ancient sculpture to use
as models in his Rome apartment, feeling that to own them was equivalent
to two years' study in Rome. Having the *Laocoön* ("the best work of art in
the world") and the *Apollo* alone, he later told Sukey, he would "possess all
that I would recommend to an Artist to Study for it is not the number of
things that an Artist Studys but thoroughly understanding those he Studys

and the principals of Art that is in them that will make him great."
Michelangelo learned "that astonishing Gusto that we see in all his works
from only the fragment of a figure. . . ." [13]

By mid-March in Rome Copley completed an *Ascension*. He sent a very
lengthy description of the work to Pelham, really a small treatise
concerning "in what manner an Historical composition is made." The
letter reveals much about his work habits and about his understanding of
current theories of history painting. His first step in making the picture, he
explained to Pelham, was to ponder the event psychohistorically. He
considered how the Apostles would be affected at the instant of Ascension.
Astonished, they would crowd together to hear what Christ said to Peter
"with vast attention in their countinances." The apostolic character,
however, demanded that these expressions of astonishment be tempered
with love and majesty. His second step was to kindle inspiration. He
recommended that the artist "Warm his Immagination by looking at some
Works of Art, in Reading, or Conversing." Next he sketched a general
idea of the whole, and made smaller sketches for particular groups. Then
he added the drapery, using as a model "a Table Cloath wet and rung
out." After about three days of this "Ideal Sketching" he drew the whole
in outline on a kit-kat canvas, hiring a model to sit for some heads. During
the drawing he frequently studied the works of Raphael and also used a
mirror to study actions and gestures.[14]

In Rome as in London, Copley quickly became a celebrity. The
engraver Giambattista Piranesi saw a colored sketch of the *Ascension* and
insisted on calling it a finished picture. Copley confided to Sukey his
pleased discovery that he was "less a stranger in the world than I
thought." The news he received from home, however, was discouraging.
Writing in February, Pelham described an alarming episode. He had
visited a mandamus councillor in Springfield, putting up for the night at a
tavern. Twenty-four drunk men stopped by after a squirrel hunt and fired
their muskets, trying to make him acknowledge his "offences aga[i]n[s]t
the Libertys of the People." Someone persuaded them to disperse. Pelham
also sent news that in January Sukey had given birth to a son.[15]

The contrast between his success in Rome and the situation of his family
in "unhappy" Boston added to Copley's perplexity. He longed to see
Sukey and his children, yet realized that he could do nothing if he
returned to Boston but "share largely in it[s] misery." His present course,
he decided, was best not only for himself and his family but finally for the
country as well: "poor America!" he told Pelham in March, "I hope the
best but I fear the worst. yet *[sic]* certain I am She will finially Imerge from
he[r] present Callamity and become a Mighty Empire. and it is a pleasing
reflection that I shall stand amongst the first of the Artists that shall

have led that Country to the Knowledge and cultivation of the fine Arts. . . ." [16] Here Copley was shrewdly prophetic, not least in fearing the worst.

28. The First Continental Congress: September–October 1774

The occupation of Boston by British troops and the Intolerable Acts virtually forced the colonies to call a Congress for the first time since the Stamp Act. Meeting in May, eighty-nine Virginia burgesses, including Washington, Jefferson, and Patrick Henry, declared their opinion "that an attack, made on one of our sister colonies, to compel submission to arbitrary taxes, is an attack made on all British America, and threatens ruin to the rights of all. . . ." [1] They asked their Committee of Correspondence to communicate with like committees in the other colonies and arrange for appointing deputies to a general Congress to consider again the rights of Americans and to set a general agreement on economic measures. By August, all of the thirteen colonies except Georgia had named delegates to the meeting, scheduled for Philadelphia in September.

Throughout the summer, the approaching Congress became a subject for speculation, advice, and some abuse. Many looked to it as an occasion of surpassing importance. *HOPE: A Rhapsody*—a broadside published in New York in July—foresaw the resurrection of Libertas in Philadelphia:

> . . . LIBERTY, great LIBERTY, yet lives,
> Lives a HEROIN *[sic]*, by Schuylkill's wat'ry side;
> Known is her worth, and FREEDOM is her pride.
> Submit your cause, obey her bold command,
> And no restraint shall bend this mighty land. . . .

"A Virginian" fantasized that the Congress might become a platform where would shine the already-celebrated oratorical powers of fellow colonists like Richard Henry Lee and Patrick Henry:

> Each orator extends his fav'rite theme,
> Each emulous his country to redeem;
> Supply'd with more than mortal grace, they plead
> And in the glorious aim may they succeed.
> Say to what better end was HENRY born?
> Why shou'd persuasive speech his lips adorn?

> Say why? But that our most invet'rate foes
> May learn, Virginia wants not Ciceroes. . . .[2]

Opponents of the Congress tried to deflate these high-flown hopes by puncturing their language. *Debates at the Robin-Hood Society* (New York, 1774), a skit taking off the verbose quibbling at a session of the New York Committee of Correspondence, dissected the phrase "Continental Congress":

> *Continent—Continent?* is not this expression rather e-qui-vo-cal, Mr. Moderator. If I misapprehend not, Mr. Johnston, in his dictionary, defines continent to be *chaste, moderate, temperate:*—An assembly of the Continent may, I humbly conceive, be taken for an Assembly of such kind of people. . . .

Trying to rescue the phrase for use, "Mr. Silver Tongue" argued that "Great occasions require great figures." In a parody of patriot rhetoric, he imagined literally the whole continent congregating in Philadelphia, "provinces, rivers, houses, cattle, men, women, and children . . . flowing on in one immense source of plenty, harmony, and liberty!"

On the radical side, this concern for tone expressed a hope that argument alone might persuade England to retreat. Versifiers offered Congress a spectrum of direct measures it might take if argument failed. At one end, the author of *HOPE* urged the delegates to imitate enraged lionesses, and to castrate Lord North, "Barbaqu'd, broil'd, his MANHOOD toss'd in air"; "A Virginian" advised that if England proved determined "From free born subjects to supplant us slaves," then Virginia must demonstrate that she has Caesars as well as Ciceros and "open in one day ten thousand graves." At the other end of the spectrum, John Trumbull, in his *Elegy on the Times*, asked Congress to act with "the manly firmness of the sage": to recommend non-importation, encourage domestic manufacture, and campaign for unity. There militancy must end:

> But, oh, my friends, the arm of blood restrain!
> (No rage intemp'rate aids the public weal)
> Nor basely blend (too daring, but in vain)
> Th' assassin's madness with the patriot's zeal.

In a note to the poem, Trumbull explained that he did not mean that Americans should not defend themselves; he only hoped to check those "who seemed desirous to let loose the rage of popular resentment, and bring matters immediately to a crisis. . . ."[3] John Adams, a delegate to the Congress with whom Trumbull was currently studying law in Boston, had similarly urged constraint. Yet the poem makes plain a conservatism in Trumbull which had already led him to blunt the satiric point of his *Progress of Dulness.*

One of the cleverest addresses to Congress came from a native of the congressional city, Francis Hopkinson. Now married into a prominent New Jersey family and performing on the spinet for family and neighbors at his beautiful home in Bordentown, Hopkinson had recently secured the political office he failed to find during his trip to England. He served as justice of the peace and councilman, also holding posts in the Library Company of Philadelphia and the American Philosophical Society. He managed at the same time to write poetry, to occasionally fill in as organist at Christ Church, and to produce in 1774 a musically conservative *Collection of the Psalm and Hymn Tunes, Used by the Reformed Protestant Dutch Church of . . . New York* (New York), nothing like the new music of Billings. As Congress adjourned, Hopkinson published an allegorical fable entitled "A Pretty Story." He used the pretty tone of children's books of the period, and built his story on the metaphor of sundered parent-child relationships, a popular simplification of the complex doctrine of submission to authority—or, as Whigs now scornfully called it, passive nonresistance to oppression.[4]

The story describes the situation which Congress must confront, and narrates its rise. England appears as a wealthy old nobleman, owner of many farms and shops, good to his children and servants. His wife (Parliament) controls his purse-strings. At one time the nobleman acquires "an immense tract of wild, uncultivated country, at a vast distance from his mansion-house," on which some of his children settle. He sends some of his servants to protect them from incursions by their neighbors and by some barbarous slaves, requiring, however, that his children reimburse him for his trouble and expense. His avaricious wife, however, sees here an opportunity for profit, "if I can persuade them, that all they possess belonged originally to me, and that I may, in right of my prerogative, demand of them such portions of their earnings as I please." She persuades her husband to send some of his most worthless and lazy servants on the pretext of defending the settlements. In fact she hopes to rid her household of these idlers and use them to check the settlers, on whom she imposes all sorts of "internal taxes." As the nobleman gets older he increasingly gives the management of his affairs to his steward (the ministry, with a verbal thrust at Lord Bute, thought by many to act for the Stuarts). Actually, the steward has debauched his wife (another shaft at Bute). Now entirely under the steward's influence, she forces her doddering husband to subject their children. Required to supply the nobleman's table, the

> inhabitants of the new farm began now to see that their father's affections were alienated from them; and that their mother was but a base mother-in-law, governed by their enemy the steward. . . . They wrote the most supplicating letters to their father. . . .

But the steward intercepts some of the letters, and decides to make Jack's family (Boston) an example, thus to frighten the other families into submission. He locks Jack's gates and sets up a gallows (the Intolerable Acts) and a hectoring overseer (Gage). The overseer's "harsh and unconstitutional proceedings" so much anger Jack and the other families (Congress) "that * * * * * *." Hopkinson leaves the conclusion of the story hanging.[5]

Congress filled in the asterisks soon after it convened at Carpenter's Hall, on September 5. Less than two weeks later it endorsed the Suffolk Resolves, drawn up by Joseph Warren and rushed to Philadelphia by Paul Revere, declaring the Intolerable Acts unconstitutional and recommending that the people of Massachusetts withhold taxes from the Crown and begin military training. The language of the resolves fairly represents the intense, high-minded tone of the entire Congress. The preamble, for instance, prophesies that

> If we arrest the hand which would ransack our pockets, if we disarm the parricide which points the dagger to our bosoms . . . if we successfully resist that unparalleled usurpation of unconstitutional power, whereby our capital is robbed of the means of life; whereby the streets of Boston are thronged with military executioners; whereby our coasts are lined and harbours crouded with ships of war; whereby the charter of the colony, that sacred barrier against the encroachments of tyranny, is mutilated and, in effect, annihilated . . . posterity will acknowledge that virtue which preserved them free and happy; and while we enjoy the rewards and blessings of the faithful, the torrent of panegyrists will roll our reputations to that latest period, when the streams of time shall be absorbed in the abyss of eternity.[6]

Before the fifty-six delegates disbanded on October 26 they passed several other decisive acts and resolutions. In a declaration on October 14 they denied Parliament the power to legislate for the colonies. In a formal Association signed on October 20 they committed themselves to non-importation, non-exportation, non-consumption, and the discouragement of all forms of extravagance. They also wrote and sent ardent addresses to the king, and to the British and American people, and agreed to meet again in May if their grievances had not been redressed.

The strong words and strong acts of the Congress evoked a like response in the public on both sides of the Atlantic. In January the declaration and resolves of the Congress were presented to Parliament. On February 9, both houses declared Massachusetts to be in a state of rebellion, giving official approval for the use of force to secure compliance with the Intolerable Acts. Benjamin West found his situation uncomfortable. He wrote to his former pupil Charles Willson Peale in February, explaining that he was not a political man and that "what I might say would have but little waight in the Scale of Opinions" but adding, perhaps with more truth, that "prudence and the times will not permit my saying anything." Despite his reservations, he ventured to say that the actions of England toward America showed "but little knowledge of that Country in the projections of them," and threatened to "brake those extensive outlines of British Empire which those Colonies alone must have procured her." Should the Americans reply with an equal lack of understanding, "both countrys are for some time undone." [7]

If West felt somberly untalkative, Patience Wright characteristically did not. The Quaker sculptress fiercely supported "the great Cause of American Safety." She sent several letters from her Pall Mall address to John Dickinson, who had drafted the Congress' petition to the king. In her view, the issue was not between England and the colonies but between the English people everywhere and a "Ministry . . . determined to Carry the Point and bring the Coloneys into a Compliance by force," if necessary by starving them: "you gentlemen of the Congress are the means and [sic] God to set free the whole English Nation on both Sides the Water." She predicted a revolution at home before October. The task of the next Continental Congress would be to

> shew the World that the wisdom and honesty of the Congress and the Coloneys all to joyn in one heart to Improve yon Land and to attend to Her Improvement of the Land and Blessing God has gave you and keep America a Land of Refuge to fly unto from opression and tyraney [sic].

She wished for several reasons to aid the cause herself. First she felt a strong attachment to the country: "I Rejoyce in being Born and Educated in America and hope soon to See that Land of Blessings and Enjoy the free undefil'd Air of a Blessed Climate and a Virtuous people." She rejoiced, too, in living at a historic if turbulent time, "to know many of the gentlemen in the Congress and am not a Silent Spectator in the grand works of Providence." "Women," she also believed, "are always useful in Grand Events." As a token of her serviceableness, she sent Dickinson some useful, she hoped, information to pass on to the Congress: A bishop was to be sent to New York, which was to have a new charter; a fleet was preparing to sail with a new model cannon (whose dimensions she gave). For Dickinson's own use, she promised to send a list of all his friends and enemies in England. She asked little in return but that he draw impeachment proceedings against Lord North.[8]

The Intolerable Acts, the closing of Boston, and the calling of the Continental Congress created not only radical firebrands but also, for the first time since the Stamp Act, a large, outspoken, literate counter-resistance. Before 1774, the bulk of political verses, skits, and caricaturas expressed the radical viewpoint. As the ever-more-unyielding tone of the radicals became adamant in the congressional debates and resolves, it catalyzed conservative derision and scorn. By early 1775, the Philadelphia printer William Bradford was writing off to James Madison hoping to get some radical verse "to counterbalance several satires that have been published this way against the Congress & the patriotic party." [9]

Many conservatives accused supporters of Congress of a disloyalty conceived in confusion. In December, John Holt replaced the nine-part severed snake on his *New-York Journal*—introduced shortly after the Port Bill—with a single snake emblematic of unity, looped over itself like a pretzel, its tail in its mouth. The body read "United Now Free and Alive Firm on this Basis Liberty Shall Stand," referring to an image inside the main loop: a liberty pillar standing on Magna Carta. James Rivington, who had ridiculed Holt's earlier device, and whose own *Gazetteer* now displayed the royal arms of Great Britain, flung back at "Neighbor HOLT" his "EMBLEMATICAL TWISTIFICATION" as an accurate image of his muddleheadedness:

> 'Tis true, JOHNNY HOLT, you have caus'd us some pain,
> by changing your HEAD-PIECE again and again;
> But then to your praise it may justly be said,
> You have given us a Notable TAIL-PIECE instead.
> 'Tis true, that the ARMS of a good *British King*,
> Have been forc'd to give way to a SNAKE—with a STING;
> Which some would interpret, as tho' it imply'd,
> That the KING by a wound of that SERPENT had died.
> But now must their Malice all sink into Shade,
> By the HAPPY Device which you lately display'd;
> And TORIES themselves be convinc'd you are slander'd,
> Who see you've ERECTED the RIGHT ROYAL STANDARD.[10]

Other radical 'twistifications' were satirized in *A Cure for the Spleen* (Boston, 1775), a skit by the attorney general of Massachusetts, Jonathan Sewall. Sewall exposed the illogic by which the lowering of the price of tea became a "mighty grievance": "who would not fight," one character asks, "rather than be deprived of the liberty of paying treble price for what they buy?" The more shrewd humor the radicals for the sake of business. A barber jests that he would *"trim Lord North"* and "rattle[s] away upon grievances, opposition, rebellion and so on, only for the innocent purpose of supporting the credit of my shop." The more pompous mouth radical confusions for the sound. In language close to that of the Suffolk Resolves, Sewall took off a besotted Massachusetts representative, lacing his tired principles with garbled Greek and doses of the forefathers:

> . . . why has not Lord *North* and Lord *Hilsboro* and that *George Greenville [sic]*
> stript us of all our constitutional charter rights and privileges—the birth-right

of Englishmen, which our pious fore-fathers purchased with their blood and treasure, when they came over into this waste howling wilderness. . . . before I'd give up our just rights and privileges, I'd take my gun, and load and fire and pull trigger like the nation and fight up to the knees in blood. . . . By your leave sir, I'll make bold to take a drink of your cyder.

Sewall traced the "epidemical frenzy" of pseudo-Whig blathering to popular leaders, who befuddle then manipulate the ignorant. "The people are told by their oracles . . . their chains are rivetted, and such kind of trumpery." By using "the language of vile seducers," the radicals hope to take the country for themselves.

Mostly the conservatives trained their newly found voice on the congressional delegates. Invariably they presented the congressmen as illiterate, ambitious, and usually drunk demagogues, hopelessly incompetent in politics, who seek to establish the form of government suited to their political incompetence, a lower-class democracy. In one verse dialogue, the political pretensions of a southern delegate are questioned by his sober wife:

> . . . I fear Child thou'rt drunk,
> Dost thou think thyself, Deary, a *Cromwel*, or *Monck?*
> Dost thou think that wise Nature meant thy shallow Pate,
> To digest the important Affairs of a State?

Another writer brought forth Liberty to warn that those who would call a second Congress were using Pennsylvania to mature the seditious imp of democracy hatched in Massachusetts:

> Can public Virtue by me stand,
> See Faction stalking through the Land?—
> Faction that Fiend begot in Hell—
> In *Boston* nurs'd—here brought to dwell
> By *Congress*, who, in airy Freak,
> Conven'd to plan a *Republick?* [11]

The liveliest execrations against the delegates appeared in *The Patriots of North-America: A Sketch*, possibly by Myles Cooper, published in New York in February by Rivington. The writer treated the Congress as blasphemers and singers of bawdy songs; "Tyrants in Garb, of Freedom clad" intent "On Rapes, Adult'ry, Spoils, and Blood"; cobblers, tinkers, and butchers who, "Form'd for the Oar, the Sledge, the Saw,/ Yet rave, of Government, and Law"; democrats who would destroy all rightful authority "Till Pow'r supreme, to Bakers devolves,/ And every Suckling, lisps Resolves." The writer's special target, however, was the delegates' oracular claim to speak in the name of the unforeseeable, to "Pierce thro' dark Night, with gummy

Eyes,/ And see an Empire, vast arise." To give authority to their futuristic rhetoric they twistify John Locke. Locke had shown that no perfect government can exist, since man is imperfect; yet the delegates

> As Casuists false, as Savage rude,
> With Glosses weak, with Comments crude,
> Pervert thy [Locke's] fair, instructive Page,
> To Sanctify, licentious Rage;
> To form, some wild, ideal Plan,
> And break the Laws, of God, and Man.

Wild-eyed idealists, the Congress condemns British government by the standard of an unattainable utopia.

Several writers lambasted the most important measure which the Congress adopted, the Continental Association. Providing for non-importation, non-consumption, and non-exportation, the Association decreased the value of English imports in America between 1774 and 1775 by 90 percent, and set a major precedent for colonial union. Here conservatives saw at work not the daft idealism of common rebels but the scheming of exploitative merchant princes. Speaking as a poor Irishman, one versifier damned the delegates as rich, college-bred snobs who do not "care a f--t" whether the Association ruins the poor or risks an Algerine takeover of New York and a consequent circumcising of the inhabitants:

XXII.

> Their merchants, they think war fine fun,
>   For they keep out of sight;
> They feel no sword, nor hear no gun,
>   But help pay troops to fight.

XXIII.

> Therefore they often, hand o'er head,
>   Into a war will souse,
> And when news comes of thousands dead,
>   They mind it not a louse.

"Bob Jingle" of New York, author of *The Association*, noted that "*of late,* Versification *is come in vogue, and now* Proclamations, Speeches, Messages, Orations, &c. *seem not to be relished in plain prose, but, to please the public* Taste, *they must be* versified." For this reason he parodied in verse each article of the Association. One article of agreement provided that the importation of slaves, and all commerce with those who continued in the slave trade, would halt on December 1. Where, Bob Jingle asked, would labor come from?

> . . . *secondly,* we do protest, vow and swear,
> That we from the Slave-Trade, will wholly forbear;

Tobacco and Indigo, Rice, we may have,
Without the Assistance of one Negro-Slave;
The *Britons* will gladly come over and work,
Tho' we use them as hard as a Jew or a Turk;
But if not, never fear, we can do well enough,
Our *poor Folks* can labour, when stript to the Buff;
And sure in the Cause of *American Freedom*,
They will not refuse to be *Slaves*, if *we* need 'em. . . .[12]

One measure adopted by the Association had serious cultural consequences. As parodied by "Bob Jingle,"

We'll see no *Horse-racings*, nor e'en a *Cock-fight*,
Our only Diversion to eat, sleep, and sh - te. . . .

He had in mind the sumptuary measure by which the Congress—seemingly inspired by an act of the Massachusetts legislature during the Townshend crisis, and perhaps aware of the resentment toward Douglass' new theatre in Charleston—moved to expressly discourage public amusements. On October 18, the delegates struck directly at the American Company. They resolved:

8. We will, in our several stations, encourage frugality, economy, and industry, and promote agriculture, arts and the manufactures of this country, especially that of wool; and will discountenance and discourage every species of extravagance and dissipation, especially all horse-racing, and all kinds of gaming, cock-fighting, exhibition of shews, plays, and other expensive diversions and entertainments. . . .

Douglass was in Philadelphia with a few of his actors during the session of Congress. The resolution was conveyed to him in a letter from the president of Congress, Peyton Randolph.[13]

Officially marked for non-consumption by the united colonies, Douglass gave up. He had closed his Charleston season by announcing that he would soon return with "a theatrical force hitherto unknown in America." Instead he added one last "hitherto unknown" to the many he had failed to deliver in a decade of frustrated trying. On February 2, 1775, he shipped aboard the *Sally* for Jamaica, for good. His customary box in the Philadelphia newspapers advertised the magician "Signor Falconi." The Company scattered. Lewis Hallam and John Henry went to London, where Henry acted Othello at Drury Lane, and Hallam appeared with his sister Mrs. Mattocks in *Hamlet*. Only Dennis Ryan seems to have stayed in America to buck the congressional resolution.[14]

Drawing together what remained of his troupe—including Nancy Hallam, recently the toast of Annapolis—Douglass opened on July 1,

1775, in Jamaica. A prologue written by the surgeon general of the island
explained the Company's migration:

> The MUSE alarm'd at the loud tempest's roar,
> Seeks an asylum on this peaceful shore. . . .

As inhabitants of another outpost of the British Empire, the audience
shared many of the hopes which activated the colonists to the north,
including the hope of Translation. They must have understood how many
flattering promises the speaker of the prologue compressed into his salute
to the Muses:

> Long may they flourish—long in vigour bloom,
> 'Till fair JAMAICA rival *Greece* and *Rome!* [15]

29. Lexington, Concord,
Bunker's Hill: April–June 1775

Following Parliament's declaration in February that some colonies were
in a state of rebellion, Lord North requested more troops for America and
further restraints on New England's trade. Lord Dartmouth urged
Governor Gage in Boston to arrest the leaders of the Massachusetts
Provincial Congress. Instead, Gage sent a secret mission to destroy the
artillery, ammunition, tents, and other military stores which the radicals
had accumulated at Concord.

Always looking out for suspicious troop movements, the radicals caught
on to Gage's operation. Joseph Warren, a prominent Boston physician
who had drafted the Suffolk Resolves, sent Paul Revere on April 16 to
Lexington, to warn John Hancock and Samuel Adams that Gage might be
planning their arrest. Two evenings later, the radical watch observed other
suspicious troop movements. Warren sent Revere to alarm Concord.
Meanwhile, in pitch darkness, about 700 troops under Colonel Francis
Smith and Major John Pitcairn set out from Boston. Near sunrise the
advance guard arrived in Lexington, where they confronted about seventy
armed men on the green. Although no one, apparently, intended it, a
battle occurred, killing eight Americans and wounding ten others in its few
minutes. Smith's force moved on to Concord, six miles away. Instead of
supplies, most of which had been hidden or sent out of town, they found
three or four hundred colonists opposing them across the North Bridge.
When the colonists started toward the bridge, with fifes and drums, the

British regulars began firing. In the brief exchange, three troops and two Americans were killed.

The real battle—at least in the rebel view—began as the British troops started to return to Boston. About a mile outside of Concord they encountered the minutemen who had earlier fought at the bridge, joined by men from other towns. Under cover of houses, fences, and trees, the colonists shot at the troops all along the return route to Lexington. At Lexington, the regulars were met by a reinforcement of 1,400 men and two cannon under General Hugh Percy. The cannon were turned on the provincials, including those sheltered in the Lexington meeting house, which came under fire. As this enlarged force retreated from Lexington to Boston, it too became prey to snipers, who raked it with gunshot throughout the sixteen-mile march. The troops reached Boston at dusk, exhausted and mauled.[1]

Night and day express riders rapidly dispatched news of the surprising chase to the other colonies. A detailed pictorial account came later in the year, from Amos Doolittle, a twenty-one-year-old New Haven silversmith and music engraver whose shop stood near Yale College. After word of Lexington and Concord reached New Haven late on April 21, Benedict Arnold, then a local bookseller, called out his militia company to join other units gathering in and around Cambridge. Arnold's company included Doolittle, who during his month's stay in Cambridge went to Lexington and Concord to sketch the locales, apparently getting descriptions of the fighting from an eyewitness. Yet when his four plates were advertised in the *Connecticut Journal* (at six shillings the set, eight shillings colored), they were said to be "from original Paintings taken on the Spot." A nineteenth-century engraver who knew Doolittle stated that these were the work of the young Connecticut painter Ralph Earl, and that Doolittle himself acted as a model for several of the figures. Not long ago one of Earl's canvases turned up, a view of Concord with Pitcairn and Smith in tomato-red uniforms and yellow breeches, standing in the graveyard. Whether Doolittle took his scene from first-hand observation of the place and secondhand knowledge of the action or simply copied Earl's paintings, his detailed engravings agree with contemporary verbal accounts of the battles. Esthetically, the engravings are crude: horses with human faces, human faces that seem cubist developments, frozenly horn-shaped jets of blood, swatches of color overflowing the outlines, the British troops scarcely more than rubber stamps. Although primitively made and now exceedingly scarce (only six sets being known), the engravings hung in American parlors throughout the eighteenth century.[2]

Numbered one to four chronologically, the plates are entitled *The Battle of Lexington, April 19ᵗʰ 1775*; *A View of the Town of Concord*; *The Engagement at the North Bridge in Concord*; and *A View of the South Part of Lexington*. Doolittle keyed important personages, groups, and buildings to a legend on each print. In the first scene, Major Pitcairn, mounted, commands a party of redcoats to fire, across the barren green, on the Lexington provincials. Doolittle effectively contrasts the ranked-and-filed troops with the sprawling, grimacing, helter-skelter dead and wounded. In the background, regular companies marching to Concord pass the Lexington meeting house. The second plate—matching the extant painting by Earl—shows Pitcairn and Colonel Smith viewing from the cemetery the provincials mustering on an east hill of Concord; they stand amid waist-high gravestones observing the minutemen through a glass. In the distance behind them lies the town, troops entering and closing ranks. At the left a detachment destroys military stores.

The third plate depicts the battle at the bridge, seen from what would later be Emerson's Old Manse (ill., p. 342). Regulars at the right and provincials at the left, each group under a bubblebath of smoke, exchange shots across the smokeless bridge. Some British troops have already begun retreating. The last print shows Smith's brigade retreating down the Lexington-Arlington road, being met by Percy's brigade. Provincials crouched behind a stone wall fire on Percy's flank guard, exposed in a plowed field. It may not be fanciful to see the hand of a music engraver in the staff-like arrangement of parallel stone walls, the British troops marching like braces of thirty-second notes across the fields. A cannon drawn up on a wooded hillock points at the Lexington meeting house; three houses in the village are afire, sending up sky-high plumes of smoke. Each print in the series gives a bird's-eye view of a large area with hundreds of diminutive figures. The result is highly objective, reportorial, apart from psychology or propaganda. Perhaps the most immediate effect is of unorganized civilians in greatcoats, jerkins, and other everyday garb, each for himself, battling vastly greater numbers of identically clothed, symmetrically ranked British troops.

If Doolittle's rendering of the event was neutral, the title of a verse broadside published in Salem made its meaning—as the rebels saw it—brutally clear: *A Bloody Butchery . . . or, the Runaway Fight of the Regulars.* Simple rustics had forced 1,800 British troops to run a sixteen-mile gauntlet, in which, by one estimate, they killed 73, wounded 174, and left 26 missing. As parodists exposed British proclamation-ese for arrogant babytalk, snipers along the march from Concord to Boston exposed British military pride for empty swagger. "Paddy" exulted in the humiliation of the troops:

> How brave you went out with muskets all bright,
> And thought to befrighten the folks with the sight;

> But when you got there how they powder'd your pums,
> And all the way home how they pepper'd your bums,
> And is it not, honies, a comical farce,
> To be proud in the face, and be shot in the a-se.[3]

One important consequence of the colonists' vindictive satisfaction was to invert the meaning of "Yankee Doodle," which from a song of derision became a song of defiance. As we have seen, the music was used as a marching tune by British troops; the earliest datable texts go back to the French and Indian War. The song had become popular during the Townshend period, when it appeared in Barton's comic opera *The Disappointment*, and was played aboard the fleet sent from Halifax to protect the Boston customs officials, and by military bands in Boston— seemingly to show contempt for provincial rusticity. It retained this meaning during the early 1770's. *The Procession*, a satire published in 1770 against the New York Son of Liberty Alexander McDougall, includes an air designated "Yankee Doodle," which compares McDougall's allegedly gross physique to "Daddy's swingeing *Hog-Trough*" and condemns his cunning use of Whig slogans:

> O *Glory* is a pretty Toy,—
> 'T is *that* for which I bawl so;
> And *Freedom*, Friends, a clever Thing,
> And *Liberty* is—*also.*
> > *Yankee doodle,* &c.

> 'T is like the Tune of Fiddle Strings,
> Or *Jotham's* Banjo rather;
> It is a SOUND worth Twenty Pound,
> "To *call the Folks together.*"
> > *Yankee doodle,* &c.

Several weeks before Lexington and Concord, the tune was played by British soldiers as they marched to Salem to destroy some powder supplies.[4] So far, "Yankee Doodle" was a British army tune.

In March, however, some troops in Boston stripped a man naked, tarred and feathered him, and paraded him through town with fife and drum, his back labeled "AMERICAN LIBERTY, OR A SPECIMEN OF DE-MOCRACY." They increased the indignity by playing "Yankee Doodle." This episode stayed in mind when, shortly after, "Yankee Doodle" was played amid the 1,400 British troops and two cannon sent from Boston to join Smith and Pitcairn. According to one newspaper account of Lexington and Concord, the troops' flight under an unrelieved hail of rebel snipers disposed them less to deride provincial manners:

> When the Second Brigade [Percy's] marched out of *Boston* to reinforce the First [at Lexington; Doolittle's Plate 4], nothing was played by the Fifes and

Drums but *Yankee Doodle*, (which had become their favourite tune ever since that notable exploit, which did such *honour* to the Troops of *Britain's* King, of tarring and feathering a poor countryman in *Boston*, and parading with him through the principal streets, under arms, with their bayonets fixed.) Upon their return to *Boston*, one asked his brother officer how he liked the tune now? "Damn them, (returned he,) they made us dance it till we were tired." Since which Yankee Doodle sounds less sweet to their ears.

Apparently the radicals began to sing and play the song as their own to emphasize the magnitude of the British defeat. The sudden reversal of meaning is caught in the title of the first published version of the music and words, *Yankee Doodle, or (as now Christened by the Saints of New England) The Lexington March.* Published in London around the summer of 1775, this is not yet the version of the song familiar to most Americans:

> Dolly Bushel let a Fart,
> Jenny Jones she found it,
> Ambrose carried it to Mill
> Where Doctor Warren ground it.

(For the more familiar version, and further evolution of the meaning see the next section.) At this stage in its history, "Yankee Doodle" may well have fallen out of use as a British marching song.[5]

The process by which Lexington and Concord transformed the political value of "Yankee Doodle" is not uncommon. The Dutch, for instance, played English tunes derisively in operations against the British in the seventeenth century. Yet the history of "Yankee Doodle" remains somewhat obscure. The colonists themselves puzzled over its origins. Jeremy Belknap recorded in 1789 having heard that it was an old English ballad, perhaps as old as "Chevy Chase." The word "doodle" may be a corruption of "do little" (i.e., a simpleton), or it may derive from the "tootling" of German flutes. "Doodle" in the slang meaning of penis survives in some gamier versions of the song, and in some modern folksongs. In *The Disappointment*, "Yankee Doodle" is sung in a brothel by a "cock-a-dandy" to his "diddling honey." In Joseph Atkinson's *A Match for a Widow*, an English play written in the 1780's, an American character claims that his countrymen are "chaste in our thoughts" and think the phrase "a *doodle of hay*, more decent than to call a thing a *cock of hay*, swamp me."[6] The meaning of "Yankee" remains similarly obscure and was similarly subject to speculation at the time. A writer in the *Virginia Gazette* in June 1775—when, like the song, the word seems to have become widely used—derived "Yankee" from a New England Indian tribe, the "Yankoos," meaning invincible. Having been subdued, the Indians "transferred their name to their conquerors." For a while New Englanders were called

Yankoos; but "from a corruption, common to names in all languages, they got through time the name of Yankees. A name which we hope will soon be equal to that of a Roman. . . ." The etymology, probably incorrect in fact, was certainly true in spirit. The penultimate stage in the history of "Yankee Doodle" was part of the larger process of retaliatory emulation— defiance and counterdefiance, song-parody-parody parodized, tit for tat—in which the colonists this time had the last word.

Many provincials who had pursued the British from Lexington back to Boston fanned out around the city. Their numbers increased when, four days after the fighting, the Massachusetts Provincial Congress voted to call 30,000 men to arms. By June the camps around Boston contained about 15,000 rebels. On June 12, General Gage issued a proclamation, written by the literary General Burgoyne, who had arrived in Boston in May with Generals Henry Clinton and William Howe. The proclamation ridiculed how the encamped rebels "affected to hold the army besieged" in Boston, and promised "fulness of Chastisement." At the same time Gage offered to pardon those who laid down their arms, except Sam Adams and John Hancock. Anyone who failed to lay down arms he proclaimed a rebel. Parodists relished still another chance to mimic Gage's (actually Burgoyne's) impudent bluster, and to refurbish the image of Gage—popular since the Townshend Acts—as at once condescending, cowardly, and murderous. In *A New Proclamation!* by John Trumbull, Gage chatters about the "little mischiefs" his troops "had done,/ But kill'd eight men at Lexington," and chides the colonists for joining in resistance:

> What dreadful crimes you've been committing,
> 'Gainst parliament and crown of Britain,
> Denied their sacred rights to these,
> Of calmly robbing whom they please,
> And trait'rously combin'd your forces
> To save your consciences and purses. . . .

Another parodist took off Gage's offer to pardon everyone but Adams and Hancock as another call, howbeit gracious, for passive nonresistance to Pope-like authority:

> . . . every other mother's son,
> The instant he destroys his gun
> (For thus doth run the king's command)
> May, if he will, come kiss my hand.[7]

Few if any of the armed provincials ringing Boston took up Gage's offer. Far from that, they received a commander-in-chief, George Washington, appointed in June by the Second Continental Congress.

Gage himself, however he scoffed at those who "affected" to besiege him, realized he was hemmed in. Early in June he decided to seize the strategic points of Dorchester Heights and Charlestown Heights. Again the radicals caught wind of his plan. On June 15, the Committee of Safety called for the occupation of Bunker's Hill, the 110-foot high point of the Charlestown peninsula, and of nearby Breed's Hill, where redoubts would threaten the British hold on Boston. On June 17, a clear summer day, British troops assaulted Bunker's Hill. Before the assault, they fired "hot shot" on Charlestown to drive out snipers, and perhaps to give the advancing troops a smokescreen. The shot set fire to the town. As Bostonians watched from their roofs and steeples, the emplaced provincials during two and a half hours of combat survived three British charges, killing many of their attackers. Some used bullets made from the melted lead pipes of the Christ Church organ in Cambridge. During the fighting, in one form or another, "Yankee Doodle" was played. Ultimately the British troops swarmed over the hill and bayoneted the provincials off. Altogether about 450 provincials were killed, wounded, or captured. British casualties amounted to over a thousand—nearly half the attacking force.[8]

At least three artists depicted the bloody battle. The Connecticut painter Winthrop Chandler recreated the action on a wooden panel, probably as a fireboard. Although crudely drawn, topographically inaccurate, and historically fanciful, it is a minutely detailed and passionate panorama, seen from Breed's Hill, of flags, steeples, riderless horses, erupting cannon, men flailing in the water or clinging to the rigging of ships, Charlestown under bombardment and already in flames. Two engravings offered a more factual account: *A Correct View of the Late Battle at Charlestown June 17th 1775*, a mezzotint by Robert Aitken, publisher of the *Pennsylvania Magazine*; and *An Exact View of the Late Battle at Charlestown June 17th 1775* by Bernard Romans, a mapmaker and military engineer present at both Lexington and Bunker's Hill. Issued simultaneously, the prints may have resulted from a deliberate collaboration. In design and detail, they resemble each other as much as do the earlier Pelham and Revere engravings of the Boston Massacre. Both give an oddly neat view of the battle. British and Americans are lined up with mechanical precision firing at each other on the hill; in the right distance smoke rises from Charlestown. Like the Doolittle series, the Bunker's Hill engravings lack propagandistic comment as well as social and psychological detail. They consist of rafts of identical sticklike figures, boxlike houses, and spidery bayonets. The result is a flat, two-dimensional effect closer to folk art than to the work of untrained professionals. Aitken shows the provincials drawn up in close order, like the more disciplined British, perhaps a deliberate reflection of the fact that Bunker's Hill already engaged some trained militia units. A month after his print appeared, however, a continental officer wounded in the battle wrote that it "ought never to go abroad— there is not a single Representation but is *very* erronious. Our little Fortification was on the right more than half way between Charlestown Ferry and Mistic River, he has placed it on the left. . . ." [9]

Bunker's Hill, many felt, at last revealed the depth of Gage's cynicism. It was he, they believed, who ordered the burning of Charlestown with its 300 houses. Actually, Howe ordered the firing and also proposed leading the troops while Gage remained at headquarters to be available for reinforcement and for dealing with emergencies. A parodist, however, took Gage's behind-scenes role for cowardice:

> I can, like *Jemmy* at the *Boyne*,
> Look safely on—fight you, *Burgoyne;*
> And mowe *[sic]*, like grass, the rebel *Yankees,*
> I fancy not these *doodle* dances. . . .

The battle produced, in addition to its comic butt, its hero—Dr. Joseph Warren. A featured speaker at public commemorations of the Boston Massacre, an official in the Masons, and a friend of the Adamses, Warren was shot through the face during the final charge on the hill and, according to Abigail Adams, decapitated by British officers, who carried his head to General Gage.[10]

Lexington, Concord, and Bunker's Hill accelerated a process of hero-formation which had surged at the time of the First Continental Congress, partly in the belief that panegyrical poems and engravings excited patriotic effort. As Americans once were offered pictures of William Pitt, the *Boston Gazette* advertised for sale on March 27 "A fine Mezzotinto Print of that truly worthy Patriot S.[amuel] A.[dams]." The unspoken message of the print was verbalized the same month when the *Royal American Magazine* published a poem "Humbly INSCRIBED to Mr. S. A - - - S": "we have Cato's, Hampden's, of our own." Warren's fate immediately produced *Lines Sacred to the Memory of the Late Major-General Joseph Warren* (Providence, 1775) and *An Elegy, Occasion'd by the Death of Major-General Joseph Warren* (Watertown, 1775). One writer in the *New England Chronicle* imagined Warren the provincial physician joining a historic company:

> Immortal Hampden leads the awful band,
> And near him Raleigh, Russel, Sidney stand;
> With them each Roman, every Greek whose name
> Glows high recorded in the roll of fame,
> Round *Warren* press, and hail with glad applause,
> This early victim in fair Freedom's cause. . . .[11]

Like the verses on Adams, those on Warren emphasized the hero's enthusiastic reception by some pantheon, as if Lexington, Concord, and Bunker's Hill, at one stroke, had dispelled provinciality and second-rateness.

Other verse on Bunker's Hill bespoke a new intensity of estrangement between Britain and her American colonies. Even with the Boston Massacre, not much blood had flowed until the events of the spring and fall, which killed and wounded as many as 2,000 people. Some Americans now perceived the British troops who fired upon them as a different race. The author of a very popular mock-British army song imagined the savage thoughts of a British soldier:

> Some People in the Town did say,
>   (Poor Rogues their Hearts were quaking)
> We went to kill their Countrymen,
>   As they their Hay were making.
> But such damn'd Whigs I never saw,
>   To hang them all I'd rather,
> Or mow their Hay with Musket-Balls
> And Buck-Shot mix'd together.

Once disinherited children, the Americans were becoming mere enemies. As their disaffection hardened to hate they blamed, for the first time, the king. Instead of picturing again a cabal of ministers intercepting colonial entreaties to the throne, "Philoleutheros Americanus" presented Lord North telling George III

> 'Tis my opinion and my great desire,
> That all America be set on fire,
> Unless they will submit to you and me,
> Though my design is lawless tyranny.

Estrangement brought with it a sense of fatefulness, reflected in the appearance of classic broadside ballads. As distinguished from songs, ballads are objective rather than subjective; instead of expressing a state of mind they narrate some memorable event, usually advancing chronologically in four-line stanzas of simple diction and close rhymes. A broadside *On the Bloody engagement that was Fought on Bunker's Hill in Charlestown*, by the minister Elisha Rich, begins in classic ballad style:

> AMERICANS pray lend an Ear
> And you a solemn Tale shall hear
> 'Twas on the seventeenth of JUNE,
> Men were cut down all in their bloom.

Flat, unadorned, concerned with telling a tale of blood rather than propagandizing it, Rich's ballad is a verse counterpart of Doolittle's engravings:

> They fought like brave MEN on both sides,
> And many a valiant HERO dy'd,
> The Earth was soaked with their blood,
> And wounded wallow'd in the Flood.

What such works convey is a new acceptance of tragic inevitability.[12]

These strains of alienation, outrage, and fatalism are blended in the best of the Bunker Hill works, Nathaniel Niles's *The American Hero: A Sapphick Ode*. First published in 1775 as a broadside in Norwich, Connecticut, and then widely reprinted, it became known simply as "Bunker Hill." It was sung to—and cannot be appreciated apart from—a beautiful and grave tune by the Connecticut singing master Andrew Law:

Probably written just after the destruction of Charlestown, the ode eloquently combines Puritan piety and Whig sentiment. The inescapable certainty of death becomes ground for ultimate political sacrifice. Since death must come, let it come in a good cause:

1.

WHY should vain Mortals tremble at the Sight of
Death and Destruction in the Field of Battle,
Where Blood & Carnage clothe the Ground in Crimson,
    Sounding with Death-Groans?

2. Death will invade us by the Means appointed,
And we must all bow to the King of Terrors.

This Puritan scorn for affliction produces a battle poem comparable to
some Anglo-Saxon and Old Scandinavian works in its grim readiness for
combat death. To the "Torturing AEther" of grapeshot, the naval
bombardment "horrible to Nature," the "Blood-Hounds, nam'd the
British Lyons," the speaker returns unflinching vaunts: "Now, *Mars*, I dare
thee"—"*War*, I defy thee." The ode resembles Anglo-Saxon verse also in
its distinctive use of alliteration. The strongly stressed d's and s's thud and
hiss like muffled drums and tambourines, "Dauntless as Death-stares":

13. Still shall the Banner of the King of Heaven
Never advance where I'm afraid to follow:
While that precedes me with an open Bosom,
    War, I defy thee.

14. Fame and dear Freedom *lure* me on to Battle,
While a fell Despot, grimer *[sic]* than a Death's-Head,
Stings me with Serpents, fiercer than Medusa's,
    To the Encounter.

15. Life, for my Country and the Cause of Freedom,
Is but a Trifle for a worm to part with;
And if preserved in so great a Contest,
    Life is redoubled.

As a rich and influential musical-literary summary of its moment, *The
American Hero* belongs with John Dickinson's "Liberty Song," CHESTER,
and "Yankee Doodle."

Its message, however, was not to be steady, trusting in God, or proud,
but to risk everything.

30. The Siege of Boston: July 1775–March 1776

Despite the mood of imminence, what followed Bunker's Hill were nine months of static confrontation. The British troops inside Boston and the armed provincials outside clashed during occasional patrol actions and exchanged cannonades. But mostly they watched each other, their numbers growing. The provincials hoped to keep the British locked in the city, preventing military adventures into the countryside; the British, uncertain what to do next, were unwilling to end the occupation lest they seem to have been driven out.

Only days before Bunker's Hill, the Continental Congress in Philadelphia had adopted the American force around Boston as a Continental Army, to be commanded by George Washington. He arrived in Cambridge on July 2, 1775, and officially took control of the troops before the Harvard College walls. Until the year before, Washington had not been prominent in the colonial opposition. As a young man he had acquired a military reputation for fighting the French in the Ohio Valley; but since the 1750's he had essentially been a businessman. It was as a planter and a holder of western lands that he became increasingly disgusted with British commercial policy. By 1774 he was bellicose. After learning of the Boston Port Bill he offered to raise a thousand-man army at his own expense and march them to Boston; before leaving Virginia as a delegate to the First Continental Congress he worked to organize a Virginia military company independent of the royal governor's militia; at the second Congress, he alone among the delegates appeared in military uniform.[1] His radicalism, his earlier military record, his impressive bearing and figure, and the fact that he came from Virginia (which might strengthen the South's attachment to New England's plight) all recommended him as commander-in-chief of the Continental Army.

Washington's new role made him, instantaneously, a magnetic symbol of patriot hopes. By the fall of 1775, Americans began naming their children "George Washington."[2] While the general became a gathering point, however, the man remained diffuse. Washington first appears in American poetry without personal qualities, as nothing more than a magical name, always set in capitals to signify its powerful preeminence. A popular song entitled, in one of its several versions, "Gen. WASHING-TON" equated the commander with the provincial military hold on Boston:

> Your dark, unfathom'd councils—our weakest heads defeat,
> Our children rout your armies—our boats destroy your fleet!

And to complete the dire disgrace, coop'd up within a town,
You live the scorn of all our host! the slaves of WASHINGTON!

Philip Freneau apostrophized Washington in 1775 as the equal of great classical warriors:

See WASHINGTON New Albion's freedom owns,
And moves to war with half Virginia's sons;
Bold in the fight, whose actions might have aw'd
A Roman Hero, or a Grecian God;
He, he, as first, his gallant troops shall lead,
Undaunted man, a second Diomede,
As when he fought at wild Ohio's flood,
When savage thousands issu'd from the wood. . . .[3]

Freneau's assurance that Caesar or Ares might have stood in awe of Washington rested on nothing more dramatic than Washington's military career twenty years ago and his organization of troops in Virginia. Indeed the assurance owed less to Washington's proven abilities than to the eighteenth-century debate between the Ancients and Moderns, in which disciples of progress often gathered evidence to show that the capacity for heroism had not degenerated in modern times. In fact, most Americans who in 1775 expected everything from Washington knew little about him. As a result, he seems in his first literary appearances at once a demigod and a nonentity.

Washington was quite aware of becoming a hero. At Cambridge in mid-December he received a poem addressed "To his Excellency General Washington," sent to him by the author, Phillis Wheatley. She explained in a covering letter that his appointment "by the Grand Continental Congress to be Generalissimo of the armies of North America" had excited in her "sensations not easy to suppress." Like Washington's other panegyrists, she commended, without specifying his gifts, her hopes for his success plus her ignorance of his character making for nebulous hyperbole:

A crown, a mansion, and a throne that shine,
With gold unfading, WASHINGTON! be thine.[4]

Washington wanted to publish the poem himself, "with a view of doing justice to her poetical genius"; but he laid aside the plan, "not knowing whether it might not be considered rather as a mark of my own vanity, than as a compliment to her. . . ." Instead he sent the poem to Joseph Reed in Philadelphia, who apparently gave it to Tom Paine, who published it in April in the *Pennsylvania Magazine*. Washington also wrote to Phillis Wheatley, thanking her for her "polite notice," praising her "poetical talents," and inviting her to camp: "If you should ever come to

Cambridge, or near head-quarters, I shall be happy to see a person so favored by the Muses. . . ." [5] She did visit Washington at Cambridge in 1776, although no record of the interview survives. The entire episode, occurring while Washington was preoccupied with shaping and maintaining an army, demonstrated a facet of the new commander's personality of which his admirers so far were ignorant: He saw himself as a patron of the arts.

Most Americans had no more definite picture of the new army. Upon arriving in Cambridge, Washington found some 16,000 troops (by his own estimate) spread in an eight- or nine-mile semicircle around Boston. They struck him as dirty, democratical, and shockingly low on public spirit, "a mixed multitude of People . . . under very little discipline, order, or Government." Others perceived the troops differently. Conservatives saw a living proof of radical illogic. Congress had legislated into being itself the most hideous bogeyman of Whig theory, a standing army:

> With poverty and dire distress,
> With standing armies us oppress;
> Whole troops to Pluto swiftly press,
> As victims to the Congress.[6]

Radical writers, however, saw essential differences between the American army and others. The difference they cited most often is dramatized in *The Battle of Bunkers-Hill* (Philadelphia, 1776), the work of Philip Freneau's Princeton classmate Hugh Henry Brackenridge.[7] The play unfolds as a series of parallel scenes in the American and British camps around Boston, culminating in the death of Warren on Bunker's Hill. The juxtapositions reveal the contrasting motives of British regulars and armed provincials. The British fight to preserve their reputation in the world; the Americans fight to preserve freedom and to deserve the sacrifices of their forefathers. Before being shot in the groin, an American officer assures his troops that the lack of a moral reason for fighting must debilitate the British: "A cause of slavery, and civil death,/ Unmans the spirit, and strikes down the soul." The Americans—who in actuality now began to insist and insist on the point—"combat in the cause of God."

In describing other differences between the two armies, radical versifiers idealized the very qualities which dismayed Washington. They glorified the American soldier's unsoldierliness. Such a contrary image existed before the Continental Army itself, shaped by the characteristically provincial preference for 'nature' above 'art.' As early as 1772, James Allen drew a "picture of the American Soldier," likening him to the Indian warrior:

> No art excites, nor martial musick's charms,
> The Soldier's soul to deeds of glory warms,

> Nor hostile Arms emblaze the pompful plain,
> Nor guards their naked front and brazen train,
> Untutor'd these in war's experienc'd school,
> By nature brave, and unoblig'd by rule. . . .

This picture endured. In 1775, Philip Freneau portrayed the American soldier's manly disdain for military dress:

> No fop in arms, no feather on his head,
> No glittering toys the manly warrior had,
> His auburne face the least employ'd his care,
> He left it to the females to be fair. . . .

While the British regular's gaudy uniform betrays effeminacy, his boasted training is merely an efficient use of his innate cruelty. The British boast, one writer said, how "under their hands, war has grown into a science, and that their youngest officers come into the field theoretically instructed in all its horrid principles." [8] The American soldier, as contrastingly seen by Philip Freneau, abhors the use of his "black, rough cannon":

> . . . deeply griev'd, the tears bedew my eyes,
> For this, the greatest of calamities;
> That our keen weapons, meant for other ends,
> Should spend their rage on Britons, once their friends. . . .

The American soldier was a man who did not look like a soldier and who had no wish to fight.

And was not, in fact, a soldier. The metaphors of Whig Sentimentalism remained powerful, casting the soldier as a lover who armed chiefly to fend off seducers, or as a peaceful farmer who yet brought to battle the hardiness and virtue of agrarian life. The author of a published letter, written at the Cambridge camp and addressed "To the American Soldiery," asked his comrades "whether we will see our wives, with every thing that is dear to us, subjected to the merciless rage of uncontrouled despotism"; those attending a dinner given by General David Wooster in New York in the summer of 1775 toasted "The daughters of America in the arms of their brave defenders *only*"; such a defender, another writer foresaw, would one day "receive for his scars and his deeds, a garland, composed by the artless hands of the village maidens." [9] Several newspapers in 1775 printed an item describing General Israel Putnam as "our American Cincinnatus," referring to the Roman farmer-patriot-warrior. The item reported that when Putnam learned of the Battle of Lexington "he was following his plough"; giving one plough-horse to his servant, he rode the other, armed, to Boston. When his opposite number, Burgoyne, was ordered to America, he was probably in "a gambling house or brothel." Thus Philip Freneau reminded the defenders of Boston that "like ancient Romans, you/ At once are soldiers, and are farmers too." [10]

The notion that the American soldier's strength lay not in hardware or training but in his good nature and moral superiority was, needless to say, unrealistic, and its prevalence made practical military legislation difficult. In fact, many of the same poems and essays which expressed this view also quietly cautioned against underestimating the enemy and offered palatable reasons for following his example. The same writer who decried the British officers' study of the "horrid principles" of war proposed that lectures on warfare be given at the American camp, on the ground that they would open "a large field of elegant amusement, [and] mingle the laurels of letters with the wreaths of the warrior." Accustomed for more than a decade to think of peace, Americans obviously found it difficult to think of war.

Among the soldiers camped around Boston were several young men with artistic ambitions. Conspicuous because of his birth and rank was the Connecticut painter John Trumbull, just turned nineteen. His mother was descended from the great Pilgrim leader John Robinson; his father had been a good classics scholar at Harvard and was now the governor of Connecticut. As a child, Trumbull imitated the drawings which his older sisters had been taught to make at a drawing school. Later he asked his father to send him to Boston to study with Copley. The governor was understanding but hardheaded: "I am sensible of his Natural Genius & inclination for Limning," he wrote, "and Art I have frequently told him, will be of no use to him." Determined on a legal or ministerial career for his son, he sent Trumbull to Harvard in January 1772. En route, we have seen, Trumbull stopped at Copley's, shortly after Copley returned from his profitable stay in New York. Trumbull was dazzled by Copley's fashionable clothes and by his painting, which "renewed all my desire to enter upon such a pursuit." [11]

Over the next few years, Trumbull's radicalism and his passion for painting fed on each other. Admitted to the junior class, he had to spend only a year and a half at Harvard. His previous training in Latin and Greek left him time to ransack the Harvard library for books on painting, and to study its set of Piranesi prints and its paintings of presidents and benefactors by Copley. When he returned to Connecticut he attempted history painting on such subjects as the death of Paulus Emilius at the battle of Cannae. Their Whiggish meaning increased his concern over the worsening political situation. "I caught the growing enthusiasm," he recalled; "the characters of Brutus, of Paulus Emilius, of the Scipios, were fresh in my remembrance, and their devoted patriotism always before my eye; besides, my father was now governor of the colony, and a patriot. . . ." [12] He organized a village military unit whose members taught each other to shoot and march. Two weeks after the Battle of Lexington a Connecticut regiment had formed and was on its way to Boston, with Trumbull as adjutant. He viewed through glasses the smoke and fire of the Battle of Bunker's Hill and exchanged fire with British troops.

Washington's arrival in July enhanced Trumbull's position. Just three weeks later, probably out of respect to his prominent father, Trumbull was appointed second aide-de-camp to the new commander. Having some experience in cartography, he drew for Washington a plan of the British works, creeping up to the enemy lines at night through tall grass to count the guns. The distinction and elegance of Washington's entourage impressed him, but he felt unequal to them. Now and later he suffered from the strain of belonging to a highly respected family whose fortune had shrunk to the point of impoverishment. Hungry for preferment, he criticized self-advancement in others. He looked with envious disapproval upon the ex–New Haven bookseller Benedict Arnold, who had received a command to go up the Kennebec and was adept at "wriggling himself into the Generals Favour." [13]

Arnold's stockjobbery, however, seemed to Trumbull typical of the entire army. He found the troops at Roxbury "in a Confus'd State— Officers grumbling about Rank—& soldiers about pay—every one thinking himself ill us'd and impos'd upon." Order did not exist, every subaltern considering himself "better than his Superiors, & can see no reason why such & such a one should be above him, & have higher pay. . . ." The troops who had been designated a Continental Army in June, moreover, were enlisted only until the end of the year. Trumbull felt that Congress would do better to enlist the men "during their Pleasure," offering a handsome bounty for the extended service. Such an army might be disciplined, "which our *summer soldiers* never can be, as they are perpetually shifting—demand^g furlows,—discharges &c.——" Like Washington, he believed the cause was better served by well-trained troops than by well-meaning ploughmen, although his concern was shot through with snobbery: "Were our Officers men of Education & our Soldiers engag'd for a number of Years we should have a power, Capable of resisting Great Britain, tho' assisted by all Europe." [14]

A few young musicians also joined the American camp, where singing was a popular diversion and morale-booster. An aspiring tunesmith named Timothy Swan, aged seventeen, was learning to play the flute, practicing with a military fifer. An aspiring singing master, Jacob French, seems to have been there too; he had been a member of William Billings' school at Stoughton in 1774, before serving at Bunker's Hill. What part they, and perhaps other New England singing masters, played in the singing at camp is uncertain, but with or without them, much was sung. One officer wrote to his wife from Cambridge in July 1775 that after the reading of orders "Corporal Clark sung Hewling's American Hearts of Oak to the sound of the drum and fife. The boys finished up with a minuet." [15] The Cincinnatus-like Major General Putnam could manage a tune as well as a plough; another soldier reported from New York that "there is not a chap in the camp who can lead him in the *Maggie Lauder* song." [16]

Many new songs were written expressly for singing by the troops, giving rise in 1775 to a new genre of 'camp songs' with such titles as *Two Favorite new SONGS at the American Camp* and *A new Liberty Song, Composed at the Camp on Prospect-Hill, August, 1775.* As the last-named title implies, the camp songs were essentially 'liberty songs' applied to 1775, justifying and inspiring the army by applying to it the long-popular themes of the forefathers, encroachment, liberty as a natural right, the ministerial plot, and the need for hand-in-hand effort. Quite in the spirit of John Dickinson's original, the song from the Prospect Hill camp explained:

> Unite, unite, New-England, unite New-England's band,
> If we divide we surely fall, if we unite we stand;
> But let our minds be all as one, and all our minds so free,
> That we had rather bleed and die than lose our liberty.
>
> IX.
> Come all you brave Americans, let's drink a loyal bowl,
> Let the dearest sound of Liberty sink deep in ev'ry soul;
> Here's a health to North-America and all her noble boys,
> Her Liberties and properties, and all that she enjoys.[17]

The above example also suggests how, like the earlier songs, the camp songs depended on refrains, marked rhythms, and boisterous singing to cultivate what John Adams called the "sensations of freedom."

The existence of the American camp provided a new subject to be set to the tune of "Yankee Doodle." The result was the text of the song which has remained closely identified with America. It seems to have come out in several undated, virtually identical broadsides, one entitled *The Farmer and his Son's return from a visit to the CAMP.* The earliest of them must have been published after July 1775, when Washington arrived at camp; almost certainly after January 1776, when he received the heavy artillery described in the text; and probably before March 1776, when the camp broke up. If so, the classic version of the song appeared around February 1776. Its distinguishing features are the visit-to-camp theme, the adolescent narrator, and the chorus:

> Yankey doodle keep it up, yankey doodle dandy,
> Mind the music and the step,
> And with the girls be handy.

The Yankee Doodle with the feather in his cap who rides a pony was a later invention, probably derived from the description in the 1776 version of "captain Washington," who wears "flaming ribbons in his hat" and rides a "slapping stallion."

The author of the 1776 version seems to have been a Harvard sophomore and minuteman named Edward Bangs.[18] He portrayed the new Continental Army through the eyes of a naive farmboy who takes a mortar for a "pumpkin shell," a drum for "a little barrel" and the bustling camp for "the world along in rows." In the darker mood of the last stanzas, he takes the "tarnal deep" trenches for graves and runs home in fright to "mother's chamber." His guilelessness produces not only comic misperceptions but also some unflattering truths. Compared with the people isolated inside Boston, the troops outside are well fed and supplied:

> And there we see a thousand men,
> As rich as 'squire David,
> And what they wasted every day,
> I wish it had been saved.

Like John Trumbull, the narrator is impressed by the finery of Washington, who "got him on his meeting clothes,"

> And gentlefolks about him,
> They say he's grown so tarnal proud,
> He will not ride without them.

The refrain has little to do with the narrator, nor even with the army. Rather, its egging-on of an exuberant country buck reflects the song's long association with sexual and romantic encounters, and gives classic expression to America's mythic youth and energy.

At the same time that the enduring text of the song appeared, the tune received a new genealogy. Americans began to think of it not as a derisive British march which they played back at the British in jubilant spite, but as an American tune originally. Two works discussed later, John Leacock's *Fall of British Tyranny* and the poet John Trumbull's *M'Fingal*, record the change. One of Leacock's characters speculates that the British at Lexington must have played "our favourite tune Yankee Doodle" not in ridicule but in pretended friendship, as a decoy: "they could never mean to ridicule a piece of music, a tune, of which such brutes cannot be supposed to be judges, and, which is allowed by the best masters of music to be a composition of the most sublime kind, and would have done honour to a Handel or a Corellius [*sic.*]" The main character in *M'Fingal* asks whether in playing an American song at Lexington, the British did not show discernment:

Outwent they not each native Noodle
By far in playing Yanky-doodle;
Which, as 'twas your New-England tune,
'Twas marvellous they took so soon?

By ironically claiming "Yankee Doodle" as a native American tune, provincials were acknowledging a narrow truth in the enemy's charge of rusticity, but now claiming it as the basis of a superiority, as if to say 'I am, and I'm proud of it.' If handsomely clothed and smartly trained British troops were oppressors, then homely things were not limitations but virtues. In its self-glorifying self-mockery, "Yankee Doodle" represents the sour triumph of the provincial injunction to 'follow Nature.'

A feeling of superiority was not unwarranted by the situation. As "Yankee Doodle" implies, the British inside Boston were in some ways worse off than the army which enclosed them. The city's population, Washington estimated, had declined from about 17,000 to 7,000, many inhabitants having fled. (Among these may have been Gilbert Stuart, who by one account departed on the last ship to sail for London before the Battle of Bunker's Hill.) The military garrison contained at top strength about 11,000 army and navy personnel. Many still suffered from wounds they had received in June, others had smallpox or scurvy. Unlike the continental troops, they were cut off from supplies of fuel and food and forced to subsist on beans and salt pork. Much criticized for his handling of Bunker's Hill, the hated General Gage had been recalled to England in October. His command went to General Howe, who had arrived in May 1775 along with the American-born Sir Henry Clinton and with "Gentleman Johnny" Burgoyne.[19]

Despite disease and deprivation in the city, the new commanders preserved something of the standards of the British officer corps. Clinton and Howe relished theatre and concert life. Burgoyne was a devoted literary amateur. After marrying the daughter of the extremely wealthy earl of Derby, he studied French language and literature in France, then served as an M.P., gambled heavily, belonged to fashionable clubs, and indulged his fondness for acting and playwriting. The same year that Burgoyne came to Boston, Garrick mounted the general's play *Maid of the Oaks* at Drury Lane. (His later play *The Heiress* [1786] was performed on the Continent and went through ten editions.) Given Burgoyne's interests, Boston would hardly seem to have been an ideal post. British troops stationed there during the Townshend period had tried to produce plays. But the city, of course, lacked a playhouse, and its contempt for the theatre was notorious. The inhabitants, said one British lieutenant, were "too puritanical a set to admit of such lewd Diversions, tho' ther's perhaps no town of its size cou'd turn out more whores than this cou'd." [20]

The occupying army, however, converted many Boston buildings to its own uses: Concert Hall, where Flagg and Selby had played, was changed into a court of inquiry for general courts-martial; Old South Church, where Copley had spoken in behalf of his in-laws, was gutted and turned into a riding school, one of its carved pews becoming a hog-trough (at Burgoyne's request), its partially completed organ stored by members of the congregation. (American troops broke into Anglican Christ Church in Cambridge; witnesses reported seeing the pipes of the church's Snetzler organ strewn in the streets.)[21]

The satisfaction of officerial tastes thus posed no special problem. "Faneuils Hall where [the radicals] used to hold yr Cabals," wrote a British captain, "is now Converted into a Play House." The conversion of Faneuil Hall was not completed until December 2, but there seem to have been performances as early as September. Tickets to the completed theatre cost one dollar for boxes and pit; what remained after paying the expenses of the house went to widows and orphaned children of the soldiers. Among the plays offered were Mrs. Centlivre's comedy *The Busybody*, Rowe's *Tamerlane*, and Aaron Hill's tragedy *Zara*.[22]

The insolent remaking of a Boston radical meeting-hall into a military playhouse was a double wound, which the British kept open. They dispatched playbills to Hancock and Washington. Burgoyne himself—the "scribbling fop," Freneau now called him—wrote a prologue to *Zara*, pointing out how the "Boston Prudes" resembled the Puritan forefathers, who under Cromwell had trammeled freedom and beauty of all kinds: "Then sunk the Stage, quell'd by the Bigot Roar,/ Truth fled with Sense and Shakespear charm'd no more." The British also performed "ridiculous plays," one Bostonian said, in which "our army and its commanders [are] turned into sport." On January 8, 1776, they gave their first performance of a farce entitled *The Blockade of Boston*. The text has not survived, but according to the diarist Dorothy Dudley, it featured "General Washington . . . represented as an uncouth countryman; dressed shabbily, with large wig and long rusty sword. . . ."[23] A bit more of the content can be glimpsed in *A Vaudevil*, a broadside published in Boston in 1776 consisting of several brief songs sung at the conclusion of the play by each of the characters. "Trumore" explains that the farce was written so the troops might "rest on our Arms, call the Arts to our Aid,/ And be merry in Spite of THE BOSTON BLOCKADE." "Fanfan," a Negress, reveals the hypocritical morals of Bostonians:

> Tho' in Public you scoff, I see many a Spark,
> Would tink me a sweet pretty Girl in the Dark.
> Thus merily runs the World on with *Fanfan*,
> I eat good [word illegible] Pork, and get kiss'd by white Man. . . .

The Boston radical leaders, "Doodle" adds, practice the same authoritarianism in politics while proclaiming freedom:

> YE tarbarrell'd Lawgivers, yankified Prigs,
> Who are Tyrants in Custom, yet call yourselves Whigs;
> In return for the Favours you've lavish'd on me,
> May I see you all hang'd upon *Liberty Tree*.

Bostonians may have found it doubly galling to hear themselves scorned from the stage, but they could do little about it. General Burgoyne was no David Douglass to be hounded out of town. Like the citizen of Cambridge quoted in the *Virginia Gazette*, Bostonians could only hope that before the British troops could present the farcical *Blockade*, "*the poor wretches* [would] *be presented with a tragedy called the Bombardment. . . .*" [24]

That very nearly happened. Once again political upheaval became indistinguishable from theatre. On the opening night of *The Blockade of Boston*, January 8, a hundred American soldiers raided Charlestown, burning some British quarters and taking prisoners. Heard in Boston, the firing in Charlestown caused a general alarm. What ensued was reported in several newspapers and diaries. According to the *Middlesex Journal*, the farce had just ended when the actors were told of the American attack,

> upon which one of them came in, dressed in the character of a Yankee sergeant (which character he was to play) desired silence, and informed the audience the alarm guns were fired; that the rebels had attacked the town, and were at it tooth and nail over at Charlestown. The audience thinking this was the opening of the new piece, clapped prodigiously; but soon finding their mistake, a general scene of confusion ensued. They immediately hurried out of the house to their alarm posts; some skipping over the orchestra, trampling on the fiddles, and every one making his most speedy retreat. The actors (who were all officers) calling out for water to wash the smut and paint from off their faces; women fainting, and, in short, the whole house was nothing but one scene of confusion, terror, and tumult.

A British lieutenant stationed in the city gave a slightly different account:

> An orderly sergeant that was standing outside the playhouse door heard the firing and immediately ran into the playhouse, got upon the stage and cried, "Turn out! Turn out! They are hard at it, hammer and tongs." The whole audience thought that the sergeant was acting a part in the farce, and that he did it so well that there was a general clap, and such a noise that he could not be heard for a considerable time. When the clapping was over he again cried, "What the deuce are you all about? If you won't believe me, by Jasus, you need only go to the door, and there you will see and hear both!" If it was the intention of the enemy to put a stop to the farce for that night [which it may well have been] they certainly succeeded, as all the officers immediately left the playhouse and joined their regiments.

By another account, the sergeant who entered the theatre said, "The rebels have attacked the lines on the Neck," or, by still another, "The Yankees are attacking our works on Bunker Hill," after which General Howe ordered "Officers to your alarm posts!" [25]

Ironically, the static confrontation between British and American troops was in fact ending. Only the day before the premiere of *The Blockade*, Colonel Henry Knox, who just a while before had been selling tunebooks at his London Book Store in Boston, arrived at the southern end of Lake George, after an arduous month-long journey from Fort Ticonderoga. He had hauled on ox-drawn sledges across ice and mountains some sixty tons of siege artillery captured at the fort in May by Ethan Allen and Benedict Arnold. With miraculous speed, the first of the forty-three cannon and fourteen mortars arrived in Cambridge before the end of January. On the night of March 4, Washington rapidly mounted the artillery on Dorchester Heights, threatening to destroy Boston and its British garrison.

Howe, unable to elevate his cannon sufficiently to hit Washington's works, concluded that Boston was untenable and decided to evacuate the city. Burgoyne and Clinton had both been urging such a move since the fall, in the belief that New York was a more central base for British operations. An informal agreement existed by which if the Americans allowed the British to carry out the evacuation, Howe would not burn Boston. Yet the departure of the troops was accompanied by a great deal of looting, by charges that they mixed arsenic with the medicine they left in the hospital, and by the blowing up of Castle William in the harbor. On March 17, Howe loaded his men onto ships, taking with him some one thousand sympathetic Bostonians to Halifax, ending the siege.[26] The same day, a detachment of American troops under General Putnam reentered Boston, John Trumbull among them.

As they had done after Lexington and Concord, Americans again rejoiced and jeered at the spectacle of a world turning upside-down—British troops in panicked flight from Yankee Doodles:

> Then hilter skilter they ran in the street,
> Sometimes on their heads and sometimes on their feet,
> Leaving cannon and mortars, pack saddles and wheat,
> Being glad to escape with the skin of their teeth.
>   Now off goes Pilgarlick with his men in a fright,
> And altho' they show cowards, yet still they show spite,
> In burning the Castle, as they pass along,
> And now by Nantasket they lie in a throng.
>   Let 'em go, let 'em go, for what they will fetch,
> I think their great Howe is a miserable wretch;
> And as for his men, they are fools for their pains,
> So let them return to Old-England again.

One of "The King's Own Regulars" tried to put a better face on the retreat:

> That we turned our backs and ran away so fast;
>   don't let that disgrace us,
> 'Twas only to make good what Sandwich said, that the Yankees—
>   could not face us.[27]

Another writer, probably Mercy Warren, answered *The Blockade of Boston* with *The Blockheads: or, the Affrighted Officers. A Farce* (Boston, 1776), an acid skit deriding the feebleness and cowardice of the British military, and the social pretensions of Americans who relied upon them for protection and advancement. The author presented not uncouth Washington in a fright wig, but General Howe ("Shallow") worn out by the impregnability of the American position and the starving times in Boston:

> My *teeth* are worn to stumps, and my *lips* are swell'd like a blubber-mouth negro's, by thumping *hard bones* against them; my *jaw bone* has been set a dozen times, dislocated by chewing *hard pork,* as tough as an old swine's ass.

(Howe, like Washington, had exceptionally bad teeth.) Frustrated and ill-fed, the British also live in fear of Yankee sharpshooters. Burgoyne ("Puff") complains that "A man can scarcely put his nose over the intrenchments without losing it." Americans who side with the British do so from self-contempt, a wish to overcome rusticity and become "great" by gaining office and position. Thus "Simple," a farmer, moves to Boston. His wife disdains "to lead my life like a *mope,* as when we were *rusty farmers*—we are now *gentle-folks*"; farming "is all *dirty stuff,* only fit for *yankees.*" She wants silk gowns, plays, and a London marriage for her daughter Tabitha. What she gets is the redcoat "Dapper," a seducer masking as a beau, and in reality impotent—a frequent element in the emerging image of British troops. Like the other British sympathizers, who vomit aboard the evacuation ship, she ends up in Halifax, cursed by her husband and daughter, living in a barn, eating salt fish. *"Burgoyne,"* one soldier concludes, "could not have contriv'd a *prettier satyr.*"

31. Outside Boston:
Spring 1774–Spring 1776

The departure of British troops ended two years of profound social dislocation in Boston, begun with the return of General Gage in May 1774. In that period, away from the snipers on the Lexington Road and the redoubts on Bunker's Hill, expectations for American culture remained high. In August 1774 and again in November 1775, the *Virginia Gazette* reprinted in its entirety Bishop Berkeley's "Prospect of Arts and Sciences." In fact, until mid-1775, the cultural progress which had brought the Rising Glory poems of 1770, *The Death of General Wolfe*, and *The New-England Psalm-Singer* showed continuing development.

The year 1775 saw the manufacture of the first American piano. Made by the Philadelphia joiner John Behrent, it was advertised as "an extraordinary instrument, by the name of the piano-forte, in mahogany in the manner of a harpsichord." [1] Although the frown of Congress sent Douglass to Jamaica, Americans wrote and published such new plays as Brackenridge's *Battle of Bunker's Hill* and John Leacock's *The Fall of British Tyranny* (Philadelphia, 1776). Presses outside of Boston printed an unusually large number of new volumes of native poetry: in Charleston, Rowland Rugeley's *Story of Aeneas and Dido Burlesqued* (1774), a sustained and accomplished satire of Dido's longing for Aeneas, rowdy and learned; in Williamsburg, Nathaniel Tucker's *The Bermudian* (1774), an autobiographical and descriptive account of a West Indian childhood; in Philadelphia, Thomas Coombe's *Edwin: or the Emigrant* (1775), a Goldsmithian study of the colonial frontier; and John Trumbull's *M'Fingal* (1776, dated 1775), probably the most popular American poem of the eighteenth century. Three days before the evacuation of Boston, the young Connecticut poet Timothy Dwight advertised proposals—ten years prematurely—for printing his epical *Conquest of Canäan*.[2] Particularly auspicious was the launching of the *Pennsylvania Magazine: or, American Monthly Museum*, easily the best literary magazine in the colonies since William Smith's one-year-lived *American Magazine* in 1757. Edited with the assistance of Tom Paine—just three months in America—it promoted the view that England now "supported Venus against the Muses" and that the future of literature lay in America. In addition to scientific and technological treatises, engravings, music, and news, the magazine included a high proportion of original short fiction and poetry by Francis Hopkinson, Phillis Wheatley, and others. With 1,500 subscribers, the fat issues achieved a larger circulation than that of any previous American magazine.

How the recourse to arms might affect Translation remained to be seen. Stunned by the example of Boston, many colonies adopted defensive measures, raising companies, seeing that available weapons worked, training civilians to shoot. Throughout 1775, publishers issued manuals on gunnery and on the treatment of wounds. The militarization reached into the arts. Sitters in portraits began to appear in uniform. Music dealers who lately sold bassoons and harpsichords began in mid-1775 to advertise "Drums of the best Quality manufactured in America" or drums "equal to any that have been imported for sound or beauty" or "all sorts of Drums and Fifes." In 1776 the Philadelphia musical amateur Michael Hillegas published *The Compleat Tutor for the Fife*—the first American work on the subject. Poets also changed their tune. "This does not seem to be the proper time for poetry," wrote one Philadelphian, "unless it be such as Tyrtaeus wrote," to spur the Spartans to victory; a like-minded Virginian announced that he would write no longer of Eliza but of Washington and Putnam: "Now Mars inspires, I cease to sing the FAIR." ³ The *Pennsylvania Magazine* ended its first year's run with a new frontispiece which made plain the replacement of the fair by Mars. Minerva with a pileus sits near a liberty tree, surrounded by maps, poleaxes, powder kegs, and cannonballs.

Americans differed on whether in this atmosphere the arts could count on or even deserved further encouragement. To the commencement audiences of 1763, who applauded the refutation of Hobbes and foresaw a "Reign of LEARNING and of PEACE," the incompatibility of Arts and Arms was axiomatic. Benjamin West, a member of that generation, wrote in February 1775 to Peale: "The polite arts are what first feels the internal disquatudes of a Nation, and from this I am afraid you must have pass'd the golden harvest in that Climet." The attitude of many Americans confirmed West's fear that in the looming crisis America would leave the arts to wither. A writer in the *Pennsylvania Magazine* equated demands for concerts and plays with indifference to the cause, denouncing those who complained, "For Heaven's sake! when will these troublesome times have an end? . . . are we to have no more plays, nor balls, nor feasts, nor parties of pleasure, nor concerts of music?—we may as well be dead and buried at once." What need for plays, when, as Francis Hopkinson said, "AMERICA is at this time a scene of desolation and distress; a theatre whereon is acted a real tragedy. . . ." ⁴

To the graduating class of 1770, however, which had witnessed both the forced repeal of the Townshend Acts and the success of their countryman's *Death of General Wolfe*, Arts and Arms seemed sprouts of one root, as the poet Trumbull asserted at the Yale commencement: "The same ardour of ambition, the same greatness of thought, which inspires the Warrior to brave danger in the conquering field, when diffused among a people will call forth Genius in every station of life, fire the imagination of the Artist, and raise to sublimity the aspiring Muse." Hugh Henry Brackenridge, a member of Trumbull's generation, prefaced his *Death of General Montgomery* with an explanation of how the Arts might serve Arms. He wrote, he said, not for the stage, but "for the private entertainment of Gentlemen of taste, and martial enterprize. . . . The subject is not love but valour. I meddle not with any of the effeminating passions, but consecrate my muse to the great themes of patriotic virtue, bravery and heroism."

At least for the moment, West was more nearly correct than Trumbull. The campaign against frivolity following the Boston Port Bill had already forced Douglass out of the country. With the outbreak of serious fighting at Lexington and Concord, other kinds of cultural activity slowed or ceased. After 1775, ads for music teachers, emigrant musicians, and concerts—and presumably the concerts and teachers as well—simply disappeared in Boston, and fell off drastically elsewhere. The May 1775 commencement at the College of Philadelphia was put together out of earlier exercises, the versifiers explaining that the flight of peace made the joys of graduation tasteless; the Yale Linonian Society suspended its annual play "on account of the black cloud that hung over our country. . . ."[5] The output of American presses declined from 852 items in 1775 to 590 in 1776. In 1775 alone, nine newspapers expired.[6] In 1776, the outstanding *Pennsylvania Magazine* folded. After 1776, the *Virginia Gazette* simply eliminated its long-established "Poet's Corner."

Only one feature of cultural life continued unaffected. The singing schools were mostly rural operations remote from scenes of conflict, directed largely at adolescents, traditionally and even inherently nonideological. They could not be abandoned or restricted, moreover, without significantly changing hallowed forms of worship. In a sermon delivered in Litchfield, Connecticut, in March 1775, the Reverend Samuel Mills acknowledged current protests against singing: "Some plead that the State of the Nation is such as rather wears a forbidding Aspect, that the Season is unsuitable for this Duty [of singing psalms]." His reply, buttressed by a dozen scriptural texts, was that psalm singing was, indeed, a duty—"Make a joyful Noise unto God, all the Earth"—and as a duty must be fulfilled:

> It is granted that the darkest Cloud now hangs over us, that ever was known. But it is not granted, that GOD is any the less worthy of Praise on this Account. Our base neglect of this Duty is rather to be considered, as one Sin among others, which provokes GOD thus to threaten us. The Way therefore for the Removal of his Judgments is not to persist in neglecting it, or any other Duty enjoined on us; but the contrary.

Justified on the ground of religious obligation, the singing schools continued despite "the ancient Observation," as Isaiah Thomas called it, "that 'Arts and Arms are not very agreeable Companions.' "[7]

Whatever their impact on the arts, the Intolerable Acts, Lexington and Concord, Bunker's Hill, and the Boston siege all spread the building realization that revolution and civil war might soon erupt. As British and American soldiers clashed in and around Boston, colonists elsewhere made painful choices. The poet Trumbull gave a sophisticated, although disengaged, picture of their deliberations in *M'Fingal: A Modern Epic Poem*, dated 1775 but published in Philadelphia in January 1776. The poem describes a town meeting at some unnamed place outside Boston just after Lexington and Concord. Torn by faction, the townspeople steer from one political side to the other:

> They met, made speeches full long winded,
> Resolv'd, protested, and rescinded;
> Addresses sign'd, then chose Committees,
> To stop all drinking of Bohea-teas;
> With winds of doctrine veer'd about,
> And turn'd all Whig-Committees out.

In this blown-about state, the meeting listens to the radical "Honorious," a figure widely taken to represent Trumbull's law teacher, John Adams. He rehearses the evolution of the crisis, in metaphors by which the colonists had been explaining British policy since the 1760's. England is old and diseased. Burdened with the "infirmities of age" while France stands ready to pick her bones, visited by distempers and strange whimsies, she is propped up only by place-seeking priests, lawyers, and merchants in the colonies. Yet decrepit as she is, she clings to fantasies of omnipotence, demanding that "all the world should bow and skip/ To her almighty Goodyship." Only the combination of dotage and imperiousness explains her perverse behavior:

> She first, without pretence of reason,
> Claim'd right whate'er we had to seize on;
> And with determin'd resolution
> To put her claims in execution,
> Sent fire and sword and call'd it, Lenity,
> Starv'd us, and christen'd it, Humanity.

Honorius is opposed in argument by the Scotsman "M'Fingal." His choplogical defense of British policy and his scriptural pseudo-exegeses are motivated by his longing for "pensions, sal'ries, places, bribes." Trumbull's choice of a conservative spokesman was dictated by increasing acceptance of the 'Scotch plot' variant of ministerial conspiracy, by which Lords Bute and Mansfield, both Scots, were using the king against America in the hope of ending his reign and restoring the Stuart pretender to the throne:

> The good Lords, Bishops, and the Kirk
> United in the public work;

Rebellion from the northern regions [i.e., Scotland],
With Bute and Mansfield swore allegiance;
And all combin'd to raze as nuisance,
Of church and state, the constitutions;
Pull down the empire, on whose ruins
They meant to edify their new ones. . . .

Honorius and M'Fingal argue back and forth whether the colonies should take up arms, in classic pros and cons. Against the remember-the-forefathers-and-posterity approach, M'Fingal argues that Britain is bigger and stronger than America and should the patriots be hanged they won't have a posterity. Honorius replies that the Americans have proven the British ineffective in arms. The last speech at the meeting goes to Honorius, who calls on the townspeople to resist the "trumpery of fear" and seek vengeance for "Encrimson'd Concord's fatal plain." M'Fingal's followers rush from their pews, fists clenched, screaming "Adjourn."

Although Trumbull shows M'Fingal to be in defense of greed and Scotch plotting, he also presents the followers of Honorius as an unstable mob, easily led and eager to tar-and-feather. He later explained that he hoped to rise above partisanship and "satirize the follies and extravagancies of my countrymen, as well as of their enemies. . . ." [8] In fact, the rollicking Hudibrastic verse does not lend itself to serious political discussion and the poem often pauses for asides on fiction, mock-epical parallels, or extraneous laughs. The result is lively and witty, but far less a political satire than a burlesque epic. Published almost simultaneously with Tom Paine's *Common Sense*, it is uncharacteristic of the mood of 1775–76.

However distant from Boston, not many other Americans could view the situation there so coolly. Unfortunately, no information about William Billings at this decisive time has survived, and there remain only glances at Benjamin West—painting a *Death of Stephen* commissioned by King George for one thousand pounds.[9] The reactions of Copley, Peale, Freneau, and of some lesser figures, however, are more fully recorded.

Copley became convinced that war was inevitable and decided, firmly now, to remain abroad. He had heard about the Lexington skirmish while in Rome in the early summer; fuller accounts containing news of the encirclement of Boston seem to have reached him in Parma early in July as he began an ambitious copy of a work by Correggio. "We are surrounded by people from farr & near," Joseph Greene wrote to him; 12,000 to 15,000 troops stood outside the town, and might attack; 2,000 Bostonians had fled. Among the refugees, Copley learned, were Sukey and his children. His half-brother Pelham, who fled with them, reported that Boston was invested by a provincial army which he estimated at 8,000 troops. Bostonians had stores enough for six months, but many had to live on salted food; all shops were closed, no business was being conducted. Pelham himself was nearly destitute and a pariah. His business had stopped, he could not collect money owed him, his property was annihilated, he had nothing but the clothes on his back and a few dollars, and for his unwillingness to "go every length with them in their Scheems however mad" he was branded "Inimical to the Liberties of America." [10] Civil war, he told Copley, had begun.

The news was not unexpected, and the artist speculated more shrewdly on the outcome than many men of affairs:

> . . . what I have greatly feared for years past has at last taken place, the War is began and if I am not mistaken that Country which was a few years ago the happyest on this Globe will for many years to come be deluged with Blood. It seems to me no plan of Reconcilement can now be formed as the Sword is drawn it must be finally settle*[sic]* by the Sword; & I cannot think that all the power of Great Briton will subdue that country if they are united as they seem at present to be. I know it may seem strange to some Man of Great understanding I should hold such an oppinion. but it seems a very evident thing to me that they will have the power of resistance till grown strong to conquer. & Victory & Independence will go hand in hand. [11]

Most of all, Copley feared for his family's safety. He urged Pelham not to arm, even if ordered, and to "be neuter at all events." For his part, Pelham wished to flee for England, but refused to leave his and Copley's mother, who refused to make the voyage. Instead, Pelham became a surveyor for Gage and Howe, convinced that the colonists were "Waging War against their great Benefactors, and endeavouring to Ruin that State to whom they owe their being." [12] Sukey, however, did sail for England in May. Fearing the effects of the crossing on the son she had recently borne, she left the infant behind, but it died soon after.

Anxiety for Sukey's arrival made Copley impatient to get to London, and almost incapable of working on his copy of Correggio; "but it must be done," he felt, "it is of too much consequence to throw it up, and if I should it would not bring about the happy moment of . . . meeting one instant sooner." As July wore on, he brooded over events, with agonized hindsight. "I was right years ago," he realized, "in my oppinion that this would be the end of the attempt to tax the Colonys." He recalled "how warmly I expostulated with som of those violent Sons of Liberty against their proceedings . . . & with how little Judgment did I then seem to speak, in the wise Judgment of these People." But the time for recrimination was past: "the Day of tribulations is now come, & years of sorrow will not dry the Orphans tears nor stop the widows Lamentations, the Ground will be drunken with the Blood of its Inhabitants, before peace will again resume her Dominion in that Country." [13] By late July he learned of Sukey's safe arrival in London, where she would soon be joined by her father, the tea-consignee Richard Clarke, and his family, from Canada. Copley hoped to get his half-brother and mother to emigrate as well, fearing that if they stayed through the winter the harbor might freeze, allowing the encircling troops to attack Boston and take prisoner those who remained, presumably British sympathizers.

Copley rejoined Sukey in London early in October 1775. Before the year was out he began work on a group portrait of his reunited family, containing himself, his father-in-law, Sukey, and his four children, and also the infant who had died in Boston, which he had never seen (ill., p. 344). (The painting was not displayed until 1777, after Sukey had borne a child in England.) Although the painting reveals a general softening in Copley's style as the result of his European tour, it remains an acute study of the differing worlds of childhood, maturity, and age. The children have a rosy hue, their fleshiness emphasized by the hold of Sukey's slender fingers on a soft breast, which it dents. Copley seems determined if tired, Sukey somber, Clarke weary, the children blithely happy despite the long ordeal the family has undergone. Early in 1776, Copley moved with his family and his father-in-law to 12 Leicester Square, a fashionable address next door to Hogarth's widow and to the auctioneer James Christie, across the square from Joshua Reynolds. London was already filling with other Americans, with Joseph Greene, Thomas Flucker, John Amory, the Salem judge Samuel Curwen—wealthy persons whom Copley had painted earlier in Boston and whom he entertained. By mid-1776, Pelham arrived via Halifax, having left his mother at home. He stayed with the Copleys in their new home.

Peale's response was less complicated, and might have been foreseen. "From the time in which G. Britain first attempted to lay a tax on America, by the memorable stamp act," he wrote later, he had been "a zealous advocate for the liberties of his Country." While studying with West he learned that Parliament had suspended the New York Assembly, and thereafter he refused to pull off his hat as the king passed by. He took no English clothes back with him to America, and upon his return immediately attended a militia muster. His feelings about the current crisis he projected onto a flag which he painted for the Independent Company of Williamsburg, depicting, in his words, "Liberty trampling on Tiranny and puting of Slavery and taking hold of Death. . . ." [14] A month after Washington took command in Cambridge, he wrote to West and to his friend the sculptor Thomas Allwood in London, blaming the crisis on the ministry, who "have dealt ungenerousely with America who is a brave and was a Loyal people." He hoped the English had had "their Eyes opened," for the next turn of events would be determined abroad: "unless something is speedily done on your side the water, the People here are prepareing for the worst." Peale was no less sure than Copley of the eventual outcome. The colonists all "declare for liberty or Death, they are much used hunting *[sic]* and are all good marksmen even our children as soon as they can carry a Gun are accustomed to shooting." Such people, settled across 1,400 miles, could scarcely be expected to "be conquered by all the Troops England can send here." [15]

While fervently convinced of the rightness of the cause, Peale was distressed by its impact on his career. He had, he felt, made a success in Annapolis and Philadelphia. He still hoped to settle permanently in Philadelphia or New York if things settled down, "which at present," he told West, "does not seem verry likely to be soon. . . ." Largely through the generosity of some Virginia planters, too, he was just beginning to clear his ever-present debts—debts in bonds at 6 percent, debts incurred when he stood surety for a brother-in-law who died insolvent. In August 1775 he wrote to his friend Edmund Jenings, lamenting that a war would catch him on the rise: "Alas! I fear I shall have no more to paint. And I well remember your once telling me that when my brush should fail, that I must take the Musket. I believe you foresaw all that has since happened." [16] Early in November he sailed for Charleston, where he had been offered the use of a house by his brother-in-law, Nathaniel Ramsay. He took with him a borrowed copy of Rousseau's *Émile* and over the month learned some French through evening "amusements of *comment vous portez vous,*" imposing fines on anyone in the family who slipped into English. He earned some money from watch repairing and cleaning. Much of his time he spent with his brother-in-law and with Charles Carroll of Carrollton, who had been appointed to try to improve the manufacture of gunpowder. Peale experimented himself, following the tips in Samuel Johnson's dictionary, mixing saltpeter and urine, and at the same time testing rifles.[17]

Philip Freneau's responses were less wholehearted and remain less clear. Twenty-three years old at the time of the Boston siege, he was moving away from his divinity studies, uncertain of his vocation, rather at loose ends. Although virtually no letters or journals by him during this period survive, he published a dozen or more poems in newspapers and pamphlets, mostly in New York, and wrote many more. Those which he published compose a gamut of scorn, sounding notes from hurt surprise to conciliation without appeasement to soberly fearless defiance:

> Who could have thought that Britons bore a heart,
> Or British troops to act so base a part?

Britons of old renown'd, can they descend,
T'enslave their brethren in a foreign land?
(American Liberty)

Hear and attest the warmest wish I bring,
God save the Congress and reform the King!
Long may Britannia rule our hearts again,
Rule as she rul'd in George the Second's reign;
May ages hence her growing empire see,
And she be glorious, but ourselves be free. . . .
(A Voyage to Boston)

If to controul the cunning of a knave,
Our freedom love, and scorn the name of slave;
If to protest against a tyrant's laws,
And arm for battle in a righteous cause
Be deemed rebellion—'tis a harmless thing,
This bug-bear name, like death, has lost its sting.
("Reflections on Gage's Letter. . . .")[18]

But Freneau had subversive feelings of a different sort as well. They also found their way into poems, but he left many of them unpublished for another ten years. In "The Distrest Shepherdess," apparently written only a month or two after the lines quoted above but unpublished until 1788, he presented "Mariana" inconsolably mourning the death of her husband "Damon," killed in the winter of 1775 in the invasion of Canada that followed the taking of Fort Ticonderoga:

O river Sorel! Thou didst hear him complain,
When dying he languish'd, and called me in vain!
When, pierc'd by the Briton he went to repel,
He sunk on the shores of the river Sorel.

As Mariana considers making a pilgrimage with their son to Damon's Canadian resting place, it occurs to her that the grave may be unmarked, even that Damon may have drowned in the Sorel—that, come to think of it, "he was uneasy when'er I complain'd." Finally,

My shepherd departed I never shall meet—
Here's Billy O' Bluster—I love him as well,
And Damon may stay at the river Sorel.[19]

Freneau possessed a deep vein of cynicism and misanthropy that gloated on thanklessness and on the short life of eternal vows. Part of him withheld devotion from the causes he espoused.

Literary aspirations also held Freneau back. Although he continues to be known as "The Poet of the American Revolution," he could be called

"The Poet Who Wrote 'The Power of Fancy' in the Year of the Boston Massacre." Even his most propagandistic verse is studded with classical allusions and designed for educated readers, those able to appreciate what an advertisement called his blend of "Ciceronian eloquence and patriotic fire." [20] His popular *Voyage to Boston* describes the British and American camps; but in doing so it uses all the machinery of the literary dream voyage. Before he can execrate the British occupation, the narrator must don a "magic vest" from "Fancy's temple" and ponder whether to reach Cambridge by horse or wind. Thus the snarling invective against Gage—"second Cortez, sent by heaven's command,/ To murder, rage, and ravage o'er our land"—is muted by the surrounding fluff:

> . . . the nimble vessel flies
> O'er Neptune's bosom and reflected skies;
> Nor halt I here to tell you how she roves
> O'er Tython's chambers and his coral groves.

Here and elsewhere Freneau refused to serve as some sloganeering proletarian firebrand; he made his abhorrence of British policy serve his wish to write the poetry of fancy.

In sum, Freneau apparently wanted both to stay and to go. His mood in 1775 is probably divulged in "MacSwiggen," a poem datelined 1775 but unpublished until 1786:

> Long have I sat on this disast'rous shore,
> And, sighing, sought to gain a passage o'er
> To Europe's towns, where, as our travellers say,
> Poets may flourish, or, perhaps they may. . . .

Freneau decided to quit the scene. An acquaintance recalled him saying in 1794 that he left America because he was "averse to enter the army & be knock'd in the head." [21] Freneau in his old age, however, insisted that he took employment on American privateers. According to family tradition, sometime in early 1776 he met in Philadelphia a Danish West Indian plantation owner who commanded his own ship and persuaded Freneau to accompany him. In any case, Freneau spent the next two years in the Caribbean.

The kinds of decisions made by Copley, Peale, and Freneau were of course being thrust upon thousands of other colonists, many of whom were identified and denounced as "Tories." Political demarcations had become quite apparent during the Stamp Act; and, as we have seen, the meeting of the First Continental Congress catalyzed a unified and articulate opposition. The Congress itself sharpened the lines of division. Under the terms of the Continental Association, it set up Committees of Safety—

often successors of local Sons of Liberty groups—to watch for and publicize violators of the non-importation agreements. Provincial legislatures gradually gave the proceedings legal sanction, imposing penalties that included the confiscation of property and even death. Patriotic demonstrations changed from burials of Liberty to window breaking and tarring-and-feathering, often on orders of local Committees of Safety.

Thus, although in use earlier, it was in 1775–76 that the term "Tory" became an issue. Recognition of a cleft in American society made "Tory" something to be discussed and defined. The New York *Packet* in January 1776 traced the term to the seventeenth century, when it was applied to dispossessed Irishmen who became outlaws, living by plundering and killing English soldiers. So a Tory was a *"highway robber,"* a man "who lived upon plunder . . . prepared for any daring or villanous *[sic]* enterprise." For Freneau, as he said in *Voyage to Boston*, a Tory abided by an unnatural, masochistic inversion of Whig principles: "Passive obedience to the worst of men"; "Slavery I love, and freedom I despise." Peale in March 1776 drew a prose sketch of "Jemmy Tory," whose hallmarks were to be "ever speaking of the weakness of our force, and incapacity to carry on a defensive war . . . proud, imperious, superficial, a mere gigan, a Silly Fop." [22] Most radicals who defined "Tory" in 1775 or 1776 meant someone who failed to actively resist the home government's directives in some way, and who thus contributed to the active exploitation and the distress of other colonists.

Like others who became identified as Tories, those involved in the country's cultural life suffered for their sentiments. Mather Byles, the Boston wit, friend of Billings, and nephew of Cotton Mather, was dismissed in the fall of 1776 by his Hollis Street congregation, which he had served since 1732. During the siege of Boston his daughters could be seen walking arm-in-arm on the Common with Generals Howe and Percy, the latter ordering his band to play beneath their window for their pleasure. Byles himself lent some British officers his field glasses to watch the erection of British works. It was charged that he took the political situation lightly. (The charge can be believed. In 1777, he was arrested for Toryism and sentenced to be exiled with his family to England; instead he was confined to his house under guard. The punster remarked that he had thereby been "guarded—regarded—and disregarded," and called his sentry his "observ-a-tory.") Another sympathizer with the British who was punished for his views was James Rivington, whose *New-York Gazetteer*, since its first issue in 1773, had reached a circulation of 3,600 and was sold throughout the colonies. With its book reviews, poetry, and essays, it made a culturally important addition to the bookshop where Rivington printed theatre tickets and pamphlet verse, displayed paintings for itinerant portraitists, and commissioned engravings from Paul Revere. At the same time, however, the newspaper had become the major Loyalist forum in the colonies, and Rivington sold Hyson tea under the counter. In November 1774, a group of subscribers withdrew support and issued a broadside explaining that Rivington was "very unfriendly, in our opinion, to the common cause of American liberty." Considered nothing more than a ministerial pensioner, Rivington was hanged in effigy; his papers and pamphlets were publicly burned. In November 1775 some patriot marauders played "Yankee Doodle" while they wrecked his printing press. Two months later he left for London.[23]

A spectacular defection to the Tories became known in the fall of 1775, with the interception of a ciphered letter borne by a woman courier. Its author, who had been acting as a spy for General Gage, was Benjamin Church, author of *The Choice* (1757), of several poems against the Stamp Act, of a satire against Governor Bernard, and of other patriotic verse—some of which he was suspected of parodying himself and publishing in Rivington's newspaper. Church's credentials were impeccably patriot: born in Mather Byles's congregation, a Harvard graduate, a member of the Boston Committee of Correspondence, the March 5 orator in 1773. Because of his background he had been placed on the Boston Committee on Safety with access to its secrets, present in 1774 and 1775 at top-secret meetings with Hancock, Adams, and Revere. Revere ran into him in Cambridge the day after the Battle of Lexington, with blood on his stocking which he said came from a man killed near him. In October 1775, he was tried before the Massachusetts House of Representatives and ultimately exiled to the West Indies. John Adams was astonished: "A Man of Genius, of Learning, of Family, of Character, a Writer of Liberty Songs and good ones too. . . . Good God!" [24]

With the identification of a large group of colonists as Tories came a large body of verse describing the peculiar distress of the blacklisted. Given the experiences of Byles, Rivington, and other known Tories in 1775, it is no surprise that little of this verse appeared in print. Much of it, undeservedly, remains unprinted. That has been the fate of the few but incisive poems of Robert Proud of Pennsylvania (a fine classical scholar who wrote an impressive *History of Pennsylvania*), and of a larger collection of Tory verse entitled "Rhapsodies," which survives in manuscript at the Library of Congress. The volume contains a group of precise and musical verses written in Philadelphia and dated between 1774 and 1778. The author(s) are not identified, but some, even all, of the poems were probably the work of the Tory versifiers Jonathan Odell and Joseph Stansbury. Odell, born in Newark in 1737, served as a surgeon in the British army early in life, but took holy orders in England and was licensed as a minister in New Jersey, where he also practiced medicine. Stansbury, the son of a London haberdasher, came to Philadelphia in 1767 at about the age of twenty-five, opened a china store, and circulated in the city's social and intellectual coteries. Stansbury and Proud were both jailed in 1776. Some letters by Odell were intercepted en route to England, and in October 1775 he was brought before the Philadelphia Council of Safety. The next year, Tories in a local jail sang one of his songs on the king's birthday, so antagonizing the New Jersey Provincial Congress that they ordered Odell confined within an eight-mile circle of the Burlington courthouse. At the end of the year he escaped to British lines and became an army chaplain.[25]

The verse of these Tory poets shows what articulate people who had lived in America a long time—Odell's ancestors settled in Concord in 1639—felt about the country and the countrymen now harassing and jailing them. Unanimously they considered the radicals a mindless mass, spellbound by "Rhapsodies" concocted by their "moon-struck Guides":

> Now Discord, the daemon of Hell, shakes the Land
> And Thousands support what they don't understand. . . .

Some Tories argued that this irrationality grew from the religious "enthusiasm" repugnant to eighteenth-century rationalism. One saw the political situation epitomized in a sermon delivered on a hot day in Philadelphia, during which a black servant vigorously fanned the preacher as he gave his "seditious Rhapsody on *Liberty*":

> . . . what can we look for, but Faction & Treason,
> From a flaming Enthusiast fann'd by the Devil! [26]

A more specific explanation, often given, was that "Forbidden Fruit's *New-England's* Choice," that the spirit of riot was only the latest outbreak of an older Puritan fanaticism. For Robert Proud,

> These Colonies of British Freedom tir'd,
> Are by the Phrenzy of Distraction fir'd;
> Surrounding Nations with Amazement view,
> The strange Infatuations they pursue,
> Virtue in tears deplores their Fate in vain,
> And Satan smiles to see Disorder reign
> The days of Cromwel, Puritannic rage,
> Return'd to curse our more unhappy age. . . .[27]

Radical alarms about encroachment, standing armies, and ministerial plots were attempts to give the semblance of reason to such "strang Infatuations." In "The General Warrant," a lawyer, a parson, and "their Wives and little Brats" are set upon by a member of a provincial congress.

Through his "Optics of Suspicion" he discerns secret letters in their "Caps & Smocks":

> Here's a Plot, he cries, how happy am I,
> Thus favor'd in Vision to see the dark Design!
> In vain shall any Tory hope to fly:
> Their Cunning is not, surely, any Match for Mine! [28]

The authors of the "Rhapsodies" saw their radical countrymen as persons with a hellish appetite for disorder, obsessed by inquisitorial frenzy.

As they saw themselves, the Tories were merely bystanders overthrown in this breaking loose of hell. Tormented, in Robert Proud's phrase, for remaining "True to our King, our Countery & our Laws," they wished nothing more than to live as they had always lived. Sociable persons averse to politics, they would rather drink in mutual harmony or idle with friends than form Associations and indite pamphlets. According to a song written for a Loyalist outing, only unreason could accuse those who detest contention of being enemies to freedom (*"Protestant"* below refers to the name of a circle of Loyalists):

> 2.
> Away from the noise of the Fife and the Drum,
> And all the rude Din of Bellona we come,
> And a plentiful Store of Good humour we bring
> To season our Feast in the Shade of Cold-Spring.
>
> 3.
> A truce, then, to all Whig-and-Tory Debate!
> *True* Lovers of Freedom, Contention we hate;
> For the Daemon of Discord in vain tries his Art
> To possess or inflame a true *Protestant* heart.
>
> 4.
> True Protestant Friends to fair Liberty's Cause
> To Decorum, Good Order, Religion and Laws,
> From Avarice, Jealousy, Perfidy free,
> We wish all the World were as happy as we!

This distaste for political strife accounts for a structural feature of Tory verse that distinguishes it from radical verse—the absence of a contrived persona. The speaker in radical poems and songs is often some ideological farmer or doodle, claiming the integrity of pastoral views or crowing over the loathed identity given him by the supercilious Briton. Tory verse is undisguisedly well-bred, and far more intimate. Instead of addressing a large public on 'issues,' it speaks to friends about the writer's personal situation. Stansbury begins his "Verses to the Tories":

> COME, ye brave, by Fortune wounded
> More than by the vaunting Foe,

> Chear your hearts, ne'er be confounded;
> Trials all must undergo.

Robert Proud writes from jail:

> In vaults with bars & Iron doors confin'd,
> They hold our Persons, but can't rule the Mind.
> Act now we cannot, else we freely wou'd,
> But calmly suffer for our Country's Good. . . .[29]

Many of the Tory poems recall the lives the poets long enjoyed before being stripped of cherished pleasures and brutally declassed. The titles alone affectingly sum up the meaning: "Sung at a Venison Feast," "Song . . . At a fishing-party, on the Delaware, near Burlington," and—dated New Jail, Philadelphia, January 1776—"Written on a Card with a Pencil, the Author being deprived of Pen Ink & Paper." Hearkening back to the time before poets were spies, when newspapers advertised harpsichords instead of drums, and artists mixed paint not gunpowder, the Tory verse of 1775–76 is a lament for the Good Old Days.

How those days ended, and what might come next, are the subjects of *The Fall of British Tyranny*, a rousingly audacious play published in Philadelphia in May 1776. Considering its date and point of view, it could be called the last work of colonial American literature. The author was John Leacock, a middle-aged gold- and silversmith associated with the Philadelphia Sons of Liberty, a friend of Dickinson, Rush, and the Franklins. In 1767 he semiretired in the countryside near Philadelphia, where he made wines.[30] It is worth reproducing here one of the large number of unusually prominent ads for his play, because it faithfully describes the action and flavor, and probably reflects contemporary enthusiasm for them:

THE FALL OF
BRITISH TYRANNY,
OR,
AMERICAN LIBERTY TRIUMPHANT.
THE FIRST CAMPAIGN.

A TRAGI COMEDY of Five Acts, containing twenty six Scenes, among which are the following, VIZ.

A pleasing scene Between *Roger* and *Dick*, two shepherds near Lexington.

[word illegible] &c. A very moving scene on the death of Doctor *Warren*, &c. in a chamber near Boston, the morning after the battle at *Bunker's Hill.*

A humorous scene between the Boatswain and a Sailor on board a man of war, near Norfolk in Virginia.

Two very laughable scenes between the Boatswain, two Sailors, and the Cook, exhibiting specimens of seafaring oratory, and peculiar eloquence of those sons of Neptune touching Tories, Convicts and Black Regulars; and between Lord *Kidnapper* [Dunmore] and the Boatswain.

A very black scene between Lord *Kidnapper* and Major *Cudgjo* [an ex-slave].

A religious scene between Lord *Kidnapper*, Chaplain and the Captain.

A scene, the Lord Mayor &c. going to St. James's with the Address.

A droll scene, a council of war in Boston, between Lord *Boston* [Gage], Admiral . . . *Elbow-Room* [Howe?], Mr. *Caper* [Burgoyne], General *Clinton*, and Earl *Piercy* [General Percy].

A diverting scene between a *Whig* and a *Tory*.

A . . . scene between General *Prescott*, and Colonel *Allen.*

A shocking scene, a dungeon, between Colonel Allen and an officer of the guard.

Two affecting scenes in Boston after the flight of the Regulars from Lexington, between Lord *Boston*, messenger, and officers of the guard.

A patriotic scene in the camp at Cambridge, between the Generals *Washington, Lee* and *Putnam* &c. &c.

With a dedication, preface, address of the Goddess of Liberty to the Congress, dramatis personae, prologue, epilogue, and a song in praise of King Tammany, the American Saint.

A truly dramatic performance, interspersed with wit, humour, burlesque, and serious matter, which cannot fail of affording abundant entertainment to readers of every disposition.[31]

The play lives up to its percussive billing. Characters and events spring up and vanish like targets in a shooting gallery. The scene leaps from Boston to London to Fort Ticonderoga to Virginia to Canada, presenting diverse military figures, literary types, social classes, religious groups, and nationalities who speak everything from Negro dialect to sailor's bawdry to Roman oratory, the action unreeling in rapid-fire vignettes conceived in exultant bitterness and crackling with violence.

For all its variety, the play has a neat overall design and a unifying argument. It treats whatever transpires, whether at Parliament or at Lexington, as a result of the Scotch plot. Dedicated in part to "the innumerable and never-ending Clan of Macs and Donalds upon Donalds," it attributes the entire crisis directly to Lord Bute, "that demon, that bird of prey, that ministerial cormorant . . . who first thought to disturb the repose of America." To eventually return the Stuart pretender to the throne, Bute decides to bribe the colonies into submission. His reason for sending the British army to America is to leave England's coasts defenseless so that 30,000 Scots soldiers can march on London.

In detailing the Scotch plot, the play offers among its other novelties a rare literary look at affairs in Virginia concurrent with the Boston siege. There Bute's design is being advanced by Lord Dunmore, the Scots royal governor of the colony, a descendant of the Stuarts. The historical Dunmore had seen an advance copy of Gage's offer (written by Burgoyne) to pardon all Bostonians who would lay down their arms, except Adams and Hancock; fearing that he would be taken as a hostage, he fled in June 1775 to a warship off Norfolk. In November, still aboard ship, he issued a proclamation offering to free all slaves and indentured servants who joined the king's forces. As Leacock depicts him, Dunmore is both unscrupulous and degenerate. He lures slaves from their masters with the promise of freedom and position: "you shall have money in your pockets, good cloaths on your backs, and be as free as them white men there. *(Pointing forward to a parcel of Tories.)*" Actually he plans to use the slaves in battle, then sell them in the West Indies. Below deck on the warship he consorts with his prostitutes, inadequately making fast, one sailor says, "the end of his small rope athwart Jenny Bluegarter and Kate Common's stern posts." [32]

Leacock divides his wrath between those who schemed the present situation and those now forwarding it. The clan of "Donalds upon Donalds" share the dedication of the play with Gage, Clinton, Howe, and Burgoyne, "Gentlemen Officers, Actors, Merry Andrews, strolling Players." They are opposed by two groups of American characters: historical personages like Ethan Allen and George Washington and literary inventions like "Dick Rifle," "Mr. Peter Buckstail," and "Mr. Freeman." The combining of real and fictional figures in the cast of Americans reflects the union outside Boston and elsewhere of identifiable heroes and nameless masses. "Dick Rifle" and Leacock's other inventions give body to an American popular spirit, strongly present in 1775–76 and becoming aware of itself through works like "Yankee Doodle." Its qualities, as Leacock imagines them, are a robust naturalness and a bold directness of language and thought, the opposites of British cunning and circumlocution. Reasoning "most justly from nature," his 'Buckstails' and 'Rifles' know that "Liberty's the right of each creature"; perfumed with bear-grease, they despise British "slip-slops and tea"; in contrast to Dunmore's "small rope" they sing of eighty-year-old Saint Tammany:

> With a pipe in his jaw, he'd buss his old squaw,
> And get a young saint ev'ry night, my brave boys.

Conceived as 'natural' men, Leacock's fictional heroes are not, however, bumpkins like Yankee Doodle. Their offspring in later national typology is the rugged, defiant, independent figure of the frontiersman.

As a historical document, the real achievement of this now-little-known but admirable play is its staccato form and manner. The nervous rhythms of the language alone proclaim that indignation has been strained to the limit: "a freeborn people butchered—their towns desolated, and become an heap of ashes—their inhabitants become beggars, wanderers and vagabonds—by the cruel orders of an unrelenting tyrant, wallowing in luxury, and wantonly wasting the people's wealth, to oppress them the more. . . ." From the opening, when a "Goddess of Liberty" orders the Congress to "Wish, talk, write, fight, and die—for LIBERTY," to the epilogue, when "Mr. Freeman" warns that "nought will do, but sound, impartial blows," *The Fall of British Tyranny* is a declaration of war. Parts must now, it says, be played in earnest:

> *The curtain's up—the musick's now begun,*
> *What is't?—Why murder, fire, and sword, and gun.*
> *What scene?—Why blood!—What act?—Fight and be free!*
>
> *. . . Come forth, ye actors, come,*
> *The Tragedy's begun. . . .*

32. The Second Continental Congress Declares Independence: Fall 1775–Summer 1776

As individuals and groups armed, fled, or found themselves in jail in response to recent events, the Second Continental Congress at Philadelphia moved toward committing the united colonies to a single response. Called in May 1775, the Congress adjourned in August, a week after creating a postal department under Benjamin Franklin, then reconvened in September. While its new army besieged Boston, it authorized a Continental Navy and launched an attack on Canada, hoping to win itself a fourteenth colony. Tory writers condemned its belligerence:

> King Cong has more hands by a Score than Briareus,
> Nine times more heads than the Hydra of yore,
> His Edicts are issued in Languages various,

> All his dark bosom is cover'd with Gore;
> From his very breath, Sir, Proceed Life and Death, Sir,
> While Thousands around him bow down and adore! [1]

On the ultimate question of independence, however, the Congress still moved cautiously, and still petitioned for reconciliation. In December, it forswore obedience to Parliament but declared continued allegiance to the Crown, even after learning that the king had proclaimed all the colonies in a state of rebellion and that he planned to hire German mercenaries.

Congressional sentiment for and against independence was forced to a test in February, however, and at the expense of Provost William Smith. Indirectly the cause was the death of General Richard Montgomery in a New Year's Eve attack on Quebec. Born in Ireland, and a graduate of Trinity College, Dublin, Montgomery had fought in the French and Indian Wars, and more recently had settled down as a gentleman-farmer in upstate New York. As second in command, he took over when the leader of the Canada advance, General Philip Schuyler, fell ill. In November he seized Montreal unresisted. Next month he moved with three hundred men through a blizzard to Quebec, where he died with two of his soldiers in an advance-guard party. Verse on his death appeared in broadsides and newspapers in Massachusetts, Pennsylvania, and Virginia, lauding him as a native (if adopted) son comparable to Cato, Wolfe, and more recent heroes like Hancock and Warren:

> When Cato fell, Rome mourn'd the fatal blow;
> Wolfe's death bid streams of British tears to flow:
> Why, then, should freemen stop the friendly tear,
> Or ever blush to weep for one so dear?

Congress itself—in an unprecedented act of intercolonial patronage for the arts—resolved to commission a statue of Montgomery from France at a cost of not more than £300, the commission eventually going to Jean Jacques Caffiéri, sculptor to the French king.[2]

For many Americans, the death of this ex–British soldier who had chosen to live among them was a powerful argument for separation. One writer, possibly Tom Paine, published a *Dialogue between the Ghost of General Montgomery Just arrived from the Elysian Fields; and an American Delegate, in a Wood near Philadelphia* (Philadelphia, 1776). The delegate opposes separation; but Montgomery assures him that it is inevitable, providential: "God did not excite the attention of all Europe—of the whole world—nay of angels themselves to the present controversy, for nothing. The inhabitants of Heaven long to see the ark finished. . . . America is the theatre where human nature will *soon* receive its greatest military-civil and literary honors. . . ." [3] Later in the year, Hugh Henry Brackenridge wrote a play presenting Montgomery's death as a climax of prolonged and unmitigated British savagery: *The Death of General Montgomery at the Siege of Quebec. A Tragedy* (Philadelphia, 1777). The play harps on the phrase "roast ox," referring to Sir Guy Carleton, royal governor of Canada. Carleton invited the Indians at Montreal to partake of a roasted ox, which he called a "Bostonian." Brackenridge treats Montgomery's death as the outcome of British bloodlust for "roast ox." In the climactic last scene—engraved for the frontispiece by the Philadelphia artist John Norman—blood-splattered Aaron Burr stands over Montgomery's corpse delivering a funeral eulogy as the wounded ghost of General Wolfe rises from the banks of the St. Lawrence. Wolfe perceives in the scene "the mighty thought/ Of separation, from the step-dame rule/ Of moon-struck Britain. . . ." [4]

The "mighty thought" was tested when Congress asked William Smith to deliver a funeral oration for Montgomery on February 14. Personally, Smith hoped for reconciliation yet was unwilling to sacrifice American rights, his moderate stance exposing him to charges both of Toryism and rebellion. For his oration, he put together an elaborate exercise with musical interludes, à la the college commencements. He recited verses from Horace and from William Collins, which a choir picked up and sang; the music was composed for the occasion, and performed by the Philadelphia music dealer Michael Hillegas, the Bremners, and other local musicians, and a third violinist brought from New York. Smith's oration on Montgomery was praised in a poem by the Tory Joseph Stansbury—a bad sign. It offended many delegates by claiming that Congress still wished for dependency on England.[5] A week after the oration, Congress considered a motion to thank Smith for the address, a motion proposed by then-opponents of independence. The motion was voted down. This vote against thanking Smith was the first victory in Congress for the forces of independence. On the last day of the month, the delegates began debating the question of independence itself.

The debate and its chief results were, of course, political events. Yet the session was a cultural event as well. It brought together intellectuals from various colonies—or states, as they were coming to be called—who otherwise rarely or never met. Among the delegates were many men of trained taste and intellect: the physician Benjamin Rush; the widely read William Ellery of Rhode Island, a Harvard graduate (and the grandfather of both William Ellery Channing and Richard Henry Dana); the learned jurist George Wythe, of Virginia; Arthur Middleton of South Carolina, a Latin and Greek scholar who read Horace during recess; James Wilson of Pennsylvania, formerly a Latin tutor at the College of Philadelphia; Thomas Jefferson, a serious amateur of books, music, and poetry; John Adams, who possessed, said Benjamin Rush, "more learning, probably, both ancient and modern, than any man who subscribed to the Declaration. . . . Even the old English poets were familiar to him"; and of course Benjamin Franklin.[6] In June arrived the president of Princeton, James Witherspoon, and his co-delegate from New Jersey, Francis Hopkinson.

Many found the ambience stimulating. En masse, the Congress attended the 1775 commencement exercises of the College, where they heard the students' joyless *Dialogue and Two Odes Set to Music*. Ellery and Wythe took up a stylish correspondence, exchanging not only political opinions but also verses, translations, epigrams, and opinions on Homer and Milton. John Adams was particularly impressed with meeting Michael Hillegas, a "great Musician," he thought, who talked "perpetually of the Forte and Piano, of Handell &c."; his stay in Philadelphia, he told his wife, Abigail, stirred longings for peace and leisure, "to amuse myself with those elegant and ingenious arts of painting, sculpture, statuary, architecture and music. . . . A taste in all of them is an agreeable accomplishment." [7]

The urbanity of the scene was enhanced by the arrival in May of Charles Willson Peale, who became virtually a delegate himself. He had long hoped to settle in Philadelphia and now wished to find out "how the People were affected, whether the Commotion should be so great as to prevent my getting any business. . . ." His politics were clear enough. Before leaving Charleston he "bespoke a Suit of Regimentals"; once in Philadelphia he continued to experiment with gunpowder, assiduously trying to sight his rifle and buying bullet molds; he practiced his shooting in the yard behind the State House, within which sat the Congress. He visited with Rittenhouse, Dickinson, Franklin, and Hopkinson, painted miniatures of William Smith and of Mrs. John Hancock, and circulated on easy terms among the delegates.[8] In May he attended the Catholic church in company with several New Englanders including John Adams, who found him a bit ostentatious, yet feeling: "He has Vanity—loves Finery—Wears a sword—gold Lace—speaks French," Adams told Abigail; but Peale was also a "tender, soft, affectionate Creature," a man "capable of Friendship, and strong Family Attachments. . . ." Adams seems to have made several visits to Peale's "Painters Room," where he thought the paintings very well done, but not so good as those of the now-expatriated Copley, "the greatest Master, that ever was in America." Yet the picture of Peale's wife with her dead infant, Adams said, "struck me prodigiously." At Peale's studio he also met Francis Hopkinson, and was amused by his appearance: "He is one of your pretty little, curious, ingenious Men. His Head is not bigger, than a large Apple. . . ." [9] By

June, Peale felt confident enough about the prospects in Philadelphia to bring the rest of his family to live there permanently.

Peale's familiarity with the delegates made it natural for Congress to turn to him when it resolved to commission an official portrait of Washington. Peale had other credentials for the task, of course. He had scored a success with his earlier engraving and portrait of Pitt, his politics were robust. He had painted Washington before, at Mount Vernon, and had developed something of a friendship with him and admiration of his qualities. In 1775 he described Washington to his patron Edmund Jenings: "a Man of very few words but when he speaks it is to the purpose, what I have often admired in him he allways avoided saying anything of the actions in which he was Engaged in last War, he is uncommonly Modest, very Industrious and prudent." [10] The commission to Peale was not exactly unprecedented, since the governments of New York, South Carolina, and Virginia had commissioned statues of King George, Pitt, and Lord Botetourt, and only three months earlier Congress itself had commissioned a monument to Montgomery. Yet Peale's commission was significant in being given by the thirteen united colonies to a native-born painter to commemorate a native-born subject. Officially, the portrait was intended to honor Washington's expulsion of the British from Boston. But it also gave prestigious recognition to the idea that art could aid in the creating of national ideals and the preservation of national events, and was therefore a concern of government.

Peale received the commission on May 19, 1776. It came from John Hancock as president of Congress, who also asked for a portrait of Martha Washington. Washington himself had left Boston a month after the British evacuation and gone to New York, in April, to establish headquarters there and to fortify the city. He visited Congress in Philadelphia for two weeks beginning on May 23. Peale began the portrait on the twenty-ninth; on May 30 and 31 Washington sat for him. Martha Washington also asked him for a miniature of her husband, which he undertook in July. (As always happened to Peale, payment for the portraits was delayed; in this case until December, when John Hancock gave him twenty-eight guineas.) Essentially a news picture, the congressional portrait shows Washington after his first military victory. A view of Boston appears in the background, with Old South and Christ churches, and smoke from burning Charlestown. Washington is shown as Phillis Wheatley's "Generallisimo," the great commander-in-chief in buff-and-blue uniform with epaulettes, green sash, huge brass buttons, and sword, one hand in his waistcoat, leaning jauntily on a walking stick, looking, for all that, somewhat embarrassed, his head seeming too small for his long, bulky body.[11]

The event which Congress chose to commemorate also helped to force a decision on separation. Beginning in mid-February, in the war fever raised by Tom Paine's *Common Sense*, and then in the wake of the British evacuation of Boston, Congress adopted one aggressive measure after another, authorizing privateers, embargoing exports to Britain, voting to disarm Loyalists, and opening relations with the French government. On June 7, Richard Henry Lee introduced a resolution calling for a Declaration of Independence. The proposal generated enough warm debate so that Congress postponed action for three weeks, meanwhile appointing a committee to draft such a pronouncement. Most of the writing was done by Thomas Jefferson, who had thought much about literature and about prose style. At the time, he was enamored of the sublimity, richness, and antique wildness of Homer and Ossian, and wholly persuaded by Lord Kames's view that taste in the arts closely resembles the moral sense. He was also a voracious and finicky bibliophile who valued literary works as possessions. Most important, he was an inquiring and imaginative student of languages, prodding his young relatives to improve their writing and suggesting how. Later he would write a lengthy "Thoughts on English Prosody" and an "Essay Towards Facilitating Instruction in the Anglo-Saxon and Modern Dialects of the English Language," and he would give the English language such words as "centrality," "grade," "sparse," "belittle," "cent," and "dollar."

In the Declaration, Jefferson seems to have striven for the senatorial prose he admired in the English statesman Lord Bolingbroke, a "lofty, rhythmical full-flowing eloquence," something with the elevation but not the pomp of oratory. The power and lasting freshness of his document result not only from its great theme but also from its thorough and subtle unity. The need to compress lofty philosophical arguments, a litany of abuses, a legal case, and a call to arms within the narrow broadside form compelled Jefferson to supercharge his language and to make each word a cooperation of sense, tone, imagery, rhythm, and design. While the congressional revision of the document generally tightened Jefferson's rough draft, his original punctuation seems more logical and artistic. In the draft, he made the bill of particulars virtually a single sentence by attaching each count to the next by a colon. Even without this grammatical welding, the published Declaration preserves the effect of a linked strain, partly through devices of repetition. The last paragraph, echoing the first in imagery and rhythm, leaves us where we began. Triplets and parallelisms abound. The ritualistically repeated pronouns "We," "They," and "He," create a pounding denunciatory chant. Key words are reiterated: In differing forms, "declaration" appears five times. The act of political severance forces itself on the ear and eye in recurrent images of connection and rupture: "dissolve" (which in various forms appears four times), "bands," "connected," "separate," "throw off," "cutting off," "ties," "absolve," "abolish." Evoking dismembered Britannias and severed snakes, the language resounds with the calamities of a decade.

A quiet alliteration also creates unity of sound:

> When in the Course of human Events, it becomes necessary for one People to dissolve the Political Bands which have connected them with another, and to assume among the Powers of the Earth, the separate and equal Station to which the Laws of Nature and of Nature's God entitle them, a decent Respect to the Opinions of Mankind requires that they should declare the causes which impel them to the Separation.

Syntax here perfectly matches content. The irresistibly steady drive of the suspended statement towards its subject expresses by other means the announced reluctance, compulsion, and tragic resignation by which the revolutionaries "acquiesce in the Necessity" of declaring their independence. Rhythmically the opening recalls such mighty suspended English openings as those of *The Canterbury Tales* and *Paradise Lost*. Jefferson's feeling for strong rhythms (visible, later, in the columns of his porticos) endows his great phrases with a repeated four-beat pulse that has the resolute solemnity of final judgment:

/ / / /
When in the Course of human Events

/ / / /
the Laws of Nature and of Nature's God

/ / / /
all Men are created equal

/ / / /
Life, Liberty, and the Pursuit of Happiness

The 'declaration' that results from these repeated images, sounds, and rhythms is a single sustained utterance, a sort of philosophic cry.

Scores of engravings, songs, skits, plays, and ringing odes had cheered or bewailed the events leading up to Jefferson's document. Yet no one in 1776 bothered to paint, engrave, or dramatize its creation, or to celebrate its meaning in a broadside poem or a piece of music. Perhaps to its first audience the Declaration only made the inevitable official. Indeed, the *New-Hampshire Gazette* published its "Ode to Independence" on June 1. Beside the full text of the Declaration the *Pennsylvania Magazine* printed in its July 1776 (and last) issue an "Ode to Independence" written by Tobias Smollett around 1765. Notable only for having been written were a song "On Independence" published in the *Freeman's Journal* in August and another song entitled "Independence" which the young tunesmith Timothy Swan, recently at the Cambridge camp, entered in his manuscript notebook. Two immediate consequences of the Declaration, however, did involve the arts: the need to imagine a corporate identity for the thirteen states, and the related need to destroy the sacrosanct identity of the king.

On July 4, as it approved the Declaration, Congress appointed Jefferson, Adams, and Franklin a committee to contrive what Adams called "a Great Seal for the confederated States." [12] New images for America had been appearing since about the time of Lexington. The March 1775 (and also final) issue of the *Royal American Magazine* featured an engraving by Revere entitled *America in Distress*. Like nearly all of his prints it closely followed an English original, in this case a *Britannia in Distress* published five years earlier. The English engraver showed a female Britannia seated on a throne, slippered, outfitted with a shield displaying the British cross and a liberty pole with pileus, one breast exposed to symbolize ravishment by corrupt members of parliament. To represent "America," Revere removed the slippers and shield, and added an Indian bow, headdress, and quiver. He thus crossed "Britannia" with the image of the Indian princess used since the sixteenth century as an emblem of the New World. Merging redskin and paleface, the image reflects many radicals' identification with Indian vigor and militancy. The country was also beginning to be conceptualized under a new name. Philip Freneau had used the name Columba in 1772, and may have been the first to use in print the name Columbia. It appeared in July 1775 in his poem *American Liberty* and again three months later in the poem which Phillis Wheatley addressed to Washington at Cambridge. The name was unfamiliar enough so that Freneau felt obliged to append several glosses explaining that it signified "America sometimes so called from Columbus the first discoverer."

The congressional committee, however, had in mind a more traditional kind of national image, known variously as an emblem or device or *impresa*. Basically it consisted of a picture plus a motto, as the *Pennsylvania Magazine* explained to its readers in December 1775: "An emblematical device, when rightly formed, is said to consist of two parts, a *body* and a *mind*, neither of which is complete or intelligible, without the aid of the other. The figure is called the *body*, the motto the *mind*." Such figures derived from an ancient and intricately codified heraldic tradition which had declined in use over the last century, so that its terms were now reduced to obscure lore and confused with each other. (The phrase "emblematical device" used by the magazine represents a confusion of forms that were once distinct, the emblem and the device.)[13] Purists continued to hold that the *impresa* should be enigmatic, to prevent interpretation by the vulgar; those to whom the tradition mattered less held that the picture and motto should be obvious and public.

Both positions had spokesmen in 1776, although most radicals seem to have favored subtlety. A writer in the *Pennsylvania Journal* late in 1775 noted that the drums of the marine corps, then being raised, bore a rattlesnake with the motto "Don't tread on me," presumably designed for "the arms of America." Such an *impresa*, he argued, must be analyzed strictly by the rules of heraldry. He pondered "the worthy properties of the animal, in the crest, borne," and interpreted every feature of the snake—its bright eye, for instance, representing vigilance, or perhaps magnanimity and courage. Several invitingly cryptic devices appeared on new issues of paper money by the states, such as a thirteen-branched candelabrum with the motto *Uno Eodemque Igne* ("one and the same fire") and a thirteen-stringed harp with the motto *Majora Minoribus Consonant* ("the greater and the lesser ones sound together"). At least one Tory versifier found the rash of radical cabalism hilarious:

5
What a depth of Design we perceiv'd thro' the whole,
When the *Newspapers* pointed out *Body* and *Soul:*
The Eagle was *Britain*—the Hawthorn bush *We*—
The Mottos, explain'd, to a Tittle agree!

6
Then *We* were a Crane, and Great Britain a Spear—
Then *We* were the Corn, which *She* thrash'd most severe—
Or We were the Harp that was ever in tune—
Then We were the Beaver—and now We're the Spoon! [14]

Congress, then, had assigned its committee a difficult chore: to create a device signifying the unity of thirteen quite different states, using the language of an ill-understood and outmoded tradition.

Two of the three committee members could claim some experience for the work, though slight. Jefferson had created a possible device in 1774 ("the Father presenting the bundle of rods to his son"), while Franklin's "join or die" snake had proved effective as propaganda. Now Franklin proposed a device expressive not of unity so much as godly resistance. He would show Moses lifting a rod to divide the Red Sea, and pharaoh in his chariot overwhelmed by the waters, with the motto "Rebellion to Tyrants is Obedience to God." [15] Jefferson proposed a double device showing on one side the Israelites in the wilderness, led by a cloud by day and a pillar of fire by night, and on the other side the Saxon chiefs Hengist and Horsa. Adams, in his own words, "proposed the Choice of Hercules, as engraved by Gribeline. . . . The Hero resting on his Clubb. Virtue pointing to her rugged Mountain, on one Hand, and perswading him to ascend. Sloth, glancing at her flowery Paths of Pleasure, wantonly reclining on the Ground, displaying the Charms both of her Eloquence and Person, to seduce him into Vice." [16] The last two devices were highly personal, Jefferson the Anglo-Saxon scholar emphasizing the continuance of 'Northern Liberty' in America, Adams the Puritan moralist emphasizing the choice between austerity and pleasure.

The committee also applied for suggestions to Pierre-Eugène du Simitière, a Swiss émigré who had made his home in Philadelphia. Passionately pro-American, Du Simitière devoted himself to retrieving the country's cultural past. He made an index of European paintings in America and collected early American poetry, culling verses from colonial periodicals of the 1720's and locating poems left in manuscript by the Dutch clergy of seventeenth-century New Amsterdam. A collector of antiquities and of natural history specimens as well, he planned to create the first American museum. By vocation, however, Du Simitière was a painter and draftsman. It was he who engraved the bombastic Minerva for the *Pennsylvania Magazine*, to which he also contributed highly skilled technological engravings and a map of Virginia. Peale visited his painting room in 1772, and found it ornamented with medals and coins, framed butterflies, and preserved snakes: "he was a Batcheler," Peale reflected, "and such was his chief amusement." [17]

Du Simitière proposed not an *impresa* but a more traditional coat-of-arms. In the past the arms of a state had nearly always been those of the sovereign or his family; these, after July 4, no longer existed, and Jefferson had privately discarded the idea. Du Simitière substituted the arms of the nations which had peopled America—England, Scotland, Ireland, Holland, Germany. To one side of the shield would stand a Libertas with pileus; on the other side, a uniformed rifleman holding a gun and tomahawk. Like the designs of Franklin and Jefferson and Adams, Du Simitière's conception was highly personal, an immigrant's conception of America's polyglot inheritance tinged with French noble-savagery.

Indeed each of the proposals was too personal for the purpose, and otherwise flawed. Du Simitière considered his frontiersman's "Armour" unique to America, but Franklin produced a book showing a Roman soldier clad identically. Adams considered his own device too complicated and unoriginal, its subject having been very popular with eighteenth-century painters. Jefferson's Hebraic-Saxon device was rather remote, and Tom Paine objected to the use of biblical scenes.[18] All of the designs lacked the support of some adequate, shared idea of America.

The design which the committee ultimately submitted to Congress on August 20 salvaged the ideas of everyone but Adams. One side of the seal would show the arms of the United States, consisting of a large shield with emblems of England and of European countries. Around these would be a chain of thirteen scutcheons, each with the name of a state. Supporting the shield would be an armored Goddess of Liberty holding a spear and cap, and the figure of Justice with sword and balance. At the crest above the group—apparently a fresh addition—would be an "Eye of Providence in a radiant Triangle whose Glory [i.e., beams] extends over the Shield and beyond the Figures." Beneath would be the motto *E Pluribus Unum*.[19] The other side of the seal would show Pharaoh in a chariot pursuing the Israelites through the Red Sea, a pillar of fire in the sky "beaming on Moses who stands on the Shore and extending his hand over the Sea causes it to overwhelm Pharaoh." Encircling the scene would be the motto "Rebellion to Tyrants is Obedience to God."

The committee thus brought back to Congress an interesting image. It stressed the unity of states and the diversity of national origins in America, it recorded the country's devotion to Libertas and Rising Glory, and acknowledged New England's Hebraism. Yet it was also overly intellectualized and very crowded, lacking in graphic punch. The committee had tried rather to honor different interests than to find a single image of mutual interest. They brought back more a visual anthology of patriotic ideas than a memorable symbol. For all the committee's work, Congress at once tabled its report for consideration again later. Meanwhile it continued its business without an official seal.

If unable to decide who they were collectively, those who in 1776 began to re-see and rename themselves differed from the dispossessed children and orphans of the 1760's. Whether buckskins, Saxon chiefs, or Old Testament patriarchs, they no longer wept at their abandonment by an adored parent. On the contrary, many rejoiced in his going. Independence, of course, was inseparable from denying the king's authority, an act with dreadful undercurrents of sacrilege, parricide, and chaos. Anniversaries of the king's birth and coronation had been, until recently, important dates in the colonies, occasions for concerts, toasts, odes, and the singing of "God Save the King" and "Rule Britannia." Now the forms remained but the content changed. Instead of singing "God Save the King," patriots sang, to the same tune, "GOD save great WASHINGTON":

> Crush all the tyrant's crew,
> Dogs that our lives pursue;
> WASHINGTON them subdue—
> Conquer them all.

The ritualistic round of toasts that formerly began "The KING and the British Parliament" now began with the Continental Congress.[20]

If Americans transferred their former devotion to the king to themselves, the transfer was nevertheless absolute, unalienable. Rumblings of criticism against the king had begun to be heard at around the time of Bunker's Hill. Soon after, the king was de-sanctified, accused, and cursed. In Tom Paine's *Dialogue*, Montgomery's ghost tells a reverential congressional delegate: "I live in a world where all political superstition is done away. The King is the author of all the measures carried on against America." In "A Political Litany," Freneau anathematized the king as a crowned dope, "a royal king Log, with his tooth-full of brains."

In 1776, effigies of the king appeared for the first time and were burned, buried, or exploded. Citizens of Savannah, Georgia, listened to a reading of the Declaration at their liberty pole, after which the light infantry and grenadiers accompanied the king to the courthouse, where he was interred with the words:

> . . . we, therefore, commit his political existence to the ground—corruption to corruption—tyranny to the grave—and oppression to eternal infamy, in sure and certain hope that he will never obtain a resurrection, to rule again over these United States of America.

After a public reading of the Declaration in New York on July 9, citizens pulled down the gilt equestrian statue of the king on the Bowling Green. It had been commissioned in gratitude for the repeal of the Stamp Act; now it was broken up and sent to women in Litchfield, Connecticut, who molded it into some 42,000 cartridges. As the statue was being overthrown, one man in the crowd sensed that the order of things was tumbling too.[21] He expressively quoted Milton's angel addressing Lucifer:

> "If thou be'st he! But ah, how fallen! how changed!"

33. New York, New Jersey, Pennsylvania: Summer 1776–Winter 1777–78

The withdrawal of Howe and a large band of Loyalists to Nova Scotia after the long siege of Boston proved not a retreat but a recovery. On June 25, three months after leaving Boston, Howe and a vanguard of his force arrived off Sandy Hook, intending to seize New York City for a new base. Washington had hastily thrown up works for the city's defense, as one Loyalist observed:

New York, in ev'ry Street, was Fortify'd:
Numbers upon each Green, & Dock beside:
The Island's width, & length, full fourteen Miles
Was full of Ditches, Forts, Redoubts, & Piles:
And still beyond; so great was Rebel Sence,
They plac'd, their Idol Fort; Independence
On each side up & down is ditch & Fort,
It seems that labour, was their daily Sport.[1]

Preparing for an attack wherever Howe might decide, Washington dispersed his forces in Long Island, Brooklyn Heights, Governor's Island, and in and around the city.

On August 27 the British engaged the Americans in the first pitched battle of the war, throwing some 20,000 invading troops against an army of 8,000, mostly raw militia, on Long Island. The Americans got some 1,500 casualties. Badly beaten, Washington decided to withdraw by night in small boats and to regroup his forces in Manhattan. His defeat was ridiculed in a spirited skit entitled *The Battle of Brooklyn, A Farce of Two Acts: As it was performed on Long-Island, on Tuesday the 27th Day of August, 1776. By the Representatives of the Tyrants of America Assembled at Philadelphia* (New York, 1776). The author depicted Washington as a whoremongering barbarian and demagogue, inwardly fearful of the American people. Even the wife of General Horatio Gates, regretful that her husband has joined him, castigates Washington for allegedly countenancing the destruction of the king's statue: "none, but a little-minded barbarian, would have suffered the Arts to be trampled under foot." (In November, British troops retaliated by pulling down and decapitating the companion statue of Pitt.) Washington's servant girl, however, thinks him "the sweetest, meekest, melancholy, sighing Gentleman"; but she at thirty dollars a night is his mistress.

In fact, Washington was in no position for dallying. In September, as Howe again readied for battle, he decided to evacuate his army to the north, receiving advice for and against burning the city as he left. Closely chased by Howe, he led the army in retreat up Manhattan Island. On September 20, by accident or design, a fire broke out on a wharf at the end of the city, spread rapidly, and ultimately destroyed nearly 500 buildings. People fled their homes in terror; Trinity Church was leveled. A Loyalist poet described the twelve hours of burning:

The engine's roar—the carman's rattling wheel—
The fireman's cry, the Soldier's glittering steel—
Grief at each heart, in every face amaze,
The town all uproar, and the heavens ablaze.
Enormous ladders scale the tottering wall;
The lofty roofs in smoking ruins fall. . . .[2]

Washington reformed his army on Harlem Heights, where he stayed for a month, moving to White Plains toward the end of October, as Howe's army again advanced upon him. In November, still pursued by the British, Washington continued to retreat across the Hudson through New Jersey, fearing that Howe, emboldened by success, might march against Philadelphia in the winter.

Howe did not. A tall, graceful, and aristocratic man, sympathetic with the Americans, he decided rather to go into winter quarters, disposing his troops in New Jersey and returning himself with an entourage to New York. His passivity has long puzzled historians, although one British soldier explained that he took his motto from the King of Prussia: "*Toujours de la gaieté.*" Knighted for his triumph on Long Island, Sir William was welcomed to Manhattan with Handellian splendor:

> HE comes, he comes, the Hero comes:
> Sound, sound your Trumpets, beat your Drums:
> From port to port let Cannon roar
> Howe's welcome to this western Shore! [3]

Howe measured up to his reputation. Instead of chasing Washington, his officers reopened the John Street Theatre. The season began on January 25, 1777, with *The Beaux' Stratagem* and Henry Fielding's *Tom Thumb*. According to Hugh Gaine's *Mercury*, the parts were taken by "gentlemen of the navy and army," who acted with "taste and strong conception of the humor." The scenery, painted by Captain Oliver Delancey, "would not disgrace a theatre, though under the management of a Garrick." The military troupe also contained William Hulett, the son of a dancer in the original Hallam company, whose dancing school stood on John Street "Fronting the Theatre." [4] The actors managed eighteen performances before Howe resumed operations in the summer, merely inaugurating what would become a sophisticated military theatre in wartime New York.

While Howe's actors readied their season, Washington, camped in Newark, was feeling the effects of his successive retreats. He saw himself in charge of an ill-provisioned army plagued by brief enlistments and dependence on the militia. Unless a new army could be recruited, he felt, "the game will be pretty well up. . . ." [5] He decided, however, to strike out across the ice-filled Delaware at the British winter quarters, particularly the isolated post at Trenton.

One participant in these desperate attacks was Charles Willson Peale, who related them in detail in his diaries. From Philadelphia he had followed the news of Washington's retreat from New York anxiously, since the escaping army included both his brother James and his brother-in-law.

At the same time he entered as a "Common Soldier" in the militia, serving guard duty at night and painting and making false teeth by day. By November, through an election in the company, he was made a first lieutenant, one of his duties being to ascertain from the troops "who will go [i.e., join the main army] and who not and their Reasons. . . ." He also wrote personally to every man in his command promising to obtain "everything they should want" and assuring their wives that "they should be supplied with necessaries while their Husbands were doing their duty in the field." [6]

Peale's military career, and Washington's attack, began with a false start. Washington arrived in Trenton on December 3, hoping to be reinforced by the troops of General Lee from White Plains. When he learned that Lee was still several days away, he was forced to cross his troops into Pennsylvania. At the same time, Peale and his eighty-one men, with the rest of the city troops, were ordered across the river to Trenton to join Washington. They no sooner reached Trenton than they were ordered back across the river with Washington's retiring army. The withdrawing forces made, Peale wrote, "a grand but dreadfull appearance. All the shores were lighted up with large fires. The Boats continually passing and repassing full of men, Horses, artilery, and Camp Equipage." As Washington deployed the troops along a twenty-five-mile front in Pennsylvania, Peale found himself sleeping in tents, alternately serving guard duty, painting miniatures for his men, and vomiting. He left a description of himself at the time:

> Peale was a thin, spare, pale faced man, in appearance totally unfit to endure the fatigues of long marches, and lying on the cold wet ground, sometimes covered with snow. Yet by temperance and by a forethought of providing for the worst that might happen, he endured this campaign better than many others whose appearance was more robust, he always carried a piece of dryed Beef and Bisquits in his Pocket, and Water in his canteen, which he found, was much better than Rum.

On December 8, Peale came across his brother James, who in the retreat from New York had lost his clothing. James was wrapped in an "old dirty Blanket Jacket, his beard long, and his face so full of Sores, that he could not clean it," so disfigured that Peale did not recognize him at first sight.[7]

On Christmas night Washington debarked again across the Delaware for Trenton, this time in hail and snow. Peale doled out rum to his men, some of whom wore rawhide moccasins which he, an ex-saddler, had fashioned. He also gave them beef, pork, and potatoes bought out of his own pocket. As part of the militia, Peale and his troops were supposed to attack the Hessians simultaneously at Burlington. They were unable, however, to move their artillery through the ice and snow. At one point they ran across Washington, who called to find out who they were. Peale, in his own words, "stepped up to him and told the Gen'l that he was giving his men something to refresh them, very well march on as fast as you can [sic]." (Peale's son Rembrandt—probably recalling a story told by his father—later wrote that at Trenton, Washington, "from a kind personal regard for the *Artist Captain,* kept him near his person, for extraordinary services. . . .")[8]

Washington had better success than Peale. In less than an hour at Trenton he took almost a thousand prisoners. On January 3, he marched toward Princeton, intending to destroy the garrison there and to take provisions. Peale and his men, marching in mud "almost over our Shoe Tops," came to within a quarter-mile of the college town, which they fired with artillery. The enemy coming upon their rear forced them into Princeton itself, together with their prisoners. In the brief fighting the Americans drove out the British regiments but lost General Hugh Mercer. After the battle Peale returned to Philadelphia. In his absence his family, only recently settled in the place, had fled and returned. Fearful of being in the line of march should the British cross the Delaware, they had left the city, taking with them all of Peale's canvases rolled up; unable to find a refuge, they had come back.[9] Washington, invigorated by his success in New Jersey, moved the army into winter quarters at Morristown.

Even as Washington settled in, a larger American victory was preparing. In February 1777, the playwright-soldier Burgoyne had proposed a plan to isolate New England from the rest of the country by holding a line along the Hudson and Lake Champlain from New York to Montreal. Basically it called for Burgoyne to move south from Canada, capture Fort Ticonderoga, and move to Albany; there Howe was to join up with him, bringing an army from New York. The actual operation began in mid-June, when Burgoyne and about 10,000 troops moved from Canada down to Lake Champlain.

Burgoyne the "literary fop" emerged when the army reached Bouquet Ferry, some forty miles north of Ticonderoga. Here Burgoyne made a speech and issued a proclamation. The first he addressed to his 400 Indian warriors assembled in council, urging restraint upon them. (Edmund Burke himself parodied the speech in the House of Commons: "My gentle lions—my humane bears—my tenderhearted hyenas, go forth! But I exhort you, as you are Christians and members of civil society, to take care not to hurt any man, woman or child.") The proclamation began in Burgoyne's highest style:

Proclamation

By John Burgoyne, Esq; etc. etc. Lieut. General of his Majesty's Forces in America, Colonel of the Queen's Regiment of Light Dragoons, Governor of Fort-William in North-Britain, one of the Representatives of the Commons of Great-Britain in Parliament, and commanding an Army and Fleet in an expedition from Canada etc. etc. etc.

William Livingston, a congressman and now governor of New Jersey, heard in Burgoyne's rodomontade the swish of a wooden sword:

> By John Burgoyne and Burgoyne, John, Esq.
> And graced with titles still more higher,
> For I'm Lieutenant-general, too,
> Of George's troops both red and blue,
> On this extensive continent;
> And of Queen Charlotte's regiment
> . . . .
> Directing too the fleet and troops
> From Canada as thick as hops;
> And all my titles to display,
> I'll end with thrice et cetera.

Burgoyne's proclamation proceeded to praise mercy as a British national trait, at the same time threatening the patriots: "The Messengers of Justice and of Wrath await them in the Field, and Devastation, Famine, and every concomitant Horror that a reluctant but indispensable Prosecution of Military Duty must occasion. . . ." If the sword was wooden, Livingston implied, the hand wielding it desired genuinely to let blood:

> I, the great knight of de la Mancha,
> Without 'Squire Carleton, my Sancho,
> Will tear you limb from limb asunder
> With cannon, blunderbuss and thunder;
> And spoil your feathering and your tarring;
> And cagg you up for pickled herring.
> . . . .
> I will let loose the dogs of Hell,
> Ten thousand Indians, who shall yell
> And foam and tear, and grin and roar,
> And drench their moccasins in gore;
> To these I'll give full scope and play
> From Ticonderog to Florida;
> They'll scalp your heads, and kick your shins,
> And rip your guts, and flay your skins,
> And of your ears be nimble croppers,
> And make your thumbs tobacco-stoppers.

At first, Burgoyne was shown to be capable of more than bluster. He quickly seized Fort Ticonderoga, crushing American morale.[10]

Burgoyne pursued the retreating American forces to Skenesborough, where he took over Fort Edward. Here again his threats turned out to be no less dangerous for being histrionic. Some of his Indian warriors seized from a house near Fort Edward a woman in her early twenties named Jane M'Crea. They shot, scalped, mutilated, and possibly tomahawked her, along with a family containing six children. Her body was identified by the scalp: She had strikingly colored (perhaps chestnut) hair, floor-length.[11]

Long and repeatedly forewarned in images of rape and seduction, the death of Jane M'Crea came with the numbing shock of the predictable. For a woman patriot in the *New-Jersey Gazette*, it confirmed how the British had "waged war against our sex." About to be married at the time of her murder, Jane M'Crea fell into the mold of the sentimental heroine. One poet described a soldier happening upon her corpse:

> A lady richly dress'd, her name *M'Crea;*
> Stretch'd on the ground, and struggling there with death,
> She cannot live, she must resign her breath.
> The cursed *Indian* knife, the cruel blade,
> Had cut her scalp, they'd tore it from her head;
> The blood is gushing forth from all her veins,
> With bitter groans and sighs she tells her pains.
> Is this that blooming fair? is this *M'Crea?*
> This was appointed for her nuptial day.
> Instead of smiles and a most brilliant bride,
> Her face besmear'd with blood, her raiment dyed;
> Instead of pleasure and transporting joys,
> There's naught but dying groans and bitter sighs. . . .

One fact, however, made Jane M'Crea's death a less-than-ideal image of American purity defiled. She was a Tory sympathizer, affianced to an officer in Burgoyne's Loyalist contingent. As a Frenchman commented later, "a death so cruel and unforeseen would furnish a most pathetic subject for a drama or an elegy; but the charms of eloquence and poetry can arouse sympathy for such a fate only by displaying the effect and ignoring the cause. . . ."[12] Indeed, not until the nineteenth century did Jane M'Crea become a folk heroine, the subject of countless poems and engravings.

Burgoyne's successes quickly turned to defeat. He had reached Fort Edward only after an extraordinarily difficult march through a trackless forest and bogs. His supplies depleted, he dispatched troops, mostly Hessians and Indians, to capture horses in nearby Bennington, Vermont.

There a pick-up force of rebels killed or dispersed most of the Indians and took about 700 prisoners. With his ranks thinned by the losses, Burgoyne learned that Howe's army, instead of meeting him at Albany, was headed for Philadelphia. He saw no alternative but to push on for Albany himself. On September 13, he crossed the Hudson River to Saratoga, where he engaged a much larger army led by General Gates and by Benedict Arnold, many of whose troops were inflamed by the Jane M'Crea massacre. The fighting was bloody; several of Burgoyne's regiments lost nearly half their men. One balladeer acknowledged the heroism on both sides:

> We fought them full six hours like valiant hearts of old
> Each party scorn'd for to give way, we fought like Britons bold
> Until the leaves with blood were stain'd, our General then did cry
> It is diamond cut diamond, fight on until we die.[13]

In the end, Burgoyne's diamond was the less cutting. After several weeks of fighting he decided to ask for terms.

On October 17, 1777, with much polite ceremony, the senior officers of both armies met for dinner. As "Gentleman Johnny's" troops marched off, the bulk of the British northern army, American military musicians apparently gave them "Yankee Doodle." One British officer recorded his reaction: "*Yankey-doodle*, is now their paean, a favorite of favorites, played in their army, esteemed as warlike as the Grenadier's March—it is the lover's spell, the nurse's lullaby. After our rapid successes, we held the Yankees in great contempt; but it was not a little mortifying to hear them play this tune. . . ."[14] Patriot versifiers toasted Burgoyne's disgrace:

> HERE's a health to the States,
>   And the brave General Gates,
> Whose conduct in history will shine;
>   In the year seventy-seven,
>   With the assistance of heaven,
> He defeated th' *important* Burgoyne.

The defeat of "Sir Jack Brag" had important effects. It jeopardized Lord North's ministry, initiated the resignation of all the British commanders-in-chief in America, and encouraged France to enter the war. It also whetted the patriots' appetite for fresh victories:

> Brave boys we'll now go & visit Lord Howe.
>   With powder and ball we will line him,
> With courage hold out & we shall without doubt
>   Before the next winter Burgoyne him.[15]

Howe did not disappoint the gleeful expectations of his Burgoyning. In

May, as Burgoyne had been preparing to enter the colonies from Canada, Howe began pulling his men out of New Jersey for an invasion of Philadelphia. Washington, deciding to stay close to the enemy, had placed his army near the British outpost at New Brunswick. When Howe tried to evacuate the post in June, the two sides maneuvered against each other, but Howe succeeded in collecting his troops. Regrouped, he led some 15,000 men and 160 ships out of New York on July 1, leaving the defense of the city to Sir Henry Clinton. Washington waited in New Jersey to learn Howe's whereabouts and intentions; news that Howe's ships had appeared in the Chesapeake convinced him that the objective was Philadelphia. Joined by Cornwallis, Howe tried to push through Washington's army to the city. Philadelphia grew alarmed. Congress ordered military stores evacuated, then itself moved hastily to Lancaster. On September 11, after suffering a thousand casualties at Brandywine Creek, Washington's army fled in confusion, bringing Howe to within twenty miles of Philadelphia. Two weeks later, Cornwallis and a column of troops took possession of the city. Howe and Washington continued dueling at Germantown and elsewhere outside Philadelphia until early December, when Washington's army settled into winter quarters at Valley Forge.

During the six months of this New Jersey campaign and the British occupation of Philadelphia, Peale again found himself rushing from his family to battle and back again. He and his men joined the fighting in June when Howe tried to withdraw his forces from New Jersey. Once more he encountered his brother James, now a prematurely gray-haired man whose wife had been raped. He also visited at camp with Washington, who promised to sit for a miniature and invited him to dine. Peale washed his linen for the occasion, but lost his horse, had to walk, and arrived too late for the dinner or the sitting. He lingered for several days, uneasy at not having heard from his family. Feeling that he "could not with any Pleasure stay to take the likeness of General Washington," he returned to Philadelphia. Here he was burdened with a "grievous task." Much to his distaste, the Executive Council of Pennsylvania assigned him to take the word of "sundry suspicious characters" that they would not aid the British. After Howe's landing in the Chesapeake, the Council recommended the arrest of several suspects, Peale being among the twenty or so charged with arresting them. Those cited included the artist James Claypoole, the college poet Thomas Coombe, the dancing master Thomas Phile, Peale's friend James Tilghman (who had enabled him to set up his saddlery sixteen years ago), and Provost William Smith. Smith was exempted when his congregation intervened on his behalf. The rest were detained in the Masonic Lodge without legal recourse, then carried in captivity to Virginia for eight months.[16]

As the British forced through Washington's army at Brandywine Creek, Peale became too worried about his family to join his troops. Leaving Rachel and the others in Philadelphia, he obtained rooms for them thirty miles outside town. When he returned, however, he learned that they had fled into New Jersey, having been warned at midnight that the British were crossing the Schuylkill. The reported invasion turned out to be rumor. Again Peale crossed into New Jersey, located the other Peales after much searching, and brought them back. But this time the British had actually crossed the river and stood at Germantown. As local patriots prepared to make some defense of Philadelphia, Peale rode out to Washington at Pennypacker Mills to ask for supplies. He told Washington of his plans to ready the militia, and received from him "as much Powder in a bag as he could well manage on horseback." He also got Washington to sit for the miniature he had planned to take in New Jersey before losing his horse.[17]

Upon Cornwallis' occupation of Philadelphia Peale removed his family to near New Town in Bucks County, and rejoined the militia as a scout and picket. He marched out on several scouting platoons, painting miniatures for soldiers to have as keepsakes, restricting himself to the small forms because they were "more portable" than canvases and could be "kept out of the way of a plundering Enemy." As winter closed in and the fighting closed down, he divided his time between his company and his family. When visiting Rachel in Bucks County he frequently slept blanketed under leaves in the woods, his dog and gun beside him, apprehensive of local Tories. One time he started from sleep to find his right hand "senseless," apparently frostbitten. He rubbed it with cold water all night, fearing the "loss of a hand to a Person who had his living to get by his labours."[18] Partly because he felt safer there, he followed Washington's army, in January, into Valley Forge.

The British army, meanwhile, had entered a desolated city. The adult male population of Philadelphia had declined to around 5,000, church bells had been removed for safety, buildings and stores stood unoccupied. All of that changed as the large army took up quarters, giving local society an animation perhaps not greater than before but probably no less, and certainly different. Taverns soon resounded with voices singing "God Save the King" and "Briton Strike Home" over punch and wine, "till the imagination is heated," said Francis Hopkinson, "and then these pot-valiant patriots sally forth and commit all manner of riot and excess in honour of their king and country." The empty stores attracted perfumers, hairdressers, and itinerant traders. The new occupation newspaper, *The Royal Pennsylvania Gazette*, advertised a startling array of luxury goods—cards, cricket bats, "Velverett" (cotton cloth with a velvet surface), "fashionable crooked combs," "Lip salve," "Purified Italian shaving powder." [19] Near the ads appeared Tory poems such as "America's Lamentation" and "The Loyalist," attacking the "stubborn soul" of Congress, denouncing Bostonians as "the dregs of Cromwell's spawn," and promising that England would protect her errant child despite her waywardness, "With all a mother's poignancy of grief." Robert Bell—publisher of *Common Sense*—began to issue a profusion of American editions of English poems and plays, announcing his wares for those who "choose to delight themselves with the more exalted and sublime Entertainments of SENTIMENTALISM." The musician H. B. Victor called for subscribers, at twenty shillings, to his *Compleat Instructor for the Violin*, promising a multilingual glossary of musical terms and an elegant frontispiece engraved by John Norman "in the present taste." [20]

The present taste required social amusements as well. One Hessian soldier found in Philadelphia so many "Assemblies, concerts, comedies, clubs, and the like" as to "make us forget there is any war, save that it is a capital joke." [21] The Southwark Theatre, vacant since the final appearance of the American Company in 1773, was reopened. Performances— followed by a ball at the City Tavern—were announced in the press and on handbills as for the benefit of the "WIDOWS and ORPHANS of the ARMY," tickets costing a dollar for boxes and pit, half a dollar for the gallery.

Seasoned by their earlier productions in occupied New York, "Howe's Strolling Players" began by advertising in December for stage managers and a clerk and treasurer, and for copies of plays, which they had trouble obtaining. The officers had to write out texts, sitting around a table on stage and copying out of a single printed play. Many of the soldiers' wives helped at the theatre, staying there all day to watch rehearsals. The players included several Philadelphia belles and a professional actress, Miss Hyde. Among the males were Dr. Hammond Beaumont (a surgeon general), Major Richard Crewe (apparently also the director of the troupe), Captain Oliver Delancey, Major Edward Williams, and the popular Major John André. As an actor, in one account, André was mediocre, albeit "very active, always hopping about the stage, and never out of humor." He also painted the company's scenery. A contemporary recalled seeing one of his sets, a "distant champagne country and a winding rivulet" with waterfall and forest; the perspective was "excellently preserved; the foliage, verdure and general coloring artistically toned and glazed." [22] Quartered in the home of the absent Benjamin Franklin, André became a favorite in Philadelphia society.

The season opened on January 19, 1778, with Mrs. Centlivre's *The Wonder. A Woman Keeps a Secret.* The prologue—based on the prologue delivered at the opening of Howe's New York theatre—declared the Southwark productions superior to those of Ranelagh, Vauxhall, or Sadlers Wells, and dazzling to the loutish Americans:

> Once more ambitious of Theatric Glory
> *Howe's* strolling Company appears before ye.
> O'er hill & dale & bogs, thro wind & weather,
> With many a hair-breadth scape we've scrambled hither.—
> For *we,* true Vagrants of the Thespian Race,
> While Summer lasts ne'er know a settled place.
> Anxious to prove the merit of our Band,
> A chosen Squadron wand'ring thro' the land,
> How beats each Yankee Bosom at our drum:
> "Hark *Jonathan,* Zounds here the Strollers come."
> Spruc'd up with Top Knots & their Sunday dress,
> With eager Looks the maidens round express:
> "*Jemima* see—An't this a charming sight?"
> "Look *Tabitha*—Oh! Lord, I wish 'twas night." [23]

Before the season ended, in May 1778, the military actors produced fourteen plays, including such standards as *Henry IV, Part I*, John Home's *Douglas*, and Samuel Foote's *The Minor.*[24]

The Philadelphia social whirl brought criticism against Howe, from both sides. His friends connected his capering with his notorious failure to pursue Washington's army. Joseph Stansbury, chosen director of the Library Company in the occupied city, tagged Howe "The Carpet Knight" for retiring after surprising Washington at Whitemarsh. Another Loyalist wondered why Sir William, with nearly 20,000 men, did not attack nearby Valley Forge. He urged:

> Awake, arouse, Sir Billy,
> There's forage in the plain,
> Ah, leave your little Filly,
> And open the Campaign.

The "little Filly" was Mrs. Joshua Loring; the wife of a Loyalist commissary of prisoners, she became Howe's mistress in Philadelphia, and attended the theatre with him. To patriots, of course, they seemed a delightful pair. When the Americans sent floating mines down the Delaware to harass British shipping, leading British troops to shoot at everything in sight on the river, Francis Hopkinson described Howe's reactions in his popular "Battle of the Kegs":

> Sir William he, snug as a flea,
>   Lay all this time a snoring,
> Nor dream'd of harm as he lay warm,
>   In bed with Mrs. L——g.

> Now in a fright, he starts upright,
>   Awak'd by such a clatter;
> He rubs both eyes, and boldly cries,
>   For God's sake, what's the matter? [25]

The matter with Howe, concluded the author of *A Tory Medley* (Philadelphia, 1777), was simply that he squandered conquest in voluptuousness:

> Howe with his legions came,
> In hopes of wealth and fame,
>   What has he done?
> All day, at Faro play'd,
> All night, with whores he laid,
> And with his bottle made,
>   Excellent fun.

The climax to the fun, and to Howe's stay in America, came with the huge pageant known as the *Mischianza* (Italian *mischio*, a medley). It was organized by André and by Captain Delancey to mark Howe's resignation as commander-in-chief, and his departure for England on May 25.[26] The day began with a regatta on the Delaware, involving 400 persons in decorated galleys and flatboats, and music boats that struck up "God Save the King." At 6:00 P.M. the regatta landed where there had been erected for the occasion a Doric triumphal arch, two small amphitheatres, and a carousel. In the amphitheatres, several colorfully dressed army bands performed martial music, followed by a parade of horses, soldiers, and heralds costumed for a mock joust. The lavishness of the women's costumes (designed by André) may be judged from a surviving description of the outfit of a "Lady to one of the Knights of the burning mountain." The headdress was a high turban and veil ornamented with "a black feather, jewels, gold lace & spangles"; the white silk gown was "flounced & Spangled," held around the waist by a silk sash tied with "Gold Strings and tassells." Supper was served in a 180-foot-long salon built for the purpose. Garlanded and chandeliered, it sported niches for buffets and music from concealed bands. A poem was to have been recited at this "feast of military love" by a plumed Mars, but was suppressed "in delicacy to the general." Tracing the chivalric motif of the *Mischianza* back to "manly sports" of the Middle Ages, it intimated that the heroism of the first English knights had been reborn in Howe.[27] The supper ended with toasts, a ball, and fireworks. The guests received expensive souvenirs (ill., p. 531).

Talked about long after, this ostentatious blend of medieval pageantry and eighteenth-century politeness brought a round of fresh criticism upon Howe. The Philadelphia Quaker Hannah Griffiths saw the *Mischianza* as a "shameful scene of dissipation," meant to dance off the burden of failure:

> Triumphal arches, rais'd on—Blunders
> And true Don Quixotes made of wonders;

The song of victory complete
Loudly reechoed from—Defeat
The Fair of vanity profound
A madman's dance, a Comus round.

In England, Howe was criticized for accepting honors due the king alone; Howe's secretary, Ambrose Searle, feared that the Americans would "dwell upon the Folly & Extravagance of it with Pleasure. Every man of Sense, among ourselves, tho' not unwilling to pay a due Respect [to Howe's departure], was ashamed of this mode of doing it." Some military authorities believe that Howe's indulgences in Philadelphia softened his army much as the 'delights of Capua' weakened Hannibal's. Such an outcome seems to have been anticipated by Benjamin Franklin. When told in Paris that Howe had captured Philadelphia, he is said to have remarked, "No, Philadelphia has captured Howe." [28]

Awareness of the gay doings in Philadelphia, just twenty miles away, induced at Washington's camp a propriety consistent with the patriots' view of their cause. The entertainments held at General Nathanael Greene's quarters allowed "no *levées* or formal *soirées,* as with the Enemy in the City," one officer reported, "only conversation over a cup of tea or coffee. No dancing or amusement of any kind, except singing. Every gentleman or lady is called on in turn for a song." [29] More than Howe's unseemly example, of course, restricted the hilarity at Valley Forge. Housed in makeshift shelters, poorly fed and clothed, an estimated 2,500 of Washington's 10,000 troops died at the camp.

Yet Valley Forge was far from lacking social amenities. Colonel Thomas Procter's excellent military band was there (see the next section), and some troops brought along instruments. In the depth of winter, a soldier named Albigense Waldo heard from the next tent "an excellent Player on the Violin in that soft kind of Musick, which is so finely adapted to stirr up the tender Passions. . . ." Dr. James Thacher and other personnel from the camp hospital even hired a dancing instructor, hoping, Thacher wrote, "in due time" to be able to "figure in a ball-room." As Washington found time at Cambridge to reply to Phillis Wheatley he found time at Valley Forge to reply to the Yale poet Timothy Dwight (now a chaplain to General Samuel Parsons' brigade), who asked permission to dedicate to the general his epic-in-progress, *The Conquest of Canäan.* Washington had not seen the poem, but he wrote back to Dwight from camp, returning encouragement as well as consent. Nothing, he said, could please him more "than to patronize the essays of Genius and a laudable cultivation of the Arts and Sciences, which had begun to flourish in so eminent a degree, before the hand of oppression was stretched over our devoted Country." Nearer to Washington but apparently unseen by him, a soldier named John Parke

In his *Samuel Adams* (oil on canvas, 50 × 40), Copley revitalized one of the Knelleresque clichés, the finger pointed to suggest authority. Here Adams points at the Massachusetts Charter, his finger archingly taut with indignation.

Amos Doolittle, *The Engagement at the North Bridge in Concord.* The action is seen from approximately the place now occupied by

Acclaimed as the first painting to depict modern history in modern dress, Benjamin West's *The Death of General Wolfe* (oil on canvas, 59½ × 84) also used the imagery of Christian martyrdom to explore emerging romantic ideals.

Winthrop Chandler, *Captain Samuel Chandler* (oil on canvas, 54⅞ × 47⅞). The open window presents a picture-within-the-picture: dead or wounded troops, a flaming house, and distant files of tiny redcoats and puffs of gunsmoke.

Winthrop Chandler, *Rev. Ebenezer Devotion* (oil on canvas, 55 × 44). To the hard
outlines and literalism of the Puritan limners, Chandler added a passionate sense
of the sitter's physical presence.

Charles Willson Peale, *The Peale Family Group* (oil on canvas, 56½ × 89¾), shown in the artist's painting room, some portrait sculpture and a picture of the three graces in the background.

By about 1770, Copley had become the most sought-after and perhaps the wealthiest painter in America. At the height of his career in Boston he painted *Paul Revere* (oil on canvas, 35 × 28½) and *Mrs. Humphrey Devereux* (oil on canvas, 40⅛ × 32).

After repeated invitations, Copley moved for about six months in 1771 to New York City, where he painted a group of distinctively subdued and simplified portraits. TOP: *Samuel Verplanck* (oil on canvas, 30 × 25). BOTTOM: *Daniel Crommelin Verplanck* (oil on canvas, 49½ × 40).

ABOVE: Frontispiece of William Billings' *The New-England Psalm-Singer*, the first volume of American-composed music. The psalm singers sit at an ordinary table in an ordinary room, reflecting the sacred-secular character of the music.

BELOW: A New England singing gallery, depicted on the frontispiece of Oliver Brownson's *Select Harmony* (New Haven, 1783). The engraved canon contains the words for a song used to open an exhibition by the singing scholars, beginning: "Welcome welcome ev'ry guest, Welcome to our Music feast."

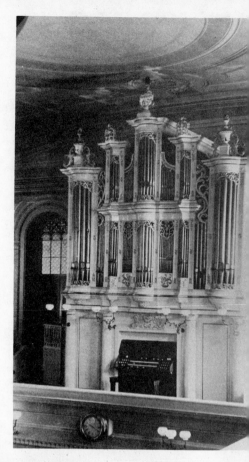

RIGHT: Organ of the Lutheran Church of the Holy Trinity, Lancaster, Pa. To one listener "it absolutely made the very building shake." David Tanneberger made the organ works; the ornate Chippendale case was carved by the cabinetmaker Peter Frick.

BELOW: Spinet built by Samuel Blyth of Salem, Mass., c. 1785–90. For a spinet he built in 1786 Blyth is known to have charged £18.

Judging by the rapturous verses addressed to her, *Nancy Hallam* was the first American star. Charles Willson Peale painted her as Imogen in Shakespeare's *Cymbeline* (oil on canvas, 50 × 40¼).

was writing classical translations and imitations, poems with conventional titles but eye-stopping datelines such as "Ode XXXI. To APOLLO. Camp. at Valley Forge, May 12, 1778." [30]

Peale, and very likely other artists too, found "some business in the miniature Painting" despite the piercing cold and pervasive sickness. During his stay at Valley Forge Peale executed small portraits in ivory of some forty officers. Chiefly, however, he painted Washington, with whom he dined and through whom he was befriended by the marquis de Lafayette.[31] Either from patriotism, admiration, or an eye to the main chance, he began at camp to turn the depiction of Washington into an industry. He brought with him in January the miniature he had made at Pennypacker Mills, for which in the growing inflation he charged the general fifty-six dollars. Colonel John Laurens saw the picture and told his father that "the visage is too long, and old age is too strongly marked in it," adding that there was another miniaturist at Valley Forge who had painted a better likeness of Washington. Peale no sooner delivered the miniature than he rode to a potter's, bought some clay, and began making a Washington bust. He also made replicas of one of his paintings of Washington, which he sold at camp to officers and troops. For such work, he used a made-to-order hinged stretcher that could be folded in three parts, fitted in a box, and carried with camp baggage without injuring the canvas.[32]

Theatre was not absent from Valley Forge either. The troops played a short season at the Bake House in April and May, although apparently without printing tickets or playbills. They put on *Cato*, and at least planned performances of Rowe's *The Fair Penitent*, Isaac Bickerstaffe's *The Padlock*, and Farquhar's *The Recruiting Officer*. *The Padlock* required a fairly elaborate musical effort, implying that some sort of theatre orchestra was available, probably Procter's military band. One performance, by contemporary testimony, played to "an overflowing audience," the parts being acted by "Officers and Ladies." According to another spectator, the May 11 production of *Cato* drew a "numerous and splendid" audience which included "Lady and Genl Washington, Lady and Lord Stirling and daughter Kitty, Mrs. Nathaniel Greene and many Officers. 'Cato' made an excellent 'die.' The scenery was in taste." If relieved to see Cato die instead of some friend, one soldier took no pleasure in the prospect of more plays being mounted. He hoped rather to be "disappointed in all these by the more agreeable Entertainment of taking possession of Philad[a]," a disappointment granted him in June.[33]

34. Excursus: Music in the Army

Miniature painting, classical imitations, and productions of *Cato* exist only as oddities in the national memory of Valley Forge, if they are remembered at all. Their mere presence is little-enough known to warrant some brief explanation. The particular presence of Colonel Thomas Procter's regimental band, more importantly, represents a new governmental sponsorship of music, which created a new corps of skilled native instrumentalists.

Obviously the playgoing, verse writing, and similar activities at Valley Forge served for diversion and to boost morale as the soldiers waited out the winter. But they were also driven by momentum, perpetuating the refinements which the country had accumulated, grown accustomed to, and striven to outdo over the last fifteen years. They received a fresh impulse, too, from conscious apprehensions that the war might reduce men swiftly from a civilized state into a state of nature. The damage sustained by cultural artifacts through looting, pillaging, and ideological fury on both sides made a long list, going back to the Stamp Act: a heart carved from Copley's portrait of Governor Hutchinson; the Chapel Street Theatre dismantled; the statues of the king and Pitt toppled; the organ pipes of Christ Church melted into bullets; South Church gutted for a stable; concerts and plays interrupted; Rivington, Copley, Stansbury, Pelham, Byles, Smith and others harassed or worse. More recently Hessian soldiers had bayoneted Matthew Pratt's large painting of Cadwallader Colden; British troops plundered several libraries in New York, offering the 60,000 or so volumes for sale on the streets; American troops in Mystic, Connecticut, destroyed the bellows and pipes of a local church organ.[1]

Such disregard for the symbols of human civility was widely condemned. The army surgeon James Thacher, among many others, protested this "warring against liberty, virtue and the arts and sciences. To make war against literature and learning is the part of barbarians." Ezra Stiles warningly recalled the "irreparable Losses sustained by the Repub. of Letters, in the destruction of the Alexandrian Library." The writing of Horatian odes, the violin playing at night in tents were in part attempts to assert human goodness despite the contrary evidence lying all around. Thus British troops built a theatre out of logs in Staunton, Virginia, in 1779. On the stage curtain they painted a Harlequin pointing his wooden sword at the words "Who would have expected this here?" A German officer explained why, in fact, "this" was "here": "The soldier wanted to show that he can rise above everything and find within himself aids in making his life tolerable and comfortable. Many things have been built by the soldiers out of spite. . . ." [2]

The wish to defy the degradation of war extended beyond Valley Forge. Indeed, in maintaining a semblance of cultural life, Washington's city of frozen huts was not odd but ordinary, typical of military camps everywhere throughout the Revolution. Any demonstration of the fact would become tediously repetitious. Enough to say that hardly a historical society from Maine to Florida lacks a military miniature or two painted at some camp, usually by an unidentified artist. Hundreds, perhaps thousands, of scraps of verse written in the field survive, of the kind traditional in all wars and all countries—lonely recollections of enlistment and tearful leave-taking, visions of groaning death. Military theatres existed in camps as scattered as Staunton and Charlottesville, Virginia; Savannah, Georgia; New Brunswick, New Jersey; Reading, Pennsylvania; and Portsmouth, New Hampshire. The Staunton playhouse, however makeshift, had three sets of scenery and offered two performances a week.[3]

In two ways, these cultural activities in the field not only maintained but raised cultural standards. First, they familiarized Americans all over with the theatre. Secondly, the armies carried into villages and open fields something confined before to the cities, and less well developed there than in the army: concerts of instrumental music.

"Nothing is more agreeable, and ornamental," Washington wrote, "than good music; every officer, for the credit of his corps, should take care to provide it." [4] Much surviving testimony justifies his concern. The Virginia tutor Philip Fithian was in camp on Long Island in August 1776 when the "To Arms" sounded; "instantly this vast body of men were at their respective posts. For one single hour, my heart fluttered. . . . horses straining every way . . . drums and fifes on all quarters making the very Air echo To Arms! To Arms!" Invigorating to one's own side, music could also be depressing to one's enemy. At the battle of New York, a British bugler played the notes of the fox chase at some American troops futilely pursuing his detachment. The taunting got to at least one American adjutant, who admitted: "I never felt such a sensation before, it seem'd to crown our Disgrace." [5] Considered inspirational, routinely used for military purposes, and always available, music was the most prevalent form of cultural activity in the army.

It was furnished by two distinct but related ensembles—the fife and drum groups and the far more splendid military bands. The fifes and drums came into existence with the organization of militia companies after 1775, but received fresh attention with the remolding of the Continental Army under Baron Friedrich von Steuben and Lafayette. In a General

Order on June 4, 1777, Steuben announced: "the music of the Army being in general very bad; it is expected, that the drum and fife Majors exert themselves to improve it, or they will be reduced." Steuben's subordinates helped to enforce his expectations. Artemas Ward of Boston ordered drum and fife majors to meet twice a week on the Common for practice, the drums and fifes of each regiment to practice separately under their respective majors until capable of joining together. He recommended that the musicians in each regiment "emulate each other in striving to excel in this pleasant part of military discipline." As a reminder, he ordered that the sentry's challenge be "MARTIAL," the countersign "MUSIC." [6] Other commanders specified how long fifers and drummers were to practice each day—four hours at Germantown in 1777, an hour at Valley Forge the next year—and also when: Drummers who practiced on their own, or outside appointed hours, sometimes confused the troops. Ultimately every American infantry company had fifers and drummers, every troop of horse had trumpeters. How many served in the army altogether is unknown, although certainly a large number. A 1783 survey of the musicians serving in twenty-three different regiments from the New England states, New York, and New Jersey lists a total of 158 drummers, 141 fifers, 22 drum majors, 19 fife majors, and 36 fife apprentices. [7]

In several ways, fifers and drummers stood out from the other troops. They perhaps made helpless targets; thirteen drummers were killed at the Battle of Bunker's Hill. Many were young, only ten or eleven years, often the sons of officers. Quite a few others seem to have been blacks, a fact apparently originating in colonial militias. One Bostonian in 1763 protested "the Musick of the Negro drum, that dins our ears on a training day." [8] American drum majors—who taught fifers and drummers—received extra pay for their work (unlike their British counterparts), although Washington warned them to improve their skill to earn it. Drummers and fifers also received extra pay: 7⅓ dollars a month for drummers in 1776, compared with 6⅔ dollars for privates. The increments for musicians obviously aroused resentment, the more so perhaps because fifers and drummers were often assigned to deal out punishments with the whip or cats-and-cord. Congress responded by ruling in 1781 that musicians must use this additional pay to repair their instruments. [9]

The instruments resembled those used by European armies. Drums meant snare or side drums, although some bass drums seem to have been used also. The thick drumheads usually were made of sheep and calf skins, which with the rather heavy sticks produced a deep sound, described by Fithian as "forceably grand." The fifes, rugged instruments without key levers or separable joints, played high to cut through the thundering drums. Brigades received large printed sheets on which to tally supplies; under the categories "Good, Bad, Wanting" they listed such items as fifes, cases, drums, drumheads, snares, cords, and pairs of sticks.[10]

The fifes and drums were used in various ways, chiefly to signal activities at camp and to give the cadence for the march. Steuben made drumbeat signals into a standard system of communication in his manual, *Regulations for the Order and Discipline of the Troops of the United States*, adopted by Congress in March 1779. Different camps, however, used their own version of Steuben's system, and the more daring drummers embellished at whim. The large number of calls included Reveille, Troop, and Tattoo, occurring nearly every day, and less frequently used calls for Cease Firing or Rogues March (to drive undesirables out of camp). The signals sometimes were misheard or misunderstood. At Germantown an American drum beating Parley (calling for a temporary suspension of battle to exchange information between sides) was mistaken for Retreat, and the troops panicked.[11] Marches were for the most part drawn from the European repertoire, those by Handel being particularly popular. Drums and fifes were also used for quasi- or non-military purposes—parades, recruiting parties, and informal entertainment at camp. Extant flute manuals used by military fifers contain jigs, reels, and minuets, and music for songs as different as "God Save the Congress," "The Sun was Set Beneath the Main," and "The Lass of Paties Mill." [12]

All of the fifing and drumming, indeed all of the music, in the Continental Army was in effect under the direction of one man—John Hiwell of the Boston 3d Regiment of Artillery. He had been at Valley Forge and knew Steuben's work there in training Washington's army during the early spring of 1778. In August 1778, after Steuben was appointed inspector general of the Continental Army, Hiwell was appointed inspector and superintendent of music, with pay and rations equal to a captain. He worked at the job with something of Steuben's singlehanded zeal. To help standardize the system of beats and signals, he personally instructed and supervised drum and fife majors, who in turn instructed regimental musicians. He personally dressed sheep and calf skins into drumheads and made sashes into drum cords.[13] Meanwhile he supervised the issuance and repair of instruments and tried to fill vacancies upon request from regimental officers. He was not always successful. Asked on one occasion to supply several musicians, he could find only a fifer and two drummers with "natural Geniuses for music." Like other army commissaries he was plagued by lack of supplies. In 1782 he complained that the army's music was in a "shatter'd situation," some regiments having ten fifers and no fifes, the drums in such disrepair as to be unplayable.[14]

The more imposing part of music in the army were the military bands—private groups of musicians employed by officers of the regiment. The so-called Band of Music grew out of the close relation between music and the military cultivated by such eighteenth-century monarchs as Louis XIV and Frederick the Great. Louis employed Jean Baptiste Lully to organize his bands and to compose music for them; Franz Joseph Haydn wrote specifically for the military band of the Princes Esterházy. Typically such bands consisted of two oboes, two clarinets, two bassoons, and two horns—the instrumentation of the classic woodwind octette. Frederick fixed the strength and makeup of the Prussian army bands at these parts, for which many marches were composed. Occasionally percussion might be added, and the players were assumed capable of also playing stringed instruments. European bands wore regimental uniforms but retained their civilian status; they were not required to perform as soldiers, nor subject to the military line of command.[15]

No Bands of Music existed in the Continental Army of 1776, although the colonists had seen them perform. They first arrived in the late 1750's, when the British sent full-strength regiments to America at the close of the French and Indian War. Some gave public concerts: The Royal Irish Regiment band performed at the College of Philadelphia commencement in 1767; in New York in the early 1770's other regimental bands gave benefit concerts, played at a presentation of Milton's *Comus*, and accompanied the songs during an intermission of *Romeo and Juliet* at the John Street Theatre. The particularly active British 64th Regiment band in Boston gave concerts in conjunction with local musicians like W. S. Morgan and Josiah Flagg. The war years greatly multiplied the number of British bands in America. Raoul Camus, the main authority on military music of the Revolution, computes that of the fifty-six British regiments serving in the Revolution, thirty-nine, at the very least, had bands, and the number was probably higher.[16]

The French allies and Hessian mercenaries brought even more elaborate and fashionable bands than the British. The *New-York Gazette* reported that the Hessians who landed in the city in October 1776 made "the Hills resound with Trumpets, French Horns, Drums and Fifes, accompanied by the Harmony of their Voices." Lord Rawdon said that the Hessians "sing hymns as loud as the Yankees, though it must [be] owned they have not the godly twang through the nose which distinguishes the faithful." A French observer noted that the quality of the Hessian bands far surpassed the musical standard of New York: "the banks of the rivers of Manhattan had never heard any [music] so perfect; the varied sounds of the flute, of the clarinet, of the hunting horns, and the bassoon. . . . Now it was a march imitated from the *Chants d'Orphée*, now one seemed to hear a shepherds' dance." [17] The regimental bands of General Rochambeau performed at several places, including Newport (where he built a dancing pavilion) and Baltimore, where en route to support Washington at Yorktown they provided the orchestra for a performance of *Humors of Ben the Soldier*. These French bands afforded Americans a hearing of the latest fashion, the janizary music then sweeping Europe, which added bass drums to the conventional band, plus cymbals, tambourines, bells, and other jingling instruments *ala turca,* as well as bizarre Turkish costumes and arm gyrations for the drummers. [18]

Such examples of musical opulence had inspired Americans to imitation since the time of the Townshend programs, when Josiah Flagg organized a militia band in Boston, followed by John Hancock, who in 1773 organized a band in his cadet company. The outbreak of war added a practical reason for emulation. Bands, even more than the fifes and drums, could directly affect morale. A military musician told Washington about a Virginia band that "had more Influence on the minds and Motions of the Militia . . . than would the Oratory of a Cicero; and, in the recruiting Business, they are at least as usefull as a well spoken recruiting Serjt." [19] With the British, French, and Hessian examples before it, the Continental Army began in 1777 to build its own Bands of Music.

How many American bands ultimately existed is uncertain. Seven are quite fully documented, many others are mentioned in contemporary diaries. The best of them was the band attached to the artillery regiment of Colonel John Crane, a former Boston Son of Liberty who led his troops in operations at Newport and at Saratoga. It owed its success to its supervisor, the inspector of music, John Hiwell. His "indefatigable endeavors to promote the science of Musick in the Army," as a colleague called them, included a special effort to obtain bassoons, clarinets, concert fifes, and other instruments for Crane's band through the quartermaster and through commercial instrument dealers in Philadelphia. The band performed at some important ceremonies, probably including the celebration near Philadelphia in 1778 honoring the French alliance. [20]

Perhaps next in importance was the band attached to Colonel Thomas Procter's Philadelphia artillery regiment. Half of its ten musicians came from Germany, including several professionals. This band accompanied General John Sullivan on his expedition into Indian country along the Pennsylvania and New York frontiers in 1779, and also played at Valley Forge for Washington (and Peale). Of the other well-documented bands, that of Colonel Samuel Webb's Connecticut Regiment included Timothy Olmstead, later a popular psalmodist; the band of "Light-Horse Harry" Lee's Partisan Corps was led by Philip Roth, a defector previously in charge of a British regimental band. Other known bands were attached to the regiments of Christian Febiger, Henry Jackson, and Philip Van Cortland.

Like the British and continental bands, the American served in various ways and on various occasions. They performed at assemblies, hangings, holiday celebrations, college commencements (including that at the College of Philadelphia in 1780), and special events. Elias Boudinot wrote that when General Charles Lee was returned to the American camp in 1778—freed from British hands in a prisoner exchange—"All the music of the army attended"; an elegant dinner that night had "music playing the whole time." (Next morning Boudinot discovered that Lee had brought with him "a miserable dirty hussy . . . and had actually taken her into his room [which was next to Martha Washington's sitting room] by a back door and she had slept with him. . . .")[21]

The bands often played background music for the officers' dinners. When Washington dined with Marquis François de Barbé-Marbois at West Point in 1779, musicians a few steps away "played military and tuneful French airs." The bands also performed at private dances, playing for instance at Morristown in the winter of 1779–80 at a ball where Washington appeared in black velvet, the foreign officers in gold lace, an outlay Washington later deplored. Some officers seem to have used the bands for serenading. An officer serving in Philadelphia reported that he and four or five other young officers "drink as hard as we can, to keep out the cold, and about midnight sally forth, attended by the band, march thro' the streets, and play under the window of any lady you choose to distinguish; which they esteem a high compliment." The bands also played on the march, to lift morale and give expression to shared emotions. When his regiment passed the site of a massacre on the New York frontier, Colonel Procter directed the band to play the standard tune for military funerals in the period, "Roslin Castle." The "soft and moving notes," one soldier said, "together with what so forcibly struck the eye, tended greatly to fill our breasts with pity, and to renew our grief for our worthy departed friends and brethren." [22]

The lack of both musical and military traditions in America posed some special problems for the Continental Army as it tried to supply its own military music. European band musicians were civilians in army costumes; but the status of the American musicians tended to be ambiguous. In 1778, Washington himself tried on his authority as commander-in-chief to have the band of Jackson's regiment forwarded to his headquarters, perhaps for entertainment in the Christmas holidays. He emphasized that he did not wish to remove the band if it had been organized at the expense of the officers, only "if it belongs to, and is supported by the public." General Sullivan, to whom Jackson's regiment was attached, replied that the instruments and musicians had been paid for by the officers, but that the principal musician in the band was also a fife major. Sullivan apparently tried to get around the situation by transferring to Washington the band of Colonel Webb, stationed in Providence. The musicians there, however, drew public pay and provisions as soldiers while the officers gave them additional pay and had hired a master to teach them. As musicians they were responsible to Webb's officers alone; as soldiers they were subject to the command of every superior. Their instruments had also been purchased by the officers, who felt that to send the musicians to Washington but not their instruments would be impolite. In the end the musicians went to Sullivan, though whether with their instruments, and whether eventually to Washington, is unknown.[23]

The scarcity of native musicians also created problems. Christian Febiger was unable to find musicians for his Virginia regimental band, "except prisoners or Deserters from the British Army, who as soon as I had two or three of them engaged one would desert me. . . ." He decided to engage a German music master to teach clarinet, violin, and other instruments to fifers and drummers whose terms of service had expired. The fifers and drummers would be rewarded by the instruction itself, permanent employment so long as he continued in charge of the regiment, and the clothing allotted to noncommissioned officers. Febiger purchased instruments for the men himself, assuming that either Congress or the Virginia government would reimburse him, since his newly trained band would be "ready taught and able to teach others." The war suggested another recruitment method: capture. Americans seized two Hessian bands at Trenton, who then performed at a July 4 celebration in Philadelphia. One delegate to Congress found the pleasantness of their music "not a little heightened by the reflection that they were hired by the British Court for purposes very different. . . ." Another band seems to have been captured at the Battle of Cowpens along with thirty-five baggage wagons.[24] At least one other British band defected, and performed in Boston.

Once found, the scarce musicians were hard to keep. Wealthier officers raided the bands of other regiments. Thomas Procter purchased music and instruments and even rented viol strings from the musicians themselves at fivepence per month. Yet he found his musicians ready to leave "from private encouragements offered to them." [25]

The Continental Army created its fife and drum groups and military bands with a sure sense of their military function and usefulness in sustaining morale. They did so, moreover, in the same spirit which animated soldiers at Valley Forge and many other camps to write verse and act plays, a spirit of competition with the enemy and of defiance against barbarism.

35. Philadelphia and New York: Summer 1778–Summer 1780

With Howe's return to England following the *Mischianza* on May 25, Philadelphia and its occupying army came under the command of Sir Henry Clinton. He did not stay long. On secret orders signed by the king, he was to abandon Philadelphia and return its garrison to New York, from there to supply expeditions to the South and to the West Indies, where America's new ally, France, was preparing to attack British possessions. In May he began dismantling defense works and evacuating heavy equipment, invalids, and a large group of Loyalists down the Delaware; on June 18 the last of the British troops in Philadelphia quietly left. Washington, at Valley Forge, directed General Benedict Arnold—severely wounded at Saratoga and still unable to take the field—to reoccupy Philadelphia, permitting no goods to be removed or sold until their ownership was decided. Arnold entered the city on the nineteenth. At the same time, Washington himself started north in pursuit of Clinton's retreating army.

Neither of Washington's moves wholly succeeded. He encountered Clinton at Monmouth, New Jersey, on June 28, a scorching-hot day on which many combatants died of sunstroke. The bloody but indecisive battle was to be the last important engagement in the North. Arnold, for his part, failed at first to establish his authority as military governor of Philadelphia. He had discussed the situation with Peale, while having his miniature taken at Valley Forge. Peale wished to ride back to Philadelphia immediately after the evacuation. Arnold refused to allow Peale or anyone else to enter the city before him. Protesting that this would delay the reunion of long-separated families, Peale went directly to Washington to get a pass for himself into town. He managed to obtain one from Washington's secretary, Tench Tilghman, but it turned out to be unnecessary. Patriots who had removed themselves from Philadelphia with the British occupation poured back in as soon as the British left.

They found the place filthy and empty, the houses stripped, some 3,000 Loyalists gone, the other inhabitants worn out. Peale described the scene:

> The city appeared very little like what it used to be, all the fences and pailing of every kind were demolished, the Houses in General in the suburbs

were puled to pieces, I suppose for fire Wood, and many in midst of the City left in Ruins. I found many lean faces. indeed it might allmost certainly be known who had staid there from those who had left.

Yet for Peale the desolation only made more poignant the joy:

What pleasure was shown in Whigs faces as they Entered the City. What shaking of Hands at their meetings who had been scattered over the face of the neighbouring Country. What variety of Salutations . . . what variety of meetings of Friends that once were Intimate, fearfull and distrustfull least they should take one by the hand who had played the Traitors part. Most of them that stayed would immediately after they Welcomed their acquaintance into the City, begin the doleful Tale of their Sufferings. how the Tories had abused them and how the whole of their Houses were taken up by either officirs or Soldiers, and they dare not say a word but they were called Rebels and threatened with the Prison and a Halter.[1]

Returning Philadelphians, Peale added, were so glad to be back in their homes that they showed no hostility toward those who had stayed in the city under the occupation.

The deserted appearance of Philadelphia changed, however, and the forgiving mood of its inhabitants disappeared. The military governor, a thirty-eight-year-old widower, entertained expensively and remarried into Philadelphia society. Congress reassembled in July, bringing its several urbane delegates, its possibilities for patronage, and visits from Washington. The unofficial Spanish minister Don Juan Mirailles and the French minister Conrad Alexandre Gérard arrived, adding something of European custom and elegance. Gérard, said an English observer, "gives a rout twice a week to the ladies . . . amongst whom French hair-dressers, milliners, and dancers are all the *ton.* The *Virginia Jig* has given place to the *Cotillon,* and minuet-de-la-cour." The new minister brought more than Paris fashions: In July 1779, St. Mary's Church offered the first festival *Te Deum* to be sung in America.[2] With a potential audience composed of Arnold, the delegates, the new ambassadors, and the American officers and troops, cultural activities in Philadelphia resumed, although constrained by economic inflation and by some groups of Congress.

The concentration of wartime celebrities made the city a painter's paradise. Peale laid plans for a whole series of engravings, "a set of heads of the principal characters who have distinguished themselves during this conflict," works capable, he said, "of exciting Emulation in our Posterity to deserve the like Attention. . . ."[3] Meanwhile he received a commission from Congress to paint Gérard. His friend Pierre du Simitière began sketching Laurens, Dickinson, Mifflin, John Jay, Steuben, Wayne, and others, with the threefold purpose of sending them abroad to satisfy French curiosity about Revolutionary leaders, of compiling a "natural and civil History of America," and of creating a museum in Philadelphia. Washingtons came forth in litters. John Norman engraved the commander for the *Philadelphia Almanack*, in full-front bust attended by an allegorical figure of Fame blowing a trumpet. Peale converted earlier miniatures into unsigned mezzotints entitled *His Excellency George Washington Esq.* and *Lady Washington*—she rather dreamy-looking, he amiable but powerful, a tall, narrow-shouldered, big-bellied man behind whom, in the distant horizon, rises a tiny radiant sun. Peale gave away copies to Paine, Gérard, and others, donated one to Du Simitière for his planned museum, and in a swoop sold four dozen to the Spanish minister.[4]

Peale also took a new, major portrait of Washington from life. It was commissioned in January 1779 by the Supreme Council of Pennsylvania for its executive chamber. At the Council's request, Washington sat for Peale in Philadelphia, sometime between January 20 and February 2. Later in February, Peale visited Trenton and Princeton to take prospective views for the background, finishing the work sometime in the spring. This so-called Trenton portrait depicts a rangy Washington, legs crossed, one hand resting on the barrel of a cannon. He seems jaunty after his victories, his self-assurance justified by the emblematically fallen flags of the Hessians and British which lie at his feet, by the file of prisoners being marched away behind him, and by the new American flag of thirteen six-point stars flying above (ill., p. 525). The painting is particularly important because Peale used it as the prototype of a signed mezzotint engraving that had a very large sale and distribution, and of nineteen oil copies, at the least. The copies differ in many details of Washington's dress and of background, some showing Trenton, others Princeton or Monmouth or the French fleet. It seems that the original went to the Pennsylvania State House, and that Peale kept one copy for his intended gallery and sent five others for sale in Europe. One of the five went in 1779 to the Maryland diplomat William Carmichael. Peale hoped to realize a good price for this copy, finding himself, as always, "in want of necessaries in painting, and clothing for my family." But the Carmichael Washington floated around Europe for the next few years, unsold, a headache.[5] Some members of Congress questioned the propriety of commissioning such a costly work in the first place, since the country was financially embarrassed.

Embarrassed or not, Philadelphia also gave birth to a wartime literary magazine, although it survived only a year. Published monthly from January to December 1779, the *United States Magazine* was the first such venture since the *Pennsylvania Magazine* had folded in July 1776, and the only magazine published in America during the period of formal conflict.

It was produced by Philip Freneau and Hugh Henry Brackenridge, in cooperation with Du Simitière. The idea probably originated with Brackenridge, who came to Philadelphia shortly after the British evacuation, prepared to invest £1,000 toward furthering his literary career. His partner and former Princeton classmate, who had left the colonies for the West Indies in 1776, had returned to New Jersey from Santa Cruz in July 1778. Unluckily, the countryside around his Mount Pleasant home had been the setting, a few weeks before his return, of Washington's bloody encounter with Clinton's retreating army. He found it ravaged. Perhaps as a result, he immediately joined the New Jersey militia. He served as a scout along the seacoast between South Amboy and Long Branch, guiding loads of arms at night through lurking privateers, trying between tours to recruit sailors for John Paul Jones. At one privateer battle he was shot in the knee. While serving in the militia he contributed to nearly every issue of the *United States Magazine*, although whether he stayed at all with Brackenridge in Philadelphia is uncertain.[6]

The editors explained their policy in a frontispiece and preface to the first issue. Du Simitière drew a large arcade receding in sharp perspective, the roof representing a united America, the pillars representing the thirteen states. Beneath the arch glided a trumpeting angel, representing Fame "Rising to the western skies." Embracing politics and the arts, the magazine would help the common man understand government, since it was necessary and desirable in America that "the greater part be moderatly [sic] instructed, than that a few should be unrivalled in the commonwealth of letters. . . ." It would also encourage "young and rising authors" and *"paint the graces on the front of war,"* convincing the world that "we are able to cultivate the *belles lettres,* even disconnected with Great-Britain. . . ." Altogether it would demonstrate what many British officers serving in America had been forced to acknowledge, not without chagrin: "that the rebels, as they are pleased to call us, had some d - mn'd good writers on their side the question, and that we had fought them no less successfully with the pen than with the sword."

According to its several aims, the *United States Magazine* published patriotic orations, military correspondence, political commentary, and the new state constitutions, as well as poetry and fiction. Boosting local culture, it printed flattering verses addressed to Peale and described a meeting in Philadelphia of some literary "whig ladies" who praised Freneau and called on American bards to honor revolutionary heroes. Almost every issue contained pieces by Freneau and Brackenridge. Brackenridge's lengthiest and most original contribution was "The Cave of Vanhest," spread serially over seven issues—the first extensive work of fiction by an American published in an American magazine. It concerns a white-robed hermit who inhabits a sumptuously appointed cave in New Jersey together with his wife, his children, and a dwarf. The cave, however, serves only as a framing device. The narrator who stumbles across it relates to the hermit and his ménage, in great detail, the story of Washington's Monmouth campaign. Obviously this bizarre use of Gothic fantasy as a pretext for journalism reflects the editors' determination to *"paint the graces on the front of war."* In this framework, however, the Battle of Monmouth comes out sounding like a story told on Halloween.

Freneau's several, ambivalent poems and essays on the West Indies suggest that the tranquillity he hoped to find there eluded him. One poem-with-essay on Santa Cruz begins with repudiation, the escapist note on which Freneau had decided to leave America: "Sick of thy northern glooms, come shepherd seek/ Less rigorous climes, and a more friendly sky." The poem goes on to disdain the sober Puritan of the north in contrast to the "cheerful Epicure" of the islands. Yet Freneau could no more abandon himself to tropical hedonism than to patriotic virtue. Slavery, he added in the essay, "casts a shade over the native charms of the country . . . and amidst all the profusion of bounties which nature has scattered, the brightness of the heaven, the mildness of the air, and the luxuriance of the vegetable kingdom, it leaves me melancholy and disconsolate, convinced that there is no pleasure in this world without its share of pain." On balance, Santa Cruz appears as a Circean place, dangerously attractive, like some of its fruits: "Enticing to the smell, fair to the eye,/ But deadly poison. . . ."

As if reconciled to acting the propagandist, Freneau also contributed to the magazine many poems on the progress and causes of the war. He updated his earlier caricature of "king Log," portraying George as not only ruthless and bloodthirsty, but now mentally unbalanced, as he may in fact have become—prey to "sullen rage," "a very idiot grown," driven less by his ministers than by "fiends of darkness." But more often than not Freneau drifted from propaganda into poetry. In "Captain Jones's Invitation," written to help John Paul Jones enlist a crew, the speaker pauses to philosophize on the illusory majesty of the sea:

> Though now this vast expanse appear
> With glassy surface, calm and clear;
> Be not deceiv'd—'tis but a show,
> For many a corpse is laid below. . . .

Hardly a beguiling 'invitation' to join the fleet, the passage illustrates how ever and again Freneau's poetical interests intruded on his political role, demanding expression even from the soapbox. Indeed, however disillusioning, his experiences in the West Indies failed to relieve his restless yearning. In "Columbus to Ferdinand" he again praised the explorer's Faustian disquiet: "An unremitting flame my breast inspires,/ To seek new lands amid the barren waves." If Freneau's personal weakness was indecision, his strength as a poet was to not rely on formulas. He gave his readers a large, stimulating variety of forms and moods and imparted to his often-ephemeral journalistic content a subsurface complexity. Whatever his poems lacked as propaganda they made up as the record of a personality.

In the last issue of the *United States Magazine*, Brackenridge explained that he had begun the publication in the beliefs that the currency would recover and the war would soon end. Both beliefs proved wrong, making him suspend after a year. (He later wrote, however, that he left Philadelphia after he "saw no chance of being anything in that city, there were such great men before me.")[7] As Brackenridge headed for Pittsburgh to begin a legal career, Freneau quit the New Jersey militia and in May 1780 entered as third mate aboard a ship named *Aurora*, bound with a cargo of tobacco and twenty guns for St. Eustacia.

An equally hopeful but even less successful attempt to revive Philadelphia's cultural life was made by some American officers, who brought with them from Valley Forge a liking for plays. In October 1778 they probably performed at the Southwark Theatre. Later in the year they published an edition of Garrick's *The Lying Valet* with a byline, worthy of David Douglass, that offered one step back for two steps forward: "Printed at the Desire of some of the Officers in the American Army, who intend to exhibit at the Playhouse, for the Benefit of Families who have suffered in the War for American Liberty." Given the recent *Mischianza*, the standing Philadelphia laws against the theatre, and the official discouragement of shows by Congress, the intention was, however charitable, ill-timed and misplaced. New England members of Congress took it for what it was, a courteously expressed threat. Samuel Adams, then a delegate in Philadelphia, growled that "in humble Imitation as it would seem, of the Example of the British Army some of the officers of ours have condescended to act on the Stage while others, and one of superior Rank were pleased to countenance them with their Presence." (The person of "superior Rank" was probably Benedict Arnold.) Such productions, he said, brought "Vice Idleness Dissipation and a general Depravity of Principles and Manners" and were "disagreeable to the Sober Inhabitants of this City."[8] Accordingly, Congress prepared a resolution recommending that the states halt performances of plays as well as horse races and other diversions.

In Philadelphia the resolution had no effect. The officers repeated their performances, Adams said, "in Contempt of the Sense of Congress," making a stronger resolution necessary. Passed on October 16, 1778, it provided for dismissal of any troops and officers who acted in or produced plays:

> Whereas frequenting Play Houses and theatrical entertainments, has a fatal tendency to divert the minds of the people from a due attention to the means necessary for the defence of their country and preservation of their liberties: *Resolved,* that any person holding an office under the United States who shall act, promote, encourage, or attend such plays, shall be deemed unworthy to hold such office, and shall be accordingly dismissed.

One contemporary explained that the new law was strictly sectional in inspiration. Southerners in Congress enjoyed diversions and regarded horse racing as a "national affair"; it was "the northern members, called the Presbyterian party, that delight in passing moral laws so as to keep their credit and rigor in full exercise." [9] But southern congressmen were not the only dignitaries deprived by "the Presbyterian party." On the very night that Congress passed the new law, the marquis de Lafayette invited the president of Congress, Henry Laurens, to attend the theatre with him. When Laurens told him what Congress had done, Lafayette stayed away, to the gratification of Samuel Adams: "The young french Marquis has discovered the Dignity of the Citizen in the Regard he so readily paid to the sentiments of those in Civil Authority on this occasion." Adams hoped that others devoted to the cause of freedom would "show as much good Sense and Attention to the Cause of Virtue." To aid them, the Pennsylvania legislature on March 30, 1779, passed a new law prohibiting the building of theatres.[10]

The congressional law succeeded in halting military theatricals in Philadelphia, but apparently nowhere else. Just five months after passage of the law, continental officers performed *Cato* in winter quarters at New Brunswick. Soldiers in Portsmouth, New Hampshire, put on *Coriolanus*, with a prologue on civic ingratitude pointedly applicable to the ill-paid troops themselves. In Reading, Pennsylvania, other soldiers gave *The Lying Valet* using local women as actresses, which in the words of one lieutenant "pleased the Dutch inhabitants exceedingly; and kept them in one continual burst of laughter." In Philadelphia itself, the effect of the ban on plays by troops was to bring the theatre-hungry of all classes swarming to theatricals at the College. At a College performance in March 1781, Martha Bland found "Governors Ladys, presidents Ladys, Chief Justices & Merchants Ladys, Tallow Chandlers and Cake Women—Shoe Makers Wives & Members of Congress. . . ." Abandoning caps, shoes, and hats in the push, they were all, she said, "Climbing up the Walls to get in—some mounted upon the heads of others . . . such a Mob, that it is impossible to discribe if Garrick had been to perform it could not have been greater." Another spectator, sore-boned from "the pressing & pounding received," decided that it was "as much like a Bull-beat as a play." [11]

Congress was no more effective, meantime, in its second effort to create a United States seal. In May 1780 a committee consisting of James Lovell of Massachusetts, John Morin Scott of Virginia, and William Houston of New Jersey reported back a fresh design. One side would depict the heraldic arms of the United States—a shield of thirteen stripes, supported by a warrior in Roman dress and a female figure of Peace with olive branch—and the motto *Bello vel Pace*. The reverse would show a seated Libertas with staff and cap, and the motto *virtute perennis*.[12] The seal was visually simpler and ideologically less obscure than the earlier Adams-Franklin-Jefferson-Du Simitière version, but at the cost of ignoring such powerful and popular emblems as the Indian warrior, the Saxon chief, and the Hebrew patriarch. Inspired by affairs of the moment, too, it emphasized war and peace *per se* rather than national belief. Indeed it confessed a continuing inability to find some essential image for the thirteen varied but concerned former colonies. Congress found the new seal unsatisfactory, and recommitted the report.

Not only cultural activities, but all forms of social life in Philadelphia were affected by severe inflation and related shortages and profiteering. The depreciation of continental currency hit bottom in the fall and early winter of 1779. In 1770 a pound of coffee in Philadelphia cost 15.5 pence; in 1780 it cost 97.5 pence. A pipe of wine jumped from £45 to £5,500; Sam Adams paid $2,000 for a hat and suit. As the phrase "not worth a continental" came into use, it applied to cultural commodities as well. The *United States Magazine* appeared at three dollars an issue, and soon rose to four. Peale more than quadrupled the price of his miniatures; for his portrait of the French minister in 1779 he received $9,333.30. Many farmers, merchants, and politicians profited from the inflation by selling to the army and manipulating prices. While visiting Philadelphia, Washington complained that "Speculation, peculation, and an insatiable thirst for riches seem to have got the better of every other consideration." [13] Arnold was tried by a military court for using his authority for financial gain, but got off with a light reprimand. Francis Hopkinson, who had been appointed treasurer of loans and judge of the admiralty, was found guilty of bestowing an office for a suit of clothes, of falsifying a writ of sale, and of collecting illegal fees from the capture of a prize ship. He was impeached from office and convicted, but ultimately acquitted by Congress.

Profiteers were not the only objects of suspicion in Philadelphia, nor the only social irritant. Most Loyalists had evacuated the city with Clinton;

many who remained found themselves estranged from their friends. One Loyalist poet tried to capture the subtleties of censure:

> Each hasty word, each look unkind,
>   Each distant hint, that seems to mean
> A something lurking in the mind
>   That almost longs to lurk unseen;
> Each shadow of a shade offends
> Th' embittered foes who once were friends.[14]

Other forms of ostracism were less subtle. As the returned patriots settled down again, their forgiving mood wore thin. They executed several Loyalists for aiding the enemy. Newspapers publicized the conservative politics of William Smith, who had barely escaped imprisonment once before. The College of Philadelphia was accused of "Enmity to the Common Cause," abolished, and reorganized as the University of Pennsylvania. Smith was forced to resign as provost and to vacate his house. He moved to Maryland to start a new school.

The punishment most often inflicted on Loyalists, however, was confiscation of their property, profits from the sale or rent going toward the war effort. This procedure had been recommended by Congress in 1777, and was eventually adopted by all of the states. A typical victim was the socialite and poetess Elizabeth Graeme Fergusson, who in the early 1760's had held literary soirees for aspiring writers and artists from the College. In 1779 her husband fled to England after serving the British as a commissary of prisoners (moving her to write a long, lugubrious poem entitled "The Deserted Wife"). His actions made her handsome estate, Graeme Park, with its three-hundred-acre deer chase, vulnerable to forfeit, even though it had been given to her by her father. In pitiful letters written during her protracted battle to retain the property she explained to authorities how her husband fell in with the British accidentally, how they "induced" him to accept the post, how he tried to get out of the British lines, how the now rundown and unremunerative estate was her sole support, and how for herself "*She* at least has done nothing to forfeit on the Contrary every thing in *her Power* to deserve from the Hands of her much loved Country." [15] Deservedly or not, her estate was confiscated, although it was in part restored to her by the legislature in 1781.

The task of seizing the property of disloyal citizens was handled by a Commission of Forfeited Estates appointed immediately upon the reoccupation of Philadelphia. The Commission was no place for a tender conscience or an overflowing heart. Commissioners often had to judge a fellow-citizen's loyalty to begin with, and sometimes had to break down doors and literally carry families out of their houses—for which dirty work they received a 5 percent return on the sold property.

To his great disgust, Charles Willson Peale was appointed to the Commission. Searching for a new house for his own family, he was ordered to evict Grace Galloway, whose husband Joseph had administered civil government in Philadelphia during the British occupation and was now in England. Like many Loyalist wives, she had remained behind to safeguard their possessions. Peale went to her house on July 28; ill though she was, he told her she must pay rent of £300 a year or move out; she agreed to leave. Three days later, however, she changed her mind. Peale returned to notify her that the house would be given to the Spanish ambassador, Don Juan Mirailles. When he returned again two days later with a party of Spaniards to take possession, Mrs. Galloway became ill, had to lie down, and sent word that she was unable to receive them. They waited until the afternoon, then locked her in the house and took away the key.

On August 20, Peale and two other men arrived to turn Mrs. Galloway out. She had shut her doors and windows, determined to make the commissioners break in. They forced open the kitchen door with a scrubbing brush. The men with Peale recited to Mrs. Galloway her husband's misdeeds and threatened to eject her clothes. Peale, however, went out and fetched a carriage for her use. Then he went upstairs, brought down two of her bonnets, and put them on a side table. He told her that the carriage was ready. Mrs. Galloway herself described her departure:

> . . . he would not hasten me I told him I was at home & in My own House & nothing but force shou'd drive me out of it he said it was not ye first time he had taken a Lady by the Hand an insolent wretch this speech was made some time in the room. . . . as the Chariot drew up Peel fetched My Bonnets & gave one to me ye other to Mrs Craig: then with greates[t] air said come Mr[s] Galloway give me your hand I answer'd indeed I will not nor will I go out of my house but by force. he then took hold of my arm & I rose & he took me to the door I then Took hold on on[e] side & Look[ed] round & said pray take Notice I do not leave my house of My own accord or with my own inclination but by force & Nothing but force shou'd have Made Me give up possession Peel said with a sneer very well Madam & when he led me down ye step I said now Mr Peel let go My Arm I want not your Assistance he said he cou'd help me to ye Carriage I told him I cou'd go without & you Mr Peel are the last Man on earth I wou'd wish to be Obliged to. . . .[16]

Peale must have found the episode unnerving, but it was only the beginning.

In the chaos of Philadelphia politics after Clinton's withdrawal, Peale became a controversial figure. Local Whigs split over the new Pennsylvania Constitution, which shifted power to previously underrepresented elements in the state. Conservative Whigs who opposed the Constitution—

including Benjamin Rush, Francis Hopkinson, and William Smith—were regarded virtually as Loyalists by radical Whigs who espoused it, including David Rittenhouse, Tom Paine, and Peale. The radicals banded together as The Constitutional Society. Besides supporting the Constitution, the Society tried to halt the depreciation of continental currency by getting Congress to issue less paper money and levy extra taxes. The Society appointed Peale its chairman; in 1779 he was also elected to the Assembly. Philadelphia, Benjamin Rush lamented, was now governed by a "mobocracy" led by "Tom Paine, Charles Wilson Peale & Co." [17]

However fond of imagining himself as the Vicar-of-Wakefield of Philadelphia, Peale began to look like the Philadelphia Robespierre. In July, Benjamin Towne's *Evening Post* published a pseudonymous essay attacking Paine and defending the financier Robert Morris, a man much scorned for profiteering. Towne was an interesting case: During the occupation he remained in Philadelphia; in February 1779, however, he announced publication of a dozen or so new patriotic songs with titles like "General Burgoyne's Defeat" and "The Female Whig." Since none of the announced works are extant, it seems probable that none were ever published. Towne may have only advertised them, hoping to reclaim his reputation. Peale chaired a meeting at which radical Whigs assembled a committee to deal with Towne. They pressured him into revealing the identity of the writer who had defended Morris and attacked Paine in his newspaper—a steel-furnace owner named Humphreys. A crowd collected at Humphreys' house threatening to drag him away. Peale tried to disperse them by arguing—Humphreys standing at his window with a musket—that the issue was not worth the risk. A delegate to Congress from Georgia, however, was living in Humphreys' house at the time and identified Peale not as a peacemaker but as the leader of the mob. Peale was brought before the chief justice of Pennsylvania, but managed to convince him that he had only tried to maintain order.[18]

In October, Peale became embroiled in what some Philadelphians regarded as an outbreak of civil war. As he recounted the incident, a group of zealous Whigs held a militia meeting at Burns's tavern, men activated by "their favourite cause" and "soured by the many insults they had met with from the Tories." They worked out a scheme to send away the wives and children left behind by Loyalist males who had evacuated with Clinton. The proposers of this asked Peale to be their commander. He refused, arguing that it would "cause much affliction and grief" and generate a backlash. Despite his refusal he was called several days later to another meeting. This time the assemblage included a party of German militiamen "most violently inveterate against all Tories." Thinking it futile to argue, Peale went home to set up his firearms. He was not present on October 4 when the militiamen paraded two suspected Loyalists up Walnut Street to the home of James Wilson—an object of radical hatred for his speculating and for his defense of price-gouging merchants. An armed band of thirty men had collected in front of Wilson's house. As the militia passed, push came to shove: Six or seven people were killed, around twenty seriously injured. The arrest of several militiamen was protested next morning by a crowd of militia officers and citizens which gathered at the Market Street Court House. Peale, who was present, sensed that they were "ripe for undertaking the release of the prisoners." He whispered to the secretary of the Council that to avoid more bloodshed it would be wise to release the men on bail. This time his role was clear. Bail was granted, cooling things off.[19]

Peacemaker or insurrectionist, Peale had made enemies. He began hanging an ash club by his bed at night and carrying it on a wrist strap by day. He called it "Hercules." He used "Hercules," too, when assaulted on the street one night, and credited it with saving his life. If imperiled by his prominence, however, he also gained by it. He bought for himself and his family one of the confiscated Loyalist properties, on Second Street. Eventually he hoped to install in the house a gallery where he could exhibit whatever portraits he had on hand, "in order that the Citizens might be amused with seeing them, a very sure method of obtaining a greater demand for the employment of his Pensil." As to the 5 percent bounty awarded to those who handled the confiscations, he reasoned that "had he applied with the same diligence in his profession as an Artist, he might have made more money than was allowed as commission on this most disagreeable business." [20]

Peale was not alone in feeling at once pleased and guilty over his situation. Most Philadelphians resumed their lives with rather furtive eagerness, relieved that the past was past but aware also of the troubled present and uncertain what might come next. With the resurgence of cultural activities came restraint and often self-criticism. In this, reoccupied cities in general differed from occupied cities, and Arnold's Philadelphia especially from Clinton's New York.

The city to which Clinton withdrew the Philadelphia garrison had been steadily filling with Loyalists from other places who preferred life under a British flag. By mid-February 1777, New York already contained about 11,000 Loyalists and better than 3,000 British troops. Clinton brought back with him an additional 3,000 Loyalists from Philadelphia, so that by 1781 New York probably contained about 25,000 civilians, and by war's end probably as many as 33,000.[21]

Whatever Clinton's qualities as a commander—most later historians regard him as jealous, hot-tempered, self-distrustful, and depressive—he was the perfect social and cultural leader for crowded and potentially lively New York. He had spent part of his childhood in the city, where his father had been governor; he wished for peace; above all, he represented the *politesse* of the British officer corps better than any other general except perhaps Burgoyne. During the occupation of Boston in 1775, he gave concerts in which he performed on the violin, one of several fiddles and bass viols he seems to have carried with him. In New York he maintained an amateur orchestra of violin, cello, and flute, and spent almost £50 on sheet music alone. He employed the printer James Rivington to bind some twenty-seven volumes of concerti, quartets, and symphonies by Bach, Haydn, Boccherini, and others. Indeed, as one authority writes, his "principal activity, to judge by his account books, was not military but musical." [22]

No doubt because of Clinton's influence, the city's musical life flourished: The John Street Theatre frequently was used for subscription concerts, for concerts to benefit refugees, or for programs of sacred music that featured parts of *The Messiah*; New Yorkers continued to learn to play instruments from established teachers like William Hulett or from locally printed editions of *A Pocket Book for the Guitar* or *New Instructions for the German Flute*, and in August 1777 a John S. Slaiffer opened a "School for Music" in Maiden Lane at which he taught violin, flute, and guitar for a guinea a month. Slaiffer's advertisements promised solace and romance:

> Few will pretend to contradict that the charm of music will sufficiently compensate for the trouble in the attainment of it. Music makes as great an impression on us as the bewitching charms of beauty; it humanizes the soul, and is in short the best companion for the gay, the wounded lover, or the drooping fair.

Convivial singing, always popular, became immensely so. New York newspapers advertised such compilations as *A New and Select Collection of the Best English, Scots, and Irish Songs . . . in the True Spirit of Social Mirth and Good Fellowship; Songs, Naval and Military;* and *Loyal and Humorous Songs . . . Calculated to promote Loyalty and Unanimity, by a Briton in New-York.* A member of the Old Church and King Club noted that Loyalists had long been compelled "in a *whisper* to toast Church & King":

> We whisper'd for fear, Sir, and faith! we had reason,
> When Honor was Baseness, and Loyalty Treason!
> And truly!, 't was no very laughable thing
> To see Faction in triumph defy Church and King. . . .

Now, however, Tories gathered at Hull's Tavern or the King's Head to sing out loyal sentiments uninhibited—secure in Clinton's protective might and relaxed by toasts "To the Pimps" (Congress):

True Souls drink and sing,
Remember the King,
  With Loyalty, good Will and fervour;
So while we can stand,
The Flaggon command,
  To GEORGE his Empire for ever.
                    A Bumper and three Huzzas[23]

Several artists, familiar and unfamiliar, settled in the occupied city as well. Among them was the Irishman John Ramage, who had set up as a goldsmith and miniature painter in Boston as early as 1775; there he joined the British forces, sailed with them to Halifax, then returned with Howe to New York, establishing himself on William Street. Known as a beauish dresser, he specialized in painting the military personnel of the British garrison and their lady friends, mostly in richly colored miniatures set in chased-gold frames of his own making. He probably painted more military men than any other artist in America. A "J. Mitchell" set up on Cherry Street to do pastel portraits and miniatures, while a Scotch soldier named John Murray engraved silver and bookplates at his own room in the 57th Regiment for "the Old Country price." [24] Still other, anonymous artists furnished decorations for Loyalist celebrations. On the queen's birthday in 1778, the King's Head Tavern was decked out with illuminated pictures of George and Charlotte, and of a Devil beside the president of Congress and the now-decapitated statue of William Pitt. For the king's birthday the same year, the tavern displayed a transparency on which a British tar trampled the thirteen stripes, "signifying that by the bravery and perseverance of the Navy, American Independence should be no more." [25]

In 1779 a more familiar name appeared in the press, advertising to paint portraits: William Williams. Some twenty years ago he had lent books and prints to Benjamin West, a young boy in Philadelphia; now he had just returned from visiting his protégé in London, where West painted his face into a monumental *Battle of La Hogue.* Williams' two sons had joined the patriot army and had been killed. A former pupil of West's, Abraham Delanoy, Jr., survived as an impoverished sign painter in Maiden Lane, a disappointing end for one of the aspiring adolescents depicted in Matthew Pratt's *American School.*[26]

The crossroads of New York's social and cultural life was the print shop of James Rivington. As mentioned previously, he had left for London in January 1776, after radicals publicly burned his pamphlets, hanged him in effigy, wrecked his press, and tried to kidnap him. He returned to New York in September 1777, welcomed with some verses by New York's other Loyalist printer, Hugh Gaine:

Rivington is arriv'd—let ev'ry Man
This injur'd Person's Worth confess;
His loyal Heart abhor'd the Rebel's Plan
And boldly dar'd them with his *Press*.

Although patriots inscribed Rivington's name with undeviating disgust, as synonymous with "Tory," the evidence strongly suggests that he was a patriot spy, gathering and passing on important information about British military plans. If so, he played out a role until his death, for he never revealed his espionage.[27]

Throughout the occupation Rivington stocked an impressive array of smaller instruments and musical accessories—German flutes, violoncellos, guitars, tabors, strings, reeds, mutes—and acted as a middleman for those who wished to dispose of chamber organs, harpsichords, and other large instruments. He also sold paintings, advertising what might appeal to the city's unique population, such as pictures of the royal dockyards or of the king and queen.[28] His greatest cultural service to New York, however, was the publication of his newspaper, *The Royal Gazette*. It advertised concerts and plays, and boosted Tory morale, though at the cost of dispensing forged letters supposedly by Washington and tonic news of Benjamin Franklin's alleged death. It was also the chief publisher of Loyalist poetry. Jonathan Odell, his New Jersey property confiscated, published frequently in the *Gazette*. When several members of Congress in Philadelphia attended the *Te Deum* at the invitation of the French minister, Odell recalled how patriots had once denounced the Quebec Act as a foretaste of popery. Who would believe it, he asked, having

Heard them foretell Religion's general wreck,
From Romish faith establish'd in Quebec:
Who, that observ'd all this, could e'er opine
That Saints like these with Popery should join?
Imagination must it not surpass,
That Congress should proceed in pomp to Mass? [29]

Scarcely a movement by the patriots went unversified. Issue after issue, poets in the *Gazette* cursed Congress as lower-class scum, baited the ragtag continentals, parodied rebel ideology, and cheered on British victories.

By far the most extravagant part of the city's cultural life was its military theatre, which outdid any of the earlier efforts by Burgoyne and Howe. Performances were advertised as being *"By Permission of his Excellency* Sir HENRY CLINTON, Knt of the Bath." For their house, Clinton's actors rented the John Street Theatre at £100 a year; refurbished with new upholstery, new lamps, new ironwork, and freshly painted and gilded, the place was renamed The Theatre Royal. Tickets up to 1779 cost a dollar for box and pit, fifty cents for gallery. Baron Wilhelm von Knyphausen, Lord Francis Rawdon, and other Hessian and British officers had season boxes, apparently accommodating eight people; Clinton also had a season box, at fifty guineas. (The officers seem to have sat together; one prologue refers to the "General's Boxes" at the side of the theatre.)[30] Tickets were sold at several taverns around town, at the theatre, and at Gaine's and Rivington's print shops. Both printers profited from the military troupe, which made large purchases of stationery, paper, and printing. Rivington, the largest single ticket seller, apparently also profited from an increased demand for printed plays; during the occupation he published American editions of several English dramas, including Sheridan's *The Rivals* and *The School for Scandal.*[31]

The schedule and repertoire of the Theatre Royal resembled those of The American Company. Most seasons ran from October or November to the next June or July. Performances usually began at seven o'clock, and usually occurred once a week, a week apart. The program offered a long tragedy or comedy with a prologue written for the occasion, a farce, and music or songs between. In the course of some 150 performances during the occupation, the players mounted such familiar works as *Mock Doctor, Flora, Douglas, The West Indian, Venice Preserved, She Stoops to Conquer, Richard II,* and *Othello.* A highlight was the American premiere of *The Rivals.* Shakespeare's plays, always very popular in the colonies, regularly outdrew the average receipts, although the most often performed works were Garrick's *Miss in Her Teens* (thirteen times) and *The Beaux' Stratagem* (twelve times). (The highest receipts during the 1779 season, however, came from Samuel Foote's *The Liar* and from *Richard III.*) The performances seem to have been very well attended. Rivington noted that an audience for *The West Indian* numbered over nine hundred people, a hundred more than Douglass' largest house in New York.[32]

"Clinton's Thespians," as they were called, consisted mostly of military personnel, but included a few professional actors and local Loyalists. Some of their names have been mentioned earlier, since the troupe actually came into being when Howe left New York on his amphibious invasion of Philadelphia. At that time, some actors from the New York theatre went with Howe and performed at the Southwark; others stayed in New York with Clinton. When Clinton took over from Howe and brought Howe's army back from Philadelphia, the two wings of the company were reunited. "Clinton's Thespians" had a succession of managers, including Colonel Guy Johnson (acting superintendent of Indian affairs, who also performed in a play by Cumberland), and the army surgeon Hammond Beaumont, in whose house at 80 King Street the theatre's account books were open for public inspection. The military actors included Lord

Rawdon, who had spoken the prologue to the production of Voltaire's *Zara* in occupied Boston; Captain Thomas Stanley, Burgoyne's brother-in-law; and Captain John André. André probably painted scenery for the theatre as well, and gave solo recitations in the city. The *Gazette* reported on January 23, 1779, that at "Mr. Deane's" André read "Love and Fashion" and "a 'Dream.' " In his dream Justice Thomas McKean of Pennsylvania appeared as a bloodhound, Congressman Silas Deane as a French marquis, John Jay as a rattlesnake, and Louis XIV as a "half-starved jackass, loaded with heavy panniers, and perpetually goaded by a meagre Frenchman." [33] The professionals in the company included a well-paid mother-and-daughter team, Anna and Jane Tomlinson, and the durable William Hulett and his son. Some roles went to campfollowers, mistresses of various officers, and local amateurs. A payment of £1 1s., for instance, survives to a "P. Shaw" covering "my Son's Performance in King Richard the Third and four Dollars for my Attendance as Steward and Stage Door Keeper for four nights." [34]

Actors accounted for only part of the company's employees and expenses. Music was provided by a fourteen-piece orchestra drawn largely from regimental bands. The instrumentalists received fifty cents a night, the price of a gallery ticket. They were conducted by a Hessian corporal named Philip Pfeil (or Phile), a versatile musician and composer who remained in America after the war. Apparently the orchestra was not always filled. A Scotch officer stationed in New York noted that musicians became scarce during the 1778–79 season, leaving the actors "chagrined to think of the injury to the play *[False Delicacy]*." One of the actors "travelled all the taverns" and at last came across a French harpsichordist. A pianoforte was located at Campbell's (a Maiden Lane music dealer), drawn by sleigh to the theatre, and kept hidden until the afternoon of the play, "when we exhibited it to the astonishment of poor André and the other players, who were delighted beyond measure." [35]

Besides costs for music the surviving account book includes payments for a scribe, a coach painter, "scene shifters," doorkeepers, boxoffice attendants, a guard of light infantry to police the gallery, and a man "for attending the fires and lights on the Stage." The managers also purchased rum, sherry, and port—probably to sell at intermissions—and lavish suppers to enliven rehearsal or celebrate an evening's performance, sometimes at the nearby Shakespeare Tavern. The largest sums went for costuming: Records of payment survive for cravats, hats, waistcoats, buckskin breeches, millinery, capes, dresses, necklaces, earrings, feathers, shoes, "two Stars," and a "Cupids dress" costing £9, as well as for washing and for wardrobe keepers—all in addition to ordinary expenses for advertising, spermaceti candles, and the like. The richness of the productions can be surmised from the accounts for the 1777–78 season, published in Rivington's *Gazette*: Costumes, repairs, and "contingent expenses" cost £3,169, not including rental of the theatre.[36]

Unlike the American troops in Philadelphia, "Clinton's Thespians" did not have to defend their taste in entertainment against a diving currency or a Samuel Adams. Yet like the Americans they stressed their charitable intent. A 1778 performance, for instance, was announced as "for the laudable Purpose of raising a Supply for the Widows and Orphans of those who have lost their Lives in his Majesty's Service." The need for such justification arose not from religious or political scruples but from the fact that the Theatre Royal was no log-cabin camp show. Set in what was then the most sophisticated city in America, it was a paying business whose profits were shared by the officer-players and whose outlay perhaps exceeded The American Company's. Some people at home thought it bad taste for "British officers to perform for hire." But an apologist explained that in New York "necessaries are so extremely dear, that an inferior officer, who has no other resources than his pay, undergoes more difficulties than the common soldier; and circumstanced as many brave men now are in America, such an exertion of their talents to increase their incomes, deserves the greatest encouragement." [37]

In fact, the officers lived well off their incomes, charging expensive clothing, meals, carriages, and liquor tabs against theatre receipts. Little made its way to charity. The total amount raised for charity in the 1778 season was £140, compared with £29 paid for costumes used in *Othello* and *The Jealous Wife*. The 1779 charity receipts amounted to £179: Of this, forty-four widows each received twenty shillings, and all but four a pair of shoes and stockings; seventy-two children received twenty shillings each; and sixteen orphans each received forty-five shillings. By contrast, the managers spent nearly £100 for headdresses and wigs, in February and March alone.[38]

The business of New York in 1779, however, was not only buying wigs. Having fought to a standstill in the North, the British decided to shift their main military offensive to the South, where they expected to find large numbers of Loyalists, whose support might bring easier victories. In December, Clinton sailed off from his Theatre Royal for Charleston.

Hopes remained, however, for a decisive breakthrough in the North. What could not be won by British arms might be gotten by American treachery.

36. The André Affair: Fall 1780

Sometime in the spring of 1779, perhaps the most able American field commander, Major General Benedict Arnold, then commandant of Philadelphia, entered into a secret correspondence with one of Clinton's Thespians, Major John André. Before the Battle of Lexington, Arnold had been a New Haven druggist, horse-trader, and bookseller; after Lexington he had been a passionate and daring soldier with a gift for command. Beside Ethan Allen in May 1775 he took part in the capture of Fort Ticonderoga. In September the same year he led a heroic march through the Maine wilderness to Quebec, where he was badly wounded in the knee. Burgoyne himself credited Arnold with his defeat at Saratoga, where Arnold was seriously wounded again. For all that, Arnold now worked out through André a deal with the British: For £20,000 he would allow them to take the strategic fort at West Point, including its artillery, its stores, and its 3,000-man garrison.

Contact between Arnold in Philadelphia and André in New York was arranged by the Loyalist poet Joseph Stansbury. Somehow he managed to survive in Philadelphia relatively unharassed under both the British and the Americans. He remained during the occupation, filled some minor government posts, and got to know André; he remained when the British left, signed an oath of allegiance to the patriot cause, and got to know Arnold. When Arnold decided to offer his aid to the British, around May 1779, he told his decision to Stansbury, who met the same month with André. André was qualified for the part: While in Philadelphia, he had become acquainted with the young socialite Peggy Shippen, who was now Arnold's wife and a collaborator in his treason; he was an aide-de-camp to Clinton; he was a highly regarded officer promoted in 1779 to major, and he was an actor.

Stansbury put into operation the correspondence by which he received information from Arnold through Peggy Arnold, and relayed it to André in New York through the Loyalist poet Jonathan Odell. The letters among them, in a cipher, contain occasional literary touches, Arnold using the code name "Gustavus," for instance, as in *Gustavus Vasa*. Arnold and the British officials discussed various plans for cooperation, and the price, for almost a year. Meanwhile, Arnold maneuvered to get command at West Point, even as he underwent investigation and trial for corruption in Philadelphia. In mid-July 1780 he informed the British that the command had been given to him. When he took over at West Point in August, a secret meeting was arranged between him and André in some woods near Haverstraw.

What followed is well known. The meeting lasted until about 4:00 A.M. During it, Arnold gave André complete descriptions of the West Point defenses, and instructions, André said, to conceal them between his stockings and his shoes. Returning to New York through Tarrytown, André ran into three volunteer militiamen, who took him and his compromising papers into custody. Minutes after learning of André's capture, Arnold also learned that Washington—as yet unaware of the plot—was an hour's ride away, approaching Arnold's headquarters with Lafayette and Alexander Hamilton. He ordered a horse and fled. Later in the day, safe aboard a British ship on the Hudson, he sent a letter to Washington explaining that he had been motivated by "Love to my country."

Of the conspirators, André alone suffered. Stansbury was arrested, apparently suspected of complicity. He had been careful, however; nothing was proved against him and he was allowed to go behind British lines. Odell, in New York, was rewarded, appointed registrar and clerk of the province of New Brunswick. André, however, was imprisoned in Tappan and tried before a military tribunal on September 29. According to Steuben, he "confessed everything." Washington directed that André be hanged at 5:00 P.M. on October 1. Several officers pleaded with him to exchange André for Arnold or even release him as a favor to Clinton. Like everyone else, Washington regretted the necessity of killing André. But with the British hanging of Nathan Hale still in public memory, with public opinion expecting that someone be punished, and with Arnold unavailable, Washington only postponed the execution until the next day.[1]

The treachery of an admired American officer and the hanging of an engaging enemy provoked more literary and graphic works than any other event since the Battle of Bunker's Hill. An age ceaselessly wary of ambition saw Arnold's act as a type of the satanic fall. A twice-wounded American officer who had vanquished the British army at Saratoga had sold his country, it was universally believed, for gain. Unexpected, unnatural, and total, Arnold's transformation created raging bitterness. In Connecticut, Benjamin Young Prime measured "the GREATNESS of his FALL" in eighteen pages of invective verse, *The Fall of Lucifer*, comparing Arnold to the once-seraphic Lucifer and to a planet deserting its fixed course, damning him as "a traitor ere the birth of time," "coward wretch!" "fiend incarnate," *"fratricide," "vagabond,"* "butcher," "BULLY Arnold," "JUDAS." [2]

Philadelphians, who had prior reasons for suspecting Arnold, held a procession reminiscent of the Stamp Act demonstrations. A cart was drawn through the city accompanied by some Continental Army officers, led on by fifes and drums playing Rogues March. On a small platform inside the cart sat an effigy of Arnold in regimental dress, his lame left leg propped on a stool. Behind him stood a black-robed Devil, shaking a purse in his ear with one hand and with the other threatening to pitchfork him into Hell. Emblematic of his treachery, Arnold held a mask and had two faces—"done to the *life*," said one witness. The faces were painted by Peale, who not long ago had been forced to resist Arnold's authority in order to rejoin his family in Philadelphia. Peale contrived the head so that a boy inside the platform could turn it toward the Devil. In front of the cart hung a large lantern with transparent panels depicting the consequences of Arnold's crime: One showed the Devil pulling him into the flames; another showed Arnold saying "My dear sir, I have served you faithfully"; a third showed two hanged men labeled "The Traitor's Reward." The front panel contained a long inscription cataloguing Arnold's wrongs, concluding, "The effigy of this ingrate is therefore hanged (for want of his body) as a Traitour to his native country, and a Betrayer of the laws of honour." After being marched through the streets, stirring fear in local Tories, the effigy was burned. Several woodcuts and engravings of the procession appeared in Philadelphia, one with the legend:

> *Mothers shall still their children, and say—Arnold!—*
> *Arnold shall be the bug-bear of their years.*
> Arnold!—*vile, treacherous, and leagued with Satan.*[3]

With similar overtones of satanic betrayal, Arnold was hanged in effigy and burned throughout New England.

As Arnold became a "bug-bear," André became a martyr. Not yet thirty at the time of his capture, well known for his social graces and artistic inclinations, he fell into the type of the sentimental hero. On the very day of his capture was to appear the third part of his mock-epical poem, *Cow-Chace* (New York, 1780), the first two parts of which had already been published in Rivington's *Gazette*. The poem dealt with a seriocomic attempt by General Anthony Wayne to storm a British blockhouse near Fort Lee, New Jersey, and to drive the cattle in the neighborhood within the American lines. The last stanza proved prophetic:

> And now I've clos'd my epic strain,
>   I tremble as I show it,
> Lest this same warrior-drover, Wayne,
>   Should ever catch the poet.

(The nineteenth-century anthologist Frank Moore claimed that he saw a copy of the poem with a new stanza added beneath, signed by André: "When the epic strain was sung,/ The poet by the neck was hung,/ And to his cost he finds too late,/ The dung-born tribe decides his fate.") André turned his execution into a triumph of sentiment, politely bowing to his executioners, blindfolding himself, springing upon the gallows cart, and remarking "It will be but a momentary pang." Joel Barlow sent his fiancée an eyewitness account of the hanging:

> A politer Gentleman or a greater character of his age perhaps is not alive, he was 28 years old, he was dressed completely and suffused with calmness & chearfulness. With the appearance of Philosophy & heroism he observed that he was buoyed above the fear of death by a consciousness that most of [the] actions of his life had been honorable, that in a few minutes he should be out of all pleasure or pain. . . . My heart is thrown into a flutter My dear at the sight. . . .

Many of the spectators wept.[4]

Some who were not present tried to imagine the event for themselves, and wept as well. One verse broadside, depicting André in prison, cast the doomed major as a genteel swain, a Damon bidding farewell to a Delia:

> How can I speak the last farewell, what
> cares distress my mind,
> How can I go to realms of bliss, and leave
> my love behind.[5]

Rivington published a *Monody* by the English poet Anna Seward, dedicated to Sir Henry Clinton. A friend of André's, she claimed to speak with "the zeal of a religious Enthusiast to his murdered Saint." Speculating that André was hanged as punishment for his *Cow-Chace*, she blasted "Remorseless Washington!" as the "cool determin'd Murderer of the Brave," and mourned the loss of André's literary and artistic gifts:

> . . . novel thoughts, in ev'ry lustre drest
> Of pointed Wit, that diamond of the breast;
> Hence glow'd thy fancy with poetic ray,
> Hence music warbled in thy sprightly lay;
> And hence thy pencil, with his colours warm,
> Caught ev'ry grace, and copied ev'ry charm.

A gallant lover as well, according to the writer, André when captured concealed the miniature of his beloved in his mouth.

Despite what contemporaries made of his gentility and artistic flair, the man who ciphered plans for the fall of West Point can hardly have been a swooning popinjay. In fact his coded letters reveal a contrary streak of cynicism. Praised as the designer of artistic costumes for the *Mischianza*, for instance, he told Stansbury that to disguise the treasonable content of some letters he might "talk of the Meschianza *[sic]* & other nonsense." To the extent that André was less feeling than he seemed and Arnold less unfeeling, the most penetrating treatment of the affair was an unpublished, and incompleted, drama in verse and prose by Philip Freneau. Entitled *The Spy*, it was presumably written shortly after André's execution.[6] Moving among West Point, Arnold's house nearby, Clinton in New York, and the apartment of André's fiancée, Lucinda, the action affords several differing perspectives on the chief actors, who try to understand each other's motives and behavior.

In Freneau's version, André seems a shrewd military tactician as he explains to Clinton the advantages of taking West Point. His intelligence, however, has become the tool of a consuming nationalism: "Had I a thousand lives, I would lay them all down for Britain and my king." Fanaticism also taints his much-applauded sensitivity. After his fiancée sings a song with the lines "I draw the sword that pities none,/ I draw their rebel blood," he remarks: "You sing charmingly, Lucinda." Freneau does not simply change André from all white to all black, however; rather he views André's fanaticism in terms of contemporary physico-theological theories of native attachments, suggesting that it is compulsive. When Lucinda protests that patriotism "need not carry us to such an idolatrous extravagance as is manifested in the little stanzas," André replies: "Nature has formed us with a principle of love to our native land."

Likewise, Arnold comes off as more than an avaricious traitor. On one side ambitious, disaffected with the French allies, and war-weary, he also fears besmirching his reputation and is tortured by guilt. He thinks of calling off the plot, but concludes:

> . . . that would be ungenerous—more than that,
> Ten thousand guineas are the offered price
> Of my desertion—more than that, perhaps
> I shall henceforward be caressed by kings
> And bear a generalship that may reduce
> These states revolted back to Britain's sway.

As the passage indicates, not even his desire to be "caressed by kings" is unequivocally selfish, since Arnold hopes thereby to return the "states revolted" to England, and he believes that Americans are not "dull republicans" by nature but favor monarchy. So far as the play has a villain it is Clinton. Pained by his failure to catch Washington—"the soul,/ The great upholder of this long contention"—he offers Arnold a double price if he can arrange to have Washington present at West Point when it falls:

> . . . let the world imagine it was Clinton
> Who schemed, who plotted, and seduced the villain;
> That by this deed more honour I may gain
> Than if I had defeated Washington
> By dint of blows on yonder Jersey plain.

Although André devises the treason, Clinton hungers to be known as its mastermind, credited with what he cannot in fact accomplish.

From Freneau's gloomy perspective, the actors in the plot appear both more and less reprehensible than they do in the many other contemporary accounts. They appear more reprehensible because they scheme more deeply and for pettier ends; less because they are driven by powerful universal forces like natural attachment, envy, and the fear of failure, and because they are wracked by a guilt that demands self-delusion as the price for self-justification.

37. The American School: 1777–1782

Despite the fighting in America, London continued to lure and to nurture American artists. Occasionally their politics aroused indignation; but none of the artists who had been popular before the Declaration of Independence lost favor for political reasons. Most managed to peaceably earn a living and to win praise without hiding their sympathy for America. They could do so, in part, because many English Whigs shared their sympathy. When Charles James Fox learned that Howe had forced Washington from New York he remarked, "What a dismal piece of news!" [1] They could do so, also, because England was waging a limited war in which sentiments of shared race and language ruled out unlimited destruction and utter alienation. Being human as well as American, they reacted individually to news from across the ocean: Some paid little attention, some followed anxiously; a few took risks, one landed in jail from the shock waves.

Londoners continued to enjoy the vigorous eccentricity and waxworks of the sculptress Patience Wright, a woman, they politely said, "of masculine understanding." Her life-sized statue of Pitt, draped with the robes Pitt wore when he made his last speech in the House of Lords, was placed in Westminster Abbey, where it remains (ill., p. 526). Her house in Pall Mall became a popular rendezvous for Garrick, West, and other artists and legislators. In 1777, the artist John Downman drew "The Famous Wax-Woman and Republican from America," clad in a decorous smock and bonnet but with a liberty pole and pileus, pug-nosed and leading with her chin.[2]

Patience Wright's politics were no less truculent than her demeanor. She called the king and queen George and Charlotte. Stories about her brazen faceoffs with English officialdom were printed in America until the end of the century. In the course of modeling a head of Lord North, it was reported, she visited North to check the likeness and steered the conversation to politics:

> She assured him of the little probability of success, and with her usual warmth declared, that if he did not immediately recall the troops, and make atonement for the blood that had already been shed, he should lose his head. He laughed, and told her, it was of little consequence, respecting himself, as long as he preserved her friendship, which at all events he should be careful to do: for you know, mrs. Wright, continued he, if they should cut my head off, *'tis in your power to make me another.*

A less good-natured response greeted a second decapitation episode. Wright's son, Joseph, a student of West's and of Hoppner's, painted his mother modeling a head of Charles I. Perhaps innocently, he included in the scene her wax heads of the present king and queen. Many who viewed the painting at the Royal Academy exhibition in 1780 perceived it not as a 'Patience Wright in her studio' but as a political threat—Patience Wright sculpting a decapitated king near heads of the current monarchs. The suggestiveness of the scene was heightened by Patience's nickname, "Sybilla," based on her claim that she could foretell political events. Reynolds was criticized for allowing the painting to be shown.[3] "And their Majesties," Walpole shuddered, "contemplating it!"

Whatever the intent of the painting, it seems likely that Patience Wright acted in London as an American spy. Apparently she undertook to fulfill her promise to John Dickinson; shortly after the First Continental Congress, she offered to supply him political and military intelligence. William Temple Franklin later revealed that as soon as "a General was appointed, or a squadron began to be fitted out, the old lady found means of access to some family where she could gain information, and thus, without being at all suspected, she contrived to transmit an account of the number of troops, and the place of their destination abroad." At least once, she was found out. In 1777, Mrs. Edward Bancroft was intercepted on a trip from London to Paris. Her husband was, presumably, an American spy working for Franklin in London. With Mrs. Bancroft were found several letters, including some by Patience Wright: One, addressed to Franklin, discounted a rumor that 5,000 troops were being sent to Howe and to William Tryon, royal governor of New York, in America; another, addressed to Bancroft, informed him that further intelligence would be relayed through his wife. Patience Wright apparently escaped recrimination for her work, perhaps because she had all along been playing into British hands: In reality, Edward Bancroft was a double agent working for the Crown.[4]

Some words of caution came from Benjamin West, who advised Mrs. Wright that *"peticoats would not protect her."* West himself remained intimate with the king, his Quaker virtue finding a common bond with George's Hanoverian propriety. The king called him Benjamin, the queen consulted him about her jewels; he painted the couple in their finery and often talked over affairs in America. Several secondhand accounts of these talks survive. In one, West had been painting the king when news arrived of the Declaration of Independence; the king was at first agitated, then became silent and thoughtful, and at last remarked to him: "if they cannot be happy under my government I hope they may not change it for a worse." In another, Lord Cathcart asked West pointedly in the presence of the king whether he had heard about the British victory at Camden, South Carolina, in 1780, which nearly annihilated General Gates's army. Cathcart said he supposed it would not please West as much as it pleased the king's loyal subjects; West replied that the troubles of his country never gave him pleasure. The king put his hand on West's shoulder and said, "Right, right, West. I honour you for it," adding to Cathcart that a man who did not love his native land could be neither a good subject nor a true friend.[5]

Yet West's devotion to America came more from blood-ties than from politics. Although he moved in 1777 into a large house at 14 Newman Street, complete with a gallery and sculpture arcade, he retained his provincial spelling and syntax, and still could barely read or write. His nephew, Leigh Hunt, discovered that he talked of the royal "Hackademy," aspirating and mispronouncing words with "puritanical barbarism."[6] Placing art anyway above politics, he received from the king around 1780 a commission for more than thirty giant paintings for Windsor Chapel, the most ambitious undertaking in religious art in the eighteenth century, considered by Reynolds the greatest examples of English art of all time. The work occupied West until the nineteenth century and eventually earned him £20,000. Intended as a history of revealed religion, the canvases were grouped into Four Dispensations. By 1781 West completed at least one of the panels, an Ascension filled with theatrically gesticulating figures, seventeen feet by ten feet.[7]

As always, West had fresh pupils from America. Gilbert Stuart, to recall, born in Rhode Island in 1755 and briefly trained by the Scotch portraitist Cosmo Alexander, had left America sometime before 1775 and made his way to England. He spent his first year in London in some poverty; by one account he became ill from having nothing to eat but a sea biscuit for an entire week. He survived by obtaining some small commissions to paint medical men and by obtaining a post as a church organist. (A serious musician, he also took flute lessons from a German member of the king's band.)[8]

Like almost everything else in Stuart's life, the circumstances that led him to West are known through later accounts that conflict. As told by Dunlap (who had it from the painter Thomas Sully, who had it from someone else), West was dining when a servant announced that someone wished to see him. West said he was engaged but added after a pause, " 'Who is he?' 'He says, sir, that he is from America.' " That was enough for West, who welcomed Stuart heartily. As told by Stuart's friend Benjamin Waterhouse, Waterhouse himself went to West to make known Stuart's financial plight, and West gave him some money. As told by Stuart's idolatrous daughter Jane, the "exceedingly well bred" Stuart went calling at West's house clad in "a fashionable green coat." [9]

The truth seems to be that Stuart first wrote to West about a year after arriving in London, in dire need. He hoped to acquire not instruction but money and care. The evidence is a letter by Stuart dated London, December 1776. It discloses someone less well-bred than Stuart's daughter believed, and calculating enough to drop some Quaker-sounding verb endings to catch West's eye:

> The Benevolence of your Disposition encourageth me, while my necessity urgeth me to write you on so disagreeable a subject. I hope I have not offended by takeing this liberty my poverty & ignorance are my only excuse Lett me beg that I may not forfeit your good will which to me is so desireable. Pitty me Good Sir I've just arriv'd att the age of 21 an age when most young men have done something worthy of notice & find myself Ignorant withoutt bussiness or Freinds, without the necessarys of life so far that for some time I have been reduced to one miserable meal a day & frequently not even that, destitute of the means of acuiring knowledge, my hopes from home Blasted & incapable of returning thither, pitching headlong into misery I have this only hope I pray that it maynot be too great (to live & learn being a Burthen, Should Mr West in his abundant kindness think of ought for me I shall esteem it an obligation which shall bind me forever with gratttude *[sic]*. . . .[10]

Deference was anything but Stuart's style, and would not last. Ever generous, West took him in.

Stuart remained with West for nearly five years as a pupil and assistant.

Given a room by himself, he was assigned important portions of West's large canvases to complete. Waterhouse says that he probably stopped writing home once he arrived in England, even though his family was jeopardized by their Toryism. Yet however unattached to his origins, Stuart resented slights on his nationality. Dr. Johnson, an Americaphobe, once remarked to West that Stuart spoke very good English, and asked Stuart where he had learned it. Stuart came back: "Sir, I can better tell you where I did not learn it—it was not from your dictionary." Like Franklin, Stuart enjoyed putting on Englishmen by playing the noble savage. Asked in a company of gentlemen where he was from, he replied, accurately: "Six miles from Pottawoone, and ten miles from Poppasquash, and about four miles west of Connonicut." [11]

In mid-1780 Stuart was joined at West's house by another pupil, John Trumbull, the son of the governor of Connecticut. Trumbull arrived nursing a grudge, the result of frustrations in his military career. After serving under Washington at Cambridge, he had served for another seven or eight months around Fort Ticonderoga, beginning in the summer of 1776. Among other duties he painted numbers on cannon-carriages and cartridge boxes and reported on the condition of the smallpox-ravaged troops who had retreated from Quebec ("I did not look into tent or hut in which I did not find either a dead or dying man"). He also presented valuable opinions on the defense of the fort which won assent from Benedict Arnold.[12] Like many others he looked on his wartime service as in part a way of getting a leg up in the world, in this case a commission as deputy adjutant general.

Trumbull looked more hungrily than others, however. He associated his advancement with repairing his family's ambiguous social standing as people of political eminence but much-diminished wealth. He did receive the commission from Congress. But it was dated September 1776 instead of June, the month when in Trumbull's eyes his actual work as adjutant had begun. Quick to see and to resent disrespect, he took the letter of commission as an insult. "I expect, Sir," he wrote John Hancock, then president of Congress, "to be commission'd from that Date, if at all. A Soldier's Honour forbids the Idea of giving up the least Pretension to Rank." Failing to get his way, Trumbull resigned. As he put it to the Massachusetts delegate James Lovell: "I lay aside my cockade and sword, with the fixed determination never to resume them until I can do it with honor." [13]

Meanwhile Trumbull took up residence in Boston. He hired the room in Queen Street that had been John Smibert's, which still housed several of Smibert's copies, especially of Van Dyck's *Bentivoglio*, Poussin's *Scipio*, and a Raphael Madonna. Finding also that "the sound of a drum frequently called an involuntary tear to my eye," he volunteered for the French-American attempt to recover Rhode Island in 1778. One mission took him through a hell of grapeshot, cannonfire, and corpses. When Trumbull returned to Boston ill, John Hancock insisted on having him removed to his own house to recuperate. Trumbull enjoyed the triumph, writing years later that the man "who had been president of Congress at the time of my resignation, and who had both signed and forwarded the misdated commission which had driven me from the service, had now witnessed my military conduct, and seen that I was not a man *to ask,* but *to earn* distinction." He resumed "daubing without profit" in Boston in the fall of 1778, selling tea and rum for a living, but satisfied that "I improve very well" and, as he put it, that "I have got my Negro." [14]

The next year some friends urged Trumbull to undertake the management of a business scheme in Europe, where he might also, they counseled, study with West. But when Trumbull arrived in Paris—in June 1778—he learned that the scheme had collapsed. He left for London, carrying a letter of introduction to West from Franklin. West, he said, "most kindly received" him and asked to see a specimen of his work. By his own count Trumbull had completed sixty-eight drawings and paintings in America, but he had brought none with him. West invited him to choose something from his painting room to copy. Trumbull picked Raphael's *Madonna della Sedia*, a choice which West thought augured well. Then West introduced him to "a young countryman of ours" working in the next room. Gilbert Stuart, who it was, helped Trumbull pick out tools and colors. The two worked thereafter in the same studio, doing joint exercises assigned by West. [15]

As it happened, Trumbull lasted in West's studio only four months before being thrown in jail, and Stuart departed about a year after. Trumbull's imprisonment came in retaliation—he believed—for the execution of Major André. Even before leaving America, Trumbull feared that his family connections and military experience would make it unsafe for him to stay in London. He secured official permission for the trip from Lord Germaine, the British secretary of state for American colonies, transmitted through the British consul general in New York, Sir John Temple, a man regarded as a neutral. Germaine gave his word, Temple told him, that he could stay unmolested in London so long as he studied art and avoided politics. Perhaps by habitual flaunting of his family name, Trumbull managed to arouse suspicion even on his voyage across. The captain of the ship concluded that he was on a secret mission from Congress to Franklin. [16]

Disregarding Germaine's strictures, Trumbull made no effort to contain his sympathies once he reached London. In July he painted, from memory, a portrait of Washington based on a copy he had made in Boston of a Washington by Peale—the general on a bank of the Hudson River, West Point in the distance. He also made clear, at least to his father, what he thought of the English. They were, he wrote home in September, hopelessly corrupt. Their rumored desire for renewed friendship and commerce was probably the treacherous prelude to new oppression. " 'Tis the Sword only that can give us such a peace," he said, "as our past glorious Struggles have merited.—The sword must finish what it has so well begun." [17] On November 20, 1780, Trumbull was charged with high treason and jailed in Tothill-fields Bridewell for eight months.

The basis for the charge was papers found on Trumbull at the time of his arrest, described by the London *Political Magazine* as "extraordinary correspondence." Trumbull said that these consisted of a memorandum book, letters to his father and to William Temple Franklin, and copies of the letters he had sent to Congress about his misdated commission. He believed himself a scapegoat, his arrest the work of American Loyalists in London who resented him, who had been spying on him since his arrival, and who found in André's execution a pretext for molesting him. News of the execution, arriving in London on November 15, "gave a new Edge to the vengeful Wishes of the American Refugees. . . . they had interest enough to persuade the Ministry that I was a dangerous person, in the service of Dr Franklin &c &c.—the Occasion united with their Wishes, & the resentment of Government mark'd me as an expiatory Sacrifice." [18]

West, Trumbull said, went immediately to the king, at once in friendship to his pupil, loyalty to America, and fear: the Loyalists, jealous of his cordial relationship with the king, might try to use against him the fact that he had lodged Trumbull in his house. West vouched to the king that Trumbull had been "so entirely devoted to the study of my profession as to have left no time for political intrigue." [19] The king, however, declared that he could do nothing since the issue was not a matter of law. He promised West, however, that Trumbull's life was safe.

Relieved that he had nothing worse to fear than a "tedious confinement," Trumbull settled down in jail, trying to extricate himself by a lawsuit while making the best of his situation. His confines were rather genteel—a parlor some twenty feet square with barred windows, the turnkey acting as his valet and the adjoining garden available for walks, at a cost to Trumbull of a guinea a week. Able to continue painting, he copied West's Correggio and other works, and received visits from friends. Gilbert Stuart painted him in his barred room. If livable, his situation was hardly ideal, and he strove to bring his case to trial. The best hope for his release, he believed, lay in a change in the military tide in favor of America, and a consequent change in English public opinion; but he attempted to make a legal case out of a proclamation of October 1778 in which the king had granted pardon for all treasons committed before that date in America. He wrote from jail to Lord Germaine citing the proclamation and pointing out that he had been charged with *"Treason committed in America,* from which I conceive myself fully protected by the proclamation."²⁰ Meanwhile, West tried but failed to obtain an interview with Germaine.

It was Edmund Burke who at last effected Trumbull's release. In May, Trumbull wrote to Burke complaining that after six months he still saw no disposition to free him. What kept him in prison, he said, was the pressure brought on the ministry by the "vindictive & malignant Arts of some of my own Countrymen," who were also, he implied, intercepting any pleas sent by him or his friends to the ministry.²¹ Burke went personally to see Germaine and visited Trumbull in jail, promising that if all "peacable & rational methods" failed he would bring the matter before Parliament. Burke secured an order from the Privy Council to have Trumbull bailed out on the surety of West and Copley, with the condition that he leave England in thirty days and not return until the restoration of peace.²²

Released on June 12, 1781, Trumbull headed for Holland, touring there and in the Basque country of Spain. Horace Walpole noted in August that, ironically, some "beautiful strokes" of Trumbull's had been shown and admired at the Royal Academy "without an idea that they came from the gloom of a prison." Trumbull returned to America in January 1782, bearing a piece of "ancient Roman cement" from a Spanish lighthouse for Ezra Stiles.²³ For the duration he stayed in Connecticut helping his brother supply the Continental Army.

Only months after Trumbull's return to America, Stuart also left West's studio. In some ways he had never really been at home there. Unlike most of West's pupils, he had not gone to England to study with West; in fact he turned to West only when his money ran out, approaching him not as a demigod but as a last resort. Later he complained that West occasionally treated him "very cavalierly" and bored him by making him labor over his *"ten-acre* pictures." A Rhode Island Yankee touched by provincial pride in going it alone, he did not look to West for instruction. One anecdote has it that Stuart was once with several other pupils when someone proposed that each student name the master he desired to follow. When his turn came, Stuart said he desired to follow no master: "I wish to find out what nature is for myself, and see her with *my own eyes.*" (Gainsborough reportedly entered while Stuart was speaking and said: "That's right, my lad; adhere to that, and you'll be an artist.") The hundreds of faces on West's huge canvases, moreover, are often little more than caricatures derived from simple line drawings in expression books of the period, supernumeraries in an epical imagining. While West's gift was for mythic overviews, Stuart's was entirely for character. He provoked West by broadcasting his deficiencies as a portraitist to Trumbull. Knowing that West stood in earshot of the painting room, he used the unaware Trumbull as a straight man, lecturing him against West's cliché technique of rendering hair with strokes in the shape of the figure three:

> "Here Trumbull," said I, "do you want to learn how to paint hair? There it is, my boy! Our master figures out a head of hair like a sum in arithmetic. Let us see,—we may tell how many guineas he is to have for this head by simple addition,—three and three make six, and three are nine, and three are twelve—"

Hearing himself mocked, West stalked in and lectured Stuart angrily back. Stuart noted, however, that no threes figured in the hair of West's next portrait.[24]

This is not to say that Stuart disliked West; indeed throughout his life he praised West's wisdom and generosity. Stuart was, rather, a satirical man, able to tolerate but not to ignore failings in his friends, fond of those he also thought boring, highhanded, or inept. In public, he and West seem to have treated each other as complements. Visitors to the studio, one Londoner reported, were "told by Mr. West that Mr. Stuart is the only portrait painter in the world; and by Mr. Stuart that no man has any pretensions in history painting but Mr. West." Others, however, began to see them as competitors and called attention to ways in which the presumed pupil excelled the master. Stuart received his first notice in the London press for a very fine portrait of West shown at the 1781 exhibit of the Royal Academy. By contrast, a portrait of the king by West, two years later, was ridiculed as a "sunburnt sign." The *St. James's Chronicle* decided that Stuart had apparently "acquired under Mr. West an art, of which Mr. West himself has shown very few instances, that of painting a good portrait." [25] Stuart's reputation was established with the showing in 1782 of his elegant full-length portrait of William Grant of Congalton, a rangy, frock-clad ice-skater upon a frozen English pond. The praise of its novel pose and design confirmed the advice of Stuart's friend, the English painter Nathaniel Dance: "You are strong enough to stand alone; take rooms; those who would be unwilling to sit to Mr. West's pupil will be glad to sit to Mr. Stuart." [26] In the spring of 1782, Stuart moved into his own quarters on Newman Street, close to West's house but not in it.

West never lacked pupils, and one and perhaps both of the vacancies in his studio were filled by two other young painters from New England. The first, Ralph Earl, belonged chronologically, temperamentally, and by place of birth with Winthrop Chandler and the Connecticut country painters who had emerged in the early 1770's. He probably painted the scenes of Lexington and Concord on which Amos Doolittle based his four famous engravings. He continued working in Connecticut during the early years of the war, painting the Yale poet Timothy Dwight and the cobbler-turned-lawyer Roger Sherman, a stiff, heavy man whom he posed in a full frontal view seated in a Windsor chair, his legs clumsily spread, a vision of uncouth Puritan severity. Earl's avowed Toryism, however, got him into trouble. His father had become a colonel, Earl said, "in the Rebel Service," and disinherited him for refusing a commission on the same side. He moved to a remote part of Connecticut "among the Friends of Governmt." [27] In March 1777 he learned of a planned descent on Long Island by American troops, and sent someone to warn the British. He was taken into custody, spared from execution only in respect to his father. Ordered to leave Connecticut or go to jail, he went to London.

Little is known about his life there. According to Dunlap, he "studied under the direction of Mr. West, immediately after the independence of his country was established," although this cannot have been before 1778 or 1779. A spendthrift and heavy drinker, Dunlap says, he "prevented improvement and destroyed himself by habitual intemperance." In 1779 he was forced to petition the Lords Commissioners of the Treasury for charity, offering a statement from Burgoyne's quartermaster-general endorsing him as "a persecuted Man in the province of Conn" who "saved a party of the Kings Troops" on Long Island. Earl later advertised himself as a student not only of West's but also of Copley's. Yet he apparently idolized Copley no more than Stuart idolized West. He considered offering one of his own works "to Copeley to coppey for his improvement." [28] In fact, Earl seems to have gravitated rather toward Reynolds and Gainsborough, from whom he borrowed the device of placing a sitter beside a window framing a landscape. This device later entered into making Earl the first important painter of the American landscape.

Whether or not Earl actually stayed with West, a far less gifted and less enigmatic young American certainly did. Mather Brown (1761–1831) came from a family illustrious in New England: His grandfather was Mather Byles, with whom he lived after the death of his mother, much as the orphaned Byles had been sent to live as a child with his uncle, Cotton Mather. Brown's artistic knack became evident before he reached his teens. In Boston he published verse, received drawing lessons from Gilbert Stuart, became acquainted with Copley and Trumbull, and helped to earn his keep by painting miniatures. By his early teens he was an itinerant portraitist working in New England, New York, and the West Indies. He saved his commissions so that he could study history painting abroad and avoid having, he said, "to go into the American Army or starve at Boston." [29] Franklin introduced him at Versailles as the "grandson to one of his most particular friends in America," and gave him an introductory letter to West, at whose studio he arrived in April 1781, while Trumbull was in jail.

His grandfather's well-known Loyalism gave Brown little reason to fear the Tory exiles in London; yet, perhaps made wary by Trumbull's fate, he extracted a promise of protection from Germaine, "upon my Assurance, how innocent I was of all rebellious and treasonable practices." Like everyone else except Stuart, he found West's example dazzling but encouraging: "While I dayly overlook Mr. West, in producing those Miracles of Historic Art," he wrote home, "I seem to feel more than Inspiration." Copley also welcomed Brown to his house and lent him pictures to study and copy. Brown visited Trumbull during his "melancholy Confinement," although Trumbull came to regard him as a facile imitator of West who desired nothing larger than a niche in the London social-artistic whirl, which he very quickly attained.[30]

Of the American artists in London, the one least given to expressing himself on American affairs was Copley. What if anything he felt about the war never issued in respectful backtalk to the king or in anything indiscreet enough to create gossip. The jailing of Trumbull and the uproar over Joseph Wright's painting of Patience may have made him cautious. In 1782, an American in London, Elkanah Watson, commissioned a portrait from Copley and asked him to include as background a ship with an American flag. Copley refused to include the flag for fear of offending the royal family, who visited his gallery.[31] The paucity of surviving anecdotes and reminiscences about Copley's opinions suggests that for whatever reasons he divulged little. He and his family continued to reside in Leicester Square, including his half-brother Henry Pelham, who profitably painted miniatures and taught drawing in the city.

Copley spent his time living up to and then surpassing the reputation which had preceded him to London. In May 1778, as American troops mounted *Cato* at Valley Forge, he exhibited a painting which won him full membership in the Royal Academy, *Brook Watson and the Shark* (ill., p. 530). The painting continues the hyperrealism of his American work in its abundance of sharply observed details and recorded accidents: the trickle of seawater on the tip of the oar; the varieties of fully rendered neckerchiefs (plaid, striped, dotted, solid) and of hair textures (the harpooneer's long, flying hair, the middle sailor's balding wisps, the Negro's thick curls). The open-shirted crew represent an even bolder use of the plebeian costuming Copley had seen fit to paint in his earlier portraits of Paul Revere and Nathaniel Hurd. Copley went even further than West in democratizing the history painting and stripping it of historicism, depicting a scene more often associated with the contemporary tabloid than with a large oil canvas. He had become, he said in 1783, "fully persuaded that modern subjects are the properest for the exercize of the pencil and far more Interesting to the present Age than those taken from Ancient History." [32] The subject he deified by pain was no longer even a heroic soldier such as Wolfe but a fourteen-year-old boy, the witness not a scarlet-coated grenadier but a black sailor staring in mute horror at the bitten body afloat near the again-lunging shark. In its concentration on man in conflict with animal violence, too, the painting dramatizes a way of conceiving nature which continues in Herman Melville's *Moby Dick*, Winslow Homer's *The Gulf Stream*, William Faulkner's *The Bear*, and Ernest Hemingway's *The Old Man and the Sea*, a line of classic American encounters with beasts.

Despite these elements of continuity with earlier and later American works, the critic in the *St. James's Chronicle* claimed *Brook Watson* for English art: "We heartily congratulate our Countrymen on a Genius, who bids fair to rival the Great Masters of the Ancient Italian Schools." [33] His feeling of kinship with Copley as an Englishman was justified. The fourteen-year-old boy in the painting had survived to become commissary general for the English armies in America, Lord Mayor of London, and a political enemy of the pro-American Wilkes. In brushwork and form, too, the work shares little with Copley's American paintings, entirely lacking their lineyness and compositional clutter. Indeed the composition is strong and calculated, the clashing horizontals and verticals heightening the feeling of violent impact. Copley's newfound passion for composition on a large scale led him to devote almost two years, 1779–80, to a *Death of Chatham* some seven and a half feet by ten feet. For authenticity, he consulted the English Shakespeare scholar Edmund Malone, who consulted with several historians and prepared a fifteen-page report on the details of the scene. Copley set up his own exhibition of the work, which drew 20,000 people in six weeks. The competition meant a financial loss to the Royal Academy's simultaneous exhibition, turning some members of the Academy against him.

Showing almost the whole peerage, the painting commemorates a moment in the House of Lords in April 1778 when William Pitt, earl of Chatham, rose to speak for a reconciliation with America and fell in a faint, to die a month later. Copley had considered Pitt once before. In the anonymous caricatura which he drew during the Stamp Act crisis, he included "W. P--t's Dog," urinating on the Scotch thistle from which a viper threatens the stricken figure of Liberty; now he induced fifty-five English noblemen to sit for life studies, including Lord Germaine, Lord

North, and the earl of Mansfield. The scene in Parliament offered many opportunities for political comment, since both pro- and anti-American members were present. Some viewers of the painting thought they could divine Copley's sympathies from his treatment of various figures. One could not do so confidently, however. Copley continued to paint robes and faces, not loyalties. Whatever his political beliefs, he saw without them.

38. Billings and Law; the Yale Poets: New England, 1777–1782

The withdrawal of Howe's army to New York after the long Boston siege of 1775–76 took the center of conflict and the crisis atmosphere out of the northeastern states. Relatively secure from the threat of invasion, New Englanders resumed some of their prewar activities. They did so, however, on much the same terms as in reoccupied Philadelphia, amidst inflation, restraints on unseemly enthusiasms, and reminders of the war still raging not far off. Still, some new figures in the arts began to establish themselves, and some established figures produced important new works.

In Boston, cultural affairs were low-keyed. Since Copley's departure the city lacked a major portraitist, and since the occupation it seems to have had no concerts. The organist-composer William Selby gave up public performances for the duration, living instead on the collections from his Boston church, and by giving organ lessons and tending a grocery store.[1] Dances with music were held, but denounced as the recreations of profiteering nouveaux riches and of others inexcusably indifferent to politics:

> Blush B[oston]! blush!—Thy honest sons bewail,
> That dance and song o'er patriot zeal prevail;
> That whigs and tories (join'd by wayward chance)
> Should hand in hand, lead on the sprightly dance. . . .

Around 1778, some Bostonians agitated for a repeal of the 1750 anti-theatre laws; they of course had no success, although in 1781 students at Harvard produced Brackenridge's *Death of General Montgomery* and other Revolutionary plays.[2] An American Academy of Arts and Sciences was founded in the city in 1781, designed to promote literature and the liberal arts, but it aroused resentment, "as though," said one Bostonian, "they were enjoying the sweetest blessings of a well established, secure peace. . . ."

One promising career was aborted not by wartime restraint but by ordinary bad luck. In October 1779, Phillis Wheatley called for subscriptions toward the publication of a new volume, dedicated to Benjamin Franklin. Patrons were promised a book of about 300 pages, containing a poem called "Niagara" and letters to Washington, Rush, and others, at the inflation price of twelve pounds. She had been freed by her former owner, John Wheatley, shortly after his wife's death in 1774. In 1778 she married a Boston black named John Peters, who worked variously as a grocer, doctor, and lawyer. His 'pretensions' (he wore a wig and carried a cane) meant social estrangement for the couple and their three children. In debt, Peters seemed to have fled to the South, taking with him the manuscript of his wife's new volume of poems. The volume was never printed, and the manuscript remains lost.[3]

Unlike professional concerts and plays, the operation of the singing schools had never really faltered. In 1779, as in virtually every year for the past fifteen years, appeared still another esthetical sermon, William Symmes's *The Duty and Advantages of singing Praises unto God* (Danvers, Connecticut), re-explaining that singing prepares the soul for grace and warning the singers once again not to become engrossed in the tune at the expense of the text. At most, the war curtailed the publication of tunebooks (perhaps because of the difficulty of getting paper) and called for revisions in the repertoire. Watts's popular rendering of the psalms, for instance, contained many flattering references to the king and to Great Britain. A revised edition was published in Newburyport in 1781, easily but cleanly bleached. In Watts's original version, Psalm 75 was *"Apply'd to the Glorious Revolution by King William, or the Happy Ascension of King George to the throne";* this became *"Applied to the glorious revolution in America, July 4th, 1776."*[4] Otherwise, a century-long defense of singing in congregational worship protected the singing school movement from serious criticism.

Such quarrels as arose in the schools concerned not political but musical propriety—whether some old tune should be scrapped, for instance, or whether the deacon should lead the singing. As more churches formed distinct gallery choirs, church members continued to resent being ousted from both the singing and their customary seats by adolescents with better voices. Involving social distinctions, generational conflict, and individual egos, the resolution of such issues called for Solomonic ingenuity. The town of Worcester in August 1779 decided one case by gathering a meeting of freeholders, which voted: "the Singers set in the front Seats in the Front Gallery, and those Gentlemen who have heretofore Set in the front seat in said Gallery have a right to set in the front body Seat & Second Seat below & that Said Singers have said Seats in the front Gallery appropriated to their own use."[5] The niceness of the quarrel and the use of a public vote to decide it both suggest that the singing schools were taken with a seriousness that insured their continued vitality during the war years.

Boston became a sort of capital of the movement. Psalm singing, John Trumbull told his brother in 1779, had become the "hobby Horse of the Town. . . ." Surely what made psalmody a favorite wartime recreation in Boston was the presence of William Billings. Lamentably but as usual, biographical details about Billings for this, as for the other periods of his life, are few. Alexander W. Thayer, the biographer of Beethoven, heard from someone who had known Billings that he was kept from fighting by his lameness, partial blindness, and withered arm: "wishing to join the army in the Revolution, he was found so far from being an able bodied man, tha[t] he was made a kind of conductor of the baggage, that being the only situation his physical misfortunes would allow him to fill." In 1778—a year otherwise marked by Washington's battle with Clinton at Monmouth and by the British evacuation of Philadelphia—the Brattle Street Church hired Billings to teach its singers. Next year Old South Church hired him for the same purpose, at £150 for two months' instruction. In 1780 he bought a house on Newbury (now Washington) Street, near where General Gage had cut down Liberty Tree.[6]

During this period Billings published in Boston perhaps his most important collection, *The Singing Master's Assistant, or Key to Practical Music*. In his 1770 *New-England Psalm-Singer* he had promised the public a new book of tunes. It was about to appear when the war erupted, "which Unhappy War," he explained, "was the sole motive that induced me to 'hang my harp upon the willows' and suppress the publication." However pleasing that volume might have been, it could hardly have been more successful than *The Singing Master's Assistant*, which came to be known as "Billings' *Best*." First published in 1778, it went through three further editions over the next three years. Containing in itself about a quarter of the most popular American tunes of the eighteenth century, it was "carried by the soldiers from camp to camp," one contemporary said, and became "popular with the multitude, and spread over the land." Billings seems to have sensed its importance from the beginning. In June 1778, apparently with *The Singing Master's Assistant* in mind, he again asked the Massachusetts legislature for a copyright, as he had done with the earlier *Psalm-Singer*. Again, however, the petition was rejected, once more preventing Billings from setting a precedent of profound consequence to American culture.[7]

The popularity of the volume and Billings' special regard for it came in part from the many patriotic songs. Tunes like PHILADELPHIA, COLUMBIA, WASHINGTON, and AMERICA in effect are musical versions of the New England view of the Revolution. Billings added four new verses to the already popular CHESTER, depicting Burgoyne, Clinton, and Cornwallis as an "Infernal League" conspiring against "New england's God." In the lengthy anthem RETROSPECT, he gave virtually a history of the war by piecing paraphrases of Jeremiah, Revelation, and Luke together with allusions to recent events: "Was not the day dark and gloomy; The enemy said, 'Let us draw a line even from York to Canada.' But, praised be the Lord! the snare is broken and we are escaped." In LAMENTATION OVER BOSTON, apparently written in collaboration with his friend Samuel Adams, Billings treated Psalm 137 in terms of the Boston siege, Roxbury Loyalists, and meetings of the Massachusetts Provincial Congress at Watertown:

> By the Rivers of Watertown we sat down & wept we wept we wept we wept when we remember'd thee O Boston. As for our Friends Lord God of Heaven preserve them defend them deliver & restore them unto us For they that held them in Bondage requir'd of them to take up Arms against their Brethren. Forbid it Lord God that those who have sucked Bostonian Breasts should thirst for American Blood Avarice was heard in Roxbury which eccho'd thro' the Continent. . . .

The blending of local place names with biblical names and phrases gives the events of the war a cosmic importance. This pious viewpoint was the basis of Loyalist cries that the patriots were Cromwellian fanatics carrying forward the revolutions of the seventeenth century. It also helps to explain why the singing schools could exist unimpeded. Works like RETROSPECT were wholly consistent with the demands of a wartime mentality, encouraging perseverance, faith, and continuity with the regional past.

Another reason for considering the volume special was that it came out of riper abilities than the *New-England Psalm-Singer*. Billings prefaced the work by admitting his disillusionment with the earlier collection:

> . . . truly a most masterly and inimitable Performance, I then thought it to be. Oh! how did my foolish heart throb and beat with tumultuous joy! With what impatience did I wait on the Book-Binder, while stitching the sheets and puting on the covers, with what extacy, did I snatch the yet unfinished Book out of his hands, and pressing it to my bosom, with rapturous delight, how lavish was I in encomiums on this infant production of my own Numb-Skull. Welcome, thrice welcome; thou legitimate offspring of my brain, go forth my little Book, go forth and immortalize the name of your Author; may your sale be rapid and may you speedily run through ten thousand Editions. . . .

Billings must have considered the earlier compositions unworthy not only of himself but also of the more adept singing produced by a decade of instruction in the schools. He appended a glossary of 140 musical terms, taken largely from Tans'ur. In his new introduction he included a more elaborate treatment of ornament than before, enlarging the section on graces of transition and adding one on the trill. Most important, he gave would-be vocalists not a set of general instructions but a systematic course of study, written in his wittiest prose. The eleven "lessons" begin with the gamut, proceed through transpositions, and end with concords, discords, and slurs, a sequence which he had found successful and which he urged other singing masters to follow, as they did.[8] The music in the new collection reflects a similar growth in versatility. Many of the tunes emphasize sectional contrast by means of changing meter, tempo, and texture; several contain *divisi* parts, providing two or three "choosing notes" from which the performer can shape his line.

Billings also went rather further than before in emphasizing the musical over the devotional aspect of performance, and in promoting a boisterous style. He commended soft-singing for training the ear and noted that singing schools, like all societies, depend on good order and a master's judgment. But he added that "it is vastly more agreeable (at least to me) to hear a few wild uncultivated sounds from a natural Singer, than a Concert of Music performed by the most refined artificial singers upon earth, provided the latter have little or no assistance from nature." Fuging-tunes he considered "twenty times as powerful as the old slow tunes" and he included ten of them, against three in his earlier collection. They required, he said, an "emphatic" performance, after the example of "a discarded Actor who after he had been twice hissed off the Stage, mounted again and with great Assurance . . . thundered on these words 'I will be heard.' " Many other tunes in the book demand if not thunder at least loud enthusiasm, such as the jolly "I am the Rose of Sharon," with its repeated proclamation that "the rain is over," and the dancy carol JUDEA, with the refrain "Then let us be merry put Sorrow away/ Our Saviour Christ Jesus was born on this Day."

The most blatantly secular piece in the collection is the raucous JARGON. This brief musical joke consists of thirty chords, only the first of which is consonant, the others being dissonant seconds, sevenths, and ninths. Billings perhaps intended the piece as a Doodle-like retort to those who criticized his harmony. In a delightful address "To the Goddess of Discord" he identified his, and Discord's, enemies as anti-American conspirators in a musical ministerial plot:

> I have . . . been informed, that some of my most implacable enemy's are some of your Majesty's privy council, and that your Majesty's Secretary at war, viz. Lord Jargon, was about to send some of your other Lords in waiting, viz. Lord second, Lord 7th, Lord 9th, alias Lord 2d, junior, with some others, to beat a tattooo upon the drum of my ear, with so great a number of contra-vibrations without the intervention of a single coincidence, and with so

much Forte as to dislocate my auditory; upon which information I called a court of Harmony, the result of which was, to repel force by force. . . .

To fight off the regulars, Billings put together *"the best piece [sic] ever composed."* To do it justice, it was necessary that an ass bray the bass, a filing saw carry the tenor, a weak hog squeal the counter, and "a cart-wheel, which is heavy loaded, and that has been long without grease, squeek the Treble." If that sounds too feeble, there may be added "the cracking of a crow, the howling of a dog, the squalling of a cat, and what would grace the Concert yet more . . . the rubing of a wet finger upon a window glass." The last "instantly conveys the sensation to the teeth"; should it fail, Billings urged adding the "most inharmonical of all sounds, *'Pay me what thou owest.'* "

The musical shriek that results paints a text beginning "Let horrid Jargon split the air" and ending "terrible as Thunder":

For all the squealing and braying, as Murray Barbour points out, the piece remains wholly singable, a tribute to Billings' unfailing tunefulness. Just the same, Billings' critics are said to have launched a counteroffensive. From the sign outside the composer's door—"BILLINGS MUSIC"—they hanged two cats by the tails.[9]

Billings' war against the musical regulars was more than an entertaining metaphor. As his influence grew, so did opposition to it. On one hand, like West, Billings was the teacher for a whole generation. By the time he settled in Boston, young musicians whom he deeply influenced were writing their first compositions, men like Daniel Read, Jacob Kimball, Jr., Jacob French, and Timothy Swan. On the other hand, one town clerk reported that he had encouraged the revival of singing in his town but was having second thoughts now that "Merry Tunes come in a pace" which put the undevout singers "into a Transport." [10] More importantly, the faint but developing resistance to the Billings idiom that already existed at this time produced a rival—Andrew Law.

Law was born in 1749 to a socially prominent family in Milford, Connecticut. A compiler more than a composer, he issued at the age of eighteen a collection of *Plain Tunes*. While enrolled at Rhode Island College (later Brown) to study for the ministry, he taught a singing school in Providence, where very likely he met Billings, who taught a school there in 1774. Law was licensed to preach but apparently abandoned the profession after issuing his first important collection, *Select Harmony* (New Haven, 1778). Like *The Singing Master's Assistant*, it contains psalms, hymns, and fuging-tunes. Whereas Billings, however, included more than a dozen patriotic songs, Law included none; whereas Billings scoffed at "refined artificial singers," Law called for "good or genteel pronunciation"; whereas Billings expanded his earlier treatment of ornamentation, Law warned that elaborate ornamentation was impractical for learners and, as currently practiced, crude and undiscriminating. Whereas Billings, above all, paid lip service to the injunction to 'sing with the understanding,' Law sought to return singing to devotional ends. As the Salem pastor William Bentley later summarized Law's achievement, he introduced a "solemn, slow & soft music" to succeed "the noise to which we had been accustomed." [11]

Law also took music seriously as a business. He first advertised *Select Harmony* as the cheapest tunebook ever offered in America. In 1782 he complained to the Connecticut legislature that the book was being widely pirated, robbing him of returns on the considerable investment he had made in printing it. Conceiving, he said, that "works of Art ought to be protected in this Country & all proper encoragement given thereto as in other Countries," he asked the legislature to grant him an "exclusive patent" on the book for five years, a right "not incompatible with the principles of a free State & not invading the rights of any individual." [12] Law succeeded where Billings failed. Impressed with his argument, the Connecticut General Assembly granted the patent, enabling Law to control—though only within the state—the second edition of *Select Harmony* (1782).

Select Harmony represents not only an important hint of the future but also a special vitality in the cultural life of Connecticut. Owing to the large number of self-taught country painters in the state, portraiture continued despite the war and despite the removal of Ralph Earl and of the painter Trumbull to London. Working in the folkish, highly patterned style of the limners, semiprofessionals like Joseph Steward, Richard Jennys, and the wax modeler Reuben Moulthrop depicted ministers, physicians, and Yale graduates amid their books and countrified households, scenes expressive of the Connecticut town-ideal. Winthrop Chandler painted several extraordinary portraits during the war, including *Colonel Ebenezer Crafts*, with a long clay pipe, near volume one of Locke's *Essays*, the words "Simple ideas" visible on the open page, and *Dr. William Glysson*, spurs on his shoes, feeling the pulse of a quarantined patient whose arm only is visible, extended from behind a curtained bed.[13]

Chandler's triumph in this period, painted around 1780, is his *Captain Samuel Chandler*, a portrait of a relative who had fought in the war (ill., p. 340). The captain wears the uniform of a Connecticut regiment, a deeply serious, rather ascetic figure with intense blue eyes and an aquiline nose, the swanlike, Hogarthian shapes of his tricorn hat and pursed lips emphasizing his tough elegance. His downturned mouth is warranted by the scene framed in the sashless window behind him, occupying almost a quarter of the canvas. Few paintings of the Revolution reflect the violence of the war except in a remote and idealized way, as in West's *Wolfe*. Casualties were, of course, far lighter than in modern wars, no battle having killed as many as 500 patriots.[14] Here, however, Chandler painted torment: bloated carcasses, a human corpse half-covered by a dead dog, a rider falling headfirst from his horse, a wounded man clutching his arm, mouth agape. The scene is made more horrible by the tininess of the figures gesticulating in anguish, and by the relative hugeness of Captain Chandler, a Gulliver, who sits unmoved, staring at the viewer with savage impassivity. Probably sometime after painting this portrait, Chandler moved to Worcester to do house painting and related work, gilding the weathervane of the courthouse but leaving no known canvases during his stay in the growing town.

Much of the cultural vitality of wartime Connecticut radiated from Yale College. In New Haven as elsewhere, patriotic sentiment diverted many cultural activities and their supporters to the schools. Charges of indifference to the war effort, or of social-climbing made possible by ill-gotten wealth, could not so deservedly be leveled at nonprofit entertainments given by adolescents, often in the name of a high purpose. Impunity made for boldness. Plays abounded, beginning a distinguished tradition of college theatre at Yale which has continued to the present. The *Connecticut Journal* reported in 1778 that a "large number of spectators" in New Haven had paid a dollar each to see a dialogue and a farce, oblivious to "the serious state of our public affairs" and in contempt of Congress. Members of one Yale literary society, the Linonian, purchased a twenty-volume set of *The British Theatre*, and apparently used it often. The president of Yale, Ezra Stiles, lamented that the students had "left the more solid parts of Learng & run into Plays & dramatic Exhibitions chiefly of the comic kind & turn'd College . . . into Drury Lane." [15]

When the threat of British raids from New York forced the students to disperse to other towns, they took Drury Lane with them. In Hartford they presented James Thomson's *Tancred and Sigismunda* plus a patriotic farce. To adequately portray Burgoyne and other British officers, a local minister complained, they "were obliged (I believe not to their sorrow) to indulge in very indecent and profane language." Worse, they gave the play during election week and, to the minister's disbelief, in the very "capital of the state, in the court house, the place where the Fathers of the Senate" met. A year later, the students attempted to mount a play commemorating the Battle of Lexington at the Hartford State House. This time, President Stiles called them in and forbade the performance, saying he "chuses not to preside at the head of a society of stage-players. . . ." [16]

Two new poets also appeared at Yale. The first was a late-blooming earlier graduate named David Humphreys. Born in Derby, Connecticut, in 1752, he was the son of a Yale-trained Congregational minister and an aristocratic, elegant woman referred to as "Lady Humphrey." He entered Yale in 1767, graduated in 1771, and afterward taught school in Connecticut and New York. Although he helped to found a new literary society at college and befriended Timothy Dwight, he did not break into print until 1780, when he published in New Haven *A Poem, Addressed to the Armies of the United States of America*. The second new poet was the less well-connected but more imaginative Joel Barlow. Born in Redding in 1754, he was the son of a farmer, the kind of student whose background John Trumbull had satirized in his *Progress of Dulness*. After studying for a while at Moor's Indian School in New Hampshire and at Dartmouth, Barlow transferred to Yale in 1774 and graduated with Noah Webster in the class of 1778.[17] Like Trumbull and Dwight he wrote and delivered a long commencement poem, *The Prospect of Peace*, published in New Haven at the height of the war. Poor and orphaned—both his parents died while he was at college—Barlow had few illusions about earning a living at present as a poet. But he believed that "some time after the settlement of peace," Americans would become "more refined" and would begin to notice and reward literary achievement. America, he believed, was a "theatre for the display of merit of every kind," the right place for people "without friends and without fortune," like himself. "If ever virtue is to be rewarded," he told Noah Webster, "it is in America." [18]

Barlow and Humphreys formed a close-knit, collaborative group with the earlier-established Yale poets Timothy Dwight and John Trumbull. As Humphreys wrote later, "no sooner had we seen each other at the place of our education, than . . . a certain similarity of genius, and congeniality of soul, connected us by the ties of an indissoluble friendship." [19] Their ties kept the young poets together not only in literary association but also on the battlefield. The crisscrossing of their lives as they shuttled between New Haven and various military camps, now writing now fighting, running into each other here and there throughout the war, makes a biographical labyrinth only a few of whose twists can be pursued here.

At one time or another all the Yale poets except Trumbull served under Connecticut's General Israel Putnam. Barlow and Humphreys joined Putnam in the fall of 1776 in New York—where he directed the American forces on Long Island—and were present at the withdrawal of the army up Manhattan Island. In the flight Barlow fell ill and had to return to Yale. Humphreys stayed with Putnam (about whom he later wrote a biography) and rose rapidly through the ranks, becoming a brigade major early in 1777, when he took part in defending Danbury against a 2,000-man British force from New York. As Major Humphreys, he served the same fall under Putnam at Peekskill, in the strategic region called the Hudson River Highlands, situated to harass British shipping along the river.

Here and at West Point Humphreys was joined by Timothy Dwight. Dwight had been appointed an army chaplain under Putnam, but found time at camp to compose patriotic songs and hymns, to ask Washington's permission for the dedication of his yet uncompleted epic, and to hike with Humphreys to the top of Sugarloaf Mountain for a view of the surrounding countryside. On another excursion, to Fort Montgomery, Dwight came on a pond of dead soldiers: "an arm, a leg, and a part of the body above the surface," the faces "monstrous," the postures "uncouth, distorted, and in the highest degree afflictive. . . . it was overwhelming. I surveyed it for a moment, and hastened away." Humphreys and Dwight split up in 1779, when Humphreys returned with Putnam to Connecticut, and Dwight's father died, forcing him to return to Northampton, Massachusetts, to care for his brothers and sisters.[20] To support his family, Dwight opened a school in Northampton, and in the summer of 1779 he hired Joel Barlow to serve as an usher.

By the time he joined Dwight in Northampton, Barlow had graduated Yale and published his long commencement poem. A month or two after his arrival he drew up an elaborate plan for a poem rivaling Dwight's in ambition. He had in mind something "rather of the philosophical than the epic kind." Using Columbus as its main character, it would deal with "America at large" as the "last and greatest theatre for the improvement of mankind in every article in which they are capable of improvement." Barlow worked on the poem at Northampton, meanwhile trying to enlist patrons from the army and the Congress. Friends had told him that as an army chaplain one might preach on Sunday, perform an occasional funeral or marriage, and still have plenty of time for writing. He crammed for six weeks in order to meet the chaplaincy requirements of the clerical association, and in 1780 was appointed chaplain to the 3d Massachusetts Brigade. Sent to New Jersey, he located near Hackensack an old Dutch house with "as good a study as ever lived," in which he could work on his poem with "scarcely any interruption." In New Jersey, too, the Yale poets crossed paths, for Barlow met up at camp with David Humphreys, himself returned from *"rustication"* in New Haven. Humphreys saw parts of the projected poem and had, he said, "an exceeding high idea" of it, rating Barlow a "very great genius" but believing that it would be a work of at least three years, during which Barlow would have a hard time supporting himself.[21]

Humphreys had something of his own to show. After only three weeks in New Jersey, he was appointed aide-de-camp to Washington. In several ways, it was a fitting appointment. The most ardently martial of the Yale poets, Humphreys had addressed his first published poem "To all the Brave Men, Whether Officers or Soldiers . . . by Their Brother Soldier." Some six feet two inches tall and weighing 230 pounds, he physically resembled Washington, whom he had long admired, even idolized. As early as July 1776, he had sent to Samuel Webb, then aide-de-camp to Washington, a poem which he had not the presumption to send to Washington himself, addressing to the illustrious hero of the Boston siege "the genuine effusions of an honest & grateful heart":

> His martial Skill our legions form'd,
> His glorious zeal their bosoms warm'd
>   And fann'd the rising flame,
> Like Fabius, he by wise delay,
> Forc'd Britain's bands to waste away,
>   Then bade them fly with shame.[22]

In his poem to the American army four years later he included what seems to be the only verse account in the period of Washington's victories at Trenton, "Where the great Chief, o'er Del'ware's icy wave,/ Led the small band, in danger doubly brave."

Once appointed aide-de-camp, Humphreys accompanied Washington everywhere, composing and delivering written and oral messages (some highly secret), dispatching his invitations, and acting in effect as his private secretary. Indeed, Humphreys' letters are one of the fullest repositories of Washington's day-by-day orders and wishes. Part of an official family that included Alexander Hamilton and the marquis de

Lafayette, he became one of Washington's most trusted subordinates, even his friend. In both capacities he very soon found himself en route to Virginia.

39. Charleston and Yorktown: May 1780–October 1781

Although the decisive shifting of the war south began late in 1779, British military planners had been attracted to the region since Independence. They saw it as a Loyalist stronghold, where the numerous Scotch settlers, restive slaves, and longstanding opponents of local governments might be translated into formidable political and military support. Clinton had launched an expedition against Charleston in 1776, but was badly defeated and forced to return to New York. When he was ordered to evacuate Philadelphia two years later, he was also ordered to send troops to Florida and Georgia, and to attempt the conquest of South Carolina again. The British captured Savannah in December 1778, giving them a solid hold on Georgia. In December 1779, Clinton himself left behind his lavish military theatre and his violins in New York. With Lord Cornwallis as second in command of his 90 transport ships, 10 warships, 8,700 soldiers, and 5,000 sailors, he sailed south.

The fighting around Charleston lasted several months against thin defenses. At one point, Clinton issued a proclamation offering to protect those who would submit—or rather those, one parodist felt, who would abase themselves:

> You shall no more for Rebels pass
> But honor'd, kiss his Royal - - -.

By May there was no longer a choice: On the twelfth Clinton forced the surrender of Charleston. Customarily, surrendering troops gave up their arms with flying colors, playing enemy tunes in derision. Clnton, however, expressly forbid the Americans to play an English march, presumably to forestall "Yankee Doodle." Thus while British oboists at the formal capitulation ceremony played "God Save the King," the Americans went off playing janizary music. Almost 5,500 armed men surrendered to the British. Some of the more rebellious Charlestonians were deported, including the city's most prominent painter, Henry Benbridge, who had studied with West and was a cousin of West's wife. He was loaded with other patriots on the British prison ship *Torbay* and exiled to St. Augustine.[1] Aside from taking the largest catch of Americans of the war, Clinton had taken the South's major port, opening a way to the conquest of the whole region.

Clinton stayed only a month or so in Charleston after the surrender, but the occupied city caught something of his tone. Concerts and dancing assemblies were held throughout the season of January–May 1781. Loyalists celebrated the king's birthday with illuminations, music, and the discharge of arms, although patriots countered with similar noises and lights on July 4. Playgoers, long famished, could find encouragement in the meeting held at a local tavern for "such gentlemen as wish to act at the theater in Charles Town," and in a startling bit of rumor which appeared in the *Gazette* in July: "the lovers of theatrical entertainment will doubtless be happy to learn, that there is some possibility of the American Company, under the direction of Mr. Hallam, being here next Winter." [2] If Hallam actually was planning a return he was also, by the logic of the situation, betting on an ultimate victory for the Crown. His willingness to perform in a captured city, protected by the British flag from the anti-theatre edicts of Congress, could be interpreted as nothing other than contempt for the patriots' chances and cause. As it happened, his return remained merely a "possibility."

Hallam would not have been alone, however, in thinking the fall of Charleston the beginning of the end. It has been called "the worst defeat in American military history until Bataan." Loyalists rejoiced. In New York, the band of the Theatre Royal moved outdoors for a celebration. To accommodate the musicians, the walk had to be widened; to do so, posts were sunk into some graves of Trinity Church, causing, a minister said, "great offense and uneasiness to all serious and still more to all godly men." [3] For patriots, the fall of Charleston made a dismal addition to the fall of Savannah, the eruption of virtual civil war between rebels and Loyalists in the South, a depreciating currency, the Arnold affair, and chronic desertions and lack of supplies.

An ominous feeling built. The famous eclipse, or "dark day," of May 19, 1780—one week after the fall of Charleston—created a scare. The Assembly meeting in New Haven broke up with "indications of terror"; thinking Judgment Day had come, some began to "preach and pray and prophesy." The writer of *A Few Lines . . . on the Dark Day* asked "What great event, next shall be sent,/ Upon this guilty land?" (Mather Byles's reply to such questions, characteristically, was "Dear Madam, I am as much in the dark as you are.")[4] Forebodings of disaster grew as in January 1781 the hated Benedict Arnold, far from swaying on the gallows like his effigies, fulfilled his first assignment as a British officer: He raided

Richmond, as Thomas Jefferson, now governor, watched helplessly from across the James River. By February, no continental soldier stood on any of the king's territory south of Virginia. By April, Washington himself felt darkly expectant: "we are at the end of our tether," he told Laurens, "and now or never our deliverance must come." [5]

Deliverance was not far off. Clinton had left Lord Cornwallis to hold the South when he returned to New York. Cornwallis did so aggressively, annihilating a large American army at Camden, South Carolina, in the summer of 1780 and marching in 1781 into Virginia. In May, Washington worked out plans with Rochambeau for a campaign against occupied New York. The campaign might be supported by the fleet of Admiral François Joseph Paul, comte de Grasse, then operating in the West Indies. Rochambeau did not like the plan, however, and had given De Grasse the option of sailing to the Chesapeake instead. On the English side, feuds and intricate, belated orders dispatched between New York, Virginia, and London led Cornwallis, in August 1781, to set up a defensive base in Yorktown, Virginia. When Washington learned of this and, the same month, learned that De Grasse was headed to the Chesapeake, he adopted Rochambeau's thinking. Abandoning plans for taking New York, he decided to move south with 2,500 American troops and the entire French force.

The long march of the armies to the northern end of Chesapeake Bay became something of a cultural event. Featuring large numbers of brilliantly clad French troops, it was broken by celebrations, illuminations, and receptions that reflected the growing, and usually welcome, influence of the French allies on patriot tastes. The upper echelons of the French expeditionary force contained several accomplished men. The marquis de Chastellux, one of Rochambeau's major generals, had arranged *Romeo and Juliet* for the French stage and written a study of progress, *On Public Felicity* (1772); Rochambeau's learned chaplain, the Abbé Robin, later wrote a fine account of his stay in America which was translated by Philip Freneau; the young marquis de Saint-Simon, leader of the troops who arrived with De Grasse, became a founder of French socialism.[6] Several of the French regiments also contained excellent bands, and they passed through Philadelphia, one observer reported, "with the military music playing before them, which is always particularly pleasing to the Americans. . . ." When Washington arrived in Williamsburg on September 14 to establish headquarters for the siege of Yorktown, he was feted by Saint-Simon's band, which played a quartet from André Grétry's opera *Lucille*; its theme, family joy produced by a returned father, was taken as a personal tribute.[7]

The band belonging to the count de Chaleur, stationed in Annapolis, found even more unusual employment. On the evening of September 20, and perhaps two days earlier as well, they supplied a theatre orchestra for the Maryland Company of Comedians, the first professional actors to risk performing in the country since the departure of Douglass. Why the company decided to take the risk can only be surmised. Probably they saw a potential audience in the French and American troops, who began moving through the Chesapeake area early in 1781. In January, Washington ordered Lafayette to lead an expedition of 1,200 men through Maryland to pursue Arnold and his troops. Lafayette stayed in Baltimore and Annapolis throughout the spring of 1781, and was honored at a ball. In the summer appeared the Maryland Company, their earliest surviving handbill being for June 14. Five of their handbills survive for September, at the height of preparations for the Yorktown campaign, increasing the likelihood that the company came into being in response to the allied expeditions.[8]

The managers of the new troupe were Thomas Wall and Adam Lindsay. Wall had played for several years with Douglass; Lindsay ran a Baltimore tavern at which a banquet was held for Washington when he arrived in the city. Their efforts displeased at least thirty-seven Baltimoreans, who endorsed a protest to the governor and Council. Their fellow citizens, they said, had "chearfully born their Proportion of Taxes" levied for prosecuting "a severe & important War"; but their ability to contribute taxes in the future would be "destroyed or diminished by what we must take the Liberty of thinking, after every consideration is duly weighed, an unprofitable Extravagance."[9] Apparently the address had little effect, for Lindsay and Wall were able to announce their performances "By Permission."

Perhaps wary just the same, the company performed in a sail-warehouse and advertised its performances as "Theatrical Trifles," a farrago of scenes from plays, the *Lecture on Heads*, demonstrations of electricity, and songs by Wall's seven-year-old daughter. At least one evening of trifles seems to have ended with a slave sale. The final items on the handbill for August 17, 1781, read:

The whole to conclude with an EPILOGUE, never performed before,
by Miss WALL
To begin at Seven o' Clock.
Boxes Half a Dollar, Pit Two Shillings and Six-pence, new
Emission.
No Persons to be admitted without TICKETS, which may
be had of Mr. Mann at the Dock, and of Mr. Wall near the
Town-gate.

TO be sold (or swop'd for a young House Wench[)], a likely
YOUNG NEGRO FELLOW, who understands Plantation
Business.

Many of the trifles seem to have been concocted for a military audience.
The same handbill promises "The HUMOURS of BEN the SAILOR"
and "An EPILOGUE, in the Character of a DRUNKEN SAILOR." On
October 3, as the fighting at Yorktown was beginning, Wall presented
"TAG, by a Person who never appeared before on the STAGE,"
performed by Lieutenant Street of the Maryland Line. Some of the cast
were local amateurs; a few, like Wall himself, had played minor roles with
the American Company; but most of the names on the bill were
unfamiliar and difficult now to identify—"Lewis," "Smith," "Brown,"
"Mrs. Elm." Perhaps to appeal to the French, Wall also used an actor
named George James L'Argeau, and a Baltimore dancing master named
"Monsieur Roussel," who performed "The Allemande," "The Fricasee,"
and comic or character dances between acts—a token of particular French
influence on American interest in dancing.[10]

A hodgepodge of stage-struck amateurs and professional bit players
managed by a local tavern keeper, the Maryland Company survived only
twenty months. In January 1782, Wall and Lindsay opened a brick
theatre in Baltimore, following the example set a decade earlier by
Douglass in Annapolis. But their receipts indicate that the house was often
less than half full. A year later they gave up the management of the
company to Dennis Ryan, formerly a prompter and minor actor with
Douglass. Ryan, we shall see, headed north.

At Yorktown, the opposing armies stood facing each other and ready for
battle by the first week of October. Many of the 30,000 or so French,
American, and English troops had already seen action in the war; together
they formed a massive military elite. The siege, once it began, lasted but a
short time. Cornwallis found himself virtually islanded in Yorktown, the
French fleet to his rear cutting off reinforcements, the allies advancing on
him by digging entrenchments closer and closer. On October 9, the big
allied batteries began bombarding, driving Cornwallis and his staff into an
underground burrow. Washington ordered the guns to fire all night. To a
German soldier sitting on the beach it "felt like the shocks of an
earthquake"; he saw "men lying everywhere who were mortally wounded
and whose heads, arms and legs had been shot off. . . ." [11] Steadily
increasing in ferocity and drawing ever closer to Cornwallis, the artillery
barrage lasted a week and destroyed Yorktown. On October 17, Cornwallis requested a truce to work out the terms of his surrender.

Part of the difficulty in arranging the surrender involved the music to be played at the formal ceremonies. Washington, in reprisal for the British surrender terms at Charleston, insisted on depriving the British of the last thrust allowed to vanquished armies—the derisive playing of an enemy tune. The final agreement directed the Yorktown garrison to march out with drums beating "a British or German March." The official ceremonies on October 20 were probably accompanied by a variety of music played by several groups, since each of the ten surrendering regiments probably had a band. The captured British military stores included eighty-one drums, twenty-eight bugles, and five French horns among the field instruments alone; the band instruments, privately owned, presumably were not seized. According to a tradition which seems to have begun in the nineteenth century, the tune "The World Turned Upside Down" was played, although it is not mentioned in contemporary accounts. The French bands performed janizary music. As the British marched out between parallel columns of the victors, they deliberately turned their heads to the French, ignoring the Americans. In reprisal, Lafayette ordered a light infantry band to strike up "Yankee Doodle." By one account, several British soldiers broke and grounded their arms in rage.[12]

40. Philadelphia:
November 1781–November 1782

News of the surrender of some 8,000 British military personnel spread quickly. A Boston poet spoke for thousands of rejoicing Americans when she proclaimed the decimation of the British army by Washington, and liberty triumphant:

> YORK-TOWN once more is freed from British chains,
> Rejoice AMERICA now FREEDOM reigns:
> FREEDOM is Our's; vain Britons boast no more
> Thy matchless strength by sea, nor on the shore.
> Great WASHINGTON doth thunder thro' the plain,
> And piles the field with mountains of the slain. . . .

But in fact, only the weakest of the three British divisions in North America had surrendered at Yorktown. The enemy still held New York, Wilmington, Savannah, and Charleston. Washington expected at least another year of fighting and believed that overconfidence would result in "disgraceful disasters." "My greatest fear," he told General Greene, "is, that Congress, viewing this stroke in too important a point of light, may think our work too nearly closed, and will fall into a state of languor and relaxation." [1] Three weeks after leaving Yorktown, he was in Philadelphia hoping to press home the need to prepare for the campaign of 1782.

The mood of Philadelphia was hard to read. Judging from the public press, Washington had little to fear. At the time he arrived, an unrelaxed and virulent propaganda campaign against the British was being waged in *The Freeman's Journal*, a newspaper begun earlier in the year. The campaign was the work of Philip Freneau, returned to America after still another period of vagabondage and vacillation, but this time returned scarred. After quitting the New Jersey militia in May 1780 he had shipped as third mate aboard the *Aurora*, bound with guns and tobacco for St. Eustacia. The ship was seized by a British frigate. With others, Freneau was handcuffed between decks and sentenced to the prison ship *Scorpion*, anchored in the Hudson River. Imprisoned for six weeks, he came down with a fever and was transferred to a hospital ship scarcely different from a lazar house. In July he returned to his home in Mount Pleasant to recuperate, hardly able to walk, a skeleton.[2] When he came to Philadelphia the following April to work on the *Freeman's Journal*, he brought along a hatred of everything British and plenty to write about.

Freneau published in pamphlet form *The British Prison-Ship*, a "Plutonian song" of hate on the keynote "Death has no charms except in British eyes." He depicted 300 famished and diseased prisoners bedded below deck on their own tattered clothing, in searing heat, brutalized by sadistic guards and kept alive on the "rotten pork, the lumpy damag'd flour,/ Soaked in salt water, and with age grown sour." He celebrated the Yorktown victory by composing another tirade which the *Journal* spread across nearly the whole front page, in keeping with its tone of exultation long drawn out: "On the fall of general earl CORNWALLIS, who, with above eight thousand men, surrendered themselves prisoners of war to the renowned and illustrious general GEORGE WASHINGTON, commander in chief of the allied armies of France and America, on the memorable 19th of October, 1781." First quoting the bitter *Titus Andronicus*, he hailed Cornwallis as "swine," "man of hell," "arch-butcher of the times," then dispatched him to "gnash your dragon's teeth in some sequester'd gloom."

Freneau sustained this vehement anglophobia while Washington was in Philadelphia. In several poems and essays he mocked the king, held up for sycophantic Loyalists the prospect of the gallows and halter, and debunked London as a place where "every man's hand is against his brother, and nothing but the extreme severity of the laws, hinders one from cutting the other's throat." He also eyed New York, whose

population had nearly doubled with British regiments returning from
Yorktown, setting in motion, predictably, a social whirl. To Freneau, the
gaiety confessed war-weariness. In February he drew up a mock will for
Rivington, stipulating:

> My fiddles, my flutes, french horns and guittars
> I leave to our heroes now weary of wars—
> To the wars of the stage they more boldly advance,
> The captains shall play and the soldiers shall dance.[3]

Here Freneau was malicious but not fanciful. Only the month before,
Rivington had advertised sixty separate plays for sale, as well as fiddles,
guitars, clarinets, and harpsichords for "the musical Season now com-
mencing." The season included the playing, on April 27, of two
"Sinfonies" by Haydn—the first known public performances of Haydn's
works in America.[4] In the wake of the British defeat at Yorktown,
"Clinton's Thespians" enjoyed perhaps their most lucrative year. For the
1782 theatrical season they extensively redecorated the John Street
Theatre and took in over £5,000.[5]

The militant Freneau managed to ignore, however, the soldiers dancing
in Philadelphia as well. The city little resembled the place to which Peale
returned from Valley Forge three years earlier, its houses stripped and
inhabitants exhausted. In the words of Pierre du Simitière, Philadelphia
had become "the Paris and the Hague of America, where the brilliancy of
our beau monde and the Sumptuosity and Elegance of their entertainments rivals those of the old world." The new French minister, Chevalier
Anne-César de La Luzerne, gave a ball one week, a concert the next.
Subscribers to the new "Philobiblian Library" could acquire "elegance of
speech from the conversation of a Cicero" or "sympathise in the distresses
of a St. Preux or Heloise." By the end of 1781 Philadelphia also contained
about 500 exiles from Carolina, including such distinguished Charlestonians as Charles Cotesworth Pinckney.[6] Their presence, added to that of
the congressional delegates, whetted a desire for diversion which had
persisted, although under restraints, throughout the war. The Yorktown
victory affected this desire so as to produce what Washington feared.

In his first month in Philadelphia, Washington found himself attending
three premature celebrations. The first occurred one day after he arrived
for a fifteen-week stay. On the evening of November 27, Charles Willson
Peale welcomed the commander by mounting at his new house on Third
and Lombard streets a display of allegorical transparencies—paintings on
varnished cloth or paper, lit from behind by lanterns. According to the
Packet, "During the whole evening the people were flocking from all parts
of the town to obtain a sight of the beautiful expressions of Mr. Peale's

respect and gratitude to the conquering Hero." Peale had exhibited part of the display a few weeks earlier to mark Cornwallis' surrender, including large pictures of Washington and Rochambeau, and of a French fighting ship. To honor Washington's visit he added a Temple of Independence around whose base ran the words Stamp Act, Duties on Tea, Boston Port Bill, Lexington, and Bunker Hill, and the motto BY THE VOICE OF THE PEOPLE. The motto supported thirteen columns, topped by a pediment allegorically depicting Justice, Hope, and Industry, and inscribed, in rays of light, BRAVE SOLDIERY. The second story portrayed Agriculture, Commerce, and the Arts. Painting, as described in the press (probably by Peale), appeared with

> . . . a pallat *[sic]* and pencils in one hand, and the other supporting a picture; she has a golden chain hanging from her neck, with a medal, on which is IMITATION: the several links allude to the many parts necessary to be studied before a whole can be produced; or the combined qualifications of an able artist; and it being of gold, to shew that the art of painting cannot flourish without it is supported by the generosity of the opulent.

Other windows at Peale's house illuminated a life-sized female Genius of America, clothed in white. She wore a purple girdle with the word VIRTUE, and a fillet with the word PERSEVERANCE as she trampled a figure of Discord.[7]

Two weeks later, on December 11, Washington was entertained, as the guest of La Luzerne, by a performance of Francis Hopkinson's *The Temple of Minerva*. Here Hopkinson drew together his talents as a musician and as a poet into the sort of mythological-allegorical-political blend of masque and oratorio fashionable at European courts. But in the creating, he told Franklin, "the Musician crampt the poet." Since everything in *The Temple* is sung, the work could be called the first American grand opera. It consists of an overture, arias, ensembles, and choruses praising the American alliance with France, with music by Handel, Niccolò Jomelli, and Hopkinson himself. In Scene I, before Minerva's closed temple, the Genius of America asks Minerva to predict whether American arms will prevail in the war. In Scene II, the temple doors open and Minerva steps forth. She sings of America's growing fame and prophesies that, in concert with France, America will triumph:

> The Gods decree
> That she shall be
> A nation great confest.

The work ends with a chorus praising Minerva, thanking France, and hailing Washington.[8]

How Washington took this can perhaps be inferred from the letter he wrote four days later from Philadelphia to General Greene. "I am apprehensive," he said, "that the States, elated by the late success, and taking it for granted that Great Britain will no longer support so losing a contest, will relax in their preparations for the next campaign." If Washington had begun to sound like a British home secretary lamenting the capers of a Clinton or Howe, Loyalists had begun sounding like latter-day patriots, deriding or sternly reproving British elegance. In January, Rivington published a parody of *Minerva* entitled "The Temple of Cloacina." Unrelentingly scatological, it transforms the overture into an "Overturd," the trio into a "TRI-OH!" and the temple into an outhouse. The prayer of the Genius of France becomes:

> Cloacina! grant her pray'r,
> Make her sh—ten sons thy care,
> To the stinking breath of fame,
> Give, oh, give the Yankie name.
> O'er her close-stools still preside,
> Wipe with nettles her backside. . . .[9]

The parody concludes with the appearance of Washington, crowned by a turd. Another New Yorker produced *Blockheads*, a parody designated *An Opera, in Two Acts*. Here the friendly Amita warns Congress that France has designs on Maryland and Virginia; fiends appear, however, and metamorphose Congress into Frenchmen "with long tails tied to their hair behind, and cocked hats, with fleur de lis as cockades." In the final scene Americana appears in chains denouncing French perfidy. As she rushes to Albion for release, she sings:

> Bless'd Albion's name, for aye rever'd,
> By thee Americana's chear'd,
> With parent fondness ease my woes,
> Assist to crush our mutual foes;
> For thee I sigh, for thee I complain,
> Haste and destroy this Gallic chain.

Two weeks after Hopkinson's production, Washington and La Luzerne were entertained at Douglass' reopened Southwark Theatre. The evening was tendered by Alexander de Quesnay, a young nobleman invalided from the army and teaching French in the city. Quesnay's students performed Beaumarchais' *Eugénie* (probably in French) and the popular farce *The Lying Valet*. Freneau contributed a prologue, which at one point addressed Washington in the audience specifically. The prologue noted that for a long time America had been "Constrain'd to shun the bold theatric show,/ To act long tragedies of real woe"; time had come, it asserted, to again indulge the comic Muse. Maintaining the French note, the performance was followed by several dances, presumably balletic. The evening ended with an illumination of thirteen pyramidal pillars. Above the middle column floated a cupid supporting a laurel crown over the motto "WASHINGTON, *the pride of his Country and terror of Britain.*" The other columns contained the names of the states and of military heroes. Attended, said the *Freeman's Journal*, by "a number of the officers of the army and a brilliant assemblage of ladies and gentlemen of the city," it was probably the most scintillating evening in Philadelphia since the *Mischianza.*[10]

It was an evening, also, expressive of an ambiguous moment. Since Yorktown, fighting in the country had virtually ceased. With opinion divided over whether England would launch a vast new offensive in the spring or evacuate New York and abandon the war, it became difficult for patriots to restrain arts in the name of arms. The alliance with the cultivated French, moreover, made it hypocritical to sneer at the enemy's plays and concerts. Both facts made for irresolution. Quesnay intended to repeat the performance of *Eugénie* a week later for the benefit of the "virtuous American Soldiery in the Barracks of Philadelphia." But he called it off—or more likely was forced to—in respect to the oft-transgressed but still existing anti-theatre laws. The ethical wobbling produced by the situation is amusingly revealed in an essay by Philip Freneau, published anonymously a week after the performance of *Eugénie*. In it, Freneau reprinted an alleged letter from "Maria Flutter," who had found the play an "enchanted world" and was disappointed that Quesnay had called off a second showing. Despite his scorn for the "wars of the stage" in New York, Freneau had written a prologue to the performance justifying the return of the comic Muse. Perhaps having guilty afterthoughts, he reminded Maria that at the moment her countrymen were "perishing in sickly prisons, dying with painful wounds . . . facing death in the field of battle." He advised her: "Have patience madam, 'till the war is successfully finished." [11]

Washington's aide David Humphreys had less trouble deciding whether high-toned festivities deserved defense or attack. He had preceded Washington to Philadelphia, bringing the captured British and German standards from Yorktown to the thronged State House; and after leaving Philadelphia with Washington in March, he wrote a malediction:

> Such are the joys that fill thy constant round
> Oh Philadelphia, 'midst the rage of War!
> Thy pride exults, as thundring o'er the ground,
> Roll the swift wheels of pleasures gilded Car!

How chang'd oh beautious Town thy simple lot,
For lo! thy sons with alter'd manners gay,
(Thy sapient founder's sober plans forgot)
Change Natures laws, & turn the night to day.
. . . .

But can the revel of nocturnal sports,
The charms of Music, or the pride of show,
Drive hostile Navies from your guarded ports,
Or sheild your Country, from the barb'rous foe?
Is this a time for feasts & flowing Bowls,
Or can ye sleep!—while yet your Country bleeds. . . .

Washington himself, however, seems during his stay in the city to have become less perturbed by signs of relaxation. Even if the public slept easily after "feasts & flowing Bowls," the congressional delegates shared his view of the need for military preparedness. He discovered to his relief, he told Lafayette, "the best disposition imaginable in Congress to prepare vigorously for another campaign." [12]

Congress supplied something else noteworthy, one of three important events which took place in Philadelphia before Washington returned for a brief visit in July. In May, a congressional committee considered a new proposal for a seal of the United States, the third submitted since the effort of Jefferson, Adams, Franklin, and Du Simitière in 1776. It was designed by William Barton of Philadelphia, a nephew of David Rittenhouse and the author of an essay on paper credit. Barton could draw, and had a knowledge of heraldry, although his elaborate designs seem influenced most by the imagery of the celebrations following Yorktown. For the face of the seal he proposed a heraldic shield with the traditional two supports: on one side a female "Genius of the American Confederated Republic" wearing an irradiated gold crown, on the other side an American soldier in uniform.[13] Atop the shield would be a flaming phoenix with expanded wings, gripping in one talon a sword with a laurel wreath hanging from the point. The obverse would feature a truncated pyramid of thirteen strata or steps topped by an eye set within a glory, with the motto *Deo Favente Perennis* ("God willing throughout the year"). Barton explained that the phoenix was "emblematical of the expiring Liberty of Britain, revived by her Descendants in America," while the obverse pyramid signified strength and duration.

The congressional committee was again not entirely satisfied with the result. Barton's design was apparently passed on in June to the secretary of Congress, Charles Thomson, a tutor in Latin and Greek at the Philadelphia Academy and a founder of the American Philosophical Society. He made several boldly imaginative changes in Barton's design. He retained the pyramid on the obverse, but replaced Barton's *Deo Favente* with a motto adapted from Vergil's *Aeneid—Annuit Coeptis* ("God has nodded at the undertaking"). He also introduced a motto adapted from Vergil's *Eclogues—Novus Ordo Saeclorum* ("A new order of the ages is born"). He made even more significant changes on the face, reversing the proportionate sizes of the small phoenix and the large shield. He made the central image of the seal a large eagle displaying a reduced shield of thirteen stripes on its chest. In its talons the eagle would grip an olive branch and a bundle of arrows. In its beak would be a scroll reading *E Pluribus Unum*. Above the eagle would hover a cloud shrouding a constellation of thirteen stars.[14] Thomson returned the design to Barton, who made a few further changes and returned it again to Thomson, who submitted it to Congress with a gloss on the symbolism:

> The Constellation denotes a new State taking its place and rank among other sovereign powers. The Escutcheon is born on the breast of an American Eagle without any other supporters, to denote that the United States of America ought to rely on their own Virtue.
>
> Reverse. The pyramid signifies Strength and Duration; The Eye over it & the Motto allude to the many signal interpositions of providence in favour of the American cause. The date underneath is that of the Declaration of Independence and the words under it signify the beginning of the new American AEra, which commences from that date.[15]

On June 20, 1782, Congress adopted the Barton-Thomson design as the official Seal of the United States.

The final seal was a radically new conception, even though most of its elements had been used before. *E Pluribus Unum* appeared in the 1776 proposal, as did the radioles; various currencies of the 1770's had used the bundle of thirteen arrows, the olive branch, and the unfinished pyramid, the last reflecting a current view of architecture as symbolic of order, thus of governance. The eagle may ultimately, and perhaps directly, descend from Ioachim Camerarius' *Symbolorum & emblematum* (Frankfort, 1654), which contains sixteen eagle figures, one of them a bald eagle with displayed wings holding an olive branch and thunderbolts. Similar eagles had appeared on Hessian banners at the Battle of Trenton, in one of Peale's 1779 portraits of Washington, and on the 1781 arms of New York State.[16]

What is remarkable is that Barton and Thomson dared to break out of the line of thinking which several committees, guided by heraldic tradition, had pursued over seven years' work on the seal. They simply scrapped what had been the central motif, repeatedly amended, of the heraldic shield with two supports, replacing it with the visually simpler and surprising eagle, levitated in space as America itself was unsupported. In concentrating national identity in the eagle—described by Thomson as an American bald eagle but in reality the German eagle of the Holy Roman Emperor—they also boldly abandoned the Whig idiom to which most of the earlier designers had committed themselves. The final seal contains no pileus, no liberty pole, no buckskinned warrior, no Columbia, no Mosaic historicist emblems. As a visual fresh start, the eagle made possible a sense of identification apart from regional variants in ideology. As a figure of self-sufficient strength and even imperial ambition, too, it befitted a country which had conquered at Yorktown and which could mount celebrations of the kind seen at Philadelphia.

A second, and not dissimilar, event took place within weeks after Washington left Philadelphia—the opening of what was advertised as "the foundation of the first American museum." It came in response to the recognition that America now had not a few, but many heroes, victories, and memorable moments. Their number demanded not an isolated engraving or commissioned portrait, but some omnibus form of commemoration. In 1781 John Eliot of Boston proposed an American biographical dictionary in eight parts: congressmen, civic officials, academics and clergymen, physicians, army officers, "Poets & other ingenious persons," "ladies that have rendered themselves eminent," and "Painters, mechanics, &c." One of the French allies, the marquis de Chastellux, suggested a way for Americans to reward their heroes without creating artificial social distinctions:

> . . . your public buildings, your *curiae*, why should they not display in sculptured relief and in painting the battles of *Bunker's Hill*, of *Saratoga*, of *Trenton*, of *Princeton*, of *Monmouth*, of *Cowpens*, of *Eutaw Springs?* Thus would you perpetuate the memory of these glorious deeds; thus would you maintain . . . that national pride, so necessary to the preservation of liberty; and you could, without offense to this liberty, lavish rewards equal to the sacrifices made in her name.[17]

The addition of Yorktown to the list confirmed the need for a comprehensive public record of the past.

The need was swiftly satisfied, for it had long been anticipated. Pierre du Simitière had been collecting American antiquities since his arrival in Philadelphia around 1768. Since 1777 he had been taking portraits of celebrated Americans and sending them to Paris to be engraved. Sets of the engravings—including Washington, Steuben, Deane, Reed, Gates, Jay, and Dickinson—arrived in Philadelphia in time for Washington's stay, but they sold poorly. Du Simitière left samples for Charles Thomson to lay before Congress, hoping, he wrote, that "that hon. body might resolve to purchase a Sett to deposit in their archives." But after two weeks they had received no more notice than "Soiling and tearring off part of the paper," and he took them back. Disappointed in the reception of his print series, but still set on becoming America's first official historian, Du Simitière opened his private collections to the public. Exactly what he chose to display is unknown, but he had amassed natural curiosities, Indian artifacts, paintings (including rococo works "in the amourous Style"), quantities of Revolutionary newspapers and pamphlets, seals, medals, prints, and such items as the sword, shield, and lance borne by Major André in the *Mischianza*. The collection could be seen three days a week at Du Simitière's home on Arch Street, beginning in May 1782. For the half-dollar admission, viewers were conducted in groups of six on hour-long tours by Du Simitière himself.[18]

The third event was the most surprising, and the richest in ambiguities. It was the return to Philadelphia of one of the American Company's stars, John Henry. Perhaps tempted by fluctuating rumors of peace, he seems to have left Jamaica shortly after the surrender at Yorktown, arriving in Maryland around January, when the Wall-Lindsay company opened its theatre. Perhaps to protect the Company's property against confiscation, he asked the Maryland Assembly to pass an act confirming Douglass' title to the 1771 Annapolis brick theatre, which the Assembly did.[19] In July, he turned up in Philadelphia, for reasons that can only be guessed. The anti-theatre laws had been violated repeatedly, and he may have felt they could be stretched enough to allow the Company to slip back into the country. He may have suspected, as others did, that the war was ending, and may have wished to survey the Company's prospects for the postwar period. It is possible, too, that a business or political rift had grown between Hallam in London, on one hand, and Douglass and Henry in Jamaica, on the other, and that Henry was considering a return of the West Indian troupe as an independent company. (Hallam's return from London, it will be remembered, had been rumored in British-occupied Charleston.)

Or perhaps, as in Maryland, Henry simply wished to confirm title to the Company's theatre. He found the Southwark out of repair, owing in taxes, and in danger of being transformed beyond use: Alexander de Quesnay had proposed dismantling the scenery, raising the pit to stage level, and turning the theatre into a ballroom. On July 1, Henry petitioned the president of the Executive Council of Pennsylvania for permission to give the *Lecture on Heads*, to pay off money owing on the theatre. He reminded him that actors had left America "at the particular request of the Honorable, the Congress"; while abroad, they continued to call themselves The American Company, a sign that they were "as firmly attached to the country (tho' absent by Command) as any residents in it." [20] The president, however, denied Henry's request. Henry seems to have gone to New York, perhaps to investigate conditions at the John Street Theatre, after which he again left the country, though whether to consult with Douglass in Jamaica or Hallam in London is unclear.

As Washington himself returned to Philadelphia in July, Benjamin Franklin in Paris had begun negotiations with the new ministry of Lord Rockingham over the terms of a peace or truce. The talks, however, were stalled over the question of a prior recognition of American independence. Washington remained wary, coming to Philadelphia to urge strong defensive and offensive preparations, and to discuss future naval operations with Rochambeau. He also remained disenchanted with his country-men. Before setting out, he wrote: "That spirit of freedom, which at the commencement of this contest would have gladly sacrificed every thing to the attainment of its object, has long since subsided, and every selfish passion has taken its place." [21] He reached the city on July 14, just in time for the joint celebration the next night of the birthday of King Louis XVI and the birth of his son, the Dauphin—a *Mischianza* à la Versailles.

Philadelphians had talked of nothing else for the last ten days. For the last six weeks they had watched the construction of the architectural and landscape arrangements, contrived by the soldier-engineer Pierre-Charles L'Enfant. Some £1,100 in tickets were distributed. As the event approached, said Benjamin Rush, "shops were crowded with customers. . . . tailors, milliners, and mantua-makers were to be seen covered with sweat and out of breath in every street." [22] The heavy demand for hairdressers forced many women to have their hair done at four o'clock in the morning on the day of the fete.

The *Dauphinade* began at the house rented by the French minister La Luzerne from John Dickinson. L'Enfant had turned the courtyard into a huge garden—cut into walks, divided by cedar branches into artificial groves, and featuring a seventy-five-foot-long hall with columns, vaults, and emblematical paintings by Matthew Pratt, one of West's first pupils. At one end of the hall was displayed the new Seal of the United States. In the morning, several odes to the Dauphin were recited to an audience of about 1,500 people. In the evening, the streets to La Luzerne's house became lined with people—10,000, by Rush's estimate—many of whom looked on at the festivities from a palisade fence placed around the courtyard. Inside the hall and around the gardens walked Washington, Dickinson, Rochambeau, Paine, Indian chiefs, faculty from the University, and, in Rush's words, "painters and musicians, poets and philosophers, and men who were never moved by beauty or harmony or by rhyme or reason. . . ." The evening started with a concert, ending at nine o'clock, when a ball and fireworks simultaneously began. After the ball, the 700-odd guests were fed by 30 cooks from the French army.[23]

Washington seems to have been embarrassed by his participation in the affair. He made a point of telling one correspondent that his presence had been "purely accidental." Having discussed with Rochambeau the possibility of an attack on New York or Charleston, or Canada, he left Philadelphia again on July 24. Rumors of a negotiated peace persisted, but the "infatuation, duplicity, and perverse system of British policy" had taught him "to doubt every thing, to suspect every thing. . . ."[24]

As the year dragged out in watchful waiting and desultory fighting, two recently prominent figures from Connecticut arrived in Philadelphia hoping to profit from the city's surging and now almost unrestrained festivity. The singing master Andrew Law opened a school on Chestnut Street toward the end of the year, where he taught five afternoons and evenings a week, selling his tunebooks through the Philadelphia dealer Robert Aitken. Already a challenger to the musical idiom of Billings, he thus carried the traditions of the Congregational singing schools outside of New England. In November, Joel Barlow arrived from West Point with fifteen letters of introduction, hoping to raise subscribers for the long poem he had been writing as he shuttled between New Haven, Hartford, and camp. His friend David Humphreys had recently enlisted General Greene, commander of the Continental Army in the South, to pass around the region a subscription list for the "great Poetical Work." Philadelphians too, Barlow discovered, "of the first and greatest character, offer the matter the warmest encouragement, and think that they and their country will be more indebted to me than I to them." On November 15 he obtained an interview with La Luzerne, who promised to promote patronage locally and to get permission for Barlow to dedicate the poem to Louis XVI. Happy with the results of his month-long stay, Barlow noted that he failed to find in Philadelphia "that extravagance, that haughtiness or idleness which I have had represented."[25]

Extravagance or no, during Barlow's visit Philadelphia acquired a large new portrait gallery, the foundation of a second museum. Its owner was Charles Willson Peale, who saw the venture as at once a monument to the accumulating accomplishment of America and a boost to business that might help to pay off his accumulating debts. Having lost his never-welcomed political power after the 1780 elections, when conservatives regained control of the state government, he also found himself "out of Blast" from building his new house—owing many tradesmen, unable to buy wood, having to send dunning letters even to Rochambeau. He found, too, that his ability to work had become impaired. For the last year or two he had fallen into a "kind of lethargy." Once, after a "frugal meal of a few roasted potatoes and some bread and Cyder," he was sitting by the fire and could not remember whether his mother-in-law was alive; another time he forgot how many children he had.[26] He also feared that his sight must soon prove too weak for him to continue painting miniatures.

In these circumstances Peale hired carpenters to build a sixty-six-foot-long structure onto the back of his house at Third and Lombard streets. The building was skylighted, the overhead windows being equipped inside with adjustable panels and curtains. When opened in November 1782, the gallery contained about thirty portraits of distinguished Americans, including Washington, Franklin, Paine, the presidents of Congress, foreign ambassadors, and most of the American generals. Peale intended to keep adding to the collection "as many of those who are distinguished by their actions or office as opportunity will serve, in full expectation that my children will reap the fruit of my labours." [27]

What extra vitality Philadelphia gained from the opening of Peale's new gallery it lost a few weeks later by the withdrawal of Philip Freneau as editor of the *Freeman's Journal*. In 1782 he had published there at least sixty-seven distinct poems and essays, many of which were reprinted in newspapers in Massachusetts, Connecticut, and New Jersey, greatly enlarging his reputation. But the special hatred of everything British which he brought to the paper had been mollified by a returning realization. "Discord and disorder," he wrote in June, "are interwoven with the nature and constitution of the human race"; not only the British, but all men are "naturally as well as habitually quarrelsome and unjust." [28] The uncertainty of the moment, the erosion of the line between patriotism and self-serving, seem to have reawakened his natural melancholy and predisposition to expect ingratitude.

In itself, Freneau's experience as editor of the *Journal* was enough to confirm his larger gloom. Radical on issues of Pennsylvania politics, the *Journal* fought a vicious verbal war with its conservative rival, the *Independent Gazetteer*, whose contributors included Rush, Dickinson, and Hopkinson. The wide-ranging political conflict found a narrow and bloody battleground in James Rivington's scatological parody of *The Temple of Minerva*. Hopkinson refused to reply in kind, professing former friendship for the parodist—whom many believed was Jonathan Odell, the Loyalist poet. Freneau criticized Hopkinson for protecting "one of the most bitter enemies to your country." Hopkinson replied that Freneau was "a general CALUMNIATOR." Freneau called him back "Francis Fiddlestick," a *"flabbergasted Musician,"* composer of "Sir-Reverential Songs" and *"Roratorios,"* a man addicted to "cringing, fawning, lying, flattering" while others with "twenty times his ability have starved to death in Grub Street." [29]

The literary war lasted nearly a year and almost brought the rival publishers to a duel. Freneau learned from it that conservative Philadelphia Whigs cared little more for him than had his tormentors on the prison ship. A typically scurrilous piece (in the *Independent Gazetteer* on September 7) depicted him being publicly flogged:

> . . . as your hide the flagellation feels,
> The *yellow* filth came trickling to your heels.
> The people crouded, soon began to stare,
> The foremost cry'd,—Lord, what a stink is there;
> . . . .
> While on the ground lay sprawling *this great wit*,
> And thus we leave him, wallowing all besh - -.

Such blasts from fellow Americans perhaps undermined the rabid partisanship Freneau brought to the *Journal*. In one of his last poems as editor, he prophesied ultimate American victory but foresaw that the Revolution would be betrayed by the stupidity and injustice meted out to himself:

> When struggling long, at last with pain
> You break a cruel tyrants chain,
> That never shall be join'd again,
>   When half your foes are homeward fled,
>   And hosts on hosts in triumph led,
>   And hundreds maim'd and thousands dead,
>   A timid race shall then succeed,
> Shall slight the virtues of the firmer race,
> That brought your tyrant to disgrace,
> Shall give your honours to an odious train,
> Who shunn'd all conflicts on the main
> And dar'd no battles on the bloody plain. . . .[30]

Early in December, Freneau resigned as editor of the *Freeman's Journal*, to work as a clerk under the postmaster general of the United States. By then, part of his prophecy was already being fulfilled.

41. 1783: Peace Returning

On what day peace returned to America is not a matter of fact but of definition. The complex negotiations abroad moved forward in September

1782, when the English ministry authorized its representative to treat with the commissioners of the "13 United States." The phrase tacitly granted the point on which the American commissioners had insisted—a prior concession of independence. On November 30, 1782, a preliminary peace treaty was signed in Paris. Reports of the signing soon reached America, but the text did not arrive until March 1783. Even so, the preamble stated that the treaty would not become operative until Great Britain and France also agreed on peace terms. Many members of Congress suspected a ploy to create distrust among the allies and within America. Washington more than anyone else remained cautious, intent on keeping the country "in a hostile position, prepared for either alternative, war or peace." On March 26, however, he received news of the conclusion of a treaty between France and Britain, activating the British-American treaty. At last he allowed himself to feel "inexpressible satisfaction." [1]

This time it was Washington who spoke prematurely. The formalities lasted another full year. A definitive treaty had first to be signed in Paris, then ratified by Congress, then the ratified definitive treaties had to be exchanged, a process which ended in mid-1784. Overlapping with what must be called the postwar period, the war for independence did not so much end as fade.

Uncertain about which one of the interminable formalities meant certain peace, Americans in one place or another celebrated them all. Philadelphians—who had been rejoicing since Yorktown—tried to raise a "Grand Exhibition" in May 1783, after Congress ratified the preliminary articles. Subscriptions were circulated to create a "Superb Sopha" mounted on a triumphal car drawn by six white horses, decorated with portraits of the "Principal Officers that have persevered in the present contest." The procession was to be accompanied by vocal and instrumental music, thirteen large torches, and "thirteen times thirteen boys drest in white." For some reason, Philadelphians failed to subscribe; a substitute plan was proposed for a combined peace and July 4 celebration. A broadside announcement called for a march from the State House to the house of the French minister in a spirit of decent gaiety instead of Roman grandeur:

> With drums and trumpets sounding,
> Liberty and joy abounding;
> Musick, strike up;
> Boys, look fierce;
> And widows, be gay;
> The road's made plain, march on, march on,
> Huzza for peace and Washington.

In December, after the definitive treaty was signed in Paris, elaborate scenery and emblematical transparencies were set up at Quesnay's French Academy, where twenty-five students dressed as shepherds gave several performances of "a BALLET representing the Return of Peace, and the Coronation of the Success of America." [2]

A more splendid celebration was planned for January, and held one week after the definitive treaty was ratified by Congress. The Philadelphia Executive Council provided a handsome outlay of £600 to Charles Willson Peale to build a Roman arch, perhaps having in mind the triumphal arches constructed for the *Mischianza*. The work was ideally suited to an artist-technologist-tinkerer, and Peale devised a clever painting-building-machine. The structure consisted of three hollow arches, the center one being thirty-five feet high, independent of the surmounting statuary. Bracketed by two lower arches, it made an edifice more than fifty feet wide, stretching nearly across Market Street. Outside, the arches were covered with transparent paper painted with revolutionary scenes and mottoes. Inside were 1,200 lamps to illuminate the transparencies, and a network of ladders and platforms from which various mechanical devices could be manipulated by technicians. The construction of the framework was assigned to a group of carpenters, while a room in the State House was turned over to Peale for a painting studio. To aid him he employed an apprentice, Billy Mercer—a young deaf mute whose father had been the much-eulogized General Hugh Mercer killed at the battle of Princeton. Peale taught Billy to paint miniatures and oils, and in return received his help in grinding paint, washing brushes, and preparing the transparencies. The arrangement did not work out well, since the boy seems to have considered his chores degrading, and the unheated room in the State House was so cold that his heel became frostbitten. [3]

Descriptions of the completed arch appeared at great length in several newspapers. They stressed how Peale had reconstructed "a building as used by the Romans," authentic down to the balustrades, cenotaphs, and Ionic pillars. [4] Among the many transparencies were representations of the French king, of various war heroes, of the various states, and of the arts and sciences, as well as a "Pyramidal Cenotaph" with the names of fallen soldiers, a tree with thirteen fruitful branches, and a picture of *"Indians building Churches in the Wilderness."* Peale rendered Washington as Cincinnatus returning to his plough, with the motto VICTRIX VIRTUS —"Victorious Virtue." The central arch was crowned with a "Temple of *Janus,"* shut to represent the close of the war, its motto echoing the new U.S. Seal: NUMINE FAVENTE MAGNUS AB INTEGRO SAECU-LORUM NASSITUR ORDO—"By divine favor, a great and new order of the ages commences."

The celebration was scheduled to begin at twilight on January 22. According to a route published in Philadelphia newspapers, citizens would march down Market Street, carriages passing through the center arch, pedestrians through the side arches. Atop the house of the president of Pennsylvania, nearby, Peale placed a figure of Peace, rigged so as to suddenly appear and to descend along a rope to the top of the arch. Here the Peace figure would ignite a central fuse, touching off the thousand lamps within a minute. As the arch and its paintings of Washington and other heroes began to colorfully glow, there would be a huge burst of fireworks from the top of the arch, opening the celebration.

The actual event was a disaster. The paper covering the arch had been varnished and oiled all over to make the paintings transparent, and was highly combustible. The fireworks, when triggered, exploded, shooting 700 rockets at the crowds on Market Street, injuring several spectators and killing one man. Stranded atop the arch in the firestorm, Peale tried to climb down the back side of the frame, which had been covered with sails to protect the candles inside from wind. Rockets bursting below him as he descended ignited his clothes; one, he feared, zoomed under his coat. Dropping twenty feet to the ground he broke several ribs. He made it to a nearby house, where he managed to extinguish his clothing, but he was badly burned. Taken home on a sleigh and bled by a surgeon, he remained in bed for three weeks and suffered from his injuries through the summer. Luckily his brother James and eldest son Raphaelle, assigned to mobilize the figure of Peace from the president's house, were unhurt. Billy Mercer also escaped, but not without having his watch and knee buckles stolen as he fled through the crowd.

Some sympathetic Philadelphians raised money to rebuild the arch, this time without fireworks. Without much enthusiasm, Peale repeated the event on Chestnut Street on May 10, 1784, two days before the exchange of the ratified definitive treaties of peace.

If not so harrowing, the peace celebrations elsewhere were equally protracted. As late as September 1784 Abraham Wood, a drummer in a Massachusetts militia company, advertised publication of a sixteen-page fuging-tune entitled *A Hymn on Peace*. Billings published *Peace*, an anthem running twelve minutes in performance and including instrumental passages, a feature in itself so unusual that he explained in a note: "Symphony is sounds without words intended for instruments." Phillis Wheatley (writing as "Phillis Peters," her married name) produced *Liberty and Peace, A Poem*, while David Humphreys praised *The Glory of America; or, Peace Triumphant over War*.[5] Looking to the past, some poets rejoiced in America's proud triumph over "Highland Clans, and Hessian Bands":

> No more their Bagpipes squeels *[sic]*
> In North America,

We made them dance such Reels
  That's danc'd them quite away:
. . . .

Now the play is ended,
  And wears a tragic face;
The farce by none attended
  But grief and foul disgrace.

Others rejoiced simply in the ending of bloodshed:

No longer thund'ring Cannons roar,
  No more the Sword we wield,
Nor slaughter'd Bodies strew'd about
  Each sanguinary Field.

Looking to the future, some savored a relaxation of wartime austerities and the return of plenty:

Hills shall be honey combs, the ocean ale,
Whipt-cream shall snow, and sugar plumbs shall hail.
Drink springs spontaneous, fit for every lip,
Grog, punch, raw-rum, and hyson-tea, and flip,
Soups, syllabubs, ragouts, and frigasees,
And nature change to chickens and green pease.
. . . .

Thus we, all fun, while faithful FRENCH defend us,
Titter and giggle at our INDEPENDENCE.

Others considered what America's example might mean to the rest of mankind:

A people social, gen'rous, and humane,
Of all the various arts and means possest,
To be within themselves completely blest:
Not niggards of that happiness *they* feel,
To suff'ring strangers they a portion deal;
Indulge the lenient, sympathetic mind,
To others' wants beneficent and kind:
And fair America can still ensure
A safe asylum to the needy poor.

As one all-but-final formality yielded to another, the terms *"Peace,"* *"liberty,"* and *"independence,"* Francis Hopkinson said, were "be-prosed, and be-rhymed" all over the country, "set to every note in the scale of music." [6]

Yearning for Mount Vernon, Washington found the drawn-out negotiations exasperating. The troops at his camp in Newburgh celebrated on April 19; an announcement by General William Heath that a peace had been arranged produced huzzas, a prayer, and a performance of Billings'

INDEPENDENCE with "vocal and instrumental music." But by June Washington was still at Newburgh and still awaiting, he said, with "great impatience the arrival of the Definitive Treaty." Delay was far from the only irritant. Troops who had been engaged for the war pressed for discharge. In March, Washington barely suppressed a virtual military coup by angry officers complaining about pay and pensions. In June, several hundred soldiers demonstrated menacingly enough before the Philadelphia State House to induce Congress to move hastily, and amid much derision, from Philadelphia to Princeton.[7] In July, to Washington's puzzlement, Congress requested his presence at Princeton and supplied him with a house at nearby Rocky Hill. With David Humphreys, he stayed there from the end of August until the beginning of November, waiting.

Washington found himself be-rhymed hardly less often than the word he waited for. A day or two after arriving at Rocky Hill he received some verses on peace addressed to him, the work of Annis Boudinot, sister of the president of Congress. The verses have not survived, but seem to have been adulatory. Amused to find "so bright a coloring" laid on his career, he wrote back to say that only cruelty would oblige the writer to make "an excellent Poem on such a subject, without any materials but those of simple reality. . . ." If the verses were more adoring than affectionate, Washington was in part responsible. His conduct of the war produced no corncob pipe, no acrid slogan like "War is Hell," no endearingly distinctive symbol of his personality. For some Americans he remained what he was when he first appeared at Cambridge in 1775, a focus of hope, featurelessly great:

> "So near perfection, that he stood
> "Upon the bound'ry line,
> "Of infinite from finite good,
> "Of human from divine.

If few Americans knew Washington's personality, however, many had an impression of his physique and character. It came in part from the many poems and songs of the war, the many paintings commissioned by legislative bodies, the many engravings published to satisfy those who were, as Benjamin West said, "curious to see the true likeness of that phenomenon among men."[8]

Visually, this "George Washington" was largely the creation of Charles Willson Peale. By 1783, Washington had been painted from life by Copley (in 1755), by Du Simitière (in profile), and probably by a few minor itinerants; but none of these works was widely replicated, copied, or engraved. Peale's 1776 portrait for Congress, on the other hand, was re-created from memory by John Trumbull in London and used as the basis for an English engraving distributed throughout Europe; was copied by the Salem painter Benjamin Blyth and turned into another engraving by John Norman in 1782; became the basis for still another mezzotint by the Boston silversmith Joseph Hiller; and was replicated by Peale himself.[9] This much from one canvas; ultimately Peale and his family turned out several hundred paintings and miniatures of Washington, so that literally thousands of pictures hanging in America and Europe depicted Washington as seen by Peale. When they imagined Washington, thousands of people thus had in view a tall, narrow-shouldered man with a rather small head and rather large belly, cutting something of the figure of a legged squash, benignly smiling and with twinkling, almond-shaped eyes. (An exception is the rather languid Washington of Peale's Valley Forge portrait.) What degree of visual likeness existed between their mental images and the real man is debatable. Washington's adopted son, George Washington Parke Custis, objected that his "manliness has been misrepresented by bulkiness." Rembrandt Peale thought his father had painted Washington's nose too small.[10]

Whether or not Peale misrepresented Washington's bulk or physiognomy, his major portraits did convey Washington's character as most of his admirers understood it. With his affable mien and stout physique, Peale's Washington suggests mildness combined with strength, a quality of benevolent power. In the Princeton portrait, smiling, he rests his hand on a cannon. A few Americans, especially in the rejoicing after Yorktown, praised Washington for naked force. A "Young Lady" in Boston, for instance, exulted in how "Great WASHINGTON doth thunder thro' the plain,/ And piles the field with mountains of the slain." But bloodletting had at best an uneasy and guilty appeal to an age of sentiment. Far more often, Washington was represented not as a scourge but as a paternal champion, "heaven approving thy exalted deeds,/ While grateful millions hail thee father, friend." Freneau explained that Washington was driven not by angry ambition but by disinterested justice:

> While *others* kindle into martial rage
> Whom fierce ambition urges to engage,
> An iron race by angry heaven design'd
> To conquer first and then enslave mankind;
> In *him* a hero more humane we see
> He ventures life that others may be free.

A manly simple person, Washington longed not for spoils of war, but for the moment when he could return to his farm:

> A chief renown'd
> (His country sav'd) his faulchion sheaths;

> Neglects his spoils
> For rural toils
> And crowns his plough with laurel wreaths:[11]

By the end of the war, most patriots had come to see Washington as a type of Christian Hero, a conqueror whose military prowess was fully matched, and thankfully tempered, by benevolence to mankind, domestic virtue, and reason.

This "George Washington," of course, had existed for a century. The smiling look and bellicose gesture given him by Peale were a political version of the dignity-without-pomp formula of earlier Knelleresque portraitists. Washington's traits were those of a long line of neoclassical heroes beginning perhaps with Addison's *Cato*, and including Godfrey's *Prince of Parthia* and the image of the new American army of 1775. Americans in 1783 praised Washington for being what they believed they ought to be themselves—kind fathers, Cincinnatus-style patriots, men of reason who preferred philosophical contentment to strife.[12] The Washington whom "millions" hailed as "father, friend" already exists in Addison's play, where Cato's daughter describes her father:

> Though stern and awful to the foes of Rome,
> He is all goodness, Lucia, always mild,
> Compassionate, and gentle to his friends.
> Filled with domestic tenderness, the best,
> The kindest father! . . .

Philip Freneau's Washington, who "ventures life that others may be free," exists full-blown in Thomas Godfrey's Addisonian prince:

> . . . this is the Hero,
> Like heav'n, to scatter blessings 'mong mankind,
> And e'er delight in making others happy.
> Cold is the praise which waits the victor's triumph,
> (Who thro' a sea of blood has rush'd to glory),
> To the o'erflowings of a grateful heart,
> By obligations conquer'd. . . .

This is not to say that Washington's panegyrists saw him differently from the way he saw himself. Like them, Washington admired Addison's play; Whig literary ideals shaped his understanding of his role. No less than Cato or Arsaces or "George Washington" he deplored power that was not permeated with benevolence. "How pitiful, in the eye of reason and religion," he wrote, "is that false ambition which desolates the world with fire and sword for the purposes of conquest and fame; when compared to the milder virtues of making our neighbours and our fellow men as happy as their frail conditions and perishable natures will permit *them to be!"* [13]

Indeed the Washington who awaited news of peace at Rocky Hill resembled his myth. The "inexpressible satisfaction" he felt on learning of the French-British treaty was in part relief that, like Cincinnatus, he would be free now "to quit the walks of public life" and to retire "under the shadow of my own vine and my own fig. . . ." The dragging negotiations, however, kept him waiting. Materials for a peace celebration were kept ready at Rocky Hill, but he feared that the bower created for the event would become unusable. He feared, too, that a peace would not be concluded while Congress remained at Princeton, where several delegates had failed to rejoin it. Privately he complained. "Congress have come to no determination *yet,* respecting a Peace Establishment," he told one correspondent; he was, he told another, in an "awkward and disagreeable situation," having "the appearance and indeed the enjoyment of peace, without a final declaration of it. . . ." [14] By mid-October he decided that he could feel safe in returning to Mount Vernon when the 'definitive treaty' was concluded or the British army left the country, whichever came first.

While waiting, Washington posed for some new portraits. The Princeton trustees, for one, asked him to sit for a portrait by Peale. They intended to place it in a frame which once held a portrait of the king that had been shattered by an American cannon ball. Congress, for another, commissioned an equestrian statue of Washington to mark the peace. This statue—ultimately made by the noted French sculptor Jean Antoine Houdon—became controversial. Congress ordered the work at the beginning of August; shortly after, it resolved to build two federal towns on the Delaware and the Potomac, where the delegates would assemble alternately. Mindful of this and probably resentful of the ignominious flight to Princeton, Francis Hopkinson proposed putting the affair on wheels so that Congress might "adjourn the statue whenever and wherever they should adjourn the house." The statue could be built large enough to transport the members themselves, with space for their "private archives" in the *"intestinum rectum."* [15] Late in August, an artist arrived at Rocky Hill to do a bust of Washington for the statue. Appropriately, it was Joseph Wright, who had shocked London by painting his mother with decapitated heads of Charles I and of the present king. Wright had left Nantes six months earlier, but had been shipwrecked and reported dead. He brought a letter of introduction to Washington from Franklin, and another from Charles Thomson asking Washington to give him "the fittest description of the events which are to be the subject of the basso relievo."

Wright's bust, however, was not used for the statue, and has since disappeared.[16]

Washington's presence at Rocky Hill proved inspiring to a seventeen-year-old painter staying nearby, William Dunlap. He had spent his childhood in garrisoned New York, helping his Loyalist father run a mirror and china shop. Although he took the part of rebel in games with his friends, he found the cultural life of Clinton's city stimulating, and profited from it. He attended Clinton's Theatre Royal, and began writing plays on Persian and Arabian history. His father, hearing him talk of West and Copley, secured art lessons for him from William Williams, West's own mentor, who gave Dunlap a drawing book and some pastels, as he had done with West some twenty-five years earlier. Dunlap began doing portraits, for three guineas a head, at the age of fifteen. At the time he met Washington, around August 1783, he had recently visited Peale's new portrait gallery.[17]

By his own account, Dunlap met Washington accidentally, while painting and staying with some local people named Van Horne. Washington occasionally visited their house. One morning Dunlap was playing the flute and heard Washington remark, in the hall, "The love of music and painting are frequently found united in the same person." Washington praised his paintings, and was asked by Van Horne to sit for Dunlap, "a triumphant moment for a boy of seventeen," but also one of "anxiety, fear and trembling." Thereafter, Dunlap recalled, he often dined with Washington and his wife and with members of Congress, finding it "delicious" to be "noticed as the young painter." He used his pastel portrait of the commander as the basis for a full-length *Washington at Princeton*, with Mercer dying in the background in precisely the pose of West's languishing Wolfe. The pastel original, however, is a murky, hazily modeled, and lifeless work, indicating, if anything, that Dunlap's vocation was rather for the theatre than for painting. Still, Washington's attentions fired him with the desire to study with West in London, as he did the following spring.

On October 31, Congress at Princeton learned of the signing of a 'definitive treaty' at Paris. Taking this as a final step, Washington delivered a farewell address to his army, and moved to West Point to prepare for the reoccupation of New York, scheduled for November 22. A display of fireworks had been held in readiness at West Point for a peace celebration. Washington ordered the pyrotechnics brought to New York, at least "such of them as have not been injured by time. . . ."[18] On November 21 he arrived at Harlem, on the outskirts of New York, where he stayed with about 800 troops for the next three days as the British completed their evacuation.

At the lower end of Manhattan, some five miles away, Loyalists were confusedly selling off property and goods. Until the very last moment, they continued to find entertainment in town. From June until August, they could see the Maryland Company of Comedians, the troupe which performed to the south at the time of Yorktown, now under the direction of Dennis Ryan. For some performances the company teamed up with the military actors to present *Douglas, The West Indian, The Fair Penitent,* and other standards. In July, a violinist named Franceschini—director of the military band which supplied the orchestra—cheered the spirits of Loyalists and departing redcoats by playing, between acts of *She Stoops to Conquer,* "God Save the King." During the evacuation itself they had been able to see the decidedly pro-British *Conquest of Canada,* performed ten years earlier in Philadelphia.[19] In departing, the nearly 30,000 troops and civilians took with them the tastes which required James Rivington to bind twenty-seven volumes of works by Haydn and Bach, which demanded portraits from John Ramage, Abraham Delanoy, Jr., and William Williams, tastes for which John André had painted scenery in a theatre that lavished nearly £100 in two months for wigs and headdresses alone.

On November 25, Washington, accompanied by Humphreys, left Harlem. Relentlessly driven from Manhattan seven years ago, he now paraded through familiar scenes and cheering crowds to lower New York. For a week he was feted at elaborate dinners, some given by returning patriots. The display of fireworks, on December 2, included a "Balloon of Serpents," a "Yew Tree of brilliant Fire," and an "Illuminated Pyramid, with Archemedian Screws, a Globe and vertical Sun," climaxed by "Fame, descending" and the firing of 100 rockets. The result, James Rivington reported, "infinitely exceeded every former Exhibition in the United States." Rivington quickly showed where his allegiances now lay (and may have lain always). He removed the British arms from his masthead, changed the name of his newspaper from *The Royal Gazette* to *The New-York Gazette,* and published adulatory verses on Washington. Philip Freneau, his longtime antagonist, was just as quick to observe the change, in "Rivington's Confessions":

> On the very same day that his army went hence
> I ceas'd to tell lies for the sake of his pence;
> And what was the reason—the true one is best,—
> I worship no suns that decline to the west:
>
> In this I resemble a Turk or a Moor,
> The day-star ascending, I prostrate adore;
> And, therefore, excuse me for printing some lays,
> An ode or a sonnet in Washington's praise.[20]

On December 4, after a farewell meeting with his principal officers at Fraunces Tavern, Washington left New York by a waiting barge.

Going home now, Washington was greeted in Philadelphia on December 8 by discharging cannon, ringing bells, and celebratory verses comparing him to Cincinnatus:

> Now hurrying from the busy scene—
> Where thy Potowmac's waters flow,
> Mayst thou enjoy the rural reign,
> And every earthly blessing know:
>   So HE who Rome's proud legions sway'd,
>   Return'd and sought his native shade.[21]

Washington stayed in the city long enough to have his likeness taken by Peale, for a transparency on the soon-to-explode triumphal arch. He also sat again for Joseph Wright, from whom he had personally commissioned a portrait as a gift to the comte de Solms (ill., p. 526). Hopkinson considered it "a most excellent copy of the General's Head" and wrote that Washington himself was "much pleased with it." Washington's family regarded it as his best likeness. What others generalized into benevolent power, Wright saw more intimately as chastened strength—a broad man with a thick nose, short silvery hair, eyebrows raised over gentle-looking eyes that lack merriment.

On December 19 Washington arrived in Annapolis, where Congress had moved from Princeton. After a round of dinners, he addressed the delegates on the twenty-third, and in a tearful ceremony formally resigned his commission. The next morning, accompanied by Humphreys, he left the city, arriving on Christmas Eve at Mount Vernon.

BOOK THREE

Virtue Against Luxury

Calendar for January 1784– April 1789

[1783]

MAY 14–15 : Commencement exercises at Washington College, Maryland; students perform the same dialogue and ode used at the College of Philadelphia in 1763

[1784]

JANUARY 21 : Lewis Hallam, Jr., returned to America, petitions the Philadelphia legislature to repeal the anti-theatre laws

FEBRUARY 22 : The *Empress of China* sails from New York, opening the China trade

In February, the Philadelphia bookseller Robert Bell advertises "Sorrows and Sympathetic Attachments of WERTER"

MARCH 10 : Sale of Du Simitière's collections, shortly after his death

MAY 14 : William Dunlap sails for London to study with West

OCTOBER 9 : John Trumbull arrives at Windsor Castle, where he is joined by Copley

DECEMBER 5 : Death of Phillis Wheatley

20 : Alexander de Quesnay proposes an "Academy of Polite Arts" in New York

23 : New York selected as temporary national capital

First recorded concert in Baltimore
JOHN SINGLETON COPLEY, *The Death of Major Peirson*
GILBERT STUART commissioned by John Boydell to do fifteen portraits
First American edition of Hugh Blair's *Lectures on Rhetoric and Belles Lettres*

[*1785*]

JANUARY 20 : ISAIAH THOMAS advertises that he has a set of musical type

MARCH : Organ played at the meeting house of the Boston First Church

APRIL 28 : ROBERT EDGE PINE arrives at Mount Vernon to paint Washington

MAY 20 : CHARLES WILLSON PEALE opens his 'moving pictures' in Philadelphia

AUGUST 10 : The *Virginia Journal* announces the return of the American Company, under John Henry, from Jamaica

OCTOBER 14 : JEAN ANTOINE HOUDON makes a life mask of Washington at Mount Vernon

27 : ANDREW LAW advertises his singing school in the *New-York Packet*

COPLEY begins work on his mammoth *Siege of Gibraltar*
TIMOTHY DWIGHT, *The Conquest of Canäan* (Hartford)
DANIEL READ, *The American Singing Book* (New Haven)
Sans Souci. Alias Free and Easy (Boston)

[*1786*]

JANUARY 11 : WILLIAM SELBY gives a "Concert of Sacred Music" in Boston, with 70 performers, to an audience of 2,000

16 : JOSEPH BROWN LADD's *Poems of Arouet* advertised in Charleston

Sometime in January, John Trumbull, working under West in London, completes a small oil version of his *Death of Warren at Bunker's Hill*, the first in a series of paintings on the American Revolution

MAY 16 : *New-York Advertiser* carries an obituary of Patience Wright, who died in March as the result of a fall

Sometime in May appears the first issue of *The American Musical Magazine*

JUNE 7 : *Poems of Philip Freneau* advertised

AUGUST : Farmers in western Massachusetts lead armed uprisings against local authorities

SEPTEMBER 25 : Anti-theatre law passed in Philadelphia

The same month appears the first issue, in Philadelphia, of *The Columbian Magazine, or Monthly Miscellany*; John Trumbull, in Paris, begins taking faces for his *Declaration of Independence*

OCTOBER 26 : First number of *The Anarchiad* appears in the *New-Haven Gazette*

NOVEMBER 2 : JOSEPH BROWN LADD dies of wounds received in a duel

New York legislature passes "An Act to Promote Literature," in effect a fourteen-year copyright

DAVID HUMPHREYS, *A Poem, on the Happiness of America* (London)
JOHN PARKE, *The Lyric Works of Horace* (Philadelphia)
ISAIAH THOMAS, *LAUS DEO! The Worcester Collection of Sacred Harmony* (Worcester)
PHILLIS WHEATLEY, *Poems on Various Subjects* (Philadelphia, the first American edition)

[*1787*]

JANUARY : First issue of *The American Museum*

MARCH 30 : PEALE advertises his mezzotint of Franklin, the first in a series of "illustrious personages"

APRIL 12 : First Uranian concert, in Philadelphia

16 : Premiere of Royall Tyler's *The Contrast* at the John Street Theatre

28 : South Carolina legislature enacts vagrancy law, classifying actors with beggars

MAY 14 : The Federal Convention scheduled to meet, but a quorum is not gathered until May 25

Sometime in May is published Joel Barlow's *The Vision of Columbus*

JUNE : First professional performance of four-handed piano music in America (a Haydn sonata) by James Juhan and the recently arrived Alexander Reinagle; Washington attends the concert

JULY 6 : WASHINGTON sits for Peale

SEPTEMBER 17 : Final draft of the United States Constitution is submitted to Congress

OCTOBER 27 : *Federalist Essays* begin appearing in New York newspapers

DECEMBER : First issue of *The American Magazine*

Ratification begins, in Delaware

ANDREW ADGATE, *Select Psalms and Hymns* (Philadelphia)
WILLIAM BROWN, *Three Rondos for the Piano Forte or Harpsichord* (Philadelphia)
DAVID HUMPHREYS, *Select Poems* (Philadelphia)
BENJAMIN WEST, sketches for *Death on a Pale Horse*

[*1788*]

APRIL 23 : *The Miscellaneous Works of Mr. Philip Freneau* advertised

JUNE 21 : New Hampshire ratifies the Constitution, insuring its adoption

JULY 4 : Grand Federal Parade in Philadelphia

18 : Quakers in Philadelphia petition for enforcement of the 1786 anti-theatre laws

23 : Federal Parade in New York

OCTOBER : JOHN SICARD's "New Constitution March" and "Federal Minuet" advertised

NOVEMBER 29 : FRANCIS HOPKINSON's *Seven Songs* advertised

[*1789*]

JANUARY 22 : WILLIAM HILL BROWN's *The Power of Sympathy* advertised

The same month appears the first issue of
The Massachusetts Magazine

FEBRUARY 4 : Electoral college chooses Washington as first
president of the United States

MARCH 2 : Philadelphia anti-theatre law of 1786 repealed

APRIL 14 : WASHINGTON officially notified of his election, at Mount Vernon

20 : WASHINGTON passes through Peale's triumphal arches en route to Philadelphia

30 : WASHINGTON inaugurated in New York

RALPH EARL, paintings of the Boardman family

Part One

American Culture between the Peace and the Constitutional Convention, 1784–1787

42. Commencement: 1783

"Whether the state of nature be a state of war?"
For the provincial audience gathered in Chester, Maryland, on May 14, 1783, for the first commencement of Washington College, it was the right, the inevitable topic. On May 17, 1763—proposed in Latin rather than English—this same maxim of Thomas Hobbes had been soundly refuted at King's College in New York. The distinguished assembly had included Sir Jeffrey Amherst, servant of a king who after seventy-five years of warfare had secured the continent for Great Britain, auguring an era of tranquility in which British culture would follow the course of empire westward to North America. By 1770, the refutation seemed less sound. The audience seated at Yale in 1770 had, to be sure, witnessed cultural progress; but it had come amidst tirades, pacts, demonstrations, and the bloody massacre on King Street, preludes, it turned out, to the expulsion of Britain itself.

Now, once more, the great word was Peace. And with Peace, everyone knew, would come progress. Appropriately, the day's events at Washington College ended with a "*prophetic* copy of verses on the progress of the sciences and the growing glory of *America.*" Next day the students and faculty marched in procession to the site chosen for the new school building. After Governor William Paca laid the cornerstone, three students dressed in shepherds' weeds delivered a verse dialogue-and-ode, surveying the current condition and future prospects of their college and state. Their rustic garb and their names symbolized undisturbed contentment, what "Philander" called a forthcoming "*Reign* of LEARNING and of PEACE!" As surely as Americans had driven forth the British, "Horatio" foresaw, the Muses might depose the powers of provincialism. America would become

> . . . a Land refin'd
> Where once rude Ignorance sway'd th' untutor'd mind.[1]

Benjamin Franklin might well have thought himself back at May 1763. Not only was the topic of debate at Chester in 1783 the same as in New York two decades earlier, but the names, the costume, and the verses of the young swains were identical with those twenty years ago at the commencement of the College of Philadelphia.

All this was no coincidence, but a deliberate reenactment staged by the resilient William Smith. As provost of the College of Philadelphia in the early 1760's, he had created a literary, musical, and artistic elite unique in the colonies; after Philadelphia radicals forced him to resign as provost, he opened Washington College in Maryland, where he had his students recite at their first commencement the verses that had expressed the hopes of 1763. The verses bore repeating because the hopes had changed only in the way that repetition suggested. They had become ritual. They reaffirmed commitment to the now-traditional purpose of acquiring in America the elements of a metropolitan culture. Significantly the place was not urban Philadelphia but one of many small towns in the United States where the process must begin anew. In an independent America progress ought not only to grow, but also to accelerate and spread.

Like the 'quiet period' dividing the Townshend period from the Tea Act, the years between the end of the war and the Constitutional Convention provide an interlude from major political and social events in which to assess the ongoing progress of the arts in America. In the wake of the War for Independence, and under the pall of a major economic depression, the country tended to itself—to its trade and debts, its veterans and Loyalists, its new western territories—looking to the time, soon approaching, when it must settle on a form of permanent government.

As in 1763, refinement was not the last consideration. Hardly was peace rumored before Americans began to demand, and receive, signs of cultural progress unprecedented in their number and ambitiousness. And, for the first time, they began to doubt that they wanted them.

43. The Art World

With the return of Peace, artistic energies pent up and long restrained by the war sprang loose. At once proposals appeared for new art schools; engravings of native scenes and celebrities decorated the many new magazines; well-known European artists migrated to the new nation. Preoccupation with military affairs gave way to contemplation again of cultural possibilities, to assessments of the progress American art had made over two decades that astonished even those who had expected much.

The first generation of American painters had realized its promise. Peale had established himself as the leading painter in Philadelphia, indeed on the continent; Copley and West were figures of fashion residing in the finest houses in London, internationally admired for their skill, ambition, and imagination, and beloved at home for being admired abroad. Of the younger generation of the 1770's—in its infancy when West first set foot in Rome—Stuart had a brilliant portrait career of his own, and Trumbull's paintings of revolutionary events were seen and praised in London and Paris alike. To an even younger generation that sought encouragement and training abroad, America had its own old masters.

In March 1783, the portraitist Abraham Delanoy, Jr., tried to lease a house in still-occupied New York that he could turn into a paint shop: "such matters will be much in demand," he thought, "if we are once more blest with Peace. . . ." [1] He was right. The ending of the war instantly brought advertisements for new drawing and painting schools, long absent from American newspapers. While encouraged by a demand for national genius and by the examples of Copley and West, such advertisements reflect a larger postwar phenomenon—the democratization and expansion of education of every sort, owing to popular theories about the necessity of universal education in republican governments.

One particularly bold proposal came from Alexander de Quesnay, who had mounted Beaumarchais' *Eugénie* in Philadelphia for Washington. In 1784 he proposed in New York an "Academy of Polite Arts"—in effect the first American art school to teach painting not alone as a social grace but also as a vocation. He offered instruction "in every branch" of painting as well as architecture, music, fencing, and dancing. Having leased the house of Lord Stirling on Broad Street, he placed several lengthy ads in New York newspapers, commending the current interest in education but observing that some branches of education, known in Europe, remained unknown in America:

> The genius of the inhabitants of these United States is susceptible of any improvement. All Europe already view, with astonishment, your abilities in the fields of war and politics, convince them also of your taste for the polite arts and sciences. A West, a Copley, evidently prove your capacity in these respects.

Mindful of the economic depression, Quesnay promised scholarships to children of respectable New Yorkers "whose private fortune may have been injured by the war, and those of officers and soldiers of the Army of the United States"; he also promised to send, after four years' instruction, three of the most accomplished painting students to Italy "to be compleated in that art." He may have planned to use live models, for he noted that any attempt to introduce prostitutes into the school would be greeted with "disgrace." [2]

The nation's financial (and moral) situation made Quesnay's scheme impracticable; the school never opened in New York. Quesnay tried in 1786 to erect the school in Richmond, where the Virginia capital had removed from Williamsburg. Again he sent out a prospectus, this time trying to raise money by offering plays at his school building, for which effort he was accused of abandoning education. Thomas Jefferson advised him to give up his painting school because Virginia was too poor to sustain it. Persistent, Quesnay went to England and France to find backers; finding none, he gave up.[3]

The fate of Quesnay's school was typical of many ambitious postwar projects, as was the fact that its failure did nothing to deter other projectors. In 1787 West's pupil Matthew Pratt opened a school in Philadelphia, teaching drawing and coloring "Upon a New Plan." In the same year, the *New-York Advertiser* offered what seems to be the first American correspondence course in painting. In learning "the Art of Drawing without a Master," students received some 250 pages of instruction, including 26 plates and engravings after Raphael, Rubens, and others.[4] Americans could also receive instruction from *The School of Wisdom or Repository of the Most Valuable Curiosities of Art*, published in 1787 by a color-shop owner named William Lawson, in New Brunswick, New Jersey—the first American book on painting technique. Like Quesnay's school, however, it represents rather the wish for cultural self-sufficiency than the reality, being little more than a pirated and retitled issue of an earlier English manual, *The School of Arts Improv'd* (London, 1776), itself compiled from several other works.

The production of native engravings, which had steadily but very slowly

grown in volume since 1763, increased swiftly and dramatically following
the war. The surge corresponded to a demand for national images, to an
explosion of new magazines (see "The Literary Scene"), and to the rise of
scientific associations. In 1784 appeared the first map of the United States
engraved in America, by the Connecticut silversmith Abel Buell, with an
elaborate allegorical cartouche depicting a seated Libertas and a Rising
Glory. Many of the new magazines featured engravings of native
celebrities and scenes. John Norman filled the *Boston Magazine* with crude
portraits of Voltaire, Franklin, and John Adams, and allegorical figures
like "A youth representing the rising Generation of AMERICA." More
skilled work came from James Trenchard, a New Jerseyan who had set up
as a watchmaker and drawing master in Philadelphia, and who served in
the militia under his lifelong friend Charles Willson Peale. Trenchard and
his pupils composed a new, distinct school of Philadelphia engravers, who
contributed at least two pictures to each issue of the new *Columbian
Magazine*. Among the eighty-seven copperplate engravings by Trenchard
himself are complex allegorical representations of the Rising Glory theme,
the first engraved portrait of Shakespeare published in the United States
(in August 1787), and many local views and landscapes which depict for
the first time the natural beauty and urban richness of the new
country—views of Independence Hall, of Christ Church, of the Virginia
Natural Bridge—works whose number marks a vastly expanded graphic
interest, and a vastly expanded pride, in the American scene. The
production of technological drawings swelled with the postwar growth of
American scientific societies. The first volume of the *Memoirs of the American
Academy of Arts and Sciences* appeared in Boston in 1785, with many plates.
In 1786 John Norman supplied thirty-nine plates for William Smellie's *An
Abridgement of the Practice of Midwifery*—the first American illustrated
medical book.[5]

As they had during the calm that followed the Boston Massacre, many
obscure foreign painters came to America after the Peace, lured by new
commercial possibilities and the desire for European commodities of all
kinds. As in 1770, ads appeared for portraits by "B. Birch" of London, or
by "a Member of the Royal Academy, from London," or by the "Canter"
in Charleston who, like countless immigrants later, had transformed
himself from the Danish Jew Joshua Canterson.[6] From Ireland with his
family came John Hazlitt, a young miniaturist who taught painting and
drawing in Boston in 1785, and gave Latin lessons to his younger brother,
later the essayist William Hazlitt, before the family moved to England.[7]
They and their many obscure predecessors—not to mention immigrants
like the organ builder Tanneberger from Saxony, the painter Cosmo
Alexander from Scotland, or the slave-poet Wheatley from Africa—intro-

duced new fashions, raised tastes, enlarged the artistic community, forwarding the progress of American culture as they altered the character of American society.

Not only commercial prospects, but equally enthusiasm for the principles of the new nation and an eagerness to see and depict its famous men brought the young English painter Robert Edge Pine. In 1784 he solicited the opinion of Samuel Vaughan in Philadelphia about "the disposition and ability of its inhabitants for giving encouragement to Painting," explaining that "I could pass the latter part of my life happier in a Country where the noblest Principles have been defended and establish'd, than with the People who have endeavored to subdue them." Pine was a friend of Garrick and one of the first painters to portray actors in character parts; encouraged to come to Philadelphia, he brought with him a full-length portrait of Mrs. Siddons as the Tragic Muse and several scenes from Shakespeare, as well as a plaster cast of Venus nude, which he kept in a shut case and showed only on request.[8] According to Peale, Robert Morris lent Pine money to build a house on Eighth Street, above Market, near Peale's museum. (Pine later built his own museum, whose collection, auctioned after his death, became the nucleus of the Boston Museum.) The competition hurt Peale financially and psychologically. After trying for a dozen years, he had just established himself permanently in Philadelphia as its leading painter; furthermore, Morris was his political enemy. He salved his wounds with Pine's failures. In Maryland, Pine received so many commissions that he would take a sitter's head alone on a small piece of canvas, which he pasted on a larger canvas when he returned to Philadelphia. He forgot, however, to sketch the torsos and could not recall them, so that, Peale said, he "made some small or slim figures, where the original was large and bulky." [9]

Peale found little more to gloat over, for Pine invaded another part of his territory. Like Peale, Du Simitière, and Trumbull, he hoped to memorialize the Revolution in a series of historical portraits. Francis Hopkinson had taken a liking to Pine, and wrote to Washington commending his "forcible Specimens of Genius" and "Zeal for the American Cause." He asked Washington to pose for Pine's series, well aware that Washington, already smothered by adulation, "would rather fight a Battle . . . than sit for a Picture." Yet, slighting Peale, he stressed that Pine was "the most eminent Artist in his way, we have ever had in this Country." Washington did not need Hopkinson's coaxing, however, since he respected Pine's credentials and was now too numbed by the adulation to shy from it. He told Hopkinson that sitting for his first portraits had made him as restive "as a colt is of the saddle"; now, many portraits later, "no dray-horse moves more readily to his thill than I to the painter's chair." When Pine arrived at Mount Vernon on April 28, 1785, Washington recorded in his diary that he had entertained "a pretty eminent Portrait and Historical Painter" at dinner. The Whig historian Catharine Macaulay saw Pine's portrait of Washington in Philadelphia and believed it "bore the strongest resemblance to the original of any I had seen." [10]

Pine's arrival involves a turnabout. In 1763, Benjamin West was setting off for England; by 1783, well-known artists abroad were setting off for America. At least some Europeans had begun to think of America as a significant western culture with its own notable figures and accomplishments. No mere province, surely, could have lured from 3,000 miles away one of the leading sculptors in Europe, Jean Antoine Houdon, who trekked to Mount Vernon in the summer of 1784.

Houdon intended to take a bust of Washington for a statue commissioned by the Virginia legislature. In itself, the commission illustrates how military events and republican ideals created a demand for public commemorative works, resulting in far wider public support of the arts than had existed in 1763 or in 1770. Houdon's own view of the public utility of art made him an ideal choice for the commission. Statues and busts could serve as educative moral exemplars, he wrote, and help "to preserve the form and render imperishable the image of men who have achieved glory or good for their country." In France, he had already completed busts of Jefferson, Franklin, and John Paul Jones, and had been employed by the Virginia House of Delegates to sculpt Lafayette as a gift for the city of Paris, a copy going to Virginia.[11]

Houdon originally planned to produce the Washington abroad. Peale was to send a full-length portrait of the commander to Jefferson in Paris, as a model for Houdon to work from. Beginning the picture in the summer of 1784, Peale included in the background a view of the British surrender at Yorktown, in case Houdon decided to add historical vignettes in bas-relief to the pedestal. Finished in October, the picture arrived in Paris in the spring of 1785, but has since become lost. In the meantime, Houdon concluded that he could not work from a picture, and, Jefferson wrote, grew "so enthusiastically fond of being the executor of this work, that he offers to go to America for the purpose of forming your bust from the life." Houdon's decision to take the bust from life may have been influenced by Jefferson himself, who, always mindful of the future, thought carefully about the statue's purpose. Ordinarily, a statue would be made slightly larger than life so that when elevated it would appear life-size. Yet Jefferson felt it important to give the work Washington's actual dimensions so that "some one monument should be preserved of the true size as well as figure, from which all other countries, and our own, at any future day when they shall desire it, may take copies. . . ." David Humphreys, then also in Paris, shared his view and gave Houdon a laudatory letter to his friend Washington promising that Houdon's exactness would make "Not only the present but future generations . . . curious to see your figure. . . ." [12]

To satisfy those generations, Houdon's enthusiasm had first to weather a hapless voyage. Just before he was to leave, Houdon became seriously ill and had to take the next boat. This time he wrangled with Jefferson, at the last minute, over his fee, asking, Jefferson said, "vastly more" than the agreed-to price. His final terms were 1,000 English guineas for statue and pedestal, plus his expenses going and coming, and 10,000 livres' life insurance for his family. Houdon at last landed in Philadelphia in September 1785, but accidentally his tools stayed in Le Havre, where they and his clothing disappeared. His miseries as he bought fresh clothing and supplies in Philadelphia were soothed by a flattering letter from Washington wishing that "the object of your mission had been more worthy of the masterly genius of the first statuary in Europe." [13]

Washington was abed in Mount Vernon when Houdon and three assistants arrived at eleven o'clock on a Sunday night.[14] Houdon cast the bust over the next two weeks. The process so fascinated Washington, however numbly he 'moved to his thill,' that he devoted some of his lengthiest diary entries to describing it. He recorded how Houdon worked the plaster of Paris into hard lumps the size of hens' eggs and larger soft pieces, baking them overnight in a superheated oven until they were calcined. Next morning the lumps were pulverized in an iron mortar and finely sifted. Then the powder was mixed with water in a basin, strained through the fingers until "thick as Loblolly, or very thick cream," and beaten with a flat iron spoon. Since the mixture hardened beyond use in four or five minutes, small batches were prepared for immediate application with a brush. The life mask of Washington itself was made on October 13, 1785, in the presence of James Madison. During his two-week stay, Houdon also took Washington's measurements before departing by Washington's barge to Alexandria, thence by stage to Philadelphia, where he left some of his belongings in the care of Pine before returning to France.

As Houdon resumed work on the statue in his Paris studio, the question of Washington's costume demanded solution. The equestrian statue of Washington commissioned by Congress—for which Joseph Wright had taken the general's head at Rocky Hill—would show Washington in Roman dress. Benjamin West, however, advised Houdon to use modern dress. Washington himself considered such questions beyond his ken, and deferred to connoisseurs. Yet the new realities of republican life, the bond between the ability of the arts to teach virtue and the need of a republican citizenry for virtue, forced Washington and many other politicians to make basically esthetic judgments. Washington's language on such occasions was more than usually circumspect, as he confessed to Jefferson that he "should even scarcely have ventured to suggest" an opinion had not Humphreys told him of West's advice to Houdon. Considering the eminence of the advice, he told Jefferson—with a tentativeness approaching reluctance—that "perhaps a servile adherence to the garb of antiquity might not be altogether so expedient, as some little deviation in favor of the modern costume." [15]

Houdon's ultimate choice of modern dress probably reflects West's innovative and "expedient" view that future generations might be taught best by viewing a near contemporary. For whatever reason, he clothed Washington in revolutionary boots and regimentals, his left arm resting on a symbolic bundle of thirteen fasces, which supports a sword and a plow, a Cincinnatean emblem of the exchange of agriculture for battle (ill., p. 526). Contemporaries approved the rendering of Washington's face. Charles Thomson (the secretary of Congress) and Francis Hopkinson both saw the model in Philadelphia: Thomson detected in the slightly uplifted countenance "one looking forward into futurity"; Hopkinson was delighted by the "noble Air, sublime Expression and faithful Likeness. . . ." [16] If Houdon's was indeed a faithful likeness, the historical Washington looked considerably more youthful and handsome than the genial, corpulent presences depicted by Peale. The completed bust was shown in Paris in the fall of 1787. After a white marble block was imported from Italy, the Virginia statue was completed in 1791, but dated 1788, and not installed in the state capitol until 1796, after which it inspired a whole school of American portrait sculptors in the nineteenth century.

If Houdon mixing "Loblolly" at Mount Vernon suggested a new, more excellent stage of Translation, Peale's prominence in Philadelphia suggested the maturation of an earlier stage. He was now, in his mid-forties, the outstanding painter in America. Although he still hurt from the injuries inflicted by his incendiary triumphal arch, he was well enough recovered by September 1784 to attend the Princeton commencement, bearing his large painting of Washington's victory, commissioned the previous year. Washington appears in full uniform as commander-in-chief, gourd-shaped, holding a sword. Behind him, Nassau Hall shows dimly through the battle smoke. At Washington's left General Hugh Mercer dies in a *Wolfe*-like Pietà, an incongruous pendant to Washington's Pealesque good cheer.[17]

For both political and commercial reasons, Peale hoped to concentrate on such public commissions of historical figures and scenes, planning also a large painting of Washington taking leave of Congress and of the capture of Major André. Important and lucrative as they seemed, however, he found them troublesome. A copy of the Princeton portrait commissioned by the state of Maryland had to be paid for through the Maryland Assembly, which contained Samuel Chase, who felt Peale had slandered him. While politics made public commissions risky, it was still riskier to paint commemorative works on speculation. Peale decided to turn his portrait gallery into prints partly because he could not afford to have forty or so unbought portraits on hand. For the same reason he put off his proposed, uncommissioned, Washington taking leave of Congress. He also discovered that he had overestimated the foreign market for American historical paintings, at least for those by him. He sent many anxious letters to William Carmichael, the overseas agent for his still-unbought Washington full-length. Their refrain is, "When you reflect on my situation, having known my difficulties and having a large family to maintain by my labours alone, you must know that the price of a whole length picture is no trifle to me. . . ." [18]

It seems likely that Peale's difficulties were owing not only to politics and his continued need to support a large family but also to the continuing distraction of his other pursuits, increased competition from much-touted painters like Pine in Philadelphia, and considerably higher standards of judgment. His weakened eyesight, too, forced him in 1786 to give over all his miniature work to his brother James. Whatever the reasons, he continued having a hard time financially, much as in 1770, borrowing coal to warm his house and money to do the marketing. He took on a variety of purse-filling chores. His apprentice Billy Mercer brought a small income from his uncle, General George Weedon of Virginia, who paid the boy's board and lodging with Peale, and such expenses as the shirt mending done for him by Peale's niece. (Rumors reached Weedon that Peale neglected the boy, prompting Peale to assure him that Billy "is treated as our Son, and Mrs Peale never Cuts an Apple or Orange without giving him a part of it.") He also worked for the Baltimore theatre, painting in 1784 the figures of Tragedy and Comedy for what the only available source calls the "Frontispiece" of the theatre.[19]

Probably to produce a decent living, Peale tried to capitalize on his inveterate love of tinkering. He installed at the end of his long picture gallery an "Exhibition of Moving Pictures." Working nonstop on the project for eighteen months, spending all his funds, neglecting his portrait business and even his sleep, he expected, he wrote, "to be amply repaid." Although he had had long experience working with illuminated transparencies, the direct source for the "Moving Pictures" remains unclear. In England, the set designer Philippe de Loutherbourg had introduced in

1781 a device called the *eidophusicon,* which used revolving screens and such new methods of lighting as Argand lamps to show clouds, sea and foam, lightning, fire, and other dramatically shifting forms. By one account, Peale read a description of this forerunner of the diorama and tried to duplicate its effects; according to John Durang, a dancer with the American Company, Peale saw a demonstration of the device by the Company and went into competition with them.[20] Whatever its origins, the show opened on May 20, 1785.

Performances, lasting about two hours, began at seven o'clock. For three shillings, nine pence admission, patrons also received a "catalogue of the views" and, in summer, air-conditioning from twelve large pasteboard fans. In his broadside advertisement, Peale described the exhibition as "NATURE DELINEATED, and in Motion." The program consisted of several gradually changing scenes: nighttime in the country changing to daylight, with singing of birds; Market Street in Philadelphia at dusk, the lighting of street lamps, and ultimately rosy dawn; a classical landscape under lowering sky, then rain and lightning, gradually fading to a rainbow; a churning water-mill near the Schuylkill; a depiction of Pandemonium based on *Paradise Lost*—featured by De Loutherbourg—with flames, smoke, lightning, Satan arising in sulfurous vapors. The most spectacular moving picture, a sort of animated history painting, showed the engagement between the American *Bonhomme Richard* and the British warship *Serapis.* In Peale's own description, the two ships were:

> . . . represented at the extreme and opposite ends of the picture in full sail with a fine breeze as represented by the waves in pleasing motion, a fleet in the distance going into Scarborough. The two ships approaching each other begin to fire, the flash and distant reports imitated. They are now close engaged, and the sails are torn in holes, the sea gradually becomes calm, and night coming on the moon rises—the fight continues, and the Seraphis *[sic]* is on fire and afterwards extinguished, her main mast falls, and then strikes her colours, the firing ceases—afterwards the day breakes, and the sea becomes agitated—The American colours are hoisted on board the Seraphis. The Bonne Homme Richard being greatly shattered begins to sink from the sight of the spectators, in a slow manner untill she gets so low as to pitch her head down & quickly passes out of sight. And then the Seraphis brasing about her yards persues her course, which ends the scene.[21]

To cover the wait between scene-changes, Peale added vocal and instrumental interludes, allowed the audience to wander free of charge in his adjoining portrait gallery, and for a while hired someone to do readings from Milton and Shakespeare. The reader, however, offended Peale by slipping in double-entendres, and the musicians proved very expensive and failed to show up. As a substitute, Peale ordered built a mechanical barrel organ capable of reproducing thirty tunes, which played between scenes, sometimes with vocal accompaniment.[22]

As always, Peale found that his work created more comment than income. Newspapers in several cities reported his exhibition. The New York *Daily Advertiser* reprinted from a Philadelphia paper an account of Peale's lighting system, brought to America from abroad by Franklin (whom Peale painted shortly after his return): The eight lamps with "treble tubes" afforded, "at a very moderate calculation . . . more light than 200 candles would." The Boston *Massachusetts Centinel*, noting that Peale believed his exhibition would make Philadelphia more agreeable and estimable to foreigners, urged Boston for the same reason to license a theatre.[23] But despite the publicity, the exhibition failed to bring in customers; it "pleases well," Peale decided, "but there is not bustle enough to make the People run mad to see it." Over the first six months of performances he made about £50 a month, less than the asking-price for his full-length Washington.[24] He began exhibiting the moving pictures only occasionally. He gave his attention to a different sort of exhibition, long-contemplated, a museum of natural history.

While Peale failed to achieve his long-sought commercial success in Philadelphia, neither had he won the adulation that now greeted each new work produced by the American artists in London.[25] To the cultural nationalists of 1783, the achievements of Copley, West, Brown, Wright, Stuart, and the promising Trumbull were artistic victories, continuations of the war by other means. Said the *Massachusetts Centinel*: "While we boast a *Washington*, as the great master of the art of war—a *Franklin* the chief of Philosophers—an *Adams*, and an infinitude of others, as statesmen and politicians whose abilities have been acknowledged throughout the civilized world; America may pride herself in giving birth to the most celebrated Artists of the present age." As American newspapers and magazines once featured anecdotes about Handel's irritability or Garrick's triumphs, they now addressed verses to "your artists, sweet Columbia," praising their genius, describing their exhibitions, gossiping about their lives and works-in-progress.[26]

Copley and West became national heroes. Their names were invoked only slightly less often and less fervently than that of Washington himself. A Baltimore newspaper boasted that "the painting of Copley and West find even in Europe, little competition," a fact which "ought to teach us very respectful ideas of American genius." The *New-Haven Gazette* proclaimed that West's huge sacred paintings for Windsor Castle would bring him ten or twelve thousand guineas, while Copley—of "the same walk of genius" and "the first class of eminence"—prospered by a huge commission from the city of London, evidence that Americans possessed "peculiarly strong talents for painting." Indeed, the cultural nationalists now elevated West and Copley to the pinnacle of world art. Some subjects, said the *Columbian Magazine*, could be done justice by "The pencil of a Raphael, or a West alone," [27] a coupling that amounted to canonization.

If not worthy of comparison with Raphael's, the accomplishments of Patience Wright elated the nationalists as well. That tall, athletic, voluble woman, whose eyes had "almost the wildness of a maniac's," who spoke of "dear America" and called the king and queen "George" and "Charlotte," had become celebrated in London as both a fiery patriot (perhaps a spy) and a sculptor of chillingly lifelike semblances. The war over, she hoped to make wax busts of notable Americans for the new public buildings planned by Congress, prepared to "go to any trouble and expense" to honor the country and, she told Jefferson, to "shame the English king." [28] In March 1786, however, she died as the result of a fall following a visit to John Adams, bringing eulogies from American newspapers and reprintings of laudatory obituary notices from London. "America has lost in her," said the *Maryland Journal*, "a warm and sincere friend, as well as one of her first ornaments to the arts." The death of this "celebrated American," said the New York *Daily Advertiser*, would grieve those "brave fellows, who during the late war were fortunate enough to escape from the arms of tyranny and take sanctuary under her roof." American readers could learn that newspapers in London also lamented the passing of "one of the most extraordinary Characters of the Age, as an Artist and as a profound Politician." [29]

Many writers and painters of the nineteenth century would rebel against such praise, which exaggerated American achievement and confused success with acceptance, making the chief proof of native genius the reputation of native artists abroad. But Americans in 1783 cherished the feeling that America had overcome the condescension or contempt with which foreigners had always viewed its cultural life. That Copley took commissions from the most hated men in America mattered less than their wanting to be painted by him. After being introduced to Burke, Fox, and the duke of Portland, John Adams was pleased to discover that "our American painters had more influence at court . . . than all of them." What mattered was the sense of parity. Indeed, the more exalted the giver of parity, the more flattering the gift. The fact that the same King Log who sent his troops to close the port of Boston now called a room in his palace "Mr. West's" room did not enrage Adams; it delighted him because it brought "so much honor to our country." [30] In the prestige of their London painters, Americans could rejoice in having overcome the feeble imitativeness and provincial backwardness of 1763. Franklin's lament over the lack of "sensible, virtuous and elegant Minds" in America no longer applied. Now America could offer "one of the most extraordinary Characters of the Age," painters in "the first class of eminence," works worthy of "a Raphael, or a West. . . ."

National pride in the past accomplishments of American painters kept growing as news arrived of their fresh successes. Now forty-five years old, rich as well as famous, Copley moved in 1783 from Leicester Square to George Street, to an elegant house with a large studio where he lived until his death. One of his first works here was a large portrait, nearly eight feet by five, of the ambassador John Adams in full court dress, looking so much a velvet-suited, portly dandy that Adams later mocked the picture as a "Bijou." If the portrait suggests some blunting of Copley's ability to penetrate character, its size makes clear his new delight in giant conceptions. Like West, he had begun canvases that dwarfed even his earlier huge *Death of Chatham* and demanded several years' work. Both his *Siege of Gibraltar* and his *Charles I demanding the House of Commons*, begun in the mid-1780's, remained unfinished until the 1790's. The *Gibraltar*, eighteen by twenty-five feet, had to be placed on rollers so that Copley could paint it in patches, his studio filled with ship-tackle, boats, and guns to paint from. Shown in special buildings, such works later rivaled in popularity the exhibitions at the Royal Academy.[31]

A less mammoth but still heroic work exhibited in 1784 was avidly reported in the American press. With *The Death of Major Peirson* Copley arrived at the height of his fame and received a commission to paint the English princesses. The work depicts a battle fought in the town of St. Helier, on the English island of Jersey, in January 1781. Twenty-four-year-old Major Francis Peirson, having crushed an insurrection on the island, was killed in the moment of his triumph, like General Wolfe (ill., p. 530). Unlike West, however, Copley depicted his hero amidst the confusion of battle. He surrounded the dying Peirson with visions of chaos: squads shooting squads point blank, paces apart; a wounded drummer appealing for help; a mother and her children fleeing in horror past another corpse. Most effective of all, Copley jam-packed the combatants, with great tension, into a tiny town square. Boxed in, unable to flee, they shriek and slaughter. Although some critics compare the painting to West's *Wolfe* as an analogue of Christian martyrdom, it seems the reverse. Unlike West's beautifully dying sacrificial patriot, the dying Peirson is held in his men's arms as on a stretcher, his torso falling backward so that his face appears on the canvas upside-down, denying the viewer any easy access to his expression and subjective state. The Copley who painted the beautifully dreamy, faun-eared *Boy with Squirrel* had no appetite for butchery. Indeed he made a powerful antiwar statement in the family escaping at the right; in his open-mouthed flight from the smoky square the delicate-looking boy barely sidesteps the crooked elbow of a corpse. This vignette itself seems to explain Copley's reasons for leaving America. (Ironically, two of Copley's own children died of scarlet fever the next year.) A highlight of the painting is Copley's depiction of a Negro in fancy cockade hat and black coat, in sharp relief to the flamingly red-coated troops, firing in retribution for the death of Peirson—the latest of several brilliantly painted black figures beginning with the sailor of *Brook Watson and the Shark.*

The Death of Major Peirson ranks as one of a great series of modern history paintings done in England in the eighteenth century, perhaps beginning with West's *Agrippina* in 1768. Much of its power results from the fact that in London Copley learned precisely what he left America in the hope of learning—composition. Despite its pandemonium, the scene is perfectly controlled by the buildings of the square; the black servant against the scarlet uniforms provides a dramatic center amidst the chaos. Indeed, the painting's arrangement of large numbers of figures, at once chaotic and unified, its brilliant coloring, its many faces, painted with great invention and care, make it perhaps the outstanding work by any American in any art in the eighteenth century, perhaps the finest painting by any American ever. The *Massachusetts Centinel*, which published a lengthy account of the exhibition, lauded the "great science" of the composition, the "fine *keeping*" in the chiaroscuro, the "skill of a master" shown in the coloring. For all that, the praise Americans lavished on Copley was ironic. By abandoning in England his earlier style of blunt portraiture Copley became, as Dunlap insisted, "no longer an American painter in feeling." [32]

Similar reproaches could have been made against the still more celebrated West, descriptions of whose ongoing career appeared widely in the American press. Yet, unlike Copley's, West's political sympathies remained clear. He had managed to spend the war years in London as both an American who favored Independence and a fashionable friend of the king. A drawing of around this time shows West and his family in the garden of their Newman Street residence (ill., p. 527); West, his wife, and his two children are expensively dressed, surrounded by shrubbery and classical sculpture, exuding domestic happiness and success. For all his London elegance, in the garden of his house West raised American corn. Hardly was the treaty signed when he congratulated his former student Charles Willson Peale, "and my Country in general, on the event of the Peace, and the fortitude they have shown during the unhappy war." He painted the American peace commissioners—Benjamin Franklin, Jay, Adams, Laurens, and William Temple Franklin—seated at the conference table, but the death of the British plenipotentiary Richard Oswald forced him to leave the painting incomplete. Immediately he planned a series of

paintings, later to be engraved, entitled *The American Revolution*. He asked
Peale for small drawings or paintings of army uniforms and military
equipment, and sent to others in Philadelphia for descriptions of flags,
military ribbons, and horses.[33] Peale supplied a hunting shirt, leggings,
and a small round hat such as worn, Indian-style, by American
sharpshooters (probably useless material to West, who had painted just
such a uniform into his *Wolfe*). He also advised West to paint the taking of
the Hessians at Trenton, and Washington's return crossing of the
Delaware ("it was a stormy morning").[34]

The difference between West's idealization of war and continued
devotion to the American cause and Copley's abhorrence of violence and
aloofness from politics was matched by artistic differences as well. Always
changing, West kept pace with new tastes. In the 1780's, as Michelangelo
began to replace Raphael as the most admired European artist, as a new
liking for Dante, for the Gothic, and for the sublime began making itself
felt, West began moving away from the bourgeois family anecdote in the
direction of the later visionary painting of Henry Fuseli and William
Blake. The *Massachusetts Spy* reported in September 1784 that his six
paintings at the Royal Academy exhibit included an *Apotheosis of Prince
Alfred and Prince Octavius* in which an angel introduced the dead princes to
each other in paradise. Around 1787 he sketched a *Death on a Pale Horse*,
exploring not the moral but the romantically apocalyptic possibilities of
the Old Testament. Competition in London exacerbated the political and
temperamental differences between Copley and West, producing some
strain and public arguments between them at meetings of the Royal
Academy. Copley received the commission for his huge *Siege of Gibralter*
over West, who had also been considered for it. Conversely, Copley had
been chosen in 1785 by Lord Sandwich to paint scriptural scenes for
Greenwich Hospital Chapel, but, at the intercession of either Lord North
or the king, the commission went to West instead.[35] The strain, however,
did not deepen into antagonism, and they continued to exchange social
visits and to circulate together in London society.

The London scene itself had been transformed since 1770 in a way
gratifying to the cultural nationalists. Then West's studio was a combined
oasis and shrine for friendless, aspiring American artists; now it was only
one of several gathering places for a large colony of transplanted
Americans—expatriate artists and art students, exiled Loyalists, and a
growing American diplomatic corps. The mixture created relationships
that were wholly unforeseen when West went abroad in 1763, leading to
public commissions for paintings and subscriptions for new literary works.

Among the diplomatic corps in London were John Adams, to whom
many young painters and poets applied for patronage, and for a while

Thomas Jefferson, who entered the circle of West, Copley, and their students. The Loyalist colony included Jacob Duché and his grandson Thomas Spence Duché. The younger Duché was studying art despite his father's warning that as a history painter in America he would probably starve. Duché and such other recent exiles from Philadelphia as the poets Thomas Coombe, Joseph Stansbury, and Jonathan Odell, and the music master Thomas Pike, passed their time at the Pennsylvania or New York Coffee House, visiting and dining with Lord Mayor Brook Watson or with Copley and West. Unfailingly hospitable to Americans, West invited them on short acquaintance to his house, where they admired his recently acquired Titian, a death of Actaeon formerly owned by King James or Charles. (West had bought it, painted over, for a small sum; cleaned, it brought him an offer of a thousand guineas.) Sometimes joined by the Copleys, West drove the exiles through Windsor forest, introduced them to the king and the princesses, and showed them his painting room in Windsor Castle.[36]

While entertaining this growing band of roving Americans, West and Copley received commissions from them as well. Their vast reputations at home made traveling Americans particularly eager to be painted by them. Mercy Warren's son Winslow, in London in 1785, sent his portrait, by Copley, to his playwright mother, who found it "a most striking likeness of a son inexpressibly dear." The future architect Charles Bulfinch, in London in 1786, hoped to hire Copley, knowing his pictures were "finished to the utmost nicety." He looked for another painter after discovering, also, that "they are *very dear*." [37]

Bulfinch did not lack alternatives, for Copley and West were now only the most prominent of several prestigious American artists in London. He hired one of them, a grandson of the also-exiled Mather Byles, Mather Brown. After studying a while with West, Brown became the first American admitted to the schools of the Royal Academy. Soon he opened his own studio, where his portrait business thrived on Americans coming to London. He painted Jefferson in a large curled wig, striped vest, and fluffy jabot, only a Libertas in the background distinguishing him from the English gentry as painted by Gainsborough; and John Adams, holding a copy of Jefferson's *Notes on Virginia*—two of what Brown described as "an hundred pictures of my Countrymen in my Room which are universally known." His aunts in Boston bruited him about, sending "Americans to see my Works when they arrive here." [38] An entirely derivative painter, Brown modeled everything he painted on Gainsborough, Copley, or his idol West, whose gallery he visited nearly every day.

However superficial and bland, Brown attracted a wealthy clientele and won commissions from the London churches and from the East India

Company for large history works. In the summer of 1783 he spent three months at Windsor Castle, often hunting with the king, who presented him with a bow. Eventually he served as historical painter to the duke of York, took over the painter George Romney's house on Cavendish Square, and became, a contemporary remarked, a "Crassus amongst artists. . . ." In his own eyes, Brown saw his success as West saw his. It proved, he wrote in 1784, that "an obscure yankey Boy" could become "as great as any of them" and "make the rays of Phoebus shine and rise from the western Hemisphere." Americans hungering for signs of national greatness also cared less about the quality or originality of Brown's work than about his reputation in London. A New York newspaper in 1785 boasted that the fame of "our countryman, Mr. Brown" was "growing with the most astonishing rapidity" and that "Connoisseurs there speak in the highest terms" of him.[39] Although Brown's works are ignored today, following the Revolution he was often braced with Copley and West in a triumvirate of American genius.

Bulfinch might also have selected the twenty-nine-year-old painter for whom William Temple Franklin sat in 1784, the one "esteem'd by West & everybody," Franklin said, "the first Portrait Painter now living: he is moreover an American. . . . He is astonishing for likeness. I heard West say—'that he *nails* the Face to the Canvass.' "[40] Gilbert Stuart, as Americans delightedly knew and repeatedly said, had developed into one of the leading face painters in London. Independent—and outrageously candid and tactless—he had moved out of West's house, but lived close by on Newman Street. A great bon-vivant and wit (though with a dark undercurrent of melancholia and misanthropy), he chatted with soldiers about warfare and with lawyers about law, using his conversational gifts to relax his sitters. With his love for essentials he had begun creating a distinctive portrait style stripped of all accessories, indeed without setting. His faces appear like busts or medallions against a blank background, absolutely without social or historical reference, lifted out of time in pure concentration upon character. The result is a series of portraits which despite a general air of upper-class refinement and poise are richly individual, inward, and finally enigmatic.

Stuart's portraits share something of Copley's intensity and seriousness, but without Copley's pitiless search for weakness or homeliness. Stuart preferred a fog color as a ground for his painting because, he reportedly said, "being of no colour it receives any colour well." Against this he cast faces notable for their sense of bone structure, of modeling from within, and for their textures and colors. He brooded on the problem of rendering flesh. "Flesh," he reportedly said, "is like no other substance under heaven. It has all the gaiety of a silk mercers shop without the gaudiness or glare

and all the soberness of old mahogany without its deadness or sadness."
Always rather jeering about West, as about many others, Stuart complained that "Benny" taught his pupils to paint "our master's flesh," a
streak of yellow here, a streak of white there. "But Nature," Dunlap recalls
Stuart saying, "does not colour in streaks. Look at my hand; see how the
colours are mottled and mingled, yet all is clear as silver." [41] It was this
silvery, all-color flesh that Stuart strove for in his own portraits, and
achieved.

With the London press praising him as the Van Dyck of his time, Stuart
got many important commissions. A notable one came in 1784, when the
print publisher John Boydell commissioned fifteen portraits for his
collection of famous personalities in the arts. These included a portrait of
West, a wonderful painting of Reynolds in sagging middle-age, and one of
Copley, appropriately in a red coat, that was displayed during the
exhibition of *The Death of Major Peirson*. Copley's son considered it the best
likeness of his father ever painted (ill., p. 527).[42]

Worldly but spendthrift, Stuart enjoyed his success and squandered his
wealth. Hiring a French cook, he gave dinner parties for upwards of forty
people, while West, said one informant, "shook his head and observed that
it would eat itself out." Passionately fond of music, he threw parties for the
best musicians in London.[43] His daughter later explained his extravagance
as a business tactic called for by the social class of his patrons, whose tone,
one gathers, Stuart had assumed himself. The provincial bare literacy of
his earlier begging letter to West—"find myself Ignorant withoutt
bussiness or Freinds"—gave way to a high court style: "I entreat that you
will be so obliging," he wrote the earl of Buchan in 1784, "as to excuse me
and to make my apology to the Ladies." While earning some £1,500 a
year, Stuart spent more, and owed £80 for snuff alone. Near the end of
1787 he had to give up his house. Apparently to escape creditors, he
simply disappeared. A London newspaper reported that he had "offers of a
very liberal kind to settle in America," a report followed by rumors that he
had gone to Paris or London. Whether he was on the run, covering his
tracks, or actually in jail, "it" did by now "eat itself out." [44]

Much of the glory of the American artists in London—their easy access
to the king, their lavish parties, splendid townhouses, and mammoth
commissions—was of course traceable to the daring, generosity, and
personal example of Benjamin West. America's Rising Glory seemed
assured as he continued to attract new pupils. Their aims, their
opportunities, even their spirit, however, differed from those of West's first
pupils in the 1770's. Peale, Benbridge, and Pratt came to him as aspiring
colonials, eager to learn coloring, composition, and portrait technique by
seeing the best European art first-hand and by receiving his direct

instruction. But his pupils of the 1780's had grown up during the war. They arrived fired with patriotic ideals and nationalistic hopes, intending to commemorate a historic struggle which they had experienced themselves. West was to them not a sympathetic countryman of recognized promise but a national hero, the creator of *The Death of General Wolfe*, the very model for the treatment of contemporary history in painting. They came, also, knowing that important business connections awaited them in Europe, where American agents were setting up a network of diplomatic and mercantile arrangements, and where a demand for some documentary record of the recent American war clearly existed.

West's most promising new pupils arrived within six months of each other in 1784—William Dunlap and, despite imprisonment as a scapegoat for Major André during his last trip to England, John Trumbull. Still inspired by Washington's sitting for him at Rocky Hill in 1783, Dunlap prepared credentials for the voyage. He painted a full-length *Washington at Princeton*, which included a languidly dying General Mercer, and a copy of *Brook Watson and the Shark* from an engraving. Probably to prepare himself for socializing in London, he also took French and dancing lessons from William Hulett. Upon his arrival in June, just eighteen years old, a friend of his father's took him to West's Newman Street studio. He found West working upon a picture of King Lear and Cordelia for the empress of Russia, and later recorded his entranced impression of

> . . . the long gallery leading from the dwelling-house, to the lofty suite of painting-rooms—a gallery filled with sketches and designs for large paintings —the spacious room through which I passed to the more retired attelier—the works of his pencil surrounding me on every side—his own figure seated at his esel *[sic]*, and the beautiful composition at which he was employed, as if in sport, not labour. . . .[45]

It struck Dunlap—and no one else seems to have remarked it—that with his powdered hair, side curls, and silk stockings, West had abandoned Quakerism. West offered moderate praise for his canvases, and smiled at Mercer dying à la Wolfe. At this, Dunlap recalled, his "thermoment rose." West gave him some plaster casts, including a *Fighting Gladiator*, to draw for practice.

Dunlap found West's studio lively but intimidating. West often worked surrounded by company and advised his pupils not to shut themselves up when painting but to invite visitors and encourage their criticism. Dunlap seems to have shunned the advice. Although his compatriot John Trumbull also lived in West's house, occupying a room at the front of West's gallery, he considered Trumbull "awfully above me" and rarely spoke with him. He also took ill during his first year, and when not ill spent his time playing music with West's son Ralph or gallivanting around London. With regret he later recalled that West made no effort to hold him to the mark. "My follies and my faults were reported, and exaggerated to Mr. West, and as he saw no appearances of the better self, which resided in me, (for there was a better self,) he left me to my fate." [46] After two years he moved, without consulting West, into a more elegant furnished apartment in Soho, before returning to America, unimproved but wiser, in October 1787.

West gave his room to the twenty-one-year-old Pennsylvanian Robert Fulton, who arrived with a letter of introduction from Benjamin Franklin and a small reputation as a painter of miniatures. Like Dunlap, Fulton found the experience disillusioning and soon left, admitting that "Painting Requires more studdy than I at first imagened." [47] Like Dunlap too, he found other talents in himself and soon gave up painting for invention.

In the return of John Trumbull, however, West had a pupil whose commercial shrewdness, well-defined ambitions, and determined energy promised the survival of his evident talent. Trumbull had spent the end of the war helping his brother, grudgingly, in the army supply business, still feeling that others knew the business world better than he, and would outshine him in it. The ending of the war and his continuing desire to be a history painter renewed his quarrel with his father, who still wanted him to be a lawyer. Even more emphatically than before, his father urged law "as the profession which in a republic leads to all emolument and distinction." Trumbull, now twenty-seven years old, the same age as the celebrated Gilbert Stuart, defended painting. He insisted, he said, "upon the honors paid to artists in the glorious days of Greece and Athens." His father complimented him on presenting a forceful case; it confirmed, he said, his opinion that his son would make a good lawyer:

> ". . . but," added he, "you must give me leave to say, that you appear to have overlooked, or forgotten, one very important point in your case." "Pray, sir," I rejoined, "what was that?" "You appear to forget sir, that *Connecticut is not Athens.*" [48]

Actually, through his unwillingly acquired business experience and his effort to recover the family's lost wealth, Trumbull had learned already that Connecticut was not Athens, and he estimated his artistic chances soberly. He decided that while the country could not yet support a history painter, it would buy cheap engravings of important scenes in its history. He would paint history pictures and convert them into popular prints. Despite his misgivings, Governor Trumbull sent his son to England with a letter explaining to the earl of Dartmouth that the young man wished "to improve his natural turn to the Pencil, which his Countryman the celebrated artist Mr. West considers as well worthy of cultivation." [49]

West greeted his returned pupil, Trumbull found, with "the same boundless liberality and the same friendship which I experienced from him formerly. . . ." He planned to stay with West two years, followed by a year or two in Rome, "without which excellence in the Historical line cannot be attain'd. . . ." [50] West brought him into his circle of aristocrats, diplomats, artists, and exiles, and entertained him at Windsor Castle, where they drove through the forest, sketched, walked, and had tea with Copley and Sukey. But Trumbull devoted most of his time, unlike Dunlap, to his training. As he described his regime to his brother, he awoke at five or six to write or to study anatomy, until breakfasting at eight; then he went to West's, where, with a lunch break at two, he painted all day. Evenings he usually spent with a friend—shunning the theatre, the opera, and other amusements—or attending classes at the Royal Academy, together with the imaginative young English painter Thomas Lawrence. Not only a determination to master history painting bound him to his easel, however. He disliked England, which he viewed as a Connecticut republican. London offered simply "no Society." People "live in a Croud.—Dissipation & pain . . . destroy all Friendship & all sober thoughts.—I study night & day that I may the sooner escape from a country & Manners which are my aversion." [51] He worked long because he wished to leave early.

Yet as Trumbull progressed in his studies he saw that he would have to stay long too. The skills required by "a tolerable degree of Eminence in my profession," he wrote to his father, "are so various & extensive; such a combination of the powers of the Mind to conceive, & facility of Hand to execute;—that nothing but incessant practice for a length of time, can acquire." He dismissed the belief held by Peale, Billings, and other provincials that nature itself was the best teacher: "No power of natural Genius can possibly suffice. . . ." [52] To return imperfectly trained to America—where no opportunities for further training existed—was to doom himself to mediocrity.

Unlike Peale or Brown, too, Trumbull feared dishonoring himself and his profession by hasty or unripe work. He gently turned down an overseas commission from Ezra Stiles to paint Governor Trumbull for the Yale library; since he was "so imperfect in my profession," he explained, his current efforts "might please my friends & myself at present: yet we should be mortified a few years hence to see so poor a monument. . . ." Given the postwar cultural situation, Trumbull's insistence on skill and quality is refreshing and impressive. The raging cultural nationalism often granted instant eminence to slight talents and mistook bombast, gimcrackery, or entertainment for art. What also steeled Trumbull against the lure of easy success was his conviction that anything less than maximum effort and maximum preparation would dishonor the splendid events which he ultimately planned to commemorate: "the great object of my wishes . . . is to take up the History of Our Country, and paint the principal Events particularly of the late War:—but this is a work which to execute with any degree of honour or profit, will require very great powers—& those powers must be attain'd before I leave Europe. . . ." [53] By the end of 1784, he had settled down to prolonged study in "a Country to which I wish never to return."

In part Trumbull supported himself from portrait commissions. He found that if he cared to, he could easily succeed as a London face painter. Money sent from his father and his brother David, however, freed him to concentrate on history painting under West. He copied West's huge *Battle of La Hogue*, making it even larger than the original, and painted a *Priam returning to his family with the dead body of Hector* in the manner of West's *Agrippina*. He sent a *Cincinnatus receiving command of the Roman armies* to the Royal Academy Exhibition, expecting it to be returned; instead, it was hung in a "very advantageous" light—a sign of approbation.[54] As he continued to work throughout 1785, with West's constant encouragement, he experienced a growing control over the complexities of history painting. By the end of the year he could report home that "the rapidity of my advances in the Art have exceeded my most sanguine expectations—and even my hopes." [55]

Steadied by a year of diligent training, Trumbull decided to take the step he had always had in view. He began "writing, *in my language,* the History of our Country." First he made small India ink sketches for paintings of Bunker's Hill and the death of Montgomery, in his view the earliest important events of the Revolution. By the end of 1785 he was actually painting the subjects, in West's room, where West, Reynolds, Copley, and other artists observed his progress. Reynolds, believing that one of the paintings was by West, remarked that West had improved his coloring. West himself called the *Bunker's Hill* "the *best picture* of a modern Battle that has been painted" and remarked that "*no Man* living can paint such another picture of that Scene. . . ." Trumbull finished a small oil version of this scene by January 1786, and a small oil of the Montgomery in late spring or early summer.[56]

Trumbull himself defined his intentions in the catalog of his works which he drew up in the nineteenth century. He hoped to illustrate decisive turns in major revolutionary battles, brought about by the deaths of key figures. The *Montgomery* depicts the moment of the general's death, as a result of which "the plan of attack was entirely disconcerted, and the consequent retreat of his column decided at once the fate of the place. . . ." The enemy is already entering as Montgomery's stunned troops watch their commander expire on the hard snow (ill., p. 529). The smoky *Bunker's Hill* records the moment when the patriots had expended their ammunition, as a result of which the British took the hill (ill., p. 528). "At this last moment of the action, Gen. Warren was killed by a musket ball through the head. . . ." Warren's friend Colonel Small—calling to a comrade who has lost power of speech—grabs the musket of a British grenadier poised to deliver Warren's coup de grâce. Around them stand patriots in defiant postures, futilely maintaining resistance with scowls and empty guns. In the center, General Putnam reluctantly orders retreat; to the right, a wounded American "attended by a faithful negro" hesitates whether to flee for safety or to aid his stricken commander.[57]

Both paintings declare the traditional theory of history painting, the innovations of West, and the London work of Copley. They are standard *exempla* depicting courageous self-sacrifice. The faces of the soldiers register varieties of fear, resolution, uncertainty, or amazement, although usually in formulas borrowed from, and widely used by, West, especially a profile mouth, downturned and open. West's *Wolfe* supplies or suggests the Christian overtones: The dying Warren and the dying Montgomery are drooping Christ-figures; the frontiersmen who behold Montgomery with outstretched, wondering hands are buckskinned shepherds from some Adoration of the Magi via West. The wounded soldier and his black servant who flee the scene in the lower right of *Bunker's Hill* are rearrangements of several elements in *Major Peirson*. In effect, Trumbull split in two the cockaded black servant who stands at the center of Copley's work, giving the cockade to a white soldier and supplying him with a black servant. Their gestures of flight derive from Copley's terror-stricken mother and child stumbling over a corpse. Trumbull also drew on Copley's baroque diagonals, bands of light and shade, and smoky confusion.[58]

Following Copley's practice in his *Chatham*, Trumbull when he could took the faces of the persons involved. For the *Bunker's Hill* he probably painted Howe and Clinton at actual sittings in London, and perhaps used Copley's portrait for the likeness of Warren.[59] The unique combination of faces taken from life, of exact rendition of military hardware and uniforms by an ex-army supplier, and of details recalled by an observer of the Battle of Bunker's Hill was no doubt what West had in mind when he said that "*no Man* living can paint such another picture of that Scene." In its documentary aspect, history painting for Trumbull was indistinguishable from historiography.

Yet Trumbull found it difficult to reconcile his documentary passion with his wish to depict raging battle. Suffering from monocular vision, his left eye almost useless, he worked best on a small scale. Seen close up, the faces of his famous men are convincingly individual, providing in many cases the best surviving graphic record of their countenances. Intent upon documentary visual accuracy, however, Trumbull often neglected the psychological drama. Many of the leading actors stare at different angles into space, as if the event enveloping them existed only to bring them together for a group portrait. Trumbull reserved psychological comment largely for the nameless spear-carriers, whom he painted from handbooks of expression. Amidst the smoke and turmoil, Howe, Clinton, and the other historical personages seem waxwork manikins, untouched by the madness around them, immaculate in their stiff authenticity.

Their petrified quality might go unnoticed in the frieze-like austerities of West's *Agrippina* or in the breathless, suspended moment caught by Copley in his *Chatham*. But in *Montgomery* and *Bunker's Hill* Trumbull had departed from the basically neoclassical conception of these works. Nearly twenty years younger than West and Copley, he was fully in touch with the developing romantic sense of nature. He set his battles in romantic landscapes—blasted trees, broken wheels, lowering skies, windswept darkling plains, as much Gothic ruins as historical sites. The tattered banner and blasted tree that occupy the upper right third of *Montgomery* are identical with the scenery he later used to illustrate Ossian's poetry. In describing the painting in his catalog, he himself called attention to how the "trees stripped of their foliage—the desolation of winter, and the gloom of night, heighten the melancholy character of the scene." Previews of Trumbull's use of nature as a correlative for action appear in the smoky confusion of West's *Battle of La Hogue* and in Copley's *Peirson.* Yet Trumbull went beyond his mentors in lending history painting a sense of the sublime, in fusing documentary realism with romantic landscape, in imparting to historical 'truth' a sense of grandeur. The combination of flashing smoky-gray skies and ultra-realistic military personnel has its literary analogue in the epic poem which Timothy Dwight of Connecticut was writing at the same time. Trumbull's paintings and Dwight's epic share a conflicting desire to satisfy the country's curiosity about its heroes while flattering its sense of glory.

The conflict also makes clear the larger importance of neoclassic historicism to the development of American culture. More and more, neoclassic historicism served as an alibi for exploring romantic sensibility, promulgating subversive ideas and esthetic forms under the guise of nobility and correctness. In their combination of heroic rectitude and *frisson,* works like *Agrippina* and *The Prince of Parthia* already contain elements which might recommend them to either Cotton Mather or Edgar Allan Poe. As the urned ashes of Germanicus gave way to the bleeding actuality of Jacques Louis David's *Marat Assassinated*, as Roman-Whig-

Puritan self-sacrifice modulated into suicidal melancholy—as expressive force overtook didactic austerity—neoclassic historicism became a major vehicle for the transformation of American Puritanism into American Romanticism.

Having completed the first two paintings of his series, Trumbull tried to find an engraver, as planned. Cheap prints would bring his work "within the power of our American purses" and, for himself, "reconcile the pleasures of Historical painting with profit"—West speculated that the prints would make £6,000.[60] Although several talented engravers now worked in America, such as James Trenchard, probably none was skillful enough to engrave Trumbull's complex canvases. On the other hand, Trumbull could find no Englishman willing to engrave them, perhaps because of the subjects. (Ironically, Dunlap noted, Bostonians resented the paintings too, since Trumbull had depicted American defeats.) He decided to have the work done in Paris.

For most American painters, Paris had been little more than a stop before settling in London with West. But the French alliance and the American diplomatic corps created an American colony in Paris, with entree to its intellectual life. In London in May 1786, Trumbull had met Thomas Jefferson, who approved of his historical series. When Trumbull went to Paris in the early fall, Jefferson invited him to stay at his home in the Hôtel de Langeac and introduced him to the Paris art world. Trumbull visited David in his studio at the Louvre and saw his just-finished *Oath of the Horatii* ("Story well told—drawing pretty good—colouring cold"), toured the salons with Houdon and his wife, attended the rue de Clery soirees of the successful painter Mme. Vigée-Le Brun, through whose husband he met "all the principal artists and connoisseurs in Paris." Although he denounced Paris to his brother as a "capital of dissipation and nonsense," in his private journal he recorded his visits to the Louvre, the Palais Royal, and the Sorbonne in a crescendo of dazzled appreciation, each sight seeming finer than the one before.[61] Paris became for Trumbull what it became for Henry James's Bostonians, a world of social and artistic refinement previously unimagined and, once experienced, transforming. He returned from seeing the king's collection of paintings, Jefferson told Hopkinson, acknowledging that "it surpassed not only every thing he had seen, but every idea he had ever formed of this art."[62]

While learning afresh that 'Connecticut was not Athens,' Trumbull did not forget his purpose. He had brought *Bunker's Hill* and *Montgomery* with him, but despite their enthusiastic reception for some reason was unable to secure an engraver even in Paris. At last he engaged Gotthard von Müller of Stuttgart to engrave *Bunker's Hill*, at the high price of £1,000; he also arranged with a Leipzig engraver to do the *Montgomery*, for £800. The arrangement proved irksome, entangling him for four years in a lengthy overseas correspondence.

After seeing Germany and the Low Countries, Trumbull returned to London in November 1786, his "brain half turned by the attention which had been paid to my paintings in Paris, and by the multitude of fine things which I had seen." Sustaining his enthusiasm, he began several new paintings for his Revolution series. He planned to follow *Bunker's Hill* and *Montgomery* with pictures of the classic demarcation points of the war, works which would be more responsible than any others for creating the popular image of the revolutionary generation. For a *Declaration of Independence* he returned to Paris to take Jefferson's head, and while at Jefferson's house took Rochambeau, De Grasse, Lafayette, and others for a *Yorktown*. He did many preliminary sketches for an ambitious *Death of Mercer at Princeton* and planned a "Death of Jane M'Crea" (that went no further than the sketches) and a *Delivery of the Standards* showing his friend David Humphreys delivering to Congress Washington's report of the Yorktown surrender and the captured flags.[63]

The series would end with a picture of the approaching Congress charged with considering a new national constitution. Part of its force, Trumbull believed, would come from showing the military figures in the preceding paintings now convened in civilian dress to establish a new government, demonstrating how "those who once wielded the arms of their Country with such effect, could also guide her Councils with equal Dignity." [64]

44. Musical Life

When Sally Franklin in 1763 tried to collect some native compositions to send abroad and found only "a few Airs," her father explained, accurately, that "Music is a new Art with us." Twenty years later, hundreds of compositions by native American composers, often protected by copyright, appeared beside European works in large collections printed by type, or in American magazines devoted solely to music; performing groups as large as three hundred sang Handel, then Billings; organs piped in Congregational churches; nondenominational vocal institutes with boards of trustees offered public training in singing; European music merchants and instrumentalists streamed to America.

"Music was before this last war," wrote an ex–army surgeon around 1784, "still quite in its infancy. Besides the organists in the towns and the schoolmasters in the country there were no professional musicians. . . . But during the war and after it straggling musicians from the various armies spread abroad a taste for music, and now in the largest towns concerts are given. . . ." [1] What the surgeon, Johann Schoepf, had in view was in fact the resumption, with doubled energy, of a rising curve of progress in public concerts that the war had halted. The German, Italian, and English musicians who migrated to the colonies in the lull between 1770 and 1773 had produced a series of concerts unprecedented in colonial experience: the first nearly complete performance of *The Messiah* in New York in 1770, the performance in Boston in 1771 of the newly introduced pianoforte and of organ concertos by the composer himself, William Selby, newly arrived from London. But there the rising curve ended. Except under the British occupation of New York and Philadelphia, as far as one can tell from contemporary newspaper advertisements, concert life after 1775 simply stopped.

When peace returned to America, there quite suddenly appeared more concerts and more musicians in more places than ever before. But this was only the visible token of a complex realignment of American musical life, an organic change that brought music out of the churches into the concert halls, that erased denominational and regional lines, and that gave music the standing of an independent profession and art.

As Schoepf reported, the increase in numbers did in part represent the "straggling" but well-trained army musicians and military bands left behind by the war. They reemerged everywhere as a new corps of civilian musicians. In Charleston Schoepf discovered "publick concerts . . . mainly under the direction of German and English musicians left behind by the army. . . ." In New York appeared the violinist Philip Phile, who as Pfeil had played in the orchestra for Clinton's Thespians in occupied New York. In New Hampshire, formal concert life apparently began in August 1783 when an American regimental band played "several Overtures, Symphonies, Military Music, several Songs, and several Duettoes on the French Horns." In Savannah, in 1785, the ex-inspector of music for the American army, John Hiwell, gave the second concert ever presented in Georgia, including two "Military Concertos," followed the next year by a concert featuring "capital Performers from Europe." [2] No doubt many other foreign and native military musicians dispersed after the war, reappearing in the Harmonic Society that gave concerts in Fredericksburg, Virginia, in 1784 or as the "John Victor" who the same year offered six months of subscription concerts in Alexandria. [3]

To the many new, trained musicians thrown into American musical life by the war was added a drove of postwar immigrants. Together with many foreign painters, they accounted for some of the 4,000 immigrants arriving yearly in America between 1784 and 1794. The commercial possibilities for musicians in the new nation were advertised abroad. The German *Musikalische Bibliothek* in 1783 promised that "Music supports her Master handsomely in America and one may speedily make a fortune through her." Musicians seeking quick fortune seem to have arrived by the boatload. The *Virginia Journal* in October 1784 announced the arrival from Rotterdam of "healthy GERMAN REDEMPTIONERS" who included bricklayers, barbers, butchers, shoemakers, "School-masters, music-masters, carpenters. . . ."⁴ Postwar newspapers swelled with ads by obscure immigrant teachers, instrument makers, and music dealers: "John Hay of Europe" teaching piano, harpsichord, and spinet; the Philadelphia teacher William Hoffmetster; the John Klipstein who taught German flute "so very easy, as to avoid every symptom of pain in the breast, which is occasioned by irregular blowing"; the Dane Hans Gram; the harpsichord and piano maker Joseph Fleming "from Europe"; the organ and piano maker Thomas Dobbs "just arrived from London"; the London organ builder Charles Tawse; the German piano maker George Ulshoefer.⁵ At least one immigrant music dealer did find fortune, although not in music. The German John Jacob Astor began selling flutes in New York in September 1784; by 1786 he operated a full-fledged music store on Queen Street that carried pianofortes, spinets, guitars, violins, flutes, fifes, clarinets, and oboes, as well as strings, music paper, and supplies. In addition, he sold the furs which he had begun to buy in small quantities, the infant stage of his millionaire nineteenth-century fur empire.⁶

Not only music teachers and merchants arrived, but also European instrumentalists, some with impressive careers. Several emigrated to Philadelphia, such as the English organist and harpsichordist John Bentley, the French cellist and composer Henri Capron, and the pianist and harpsichordist William Brown (his name probably anglicized from Braun), who gave the first recorded concert held in Baltimore. Beginning in the fall of 1784, the trio joined in a series of fortnightly City Concerts designed to please what they called "the rising taste for music, and its improved state in Philadelphia. . . ."⁷ In 1786 arrived the most distinguished European performer to migrate to America before the nineteenth century, the pianist Alexander Reinagle (1756–1809). A student of Raynor Taylor in Scotland, he had been praised by his intimate friend K. P. E. Bach, and probably had performed in the first of the great Handel festivals. One spectator who heard him late in the century recalled his Shubertesque appearance, his "bushy, powdered hair, large high forehead, and round full face, illuminated by silver mounted spectacle glasses, a perceptible smirk at all times about the mouth, and an extraordinary

depth of dimple in his cheek. . . ." [8] Arriving in New York, Reinagle
offered instruction on several instruments and performed in concert with
Maria Storer of the American Company and with the immigrant violinist
Philip Phile. In Philadelphia, he joined up with Capron and Brown in a
concert series at the City Tavern. He also introduced to American
audiences a new repertoire of piano works. Devoted to Haydn (and
responsible for the first American publication of Haydn's works, in 1789),
he offered a Haydn trio, Haydn sonatas, and (with Alexander Juhan)
Haydn piano works for four hands.[9]

While Reinagle himself represents a new grade of professionalism in
American concerts, his popularizing of Haydn reflects other changes that
were bringing about a larger, kaleidoscopic transformation of the pattern
of American musical life. As the most prominent musicians in America
had been organists but were now pianists, the piano itself had begun to
replace the harpsichord in fashionable drawing rooms, and as a favored
instrument for concert performance. Its ascendency can be traced from the
first American piano concert (1771) through the first ads for piano lessons
and for American-made pianos (1774) to the publication in Philadelphia
in 1787 of William Brown's *Three Rondos for the Piano Forte or Harpsichord*,
claiming to be "the first attempt of this kind made in America." (Reinagle
the same year, also in Philadelphia, published a group of Scots tunes with
variations for piano, *A Select Collection*.) By the early 1780's, Philadelphia
had several piano dealers. One, named Jackson, offered "perhaps the very
best instrument that ever came to this Country whether it be considered
for the elegance of it's workmanship or the sweetness of it's tones." [10]
Chronic problems with imported instruments encouraged native piano-
building, as did the new cultural nationalism, which honored evidence of
self-help. In 1787 the *Worcester Magazine* flaunted a two-page, double-column list of items now manufactured in America which included not only
metheglin and starch but also history paintings and "Musical Instruments." In 1783, James Juhan (probably the father of Reinagle's
accompanist) manufactured and advertised in Philadelphia "the great
North American forte pianos, the mechanical part of them being entirely
of his own invention, and so simple, that it is the easiest thing in the world
to keep them in order and to tune them." [11]

Even more potent than sheer numbers of musicians or new instruments
in transforming American concert life was the merger in performance of
secular professionals, Anglican organist-composers, and New England
singing masters.[12] In part, this confluence of musical traditions that had
been kept distinct by strong denominational affiliations was made possible
by the erosion of Congregational resistance to church organ music, itself
prepared by the growing sophistication of the singing schools. Although in

1770 an organ had been installed in Ezra Stiles's Congregational Church in Providence (it was lost during the war), most Congregational churches had considered the instrument anathema. By 1783, however, after a long history of debate within the churches and after the entering wedge in Providence, given the musical training in the singing schools and the postwar desire for a little entertainment, many could no longer take the issue seriously. *A Collection of Funny, Moral, and Entertaining Stories* (New Haven, 1787)—one of many postwar jokebooks—told about a bill brought to a New England assembly for the purpose of *"organising"* a militia. "A venerable old man arose and opposed the Bill, for, says he, our Militia had good *Drum's* and Fifes, and therefore I think it needless these hard times to be at the expence of purchasing them *Organs.*" Such 'venerable old men' could no longer hold out against the younger congregations.

In March 1785, an organ was played at the most revered meeting house in America, that of the Boston First Church, formed in 1630 under the Puritan patriarchs John Wilson and John Cotton. It was installed at the insistence of the congregation, and against the wishes of their ancient minister Charles Chauncy, who told them "that it would not be long before he was in his grave—he knew that before his head was cold there, they would have an Organ. . . ." Instructed by the congregation to obtain £500 for the organ from London, Chauncy obtained instead *A Tractate on Church Music* (London, 1786), 500 copies of which were circulated to the congregation. Dedicated to Chauncy, it warned that "instrumental music is not fit and proper for the public worship. . . . The Christian Religion shines brightest in its own dress; and to paint it, is but to deform it." Deformative or not, the organ was first played at the meeting house to accompany "the best masters in town" in Billings' anthem "I was glad when they said unto me, we will go into the house of ye Lord." According to one listener, the new instrument was "a very great help to the singing" and pleased everyone "excepting a few who retain their ancient prejudices, and who had rather hear this pleasing part of devotion performed by a small number of screaming voices." [13]

As Congregational churches began admitting organs, Anglican churches, in a similar spirit of interdenominational union, began admitting Congregational tunes. In 1782, Trinity Church in Boston decided to commission a hymn tune, with organ accompaniment, from William Billings. The two musical traditions joined in ambitious, nationalistic concerts that featured works of native composers side by side with works of Handel and Vivaldi, according them a single standard of performance and implicitly a single regard. The crossing of denominational lines and of musical and national traditions is epitomized by the alliance in postwar Boston of the Anglican organist William Selby and Billings the Congregational singing master. Selby, to recall, had been organist in London's distinguished Holy Sepulcher church before arriving in Boston in 1771 as organist of King's Chapel. Between 1771 and 1775 he gave several concerts in Boston and Newport, playing his own organ concertos but featuring the works of Handel. With the departure of British troops in March 1776, King's Chapel ceased holding services and concert life in Boston ended. For the duration, Selby gave no concerts; he occasionally served as a church organist but mostly kept a grocery store, vending wines, tea, and soap.[14]

Just three months after Cornwallis' surrender, however, Selby launched the first important concert in Boston since 1776. Advertised as *Musica Spiritualis, or Sacred Music*, it was given at King's Chapel for the benefit of the Boston poor. At the door, concertgoers could buy "Music books" containing texts of the pieces. These included selections from Handel's *Samson* and *Joseph*, a solo based on *Paradise Lost*, a dirge by Thomas Arne, a solo by Thomas Stanley (the English musician who had tested the King's Chapel organ in England before it was shipped to Boston in 1754), and an organ concerto and a four-part setting for the Hundredth Psalm by Selby himself. With these, Selby performed a lengthy anthem by Billings ("And I saw a mighty angel") based on Revelation and containing a Hallelujah chorus.[15]

The coupling of Billings and Handel gave a significant recognition to Billings' gifts and to a musical tradition that if not indigenous exactly, had distinct local elements and strong associations to the place. The coupling also indicates—though the surviving biographical information is skimpy—that Billings and Selby had come together in the musical life of Boston, in mutual recognition if not in direct collaboration. Their alliance was probably eased by the fact that in 1782 King's Chapel was used in the mornings by Anglicans and in the afternoons by the congregation of the disused Old South Church. Indeed, when Old South reopened in March 1783, the Anglican Selby himself wrote an anthem for the occasion. The connection between the two musicians continued through the decade: In 1785, Billings gave singing lessons at Selby's church; at a concert in 1787 Selby performed two of Billings' works and in 1790 gave another concert for Billings' benefit.

The church concerts of 1783 differed from those of 1763 or 1773 not only in their programs but also in their size. A public hungry for music formed into new organizations like the Boston Musical Society and the Private Musical Society, which offered enthusiastically reviewed concerts of their own and sponsored secular concerts by Selby at Concert Hall; this public went to hear the itinerant "Dr. Moyes" lecture at Faneuil Hall on "The

Cause and the Properties of Echo, the Theory of Musical Tones, and the Effects of Music on the Human Mind." [16] It must have read longingly the detailed reports in Boston newspapers of the Centenary Commemoration of Handel held in Westminster Abbey in 1784 and repeated over the next few years, involving more than 500 performers and an audience of 4,500. Handel, since before the Peace of 1763, had been the most popular composer in America, his biblical oratorios pleasing the same historicist taste that relished the biblical and classical moral dramas of West. Attending one of the Commemoration concerts, Abigail Adams "could scarcely believe myself an inhabitant of the earth. I was one continued shudder from the beggining to the end. . . ." [17]

Selby tried to translate this splendor from London to Boston. In January 1786, with the sponsorship of the Boston Musical Society, he produced a liturgical musical festival based on the Handel Commemorations and grander than anything seen before in America. He presided at the organ over 70 performers, including a band of instruments, before an audience of 2,000. Mixing the church service with vocal and instrumental works, he alternated the chanting of *Te Deum*, the reading of the Apostle's Creed, and the offering of a prayer for Congress with anthems, overtures by Bach and Handel, solos from *The Messiah* (accompanied by strings), songs from *Samson*, Handel's second organ concerto, and organ and vocal works by himself and others—nineteen items in all. Proceeds from the tickets, at three shillings each, were collected by local ministers, who turned them over for the relief of imprisoned debtors. In imitation of the London concerts, Selby repeated the festival the next year, with different music. [18] One newspaper rated the instrumental part "excellent," the vocal part "super-excellent." Another raved at the "overpowering pathos of *Handel.* . . . *Handel! Handel! Handel!*" adding that it could not well describe "the surprise and astonishment of the audience, at the performance of this divine Chorus . . . especially . . . where the *drums* so unexpectedly thundered in and joined in the glorious Hallelujahs" [19] (ill., p. 533).

Reported in newspapers in New York and Philadelphia as well as Boston, Selby's innovations set a new standard to be emulated and then surpassed. In May 1786, the Philadelphia singing master Andrew Adgate mounted a "Grand Concert of Sacred Music" that was interdenominational à la Boston and, innovatingly in its own right, national, or at least not regional, mixing the musical traditions of Boston, Philadelphia, and New York. In addition to playing works of Aaron Williams and Handel alongside Billings, he included a violin concerto by Juhan and a flute concerto by Brown, both of Philadelphia, and an anthem by the organist Tuckey of New York. Strikingly, he included an anthem by James Lyon, the Princeton graduate whose *Urania* in 1761 was the cornerstone of the new church music. Adgate's "Grand Concert" was thus a retrospective of American music over the last quarter-century.

A year later Adgate went further. In honor of Lyon, but inspired by Selby, he presented "The First Uranian Concert." Noah Webster, who attended, estimated the number of performers at 300, a larger contingent than Selby's and probably the largest performing group yet assembled on the continent. Alexander Juhan led the fifty-piece orchestra. The program, or "Syllabus," included works by Arnold, Arne, and Williams, a flute concerto by "Ponceau" (probably Giuseppe Ponzo), an overture by Giovanni Martini, a violin concerto performed by Philip Phile, an anthem by Tuckey, a piece by Lyon, and three anthems by Billings, the whole climaxed by Handel's "Hallelujah Chorus." [20] Bringing together Anglican and Congregational, English and American, vocal and instrumental, New York, Boston, and Philadelphia music, Adgate and Selby gave American concerts a new richness, made them symbols of widespread and long-developing national accomplishment so that music no longer seemed "a new Art with us."

Many of the 300 performers in Adgate's First Uranian Concert were his own pupils. Indeed, the progress of concert life was inseparable from that of the singing schools. The two underwent identical transformations in character and size, crossing sectarian and regional lines and enlarging their ambitions. The schools of 1770 had been local New England affairs attached to Congregational churches. But with the end of the war, several New England singing masters began carrying their methods and repertoire southward. Adgate, born in Norwich, Connecticut, opened a school in 1784 in Philadelphia. No knot of adolescents gathered in the public room of some tavern to sing over sawhorses, it aspired to the impressiveness of Alexander de Quesnay's postwar painting academy. It was called *Mr. Adgate's Institution for diffusing more generally the Knowledge of Vocal Music.* Adgate published tunes by Billings in his *Philadelphia Harmony* (1789) and was probably responsible for advertising a separate Philadelphia publication of Billings' anthem "I am the rose of Sharon," a performance of which Adgate directed at the College of Philadelphia in 1788.[21]

The results of extending the New England schools outside the region can be glimpsed in a *Discourse on Psalmody* by Samuel Blair, a New England–style defense of psalmody published in 1789 in Philadelphia, and delivered at a New England–style singing school concert held in Neshaminy, Pennsylvania. Blair praised Adgate for improving singing in Philadelphia, and described the performance, which was attended by more than a thousand people:

> . . . we had about two hundred and fifty singers; who were arranged in the order of the art, on the front floor of the gallery. They were all, I may say, well

dressed; that is, in rural simplicity and elegance. . . . They all, indeed, seemed to be well taught and practised in the tunes, and different kinds of music, which they sang; and many of their voices were remarkably fine. The several parts of counter, treble, tenor, and bass were so judiciously adjusted and proportioned, and the time was so accurately observed, that not a jar, or any kind of insipidity, or dissonance, offended the ear.

Further south, the Springfield musician Lucius Chapin began teaching as early as 1787 in the Shenandoah Valley. In 1785 Noah Webster of Connecticut taught singing school in Baltimore.[22] His close friend Andrew Law, after working as a singing master in Philadelphia and New York, opened a school in Charleston, South Carolina.

The spread of the schools was encouraged by the postwar academy movement, with its ideal of public singing education. What the age called the "power of music" seemed to some pedagogues a means of producing the empathy necessary for republican life, inducing people to place the public good above their own. In his essay "On the Mode of Education Proper in a Republic" (1784), Benjamin Rush wrote:

> To those who have studied human nature, it will not appear paradoxical to recommend [in education] . . . a particular attention to vocal music. Its mechanical effects in civilizing the mind, and thereby preparing it for the influence of religion and government, have been so often felt and recorded, that it will be unnecessary to mention facts in favour of its usefulness. . . .

This belief in the public utility of universal training in music probably explains several further innovations in the postwar singing schools. Adgate offered instruction to pupils of all denominations, and opened his school gratis. He planned to depend for support on a board of trustees, who would raise subscriptions at eight dollars each for twelve vocal concerts to be given by the pupils. The trustees raised enough subscribers to enable him to begin instruction, free, at the College of Philadelphia. Law tried unsuccessfully to open a similarly subsidized school in New York, interdenominational and, if not free, inexpensive.[23] Probably also influenced by the movement for public education, Law began trying at this time to simplify musical notation, doing away with the musical staff and inventing shape notes to represent the fasola syllables. He was unable to publish his method because of the difficulty in printing it. Anyway, he had been anticipated by Benjamin Dearborn of New Hampshire, who in 1785 published in Portsmouth *A Scheme, for reducing the Science of Music*, a system of notation using standard alphabet letters, numbers, and punctuation marks.

Attention to the uses of music in a republic perhaps also explains its much-expanded place in the American colleges. The Act of Incorporation opening Phillips Exeter Academy in 1781 specified "Musick & the Art of Speaking" as part of the curriculum. At Yale in 1786 students formed their own "Musical Society" (which performed during intervals at the Yale commencement) and created an elaborate Christmas ode for three groups of shepherds and a chorus of angels, later printed.[24] One young member of the Yale singing school, Chauncy Langdon, gathered for its use works by Billings and other New England composers and published them as *The Beauties of Psalmody* (New Haven, 1786), a tunebook which has been called "one of the most aesthetically pleasing compilations of early American music ever made." Harvard had a "Singing Club" by 1789, and probably as early as 1786, when at the commencement, one observer reported, appeared "2 French horns, clarinets, etc., which go into the meeting-house and file off at the pulpit, go into the gallery, and there are joined by seven singers, and continue till the people are seated and the house filled." [25]

Benjamin Rush discouraged the teaching of instruments because the state of American society allowed few the time to master them; harpsichords, he said, would likely "serve only as sideboards for their parlors." Yet, as in the churches, instrumental music followed vocal music into the colleges, beyond the playing of an organ or flute that had often accompanied prewar commencements. In 1784 the College of Philadelphia exercises included musical interludes of three to five minutes each with bassoons and clarinets, while at the Yale Quarter Day ceremonies in 1783, Ezra Stiles reluctantly noted, "For the first time I admitted a Flute in Chapel with the vocal Music." [26]

The changes in concert life and the singing schools are echoed in the many new postwar tunebooks, whose very number is the single most dramatic evidence of progress in American music. The years 1782–1786 produced as many collections of psalm tunes as the whole previous decade. Most came from compilers and composers who had grown up during the war under Billings' influence, and in some cases under his instruction. Outstanding among them were Simeon Jocelin's *The Chorister's Companion* (New Haven, 1782), Oliver Brownson's *Select Harmony* (New Haven, 1783), Andrew Law's *Rudiments of Music* (Cheshire, Connecticut, 1783), Daniel Read's *The American Singing Book* (New Haven, 1785), and Isaiah Thomas' *LAUS DEO! The Worcester Collection of Sacred Harmony* (Worcester, 1786). Several of the collections introduced new tunes that stayed popular well into the nineteenth century. Read's book went through five editions, Thomas' through eight before 1803.

Like the postwar concerts and singing schools, the new tunebooks were eclectic and ambitious. Thomas' collection, the most popular of the later eighteenth century, mixed works by Billings with traditional Protestant tunes like OLD HUNDRED with a chorus for five voices by Handel with a doxology by Selby. Law's *Rudiments* included both Congregational psalm tunes and music for Anglican chants. A startling marriage of religious and musical traditions appeared in the *Compilation of the Litanies and Vespers, Hymns and Anthems as they are sung in the Catholic Church* (Philadelphia, 1787), by a recently arrived Scottish engraver named John Aitken. The only Catholic tunebook published in America before the nineteenth century, it contained instructions on ornament taken from Tans'ur and a selection of Anglican anthems.[27] The eclecticism was geographic as well as religious and musical. The tunes in *LAUS DEO!*—Virginia, Amherst, Maryland, Philadelphia, Annapolis, Georgia—form a virtual atlas of the thirteen new states. The titles register both the spread of the singing schools and the spirit of national unity, as does the complexity of some of the music. Thomas ventured to print in *LAUS DEO!* an unaccompanied version of Handel's "Hallelujah Chorus," although, as he remarked, some thought it "too hard to be learned, and too delicate to be sung, even by the best performers in this country." He pointed out, however, that America now had singers "at least equal" in skill and judgment "to some of the best singers in Europe."

The postwar tunebooks printed for the first time a large number of new works by new American composers, dramatizing the remarkable growth of native music over the period of the war. In his preface, Thomas paid tribute to Billings as the progenitor of a whole school of native composers:

> Mr. WILLIAM BILLINGS, of Boston was the first person we know of that attempted to compose Church Musick, in the New-England States; his musick met with approbation. . . . Several adepts in musick followed Mr. *Billings's* example, and the New-England States can now boast of many authors of Church Musick, whose compositions do them honour.

Jocelin's collection, whose index has a column headed "American Authors," was the first to identify works by native composers. Following Jocelin's lead, Brownson also specifically identified American as distinct from European works. The tunebooks justified the distinction by publishing an impressive number of new native composers. Among them was the Berkshire Mountain blacksmith Lewis Edson. Apparently self-taught, he became known as "the great singer" and ultimately was considered by many contemporaries comparable to Billings himself.[28] Jocelin published in the *Chorister's Companion* three of Edson's tunes, which were reprinted by Brownson, Read, and Thomas, and thereafter appeared in nearly every tunebook until the early nineteenth century, and remain popular today: Greenfield, Lenox, and Bridgewater. The tom-tom rhythms of Lenox mesmerized Billings' younger contemporaries and pulse through many later tunes. The new tunebooks also printed works by Jacob French, who had been a member of a singing school taught by Billings in Stoughton in 1774. French served in the army throughout the war, present at Bunker's Hill, Ticonderoga, and possibly Saratoga. Thomas published his "The Heavenly Vision," an anthem based on Revelation.

Brownson, Thomas, and Read also introduced works by Timothy Swan of Worcester, an admirer and acquaintance of Billings. Although pressed by his father to enter business, his experience at a singing school awakened his interest in music; while with the army at Cambridge he learned to play the fife. Eventually, his daughter said, he could play "(but ordinarily) on any instrument he ever saw." Apprenticed to a hatter, he began to compose, circulating his hymn tunes in manuscript, from which they were widely sung. In 1779, at the age of twenty-one, he moved to Suffield, Connecticut, where he wrote most of his music and dabbled in verse, some in imitation of Robert Burns. Brownson seems to have sought him out in Suffield, telling him that "from your reputation as a composer, I supposed you to be a man well stricken in years, with a Wig and a cock'd hat." [29] Brownson printed in his collection Swan's immensely popular tune RAINBOW.

Perhaps the most important new composer was Daniel Read (1754– 1836), one of eleven children of an Attleboro, Massachusetts, farmer. According to his son, he walked ten miles into Providence to buy his first singing book. Beginning to compose in his teens, he served in the army in Long Island before moving in 1782 to New Haven. He taught singing school in and near the town, and also traveled into New York State for his health, bringing New England psalmody to both sides of the Hudson around Fishkill.[30] Ezra Stiles gave him a letter of recommendation as "an uncommon proficient in the art of vocal music." [31] In New Haven Read became partners with Amos Doolittle, the engraver of the Concord and Lexington prints. In 1785 they issued the nationalistically titled *American Singing Book*, intended as a new guide to psalmody. Although only seventy-two pages long, it went through six editions. Its popularity led Read to issue a twenty-five-tune *Supplement to the American Singing Book* (New Haven, 1787), including works by Billings, Edson, Swan, himself, and others, in order to further "the prosperity of the science of music in America."

Read's own tunes became extremely popular. Of the thirty-eight most reprinted American tunes of the eighteenth century, nine were by Read, compared with eight by Billings. Read's SHERBURN, reprinted more than fifty times before 1810, was sung in the North until the Civil War and continues to be sung in the South, where it appeared in print as recently as the 1970 edition of the *Original Sacred Harp*. His MORTALITY, included in the *American Singing Book*, is one of the half-dozen best tunes written in

America in the eighteenth century. This "tiny masterpiece," as Irving
Lowens calls it, is set to Isaac Watts' paraphrase of the ninetieth Psalm:

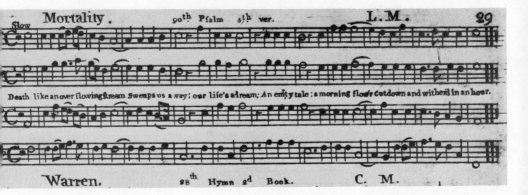

Death like an overflowing stream
Sweeps us away; our life's a dream;
An empty tale; a morning flow'r
Cut down and wither'd in an hour.

A deeply mournful tune, MORTALITY combines the stark New England
idiom with a tremulous melancholy.

Read also contributed to America's musical progress an important first.
In 1786 he issued in conjunction with Doolittle *The American Musical
Magazine.* William Selby in Boston had tried to launch something like a
periodical in 1782, when he printed proposals for a monthly *New Minstrel.*
He promised that each number would contain an essay on "musical
expression" plus at least one piece for harpsichord, piano, or spinet, one for
guitar, one for German flute, two songs in English, and one in French—
revealing again the influence, as Selby put it, of America's "acquaintance
with a nation far gone in politeness and fine arts." Not only the cultivated
tastes of the liberty-loving French, he noted, legitimated his project;
America had made startling advances culturally which it was time to
acknowledge: "The promptness of this young country in those sciences
which were once thought peculiar only to riper age, has already brought
upon her the eyes of the world. . . . And shall those arts which make her
happy be less courted than those arts which have made her great? Why
may she not be 'In song unequall'd as unmatch'd in war'?" [32] But the *New
Minstrel* never appeared, leaving it to Read and Doolittle to publish the

first American musical magazine. In terms of 1786, their venture represents only one volley in what was an explosion of magazine publishing (see "The Literary Scene"). The first volume consisted of some thirty-four distinct pieces in twelve monthly fascicles. Each fascicle contained four very clearly printed folio pages with more than usual numbers of incidentals and dynamic indications. Doolittle and Read promised their subscribers "the works of the best American and European masters" and did give them in addition to psalmody such secular works as a minuet and "The Pastoral Nymph" for voice, harpsichord, and violin. Pieces in the magazine were tested out by pupils in the Yale singing school.

In bringing together the signs of musical progress in the decade since Billings' *New-England Psalm-Singer*, Read and the other compilers added a further sign. They acted with a professionalism foreign to the original singing school movement. When Jocelin in 1787 proposed an "Improved" edition of his *Chorister*, he wrote to Swan asking permission to use his tunes and publicly announced, in the spirit of the copyright laws secured by Andrew Law, that "No new Tunes will be printed that are incorrect nor without Leave from the Composer." [33] Thomas announced that he was printing his *LAUS DEO!* not from engraved copper or pewter plates, like every earlier New England tunebook, but from musical type, "by which he is enabled to print any kind of CHURCH, or other MUSICK, in a neat and elegant manner, and can afford to do it cheaper than such work has been heretofore done in this country. . . ." Not only did such tunebooks cost less, but more copies could be printed without wearing down the type. By contrast, Andrew Law had printed his *Select Harmony* in the family backyard, while Timothy Swan had had his music engraved by a West Springfield farmer.[34]

Yet the new professionalism, as Richard Crawford discerned, contained a trap. Typesetting demanded a large run and involved a large financial risk. Printing by engraved plates cost less, enabling little known or poor composers to bring out small editions of their works for local circulation. The tunesmiths had flourished in such informal circumstances, writing music betwixt farm chores, blocking hats, or inspecting leather. Having not much to lose financially, they composed as they wished and published when they pleased. The transition to typesetting diminished rather than increased the amount of musical publication, concentrating it in the hands of a few printers and squeezing some gifted amateurs out of business. The copyright laws which came into being at the same time covered American but not European works, resulting in more reprinting of European music. While typeset tunebooks and copyrighted music delighted the cultural nationalists, they contributed to the decline of the tunesmith tradition.

Even in strictly musical terms, this decline was already evident in the postwar tunebooks. Billings' eminence continued undiminished as he continued to publish, to instruct singers at the Old South Church, to concertize with Selby, to see his works reprinted and performed outside of New England, to be praised as "the rival of Handel." [35] His latest collection, *The Psalm-Singer's Amusement* (Boston, 1781)—published when he was thirty-five—all but boasted that the singing schools were social, not sacred institutions. Promising *Amusement* rather than pious edification, he included a large number of flamboyant anthems designed for accomplished singers who were adept at text painting and inclined to musical joking. One anthem, disdaining Billings' own definition of the form as a "divine song, generally in prose," musically imitates storm, wind, and waves, while another imitates a drunken sailor. In MODERN MUSIC the singers describe the concert they are about to give, beginning:

> We are met for a Concert of modern invention
> To tickle the Ear is our present intention. . . .

Each voice enters describing its unique activity, the bass first singing "Let the Bass take the Lead"; at each of the numerous shifts in tempo the singers sing "Then change to brisker time" or "six four is the movement that pleases us best"—the song passing through many moods, rhythms, and voices, the text describing the musical changes as they occur. As music about music, it is one of Billings' gayest and wittiest pieces. As music for use by latter-day Puritans, it seems to flout, to blaspheme, Calvin's warning that "songs composed merely to tickle and delight the ear are unbecoming the majesty of the Church. . . ." [36]

'Ear tickling' was precisely what many of the new compilers and tunesmiths opposed. Even while acknowledging their obligation to Billings' music, several had begun leaning away from it. Most of the new music—as the places of publication indicate—came by no accident from Connecticut, where the proprieties of the older Puritan orthodoxy were vigilantly maintained. Count Miranda, a reliable judge, visited the New Haven Congregational Church in 1783 and found the singing in its school "the most solemn and ecclesiastic I have heard until now on this continent." [37] The same solemnity activates the intensity of Winthrop Chandler and the Connecticut country painters, as it activated Timothy Dwight to portray revolutionary Washington as Hebraic Joshua in his *Conquest of Canäan.* Many of the new compilers shared this sensibility and expressed uneasiness over Billings' music. Jocelin, significantly subtitling his collection *Church Music Revised,* noted the "considerable revolution" in American church music, consisting of the supplanting of older tunes by "those of a more lively and airy turn." Singing had improved, he said, but at the cost of bringing into worship "light and trifling airs, more becoming the theatre or shepherd's pipe." Brownson repeated with new insistence the byword of tunebooks in the early 1760's: "The Music should bend to the words and not the words to the music." Omitting instruction in graces, he reminded his readers that the main grace is to sing "with hearts deeply affected with a sense of the great truths we utter."

Andrew Law's answer was to oppose Billings with a new gentility. In his *Collection of Hymn Tunes from the Most Modern and Approv'd Authors* (Cheshire, Connecticut, 1783), "Modern" and "Approv'd" connote the recent Italian-style hymn tunes of Martin Madan and other English composers meaningful to Law because of their orthodox harmony. In his *Collection* Law broke decisively with some earlier Congregational traditions. Billings regularly scored the melody for the tenor voice; Law scored it for the treble. Giving the melody to the treble, he explained, was "most agreeable to the principles of harmony"; the tenor should serve to "fill up and perfect the harmony." [38] Law thus took the melody away from the male singers and gave it to the female singers, replacing the 'bottom-heaviness' of the earlier Congregational sound with a genteel 'correct' sound.

Not until the 1790's would Law evolve a reformist ideology to explain and promote his shift in musical idiom. Just the same, he was onto something new, something suited to "pretty, curious" Francis Hopkinson of Philadelphia, something that would prevail over bluff, always faintly agonized William Billings of Boston.

45. The Literary Scene

Twenty years after his search for "sensible, virtuous and elegant Minds," Benjamin Franklin would no longer have found the literary scene discouraging. In 1763 the Muses seemed little inclined to migrate west. The British colonies in vast America supported not a single magazine; no one earned a living by writing; no one who could be called an American had ever published any work in any of the longer, major European literary forms. The few poems of 1763 came mostly from anonymous writers of broadsides and newspaper verses stirred by local political conflicts, and from the colonial colleges, where young men turned out genteel lyrics that displayed their provincial highmindedness. By 1770, the country still lacked many distinctive features of metropolitan literary culture. Yet increased study of modern literature in the colleges, a feeling of self assurance after the forced repeal of the Stamp and Townshend acts, and such evidence of cultural progress as the celebrity of Phillis Wheatley had all produced a new generation of poets who theorized, in long poems that made their theories believable, that literature in America must rise as inevitably as the sun.

By 1783, that sun was shining unmistakably. Literature had become, if not yet a profession, professionalized. Writers could count upon mushrooming literary magazines, copyright laws that protected their work from piracy, new sources of support and patronage. Matured during the war, the Rising Glory poets produced America's first epic poems. The first works of American fiction appeared. A new generation explored the romantic cult of feeling and pondered the need for an independent American literature. While dozens of volumes of American poetry issued from the presses, dozens of American writers were noticed and published around the world.

"At no time did Literature make so rapid a progress in America, as since the peace," reported the Massachusetts Centinel *in 1785. "It must afford real pleasure to every son of science, that our swords are* beaten into ploughshares, *and that the torch of Learning now shines with such lustre in this western hemisphere."* [1]

The desire to renew peacetime pursuits released a deluge of verse. Extremely varied in kind, but equally remote in subject from the propaganda blasts at General Gage, it ranged from book-length epics to murder ballads and new American editions of English poets, from translations by Americans of Sophocles' *Electra* to children's verses on Tom Bolin's sheepskin breeches ("The flesh-side out, and the wool-side in,/ They are charming and cool, says TOM BOLIN").[2] Whereas in 1763 American presses had issued roughly 7 items of belles-lettres, and in 1773 roughly 45 items, in 1787 they issued 105 items. Between 1773 and 1792, the number of persons and firms involved in the book trades in the major American cities doubled.[3]

Print not only increased, but like the singing schools and tunebooks it also spread across the country. As the cap and pike of Libertas gave way on mastheads and frontispieces to thirteen candles, thirteen pillars, or thirteen hands, poets no longer addressed local audiences on local issues, but pointedly referred to all thirteen states; subscription lists numbered persons from every region. Edward Taylor's poem *Werter to Charlotte* (1787) appeared in separate editions in Baltimore, New York, and Philadelphia; Philip Freneau's "The Hurricane" was published in no fewer than eight newspapers and magazines; Joseph Brown Ladd's "Prospect of America" was extracted in Philadelphia and New York and depicted in transparencies in Edenton, North Carolina.[4] Literature spread upward and downward through society as well. In Philadelphia, the bookseller Robert Bell argued the need of book auctions and book exchanges to make reading available to "every SON of ADAM, Farmer, Mechanic, or Merchant," particularly the "middling Class, (who cannot afford to keep large Collections of Books)." [5]

Magazine publishing, a telltale lack in 1763 and 1770, boomed. The lives of such excellent periodicals as the *Pennsylvania Magazine* (1776) and the *United States Magazine* (1779) had been ended after a year by political and military struggle. Now, however, the number of new magazines appearing in the two years 1786–87 exceeded the number that appeared in the twenty years from 1763 to 1783. (The boom continued; in 1789 alone, six new magazines appeared.) Not all of the new magazines were literary: Read and Doolittle's *American Musical Magazine*, discussed earlier, essentially reprinted music; the *American Monitor* (begun 1785) promoted commerce; the mediocre *New-Jersey Magazine* (begun 1786) published a bit of everything. Other new magazines combined the literary-scientific review with the newspaper. Among the best of these hybrids was the *New-Haven Gazette, and the Connecticut Magazine*, an eight-page weekly begun in 1786 by Josiah Meigs, a Yale tutor and classmate of Joel Barlow. Intensely nationalistic, it published and praised verse and essays by Dwight, Barlow, and Humphreys, offered self-satisfied accounts of West's successes in the Royal Academy, reprinted flattering English reviews of American works, and introduced poets of the new generation such as Peter Markoe and Joseph Brown Ladd. William Billings, who so far had confined his considerable literary talent to instructional prefaces and song texts, ventured to edit the first issue of *The Boston Magazine*, run by the engraver John Norman, who had cut his *Psalm-Singer's Amusement.* The issue, in October 1783, featured engraved music, an essay "On the Seduction of Young Women," and a tale of "The Life of Sawney Beane," probably by Billings. The hero of the story and his sons and grandsons have "their private members cut off, and thrown into the fire" in full sight of their wives and daughters, all of whom were "begotten in incest." "Never was anything more wretched than this first number of Mr Billings' undertaking," complained one reader.[6] In the next issue Norman profusely apologized that Billings' work had not been "correct enough for the Public Eye," and led off with a "*Disquisition on* rational Christianity." It is unclear whether readers found Billings' editorial work risqué, sloppy, or unorthodox, but in any case he returned to composing. After his departure the magazine offered a diet of Harvard writing, discourses by Reynolds, literary criticism, short fiction, and works by Byles, Dwight, Warren, Wheatley, Humphreys, and others, as well as Norman's own crude engravings of Voltaire, Franklin, Adams, and allegorical subjects.

The outstanding magazines of the immediate postwar period, however, were *The Columbian Magazine*, begun in September 1786 at a yearly subscription rate of $2.66, and *The American Museum*, begun in January 1787 at a rate of $3.33. Both were published in Philadelphia by an Irish immigrant named Mathew Carey. He had worked as a journalist in

Ireland, from which he escaped in female dress to America in 1784, twenty-four years old. Washington himself encouraged Carey, in the belief that magazines aided republicanism by disseminating knowledge: "I consider such easy vehicles of knowledge," he told Carey, "more happily calculated than any other, to preserve the liberty, stimulate the industry and meliorate the morals of an enlightened and free People." [7]

Modeled on the leading English magazines, Carey's *Columbian Magazine* was the most ambitious periodical yet published in America. Its declared policy was to add to evidences of American success in arms "cotemporary evidence of the progress of literature and the arts among her citizens. . . ." [8] Gathering such evidence from agriculture, natural science, chess, music, literature, and architecture, it printed the best currently being thought, written, invented, or investigated in America—essays on Francis Hopkinson's new method of harpsichord quilling, extracts from Jefferson's *Notes on Virginia*, early notices of the architecture of Charles Bulfinch, puffs for West and Copley, and a monthly section called "The Columbian Parnassiad" devoted to native poetry. Owing to the engravings of Carey's partner, James Trenchard, the magazine was also by far the best graphically to have existed in America.

For some reason, Carey withdrew from the *Columbian Magazine* after several months and began *The American Museum, or Repository of Ancient and Modern Fugitive Pieces, Prose and Poetical.* As the subtitle suggests, the magazine specialized in printing or reprinting American writing of the past and present, especially long works. The first issue ran ninety-six pages. In this ample format Carey could print works whole that other magazines reduced to snippets or serialized. He reprinted all of *Common Sense*, devoted twenty-three double-column pages to David Humphreys, and gave thirty double-column pages to reprinting Trumbull's complete *M'Fingal*. He performed one other unique and extraordinarily valuable service. In both magazines he printed earlier American poetry, keeping alive a sense of American literary tradition—poems by Godfrey and Evans, the *Carmen Seculare* of the early eighteenth century Maryland poet Richard Lewis, the lengthy poem *New-England* by William Morrell, first published in 1625. The *Museum* also featured a section of "Select Poetry," often of ten double-column pages, including shorter verse by Hopkinson, Ladd, Freneau, Dwight, Humphreys, Tucker, and others. Together with its very large and judicious assortment of native poetry, the magazine reprinted lengthy political works of consistently high quality and in a high-republican tone. Carey's serious political and literary intent impressed the French traveler Brissot de Warville, who considered the magazine "equal to the best periodicals of Europe." [9] In providing a "Museum" for the preservation of past American poetry and a showcase for the best American poetry of the present, Carey made the abundance of sensible and elegant American minds impressively visible.

The many new postwar magazines not only made available and kept in print vastly more American poetry than ever before; they also gave American poetry a wider market and larger audience than ever before. Literature was becoming a business. With the restoration of peace came a turning-point in the continued agitation for copyright laws. On March 17, 1783, Massachusetts passed "An Act for the Purpose of securing to Authors the exclusive Right and Benefit of publishing their Literary Production, for Twenty-one Years." [10] In Connecticut, a decisive battle was brought on by a second edition of *M'Fingal* published in Hartford in September 1782. The work was pirated by another Hartford printer, who purveyed an incorrectly printed text at a third less than the original half-dollar price, cheating Trumbull of a financial return and jeopardizing his reputation. Outraged, Trumbull's friends began a campaign to protect literary property.

Timothy Dwight brought the matter before the Connecticut General Assembly in the spring of 1783 and managed to have passed "An Act for the Encouragement of Literature and Genius," securing to authors in the state a fourteen-year copyright, renewable for another fourteen years should they continue to live. Joel Barlow also took up Trumbull's cause, the more passionately because of his own experience. Orphaned, poor, and struggling to establish a literary career, he believed that the paucity of wealth in America made a copyright indispensable: "As we have few Gentlemen of fortune sufficient to enable them to spend a whole life in study, or enduce [sic] others to do it by their patronage, it is more necessary, in this country than in any other, that the rights of authors should be secured by law." Barlow sent a copy of the Connecticut law to Congress, which gave it to a committee, including James Madison, for consideration. The committee reported back just two weeks after ratifying the peace treaty, recommending that the states pass legislation granting copyright of not less than fourteen years, renewable for another term, "to secure to the authors or publishers of any new books not hitherto printed, being citizens of the United States." [11] Several states followed the lead of Massachusetts and Connecticut. Noah Webster managed to secure a Maryland copyright for the works of his friend Andrew Law. In 1786 the New York legislature passed "An Act to Promote Literature" providing, like Connecticut, a fourteen-year copyright with a fourteen-year renewal.

Legal recognition of literature as property gave literary dealings a brusque, no-longer-dilettantish tone. In his *American Magazine* Noah Webster served notice that "this publication circulates as the Editor's property," and threatened suits for infringement. When Carey asked permission to reprint *M'Fingal*, Trumbull's response was no blush of thanks: "I should have no objection to the sale of the copyright, and would give you, if you wish it, the first offer of the purchase." Jeremy Belknap received a guinea for each three printed pages he contributed to the *Columbian Magazine*. As a contributor also to the *American Museum*, the *American Magazine*, and the later *Massachusetts Magazine*, he became probably the first free-lance magazine writer in America, sought by competing editors who wished to publish parts of his large collection of literary and historical documents.[12]

Literary sales were boosted by public endorsements and by new sources of patronage. The creation of such luminously heroic names as Washington in turn created and sold new volumes of poetry. As Timothy Dwight told John Adams, "literary merit forms a species of claim, from necessity, to the fostering influence of eminent personages." [13] The claim was justified not only by "necessity," however, but also by familiarity, acknowledging the fact that poets of the period like Humphreys and Barlow moved easily in military and political circles, just as politicians and soldiers like Jefferson and Lafayette moved easily in artistic ones.

Many writers sought patronage from revolutionary figures, but particularly from Washington. Noah Webster stressed to the former commander that his support for the arts would be "a continuation of your public utility." Washington himself was entirely willing to become an American Maecenas, certain that "every effort of genius, and all attempts towards improving useful knowledge ought to meet with encouragement in this country." [14] His desire to encourage was gratified in the many who desired his encouragement. To Dwight, Barlow, Humphreys, and the other poets who dedicated works to him, Washington represented not only Cincinnatus but a soldier-scholar who had protected the arts during the war. In dedicating his *Lyric Works of Horace* (Philadelphia, 1786) to Washington, John Parke observed that "The whole circle of arts and sciences, is bound to you, by every sacred tie of gratitude and affection. It was your influence that encouraged, and your arms that supported the drooping spirit of learning, through the toils and perils. . . ." The addition of Washington's name to the subscription list of some proposed magazine or poem became at once an imprimatur of correct republican sentiment, a mark of the country's willingness to go its own way, and no doubt a goad to others to subscribe their own names. The *American Museum* flaunted the names of Washington, Franklin, Hamilton, Madison, Peale, and Jefferson at the head of a list of hundreds of prominent subscribers; in his *Vision of Columbus* (discussed later in this section) Barlow included, largely in double columns and small print, an eleven-page list of subscribers headed by Washington, Lafayette, Franklin, and Paine.

The proliferation of literary magazines and the possibility of patronage encouraged young writers and gave them not only an audience but a market such as had not existed for the Rising Glory poets of the 1770's. Among many of these new writers, however, the sentimentalism of the 1760's and 1770's—the patriots beweeping "fair Liberty," the affectionate presences in Peale's family groups—had ripened into a romantic cultivation of feeling for its own sake. Perhaps the war, with its scenes of real distress and real tears, postponed the appearance of romantic sensibility in America. The war over, however, a new generation exulted in unhappiness, greatness of soul, and alienated genius.

The idol of the young was no longer the gallant, languishing Wolfe, but his offspring, The Man of Sorrow. A pivotal date was February 1784, when Robert Bell advertised for sale in Philadelphia Goethe's "Sorrows and Sympathetic Attachments of WERTER." As Goethe himself described it, the novel concerns "a young man, gifted with deep, unspoiled sensitivity and penetrating insight, who loses himself in visionary dreams, undermines himself by empty speculations until finally, deranged by unhappy passions he experiences, especially an unending love, he puts a bullet in his head." _The Sorrows of Young Werther_ (Werter) affected American society and literature in the 1780's quite as much as _Cato_ two decades before. As young diarists in the sixties recorded the exchange of pastoral verses by "Damon" and as those in the seventies recorded rousing liberty songs, the young merchant Robert Hunter visited a southern plantation in 1786 and recorded reading to a young woman the "interesting but unfortunate story" of Werter.[15] Carey published selections from _Werter_ in his _Columbian Magazine_. The Irishman Edward Taylor's _Werter to Charlotte. A Poem_ went through three American editions in 1787, allowing American readers to understand "pleasing pain" and "fierce sensations." _Werter_ was advertised on the back of Thomas Coombe's _The Peasant of AUBURN_ (Philadelphia, 1784 and 1786), which itself contained "The Highwayman's Soliloquy" on the twin themes of the despair of the poor ("Oh stain, to human sensibility!") and of the noble criminal.

The young poet of the 1780's most directly in the line of American literature that was to develop through Charles Brockden Brown, Edgar Allan Poe, and Herman Melville was Joseph Brown Ladd, born in Newport in 1764. He wrote his first poem at ten (published in the _Newport Mercury_), studied medicine with a Rhode Island physician, and opened a practice in Charleston, where in 1786 was published his _Poems of Arouet_. The volume included several poems on Werter, "the son of _Sorrow_ and _Distress_," to whom nature gave "passions, as she virtue gave;/ But gave not power those passions to suppress." Ladd showed the result of Werter's too-great feeling in his wrenching suicide:

CHARLOTTE I go!—my pistols have their load:
My last, my dying thoughts are fix'd on you!
I go! I go thro' death's untrodden road;
Once, and forever, CHARLOTTE—Oh! Adieu!

As the chief American exponent of extreme, Goethean sensibility, Ladd was immensely popular. Carey devoted the whole of a "Select Poetry" column to his verse. Ladd displayed sensibility in his own life. Too sensitive to "be deaf to the distressed invalid," he provided two hours each day of free medical care for the poor, announcing that *"The pleasure of doing good is . . . the only enjoyment that can reconcile us to the woes and miseries inseparably annexed to human life."* [16] After his leg was shattered in a duel with another Charlestonian, Ladd died, at the age of twenty-two, consummating his role as the first American romantic poet.

What further distinguishes the literary scene of 1783 from that of 1763 or 1770 is the dawning of genuine literary nationalism. The magazines, the long subscription lists, the arrival of distinguished foreigners like Houdon, Pine, and Reinagle, the new poets, the sheer weight of print had of course been prophesied for the last fifty years. To older observers they simply represented the inevitable fulfillment of the theory of cultural progress. What seemed in 1763 a consoling hope was now an accomplished fact; Bishop Berkeley had been right. As one versifier put it, commenting on the visit to Boston of the learned English Whig historian Catharine Macaulay:

BERKELEY the wise, deep skill'd in fates dark lore,
And distant times mysterious sybil page,
With brighten'd optics, saw from Albion's shore
Retiring Genius quit the dawning age.
. . . .
She [Mrs. Macaulay] comes, she comes, see pensive Britain weep,
Her arts, her arms, adorn this infant clime.

The empire to the east lay abandoned. "England was," reported the *Massachusetts Centinel*, "in days of yore, the seat of philosophy, and the most distinguished of all the Arts and Sciences; but now it is become the asylum of vagabonds and imposters. . . ." In 1786 John Adams summed up the drift of the last two decades: "The Muses," he wrote, "have crossed the Atlantic. . . ." [17]

Americans, to repeat, had been charting the process of Translation since the 1760's, and before. But while the Rising Glory writers of 1770, after examining the dynamics of history, had looked forward to American writers of excellence in a transnational Republic of Letters, those of 1783 looked forward to writers both excellent and different. The arts must not only cross the Atlantic; they must, like the migrants themselves, become Americanized. "Let the learned of our Country," demanded one broadside in 1787, "no longer shine in borrowed . . . but in their own native Lustre. . . . Let us encourage literary Genius wherever we find it. Let us think for ourselves, and make our own Books. . . ." [18] In calling for an end to "servile Imitation," some literary nationalists had in mind the fact that the war had created a precious and memorable common experience which those outside the country could neither appreciate nor fully understand. The author of *Female Fortitude; or, the Powers of Love . . . Found amongst the Papers of a brave Officer, who was killed at the General Captivity of York-Town* (Philadelphia, 1784) appealed especially to the "patriotic Sons of America, who have drawn the Sword of Liberty" as the persons who "will feel a Sympathy in the perusal of these Scenes, as they pourtray the various Vicissitudes of INVASION, CIVIL-WAR, LOVE, DANGER and DISTRESS, from which we were lately and happily relieved." Not only would those outside the country misunderstand what Americans had lived through and needed to write about; a moribund Europe that could not support its own writers would plainly be too envious to support or praise American writers, who were in part responsible for its decline. "The United States must encourage their own Poets as well as Warriors," John Adams told Joel Barlow, "or they will be discouraged—all Europe is too jealous of both to do this Duty for us." Americans, said the *New-Haven Gazette*, must "be taught to revere themselves. . . ." [19]

These bold demands suggest a concerted program, yet they came from a mixed chorus of poets and ideologues who had varying conceptions of "American" and differing kinds of interest in literature. Many who had lived through the war conceived the nation as some vague superpower containing their ex-colony, Congress, the Crown, Washington, and a group of united states. Cultural nationalism, also, is by definition as much a political as an artistic stance. In calling for an American literature, most political nationalists required little more than that writers style themselves "American." Others dimly hoped that claiming a national identity might help to create one. The more purely literary—precursors of the searching nationalism of the nineteenth century—sensed that American writers might have to have their own language, subjects, and forms. Yet the several kinds of nationalists, from the purely jingoistic to the seriously literary, summed up their different expectations in the same demand that Americans "make our own books." Containing husks of the theory of Rising Glory, germs of romantic nationalism, and virulent demands for ill-defined greatness, the nationalism of 1783 was diffuse and protean, like the shapeless power in the mind of its advocates.

Responses to the call for works about, for, and praised by Americans also varied in seriousness, clarity, and intent. One response was a relentless invocation of the word "American." From American presses came the *Lyric Works of Horace . . . By a Native of America; Select Poems . . . chiefly American; Winter Display'd, A Poem . . . By an American; Effusions of Female Fancy. By a Young Lady, of America*; and *Lessons for Lovers* by "Ovid Americanus." The publisher of Ladd's *Poems of Arouet* appealed to "AMERICANS!" to buy a work *"produced by one of the earliest of the American bards. . . ."* Carey promised American poems on "neat paper, of American manufacture," with engravings "by an American artist." [20] The Americanness of such works often stopped at the byline. The scenes of civil war and distress promised in *Female Fortitude*—the work which asked special understanding from the "Sons of America, who have drawn the Sword of Liberty"—turn out to have occurred in the time of King Canute and Ethelred the Unready.

If often nominal, "By an American" was a powerful slogan that excited the market for American poetry, multiplying the number of American poems in print and prompting the publication of collected editions of earlier American poets. Shortly after the Peace appeared the first American edition of Phillis Wheatley's *Poems on Various Subjects* (Philadelphia, 1786, originally published in London more than a decade earlier); David Humphreys' *Select Poems* (Philadelphia, 1787); and the *Poems of Philip Freneau Written Chiefly During the Late War* (Philadelphia, 1786), a 407-page work whose sustained vigor and fertile imagination make it the first esthetically interesting volume of collected poems by an American to be published in America. Motions were made toward compiling the first anthologies of American poetry. Carey undertook an anthology of "all the American poets of reputation," while some Connecticut writers planned what Barlow called "a collection of American Poems, somewhat in the manner of Dodsley." [21] What they meant by "manner" is unclear, but the English publisher Robert Dodsley's *Collection of Poems by several hands* ran six volumes.

Feeling that Europeans could not understand American works and would be too envious to praise them, American poets praised each other. Dozens of postwar poems by Ladd, Barlow, Humphreys, and others unrolled long catalogues of the American poets, and often the painters, deserving admiration, characterizing the work of each and offering the list as proof of cultural progress. John Parke praised Philip Freneau's "soul-cutting pen" for exposing the "star-garter'd villain, the scoundrel in pow'r," and placed him in the line of patriot-writers made famous by their commitment to liberty:

> Your name to bright honor, the spirits shall lift,
> That glow'd in the bosoms of Churchill and Swift.

In his *Vision of Columbus*, Joel Barlow devoted a paragraph each to praising Trumbull's "skillful hand," which "Hurls the keen darts of Satire thro' the land"; "seraphic" Dwight, whose "voice divine revives the promised land"; and gallant Humphreys, who "Roused the sad realms to urge the unfinish'd war." Humphreys in turn lauded Barlow's "conscious genius bold," which "sings the new world happier than the old." The death of Phillis Wheatley in 1784—at about the age of thirty and shortly after the death of her two children and the jailing of her husband—brought eulogistic praise from Joseph Brown Ladd, who placed her with Barlow and Freneau for the "force of numbers, in her polish'd lines." [22]

These and scores of similar tributes were as much political as literary. No one praised James Rivington, who had printed the best Loyalist verse of the war. Indeed he was forced to close down his newspaper and even his printing office, which had served for several decades as an outstanding music shop, bookstore, and painting gallery. Unable to support his eight children, he spent time in debtor's prison. When the Loyalist poet Joseph Stansbury returned to Philadelphia in 1785, the Philadelphia press reported that this "attainted and proscribed character" was about to be "constituted *Poet Laureat*" to "*Canaille*, lately imported from the *three Kingdoms*." [23] He was driven away.

Not all of the literary nationalists limited themselves to praising Whig works printed on American paper. A few began dealing with problems of language and subject, although without the profundity or urgency of the great American romantic writers. How should the language of an independent America differ from British English? What should Americans, lacking a highly evolved social life and artistic traditions, write about? For several reasons, these questions were more difficult to answer in 1850 than in 1783, before a central government had been established and before significant westward expansion. The desire for an American English was satisfied merely by nationalizing the emerging romantic creed of simplicity and informality, while a shared reverence for events that were at once heroic and domestic satisfied the desire for American subjects.

The postwar call for an American language was only the latest stage of older, independent developments in education and politics. Since midcentury, prominent colonial educators had tried to supplant the classical curriculum by the study of modern literature. The war politicized the distinction: Many Whigs equated Latinity with monarchy, Saxon plainness with liberty. John Witherspoon, president of Princeton, observed that "Absolute monarchies, and the obsequious subjection introduced at the courts of princes, occasions a pompous swelling and compliment to be in request, different from the boldness and sometimes ferocity of republican states." Another writer in 1776 claimed that "since the Declaration of

Independence, the colonies have divorced monarchy forever, and become free, independent states. It becomes then necessary to adopt the simple language of free governments." The postwar nationalists continued this older attack on classical study and a high style, but in the name of Americanness. In an oration "On the Learned Languages" in 1786, Francis Hopkinson told Americans to use plain names, since the mere sounds of *"imperial crown"* and *"lord chancellor"* created Tories. Joseph Brown Ladd blasted the great English Tory Samuel Johnson for his "swelled, pompous, bombastical language . . . affected structure, and verbosity of style." Students reared in the new federal university proposed by Benjamin Rush would hear no lectures about Palmyra and Herculaneum or any other "offal learning." [24]

The desire for a utilitarian, democratic style intelligible to all, hence appropriate to American life, was largely met by Hugh Blair's *Lectures on Rhetoric and Belles Lettres* (1782), first published in America in 1784. Its stated aim was "to explode false ornament, to direct attention more towards substance than show, to recommend good sense as the foundation of all good composition, and simplicity as essential to all true ornament." [25] Blair became the bible of linguistic nationalists. Widely extracted in the postwar magazines, his book was adopted as a text at Yale in 1785 and at Harvard three years later. Before 1835 it went through some forty editions and abridgments, shaping the prose of several generations of rising lawyers, ministers, and poets. The question of an American language, of course, involved more than simplicity, and was not settled until the time of Emerson and Whitman, if then.

Writers of the 1780's just as readily solved the question of indigenous subjects, since they felt no lack of native materials. Many believed that the country possessed two great, unique subjects: American nature and the American Revolution. If the country had no pyramids and ruins to inspire its poets, it did have a majestic, no less inspiring landscape, as one literary nationalist explained in 1786:

> The face of nature, throughout the united states *[sic]*, exhibits the *sublime and beautiful,* in the most exalted degree. In almost every part of this country, we are surrounded with objects calculated to inspire the most elevated conceptions of the imagination. Our mountains, vallies, plains, and rivers, are formed upon a great scale; the extent of the country itself is great; and the whole is rendered magnificently beautiful, by the creating hand of the almighty architect.

The task of American poets would be to hallow the American landscape by revering it themselves, by affording it deserved recognition as equal to the legendary places of the Old World. "Lycurgus" proposed creating an

"American Poet Laureat" who, "warmed by the charms of nature in his rural abode," would attempt to "raise a new Parnassus on the Allegany mountains, and open a second Helicon at the source of the Potowmack." [26] In asserting the sufficiency of American nature for the purposes of high art, the postwar nationalists at least started down the road of the later romantics, who did elevate the country by drawing inspiration from pickerel at Walden Pond and leaves of grass on Long Island.

The recent American past also seemed to many nationalists a store of dramatic themes and images:

> . . . if we contemplate the eminently dignified part that has been recently acted on the vast national stage; with the scenes of magnanimity, wisdom, and patriotic virtue, which our gallant countrymen have exhibited thereon: we must allow, that nothing can afford more noble themes for our native bards.[27]

Indeed, the Revolution had already provided the factual base for much well-known American writing of the next seventy-five years—the Jane M'Creas, the Spys, the George Washingtons who would act in tales by Hawthorne, novels by Cooper and Melville, poems by Longfellow. The innumerable heroes, villains, and exploits already existing in print and in memory were increased by new histories and travel books like William Robertson's *History of America* and Abbé Robin's *New Travels Through North America* (both advertised in 1784), by quantities of engravings, tracts, biographies, pamphlets, and anecdotes of the war pouring from the press, and by dozens of songs and poems freshly written to celebrate Independence Day, Washington's birthday, and the like.

Out of this wealth of material came the first American fiction. Before the war, nothing that could be called a novel had been written in America, while only five pieces of extended fiction had appeared in American magazines—results partly of the relatively high cost of publishing new novels and the ease of pirating or importing them. A market for fiction clearly existed, since prewar journals and letters record widespread reading of novels. The question of whether novels made desirable reading was frequently argued in the prewar press, and had many proponents. Thomas Jefferson told his nephew in 1770 that fiction surpassed history as a moral instructor because it offers more lessons than history and arouses the "sympathetic emotion of virtue," making us feel for others. On the other hand, a considerable body of opinion since colonial times insisted that novel reading was harmful. Echoing English detractors of fiction, the critics held that novels inspired romantic expectations in the young, whose time was better spent otherwise, and whose powers of discernment were overtaxed in sorting out the images of vice and virtue which fiction presented. The lawyer Alexander Graydon, for example, told of reading

Samuel Richardson's *Clarissa* for relief from his law studies and finding
that the seducer Lovelace's "unrelenting villany . . . was so relieved by
great qualities . . . that the feeling of detestation was intermingled with
admiration and respect"—inspiring a friend of his not to revulsion but to
imitation.[28] John Trumbull in his *Progress of Dulness* (1772) also complained against sentimental novels for teaching not the wages of sin but the
arts of seduction:

> Thus *Harriet* reads, and reading really
> Believes herself a young *Pamela*,
> The high-wrought whim, the tender strain
> Elate her mind and turn her brain:
> Before her glass, with smiling grace,
> She views the wonders of her face;
> There stands in admiration moveless,
> And hopes a *Grandison*, or *Lovelace*.

Such complaints, coupled with the risk and cost involved to publishers,
clearly retarded the appearance of American works of fiction.

With the postwar literary boom, however, American magazines began
publishing a plethora of short and medium-length fiction. In stories like
"The Castle of Costanzo," American writers began to explore the weird
natural phenomena, castles, and tombs associated with the Gothic aspect
of sensibility,[29] while in other works appeared the republican farmer, the
slave, the Yankee, the Irish immigrant, and other native types. The
Columbian Magazine in 1787 began serializing two interesting native works
of fiction, although neither is long enough to be called the first American
novel. In *The Foresters, an American Tale*, Jeremy Belknap created a satirical
allegory of American relations with Britain, from the time of Elizabeth
through the Revolution. His narrative concerns "John Bull," whose
mother (the Anglican church) decides that "every one of the family must
hold knife and fork and spoon exactly alike; that they must all . . . sit,
stand, walk, kneel, bow, spit, blow their noses, and perform every other
animal function by the exact rule of *uniformity*." As a result, "John
Codline" (the Massachusetts settlers) moves to the "forest" (America).
Envious of what John Codline accomplishes in the forest, John Bull thinks:
"Those fellows live too well in the forest; they thrive too fast; the place is
too good for them; they ought to know who is their master; they can afford
to pay more rent. . . ."[30] The result is the Stamp Act, then the
Revolution. Belknap produced a comic history of America similar in
technique and spirit to Washington Irving's *Knickerbocker History*, which it
probably influenced.

More sentimental use of revolutionary material was made by the
anonymous author of *Amelia: or the Faithless Briton*. This "history of female

affliction" recounts private tragedies such as "the historian has neither leisure nor disposition to commemorate." It proved very popular, appearing in several magazines besides the *Columbian*, and in several separate publications later, including a German translation in Baltimore.[31] The action concerns a dissolute British officer of noble birth. Through pretended sensibility he lures a seventeen-year-old American girl named Amelia into a staged marriage ceremony. Pregnant and abandoned, she pursues him to England, where he scornfully reveals the hoax, causing her to give birth prematurely in a London hovel. Only the miraculous intervention of her father—who has followed her from America—stays her from swallowing a vial of laudanum. Amelia's brother challenges the seducer of his now-deranged sister, kills him, and returns to America in time for the Battle of Monmouth, where he dies. In its fifty or so pages, *Amelia* represents the most ambitious work of American fiction so far. Its adaption of revolutionary materials to the moral tale betrays a growing disengagement from the political concerns that preoccupied writers throughout the last decade. More and more during the 1780's, atrocities and escapades that had been used for propaganda became used simply for plot.

Two other American works of fiction were written at around this time, but published later. *The History of Maria Kittle*, written toward the end of the war, remained unpublished until 1790. Its author, Ann Eliza Bleecker, lived in an exposed upstate New York settlement, where she lost a daughter, a sister, and her mother in Indian attacks.[32] Her *History*, for all its Gothic and sentimental overtones, is a violent shoot-'em-up. In one episode of vivid butchery, the Indians first kill a man, then

> . . . mangle the corpse, and having made an incision round his head with a crooked knife, they tugged off his bloody scalp with barbarous triumph. While this was perpetrating, an Indian, hediously *[sic]* painted, strode ferociously up to Comelia, (who sunk away at the sight, and fainted on a chair) and clift her white forehead deeply with his tomahack *[sic]*. . . . His sanguinary soul was not yet satisfied with blood; he deformed her lovely body with deep gashes, and tearing her unborn babe away, dashed it to pieces against the stone wall. . . .

Fiction of another order, indeed one of the best early American works, is the *Journal of Llewellin Penrose, a Seaman*. Although it carries the date-line "New York May 2, 1783," it was not published until 1815. The work is doubly revealing as the product of the portraitist William Williams, one of Benjamin West's first teachers. The story is told through the supposed journal of a Welsh sailor marooned for twenty-five years on an island off Nicaragua. Between moral commentary on the inscrutability of Providence and the need to reconcile oneself to circumstances, Penrose records his marriages to native women, the birth of his mulatto children, his handling of interlopers, his painterly impressions of cashews, parrots, yams, and other tropical flora and fauna. The *Journal* shares with Williams' family groups and conversation pieces a benign view of human pretension and awkwardness that always stops short of satire. Williams' sincerity and affection give the work an uncanny verisimilitude. Lord Byron stayed up half the night reading it, finding that it had "all the air of truth. . . ." [33] The illusion of a real, not a contrived, journal derives also from Williams' unexpected skill in rendering dialect and conceiving his characters, while the felt and touchingly conveyed deaths of Penrose's wives and children perhaps draw their power from Williams' loss of his sons in battles of the Revolution. Penrose's descriptions of his exotic surroundings constantly recall the Caribbean poems of Philip Freneau, with whom Penrose shares a desire to escape a barbaric world. But pirates, warmongers, and slave drivers keep intruding on the idyllic moonlit turtle hunts and merry marriage nights. These disruptions give the work a deeper moral quality that surfaces toward the end, with the introduction of a black hermit from Guinea, whose hate-filled tale of harrowing removals from one slave master to another is a malediction on white civilization.

However gladdening the abundance of new magazines, volumes of poetry, and native fiction, the showpiece of the new nationalism was the epic poem. As the literary form generically concerned with national origins, the epic was itself an outgrowth and a mark of nationhood. Since it was the most difficult and ambitious literary form as well, so long as the country lacked an epic the Muses could not be said to have crossed the Atlantic. Even the first visions of *Translatio studii* foresaw the creation of an epic of the New World, Berkeley himself prophesying

> There shall be sung another golden age,
>   The rise of empire and of arts,
> The good and great inspiring epic rage. . . .

Several generations later, the college Rising Glory poets of the 1770's still looked forward to America having—as a Dartmouth speaker described the epic—"the noblest Production of Man. . . ." In 1785, John Adams still was hoping, as he said, "to see our young America in Possession of an Heroic Poem, equal to those the most esteemed in any Country." [34]

What perhaps supplied the commitment and the lasting drive needed to fulfill this half-century-old hope was a general heightening of ambition during and after the war, a feeling that great things had been and could be accomplished. As Thucydides pointed out, revolutionary times demand no other qualities so much as energy and boldness. Boldness and energy characterized much of postrevolutionary society—the many large magazines, the large new tunebooks, the opulent peace celebrations, the huge, larger-than-life canvases of West and Copley, the festival concerts of Adgate and Selby, the new scale of effort. What Ezra Stiles noticed about divinity students at Yale in 1787 was true, in their own way, of many postwar musicians, painters, and writers: "They all want to be Luthers." [35]

The first American epic poem was Timothy Dwight's *The Conquest of Canäan*. It was in progress throughout the Revolution, being written at military camps and in New Haven, Hartford, and Northampton.[36] By 1776, Dwight had completed a first draft, and had printed proposals for its publication, which the imminent Revolution made impossible. A second stage of composition began when Dwight returned to Yale as a senior tutor in 1777; he then inserted into his completed epic two whole new books, Three and Five, comprising the romance of Irad and Selima, irrelevant except as a gift to his new bride. Shortly after, Congress approved Dwight as chaplain to Parson's Connecticut Brigade at Peekskill. Here the poem underwent additional revision as his camp experiences inspired panegyrics to various revolutionary heroes. The poem remained unpublished even at the conclusion of the war because Dwight wished to secure copyright protection before releasing it. Meanwhile he settled down as pastor of the church in Greenfield Hill, Connecticut; thirty years old, he earned a reputation in some quarters as a superb preacher and in others as "a compleat bigot on the plan of his grandfather, Mr. Edwards." [37] The poem finally appeared in Hartford in 1785, dedicated, inevitably, to Washington: "Commander in chief of the American Armies, The Saviour of his Country, The Supporter of Freedom, And the Benefactor of Mankind."

Essentially *The Conquest of Canäan* recounts the Israelite battles against the peoples of Ai and Gibeon as related in the central chapters of the Book of Joshua, culminating in Joshua's victory over the Canaanites. The biblical action, occupying only four short chapters, is filled out into eleven books of closed couplets—by far the longest poem yet written and published in America—by the addition of lengthy speeches, protracted battle scenes, epic devices, testimonials to American heroes, poets, and painters, and the love story. Although Dwight knew Homer first-hand, and saw carnage close up, it was from Pope that he drew his battle scenes. He extensively copied the Miltonic manner and tone, bringing many of his epic characters onstage with some variation of Milton's celebrated picture of Satan in *Paradise Lost*, Book Two: "High in the van exalted Irad strode"—a formula used by poets throughout the Revolution to introduce Gage, Hutchinson, or some other detested Englishman. The structure as well as the language of the *Conquest* is Miltonic. Dwight's consultation of the leaders of Israel—like many Revolutionary verse treatments of the ministerial conspiracy—parallels Milton's infernal council.

Like the painter John Trumbull, Dwight found room in his battle scenes for expressions of romantic sublimity. Unrestrained by Trumbull's sobering concern for documentation, however, he piled up storm-tossed oceans, earthquakes, tempests, thunder, trembling heavens, whirlwinds, gales, blood-red skies, and hosts of murmuring widows, lending his hundreds of lines of battle-description the roaring fury of elemental nature:

> As when two seas, by winds together hurl'd,
> With bursting fury shake the solid world;
> Waves pil'd o'er waves, the watery mountains rise,
> And foam, and roar, and rage, against the skies:
> So join'd the combat; ranks, o'er ranks impell'd,
> Swell'd the hoarse tumult of the hideous field;
> Black drifts of dust becloud the gloomy ground;
> Hoarse groans ascend, and clashing arms resound.
> And now, where Zimri broke th' embodied war,
> Imperious Hoham drove his sounding car;
> Like flames, his rapid courses rush'd along,
> Forc'd a red path, and crush'd the thickening throng. . . .

This flood of bombast rushes the reader unawares past many unprepared and inexplicable shifts in point-of-view, the results of Dwight's addition to the completed poem of the romance of Irad and Selima. Dwight masked the irrelevance of this sentimental subplot by involving his lovers in a half-dozen harrowing skirmishes, written in the sublime style, and padded with didactic asides on art and nature. The swollen, repetitious verse serves to disguise the otherwise glaring mismanagement of the action, and the result is by turns tiresome and bewildering.

Most of Dwight's contemporaries read the poem as an allegory of the Revolution, with Washington represented by Joshua. This interpretation irked Dwight, who denied any allegorical intent. It was absurd, he said, to imagine "the *Conquest* of a country a proper event, under which to allegorize the *defence* of another country." Nevertheless, that is approximately what Dwight did. American affairs had been treated in the guise of biblical narrative since the Puritans, to whom the story of the flight from Egypt seemed a glowingly meaningful type of their own migration to the New World. Revolutionary writers, particularly in New England, gave these traditional parallels new life. After the British evacuated Boston in 1776, for instance, a Cambridge minister preached a sermon before Washington on Exodus 14:25: "And we took off their chariot wheels, that they drave them heavily; so that the Egyptians said, Let us flee from the

face of Israel, for the Lord fighteth for them against the Egyptians."
Broadside verses on General Burgoyne a year later compared the salvation
of America to the parting of the Red Sea:

> 14. Had not the Lord for us appear'd,
> When George the tyrant frowned,
> We should have been, 'tis to be fear'd
> Like Pharaoh's army drowned.[38]

A biblical poem on a patriotic theme would have been no novelty in
revolutionary America, or in America at any time since 1630, or indeed in
an age which produced West's painting of *Saul and the Witch of Endor* and
Handel's *Judas Maccabeus*. *The Conquest of Canäan* is simply an ambitious
historicist attempt to body forth current ideals. Dwight's disavowal is
probably owing to the fact that he intermittently dropped and renewed his
design of matching the American and Israelite causes, as the biblical
narrative allowed.

Like West's Agrippina, then, Joshua-Washington is, one and inseparable, an Ideal Republican and an Ideal Spouse. Dwight transformed the
warlike Old Testament Joshua—who at one point leads Israel in stoning
and burning a Canaanite family to death—into a caring consort, notable
for practical temper and clear judgment, soberly Calvinistic in his estimate
of human personality. What fits Joshua for leadership is not some fanciful
political vision but his exemplary family life. He extends the tried methods
of domestic government to the whole nation: "At once his friends, his race,
his Maker, serv'd;/ At once his own domestic bliss preserv'd." His military
genius consists not in desperate sallies but in levelheaded plans that enable
him to capitalize on the enemy's "childish rage." Joshua is a teacher whose
self-governance, reverence for God, and sobriety set a precedent for
American character and teach the nation how to rule.

Dwight came closest to identifying the Israelite and American causes in
the debate between Joshua and Hanniel in Book One, which reenacts the
prewar debate over Independence. Hanniel, an Old Testament Tory, lists
the advantages of monarchy: Regal trappings enhance authority; tribute
is justified because the Crown will protect Israel-America from the
imperial designs of other nations, and "who share the blessing must the tax
supply." Joshua, a radical Whig patriarch, warns that despite Hanniel's
theory, the purely practical consequences of returning to Egypt must be
disastrous. History empirically exposes the failure of monarchical rule:
"Scarce can each age a single king confess,/ Who knew to govern, or who
wish'd to bless." Returned to Egypt-England, Israelite children, sharing
the corruptible nature of men, would copy Egypt's corrupt manners and
debased worship. In the prosperity of its alien minority, an envious Egypt
would see its own ruin, and would seek revenge against Israel. He answers

Hanniel's doubts that the disparate Israelite tribes can unite, without faction or tyranny, by asserting that the Israelite-Americans are inspired by a single character, a communal will:

> By friendship's ties, religion's bands combin'd,
> By birth united, and by interest join'd,
> In the same view our every wish conspires,
> One spirit actuates, and one genius fires;
> Plain, generous manners vigorous limbs confess,
> And vigorous minds to freedom ardent press. . . .

To this vigor and plainness, monarchy is repugnant and humiliating.

The Conquest of Canäan begot the largest critical response yet afforded any American poem. Most English reviewers disliked it. Thomas Day defied "the most resolute reader to wade through it without yawning an hundred times." Such comments confirmed the nationalists' belief that American writers could not look overseas for praise. For many Americans, the appearance of Dwight's poem was a *rite de passage* in which they attained full cultural maturity. The poet Trumbull—although he accused Dwight of prolixity—compiled a list of epic poets in which Homer and Milton shared the first place, and on which Dwight appeared eighth, after Edmund Spenser and Ossian but before Lucan and Statius. The painter Trumbull began drawings based on passages from Dwight's epic, one showing a skeleton Death brandishing his spear amidst sprawling corpses, entitled "Joshua Attended by Death at the Battle of Ai." Satisfying an old hope for a heroic poem of the New World, *The Conquest of Canäan* was the literary equivalent of "a Raphael, or a West." "Excepting Paradise Lost," John Adams boasted in 1786, "I know of nothing Superiour in any modern Language." [39]

Dwight translated into the events of ancient history an ideal of American character, a sense of the personality appropriate to republicans. To be an American, he and others felt, was to have new feelings; he filled his poem with unembodied but representative emotional states, with postures usually declaring benevolence plus courage, reason plus endurance, democracy plus righteousness. But the true hero of the poem is Dwight himself, the epic poet. The publication of *The Conquest* showed that only two years after a great war the country could call forth such noble feelings at such length in language of such sublimity, that its homely ways could inspire in one of its citizens such consequential feelings, that its long dream of Rising Glory had fleshed. Nearly the most important part of the poem is the understated avowal of Dwight's preface that expresses his wish to throw "in his mite, for the advancement of the refined arts, on this side of the Atlantic." *The Conquest of Canäan* is a gesture of cultural maturity whose inmost subject is the writing of an epic poem by an American.

The Literary Scene ii: Was America a Mistake?

Not all Americans were confident that their new nation would continue to rise in glory. To many, in fact, America seemed to have become diseased.

The painting schools, the festival concerts, Peale's moving pictures, the new magazines and epics appeared amidst blatant and widening social inequities. While a huge public debt accumulated, while the numbers of poor mounted and soldiers begged in the streets, the young and newly rich sported fashionable clothes, patronized French hairdressers, devoted themselves to card parties. Boston, once noted for fiery resistance, was noted now for its schools of French dance: "even the Negroes have theirs," count de Miranda discovered in 1784, "which they attend twice a week from seven miles away. There is not a mechanic who does not send his daughters . . . to this important branch of democratic-American education." The situation was startling enough to make news as far away as Kingston, Jamaica, where a newspaper reported in the same year: "The Bostonians, from being puritannical, are become the politest people in the world; for besides the theatre which they hope will be established, they have assemblies and dances every week." [40] The clearing battle smoke revealed a country that hardly seemed worth fighting for.

How fast and painfully the revelation came appears in Richard Price's *Observations on the Importance of the American Revolution* (1784). Price began his work asserting: "next to the introduction of Christianity among mankind, the American revolution may prove the most important step in the progressive course of human improvement." During the time he spent writing the book, the country and his feelings changed. Toward the end he found himself, he told the reader, "mortified more than I can express by accounts which have led me to fear that I have carried my ideas of them too high, and deceived myself with visionary expectations":

> Should they lose those virtuous and simple manners by which alone Republics can long subsist—Should false refinement, luxury, and irreligion spread among them; excessive jealousy district their governments; and clashing interests, subject to no strong controul, break the federal union—The consequence will be, that the fairest experiment ever tried in human affairs will miscarry.[41]

Postwar America filled many not with satisfaction over cultural progress but with forebodings of cultural collapse.

Foreboding was the response dictated by the theory of republicanism which had evolved in America over the last century. Rooted in Puritan ideas of regeneration and in Whig Liberty, its chief article of faith came from Montesquieu, a prose slogan reprinted quite as often as Bishop Berkeley's poem. *"Montesqueu [sic],"* as the *New-York Packet* reminded its readers in 1786, "pronounces VIRTUE to be the leading principle in a republic." "No virtue," as another writer condensed the slogan, "no Commonwealth." The essence of republicanism was an insistence on the literal meaning of the term: *res publica,* the public thing. According to Montesquieu himself, "virtue, in a republic, is the love of one's country, that is, the love of equality." [42] Republics survived only by altruism: They required mature, self-disciplined citizens willing to sacrifice private interests for the public good—in short, virtuous. It was this command for an exceptional caliber of public moral character that, as Gordon Wood says, gave the Revolution its "socially radical character," for it implied a regeneration of human nature. Americans dramatized the ideal in various forms, from the Cato who commits suicide in the name of the Republic to the Joshua-Washington in Dwight's epic who abandons family and friends to lead his country. To the imported Roman and Whiggish conceptions of republican virtue they added an older, indigenous Puritan-Hebraic conception that made a formidable merger, giving the term a religious dimension that Montesquieu never intended.[43]

As Virtue, the sacrifice of private interests to the public good, was the lifeblood of republicanism, its opposite, poisoning the body politic, was self-indulgence, Luxury. Since the time of Herodotus, Luxury had been cited as the cause of cultural decay. Luxury was the destructive agent in many popular studies of the inevitable rise and fall of empires, such as Charles Rollin's thirteen-volume *Ancient History of the Egyptians, Carthaginians, Assyrians, Babylonians, Medes and Persians, Macedonians, and Grecians* (1730–38). The message that love of refinement and hunger for distinction portend decay can be traced in America back to the writings of John Smith, and was endlessly retold in the Rising Glory poems, in Bishop Berkeley's ever-present "Prospect," in the arguments for non-importation in 1769. Many saw English Luxury as the seed of the Revolution itself, as did the *Virginia Gazette* in 1778:

> Genealogy of the American War
>
> Luxury begot Arbitrary Power.
> Arbitrary Power begot Oppression.
> Oppression begot Resentment.
> Resentment begot Revenge.

It was this very Luxury, this Luxury just fought to the death, that Americans began seeing all around themselves: "are we not precipitating ourselves into the imitation of every species of Luxury & refinement?" the painter Trumbull asked his father, "& does not all this tend to the inevitable destruction of republican Virtue & national Character?—I fear so." [44]

Harbingers of Luxury, of course, had been detected and condemned during the war years. Despite calls for restraint, despite the death and sacrifice on distant battlefields, American troops in Philadelphia had tried to open up the Southwark Theatre; Boston Whigs and Tories had mingled at dancing assemblies; Yale students had given plays at the state capital during election week. The Peace put an end not only to the war but also to whatever had existed of wartime forbearance. With Peace had come a letting loose, a binge. To many Americans, the term "Luxury" now summed up the way their society was moving and growing.

Luxury expressed itself in a rich assortment of mutually stimulating kinds of behavior that became the subjects of numerous postwar satires and jeremiads: a passion for foreign goods, amorous trifling, ostentatious wardrobes, card playing, indifference to suffering, aristocratic longings, preoccupation with *tone*. The *Philadelphiad* (1784) sneered at the dogskin shoes and mincing steps of the postwar fop:

> His scarlet coat, that ev'ry one may see,
> Mark and observe and know the fool is he,
> With buttons garnish'd, sparkling in a row
> On sleeves and breasts and skirts to make a show,
> His waistcoat too with tinsel shining o'er,
> His cravat knotted in a bow before,
> His empty head with powder loaded deep,
> Wings to the same of formal cut and sweep,
> With three-cock'd hat and loop and button bright,
> And open mouth to shew his teeth are white.

Unrepublican preening was organically related to another symptom of Luxury, a lowering of sexual standards. Breasts, Ebenezer Hazard complained, were now "almost as much exposed as the face. . . ." "Republican" warned the virtuous to "pull down those *false bosoms* which appear to every modest person as objects of temptation for the gentlemen" and which make them appear "more like dissipated depraved Europeans, than plain, simple Americans." [45] To the tastes of newly fashionable and loose Americans is probably owing another significant first during the postwar period. Around 1787, the printer Isaiah Thomas apparently tried to bring out, concurrently with *The History of Little Goody Twoshoes*, an American edition of *Fanny Hill*.[46]

As "Republican" warned, Luxury signaled a relapse to the ways of "dissipated depraved" Europe. At the very time that America had become politically free, her moral weakness was forging a new social dependence. Americans had exposed, John Trumbull feared, "an unfortunate trait in their national character," an "endless itch of imitation." Fond American parents sent their children abroad hoping to improve their minds and manners, but in practice to exchange happiness for splendor, feeling for corruption, virtue for brothels, cards, and atheism. Timothy Dwight deplored how this "travell'd Ape" gave his republican birthright for monarchic pottage:

> With eye estrang'd, from fair Columbia turn,
> Her youth, her innocence, and beauty scorn;
> To that foul harlot, Europe, yield his mind,
> Witch'd by her smiles, and to her snares resign'd;
> To nature's bloom prefer the rouge of art,
> A tinsell'd out-side to a golden heart. . . .[47]

Worse, the road from New Haven to Paris also led from Paris to New Haven. The postwar flood of immigrants, many believed, carried Luxury in. It alarmed even the internationalist Jefferson to think that foreigners "will bring with them the principles of the governments they leave, imbibed in their early youth; or, if able to throw them off, it will be in exchange for an unbounded licentiousness. . . ." The French had brought not only love of liberty but also hairdressers, whited sepulchers of vanity and lust:

> Ye, Gentlemen, who of French fashions are fond,
> Who admire the gay croud, and compose the *beau monde,*
> All humours, all scabs in your heads shall be heal'd,
> By bear's grease, pomatum, and ointment congeal'd;
> . . . .
> I'll fill up all marks and so polish your skin,
> All without shall seem fair—tho' polluted within;
> 'Twill make false hair take root, I can easily shew,
> Where nature intended none ever should grow;
> All which I perform near the sign of Queen Charlotte,
> A dollar's the price—for b - - d, st - - mp - t, or h - rl - t.

Besides delighted notices of the arrival of a Reinagle or a Houdon, newspapers jeered the arrival of "*convict rogues* and *refugees*" who would contaminate Americans:

> Let *Dutchmen* come and drain your bogs,
> Let *Frenchmen* dance and feast on frogs,
> Let *Jews* among you toil and sweat,

Let stout *Hibernians* children get
. . . .
The eggs are citizens if you please,
The rotten ones are *refugees*.
A single rotten egg shall spoil
The largest custard you can boil. . . .[48]

To some, the purchase of foreign goods brought economic ruin along with
moral rot. A skit entitled *The Double Conspiracy* (Hartford, 1783) traced to
the feverishly vengeful Benedict Arnold a twofold plot to expose bosoms
and cause a depression. To distress the country it could not conquer,
England would dazzle America with European fineries, undermining
American character while draining away American specie. In the skit, a
too-discriminating Connecticut father hurls a cup of cider in the face of his
son merely because the boy drew it from the wrong barrel; his daughter
tries to seduce a "spark" who, it turns out, is a British spy—proofs that
imported merchandise produce vicious nicety and blinding lust.

Luxury also meant affectation, airs of superiority that foreboded the
return of aristocracy to America. The group of army officers who in 1783
formed the Society of the Cincinnati adopted elaborate badges and
ceremonies which seemed to many the trappings of a hereditary peerage.
Americans rushed to join the professional and intellectual classes, neglecting agriculture and what it implied about the virtuous life. "Thousands
are unnecessarily crowding themselves into the polite stations," the
Connecticut Journal observed, "while the profitable and beautiful culture of
the fields is meanly neglected—Physicians, merchants, judges, attornies
. . . are seen doubling their revenues (as they are pleased to say) to *support
themselves in decency*." Fears of a revival of aristocracy were often based not
so much on concern for *respublica* as in desires for social exclusion. A
nouveau-riche scum was rising to the top, bringing from as far off as China
gowns and gewgaws that would suggest its eminence while disguising its
ill-grace and ignorance:

. . . silk-clad *John*, with beauish grace,
To silk-clad *Nell* presents the vase,
Who screams aloud "what handsome features!
These *chany-men* are charming creatures!
What chubbed cheeks, and little eyes!
Pray, tell us, sir, where *Chany* lies?"
The beau, whose matchless impudence
Supplies the want of wit or sense,
At once replies (less taught than lucky)
" 'Tis on the main road to Kentucky."

The *Freeman's Journal* described a local after-dinner "drum" where the gaucherie of the hostess exposed itself despite her hired fiddlers, coachmen, and black servants:

> One party at cards and another at dice;
> And Sukey complaining that things were not nice,
> For these nasty black *negars*, says she, are so dull
> That there's *no driving nothing* genteel in their skull. . . .

Displays of gentility offended not only democrats fearful of granting privilege and an elite fearful of losing it, but also the rising romantic subjectivism, with its emphasis on sincerity. Opponents of Luxury had a powerful ally in young Werther, champion of authentic personal feeling, whose admirers joined in attacking the "affectation of fine breeding. . . . Dissimulation and insincerity are connected with its tenets. . . ."⁴⁹ In essays and letters to the editor, American newspapers and magazines denounced Lord Chesterfield's *Letters to His Son* for teaching artificial manners and mechanical breeding.

The variety of social ills comprehended under Luxury—fashion, loose morals, Europeanization, aristocracy, false gentility, and the rest—are most vividly examined in *Sans Souci. Alias Free and Easy: or an Evening's Peep into a polite Circle*, a three-act play published in two editions in Boston in 1785, and possibly written by Mercy Warren. A slight play but an essential document of postwar society, its technique closely resembles that of *The Defeat, The Group*, and many earlier propaganda skits. It depicts the operation of an actual club called the Tea Assembly which met every other week in Boston to drink wine or tea, dance, and play at forty card tables set up at the Concert Hall. The members were principally young, new gentry like Harrison Gray Otis, then about twenty years old, and Sarah Apthorp Morton, a poetess who published in several Boston newspapers as "Philenia." Samuel Adams, John Hancock, and other notable Bostonians joined in a violent, even frenzied, controversy over the club that suggests how Luxury grated at the root of many sensitive nerves, especially in New England. It seemed that Warren had bled to death on Bunker's Hill only so that a mixed group of unchaperoned teen-agers could drink, gamble, and ape British manners. An evening spent at the Assembly, wrote the *Independent Chronicle*, corrupted republican character worse "than an evening spent in a *back chamber* of a tavern, among a group of wretches." John Eliot equated it with the organ lately introduced into Charles Chauncy's Congregational church. Its purpose was "to encourage the rising generation to throw off all restraint, & to learn the science of cards. And this in order to know life and manners, & be fit companions for the French. . . ."⁵⁰

The chief characters in *Sans Souci* are Mr. and Mrs. Importance—representing "Philenia" and her husband—and such anti-republican types as "Madam Brilliant," "Mr. Bon Ton," and "Doctor Gallant." They are denounced by "Republican Heroine," representing the Whig historian Catharine Macaulay, who visited the club during her stay in Boston and took it as a symptom portending America's infant mortality. The first two acts consist mostly of soliloquies by the major characters, like those in which Hutchinson, Gage, or Arnold reveal their inner uncertainties; the third act brings the components of Luxury together at a climactic card party.

The play stresses the appeal of Luxury to the young. Born in a more cosmopolitan and secular Boston than their forebears, they rebel against being known for "singing psalms, and going to Thursday-Lectures." Too young to have fought in the war, many have already become detached from their ancestors' ideology, or willfully misconstrue it. Mr. and Mrs. Importance—who want to introduce a theatre in Boston—defend the Assembly as an updated version of "the ancient republican spirit" and of "staunch Calvinism": "we have modernized them, and united them with the court stile of taste and fashion." Bored with high-toned debate over republican ideals, "national manners—national debts—oeconomy—industry and such disagreeable subjects," they and their friends declare a mock-independence:

> D——n the old musty rules of decency and decorum—national characters—Spartan virtues—republican principles—they are all calculated for rigid manners, and Cromwelian days;—they are as disgusting as old orthodoxy:—Fashion and etiquette are more agreeable to my ideas of life—this is the independence I aim at—the free and easy air which so distinguishes the man of fashion, from the self-formal republican—the court stile—*je ne scai quoi* *[sic]*—give me but this, and away with all your buckram of Presbeterianism *[sic]*.

By dismissing or perverting religion, morals, and revolutionary ideology, people like Mr. and Mrs. Importance hope to repel the "levelling spirit of republicanism" and to establish an aristocracy of tone. The reality of the European high life they desperately try to emulate appears in Act II, when Mr. Bon Ton sits down for cards—a silent, unamusing Frenchman out for blood and money. The "Republican Heroine" weeps when she sees the "publick card playing," whose meaning is clear.[51] Americans have simply "copied the vices of that nation which we have so lately opposed." They have not revolted but reproduced.

To the extent that its opponents saw Luxury as a return to the corruption of English life, they stood together with the cultural nationalists, united in xenophobia. But Luxury came not only from England or France; it was an ever-threatening, ever-recurrent disease of republics. And it was often accompanied and encouraged, many believed, by cultural progress. Were the exposed bosoms, the games of whist, the rush into the professions and to Europe born of the same energies that inspired the festival concerts, the painting academies, the new magazines? Had Luxury, of necessity, arisen beside Glory? Whiggish poets like Thomson and Milton, often cited by Americans, argued the absolute dependence of the arts on freedom, and of freedom upon roman austerity and self-sacrifice leavened by altruism. But a quite opposite body of theory existed of which Americans were also aware. The English social theorist Bernard Mandeville argued that Luxury, far from producing decay, actually produced progress. The philosopher David Hume found that while a republic favored the sciences, the arts were fostered most by "civilized monarchy": Activities in a republic are legitimized by public acceptance, which encourages utility; in a monarchy, value is conferred by the court, which encourages wit and civility. Rollin warned in his thirteen-volume history of empires that a "taste for statues, pictures, and other rare curiosities of art, may be very commendable in a prince, and other great men, when indulged to a certain degree; but when a person abandons himself to it entirely, it degenerates into a dangerous temptation, and frequently prompts him to notorious injustice and violence." [52]

Many Americans outdid Rollin in asserting that the arts partook of whatever rotted republican spirit. They enervate: A "delicate taste in the fine arts too often degenerates into a sickly refinement," one writer noted; a "false sentimental luxury" makes people "slaves, not lovers of the muses" and discontents them with their "best fellow creatures." The arts threaten religion and the home: *"Novels, Comedies, and London Magazines in greater demand than Bibles, Testaments, and Psalm Books—"* lamented another writer, *"Umbrellas more in use than the thimble or knitting needle. . . ."* They introduce idleness and foreign vagrants: Among the "unprofitable labourers" in the state of Massachusetts, one writer included "painters, (particularly inside, house, miniature and portrait painters), hairdressers, tavern keepers, musicians, stage players, buffoons and exhibitors of birds and puppets"; a Charleston newspaper greeted the arrival of some immigrant "husband-men" by noting that this "species of importation is undoubtedly of more substantial utility to our Country, than the swarms of dancing-masters, fiddlers, musicians . . . which have poured in upon us from Europe since the conclusion of the late war." The arts are useless: "only tell me what is the best scene of the last play you have read, where the author errs in the management of a novel, or what lines of a certain poem might be improved," another writer warned republican women; "if that be all you have learned, I think your reading hours and all your life would have been employed as profitably in clear-starching, knitting worsted stockings, or making balloon hats." [53]

Others attacked not art or artists, but the Luxury-loving social groups, the "literary, musical, and gay circles" that supported them.[54] When in 1785 a "Boston Orchestra" attempted to establish itself at the Pantheon, in a city that had recently seen the Handellian festival concerts of William Selby, stones were thrown at the theatre. Newspapers derided the conductor, J(oshua?) Eaton, as a "modern *beau Nash*" and his patrons as "the *mezotinto gentry*," "gay, improving circles of *taste and etiquette*," who would attempt to decorate the building "in the Chinese taste," threatening industry and frugality and crushing the possibilities of republican life. Shops would close early so storekeepers could attend. No hats would be admitted under three feet in diameter, no man without "an umbrella of English manufacture." Since strangers were encouraged to attend, subscribers would bring "our *Halifax friends*," i.e., flown Tories:

> We may now expect a trial of the Italian opera;—The Boston Orchestra! the exalted characters, who are at the head of this capital amusement promise the publick the highest refinement in this soft enchanting entertainment; the *gentlemen conductors* appear possessed with every grace of *Chesterfield;* their *easy deportment* is a perfect lesson to all who are blessed with their *familiar acquaintance.* . . . the influence which [the Orchestra society] are likely to acquire from their *musick,* may prove destructive to our young republicks, as their *luxurious entertainment,* in which the *whole soul* will be absorbed, is too apt to introduce so great a degree of *dissipation* and *effeminacy* as totally to *enervate* every *manly faculty.*[55]

To the assertion that the arts would glorify, instruct, and unify the new republic, came the rejoinder that they could only impoverish, European-ize, and emasculate it.

Another feature of postwar society, related to Luxury, also cast a subduing light on the claims and hopes of the cultural nationalists. In an essay on the "Influence of the American Revolution" in 1789, Benjamin Rush observed that the Peace did not quench revolutionary ardor. An "excess of the passion for liberty, inflamed by the successful issue of the war," lingered on, producing irrational opinions and conduct, indeed a "species of insanity" which Rush called *"Anarchia."* The symptoms of this disease were gathering mobs and a rising crime rate:

> Such thieving, murd'ring, desp'rate deeds,
> As nearly all belief exceeds
> The Negroes too from massa free,
> Teel [steal] ebbry day for LIBERTY,

A little pig, or barn door chick,
Or what the devil they can pick. . . .

Stolen chickens were only a danger signal of *Anarchia*. That the new republic might be mortally afflicted did not appear until August 1786, when some poor farmers in western Massachusetts led armed uprisings against local authorities. Complaining of the scarcity of money and the weight of taxation, they asked that more currency be placed in circulation and that the cost of government and the courts be reduced. For immediate relief they asked for suspension of civil actions against debt. They were charged with wanting no courts at all, thus with anarchy. Captain Daniel Shays of Pelham became identified as their ringleader when, in December, he led 300 men into Springfield to prevent the sitting of the county courts, provoking George Washington to remark that "notwithstanding the boasted virtue of America," his countrymen differed little from the English in "dispositions to every thing that is bad." [56]

The anarchic rebellions in western Massachusetts particularly shocked the Connecticut Rising Glory poets of the 1770's. Several of them were lawyers, a group the farmers hated; some belonged to the Society of the Cincinnati, thus strongly preferred continental currency (which had been used to pay the continental troops) over local currencies, which favored the debtor classes. All of them feared the spread of *Anarchia* to Connecticut, where similar problems festered and might similarly erupt. In the fall of 1786, Barlow, Trumbull, Humphreys, and lesser poets like Lemuel Hopkins discussed and jointly wrote articles and poems on Shays' Rebellion and on paper money. Their aim, Humphreys told Washington, was to attack "the Anti-federalists & Advocates for Mobs & Conventions" (i.e., extralegal meetings).[57] Their efforts appeared serially between October 1786 and September 1787 as twelve numbers of *The Anarchiad*. Originally published in the *New-Haven Gazette*, they were picked up and reprinted in Massachusetts, New York, and elsewhere, giving wide notice to the Connecticut writers as a group at the same time that their epic poems appeared, gaining them such titles as The Connecticut Wits, The Hartford Wits, or The Connecticut Triumvirate, names by which they continue to be known. So popular did the series become that Humphreys was unable to find extra copies to send to Washington.

The twelve installments of *The Anarchiad* constitute a small anthology of popular forms of the day—songs, Popean satire, Miltonic epic verse, Rising Glory poems, newspaper doggerel, execution speeches, patriotic odes. Whatever the form, however, the subject is the ravages of anarchy. As depicted by the Wits, the armed groups who succeeded in closing down the Springfield and Northampton courthouses to stop proceedings against debtors were a subhuman swarm, lawless and unreasoning woodchucks, locusts, frogs, bears, owls, or fish blighting the newly created states:

> LO, THE COURT FALLS; th'affrighted judges run,
> Clerks, Lawyers, Sheriffs, every mother's son.
> The stocks, the gallows lose th'expected prize,
> See the jails open, and the thieves arise.
> Thy constitution, Chaos, is restor'd;
> Law sinks before thy uncreating word;
> Thy hand unbars th'unfathom'd gulf of fate,
> And deep in darkness 'whelms the new-born state.

Several of the poems deal with the emissions of paper money which the farmers desired to pay off their debts. Creditors argued that paper money quickly depreciated, and would not be a real return of money owed to them. The Wits saw the issue as an effort by shrewd farmers to impoverish the creditor class:

> The crafty knave his creditor besets,
> And advertising paper pays his debts;
> Bankrupts their creditors with rage pursue,
> No stop, no mercy from the debtor crew.

The farmers claimed (and several later historians agree) that they were being overtaxed by an insensitive government which left them simply unable to pay their debts. But the Wits (and others) treated their claim as hypocritical. The cause of the farmers' plight, said the Wits, was that they ate too well, drank too much, dressed above their station in foreign clothing, sent their children to college instead of to the plough, and were accomplished seducers. Many poems in *The Anarchiad* draw on older Whig associations between political and sexual license to suggest that the farmers were not impoverished by taxes but ensnared by Luxury. "Long on the lap of softening luxury nurst," they turned the "bliss of freedom" into "wanton change" and made Liberty a "fair fugitive."

The farmers of *The Anarchiad* are probably the first group in the country's history to be accused of un-American activities. The Wits perceived their call for paper money as a defiance of the main commandment of republican life, a placing of "jealous, local schemes" above "union'd empire," private above public interest. Their closing down of the courts and defaulting on debts represented, like Luxury, a subversion of the Revolution, a desecration of Mercer, Warren, and Montgomery: *"In vain they conquer'd! and they bled in vain!"* In Shays' Rebellion the Wits saw the grotesque negative of the hopes for progress of 1770. They recorded their feeling of betrayal in a black parody of the Rising Glory poem itself, tracing the ascent not of arts and science but of the demon Anarch:

Here shall my best and brightest empire rise,
Wild riot reign, and discord greet the skies.
Awake, my chosen sons, in folly brave,
Stab Independence! dance o'er Freedom's grave!

From the best, it seemed, had come the worst.

Americans found no comfort in knowing that their alarm over native Luxury and Anarchy was publicized abroad. Traveling in Europe in 1785, David Humphreys became aware of a "belief throughout the Continent that the United States are on the brink of perdition." [58] The reports that reached European intellectual circles played into two standing controversies about America. In 1750, the Academy of Dijon had offered a prize—won by Jean Jacques Rousseau, who argued the negative—for an essay on whether the revival of sciences and arts had improved or worsened morals. The question involved the largest issues in European culture—nature versus civilization, romanticism versus naturalism, the physiocrat emphasis on agriculture versus the mercantilist emphasis on commerce. As Europeans continued to argue the value of progress and of civilization itself, they made a test case of America, the country whose development resulted from the European spirit of exploration and expansion which was the very medium of progress in the civilized world. Postwar conditions in America offered proof of what the opponents of progress had asserted for a quarter of a century: that wherever Europeans expanded they brought war, introduced slavery, caused the slaughter of innocent natives, substituted love of gold for love of honor, and spread enervating luxuries. The question 'Whether progress in science and the arts improves morals?' took a new form. In 1782 the Academy of Lyon offered an essay prize on the topic 'Was America a Mistake?'

Native attacks on Luxury and Anarchy also supported the theory of degeneration propounded by the French natural scientists the comte de Buffon, Guillaume Raynal, and Cornelius de Pauw. In 1768 De Pauw published his *Recherches philosophiques sur les Américains*, proposing on quasi-scientific grounds that the climate of America stunted domestic plants and livestock but caused viperous animals and noisome plants to thrive. Some radical vice in the American climate stunted propagation, conceiving ugly animals, poisonous trees, and syphilitic air. America's food animals and plants were thus abnormally scrappy, its animals of prey and its useless plants abnormally gross. De Pauw reported that frogs in Louisiana grew up to thirty-seven pounds and bellowed like bulls, while plants that in Europe were tender became woody shrubs in America. (American wood ash used for bleaching clothes instantly shredded them.)[59] From their evidence of diminutive cows and giant gnats, the naturalists divined a comparable sterility or savagery in the whole quality of American life. American history was victimized, they said, by harshness and violence; because of their climate and soil Americans were incapable of genius.

Atop native diagnoses of Luxury and Anarchy, foreign dissections of the republic as a specimen of the decadence brought by civilization and the degeneracy bred by swamps made a formidable discouragement to further hopes for progress. Despite the glamorous subscription lists, the epic poems, the new magazines, Robert Morris arose in the Pennsylvania Assembly in 1785 and announced, quoting the comte de Buffon, "America has produced nothing yet like a poet." [60]

In several of its results, this discouragement was healthful. Many cultural nationalists simply battled back with reassertions of American genius. A proposal for *A Poem, on the Prospects of America* urged that the work would shatter the theory that "the human Mind depressed in America," and would "convince Europe that the Abbé [Raynal] was mistaken." More important, discouragement brought self-examination. College orators debated "Whether Monarchy or Republicanism most friendly to the Sciences & Literature?" *"Whether sumptuary Laws ought to be established in the United States?"* "Whether the Discovery of America had been beneficial to Mank[in]d?" [61] Americans began to consider the place of the arts in their society, and whether cultural progress might proceed without social decay. They raised questions which they failed to resolve, and which remain unresolved, questions of how to encourage an egalitarian spirit while recognizing excellence and of how to justify esthetic experience in a society committed to utility.

Some writers drew distinctions to suggest that depending on the circumstances the arts might promote either Luxury or Virtue. In a long essay on "The Progress of the Arts and Sciences in America," the marquis de Chastellux argued that the arts could actually preserve a nation "from the excesses of luxury and the caprices of fashion" by making wealth no longer a source of social friction. People who put their money into statues, paintings, or music would arouse less envy in their neighbors than those who maintained horses and a pack of hounds: *"as long as a taste for the Arts can be reconciled with rural and domestic life, it will always be advantageous to your country, and vice versa."* Some distinguished the art from the audience. A reviewer of William Selby's 1786 festival denied any necessary connection between concerts and fashionable concert-going, calling attention to the fact that despite a gathering of 2,000 persons, none of the ladies present wore "those *mountains* of feathers, diamonds and flowers, which the *ton* of the times, to the great detriment of our country, has rendered customary. . . ." Others distinguished among various artistic forms. While "fiddles, plays and assemblies" do corrode republican principles, vocal music tends "to refine our passions, soften the ruggedness of our natures, and improve all the delicate feelings of social life," thus creating "humane citizens." [62]

The sentimental tradition, of course, virtually equated the feelings aroused by art with Christian benevolence and charity, the twin of republican Virtue. The new literature of sensibility, however, threatened to undo the equation by valuing feeling for its own sake, recommending an indulgence in self that was but a subjective form of Luxury. Another writer distinguished virtuous sensibility, directed toward the country, from luxurious sensibility, given indiscriminately: "there then should be a distinction made, where the tears of sensibility flow over every urn, and the big drop which falls upon the tomb of the patriot—or swells the eye, where the countenance is animated with beholding a nation covered with glory." A republican might be not at all touched by "EXQUISITE sensations" when reading a sentimental novel, yet be "agitated" to contemplate "a WASHINGTON . . . saluted as the Deliverer of his country." [63] Kept distinct from self-indulgence, the arts could foster the sympathy essential to republican life.

Many writers, of course, were at the same time fiercely protective toward the newly independent nation and outraged by its drift. As David Humphreys admitted, "I detest to hear any body abuse our Country but myself." Those who shared his qualms could be called negative nationalists. They faced the delicate task of denouncing America to itself while defending it from aspersions, of conducting a family quarrel in public, correcting without disgracing. Humphreys himself was an important purveyor of this negative nationalism. Never less than ardent about America, one of very few men who addressed Washington as "my dear friend," he was yet one of the writers of the angry *Anarchiad*. Since the Peace, he had been appointed secretary to a commission consisting of Adams, Franklin, and Jefferson that was sent abroad to negotiate treaties of amity and commerce with European powers. Distressed that the English press depicted America teetering "on the brink of perdition," but sharing that opinion, he wrote and published in London in 1786 a *Poem, on the Happiness of America; Addressed to the Citizens of the United States* (rpt. Hartford, 1786). He intended to show America's "superior advantages for happiness over all the rest of mankind, whether considered in a physical, moral, or political point of view." [64]

Fifty-one pages long, the poem reflects the epic aims of Humphreys' Connecticut friends, and of the postwar period generally. Much of it concerns recent depredations of American shipping by pirates off the Barbary coast; the rest, in Humphreys' modest, thoughtful manner and from his unique soldierly slant, discourses on Washington, agriculture, commerce, the place of women in society, and other features of postwar America. Throughout, Humphreys tries to reconcile the conditions of progress with those of republicanism. In place of the forests of masts and spires, the teeming ports and villages desired and foreseen by the Rising Glory poets of the 1770's, he offers an America of the middle landscape, a place neither dull nor dazzling which can avoid Luxury while attaining greatness:

> Here holds society its middle stage,
> Between too rude and too refin'd an age. . . .

The basis of this "middle stage" is a sort of Washingtonian agrarianism, a peaceful, bountifully fed, independent, and vigorous American yeomanry devoted—in the key words of the poem—not to "art" but to "nature."

To correct without disgracing, Humphreys treats the ideal as the real. Denunciation of what does exist appears rather as nudging praise for what might exist. "Ought" becomes "is," allowing insiders to read as solutions what to outsiders must seem a lack of problems. Instead of Europe's fetid cities crowded with and indifferent to the beggaring poor, American nature provides (can provide) abundant land that both feeds its citizens and cultivates charity:

> Here hamlets grow—here Europe's pilgrims come
> From vassall'd woes to find a quiet home—
> The eye no view of waning cities meets,
> Of mould'ring domes, of narrow, fetid streets:
> Of grey-hair'd wretches who ne'er own'd a shed,
> And beggars dying for the want of bread:
> But oft in transport round th' horizon roves,
> O'er mountains, vallies, towns and stately groves;
> Then dwells best pleas'd on cultivated plains,
> Steeds, flocks, and herds commix'd with lab'ring swains.

Yet the same nature which promotes stability by providing for all also promotes progress by instilling "native force." The "lab'ring swains" become "Men of firm nerves." Nature sends "gallant youth, inur'd to heat and cold" to whaling boats after "the wounded monster plunging," encouraging American shipbuilding, commerce, exploration—and poetry. For the great whales, the great mountains, Niagara Falls also inspire (can inspire) fresher songs than can Europe's decayed monuments and neoclassical relics:

> What tho' no splendid spoils of other times,
> Invite the curious to these western climes;

No virtuoso with fantastic aim,
Here hunts the shadow of departed fame;
No piles of rubbish his attention call,
Nor mystic obilisk or storied wall:
No ruin'd statues claim the long research,
No sliding columns and no crumbling arch,
Inscriptions half effac'd and safely read,
Or cumbrous relicks of th' unletter'd dead.
Yet here I rove untrodden scenes among,
Catch inspiration for my rising song;
See nature's grandeur awfully unfold,
And, rapt in thought, her works sublime behold. . . .

America's happiness, in short, lies "Within the compass of your little farms,/ Lodg'd in your breasts, or folded in your arms." Humphreys' rather nostalgic solution for achieving progress without Luxury was to somehow unbuild the growing cities and return America to the land, guarding against fops in dogskin shoes but spurring commerce and poetry.

Joel Barlow dealt with the postwar crisis differently in his philosophical epic *The Vision of Columbus*. While with Timothy Dwight at Northampton in 1779 he had outlined the first nine books, then drastically revised the plan to include a history of the Revolution. He kept writing at military camp. By July 1782 he had printed proposals for publication, and took the manuscript with him to Philadelphia hoping to interest subscribers. But he continued revising at least to the end of 1785, well into the period of clamor over Luxury and Virtue. To support himself he opened a store where he sold books and household goods, simultaneously trying to secure copyright protection for his epic and permission to dedicate it to the king of France. John Adams—to whom he sent a manuscript copy in England—warned that such a dedication would offend English readers and spoil the sale. Lafayette, however, wrote on Barlow's behalf to the comte de Vergennes, and Barlow wrote directly to the king himself. On January 8, 1787, the book was advertised in the *Connecticut Courant* as ready for sale in six weeks, for a dollar and a third, "bound, gilt and lettered by an Artist equal to any in America, and perhaps not inferior to any workman in London." [65]

Publication was apparently delayed until May, but came as an event. The subscription list contained 769 names headed by Louis XVI (who ordered 25 copies), Lafayette, and Washington. In a year almost all of the copies were gone, and a second edition was advertised. Barlow grossed over $1,500 on the publication, the strongest indication so far in its history that America might support professional writers. But Barlow's success was more than financial. *The Vision of Columbus* is the most serious American poem of the eighteenth century, the work of a forceful imagination bent on integrating its complex preoccupations, the one ambitious poem of the period which comes at all close to achieving what it projects.

Although Barlow had worked on the *Vision* since 1778, its atmosphere and much of its action are postrevolutionary. Like Humphreys, he hoped to counteract foreign criticism of Luxury and Anarchy, to see America, he told Jefferson, "vindicated from those despicable aspersions which have long been thrown upon us and echoed from one ignorant Scribbler to another in all the languages of Europe." [66] Quite specifically, his poem was a reply to the question 'Was America a Mistake?' He dramatized his reply in a central image to which the poem owes much of its success, an image at once memorable, esthetically unifying, and complexly expressive of the postwar cultural situation and its inverted nationalism. The poem opens with, and relates everything to, Christopher Columbus in prison, unremembered and overwhelmed with failure. The vision that follows is an attempt, as Barlow says, to "gratify and sooth the desponding mind of the hero." It shows him that he is the author not of a mistake but of "extensive happiness to the human race."

The case is presented by a tall angel-like creature with ringleted hair, who appears to Columbus in prison and describes to him the results of his discovery. He keeps in Columbus' view a double perspective, setting his account of the spiraling rise and fall of civilization in the Americas within a universal progress toward human unity and enlightenment, causing Columbus to alternately groan and take heart. The Seraph's chief characters are the succession of "imperial heroes" who founded ordered societies—Moses, Manco Capac, Columbus himself, Washington. As he pauses to speculate on matters raised by the account, the poem traverses many political and philosophical issues within its narrative frame: the basis of the social compact, the origin of North and South American Indians (respectively from Asia and from the Mediterranean), the effects of climate on race, the role of art in civilization, mercantilist theory, the geological formation of coastlines, the achievements of American heroes, poets, and painters.

First the Seraph takes Columbus to an imaginary height, from which, in twenty pages of topographical verse, he surveys the beauty and immensity of the Americas—a swooping vision of volcanoes, sparkling rivulets, and plunging canyons from the Andes to the Catskills. In Book Two the Seraph describes the settlement of the Americas by Indians. His account of the destruction of Mexican civilization by Cortez appalls Columbus, who broods over the havoc accompanying the growth of the New World. The Seraph heartens him by relating the ascent of Peruvian culture under the visionary constitutionalist Manco Capac, who "Bade, in the wild, a growing empire rise." Book Three, however, details the inevitable collapse of Capac's empire. This and the other purely narrative sections of the poem consist of monotonously effulgent battle scenes—glowering skies, military sublimity, pandemonium, and carnage—clearly influenced, indeed carried away, by Timothy Dwight:

> Now meet the dreadful chiefs, with eyes on fire;
>   Beneath their blows the parting ranks retire:
> In whirlwind-sweep, their meeting axes bound,
>   Wheel, crash in air, and plough the trembling ground. . . .

The agonized scene again makes Columbus groan. But again too the Seraph describes the compensating Reformation in Europe and the Elizabethan period of exploration. The overthrow of superstition and the papacy gives rise to a new era of questing: Raleigh and the English voyagers, Penn, Baltimore, the Pilgrims, the settlement of North America. In Books Five and Six the Seraph shows Columbus the unfolding of the American Revolution from the French and Indian Wars to the Peace of 1783, a kaleidoscopic view of major campaigns and major heroes.

With the restoration of peace, the Seraph returns in Book Seven to primeval America to plot the progress of arts and sciences in the New World. As in the earlier books he described the evolution of social and political institutions, he now describes the emergence of schools, universities, science, and technology, climaxed by apostrophes to Franklin, Copley, Dwight, Humphreys, Wright, and the entire pantheon of postwar cultural nationalism. At this point Columbus questions the "progressive labouring search of man"; why have knowledge and reason developed more slowly than civilization itself, so that man destroys what he builds? The Seraph answers with a long history of the struggle between fanaticism and enlightenment (see below). Finally, in Book Nine, he allows Columbus to see the ultimate destiny of mankind, a vision of humanity united in manners, beliefs, and language, peaceable citizens of "one great empire." Columbus sees that he has contributed toward this universal kingdom a momentous act of spanning and connection.

The originality of the *Vision* is undeniable, but it is also largely synthetic. Barlow formed his response to specific postwar issues out of material then at hand but now virtually forgotten. Several long English poems of the period used ancient America as a vehicle for primitivist ideals, such as Edward Jerningham's *Fall of Mexico* (1775) and Helena Williams' *Peru* (1784). Frederick the Great wrote an opera about the Incas, using the American scene for an Enlightenment attack on Christianity, represented by the tyrannical Pizarro. The 'Was America a Mistake?' controversy, moreover, treated the Americas as a single place, and often invoked

Columbus, as well as the charge that two of his companions had introduced venereal disease to Europe. Barlow's choice of Columbus as a protagonist also had behind it a considerable literary tradition. As early as 1614, Columbus had appeared as a dreamer mocked by the world in Lope de Vega's play *El Nuevo Mundo descubierto por Cristóbal Colón*; several other works depicted him as a providential instrument for spreading the Gospel.[67] In prerevolutionary America, Columbus perhaps first appeared as a character during the Townshend Acts crisis in the poem *Liberty* by "Rusticus" (see section 16); Freneau also had written a poem about Columbus in prison. Barlow derived most of his knowledge about Columbus, however, and material on Central and South America, from Robertson's four-volume history of America, then recently published. Despite these precedents, he made Columbus a figure of his own imagination and place, a man of questing fancy, Franklinian intellect, and Washingtonian honor, called by turns "the hero," "the Sage," and "the Chief."

Yet to consider the poem in narrative and dramatic terms is misleading. The *Vision* is as much a treatise on social evolution, a loosely narrative handling of what would now be called cultural anthropology. Like history painting it claims to be both history and art, sometimes applying to history the methods of natural science and at other times subordinating history to a desired dramatic effect. In this respect, the *Vision* is a logical exaggeration of the Rising Glory commencement poems of the 1770's. They adapted Vergilian prophecy to the 'theoretical history' that had become popular among Scottish philosophers like Adam Ferguson, so as to foretell on quasi-scientific principles the future development of American society. The result was a moral-naturalistic-historical paean to the present moment of American culture as a fruition of the past and harbinger of the present, rich in instances of comparative cultural analysis and in attempts to understand the laws of society.[68] The difference between the Rising Glory poems and Barlow's *Vision* is that the poets of 1770 wrote when for the second time the colonies had forced England to back down on its tax measures, a moment of self-confidence; Barlow wrote at a moment of self-doubt and damaged hope.

Also, the college poets posited an end to history that made the past and present comprehensible as a tendency, namely the Christian Millennium. But Barlow no longer comfortably accepted the Millennium as the end and design of things. Frowningly, Noah Webster jotted in his copy of the poem, beside Barlow's phrase "fair fountain of redeeming love": "the author has adopted the system of Epicurus." Another contemporary censured the edition of Watts's *Psalms* which Barlow prepared in 1784: "You've tried the word of God to alter,/ And for your pains deserve a halter." [69] Barlow had already begun the religious and philosophical transformation for which Timothy Dwight would later take down his portrait at Yale University. In the *Vision*, what justifies things is not the Millennium but the principles of deism and mercantilism. These explain how the social ills which cause Columbus to despair over his discovery are necessary stages in human development, how the evils of history also serve the cause of Progress.

Perhaps the ruling idea of Barlow's epic is Cosmopolitanism, the deist belief in the unity of mankind.[70] For Barlow, the woes of present America become comprehensible as steps toward a new social order designed by the deistic "creative Power" or "Source." This order, revealed to Columbus in the final book, is "one great empire." On a planet interconnected by shipping and canals, all of humanity shall speak the same language, abide by the same natural morality, be governed by a "general council" of the "fathers of all empires." Violence-breeding nationalism shall give way to universal love, making "patriot views and moral views the same."

Barlow divines three distinct stages in this spreading social compact: (1) an early stage of "savage tribes" with "few strong passions"; (2) an era of nationalism marked by "social bands" strengthened by "local views" that produce "Eternal bickerings" leading to conquest and commerce that produce (3) the universal empire:

> See, thro' the whole, the same progressive plan,
> That draws, for mutual succour, man to man,
> From friends to tribes, from tribes to realms ascend,
> Their powers, their interests and their passions blend;
> Adorn their manners, social virtues spread,
> . . . .
> Till each remotest realm, by friendship join'd,
> Links in the chain that binds all human kind,
> The union'd banners rise at last unfurl'd,
> And wave triumphant round the accordant world.

The controlling events of history are explorations, migrations, even warfare, whatever has brought separated peoples together. Understood as approaches to human union, what in human history seems wayward and destructive thus becomes ameliorative, brings good from evil. The Seraph explains how the "monkish fury" of Cortez ultimately annihilated itself, for his rape of Mexico inadvertently brought European and Indian culture face to face, inadvertently opened mines of gold that stimulated new human commerce, inadvertently created disrespect for Catholicism that insured the collapse of superstition:

> Tho' impious ruffians spread their crimes abroad,
> And o'er these empires pour the purple flood;

> Tis thus religious rage, its own dire bane,
> Shall fall at last, with all its millions slain,
> And buried gold, drawn bounteous from the mine,
> Give wings to commerce and the world refine.

Similarly, the devastation of Peru poured new gold into Europe, creating envy and imitation among rival states, leading to fresh war and conquest. But conquest brought under a single hand realms that had lain distinct:

> . . . from the blazing mine, the golden store,
> Mid warring nations, spreads from shore to shore,
> With new ambition fires their ravish'd eyes,
> O'er factious nobles bids the monarch rise;
> Unites the force of realms, the wealth to share,
> Leads larger hosts to milder walks of war. . . .

Every seeming impediment to progress—superstition, rapine, war—serves progress itself.

Barlow argues in his long prose digression that, so far, history has been a seesaw contest between Reason and Power—or, more accurately, between their socioreligious forms, Superstition and Skepticism. Harsh, tyrannical periods dominated by "rites absurd" have rotated with faithless, anarchic periods of "learned doubt," both contributing to the single world order. In at least one unusual effort of consciousness, however, mankind transcended this dialectic of inadvertently progressive violence. Barlow devotes a large section of the poem to "Immortal Capac," who balanced "rites absurd" and "learned doubt" in his passion to civilize the world. While Montezuma wished to make his people merely brave and powerful (and ended by making them superstitious and ferocious), Capac wished to make his people humane and happy. He invented an entire civilization that prospered for several hundred years in peace. The ground of its success was a constitutional system that in Barlow's view remains "the most surprizing exertion of human genius to be found in the history of mankind."

Barlow's long prose digression on the "Genius and Institutions of Manco Capac" is rife with suggestions for the soon-to-be-convened Constitutional Convention. In effect Barlow asks that the delegates look to Capac for a model rather than to the much-admired but far less durable classical constitutions. Capac ordered government and society in a way that made them progressive but stable, adjustable to advances in knowledge and changes in circumstance without endangering their permanence. Barlow commends three of Capac's measures in particular: Capac officially recognized a benign deity (as opposed to the Christian God of affliction), to whom he attributed his own wisdom and the constitution, imbuing his people with a righteous loyalty to both governor and government; he gave

Charles Willson Peale's *George Washington* (oil on canvas, 95 × 61¾) shows the American commander-in-chief after his victories at Trenton and Princeton, in which Peale participated.

ABOVE, LEFT: Washington's family felt that Joseph Wright, son of the wax sculptor, had painted the best likeness of Washington (oil on canvas, 48 × 40). RIGHT: Jean Antoine Houdon came to Mount Vernon from France to cast a life-mask for this marble statue of Washington.

BELOW, LEFT: In retaliation for the destruction of the statue of King George, British troops in occupied New York decapitated Joseph Wilton's companion statue of *William Pitt*. RIGHT: Pitt as rendered by "The Famous Wax-Woman and Republican from America," Patience Wright.

RIGHT: Gilbert Stuart, *John Single-ton Copley* (oil on canvas, 26½ × 22¼). Unlike most American painters who went abroad to study, Stuart had no desire to do history painting.

BELOW: In sketching his family and pets in the garden of their imposing house on Newman Street, Benjamin West gave no hint that the American Raphael had once been a barely literate Pennsylvania Quaker (pen and wash drawing, 7¼ × 9⅛).

John Trumbull, *The Battle of Bunker's Hill* (oil on canvas, 25 × 34). Above the butt of the musket which points at Joseph Warren appear the British Generals Sir William Howe and Sir Henry Clinton (bareheaded, with raised sword).

Trumbull's *Death of General Montgomery in the Attack on Quebec* (oil on canvas, 25 × 36) combines documentary realism with romantic sublimity, linking *The Death of General Wolfe* with the landscapes of Washington Allston.

ABOVE: John Singleton Copley, *Brook Watson and the Shark* (oil on canvas, 72⅛ × 90¼). Outstretched and naked, Watson recalls the stricken figure of Liberty in Copley's earlier Stamp Act cartoon. BELOW: The day before being exhibited, Copley's *The Death of Major Peirson* (oil on canvas, 97 × 144) was sent to Buckingham Palace, where the king reportedly studied it for three hours.

LEFT: Decorative cutout supposedly painted by Major André for the *Mischianza*. BELOW: John Durang, the first native American dancer, sketched himself performing his celebrated hornpipe.

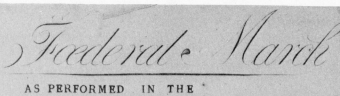

Alexander Reinagle, one of many European musicians who emigrated to America after the war, wrote this *Foederal March* for the parade in Philadelphia marking the ratification of the Constitution. Note the liberty staff and *pileus*.

THE FIRST MUSICAL FESTIVAL IN NEW ENGLAND, KING'S CHAPEL, BOSTON
January 10, 1786

ABOVE: Nineteenth-century engraving of William Selby's concert at King's Chapel, January 10, 1786, featuring more than seventy vocalists and instrumentalists.

BELOW: Banner borne by the pewterers in the New York City federal procession, July 23, 1788.

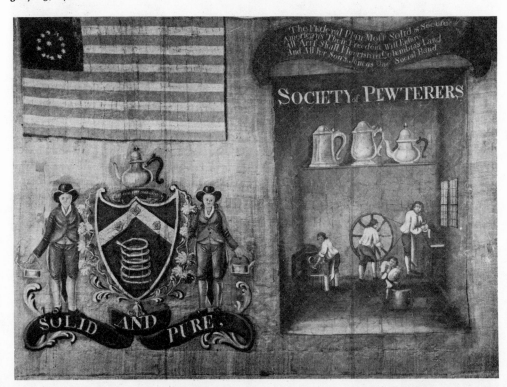

Ralph Earl, *Major Daniel Boardman* (oil on canvas, 81⅝ × 55⁵⁄₁₆). Earl was the first American painter to treat the local scene as a subject for art.

state recognition to agriculture not as a low employment but as a divine art; and he balanced powers in the state by creating a caste of nobles, distinguished by natural talent or ancestry, to act as judges in peace and as commanders in war. In sum, Barlow saw in Capac the machinery of a deistic agrarian aristocracy where the Society of the Cincinnati might live at peace with Daniel Shays under the king of France, in effect what Connecticut Federalists later thought Jeffersonian Republicanism to be.

The negative nationalism of Barlow's poem—its view that national states are but secondary stages of the "one great empire"—extends to its description of America's cultural progress. On the one hand, against the naturalists' charge that Americans were incapable of producing genius Barlow cataloged the accomplishments of American worthies: Franklin, who "holds the imprison'd fire"; David Rittenhouse, who "Copies creation in his forming mind"; his friends "seraphic" Dwight, "skillful" Trumbull and "heart-felt" Humphreys. He addressed long tributes to West and Copley, choosing the *Death of General Wolfe* and the *Death of Chatham* as illustrative of their careers. Spurning "cold critic rules," West freed the Muse:

> No more her powers to ancient scenes confined,
> He opes her liberal aid to all mankind:
> She calls to life each patriot, chief or sage,
> Garb'd in the dress and drapery of his age. . . .

On the other hand, the arts cannot escape history. So far, they have accompanied conquest and been misused to "raise a tyrant's name" or arouse men to war. Barlow's deistic pacifism forces him, despite his praise for West, to regard the heroic dying of *Wolfe* as the mirror of incomplete development, of the unconscious collaboration of art in human fragmentation. With growing human connectedness,

> . . . milder themes shall wake the peaceful song,
> Life in the soul and rapture on the tongue;
> To moral beauties bid the world attend,
> And distant lands their social ties extend. . . .

Similarly, Barlow's vision of world unity gives only temporary value to nationalistic calls for a simple American English, freed of monarchical Latinity. Instead, Barlow calls for a universal tongue shorn by definition of barbarisms, available to all humanity, impressing upon mankind a single standard of benevolent virtue:

> No foreign terms shall croud with barbarous rules,
> The full, unmeaning pageantry of schools;
> . . . .

One living language, one unborrow'd dress
Her boldest flights with happiest force express;
Triumphant virtue, in the garb of truth,
Win a pure passage to the heart of youth,
Pervade all climes. . . .

While defending postwar America and answering its critics abroad, *The Vision of Columbus* offered the more rabid nationalists little support. Barlow justified the new nation by renouncing the idea of nations. Viewing history as the troubled progress of Cosmopolitanism, he showed that America's ills were temporary and creative, but implied also that its boasted triumphs were impure. Yet triumphs they were. To see Columbus as the author only of open bosoms and closed courts, of Luxury and Anarchy, was to take a limited view. By the end of the poem the explorer understands that his discoveries have extended commerce and civilization and have "unfolded to the view of mankind one half of the globe," bringing the hemispheres together so that the human circle can be closed.

Like the America it defends, Barlow's epic is an impure, embryonic work, seen most clearly in hindsight. It is the first of those feats of encompassment which characterize later American culture, works like Walt Whitman's *Song of Myself*, William Carlos Williams' *Paterson*, and Hart Crane's *The Bridge*, which try to embrace the great diversity of American life, which in their search for national good amid national decay trace ultimate patterns in American, and human, history. If seen most clearly from the future, however, it is seen most flatteringly in its own moment, the seriousness of its conception alone suggesting how much the country had achieved in a single generation.

46. The Theatre

In the attempt of the American Company to return to the United States, the clash between Rising Glory and republicanism became open war. Congressional disfavor toward "shews, plays, and other expensive diversions" in 1774 had exiled most of the actors for the duration, ending a decade-long program of refurbishment by which they had tried to win over a country that more often scorned them than cheered. The place to which they now tried to return had changed in ways that posed new problems but offered new opportunities. On one side, they faced an economic depression, outcries against Luxury, suspicions of Loyalism, and several new, competing troupes. On the other side, they might profit from a more indulgent moral atmosphere, a public grown used to military and college theatricals, and cultural nationalists anxious for America to display its dramatic, as well as its musical or artistic, genius. Lewis Hallam, Jr., and his new partner, John Henry, maneuvered to finally establish themselves as the one and only American theatre. They introduced the latest London hits and stagecraft and hired outstanding new performers; but they did so against a redoubled assault of petitions, riots, insults, threats, and political infighting. The first result of their return was a fresh round of anti-theatre legislation that left them an even smaller audience than they had in 1763.

The American Company had been gone from the country for eight years by the time Americans learned that they were coming back. In April 1783 newspapers in Providence and several other cities published an item from London datelined February 8, four days after Britain proclaimed a cessation of hostilities:

> Mr. Hallam . . . has lately had a letter from America, inviting him to the direction of three theatres in the principal cities in America, vz. New-York, Boston, and Philadelphia. Mr. Henry, joint manager with Mr. Hallam, is now in town, raising some theatrical troops for the company, at handsome salaries.—Mr. Hallam, at the beginning of the war, having an intimation from Congress, that he and his company would be dispensed with in America, went to the West-Indies, where he has since mostly remained; but the war being now over, he has received a genteel invitation, to recompence him, in some measure, for his honorary banishment.[1]

With its tone of affronted but forgiving dignity, its ingratiating reference to "theatrical troops," and its face-saving distortion about "honorary banishment," the item made it clear that in their absence from America the Company had become no less artful dodgers than they were before.

Nor had their announcements become any more dependable. David Douglass had turned over his management of the Company to Hallam and Henry, as the item implied, having found such wealth and respectability in Jamaica as a judge and councilman that he decided to retire from the stage. But when Hallam reappeared in America, around January 1784, he advertised his performances for a year and a half as under the management of "Messrs. Hallam and Allen," his associate being an obscure actor formerly with Douglass. Quite as if Hallam and Allen did not exist, the *Virginia Journal* in the fall of 1785 announced the return of the American Company from Jamaica—under John Henry.[2] It is unclear whether Henry had chosen to claim leadership of the Company independently from Hallam or whether Allen was only acting as co-manager temporarily. In either case, the new Hallam-Henry American Company whose arrival was heralded in the spring of 1783 did not appear until the end of 1785.

The Company opened in New York with Mrs. Centlivre's *The Gamester* and Charles Macklin's *Love a-la-Mode.* Henry lost no time in explaining that he and Hallam had never wanted to leave America and that they would now do their best to stay. On opening night he delivered a speech affirming the actors' loyalty to the principles of the Revolution: The Company had played happily in the colonies until "the black cloud that threatened the liberty of America rendered it necessary for the sons of freedom at their joint meeting to prohibit during that awful period all public amusements." Although the prohibition "struck at our very existence" the players submitted to the public good. Exiled for ten years in Jamaica, they "languished in absence from this our wished for, our desirable home," dutifully refusing invitations to return to British-occupied New York. (Henry neglected to say that he had performed the *Lecture on Heads* in the last days of the occupation.) Having spent the "spring and summer of our days in your service," the Company asked only to be allowed to peaceably spend "the evening of them under the happy auspices of your protection." ³

To deserve such protection, Hallam and Henry could offer, first of all, themselves. Since making his stage debut in Williamsburg at the age of twelve, when he ran from the stage in tears, Hallam had aged badly. Often ill, he was dressed for one Baltimore performance when he had to be rushed to a nearby house, "with little prospect of Life," he told a friend, "the Disorder a kind of Vertigo of the most Alarming Sort—the Blood . . . Rushing to the Head and Heart." Although an occasional reviewer still referred to his "elegant person," the more general critical response was that "the animation, the fire, had left the withered body." Some Americans still resented him for having returned to the London stage after the congressional prohibitions, when the rest of the Company retired to Jamaica.⁴ John Henry, on the other hand, had become neither debilitated nor stigmatized. A large, handsome man, he continued to be praised for his charm and his fine voice. General Otho Williams of Maryland entrusted to him a package of papers regarding the Society of the Cincinnati for delivery to ex-general Henry Knox, a responsibility worthy of David Humphreys. That Henry cultivated such trust more in the interests of business than of patriotism is suggested by *The School for Soldiers,* Henry's own adaptation of a French play. He gave the work in two versions, one pro-British the other pro-colonies. As acted in Jamaica, it extolled British troops and reproved the American cause; revised for American audiences, it was performed in honor of Washington's birthday.⁵

Hallam, however, considered his shrewd partner a blunderer, and quarreled with him over company business. In 1786 Henry oversaw the erection of a new theatre in Baltimore, which on an average took in only

£10 nightly. Hallam blamed him for the miserably low receipts. "Henry by a Gross Error in Judgment has so Plac'd" the theatre, he wrote, "that even in the Best of Weather it must be attended with the greatest inconvenience to the audience, but in bad its Distance and Situation render it almost impracticable to come at." The friction between them was probably aggravated by the fact that Hallam was the stepson of David Douglass, with whom Henry had once fought over billing. Douglass, moreover, still owned shares in the Company's American theatres and property, and had signed over to Hallam his power of attorney.[6] Nor, apparently, did Henry and Hallam leave their rivalry backstage. In December 1785, shortly before the two companies recombined, Henry offered an important premiere, the first American performance of Sheridan's *School for Scandal*. Henry had been a pupil of Sheridan's father, a well-known elocutionist. His tie to Sheridan led to perhaps the most important American edition of the eighteenth century: The first authoritative printing of *School for Scandal* (as opposed to corrupt acting editions) appeared in New York in 1786, subtitled "from a manuscript in the possession of John Henry, Esquire, joint manager of the American Company, given him by the author." Yet Henry refused to wait what was probably only a few days for Hallam to join him before mounting the play, so that Hallam failed to appear in its first American production.[7]

The Company that Hallam and Henry brought back to America contained the nucleus of the Company that had left it in 1775. Although Dennis Ryan now led a company of his own and Sarah Hallam now ran a boarding school in Williamsburg, the cast of about seventeen included such prewar favorites as the Morrises, Miss Tuke, and Maria Storer. Sometimes billed as "Maria Henry," she was the third of the Storer sisters to become John Henry's mistress. American newspapers continued to recall that she had achieved an "exalted reputation" in the chief English cities for her solo performances in Handel oratorios. Upon her return to the American stage, in Isaac Bickerstaffe's popular *Maid of the Mill*, 200 people had to be turned away at the boxoffice. One reviewer rated her performance "infinitely beyond anything ever heard on this side of the Atlantic." Hallam and Henry also retained Douglass' leading scene painter, Jacob Schneider, even though he was now crippled by rheumatism.[8]

To this remnant of the original American Company, Hallam and Henry added some new personnel. They employed several of the recent musical emigrants, probably enlarging the theatre orchestra: the French violinist Henri Capron, the German Philip Phile, and the English harpsichordist John Bentley, who later conducted the orchestra. The Kenna family was "imported at a great expence by the managers," who also greatly misjudged their appeal. One critic offered sympathy to Mrs. Kenna for "being connected with a husband who guzzles fat beef,—with a gawky son whose eyes pass and cross under his nose, and whose tongue is tied, and with a daughter who ought to beat hemp in Bridewell [a forced-labor prison]." Mrs. Kenna's own reception topped her family's. Her appearance in George Colman's *The Clandestine Marriage* produced a first, at least in the experience of one theatregoer. It marked the first time in America, he said, that an actress had been hissed.[9] The Kennas soon left the Company.

Hallam and Henry judged better in hiring John Durang of Pennsylvania, who became the first important native American dancer. When he joined the Company in New York during its 1785–86 season, Durang was seventeen years old. Later he wrote a valuable memoir of his career, including watercolor sketches of himself as various characters (ill., p. 531). By his own account, he aspired to the stage after hearing the band of some British officers, prisoners of war who boarded at his father's house in Lancaster (a further hint of the influence exerted by the foreign military bands). After the British evacuated Philadelphia, Durang's family moved to the city, enabling him to see several dancers at the Southwark Theatre, especially the popular Roussel. He got Roussel to board at his father's house and to teach him "the correct stile of dancing a hornpipe in the French stile, an allemande, and steps for a country dance." Hallam hired Durang in 1785, after seeing him dance at a ball in Philadelphia. A three-foot-tall dwarf named Hoffmaster composed a special hornpipe in which Durang bounded on stage from the wings by means of a trampoline. "Durang's Hornpipe" became a starring vehicle and survived well into the nineteenth century as a popular theatre piece:

> My dress was in the caracter of a sailor, a dark blue round about full of plated buttons, paticoat trousers made with 6 yeard of fine linnen, black satin small clothes underneath, white silk stockings, a light shoe with a hansome set buckle, a red westcoat, a blue silk handkerchief; my hair curled and black, a small round hat gold laced with a blue ribband, a small rattan.

In his several other dances—some of them performed before Washington —Durang imitated the costume of the celebrated English dancer Gaetan Appoline Balthasar Vestris, or appeared in harlequinades as Scaramouche, or accompanied himself on the pipes of Pan. A versatile showman and performer, he also painted scenery, devised transparencies, acted minor dramatic roles, did acrobatics, played the violin, and built a miniature theatre where he performed some of the American Company's repertoire using puppets.[10]

Another boon to the returning Company were the comic gifts of

Hallam's cousin, Thomas Wignell. Wignell had been with Garrick's Drury Lane Company, the very standard of theatrical excellence. This was his second visit to America, but his first appearance on the American stage. According to one story, he had just arrived in New York in 1774 and was seated in a local barber's chair when news came that Congress had officially discouraged plays. A rather short, slightly stooped, athletic man with very small feet and large blue eyes, he was considered an intelligent comic actor who respected the script and shunned easy clowning. His immense success came in William Shield's and John O'Keeffe's recent *The Poor Soldier*, a comic opera about the love between a common soldier and the fiancée of an officer. With its many lively songs it ran an unprecedented eighteen nights during the Company's return season in New York and became Washington's favorite opera. Wignell's success came in the role of the comic Irishman Darby, in which he matched Hallam's success as Mungo in *The Padlock*. No doubt partly because of Wignell's performances, the texts of the songs were widely reprinted in American newspapers and an edition of the work was published in 1787. Appearing also in such comic leads as Joseph Surface in *School for Scandal*, Wignell became a popular and skillful addition to the Company.[11]

Obviously the successes of Durang and Wignell were made possible by changes in the Company's repertoire, which in turn mirrored changes in American society. Receding in time, circumstances that once provoked outrage and defiance now provoked sentimental memories and even satire. Prewar neoclassical favorites like *Douglas* and *Cato* gave way to *The School for Soldiers* and *The Poor Soldier*, their Roman-Whig ardor replaced by a lighter social realism. (Simultaneously, Thomas Arne's "The Soldier Tired of War's Alarms" became the favorite bravura song of concert singers.) Hallam and Henry gave scope to Durang's talents merely in feeding the taste for theatrical opulence which had grown in the country during the war, whetted by the *Mischianza*, the *Dauphinade*, the huge outdoor transparencies, and Peale's triumphal arches. The Company offered *Les Grandes Ombres Chinoises* and *Petites Ombres Italiennes* (moving silhouettes popular in France) and in 1785 advertised "a Superb Pantomimical Fete, in which the Powers of *Music, Machinery* and *Painting* are combined to cause the most pleasing effects"—apparently scenes of a storm and of a shipwreck based on De Loutherbourg's *eidophusicon* (mentioned earlier).[12] Hallam and Henry also mounted many masque-like patriotic entertainments, such as "*Columbus*; or, the Discovery of America, with Harlequin's Revels," "A *Rondelay* celebrating the Independence of America. Music, Scenery, and other Decorations," and *A Monody in Honor of the Chiefs Who have fallen in the Cause of American Liberty*.[13] The last takes place in an ancient abbey cluttered with transparencies, urns, and sculpture, and emblazoned with patriotic mottoes, in which setting a chorus of women sing about Saratoga, Yorktown, and Princeton. On July 4, 1786, the Company in effect sponsored a patriotic celebration at the Philadelphia theatre, consisting of two twenty-foot-high pillars wreathed with flowers and a flame-capped "grand Obelisk" illuminated with emblems, trophies, Liberty figures, and the American seal.[14]

Corresponding to the changed repertoire, American audiences seem gamier and more demanding than those before the war. A Charleston reviewer noted that at one performance a "demi-rep sported her person in the first row"; a New Yorker also spotted women of "ill fame" at the John Street Theatre, "alluring the unwary youth. . . ." Anxious to satisfy whatever taste prevailed, Hallam and Henry produced such risqué plays as Farquhar's *The Recruiting Officer,* and ventured some bawdy stage business. In one performance several actresses appeared as Amazons with, said one newspaper, "the right bosom exposed." If it wished to be titillated, however, a country that boasted "a Raphael, or a West" also expected to be wooed. Another New Yorker criticized the Company for allowing the stage to contain a drop depicting a street within side scenes showing a forest, and frowned on the musicians for ducking between acts into "tippling houses." "Tho' we do not look for a theatre here conducted in so regular a manner as those in Europe," he said, "yet a proper respect to the audience, and decent and proper scenery, is and ought to be expected." [15]

Postwar audiences perhaps demanded more because they had more to choose from. Hallam and Henry no longer monopolized the American theatre. Like tunebooks or magazines, the number of actors in the country had multiplied. The Maryland troupe which had performed during the war in Hallam's absence hung on after the Peace to compete with him. They had been taken over by Dennis Ryan (a member of the prewar Douglass company) and renamed The American Company of Comedians. Benjamin Harrison, the governor of Virginia, granted Ryan permission to play in the state in the spring of 1784, and gave him a recommendation to the governor of Georgia (which Ryan's servant stole on the road, together with his valises and horse). Ryan saw some opportunities in the newly flourishing town of Richmond, which in 1779 succeeded Williamsburg as the state capital—one of many new towns whose growth in part explains the heightened demand for painters, musicians, and actors. In 1784 it consisted of no more than two or three hundred houses, the capital building a mere barn; yet John Marshall, James Monroe, Governor Harrison, and members of the legislature lived there, the core of a discerning audience that meant new business. Timing his tour to coincide with the meeting of the legislature, Ryan opened "Dennis Ryan's New

Theatre" with a surefire bill of *Douglas* and *The Padlock*. He also took his company into Dumfries, Bath, Baltimore, and Charleston.[16] Only ill health prevented Ryan from replacing Hallam in the South. After his death in March 1786, his wife advertised for someone to take shares with her in managing the company and its Baltimore theatre; instead, Hallam and Henry moved into Baltimore a few months later and set up a theatre near Lombard and Albemarle streets.[17]

While Ryan was performing in Charleston in 1785, however, one of his own actors split off to form a separate troupe which remained in competition with Hallam after Ryan's death. The upstart was James Verling Godwin, a theatrical dancer who like Ryan had appeared with Douglass in the 1760's, before organizing a prewar "Virginia Company of Comedians." With his partner, a dancing master named Kidd, he opened a theatre in August 1785, in Savannah, Georgia, where British troops had given plays until they evacuated the city three years earlier. Offering standard fare—*Cato*, *The Revenge*, *The Roman Father*—Godwin and Kidd had no great success, and moved on to Charleston. In the summer of 1786, borrowing the tactic Douglass had used for the Southwark Theatre, they built a new theatre outside the city, skirting the fee for a theatrical license within city limits. Named Harmony Hall, it impressed Charlestonians with its beauty, airiness, brilliant lighting, and refinements: Twenty-seven boxes circled the pit, each box with a key. The opening, reported as far away as New York, consisted of a three-hour "Grand Concert of Music, in Three Acts" including 'heads,' patriotic transparencies, a farce, a hornpipe, a pantomime, and a harpsichord performance by a "foreign Gentleman, lately arrived in this City. . . ."[18]

To undo some of this competition, Henry and Hallam changed their name to The Old American Company. Clearly they hoped to claim a more prestigious ancestry than pretenders like Ryan's "American Company of Comedians," Godwin's "New American Company," or the "Real American Company of Comedians," titles by which their smaller rivals tried to capture Douglass' prewar audience. They also tried political savaging. "An Old Citizen," in the *New-York Packet* in September 1785—very likely Hallam or Henry—prayed that when theatre came again to New York, the bringers would not be *"British strangers"* but the long-familiar actors of Douglass "who have a claim to remembrance, not only for having lived long amongst us, but for conducting themselves, by a compliance with the desires of the first committee in the beginning of the revolution [i.e., the congressional anti-theatre acts], perfectly consonant to the wishes of the city."[19]

Appeals for loyalty to the original company became confusing, however, as competition started from within the company itself. Perhaps the general aspiration which turned all divinity students into Luthers and all versifiers into Homers encouraged ordinary actors to become impresarios. Whether ambitious or just disgruntled, Allen—Hallam's partner before the merger with Henry—split with the Company late in 1785, taking along the harpsichordist Bentley and some others. They traveled to Montreal, playing en route in two rooms of the Albany hospital. The Kenna family, viciously criticized in New York, roamed as a troupe to Alexandria, Virginia, where newspapers berated the hapless Mr. Kenna again, this time for giving a "shameful display of his talents for ribaldry" (he seems to have sniffed a garter on stage).[20] Maria Storer followed her triumphant appearance in New York with a tour of the South, singing with the St. Coecilia Society and giving selections from *The Messiah* at St. Michael's Church. (A collection was taken at the church door, which many suspected was for her. Noah Webster deplored the mixture of show business and religion—"Very odd indeed! A woman sings in Public after church for her own benefit!"—but he put a quarter in the plate.) Hallam's own son Mirvin went off to play in Fredericksburg, Norfolk, and New Bern.[21] With these and more obscure companies playing in Albany, Savannah, Richmond, Petersburg, Quebec, Portsmouth, and elsewhere, the country, once a branch of the English provincial theatre, had sprouted a distinct provincial theatre of its own apart from and outside of the large urban centers.

A different kind of competition to Hallam and Henry came from the schools. By the time of the Peace, school productions differed little in kind or quality from prewar professional productions—the result, perhaps, of their having filled the place left by the removal of the American Company from the scene. Apart from continuing productions at Yale, Princeton, and the College of Philadelphia, students at Dickinson College in 1786–87 mounted such standards as James Townley's *High Life Below Stairs* and Samuel Foote's *The Mayor of Garrett* (over the opposition of the trustees and faculty), students at Rhode Island College gave Edward Young's *Revenge* and Thomas Otway's *Cheats of Scapin* (based on Molière), and George Washington was appropriately feted at the new George Washington University with a production of *Gustavus Vasa*.[22] Theatricals had become an established feature of the lower schools also. To choose from among many examples, *Cato* was produced at a school in Worcester in 1787 (the first dramatic performance in the town), while students at a Salem school gave (and perhaps wrote) *The Distracted Mother* with two fiddles and a drum, to an audience of a hundred.[23] At the same time appeared what seems to be the first American collection of school plays, *The Theatre of Education* (Philadelphia, 1787), euphemistically subtitled *Moral Instructions in the Form of Short Comedies.*

In effect, the postwar colleges sponsored a semiprofessional theatre. Richard Randolph, a student at the College of William and Mary, told his mother that the inhabitants of Williamsburg considered a recent student play "much better done than they ever saw it by Douglas's *[sic]* company." The caliber of college productions belied older attempts to justify them as instruction in public speaking. Far from learning elocution, warned the *Providence Gazette*, youths who participated in plays at Rhode Island College lost all "relish for substantial learning, but attached themselves to some strolling actors passing through the country. . . ." [24]

Some schools not only imitated professional companies but employed them. In 1786, Alexander de Quesnay (who had produced *Eugénie* for Washington and the French minister at his Philadelphia school) opened an academy in Richmond, intending to finance it by producing plays. Actually, he assigned the larger part of his academy building to the theatre, which by one account sat 1,600 spectators, had a floor with trap doors in it, and was valued at £3,000. Much as postwar singing masters joined with professional musicians, Quesnay contracted with Hallam and Henry to perform at the academy for two months each year over the next four years. The receipts, he argued to local critics, would enable him to attract "able Masters" without boosting tuition charges. The arrangement failed, Hallam and Henry playing at the school only one year, Quesnay returning to France; but the idea seems to have caught on. In 1785, the classical scholar Walker Maury tried to raise money for alterations in his Williamsburg grammar school by scheduling a series of student plays during the session of court. [25]

If the college plays and the several new troupes narrowed Hallam's territory, they owed their existence to an enlarged postwar audience whose size and enthusiasm offset the disadvantages of increased competition. Hallam's professional rivals, besides, suffered equally with him under a three-sided attack: from the old anti-theatre laws, from the still-standing congressional discouragement of plays, and from the postwar assault on Luxury. Wherever they wished to perform, managers had to petition local legislatures—as once they appealed to royal governors—for permission. Each petition triggered a newspaper war lasting several months and counterpetitions from anti-theatre groups, ending in legislative action that usually reinforced existing laws. New York, Philadelphia, Albany, and Charleston were rocked by major debates on the theatre between 1784 and 1787; Boston, Portsmouth, and several other cities reverberated with lesser debates.

Because the controversy involved the train of related social ills called Luxury—loose morals, fashionableness, Europeanization, false gentility— as well as the political ideals comprehended under Virtue, the theatre became a battleground of ideologies. Throughout the long, animated, and often intelligent arguments in the press, in popular assemblies, and on the streets, defenders and attackers alike claimed to speak as the legitimate Americans, in behalf of the genuine principles of the Revolution. They quarreled, that is, as much about America as about the theatre, about whether the United States was one country, whether that country wished to encourage refinement at the cost of social inequity, whether it was obliged to purge its citizens of Old World corruption or to allow human nature unlimited expression. The test to which they held the theatre became the test for all of the arts throughout much of later American history: It must stand or fall by its relevance to the purposes of the nation.

Given their by-now-traditional relish for public debate, Americans turned the theatre issue into a public forum. The pattern of dialogue, indeed, did not differ from earlier controversy over the Paxton affair or taxation. Charges were raised one week in some skit or broadside, answered the next week in some poem or essay, and re-countered the week after that, resulting in a sharpening and clarification of basic issues of republican life. Wherever the debate raged, it became entangled with local gripes and personalities, so that only a city-by-city study can suggest the intricacies and flavor of this passionate, four-year-long, nationwide dispute. As the several full-scale debates, the many local issues, the many writers, and the hundreds of documents involved deserve a distinct (and lively) book, what follows can only synopsize the main arguments on both sides, ignoring the many local, personal, and chronological emphases.

Many of the anti-theatre spokesmen merely repeated familiar prewar arguments. As opponents of the theatre had argued in Philadelphia in 1766 and in New York in 1768, they argued again nearly two decades later that the theatre threatens morals, diverts apprentices, subverts religion, and spawns brothels. Again they denounced actors, whose "lives are spent in every species of irregularity and debauchery"; again they attacked plays, which teach "running away with an only daughter—violating the chastity of a friend's wife—separating a married pair—putting matrimony out of countenance"; again they warned that "where a Theatre is established there stews are immediately introduced." [26] In a mock lament over the anti-theatre laws, one versifier cataloged the playgoer's lost opportunities for stimulating lust, learning arts of seduction, squandering money, and contracting venereal disease:

> No more the fond theme of unlawful desire,
>   Shall rouse the dull feelings of man;
> No more set the cheek of the virgin on fire
>   With the luscious lewd strokes of the pen.

No more shall the libertine, learn from the stage,
  The artless poor maid to delude,
Dull virtue may reign in this Saturnine age
  And vice never dare to intrude.
No more shall dear "Congreve," with smutty keen wit,
  Nor "Dryden" that *chastest* of men,
No more they'll excite the lewd leer of the pit,
  Or set the whole house in a grin.
The harlots, alas! now their stations may quit,
  Nor patches nor breasts need expose,
To catch heedless youth, just emerg'd from the pit
  At risque of both money and nose.

Postwar defenders of the theatre, as they also had argued twenty years ago, insisted that the stage commends virtue and chastizes vice; that it gives examples of eloquence useful to the pulpit and bar; that its antagonists are usually gloomy and superstitious fanatics; and that youths deprived of "rational amusement" will head for taverns, gaming houses, or brothels.[27]

Drillingly repeated in the newspapers of the early 1780's, these were textbook arguments, articles of faith. But the war and its aftermath armed both opponents and proponents with powerful new arguments. The bawdy stage business by which Hallam and Henry probably sought to profit from the relaxed moral atmosphere stiffened the older arguments against license. The Company's performance of *The Recruiting Officer*, in which several actresses took male roles, brought infuriated scorn. The managers had mounted Farquhar's "most obscene play" in "compliance with the depraved taste of the town"; they had "put the Ladies into confusion"; actresses had appeared dressed as men in parts "so obscene and immodest. . . . so indelicate and masculine," as to disgrace "a Republican City, where delicacy and innocence of manners should prevail." [28] Others were newly outraged by the mindlessness of the Company's fashionable spectacles and pantomimes. Lacking talent and prevented by law from promulgating smut, the managers fell back on "rank nonsense." Instead of "tragedies, abounding in excellent morals," complained one New York writer, they presented the "Genii of the Rock, the Witches, Harlequin in the Moon, with a thousand other pantomimical mummeries at which common sense stands aghast." Another writer illustrated the situation by quoting from Samuel Arnold's *The Castle of Andalusia*:

Ditherum, doodle adgety,
Nagity, tragedy rum,
Goostnerum foodle fidgety
Nidgedy nagety mum.

Could "people with any refined sensibilities," he asked, be "entertained by such stuff as this"? Such works were "abhorrent" to the "august genius of the republic." [29]

The company's supporters battled back with new candor. Many admitted enjoying a climate that could produce stage-Amazons with exposed breasts and the first American edition of *Fanny Hill*. They castigated "our rigid guardians" and objected to any censorship by which "English comedy is reduced to the insipidity of a Presbyterian sermon." Publicly they expressed pleasure in a theatre no longer confined to *"dull* lectures, and *squaretoed* essays." [30] As anti-theatre petitions circulated among the Protestant churches of New York, "Civis" suggested circulating a petition to shut up the nightly Methodist meeting, "setting forth that there are more assignations made, more young women debauched, and more run-away matches concluded upon there than any where in the city."

Indeed, many argued that, considering the mushrooming of cheaper iniquities, the campaign against the theatre was a diversion. While the foes of vice concentrated their forces against the playhouse, *"private* carousing, wenching, gaming, drinking, rendezvouses are suffered, with impunity, to corrupt the morals, and ruin the constitutions of youth." The real friends of Virtue, "Roscius" said, ought to demolish the 800 taverns in New York: *"every tavern is more pernicious than twelve play-houses. . . .* while an evil of such magnitude exists in the state, I would wish you to treat with becoming indignity a petition against *the stage,* forwarded by men who wish to acquire credit by *only plucking the leaves off the tree of evil,* without . . . a stroke at its *root."* [31] To attack the theatre without smashing card-parties and dancing assemblies was ineffectual hypocrisy.

The postwar depression gave the theatre controversy a new note of complaining bitterness. Many railed against the theatre as a cruelly flagrant, public witness of the social inequality produced by the war. Within were Haves, outside Have-Nots. In 1785 the New York City Council denounced Hallam for performing "while so great a part of this city still lies in ruins, and many of the citizens continue to be pressed with the distresses brought on them in consequence of the late war." As the streets filled with the poor and destitute, "bucks" at the theatre thought nothing of spending "sixpence for a half rotten apple, a shilling for three cakes as big as a childs thumb, or two shillings for a sower orange." While families who felt the pinch most were on the verge of starvation, others made the theatre a conspicuous consumption to enhance their station: "the more extravagant the entertainment," one Carolinian observed, "the more crowded we always find the company. An amusement is reckoned vulgar in proportion to its cheapness and those only are followed with any kind of avidity at which the charges of a single evening would afford a week's decent provision for a middling family." [32]

The omnipresent signs of national debt, scarce cash, and deranged trade reduced theoretical moral issues to harsh practicalities. Henry replied that those who thoughtlessly wished to legislate the theatre out of existence would only increase the army of poor, "depriving seventy-two innocent persons, employed about the *Theatre*, of their daily bread. . . ." Others believed that a flourishing theatre would even ease the economic situation by employing indigent families and by attracting foreign visitors and their wealth to American cities. To the charge that actors were little better than swindlers who "pretend to stay but a short time amongst us . . . but in reality will drain us of our money," Joseph Brown Ladd replied that actors "are generally profuse in living; they seldom deprive a country of its cash. Hence, money in their hands is not lost: on the contrary, it is put in circulation." [33] A few writers even questioned whether the depression was real or only psychological. During the Company's performances over the last two years, noted one ironist, "such was the *'prodigious scarcity of money,'* that their audience seldom exceeded 200." A New Yorker traced the anti-theatre campaign to the poormouthing of actually rich men, to whom petitioners against the theatre deferred "from a kind of servile fear of displeasing those gentlemen who plead poverty under a silk gown, and an enormous white wig." [34]

Questions about bawdiness or class exclusion were not simply additions to an older debate that had been interrupted by the war and renewed by the Peace. The pre- and postwar theatre controversies differed at the heart. Narrowly moral concerns were absorbed into a larger, vital political question. 'Do plays destroy morals?' became 'Do plays destroy republics?'

As in the broader debate between Luxury and Virtue, behind the view that the theatre was counterrevolutionary lay a body of theory which connected plays with the collapse of ancient republics. According to the historian Charles Rollin, a love of the theatre had been "one of the principal causes of the decline, degeneracy, and corruption of the Athenian State." Montesquieu had demonstrated that republicanism rested on Virtue; in corrupting morals, therefore, the theatre undermined all that the Revolution had built. According to one Philadelphian, the underlying cause of the Revolution itself was the English theatre: "The American war may be fairly traced up to this great source of national depravity; for the young people in that country, instead of obtaining the knowledge of history, politics, the laws of their country, the principles of general liberty" had instead made themselves "acquainted with the characters, the abilities, the fine voices, &c.&c. of the stage-players." The ministry forwarded its plot unobserved by a vitiated nation that sat drugged at "Ranelagh, Vauxhall, the opera, the play-houses, Sadlers Wells, Astley's feats of horsemanship, and the masquerade." [35]

By the same reasoning, those who wished to reintroduce the stage into America were Tories or even Englishmen hoping to take by means of a theatrical license what they failed to take by the sword. A four-act anti-theatre play in the *Freeman's Journal* in 1784 revealed that the local pro-theatre forces were commanded by the counterrevolutionary "Baron Loveplay" and the "Marquis of Downclown." They land five British regiments at Newcastle while "Kingley" soliloquizes:

> I'll wear a sceptre or sink in the conflict. . . . I have led the giddy throng into the vortex of royalty. . . . Fools that they were, to think I meant their amusement merely, when I declaimed on the virtues of the stage, and ridiculed the idea of its corrupting their morals. I baffled the heedless multitude, established the theatres both in town and country, gradually poisoned their minds by the fascination of imaginary pomp, ruined their fortunes by dissipation, and bought their leaders for a trifle.

Americans all over were alert to these republic-destroying fascinations. "Plays," warned "Janus," "have so bewitching a tendency, that few men ever attended the theatre when great and illustrious characters have been represented, without a secret wish to possess the state grandeur and power displayed before them. Let but our eyes and ears become familiar to the characters and titles of kings, dukes, and lords, and the antipathy will soon wear off; accustomed to see them daily on the stage, we shall be gradually prepared to admit their real existence amongst us." The argument that plays narcotize a people against encroachment became the main line of attack among the postwar anti-theatre forces. European countries allow plays, "Janus" claimed, not for improvement but "because they employ the leisure hours of the populace, who in great cities might associate more than they now do, into knots and clubs, and canvas the affairs of the state and the management of ministers, and ultimately overturn the realm." "Attendance on public Stages," "Chilo" protested, "intoxicates a populace and diverts their minds from what ought to be the grand object of their study, the public good." [36] The Southwark and John Street theatres were no longer mere vice dens but brainwashing cells.

To complete the process of de-republicanization, the stage would make innocence shameful. Flashily dressed players would portray republican simplicity as rusticity:

> 1st Player. . . . I'll sweat you, old gentleman, and all your stiff rump'd musty neighbours. I'll write a farce myself that shall make your ears burn like a Glow-Worm—your old greasy breeches and rusty shoes with canker'd round brass buckles shall put the gallery in a roar—I'll shew them how you wipe

your bacon smear'd knives before you cut your cheese, that the grease may
remain in the family as long your shining buckskins can hold together. . . .

Such protests no doubt sprang from resentment among farmers and the
'meaner sort' over the growing opulence and European tastes of the cities.
The view that theatregoing corrected provincial awkwardness offended
anti-theatre petitioners in Albany, who complained to the mayor that "the
inhabitants are suspected of rusticity and want of politeness." By refining
the tastes of the few, others continued, the theatre would increase the gap
between classes, contrary to the nature of popular government, which "if
not carefully counteracted, will, one day, produce a revolution." If the
stage did not exaggerate inequalities of wealth and position in a republic it
might, even worse, spread corruption through all classes equally. "Let no
person alledge that the influence of the stage will be confined to the city or
town where it is established. . . . In a free state, where the citizens stand
all on a level in point of privilege—where there is a free intercourse
between city and country—between the merchant, the farmer, and the
mechanic, it is vain to think of preventing a spirit or disposition which
prevails in one place, from spreading to another. . . ." [37] The effect would
be to debauch the state and deafen citizens to the clanking chains of
slavery.

To many Americans who opposed the theatre, Hallam and Henry thus
represented enemies of the state. The issue was sharply drawn, black and
white. On one side, said a New York newspaper, stood "the pleasure-rid-
den dupes of dissipation"; on the other stood "those who chuse to favour
the prosperity of our Republic." One writer summarized the dispute in a
single cry: "*Oh the Theatres!* Oh my country." [38]

The theory of republicanism clothed longstanding anti-theatre sentiment in political rectitude. But the shining armor did not go unchallenged
by defenders of the theatre, who had their own version of what the
Revolution had accomplished and of its legacy to them. Many questioned
the unevenness of the anti-theatre laws. In a group of states recently united
as one against a single enemy, why should plays be allowed in Annapolis
and not in Philadelphia? Why had Congress prohibited plays for
Americans but tolerated them for the French allies? Was not every
American entitled to "such amusements that inclination naturally may
lead him to," compatible with public peace and government? The writer
who asked this question, a New Yorker styling himself "Theatricus,"
answered it by stating a principle that was very often and ever after
repeated. It is, he said firmly, a "free country." [39]

Defenders of the theatre challenged point by point their opponents'
version of republican theory as well. In the cry "*Oh the Theatres!* Oh my

country" they heard not a profession of Whig principles, but ignorance of
the great Whig literary tradition. Playwrights like Addison and Rowe,
after all, had been among the champions of republican ideals. The author
of "The Political Critic" (possibly Freneau) portrayed one theatre-hater as
a tippling, ignorant merchant's clerk declaring in his cups that the stage is

> . . . scarcely worthy of a Turk,—
> These Addison's, and Moore's, and Rowe's,
> To liberty were sworn foes;
> They lived in Greece, and all was try'd
> For horrid treasons e'ere *[sic]* they di'd. . . .

Others dismissed as ludicrous the belief that theatres had felled republics.
Empires decline from Luxury, the product of wealth, which has more often
been the product of a priestly class. Several writers quoted Lord Kames to
show that theatre, like all the arts, actually prevents Luxury by diverting
wealth to itself.[40] Many viewed the equation of the stage with Luxury as
part of a dogmatic formulaic republicanism that had hardened into
humorless cliché. The *Philadelphiad* depicted an anti-theatre advocate
mechanically "quoting Roman luxury of old," denying reality by his
"Idioms and blunders":

> "We the *Gardeens* of all the state," he said,
> Then cough'd and haugh'd and strok'd his brainless head,
> "Should banish taste and luxury from hence,
> "And plays of course . . . these shock all common sense;
> "Rome, Sir, was great, 'till plays reduc'd her fame;
> "Her modern sons are nothing but a name. . . .

To the argument that the stage excited imitation of aristocrats and
denigrated common life, defenders replied that few English plays besides
Shakespeare's actually depict princes, and then to show the rewards of
virtue or the punishments of vice; one might as reasonably forbid ministers
to use texts with the words 'king' or 'prince.' Satire of common life,
moreover, encourages people to reach beyond their present level of
existence. Seeing himself derided, a tradesman or farmer "laments his
want of information, and, at last, being conscious of his own imperfections,
he studies to improve, desires to amend, and aims at something above
mediocrity." [41] In making provincialism shameful, the stage promotes
self-transcendence.

Indeed, a rise in the general welfare was only one role claimed for the
theatre in republican life. Far from producing a moral slumber that
permitted encroachment, the stage might serve as a safety valve that
insured domestic tranquillity. Where, one writer asked, did *Anarchia*, did
Shays' Rebellion originate?

Witness the factions and animosities that subsist in our own commonwealth—witness, also, the dangerous insurrection and rebellion that have enkindled throughout almost every part of the commonwealth of Massachusetts-bay, destructive of order and subversive of all law and government.—And what does all this anarchy proceed from? From the want of theatres, dances, shows and other public amusements.

The stage gives the mind an outlet for its native restlessness that is a friend to liberty and order. Could not the stage perform in America the same function that, mourners of fallen empires to the contrary, it had performed in the great classical republics? In Athens, eloquence accompanied learning and led to liberty. Ancient actors "subdued a mighty nation to elegance and virtue," exhibiting "the same delicacy of thought and morality of life; the same humanity of heart and sweetness of affections, that could at once constitute the Patriot, the Hero, the Lover, the Friend." The very fact, another writer said, that "those virtuous people of antiquity" patronized the theatre suggested that an American theatre should be encouraged by "men of genius, (for such I trust we have)." [42]

This defensive "trust" gave defenders of the theatre a final powerful weapon. "Have Shakespear and Johnson written to be admired by all Europe, and be forgotten, or neglected," asked one cultural nationalist, "by the Philadelphians?" "Have the Americans presented no object for the admiration of the world? And shall they be behind hand in refinements?" For the country to exist without a theatre was to confirm what Europeans hoped to believe, that Americans were culturally impotent. Anti-theatre laws, another writer complained, amounted to an "embargo" on American genius, disclosing to a watching world that "genius meets with so little encouragement in a land of liberty." How long must Americans suffer the taunts of English beaus, smelling bottles in hand, exclaiming at the John Street or Southwark theatres, "Oh la! 'tis nothing to what we have in England; pon honor I never saw such rascally acting, quite surfeiting truly. . . ." [43]

America needed not only its own theatres but its own plays as well, for the same reasons it needed epic poems and historical paintings. The country had accumulated a rich past that deserved telling, and noble leaders who deserved fame. A prologue intended for the 1786 opening of the New York theatre observed:

> The time is come, and this eventful land,
> Demands the skill of many a master's hand.
> The theme is ready. . . .

The theme was not only ready but also useful. Brought to life on the stage, scenes from the American past could teach history to people too lazy to read about it, and inspire the young with the example of "matchless *Washington*" and other republican heroes. There seemed little danger that, if encouraged, an American dramatic literature could develop in the direction of Farquhar. As a Charlestonian speculated, the "morals and the manners of this country are too chaste to leave reason to apprehend that any improper plays will be written here for perhaps centuries to come." [44]

Out of this strident atmosphere of argument and rejoinder came petitions and counterpetitions that in several cases forced legislative action. In itself, the recourse to legislative bodies is significant of the country's political mood. A few dramaphobes threatened to riot, but no one pulled down playhouses or assaulted actors, as they had in the 1760's. When some irate New Yorkers threatened to dismantle the John Street Theatre, they were stopped by the local clergy, who advised them to settle the issue by "the proper constitutional mode" of petitioning the legislature for an anti-theatre law. [45] Several of these petitions survive. An Albany petition with seventy signatories was defeated on the grounds that the mayor lacked "a Legal Right to prohibit" Allen's actors. In Savannah, Georgia, in 1786 a presentment was made to the Grand Jury "against the toleration given to all theatrical performances, which tend to injure the morals of the people, already sufficiently corrupted. . . ." Between November 1785 and April 1786, while the state legislature sat in New York, two petitions circulated and were endorsed by many leading citizens before being sent to the lawmakers. The second petition, submitted in the spring, contained over 700 signatures. It condemned brothels, taverns, and the John Street Theatre as unfriendly to republican virtue and to "that frugality and oeconomy which are so essential to the prosperity and honor of our country." [46]

Not surprisingly, the most righteously insistent petitions, and the most determined counterpetitions, appeared in Philadelphia, precipitating a formal debate in the Pennsylvania legislature which lasted three days in November 1785. The debate focused on one section of a proposed "Act for the Prevention of Vice and Immorality," imposing a large fine for attempted stage productions. The section was the work of Robert Whitehill, representing the Calvinistic Scotch-Irish Presbyterians of the Pennsylvania frontier. The army surgeon Johann Schoepf, present for legislative debates on the theatre in 1783, believed that the sides were drawn between those in the city who enjoyed its sophisticated immigrant culture and an alliance of back-country agrarians and city Quakers:

> . . . the long sojourn of many foreigners, military men and others, has greatly changed manners, taste, and ideas, widening and increasing a disposition for all pleasures. A great part of the modernized inhabitants [of Philadelphia]

desired that plays should go on, which the others vehemently opposed as an unlawful and immoral innovation. . . . [Most members of the Assembly] have been born and brought up in the country, have never seen a play, and therefore have few and wrong ideas as to the morality of the matter, or [are] on the other hand Quakers and other sectarians who from their religious principles frown on all the pleasures of the rest of the world. . . .[47]

The chief defenders of Whitehill's section (hence opponents of the theatre) were Whitehill himself, Dr. George Logan (a prominent local physician), and two delegates named Finley and Smiley. The chief opponents of the section were the merchant Cadwallader Morris; George Clymer, a friend of Franklin and a signer of the Declaration; and General Anthony Wayne, the hero of Stony Point and evidently a personal acquaintance of Hallam—one of many military officers who had learned to enjoy plays and outspokenly supported the theatre. During the three days of debate, each rose to speak several times, their exchanges punctuated by briefer comments from lesser speakers.

Sectionalism did figure in the debate, Morris in particular arguing that the issue came down to the country wishing to deprive the city of its amusements. But most of the floor exchanges developed out of the ongoing newspaper controversy and similarly posed larger questions about America. Logan and Smiley repeatedly argued that plays suited only monarchies and despotisms. To the suggestion that the existence of a theatre in Philadelphia would induce Congress to resume its sessions in the city—"as there are many young fellows in that body, who do not choose to be debarred from such an innocent relaxation"—Smiley retorted that this merely demonstrated how the theatre draws attention away from politics. Speaking for the other side, Morris asserted that even in a republic, not everyone must devote all his time to public affairs. On the authority of his many daring battlefield victories, Wayne gave his opinion that congressional discouragement of the theatre had been "an ill-timed measure, as the representation of Cato and such other tragedies, in the foederal camps, would have been an additional stimulus to the officers to heroic actions." Plays could remain useful as deserved reminders of revolutionary sacrifice. "I trust," he said, "we shall never agree to a measure whereof the tendency is to prevent justice being done to the heroic actions of our soldiers. . . ." Clymer, the spokesman for cultural nationalism in the affair, described the theatre as a necessary condition of independence, and reminded the other delegates that Philadelphia's second greatest boast—Benjamin West— lived abroad: "We are now an independent people.—Are we to be forever indebted to other nations for genius, wit and refinement? . . . In England, some of the best and most celebrated painters and artists, are Americans, who here could meet with no encouragement." Smiley replied that, lacking a theatre, Americans could still commemorate their past in odes, epics, pastorals, and histories.[48]

Following the debate, Wayne submitted a second bill. It seems likely that he drew it up with Hallam's cooperation, for the bill closely resembled a memorial which had been sent to the legislature earlier by Hallam himself.[49] The bill licensed Hallam to open a theatre in Philadelphia or its suburbs, but nowhere else in the state. For the privilege, Hallam would pay an annual fee of $2,000 and devote two performances annually for the relief of the poor or of jailed debtors. His theatre would be closely regulated. The Philadelphia Council would approve or disapprove the repertoire he submitted to them, and would fix his prices. No doubt these restrictions were intended as a sop to delegates who were inclined to vote for Whitehill's bill, which abolished theatre altogether. Further debate amidst much other important business prevented a vote until next fall.

Whitehill's anti-theatre bill passed. The legislature added to its "Act for the Prevention of Vice and Immorality"—covering swearing, Sabbath breaking, cock fighting, pool shooting, and other infractions—a section on plays:

> . . . if any person or persons whatsoever shall erect, build or cause to be erected or built, any play house, theatre, stage or scaffold for acting, showing or exhibiting any tragedy, comedy, tragi-comedy, farce, interlude, panto-mime, or other play, or any scene or part of any play whatsoever, or who shall act, show or exhibit any such play or any part of a play or shall be in anywise concerned or employed therein, or in selling any ticket or tickets for that purpose in any place within this commonwealth, and be thereof legally convicted in the court of quarter sessions of the peace, or of oyer and terminer and general gaol delivery of the city or county wherein the offence shall be committed, shall forfeit and pay the sum of two hundred pounds for every such offence, and every such person after conviction as aforesaid shall be holden in recognizance with two sufficient sureties to be of his or her good behaviour and if such person offend again in like manner such offence shall incur the forfeiture of such recognizance.[50]

The act ended professional theatre in Philadelphia.

Devastating as this statute must have been to Hallam's hope of reestablishing his company, painful as it must have been when recollecting his father's determination thirty-five years ago "to try his fortune in America," the Philadelphia act was only the most complete and severe of a batch of postwar anti-theatre acts growing out of the petitions and newspaper controversies. They left the theatre at its nadir in America during the eighteenth century. In 1786 the South Carolina legislature refused Hallam's petition to rebuild his Charleston theatre (accidentally burned during the war) as inconsistent with the "present distressed State of the country." Petersburg, Virginia, in 1785 voted to allow no play without the express permission of the mayor or some magistrate, and taxed each performance three guineas. The city of Richmond voted the same year to regulate the number and price of theatre tickets. After passage of the new Pennsylvania law, the South Carolina legislature followed suit by enacting a Vagrancy Law which classified actors with beggars, peddlers, and fortunetellers, effectually ending theatre in the state. Boston, which needed no encouragement, reenacted its prohibitory act of 1750 in 1784, and again in each succeeding year until 1791.[51] These laws cornered the theatre. With their eidophusicons, with Wignell as Darby and Durang in his hornpipe, with their instant productions of London hits, Hallam and Henry had no place to go but Maryland and New York. Everywhere else, by law, 'The American Company' was a contradiction in terms.

So far as the resolution of this contradiction could be glimpsed in the mid-1780's, its indicators were Hallam's persevering resourcefulness and the appearance of a single play. During his travels in America Hallam had mastered two necessary skills: evasion and ingratiation. Immediately he replaced plays with 'concerts,' 'music,' or the perennial *Lecture on Heads* or *Lecture on Hearts*, outdoing himself in impressing upon local officials his decency and benevolence. The 1786 Philadelphia law was not to take effect until August 31, 1787, probably in deference to the tastes of the men who would convene there in June for the Constitutional Convention. In the period of grace the Company solemnly gave "Strictures upon the most eminent Dramatic Authors" or "a mixed Entertainment of Representation and Harmony," no doubt smuggling in themselves and their repertoire. Durang presented *The Poor Soldier* as a puppet play, the regular actors supplying the dialogue and songs. By specifically forbidding "tragedy, comedy, tragi-comedy, farce, interlude, pantomime, or other play, or any scene or part of any play," the 1786 theatre law tried to halt such dodges, but Hallam apparently forged ahead. One Philadelphian protested early in 1787 that in defiance of the new law playbills were "stuck up on every corner"—a dangerous precedent, since in "a government, so new as ours is, the laws should be enforced with severity."[52]

Hallam also became prodigal in well-publicized contributions to the poor. One friend to the theatre—probably himself—commented that his charities would warm every "friend and patron of the stage that 'shining supplement' to the pulpit." (John Henry, who did not lack a sense of humor, privately referred to the Southwark as "the Philadelphia Conventicle."[53]) Such donations could only be arranged with the help of sympathetic local officials, who in the wake of the new laws had become cautious. In 1784 Ryan, hoping to obtain a license to perform in

Richmond, offered to play a benefit for the city which may have involved a bribe to some overseer. His offer was declined with the statement that the city fathers, grateful for his attention to the city, did not "conceive themselves at liberty to apply any part of the produce thereof to the emolument of the Corporation." The next year Hallam offered a commissioner of the New York almshouse forty pounds for charity; a few weeks later the City Council ordered the money returned to him.[54]

Ultimately the fate of the theatre depended not on evasions or disguised bribes but simply on the momentum of cultural energy, upon a steady progress in the arts that in surmounting bloodshed, looting, economic failure, and provincial backwardness had proven itself irresistible. Now it brought forth the best play yet written in America, by America's first successful dramatist, a production to delight and encourage the many who called for an American literature, a work to set beside *The Vision of Columbus*, the historical paintings of Trumbull, and the Handel-Billings concerts as a symptom of the health of American culture and a proof of what it had achieved in the quarter-century since the Treaty of Paris.

This was *The Contrast*, first performed by the American Company at the John Street Theatre on April 16, 1787. It came unexpectedly, from a new figure on the literary scene. Royall Tyler (1757–1826) graduated Harvard in July 1776 and began studying law in Cambridge and Boston; with the painter Trumbull, he discussed literature and politics at John Smibert's studio on Scollay Square, gaining a reputation for wit and perhaps fathering an illegitimate child. During the war he enlisted in John Hancock's Independent Company of troops (together with Trumbull) and served as aide to General John Sullivan in Rhode Island. Admitted to the bar in 1780, he opened an office in Braintree, where he courted seventeen-year-old Nabby Adams, the daughter of John Adams. Adams disliked Tyler's "gaiety" and wished his daughter to marry someone devoted to study and business. "I am not," he said, "looking out for a Poet." Nabby was sent to England. After the war Tyler settled into a law practice in Boston. He joined an expedition against Daniel Shays and proved so useful in negotiations that the Boston Council asked him to conduct some official business in New York in March 1787. Five weeks later he had written *The Contrast* and seen it performed.[55]

The Contrast is a five-act sentimental comedy laid in postwar New York. The main plot concerns an arranged marriage between the foppish Billy Dimple and the delicate, sentimental Maria. This mismatch is largely the work of Maria's gruff but straightforward father, the businessman Van Rough. The arrangement, however, is disturbed by the arrival in New York of Colonel Manly. Currently helping to put down insurgents in western Massachusetts, he has come to the city to ask Congress to provide pensions for the men who served under him during the war. The patriotic Manly is introduced to the chaste Maria by his sister Charlotte, a coquette. The "two penserosos," as Charlotte calls them, fall in love, but their sense of honor and obedience keeps them from trying to alter Van Rough's marriage design for Maria and Billy Dimple. Dimple himself, however, no longer desires to marry Maria. Heavily in debt to two English lords, he hopes to break the engagement and marry the wealthy Letitia, another coquette, meanwhile pursuing Manly's sister Charlotte. Manly discovers Dimple's scheme when, closeted in Charlotte's library, he overhears Dimple first proposing to Letitia, then, after she leaves, attempting to seduce Charlotte. He rushes out to his besieged sister with a drawn sword given him by the marquis de Lafayette. With Dimple unmasked, Maria's father willingly dissolves the engagement and accepts Manly as his son-in-law. An elaborate comic subplot in the play involves Manly's Yankee servant Jonathan and Dimple's Frenchified servant Jessamy. Jessamy proposes to polish Jonathan's manners by having him seduced and then made elegant by the cook Jenny, "as Madam Ramboulliet, did young Stanhope."

That Tyler should have written the play during a visit to New York is understandable. The main source for its plot, characters, and dialogue is the repertoire of the American Company, to which his characters often refer. Indeed the play reads like a garbled transcription of several weeks' enthusiastic attendance at the John Street Theatre. Characters named "Manly" appear in William Wycherly's *The Plain Dealer* and in Farquhar's *The Provok'd Husband.* Tyler's colonel is only the latest of the sentimental-soldier types that had become popular on the postwar stage in such plays as *The Poor Soldier* or John Henry's own *School for Soldiers.* The prototypes of the sentimental Maria and the hypocritical Dimple exist in the sentimental young ladies of *The Rivals* and in Joseph Surface of *The School for Scandal.* Jonathan's down-home exclamations—*"Maple-log seize it!"*—first come out of the mouth of farmer Fairfield in *The Maid of the Mill,* exclaiming "murrain take it." The moral duel between the sentimental Maria and the coquettish Charlotte is fought earlier between the sentimentalists and anti-sentimentalists of Kelly's *False Delicacy.* Tyler's traveled apes, helpless females, and intolerant fathers are literary creatures formed out of characteristics and bits of dialogue taken here and there from Hallam's offerings.

Yet by casting his borrowings into postwar social forms, Tyler created the most distinctively American literary work of the eighteenth century. He transformed the sincerity-hypocrisy conflict of conventional social comedy into a rich satire on the debate between Virtue and Luxury. The "contrasts" between Manly and Dimple, Maria and Charlotte, Jonathan and Jessamy dramatize the forms of behavior and social life which the terms embrace. They pit revolutionary stoicism and high-mindedness against the new spirit of display and fun, republicanism against aristocracy, country against city, soldier against beau, Boston against New York, marriage against seduction, homespun against lace, the language of the heart against Frenchified elevation, American simplicity and sincerity against European affectation and preoccupation with fashion. The characters work out these issues, moreover, wholly in the contemporary terms that were their concrete forms. Their dialogue teems with references to French hairdressers, exposed bosoms, Shays' Rebellion, Chesterfield's letters, education for women, the marquis de Lafayette, the Handel commemorative concerts, the New England singing schools, the New York statues of the king and Pitt, the "late glorious contest," the Society of the Cincinnati. In dramatizing the debate between Luxury and Virtue, *The Contrast* makes fuller use than any other work of its time of American manners. The stock characters and bits of dialogue that Tyler's imagination absorbed at the John Street Theatre become merely a dramatic vocabulary through which he reproduces his vision of postwar American life.

Because of Tyler's enthusiastic commitment to the unique social reality of 1787, *The Contrast* is as much a work of social and cultural history as it is a play. Not even the diaries and journals of the period bring together so many specific political, social, and local issues, restore the reader so intimately to a once-actual world of buckles and hoops and soldiers in musty uniforms. No other writer of the eighteenth century gave Americans so perfect a glass of their existence. Audiences must have viewed the play's many contemporary vignettes with a sense of delicious recognition: Charlotte and Letitia gushing about New York fashions; the genteel Maria singing "Alknowmook," the death song of a Cherokee chieftain; the merchant Van Rough minding "the main chance" and fulminating against English novels; Jenny attempting to seduce Jonathan, who knows no love songs and "can't sing but a hundred and ninety verses" of Yankee Doodle. As cultural history, the most informative and revealing episodes in the play concern postwar theatregoing. Charlotte's description of a New York theatre party is the closest we can come to glimpsing the suggestive mating games within the playhouse that must have prompted some of the anti-theatre protest:

> . . . the curtain rises, then our sensibility is all awake, and then, by the mere force of apprehension, we torture some harmless expression into a double meaning, which the poor author never dreamt of, and then we have recourse to our fans, and then we blush, and then the gentlemen jog one another, peep

under the fan, and make the prettiest remarks; and then we giggle and they simper, and they giggle and we simper, and then the curtain drops, and then for nuts and oranges, and then we bow, and it's pray, Ma'am, take it, and pray, Sir, keep it, and oh! not for the world, Sir!; and then the curtain rises again, and then we blush and giggle and simper and bow all over again.

The bumpkin Jonathan—who mistakes the playhouse for a meeting house—provides a brief but unique account of the operation of the John Street Theatre itself. Present for "The School for Scandalization" featuring "Wig—Wag—Wag-all," he tells of seeing "a power of topping folks, all sitting round in little cabbins, 'just like father's corn-cribs'; and then there was such a squeaking with the fiddles, and such a tarnal blaze with the lights, my head was near turned." Finally they "lifted up a great green cloth and let us look right into the next neighbor's house." In the fullness of its reference to local behavior and issues, *The Contrast* fills the claim of its prologue: "this night is shewn/ A piece, which we may fairly call our own."

The uninterrupted flow of local references makes the characters seem national rather than literary types. Billy Dimple emerges not as the stock hypocritical rake but as the Europeanized American, the very embodiment of the attempt to bring the country down by introducing Luxury. His fickle hopping from one coquette to the next is only one feature in a larger ideological portrait of the postwar nouveaux riches, his name changed to Dimple from Van Dumpling, his Chesterfieldian foppery acquired during an English tour. Colonel Manly's role, similarly, is less that of the stock sentimental soldier than of the postwar doctrinaire republican. A paragon of self-sacrificing Roman-Puritan virtue, he stands on "probity, virtue, honour," referring to his parents as "the venerable pair" or the "authors of my existence," denouncing Mandeville, dissipation, private interest, dueling, and the fall of empires, essaying not to seduce woman but "to rectify her foibles." Mindful of the country's difficulty in supporting its credit, he retains uncashed the notes issued to him for his military service and still wears his regimental coat. Unashamedly provincial, he commends the "laudable partiality which ignorant, untravelled men entertain for everything that belongs to their native country." To the luxurious fops and coquettes he seems both alien and preposterous, a Cato on Beekman Street. Even his sister thinks him "a player run mad, with your head filled with old scraps of tragedy."

In creating Jonathan, his most inspired character, Tyler likewise transformed the stock comic servant into the archetypal Yankee.[56] The purest democrat, contemptuous of servitude and of social distinctions, when called a "servant" by the effete Jessamy, he snaps "Servant! Sir, do

you take me for a neger,—I am Colonel Manly's waiter." Unaware of any
reality but his own, he blunders into the play blind to urban niceties,
mistaking playhouse for meeting house and arts of seduction for invitations
to sing "Yankee Doodle." Independent, boastful, nosy, impudent, brave,
and moral, he represents a new but later familiar cultural type, the
American as Adam. Despite his literary antecedents, he is a man utterly
cut off from and ignorant of the assumptions of European culture, "a true
born Yankee American son of liberty" whose impercipience is a form of
rebirth.

American theatregoers recognized that Tyler had written the first
significant realistic comedy of American life, "A piece, which we may
fairly call our own." With Wignell as Jonathan, Henry as Manly, Hallam
as Dimple, and Mrs. Morris as Charlotte, the play became a celebrated
success repeated several times in quick succession after its premiere.
Proposals were issued for printing it as "the first dramatic production of a
citizen of the United States," a work "honorable to American genius and
literature." It became the first American play to garner many reviews;
indeed it occasioned the first genuine theatrical criticism in America. Most
reviewers saw the action as a mirror of the prevailing ideological debate
and applauded its republican stance:

> The striking *Contrast*, in this piece, is between a person who had made his tour
> of Europe, studied the *bon ton,* acquired Chesterfieldian gallantry, and
> possessed that *J'aine sais quois [sic]* which ever proves irresistible by those who
> are generally stiled *la belle monde,* with his *galloned attendant*—and an heroick,
> sentimental American Colonel, with his *honest waiting man.* The several acts
> concentre in this important point—to render superlatively ridiculous the
> cox-comical extravagance of the age, and the subversion of *natural simplicity,*
> into the *imp of luxury*—and holding high to view, in letters of the purest gold,
> all the virtues of the human heart.

The cultural nationalists installed *The Contrast* beside *The Vision of Columbus*
and the paintings of Copley. In the opinion of the *Independent Journal*, it
"must give sincere satisfaction to every lover of his country to find that
this, the most difficult of all the works of human genius, has been
attempted with such abundant success . . . America may one day rank a
Tyler in the Dramatic Line as she already does a *Franklin* and a *West* in
those of Philosophy and the Fine Arts." "These blossoms of the comic
muse," said the *Pennsylvania Herald*, "wear every mark of vigor and are an
additional specimen in proof that these new climes are particularly
favorable to the cultivation of arts and sciences." [57] Manly had triumphed
not only over Billy Dimple but over the Abbé Raynal as well.

In their praise of Tyler for portraying Virtue "in letters of purest gold," the reviewers paid no attention to his prologue, an invocation of Thalia, the *"laughing, useful"* Muse of satire. Only the critic in the New York *Daily Advertiser* bothered to say that Manly's patriotic speeches seemed overlong and unnatural. With its own variety of negative nationalism, the play wavers between jingoism and satire, between flattery of the country and "light Censure on your faults." Manly is not merely a republican hero but a stuffy fool, repeatedly and justly mocked in the play for his doctrinaire magniloquence, his overpunctilious and antiquated bearing, "like an old maiden lady's bandbox." Tyler stays faithful to his satirical purpose, lightly censuring all faults, including provincial pomposity however right-minded. It is by no means clear whether he intended Manly's oration on the dissolution of empires seriously or as a parody of Catonic delusions of grandeur. In *The Contrast*, Tyler stands further away from the events of the Revolution than does any other writer of the period. The point-of-view makes apparent a ridiculous grandiosity in the Roman sentiments that once in all seriousness sustained the cause. A comic realist rising above the battle, Tyler is less the offspring of theatrical patriots beweeping "fair Liberty" than the forebear of Washington Irving, eying the debauched Dimple and the stoical Manly with cosmopolitan detachment and the faint cynicism of nostalgia.

Indeed the more lasting cultural conflict in the play is not between Luxury and Virtue, but between Manly and Jonathan, a contrast within the contrast. Neither the sober, Washingtonian republican, whose formalism sounds hollow, nor the bumptious, untutored Yankee, whose rustic ways look foolish, serves for a cultural ideal. Tyler's culture, itself groping for an identity, gave him no single model of the American. The country would wait another fifty years for Emerson and Whitman to suggest how an American might be both idealistic and natural, elevated and downright, grandiosely republican and unselfconsciously Yankee.

But those were growing pains, not birth pains. With its exchanges on the singing schools, the continental soldier, the John Street Theatre, the Chesterfieldian possibilities of New York, *The Contrast* records the jelling of the twenty-five years of accelerating progress that made it possible, the emergence of American society in vivid wholeness. Tyler was perhaps the first imaginative writer to whom America was not a future possibility but a present circumstance. His unquestioning decision to treat the country's foibles with amusement rather than anxiety rested in the profound new assumption that there now existed a country substantial enough to withstand laughter.

Americans viewed their cultural life in 1785 with either astonished pride or dismay. One newspaper writer asserted what many of them felt about their country's artistic accomplishments: "Of no other nation can so honourable things be mentioned, at so early a period of their existence." [58] But other Americans believed that with these "honourable things" had come the affectation, self-indulgence, and moral laxity which endangered republics at the core and spelled their decline. Whereas some Americans saw concerts on the scale of London, others saw the gaudy umbrellas of concertgoers; whereas some saw the American premiere of *The School for Scandal*, others saw a crowd of demi-mondes; where some saw ennobling, Wertherean sensibility, others saw Mr. and Mrs. Importance strutting. Some saw glory, others saw decay.

Looked at two centuries later, however, the debate between these contending perceptions seems extravagant and ironic. Few in a society unaccustomed to having celebrated painters, epic poets, and festival concerts perceived how vastly what they boasted as progress or denounced as Luxury differed from the riper standards of European culture. *The Contrast*, to be sure, remains a delightful and actable play. But it by no means rivaled, as the *Pennsylvania Herald* claimed, "the most celebrated productions of the British muse." John Durang, looking back in successful old age on the eidophusicon sea-fight and other moving marvels of his youth, considered them "all bad enough, but anything was thought great in those days." [59] Only provincials who had just won a war and had witnessed a very rapid cultural development over two decades could have argued whether America really needed Miltons, Raphaels, and Handels, when they had in mind Barlow, West, and Billings.

What makes the postwar debate also ironic is the fact that it took place at a moment when the kind of progress Americans had expected for half a century had reached its limit. Like the Roman-Whig-Puritan Virtue to which it was closely related, the hope for continued Translation was being distracted by practical problems of representation, territory, and slavery, transformed by new intellectual fashions, questioned by a widespread distrust of highflown hopes, and made to sound banal by repetition. Given what would then have been called its 'state of society,' too, the country had gone as far as it could in re-creating what it imagined to be the culture of metropolitan Europe. Its available wealth and talent had done all they could to make Philadelphia, New York, and Charleston into a new Athens and Rome, the habitation of history painters, composers of oratorios, epic poets, planners of triumphal arches, and Catonic heroes.

The fact that a limit had been reached was highlighted by postwar euphoria and laid naked by foreign travelers. After a successful revolution, Tocqueville noted, "nothing seems impossible to anyone." Americans carried over from the War for Independence a sense of easy triumph, even of omnipotence. For those who cared to see, their overreaching began to show, especially in the performance arts. Andrew Adgate quarreled with Alexander Juhan before the first Uranian concert, charging that the works he wanted to perform surpassed the performers' abilities. Attending a concert in Philadelphia in 1783, the count dal Verme judged the instrumentalists "competent, but the music was too difficult for most of them." The many cultivated foreigners who visited the country after the war left little doubt that America's best was not good enough. An English merchant who attended the John Street Theatre in 1785, during an evening graced by Steuben and Washington, saw neither glory nor decay, but a small shabby house and a performance that was simply "wretched. I would not go a second time without a party of ladies if anybody would pay me for it." A Frenchman who had visited Philadelphia found that when he returned home a "very moderate exhibition at the Louvre" struck him, compared with the works of Peale, as "a group of Raphaels, Titians, and Vandykes." [60]

Philip Freneau, unique among his countrymen, also insisted that American culture was mediocre, and added that it was unreal as well. Continuing to drift from place to place, he viewed Philadelphia not as a new American Hague or Paris, but as "a city where there are not three persons possessed of elegant ideas!" While his contemporaries boasted the plethora of new magazines, fiction, and poetry, he found "few writers of books in this new world, and amongst these very few that deal in works of imagination, and, I am sorry to say, fewer still that have any success. . . ." As others debated Luxury against Virtue, he wrote indignantly about those the categories shut out, the many Americans who could afford to be neither carefree nor self-sacrificing: the begging soldier, out of drink and "bespatter'd around/ With the grog he had vomited up"; patriots like Joseph Reed, unmourned by "this ungrateful age"; debtors lying for nine unpaid shillings in jail "Appointed by the wisdom of your State/ To shut in *little* rogues, and keep out *great*." He slashed the much-praised commemorative portrait galleries and the heroic poems of the Connecticut writers because they failed to depict "a naked soldier, perishing with cold." Instead they offered Americans (as he satirized Dwight's *Conquest of Canäan*) "THE FALL OF ADONI-BEZEK," a twelve-book epic of "that mighty chief, who vex'd by foes,/ At length was robb'd of *both his thumbs and toes.*" [61]

Freneau found so much shallowness, of course, because he searched for it, overlooking whatever did not confirm his implacable dissatisfaction. Yet the very success of the process of Translation, paradoxically, was itself beginning to force a more sober estimate of what Americans had achieved. The ever more numerous accessions of European culture made the works of the recent past and the resources of the present seem ever more inadequate. The eclectic, nationalistic tunebooks of the early 1780's, the playing side by side of Billings and Read with Handel and Madan, gave the tunesmiths a titular parity with the best English and European composers but also exposed their shortcomings. One Philadelphian complained against a local concert manager for "producing some of his own compositions, which, after Handel's, was nearly similar to a low farce after a fine tragedy." [62] As cultural standards rose, today's evidence of Translation became tomorrow's evidence of provincialism. Like all theories of progress, the theory of Translation doomed the past to diminishment. By 1785 a process of repudiation had already begun whose outcome most Americans at the time would probably have found inexplicable and wounding. Fifty years later their ardently prized epic poems, their celebrated oratorios and festival concerts, most of their playwriting and a good deal of their history painting had been either dismissed as trifles or, for the greater part, entirely forgotten, as they remain today. Like the commencement poets of 1763, Emerson and his contemporaries would imagine themselves as having to create a culture where nothing had existed before.

By 1785, a limit had been reached economically as well. Rinsed of political moralizing, the arguments against Luxury contained the clear truth that the country could not support the arts any more lavishly. The progress of and the desire for the arts had so much boomed and accelerated as to have outstripped the growth of wealth. By 1789, the French-language *Courier de Boston* was warning artists abroad who planned to emigrate that few Americans were "wealthy enough to live unemployed on their revenue, or to pay the excessive price given in Europe for paintings and sculptures, and for the productions of arts more curious than useful." [63] America could no longer support the many foreign musicians who poured in atop the many established ones, the many magazines that kept appearing, the many engravings offered, the many acting companies. They had all begun to hurt each other by competing in a depressed market.

Both the cultural nationalists and the doctrinaire republicans neglected to say, or did not know, that the artists in America whom they boasted or denounced were barely managing to survive. While in 1763 modest schemes to raise subscriptions for some organ works or singing school failed, Peale's moving pictures or Quesnay's painting academy now failed more grandly. For all his collection of over one thousand prints and his devotion to America, Du Simitière failed to get support from the legislature to whom he applied; a finger of his left hand amputated, he died a pauper.[64] While music masters sponsored "Vocal Institutes," their low state had already become a standing joke, like the "Isaac Fac-Totum" sketched in the *Virginia Journal*, who barbers, lights lamps, and does "psalm singing and horse-shoeing . . . makes and mends all sorts of boots and shoes, teaches the hoboy [oboe] and Jew's-harp, cuts corns, bleeds and blisters on the lowest terms." When Andrew Law went to New York after abandoning his Philadelphia singing school, he found that his prospective clientele had been taken by a competitor, a black singing master whom he had trained himself. When he opened the school, he wrote, "very few attended. Frank the Negro who lived with me has about 40 scholars which he engaged to give up when I came, but he does not incline to now. . . . Every one to whom I bestow favours takes the bread out of my mouth." Law opened a school in Charleston instead, which apparently also failed. After applauding the "overpowering Pathos" of Selby's 1787 Handelian festival, Boston newspapers noted that because of the scarcity of money it was not well attended and earned only $151. The *American Magazine* and the *American Musical Magazine* lasted only a year, while the *Town and Country Magazine* lasted eight issues, the *New-Jersey Magazine* three issues, the *American Monitor* one issue. During his editorship of the more durable *American Museum*—supported by Washington—Mathew Carey complained that he lived in "intense penury," unable to pay his grocer.[65] Joel Barlow, while dedicating his epic poem to the king of France, was selling flax seed and coffee. Everywhere the supply of cultural commodities had outgrown the ability to pay for them.

Few Americans who had lived through the war, of course, cared how a Peale looked beside a Titian or whether their Vergil ran a store. What mattered was that twenty years ago they had no portraits by Peale and no American epics. As the country expanded westward, the process which delighted them would be repeated in places like St. Louis, Chicago, and Los Angeles, whose inhabitants would again record, with a sense of destiny, their first theatre, their first symphony orchestra, their first museum or important poem, taking for their standard of comparison not Athens or Rome, however, but the older established cities of the American East.

As the revolutionary period ended, the idiom of cultural translation was chorused more exuberantly than ever before. It was, nevertheless, falling out of use, and in large part because it had succeeded so well. The sun had indeed risen, the plant had bloomed, the drama was closing.

Part Two

<hr style="border: 1.5px double black;">

Parades—American Culture 1787–1789

Between 1787 and 1789 the United States devised, adopted, and began to live under their own form of government, events which seemed to many Americans the momentous final acts of the American Revolution and the prologue to a new future.

From May to September 1787, a Federal Convention meeting in Philadelphia worked out a written Constitution to be submitted to the states for ratification. Amid the public debate which followed the Convention, citizens of every class, trade, and profession paraded through American cities trailing federal banners, playing federal marches, and distributing federal verses in order to celebrate and promote the new scheme of government, which was ratified in June. An election for the first president and vice president of the United States was set for January and February 1789. Simultaneous with its unfolding appeared the first collection of American art songs, the first American novel, and possibly the first American landscape paintings. In March, the longstanding Philadelphia anti-theatre laws were repealed forever.

Congress announced the election results in April, after it convened for the first time under the Constitution. That the electors would necessarily choose Washington as president was obvious to almost everyone but Washington himself. Wishing nothing more than to remain in retirement on his farm, he resisted, protested, and at last acquiesced to serve. Jubilant thousands honored "Columbia's Favourite Son" with music, transparencies, triumphal arches, and congratulatory odes, lining the route and swelling the guard during his week-long procession from Mount Vernon to New York, the first national capital, where he was inaugurated on April 30, 1789.

47. The Constitution: May 1787–June 1788

On May 14, 1787, a Federal Convention was scheduled to meet in Philadelphia to devise a written Constitution for the United States. Many Americans believed that a stronger central government was necessary, one, moreover, which would realize the ideal of the people as a constituent power, able fundamentally to change their form of government without resorting again to the streets. As the Convention met, its president, George Washington, invoked the visionary language of his generation to suggest that the delegates' task was to direct mankind in a role the most appropriate to its possibilities: "a greater drama," he said, "is now acting on this theater than has heretofore been brought on the American stage, or any other in the world. We exhibit at present the novel and astonishing spectacle of a whole people deliberating calmly on what form of government will be most conducive to their happiness." [1]

A quorum for the Convention was not gathered until May 25, although eventually fifty-five delegates attended. They formed a political counterpart of the country's impressive cultural growth. Only a week or so before the first session, Joel Barlow had published his *Vision of Columbus*; only a few weeks before that, New Yorkers had seen the first performance of *The Contrast*; and in the preceding twelve months Americans had acquired their first musical magazine, Charles Willson Peale's "moving pictures," *The Poems of Philip Freneau*, concerts by Alexander Reinagle, and the *American Museum* and *Columbian Magazine*. The Convention provided a comparable symbol of modest but solid achievement. Washington and eighty-one-year-old Benjamin Franklin, of course, were international celebrities. Among the other delegates were Samuel Johnson, the first president of King's College; William Livingston, author of *Philosophic Solitude*; George Clymer, who had supported the American Company in its recent fight in the Pennsylvania legislature; James Wilson, formerly a tutor of Latin at the College of Philadelphia; John Dickinson, author of the original "Liberty Song"; George Wythe, professor of law at William and Mary; and Philip Freneau's Princeton classmate and fellow-satirist, James Madison.

As happened during the earlier Continental Congresses, the presence of a large group of sophisticated men in Philadelphia stimulated cultural activities of all kinds. David Humphreys and Andrew Law both came to town, Law to join his friend Noah Webster, Humphreys to meet with the Society of the Cincinnati and to join Washington. In July, Alexander Reinagle performed one of his own sonatas before Washington, as well as four-handed piano music in conjunction with James or Alexander Juhan.[2] Since the stringent anti-theatre law of 1786 did not take effect until August 31, 1787, the American Company managed to play until the last two weeks of the Convention. They trod lightly but surely, referring to the Southwark Theatre as the "Opera House" and advertising "a concert of music and lectures." Probably to gain support from the Society of the Cincinnati, they opened with a benefit for American seamen who had been captured by Barbary coast pirates.[3] The law stood, but the Company succeeded in establishing its patriotic credentials. During the last week of the Convention, the Philadelphia *Independent Gazetteer* published a "THE-ATRICAL QUERE" first printed in 1782, allegedly written by some soldiers:

> A NUMBER of the Officers in the Army would be glad to know why Congress are pleased to forbid ALL Public Diversions in this State, particularly the acting of Plays, which is so much approved and admired in all Parts of Europe, when our Sister States have Permission to fix Theatres, &c. for the Entertainment and Instruction of their Inhabitants?

Washington himself attended the Southwark at least three times during the Convention, witnessing concert versions of *Love in a Camp* and of Dryden's operatic version of *The Tempest*.[4]

The presence of the delegates also gave Charles Willson Peale a chance to reopen his moribund "moving pictures," and to test an even more ambitious entertainment. He had revived the show briefly in February but failed even to make expenses. In May, with the arrival of the delegates, he offered a special showing to the Society of the Cincinnati and issued a separate invitation to Washington. Washington attended, but ordinary citizens still did not. Peale had been nurturing, however, another venture. As he informed Benjamin West, his moving pictures had "injured my health and straightened my circumstances, and after a full essay, I have quitted that for a new, but no less arduous undertaking, that is the preserving of Birds & Beasts etc to form a Museum. . . ."[5]

Peale had begun work on the new museum just after the war. In 1783, a naturalist named Christian Michaelis visited Philadelphia, curious to see some giant bones found in Ohio which were in the collections of Du Simitière and of Dr. John Moran. Moran gave him permission to have drawings made of the bones, which were taken to Peale's studio for the purpose. Peale found that they brought in visitors. Sensing the business prospects, he began in June 1784 to form a natural history collection. Its growth was slowed by the building of his moving pictures, although in Peale's mind the two projects were not separate. As a deist, Peale was devoted to nature. He designed his motion pictures, he wrote, to imitate "those wonderful and pleasing presentations which divine nature so frequently offers to our view." [6] The new natural history museum amounted only to a more realistic imitation of the nature he adored.

Peale gathered materials for the museum throughout the early postwar period, collecting more energetically as his motion pictures failed commercially. He obtained silk grass from Beale Bordley of Maryland, wrote to Dr. Ramsay in Charleston for an alligator skin, began a collection of wild ducks to dispose on an artificial pond, personally pried loose from a ship's hull the sword of a swordfish, stuffed a Chinese gold pheasant sent him by Washington.[7] At the same time he converted his picture gallery and movie room into a natural history museum; removing the partition between the two, he had a single hall some seventy-seven feet long. The motion picture room became a rocky grotto for the display of snakes and reptiles, mirrors representing the water. By the winter of 1786 he believed that his museum would be considered of "more consequence than any thing of this sort in America." [8]

Peale opened the partly completed museum during the Convention. Several delegates visited it, including Washington.[9] What they saw was described in detail by the Reverend Manasseh Cutler, a representative of the Ohio Company, who was in Philadelphia in July, hoping to prosper from the opening of the new western territories. Cutler recalled being led into the room by a boy. Through a glass window, he saw Peale drawing with a pencil on a sheet of ivory. Believing that Peale was busy, he began going out—and was greeted from the door he had entered by Peale himself, who explained the joke. What Cutler had seen was a trompe-l'oeil wax statue that looked "*absolutely* alive." Cutler described the museum:

> It is very long but not very wide, has no windows, nor floor over it, but is open up to the roof, which is two or three stories, and from above the light is admitted in greater or less quantities at pleasure. The walls of the room are covered with paintings, both portrait and historic. One particular part is assigned to the portraits of the principal American characters who appeared on the stage during the late revolution. . . . To grace his collection, he had a number of the most distinguished clergymen in the middle and southern states who had, in some way or other, been active in the revolution. In other parts were a number of fine historic pieces, executed in a masterly manner. At the upper end of the room, General Washington, at full length and nearly as large as the life, was placed, as President of this sage and martial assembly.

Facing the large portrait of Washington, at the other end of the hall, were the natural history exhibits, beneath a small gallery:

> There was a mound of earth, considerably raised and covered with green turf, from which a number of trees ascended and branched out in different directions. On the declivity of this mound was a small thicket, and just below it an artificial pond; on the other side a number of large and small rocks of different kinds, collected from different parts of the world, and represented the rude state in which they are generally found. At the foot of the mound were holes dug and the earth thrown up, to show the different kinds of clay, ochre, coal, marl, etc., which he had collected from different parts; also, various ores and minerals. Around the pond was a beach, on which was exhibited an assortment of shells of different kinds, turtles, frogs, toads, lizards, water-snakes, etc. In the pond was a collection of fish with their skins stuffed, water-fowls, such as the different species of geese, ducks, cranes, herons, etc.; all having the appearance of life, for their skins were admirably preserved. On the mound were those birds which commonly walk on the ground, as the partridge, quail, heath-hen, etc.; also, different kinds of wild animals—bear, deer, leopard, tiger, wild-cat, fox, raccoon, rabbit, squirrel, etc. In the thickets and among the rocks, land-snakes, rattle-snakes of an enormous size, black, glass, striped, and a number of other snakes. The boughs of the trees were loaded with birds, some of almost every species in America, and many exotics.

Peale accompanied Cutler on the tour, providing "every information we desired." [10]

With Washington in town, Peale did not ignore the opportunity of taking a fresh likeness. In May he asked Washington for a sitting, explaining that "it gives me pain to make the request," but that he was moved by "the great desire I have to make a good mezzotinto print, that your numerous friends may be gratified with a faithful likeness (several of whom I find is not satisfied with any of the portraits they have seen.)" (Later he confided that a good print might also get him out of debt so that "on the success of this undertaking depends much of my happiness.") For Washington's convenience he suggested bringing his gear to Robert Morris' house, where Washington could sit at leisure but look after any pressing business that might arise. The painting, however, seems to have occurred at Peale's house, Washington posing on three mornings in early July, before attending the day's session. Peale turned the painting into a mezzotint which he advertised for sale just ten days after the Convention ended. It seems to have sold poorly, for shortly after its appearance he cut the price from one dollar to two-thirds of a dollar.[11] Americans were evidently growing weary of somber memorials to the war, and of gazing on still another Washington, another having appeared, by James Trenchard, early in 1787.

Delegates to the Convention shared something of this detachment from republican Virtue. Shays' Rebellion and postwar Luxury suggested that the citizen of the new nation was not a paragon of charity and benevolence. Those who debated the future of the republic, as James Madison recorded their words, occasionally likened the state to a diseased body in need of remedy, or compared the thirteen states to so many streams rushing to an ocean. But for the most part, they spoke without metaphor, designing a government that would not so much liberate the potential in defenders of "fair Liberty" as quell the factiousness of average sensual men minding the main chance. In this twilight of classical politics and of the neoclassical idiom, they paid little attention to the future of the arts in America, despite the earlier Whig view of the bond between Liberty and Learning. They did touch on such peripherally related problems as immigration, Madison himself arguing that the "part of America which had encouraged them [immigrants] most had advanced most rapidly in population, agriculture & the arts." Late in the proceedings, George Mason and Robert Morris briefly argued the need for sumptuary laws, an issue likely to affect the theatre. Morris held that sumptuary laws would freeze present levels of affluence and in effect create a landed nobility; Mason called attention to "the extravagance of our manners, the excessive consumption of foreign superfluities, and the necessity of restricting it. . . ." [12] A committee was appointed to report back on the question, but never did so.

The Convention came closest to dealing with matters vital to the arts in its debate on a copyright law. In 1783, Joel Barlow had sent to Madison a copy of the Connecticut copyright statute. Shortly before the Convention, Madison wrote an essay on the "Vices of the Political System of the United States" in which he listed among other defects in the Articles of Confederation the lack of uniformity "in the laws concerning naturalization & literary property. . . ." In August he submitted to a committee of detail a power for Congress to "secure to literary authors their copy rights for a limited time." It came back from committee far narrower; the version finally approved on September 12 read: "To promote the progress of science and useful arts, by securing for limited times to authors and inventors the exclusive right to their respective writings and discoveries." [13] The promotion of "science and useful arts" offered no help to writers of plays, verse, or music.

Given the Convention's neglect of the arts, the celebrated remark made five days later by Benjamin Franklin was unwittingly ironic. As George Washington and thirty-eight delegates signed the new Constitution, he looked toward the radiant sun painted on Washington's chair. Painters, he observed, "found it difficult to distinguish in their art a rising from a setting sun. I have . . . often and often in the course of the Session . . . looked at that behind the President without being able to tell whether it was rising or setting: But now at length I have the happiness to know that it is a rising and not a setting Sun." [14]

Three delegates at the Convention refused to sign the Constitution, foreshadowing a campaign against its acceptance which lasted until July 1788. While each of the states except Rhode Island called ratifying conventions to consider the document, debate over its meaning filled the presses. On one side, anti-Federalists saw the Constitution as a betrayal of the war for Independence: Ignoring Montesquieu's dictum that republicanism was impossible in a large territory, it sacrificed the rights of states to an overweeningly powerful central government; providing for infrequent elections, and overlapping judicial and executive functions, it gave political power to a social elite in the hope of containing *Anarchia*. In the words of a typical anti-Federalist account, the document had been framed by a *"dark conclave"* of "monarchy-men," "bold conspirators" who had devised a government "composed of an *elective* king and a standing army, officered by his sycophants, the starvelings of the Cincinnati, and an aristocratical Congress of the *well-born*. . . ." For their side, the pro-Constitution forces had such persuasive spokesmen as Hamilton, Madison, and Jay, whose eighty-five essays, later *The Federalist*, appeared in New York newspapers in 1787–88. They answered anti-Federalist charges and justified with retrospective symmetry and system what the Convention had wrought out of improvisation and expediency. In their concern over the dangers of power, both sides occasionally revived the expiring idiom of "fair Liberty." Anti-Federalists warned that the Constitution pointed "the dagger of Ambition . . . at the fair bosom of Liberty. . . . Shall we not recoil at such a deed, and all cry out with one voice, 'Hands off!' " In kind, the writers of *The Federalist* warned against idle schemes to preserve the Articles of Confederation, "which would seduce us into an expectation of peace and cordiality," and against "the fatal charm which has too long seduced us from the paths of felicity." [15] In drawing on the language of Whig Sentimentalism, both sides claimed to speak for the authentic tradition of the Revolution.

The arts entered the debate with their own means of persuasion and propaganda. Sometime shortly after the Convention, Matthew Pratt painted a large sign for the tavern opposite the Southwark Theatre, depicting the assembled delegates. Philadelphians paused to point out likenesses of Franklin, Washington, and others, and to consider the verses beneath: "Those 38 great men have signed a powerful Deed/ That better times to us, should very soon succeed." For the January 1788 issue of the *Columbian Magazine*, James Trenchard engraved Fame holding a copy of the Constitution and pointing to a classical temple. In April, the American Company advertised in New York "A Serious Pastoral . . . by a Citizen of the United States, called The Convention, or the Columbian Father. . . . In Act 1st, a Procession of the Thirteen States, From the Temple of Liberty." The image of the Constitution as architecture, and of its government as a new structure, was elaborated by Francis Hopkinson in an allegorical tale entitled "The New Roof." Hopkinson dramatized many constitutional issues in terms of a family needing a new roof for safety and comfort. He argued the case for hard currency to replace paper money, for instance, by observing that the old shingling "had not been secured with iron nails, but only wooden pegs, which swelling and shrinking by successions of wet and dry weather . . . [had become] so loose, that many of them had been blown away by the wind." In "The Raising: A New Song for Federal Mechanics," published in March 1788, Hopkinson tried to suggest the democratic basis of the Constitution in the face of anti-Federalist insistence on its essentially aristocratic thrust:

> COME muster, my lads, your mechanical tools,
> Your saws and your axes, your hammers and rules;
> Bring your mallets and planes, your level and line,
> And plenty of pins of American pine:
> *For our roof we will raise, and our song still shall be,*
> *Our government firm, and our citizens free.*[16]

On the other side, *The Times* and *The Storm* (Philadelphia, 1788) by the Philadelphia poet Peter Markoe leagued the Federalists with Luxury and deism, and showed that they sought to dupe the common people with a baffling scheme of checks and balances which required a standing army.

Weary of still more suspected plots and divisive storms, other Americans regarded the proposed Constitution with the comic detachment of *The Contrast*. As Bostonians rejoiced over ratification by Massachusetts in February 1788, the Philadelphia *Gazetteer* reminded them that the vote had been carried by a scant majority of nineteen:

> There they went up, up, up,
> And there they went down, down, downy,
> There they went backwards and forwards,
> And poop for *Boston* towny!

Another Philadelphia newspaper proposed its own version of the proceedings at the Massachusetts ratifying convention, which was copied in more than thirty newspapers and issued as a separate broadside. In thirteen verses it reduced the delegates' flights about Virtue and representation to Yankee "notions," much as Bostonians themselves had recently reduced the proclamations of Gage or Burgoyne:

Then 'squire *Hancock*, like a man,
  Who dearly loves the nation,
By a concil'atory plan,
  Prevented much Vexation.
            Yankee doodle, &c.
He made a *woundy* Fed'ral speech,
  With sense and elocution;
And then the 'Vention did beseech,
  T'adopt the Constitution.
            Yankee doodle, &c.
. . . .

The *Boston* folks are *deucid* lads,
  And always full of notions;
The boys, the girls, their mams and dads,
  Were fill'd with joy's commotions.
            Yankee doodle, &c. . . .[17]

The most lighthearted debunking of the solemnity on both sides of the constitutional debate appeared in *The Politician Out-Witted*, a five-act comedy written in 1788 by twenty-three-year-old Samuel Low of New York and published the next year. Low seems to have offered the play to Hallam and Henry, who rejected it—with good reason, since although it begins very well, its unmanageable comic and romantic complications end in confusion. Influenced by *The Contrast*, the play contains a Jonathan-like bumpkin named Humphry Chubb, a coquette named Maria who enjoys "a walk in the Broad-way, Pharisee like, to be seen of men," and a Europeanized fop named Worthnought, *"foy d'Homme d'Honneur,"* all of whom exchange lively repartee about Chesterfield, novels, barbers, and other features of postwar society in New York.

The main action of the play, however, involves "Trueman" and "Loveyet," whose feuding over the Constitution nearly prevents the marriage between their offspring. Trueman, the Federalist, is a Latinate blatherer who defines the Constitution as "a concatenation or coacervation of simple, distinct parts, of various qualities or properties, united, compounded, or constituted in such a manner, as to form or compose a system or body, when viewed in its aggregate or general nature." His rhapsodies over the new government are mishmashes of the once-glorious emblems of progress:

> . . . this [ratification by Massachusetts] is the sixth grand column in the federal edifice; we only want three more to make up the lucky nine; and then the nine Muses will make our western world their permanent abode; and HE who is at once their *Favorite* and *Patron*, will preside over the whole: then we shall see another Golden Age; arts will then flourish, and literature be properly encouraged. That's the grand *desideratum.* . . .

Loveyet's apoplectic reply to this is that Federalists want to "cram their unconstitutional bolus down our throats, with latin;—you and your vile junto of perfidious politicians, want to *latin* us out of our liberties." Loveyet, however, is no less a fool than Trueman, a crotchety, penny-pinching, superannuated merchant who turns out to be in love with the coquette Maria. His anti-Federalism is seen as simply an aspect of his vanity and libertinism, much as Trueman's cosmic Federalism is seen as an outlet for his foggy pedantry and bewildered erudition. The villain of the play is the surrounding debate on the Constitution, which divides families, prevents likely marriages, and raises tempers. The gist of the play is that political strife however fateful-sounding is temporary. Loveyet's son is correct to "think of no Constitution but that of Love and Matrimony."

Amidst the public debate, legislative action on the Constitution continued. By May 1788, eight states had ratified the document, one short of the number required for adoption. Rhode Island had refused even to call a ratifying convention; Virginia and New York contended against strong anti-Federalist opposition. In June, however, New Hampshire ratified, giving the United States a new form of government. Virginia followed later the same month, New York in July. As each state fell in line, its citizens celebrated the federal union with public festivals combining parades, community banquets, poetry readings, concerts, plays, and much else. Spectacular processions followed the official announcement by Congress, on July 2, that the Constitution had been adopted.

Newspapers of the day praised the decorum and harmony which prevailed at these festivals. But antagonisms between the Truemans and Loveyets remained. Rhode Island Federalists, angered by the failure of their state to call a ratifying convention, attempted to celebrate ratification by New Hampshire. They were surrounded by several hundred armed anti-Federalists who would allow them to drink thirteen toasts or fire thirteen salutes but not nine. Francis Hopkinson suggested that anti-Federalists might hold an anti-procession. It could take place on July 5, start at ten at night with toasts, display emblems of Anarchy and a liberty cap of green crocus, and feature a "Band of Music consisting of four Hurdy-Gurdies, two Jews Harps and a Banjoe-playing the *dead March* in Saul." [18]

For those who welcomed them, however, the festivals vividly and complexly expressed what the members of the new nation thought of themselves and of each other. In an oration delivered from a float after the Philadelphia procession, James Wilson explained the nature of the event in which the citizens had just participated, and three ways in which future processions might serve the government:

> They may *instruct* and *improve*, while they *entertain* and *please*. They may point out the elegance or usefulness of the sciences and the arts. They may preserve

the memory, and engrave the importance of great *political events*. They may represent, with peculiar felicity and force, the operation and effects of great *political truths*.[19]

To point out the importance of the arts, the processions employed poets, musicians, painters, and actors in the creation of odes, marches, floats, and skits. Indeed, the participation of so many cultural figures in the political rejoicing marks the fullest expression in eighteenth-century America of the Whig view of the reciprocal relation between liberty and the arts.

To dramatize and reinforce the meaning of "great *political events*," the processions hoisted portraits and effigies of Washington and other now-national heroes through the streets. The processions held after July 2—combined July 4 and ratification ceremonies—deliberately arranged pictures, floats, and costumes so as to present the Constitution as the last link of a long historical chain, beginning in at least two parades with a marcher dressed as Columbus. Benjamin Rush described the effect:

> The connection of the great event of independence, the French alliance, the Peace, and name of General Washington with the adoption of the Constitution was happily calculated to unite the most remarkable transports of the mind which were felt during the war with the great event of the day, and to produce such a tide of joy as has seldom been felt in any age or country. Political joy is one of the strongest emotions of the human mind.[20]

Less directly, the processions jogged memories of earlier demonstrations, and their poignant circumstances. The Burial of Liberty rites, the *Mischianza*, the *Dauphinade*, the Peace celebrations, Peale's triumphal arch—each strove to surpass, and thus recalled, the last public event in memory. The constitutional processions surpassed and recalled them all. Newspaper after newspaper gave the sizes of crowds, the lengths of floats, the height and width of flags and standards, the weights of oxen to be slaughtered for public consumption—the impressive numbers testifying like massive oaks to the miraculous burgeoning power of the seed.

In representing *"political truths,"* the procession argued the Federalist case as forcibly as did the recent essays of Madison, Hamilton, and Jay. Blacksmiths, sailors, citizens, merchants, scholars, painters, aldermen all marched together, their places usually assigned by lot, a living image, in Wilson's words, of *"A people, free and enlightened, establishing and ratifying a system of government which they have previously considered, examined, and approved!"* Contemporary commentators unfailingly remarked that the processions stood not for a part of society but for a *"whole People,"* a "Commixture of all descriptions," a federal union in which the parts, *E Pluribus Unum,* were equal however diverse.[21] In marching side by side, the various classes, professions, and trades demonstrated—and experienced—the amity and indifference to rank vital to republican life. Their "harmony and respect for each other," Benjamin Rush observed, argued that "they were all necessary to each other and all useful in cultivated society." The message of public consent and cooperation was reiterated on the maxims displayed on flags and floats and in odes written for the occasion, making, Rush added, "such an impression upon the minds of our young people that 'federal' and 'union' have now become part of the 'household words' of every family in the city."

The processions owed their impact, however, to more than demonstrations of Rising Glory and of political truths. Jacques Louis David, who later arranged plebeian fetes for the French republic, explained that "National festivals are instituted for the people; it is fitting that they participate in them with a common accord and that they play the principal role there." [22] Those who witnessed and who comprised the flowing vision of a past tied inexorably to the present were not merely the arguers but also the argument, not merely the spectators but also the actors, observing themselves in the process of defining themselves. In their self-proclaiming excess, they were giving early form to a distinctive American popular culture. Deriving its intent from the opulent visions of Rising Glory and its spirit from the ebullience expressed in "Yankee Doodle," its later products are Broadway and Disneyland, Rose Bowl Parades and Super Bowl spectaculars, the films of Cecil B. De Mille and Busby Berkeley—the creations, for better or worse, of an exuberant love of superfluity.

The first sizable celebration took place in Boston on February 8, just two days after ratification by Massachusetts. Marchers drew across the snow-filled streets what became a standard feature of later parades—a ship representing the Constitution. One versifier pictured the affair to "Yankee Doodle":

> So straightway they procession made,
>   Lord! how *nation* fine, Sir!
> For ev'ry man of ev'ry trade
>   Went with his tools—to dine, Sir!
>   *Yankee doodle*, &c.
>
> *John Foster Williams* in a ship,
>   Join'd in the social band, Sir,
> And made the lasses dance and skip,
>   To see him sail on land, Sir.
>   *Yankee doodle*, &c.
>
> Oh then a *whapping* feast begun
>   And all hands went to eating;

> They drank their toasts,—shook hands and sung,
> Huzza'd for 'Vention meeting.
> *Yankee doodle,* &c.[23]

Maryland ratified on April 26. Two days later, 200 people sat down to dinner at Mann's Tavern in Annapolis. At the fifth toast—to Washington —curtains were drawn back, revealing a portrait of Washington by Peale. For other festivities in Annapolis Peale painted, at his own expense, a nine-foot-square transparency of a female Genius of America, putting Anarchy away with her left hand and pointing with her right to the consequences of good government—science, agriculture, commerce, and the arts. Above her a figure of Fame with two trumpets heralded the "NEW CONSTITUTION." Peale showed the transparency also in Baltimore, where, on May 1, about 3,000 people celebrated.[24] Carpenters built a tower for the event, supported by seven architects (the seven so-far ratifying states), and having thirteen each of stories, pillars, arches, pediments, and spires. Thirty-nine guns (three times thirteen) saluted. Painters in the 'mixed' procession carried a painted figure of Michelangelo sketching on a piece of canvas. Local merchants built a ship called "Federalist," which after the procession they sent down the Potomac to Mount Vernon as a gift to Washington.[25]

As adoption proceeded through the late spring and summer, the festivities in cities and towns of the ratifying states often declared the importance of the arts in the new republic. Charlestonians held a procession, shortly after ratification by South Carolina, on May 27. Among them was the city's chief portrait painter, Henry Benbridge. Exiled to St. Augustine shortly after the fall of Charleston in 1780, he had been welcomed back by the *Gazette* with hopes for "the Progress of the ARTS, which we trust soon to see flourish in our State." Now, to represent his trade, he carried "tools decorated with ribbons" as he marched in a platoon of limners. The parade at York, Pennsylvania, contained another group of painters, who toasted: "The new constitution in its true colours, neither caricatured nor flattered; and may the brush of investigation correct the glare of light given by its friends, and the profusion of shade thrown on it by its enemies." [26]

The specially significant New Hampshire parade, on June 26, seems to have introduced the idea of drawing a printing press through the streets to strike off poems written for the occasion. In New Hampshire, the press produced an ode sung during the march to the tune of Handel's "He comes, he comes":

> It comes! It comes! high raise the song
> The bright procession moves along

From pole to pole resound the Nine [states]
And distant worlds the chorus join.

As a procession moved through Trenton on July 4, a poem was distributed
to the crowd, prophesying that the Constitution would repress *Anarchia*:

This government will order bring
Out of our sad confusion,
Then let us all rejoice and sing—
Huzza, the Constitution!

On the same day, a procession wound through New Haven, containing a
federal ship and a contingent of 200 Yale students who were all, said the
Gazette, "carrying various books which they were reading, from the
New-England primer, to the Works of Vergil and Homer." After parading
for nearly two miles, the marchers entered the meeting house, where they
heard anthems, a singing of Barlow's version of the Sixty-seventh Psalm,
and a federal hymn composed by the Yale tutor Barnabas Bidwell,
followed by a reading of the Declaration of Independence.[27]

The climax to these events came in Philadelphia and New York. The
Philadelphia spectacle is unusually well documented in very lengthy
accounts by Rush, Hopkinson (the chairman of the organizing committee), and others. One of its producers, appropriately, was Charles Willson
Peale. He helped to plan the route, turned pasteboard and silver paper
into armor, decorated the beeves carried by the butchers and later given to
the poor, painted the water on the ship-float representing federal union,
and tackled the problem of how to negotiate the ship around street
corners.[28] He also painted the figures for, and may have helped design,
"The Grand Federal Edifice" that was the main float of the parade—a
domed building with many emblems and devices supported by thirteen
Corinthian columns, three columns left uncompleted to symbolize the
present state of adoption. Some thirty-six feet high in all, the float was
drawn by ten white horses.

In Hopkinson's account, the day began with a full peal of bells from
Christ Church steeple and a discharge of cannon from a ship, anchored off
Market Street, named *Rising Sun*. Groups began assembling at eight in the
morning at South and Third streets and were marshaled in an order
determined by lots, by nine directors with speaking trumpets. (One of the
directors was Thomas Procter, now a colonel in the Philadelphia cavalry,
but recently a prominent military musician whose band performed at
Valley Forge.)[29] Hopkinson estimated that there were 5,000 marchers,
forming a procession about a mile and a half long that took three hours to
pass by. Large broadsides were distributed identifying the passing groups
and giving the parade route, which stretched from Third Street to Union

Green, a distance of about three miles. Along the whole line of march streets had been swept and trees lopped.

At nine-thirty in the morning the procession began moving. Twelve "axe-men" in white frocks headed the march, symbolic of pioneers or foresters. They were followed by a troop of light dragoons and a flock of emblematic flags—Independence, the state conventions, the peace treaty, Washington—borne on horse and foot. One rider wore a liberty cap and carried a flag with the words Fourth of July 1776. The bearer of a flag signifying the French alliance rode the horse which Rochambeau had ridden at Yorktown. A herald crying aloud "a new aera" carried a flag with the verse:

> Peace o'er our land her olive wand extends,
> And white rob'd innocence from heav'n descends;
> The crimes and frauds of anarchy shall fail,
> Returning justice lifts again her scale.

Amidst this array marched groups of soldiers and a band performing Alexander Reinagle's new "Foederal March," written for the occasion (ill., p. 532).

Behind the emblems came the Constitution float, drawn by six horses and mounted on a light blue carriage some twenty feet long whose hind wheels were eight feet in diameter. Decorated with liberty caps, the float displayed a framed copy of the Constitution over the words "THE PEOPLE." The centerpiece was a thirteen-foot-high eagle emblazoned with thirteen silver stars in a blue field, talons gripping an olive branch and thirteen arrows. Behind it marched Hopkinson (dressed as an admiralty judge) and other dignitaries, followed by "The Grand Federal Edifice" with its motto "IN UNION THE FABRIC STANDS FIRM," followed in turn by 450 architects and carpenters with insignia of their trade, the Cincinnati, and a large contingent of emblem-bearing farmers, including a sower tossing actual seed in the streets.

The two hundred or so manufacturers and mariners who came next had devised elaborate dumb-shows. Onto a thirty-foot-long carriage hauled by ten horses were crammed a carding machine, a spinning machine, several looms, and an apparatus for printing muslin—in effect an entire factory, kept in operation throughout the procession by about a dozen people: Two men carded cotton at the rate of fifty pounds a day, a woman drew cotton on the eighty-spindle machine, muslin was designed, printed, and cut by workers dressed in their own products. Mariners carrying spyglasses and charts preceded the thirty-three-foot-long "Federal Ship *Union*," its wheels and machinery hidden under a sheet of canvas painted by Peale as the sea. The bottom of the ship was a barge taken from the *Serapis* captured by

John Paul Jones. Aboard were twenty mounted guns, and a crew of twenty-five sailors demonstrating nautical skills. Other floats in their wake demonstrated shipbuilding, nearly completing in the course of the procession the construction of a thirteen-foot boat.

Behind this, with another "band of music-conductors," moved a throng of more than forty distinct trades, most with their own float and demonstration of skill—coach painters, porters, gilders, blacksmiths, hatters, glovers, bookbinders, stone cutters, barbers, tobacconists, makers of instruments, of clocks, of cabinets, of bricks—a cross section of a theoretically classless society of rich potential, self-sufficient and populous. The carvers displayed busts of Washington and Phidias. The printers' float, a nine-foot-square platform drawn by four horses, supported an operating press which struck off an ode by Francis Hopkinson:

> Behold! Behold! an Empire rise!
> An AEra new, time as he flies,
> Hath entered in the book of fame.
>
> . . . .
>
> Science shall flourish, genius stretch her wing,
> In native strains Columbian muses sing. . . .

Copies of the ode (and of another written in German) were distributed to the crowd as the platform passed. Ten small packets containing Hopkinson's lines and toasts for the day were dispatched to the ratifying states, with inspired novelty, by air. Atop the printers' platform stood the dancer John Durang, dressed as Mercury in a flesh-color costume with wings of feather.[30] The ten packets were tied to pigeons which at intervals—and "amidst the acclamations," Hopkinson noted, "of an admiring multitude" —lifted off from Durang's cap.

At the tag end of the procession came members of Congress, civic officials, lawyers, physicians, a band, the "clergy of the different Christian denominations, with the rabbi of the Jews, walking arm in arm." Distilling the meaning of the whole, the last contingent—followed only by a county troop of horse to bring up the rear—consisted of students from the University of Pennsylvania and from other schools in the city. Led by professors, masters, and tutors, they marched behind a flag inscribed *"The rising generation."*

When the last of the procession reached Union Green, some 17,000 people—nearly half the population of Philadelphia—sat down to dinner. A circle of tables had been built, within whose 500-foot diameter had been brought the "Grand Federal Edifice" and the "Federal Ship *Union*." Hogsheads of American porter, beer, and cider lined the inner circumference. Announced by trumpets and answered by cannon from the ship

Rising Sun, ten toasts were drunk, first to "The people of the United States," last to "The whole family of mankind."

The New York procession, on July 23, went on even though ratification by New York was still being debated with bitterness in convention at Poughkeepsie. The organizers presumably hoped that the parade would influence the upstate proceedings, as it probably did; three days later, the convention ratified. Citizens were asked to sweep and water their streets on the morning of the event, which began, symbolically, with the firing of thirteen guns at ten o'clock. In ten divisions, seventy-six groups of marchers moved down Broadway toward Bowling Green—where New Yorkers had toppled the statue of George III thirteen years before.

The New York procession was smaller than Philadelphia's, but no less heartily ingenious. As in Philadelphia, the line began with "4 Foresters in Frocks, carrying Axes," and ended with a corps of students, from Columbia College (renamed in 1784 from King's College). Second place, however, went to a personage who did not appear on Market Street, "Columbus in his Ancient Dress—on Horseback." Squads of tradesmen, from chocolate makers to silversmiths, carried flags with emblems and mottoes, before and behind floats that enacted American accomplishment and self-sufficiency. Instrument makers carried a figure of Apollo playing a lyre; tinplate workers built a "Federal Tin Warehouse"; farmers ran a threshing machine; bakers displayed a "Federal Loaf" risen from a whole barrel of flour; furriers appeared with Indians in fur-trimmed garments. The printers' standard portrayed Libertas holding a pileus above the head of Benjamin Franklin; their float struck off for distribution to the crowd an ode by Samuel Low hailing "An AEra, greater than the golden age/ Of which the Poets dream." Noah Webster and William Dunlap marched with the New York Philological Society, a band of linguistic nationalists dressed uniformly in black. The secretary of the Society held a scroll "containing the principles of a *Federal* language"; the librarian, behind him, carried a treatise on language by the English radical Horne Tooke; Dunlap, recently returned from England, bore a standard with several complex emblems, one of which signified "the *obvious* origin of the American language from the Gothic." [31]

New York's failure to ratify gave the procession an undercurrent of exhortation. Many banners, floats, and skits were contrived less in a spirit of celebration than of imprecation or cheerleading. On the coopers' float, barrelmakers implied the uselessness of the Articles of Confederation by trying to put back together an old keg; unable to, they built a new, tight, ironbound keg labeled "New Constitution." Other paraders called on New York to join the other ratifying states. Sailmakers in the course of the march made a sail, under the banner "Fit me well, and rig me neat,/ And join me to the Federal fleet." The pewterers' silk banner (ill., p. 533) promised that Liberty and Learning would thrive in a united Columbia:

> The Federal Plan Most Solid & Secure
> Americans Their Freedom Will Endure
> All Arts Shall Flourish in Columbia's Land
> And All her Son's Join as One Social Band

The twenty-seven-foot-long Federal Ship—a thirty-two-gun frigate manned by sailors and drawn by ten horses—took on a pilot when it reached Beaver Street. He arrived on an eighteen-foot-long, horsedrawn boat and halloed the captain:

> PILOT: From whence came ye?
> CAPT. M. [athewman]: From the old Constitution
> PILOT: Where bound?
> CAPT. M.: To the New Constitution.
> PILOT: Will you have a pilot?
> CAPT. M.: Aye.
> PILOT: I'll board you on the star board bow.[32]

Upholsterers made an intricate case for ratification on a blue, railed stage containing a seven-foot-high Federal Chair. Covered with blue satin, the chair was decorated with oak and laurel leaves—symbols of strength and "proof against vice, being ever green." To one side stood a liberty-capped boy holding a parchment entitled "Federal Constitution"; on the other side stood a boy with sword and balance representing Justice; behind stood two genii, emblems of achievement, with the motto "The reward of virtue." On the chair itself sat a genie with the word "wisdom" on his breast. A verse interpreted the tableau:

> None but the virtuous, wise and great,
> The Federal States shall e'er dictate.
> Virtues genii, wisdom show
> That laurels are the worthies due.

The canopy over the chair showed ten gold stars and two watchful tigers, "emblematical of our native strength and watchfulness over our country." A dome—apparently roofing the stage—depicted thirteen star-tipped gold rays, and supported a globe topped by an eagle "with expanded wings ready to fly away the moment her liberty is invaded." Somewhere on the stage, a boy dressed as an Indian to represent America held a standard with the words "May the Federal Constitution be supported as is the canopy and chair of state." Beside the float walked thirteen upholsterers wearing blue and white cockades with the initials "F. C." [33]

The New York procession ended with a banquet for some 6,000 persons, held in a pavilion designed by Pierre L'Enfant, the architect of the 1782 Philadelphia *Dauphinade*. The diners sat at ten rows or colonnades of tables, each 440 feet long, arranged like spokes of a fan. At the gathering point was a dome surmounted by a figure of Fame—the symbol of achieved progress—her trumpet proclaiming a new era.

48. Late Developments During the First Presidential Election. The First American Songsters; the First American Novel; the First American Landscape Paintings; the Repeal of the Anti-Theatre Laws: November 1788–March 1789

Immediately after adoption of the Constitution, Congress appointed a committee for putting the new government into effect. It selected New York as the first national capital and set a timetable for the election of the first president. Electors would be chosen in the different states on the first Wednesday in January 1789, and would vote in designated cities of the ratifying states on the first Wednesday in February. Congress would convene for the first time under the Constitution the first Wednesday in March, and formally announce the names of the two men picked by the electors.

Some striking cultural events accompanied the unfolding of the electoral process. Occurring within three months, they can be thought of as either the last cultural accessions of British America or the initial achievements of the United States, for each event spanned old and new and bore the likeness of broad political and cultural changes of the moment.

The first happened on November 29, 1788, when the Philadelphia *Federal Gazette* announced the publication of Francis Hopkinson's *Seven Songs for the Harpsichord or Forte Piano*, "the first Work of this kind attempted in the United States." [1] Consisting of lyrics and accompaniments for young or inexperienced players, it was the first published collection of American art songs. Collections like the *American Mock-Bird* (New York, 1764) had existed before the Revolution, indeed since the 1730's; but they were merely American anthologies of English songs. A swelling taste for secular songs in the late 1780's brought with it a spurt of such works: *The American Songster, The Charms of Melody, The Philadelphia Songster, A Collection of Favorite Songs,* and *Twelve Favorite Pieces,* all except the first being published in Philadelphia, in 1788 or 1789. But these still contained mostly English works, with a scattering of American. Cultural nationalists found the imbalance galling. A character in *The Better Sort* (Boston, 1789) complained: "Must we be obliged to sing *English songs* forever—I heard a person some evenings since sing a song about *Auld England's glory*—what have *Americans* to do, in the name of *Phebus [sic],* with *'Auld England's glory'?*" Hopkinson's *Seven Songs* was in part a response to his query: "Ought not a *new nation* to have *new songs?*"

The response was ironic in two ways, however. In spirit and style, Hopkinson's songs differed little from English and European songs. Moreover the outburst of American secular songs compounded the problems of the New England singing schools, which had in fact produced an indigenous music, an art grown out of village worship, designed for people suspicious of art. The ability of the schools to occupy an unstable middle ground between devotion and recreation was already undermined by those who had grown impatient with their gaiety and estheticism. The popularity of the new songsters represented an attack from the other side, from those who had grown impatient with the schools' austerities. Philip Freneau dramatized the change of taste in his *Journey from Philadelphia to New-York* (Philadelphia, 1787), in which "Bob," a ballad singer, detects that his time has come:

> That the tunes which the kirk or the curates had made
> (And which always had ruin'd the balladman's trade)
> Were wholly disus'd, and that now was the time
> For singers of catches and dealers in rhyme
> To step from their stalls, where they long were disgrac'd,
> Reform the old music, and fix a new taste.

Some Protestant church musicians accommodated themselves to the "new taste": The "Absalom Aimwell" who compiled the *Philadelphia Songster* was in reality Andrew Adgate, the Connecticut-born singing master. A benefit concert given for William Selby in Boston in 1788 featured not the usual mix of Handel, Billings, and Selby but Selby's Organ Concerto, a Mr. Deverell singing *"Je pense a vous"* and a "Master *Brewer*" doing "Song in the Country Courtship." A concert by the Aretinian Society the same year coupled works by Billings with "Major André's Farewell." [2]

The new taste that threatened to overwhelm the schools manifested itself in other forms as well. In Providence in 1788 appeared John

Griffiths' *Collection of the newest and most fashionable country dances and cotillions*—the first dance book published in America. Magazines of the late 1780's suddenly began printing with regularity what amounts to the first serious American music criticism—articles such as "The Power of Musick," "On Vocal Music," "On the Power of Sound," "Music Physically Examined," "Origin of Musical Notes," "Vocal and Instrumental Music."[3] Readers of such essays could hardly escape seeing more clearly than before the crudities of the New England singing schools, and seeing less clearly their great achievement, which was their perfection of provincial possibilities.

The second telling event occurred two months later, shortly after the states chose their electors. On January 22, 1789, the Boston *Independent Chronicle* advertised for sale at six shillings what it called "The First American Novel." It was *The Power of Sympathy: Or, The Triumph of Nature. Founded in Truth.* Its publication marks the beginning not only of the American novel, but of a huge vogue for novel reading in America. Between 1744, when Franklin reprinted *Pamela,* and 1789 there had been 56 American reprints of foreign novels; between *The Power of Sympathy* and 1800 there were 350 reprints.[4]

Like Hopkinson's *Songs,* however, *The Power of Sympathy* was as much a culmination as a beginning, developing earlier tendencies to a point where they seemed a fresh start. The late 1780's sped the growth of a native school of sensibility, whose emergence we have traced in the first postwar publication of Goethe and in the poems of Joseph Brown Ladd. By 1789, American readers and writers, particularly those under twenty-five, were gorging themselves on wretchedness. The cover of the *Massachusetts Magazine* revealed Thisbe, a sword partly driven into her breast, ready to deliver her own coup de grâce by falling upon her slain lover. Joseph Hazard's *Juvenile Poems* anatomized *"Depression of Spirits"*:

> These nerves, unstrung, their wonted task disclaim,
>   Nor more the sympathetic aid dispense,
> To shoot the rapture thro' the kind'ling frame,
>   Or waft the transports of the thrilling sense.

Instead of *Common Sense,* the eighteen-year-old Philadelphian Charles Brockden Brown offered *The Rhapsodist,* the mental wanderings of a solitary man attuned to physical nature but contemptuous of "the practice and opinions of the multitude"—an archetypal, and anti-republican, romantic hero.[5]

The Power of Sympathy was thus only the lengthiest of many new works of overheated imagination. Its author was twenty-four-year-old William Hill Brown, a half-brother of the painter Mather Brown.[6] He closely based his plot on a tragic and notorious scandal in the family of his neighbors, the Mortons, who tried to prevent publication of the novel.[7] Both scandal and novel gave substance to the forebodings of the foes of Luxury, since they both involved the same couples who had been satirized in 1785 in *Sans Souci. Alias Free and Easy*. The author of that skit had modeled the characterizations of "Mr. and Mrs. Importance" upon Perez Morton (author of the text for Billings' "When Jesus Wept") and his wife Sarah Apthorp Morton (the poet "Philenia"). As things turned out, Perez seduced his wife's younger sister, who in August 1788 committed suicide. This tragedy forms the core of Brown's novel, which he dedicated to "the Young Ladies of United Columbia . . . to Expose the fatal Consequences, of Seduction." [8] In Brown's version of the affair, Harrington, a seducer, is transformed by his love for Harriot into a genuine lover desirous of marriage. But, as their names might have intimated to them, Harrington and Harriot are in reality brother and sister, products of their father's disordered life. Deeply in love when the incestuous relation is revealed to them, Harriot languishes and dies, Harrington kills himself beside a copy of *The Sorrows of Young Werter*.

Brown seems to have been sensitive to the postwar criticism that extreme sensibility was anti-Republican, a source of selfishness and isolation. In his novel he deliberately tried to connect exaggerated feeling with the social and moral principles underlying Republican Virtue:

> HAIL *Sensibility!* Sweetener of the joys of life! Heaven has implanted thee in the breasts of his children—to soothe the sorrows of the afflicted—to mitigate the wounds of the stranger who falleth in our way. *Thou* regardest with an eye of pity, those whom *wealth* and *ambition* treat in terms of reproach. Away, ye seekers of power—ye boasters of wealth—ye are the *Levite* and the *Pharisee*, who restrain the hand of charity from the indigent, and turn with indignation from the way-worn son of misery. . . .

In learning how to feel deeply, Harrington becomes not only a reformed rake but also a reformed anti-republican, reclaimed from snobbery and social indifference to concern for social equality, the condition of slaves, the equality of women, the superiority of Dwight and Barlow to Lord Chesterfield, and the worth of the new United States Constitution.

Yet *The Power of Sympathy* is an equivocal work. It commands the reader's attention, as Leslie Fiedler has said, not by its many salubrious lessons on the moral-political power of sensibility, but by its distraught style and enveloping shadow of incest and suicide. The tendency of deep feeling to detach itself from didacticism is already apparent, of course, in West's *Death of General Wolfe* twenty years earlier; but there the note of national and Christian self-sacrifice still predominates over the languorous beauty of Wolfe's expiring. What predominates in *The Power of Sympathy* is the thrill. The sensibility or "Sympathy" that theoretically leads to fellow-feeling and republicanism leads Harrington instead to kill himself. In fact, Harrington's plight cannot be understood in social or political terms. Like the later great romantic heroes, he suffers from oversensitivity: "Ah! poor well natured, warm hearted, hot headed youth. . . . the dupe of Nature, and the sacrifice of Seduction." The "and" is significant, for Brown alternates between ascribing Harrington's fate to Nature or to Seduction, between seeing him as a victim or as a criminal. In *The Power of Sympathy*, republican principles have become problems because the equation of feeling and benevolence has come apart. Like the framers of the Constitution, Brown doubted that human nature left to itself would produce order. While too abstract and too naively overwrought to be called a good novel, and while lacking the later romantics' awareness of the paradoxes of sincerity, his book seems to belong less to the age that produced *Wolfe* than to the age that produced *Moby Dick* and *Pierre*, in which other ambiguously criminal-victim 'dupes of Nature' suffer precious but self-destructive struggles to express their most feeling selves.

The third important event occurred sometime in 1789, although exactly when is uncertain. Chronologically it may not have fallen within the period of Washington's election, yet it belongs with Hopkinson's *Songs* and *The Power of Sympathy* for what it shows about the general metamorphosis of intellectual and artistic values. In 1785, the enigmatic Connecticut artist Ralph Earl returned to America after about seven years abroad. His return was heralded by ads in New York, Boston, and Connecticut newspapers (quite likely by himself), promising that he was "a very capital Portrait Painter . . . of great eminence" who had studied under Copley and West and would probably "soon take a very capital lead" in American portraiture.[9] A spendthrift, a heavy drinker, and probably a bigamist as well, Earl was within two years of his return imprisoned for debt. His release was obtained by Alexander Hamilton and some other New York lawyers, in return for his painting their wives and children.[10]

Freed from jail sometime in 1788, Earl returned to Connecticut, where in Litchfield, Sharon, Hartford, and other towns he painted what amount to the first American landscapes. Whereas most earlier American portraitists depicted their sitters beside bookcases or burnished desks in plushly curtained interiors, or against sketchy trees and blank expanses of sky, Earl brought his subjects into a specific Connecticut countryside of white buildings and thick foliage, painting them with a romantic feeling for the spaciousness of nature while preserving the air of order and learning characteristic of New England. In 1789 he painted particularly scenic pictures of the Boardman family of New Milford, the pious, tasteful descendants of a long line of Connecticut Puritans. *Esther Boardman* appears seated on a gently sloping hillside in a leafy grove, holding a reddish-covered book on her lap, before a detailed prospect of houses, fences, churches, and hills. *Major Daniel Boardman* shows a jaunty young man with a Malacca cane, dark blue coat, and yellow breeches, standing by a tree (ill., p. 534). Behind him loom the town of New Milford and the Housatonic River. It is as if the tiny background occasionally seen in earlier works of the period, usually through a window, had suddenly been brought up to the viewer, made a large and integral part of the painting. Earl's realistic depiction of the local rural scene on a canvas almost the same size as *Wolfe* (nearly 5′ x 7′) was a precedent quite as important to the future of American art as West's work, and quite as daring. The miles of white fences, the steepled church, the clapboard buildings amidst the rolling hills reflect a new willingness to treat the humble local scene on its own terms, a love of the American landscape for its own sake, proclaiming the rather elegant subject a citizen of this pleasant valley and no less stylish for the association.

From the viewpoint of America's early cultural development, however, it is the last event which makes the late 1780's seem most clearly a boundary, and which seems both a decisive climax and a decisive beginning. On March 2, 1789—as the first Congress to meet under the Constitution gathered in New York to tally the first vote for an American president—the Pennsylvania Assembly repealed the standing anti-theatre laws, a first step in the legalization of theatre throughout the United States.

The repeal ended nearly eight months of public contention in Philadelphia, beginning shortly after the 1788 ratification parade. The American Company had continued to flout the stringent anti-theatre law of 1786. The law's quite narrow definition of 'plays' unmistakably ruled out their favorite dodges, yet Wignell gave a reading of *The Contrast* at the City Tavern and *She Stoops to Conquer* was offered as "A Lecture on the Disadvantages of Improper Education." Now flagrantly illegal, these standbys provoked the Quakers to petition the Executive Council on July 18, 1788, to get rid of theatre in the city once and for all. The dignity of government, they said, was "insulted by the open contravention of the Law in the exhibition of Stage Plays, under whatever evasive name disguised. . . ." The Council appointed a committee "to consider of the most proper measures for giving effect to the act of Assembly . . . of September 1786. . . ." [11] At nearly the same time, however, Hallam and Henry applied directly to the Assembly, where they had many supporters, to have the 1786 act repealed. The committee that weighed their claims was friendly, and cultural-nationalist. In reporting to the Assembly it explained that it had felt obliged to consider not only moral issues but also to "contemplate the stage as the great mart of genius, and as such, a natural and necessary concomitant of our independence." It recommended that the Assembly repeal the 1786 statute: "We have cast off a foreign yoke in government, but shall still be dependent for those productions of the mind, which do most honour to human nature, until we can afford due protection and encouragement to every species of our own literature." [12]

In February 1789, quite as if the 1786 anti-theatre law had never been passed, the entire question of a legal theatre was again brought up in the Assembly for a vote. A "Dramatic Association" had formed in Philadelphia, headed by William Temple Franklin, Robert Morris, General Anthony Wayne, and other prominent citizens. On February 6, a petition with 1,900 names, calling for repeal, was presented to the Assembly but tabled.[13] Ten days later a delegation from the Dramatic Association, headed by William Franklin, appeared at the Assembly to argue a lengthy defense of the petition. They disposed of the moral issue entirely by relegating it to "speculation": "we do not admit, that a Theatre is the temple of vice, we presume not to insist that it is the school of virtue." The real issue, they insisted, was political. To deprive people of the right to attend a theatre was to "abridge the natural right of every freeman to dispose of his time and money, according to his own taste and disposition. . . ." At stake was liberty itself: "the same authority which proscribes our amusements, may, with equal justice, dictate the shape and texture of our dress or the modes and ceremonies of our worship." [14]

On the same day that the Assembly listened to the Dramatic Association's defense, however, it received a new anti-theatre petition with 3,446 subscribers. (The other side claimed that many of these were "Boys, bound Servants and Negroes . . . Girls, Apprentices and Mulattoes.")[15] The *Gazette* estimated that the several petitions now before the Assembly contained about 6,000 signatures in favor of the theatre and about 4,000 against. On February 20, members of the Assembly voted on whether a committee of city members should be appointed to draft a bill repealing all existing anti-theatre laws. The House divided thirty-five in favor, twenty-nine against, its decision bringing, the *Gazette* said, a "joyful acclamation." [16]

As the committee drafted its bill, the controversy moved into the city's newspapers. Much of it followed the lines of argument established in the first postwar theatre debates, both sides speaking from a high ground of Independence and republicanism through which ran a gritty undercurrent of local politics. Events since the calling of the Constitutional Convention injected some new issues, however. The ongoing presidential election aggravated the sense that Philadelphia had failed to make itself felt in the new nation. Many inhabitants of the city still brooded over the removal of Congress, believing that it had dimmed Philadelphia's brilliance and its prospects. "Those who wish to see this city flourish, and become the residence of Congress," one writer warned, "will doubtless exert themselves in favor of the Drama." Another writer complained that the southern states were about to give the union a president, the northern states a vice president, while Philadelphia was contributing only a paradise of saints.[17]

Inevitably, Hallam's case was argued afresh in terms of constitutional rights. "Candidus" drew up a pamphlet-length legal brief, published over three issues of the *Pennsylvania Packet*. He observed that some of the actors had lived in America as "good citizens" for twenty-six years, contributing their "proportion" towards the expense of government, doing "what the constitution of their country required of them," and, most important, operating under the law. Before the Revolution, only the provincial governor was empowered to grant licenses; he had licensed the actors to build the Southwark Theatre, which they did "in the fullest confidence of being protected, to their profession and property." The governments formed under the Confederation sought to preserve the legal guarantees intended by the provincial governments. Thus to close the Philadelphia theatres was to revoke the provincial license and abrogate the promises of the Confederation, *"without even the shadow of a trial."* Candidus complimented the Company for performing in defiance of the anti-theatre laws: "They have persevered from a laudable motive—they have persevered to assert their rights." [18]

Hovering palpably but indistinctly over the war of words was the spirit of *Sans Souci*. An ultimate weapon, it was rarely used forthrightly; yet the entire debate resonated with the unspoken argument that people secure in their republican faith can afford to have a good time. Like Tyler's *Contrast*, this final clash of pro- and anti-theatre forces took place at a remove from the historic struggle between republicans and monarchists, whose lofty earnestness already smacked of insecurity and provincialism. Many of those who defended the theatre raised constitutional and political points only to legitimize their own devaluation of politics. They spoke for property rights and freedom of choice only to establish their moral credentials, preliminary to asserting that the theatre provides "a pleasing relaxation from the fatigues of business" or "a rational amusement to an enlightened community" or recreation from "incessant toil and continual fatigue." The more direct "CIVIS" recommended that the whole issue be decided as a country judge in England resolved a dispute about a Maypole. Half the village wanted it, the other half did not. "You grave folks who are against a *May pole* shall have none—," the judge ruled, "but you gay folks who are for a *May pole* may set one up as soon as you like." [19]

The committee appointed by the Assembly brought in its bill on March 2, 1789. The same day, fifty persons from Franklin County petitioned the legislature protesting that a theatre "is incompatible with the true principle and Spirit of a republic, the existence and happiness of which depend upon Simplicity of manners, purity of morals, industry and frugality." [20] It was a last-ditch effort. The Assembly passed the bill the same day, giving legal recognition to the theatre in Philadelphia.

In repealing the earlier laws, the bill recognized the force of current cultural and political arguments in favor of a theatre. Its two main grounds were, first, the Assembly's hope "of promoting the interests of genius and literature by permitting such theatrical exhibitions as are capable of advancing morality and virtue and polishing the manners and habits of society"; second, the idea that it was "contrary to the principles of a free government to deprive any of its citizens of a rational and innocent entertainment. . . ." In deference to the anti-theatre forces, the Assembly amended the bill of repeal by including measures for regulating the theatre. Acknowledging that "respectable citizens" feared lest the theatre be "abused by indecent, vicious and immoral performances" the bill provided that for the next three years the president of the Executive Council, the chief justice of the Supreme Court, and the president of the Court of Common Pleas for Philadelphia would have the power "to permit and license such theatrical exhibitions only as shall in the opinion of him who shall grant such license be unexceptional." [21] Persons who performed without such a license would be fined up to £200 and face imprisonment. The bill, however, set up no machinery for the licensing procedure; in fact, it conceded nothing which Hallam himself had not long advocated in trying to appease the moralists.

On March 7, the *Gazette* announced a performance of *The Roman Father*, a hornpipe by Durang, and a "celebration over the victory of the theatre." For the first time in Philadelphia in fifteen years, the Company published its cast for the evening "By Authority."

With the repeal of the Philadelphia laws, the even older and previously ironclad laws of New England began to give as well. One month after the repeal, a writer to the Boston *Herald of Freedom* urged the licensing of a theatre in his city, on the grounds that it would make enough money to support the poor in the almshouse and would prevent youth from going to worse places. A writer to the *Massachusetts Centinel* pointed out that the absence of a theatre made Boston seem dull:

> It is the just remark of almost all strangers who resort to this place, that there is no town in America so large as this, that has so few public amusements. By

encouraging this establishment, we should prevent this in the future; and at the same time the building of a Theatre would give employment to a number of deserving citizens, it would be greatly ornamental to the town.[22]

Hallam and Henry were quick to exploit these stirrings. In the summer of 1789, after passage of the Philadelphia bill, Henry paid a visit in Boston to Samuel Adams, whose favor would probably have led to permission for a Boston theatre. During the war, Adams had been outraged by the efforts of American troops to produce plays in Philadelphia, and had helped to snuff them out. Henry approached him with a letter of recommendation from Adams' friend Elbridge Gerry, a member of the Constitutional Convention who had lived in New York and developed a taste for the stage. Gerry tried with conviction and at length to persuade Adams that a "well regulated" theatre would benefit the city and the nation. It would polish American manners and display to foreigners the country's "comparative liberality of sentiment." A powerful institution in "forming a national character," it would create democratic sentiment but preserve good order: All ranks may partake "without destroying the necessary distinction of ranks. . . . all ranks are pleased at the theatre, and participating alike in the pleasures appear to be of the same family and society uninterrupted by envy or malice." Massachusetts, he said, must not stand apart from the rest of the union in prohibiting the stage. Neither Henry's visit nor Gerry's letter moved Adams, however. He told Gerry that he and Henry had had "a free and candid Conversation" but that Henry's reasons "were not powerful enough to convince me of the Utility of his Design in this Commonwealth." He still considered the theatre opposed to two fundamental characteristics of a republic: "*Sobriety* of Sentiment and Manners and a Spirit of *honest* Industry. . . ." [23]

But by 1789 Adams' opposition meant little. New England towns previously nailed shut against the theatre were opening up. On January 19, 1789, the *Connecticut Courant* advertised the first professional theatrical performance to be given in Hartford, a *Lecture on Heads* and a reading of two scenes from *The Contrast* ("Written by a Citizen of Boston"), offered by an actor named McPherson. In October, the wife of the recently deceased Dennis Ryan appeared in Salem, Massachusetts; with her two children and Miss Wall she offered *Douglas, The Beggar's Opera*, and *George Barnwell*.[24] These efforts to provide theatre in New England remained low-keyed until 1791, when a group of Bostonians raised the theatre issue at the town meeting. They triggered what turned out to be the most violent theatre controversy of the eighteenth century, which resulted in the opening of the Federal Street Theatre in Boston in 1794, and of a legal theatre in Providence a year later.

The breaking of the Philadelphia laws in March 1789 and the intrusion of theatre into New England were preconditions for giving the stage a fairly stable and respectable place in American cultural life. Several thousand people had also said something about the kind of country America should be, and about who ought to decide. As Thomas Jefferson recognized, writing about the theatre in 1788: "The utility of this in America is a great question." [25] Throughout the existence of America, the theatre had maintained a marginal existence, touching sensitive political, domestic, and religious nerves, as comparable issues like sex education and pornography still do. With their ancient reputation for luxury, bawdry, and bunkum, actors deeply offended many provincials, who were by and large poor, pious, and wary. Every commercial and financial crisis in the colonies and the United States brought fresh outcries against itinerant Englishmen who breezed through town, many felt, to pick their pockets and depart, enriched by money that the charitable had given to the distressed or that prostitutes had charmed from idle apprentices.

These outcries became ineffective through an intricate combination of circumstances. Despite open hostility, Douglass, Hallam, and Henry had persisted in keeping the theatre alive. They managed to do so because, among other things, a sizable audience for the theatre had always existed in the colonies, because many plays in their repertoire advocated Whiggish ideas in popular form, and because they cultivated friends in high places. Their Company, moreover, had acted in America since the time of Lewis Hallam, Sr., nearly fifty years. Philadelphians were stating a fact when they argued that to maintain prohibition was to deprive Hallam of his rights as a citizen: The American Company had become an institution, part of the American cultural landscape. Its members had married Americans and been buried in America; it gave plays by Americans with American actors and dancers; thousands of Americans had seen them perform.

The war that sent the Company out of America greatly increased its audience and weakened its critics. Exempt from congressional prohibitions against wartime shows, college students filled the gap left by the departure of the American Company, mounting more and more (and more and more professional) productions. At the same time, troops who perhaps had never seen a play before both saw and produced them at army camps from Florida to New Hampshire, sometimes emulating the metropolitan standards introduced to America by Burgoyne, Clinton, Howe, and other cultivated French and English officers. While more Americans than before saw plays, fewer Americans than before were able to challenge them. Nonprofit and often high-minded, college productions were relatively immune to charges of idleness and immorality. The attendance of irreproachable persons like Lafayette, Wayne, and Washington made the productions themselves irreproachable.

This more numerous and more sophisticated audience remained when professional theatre resumed after the war. To it was added a young generation which had not experienced the ministerial plots and Scotch maneuverings that gave vitality to Whig maxims. Times were changing: many sought pleasure and relaxation unblushingly. The avoidance of the issue of sumptuary laws by the Constitutional Convention, too, probably stimulated opposition to the anti-theatre laws, since it withheld federal recognition from the several state prohibitions. More than anything else, finally, the sanctioning of the theatre was simply an ingrained branch of America's larger cultural flourishing, irresistible as the rising sun.

49. The Inauguration of Washington: April 1789

On April 6, 1789, a month after the Philadelphia General Assembly repealed the anti-theatre laws, the United States Congress seated in New York opened the sixty-nine votes cast by the electoral college for the first president of the United States. George Washington received all of the votes. The classical scholar Charles Thomson, a designer of the U.S. Seal, was dispatched to Mount Vernon to announce the results.

Many Americans looked upon Washington's inauguration as both the close of the revolutionary period and the beginning, in the favorite phrase of the day, of a "New AEra." From their viewpoint, the events climaxed and completed the culture that had grown in America over the last quarter-century. In that time, the population of the country had risen from nearly 2 million to nearly 4 million. In the same time, the country had produced its own celebrated painters, its own epic poets, its own composers, its own playwrights, its own magazines, songs, pianos, organs, museums, its own government. Now it had its first national governor. A national existence in the style of longer-established countries could commence. "Culture's bright star, and learning's morn," as one versifier wrote, had reached the "ZENITH OF GLORY." [1]

Not all Americans shared this viewpoint, however. With its triumphal arches, Handelian odes, and allegorical transparencies, the Inauguration was perhaps the last large public expression in America of a style that now began to seem not only stale but also undemocratic. When John Adams arrived in New York to assume the vice presidency, local newspapers lauded him as the deciding voice in producing a Declaration of Independence: "Lo! Adams rose! a giant in debate/ And turned the vote which fix'd our empire's fate." A writer in the *Boston Gazette* bristled at this: "FLATTERY is the bane of freedom, the thief of liberty." John Trumbull detected "the odour of incense" at the inaugural celebrations and regretted that while launching its first executive the country had idolatrously "gone through all the Popish grades of worship at least up to the *Hyperdoulia*." [2]

Even apart from the crosscurrents and tensions at the time, Washington's inauguration represents something highly mobile and complex. Its great power as a symbol of completion and of birth was owing to the reality of cultural progress, the broad change in values, the initiation of a new form of government. Yet this power should not be allowed to obscure the ongoing character of the arts at the moment. From the viewpoint of America's later cultural evolution, April 1789 was a commingling of endings, continuations, beginnings—a flow.

By 1789, several of the major figures in this history had done most of their work. Timothy Dwight, the author of America's first epic, would shortly settle into the Yale presidency, stop writing poetry, and become one of the bitterest foes of Jeffersonian republicanism until his death in 1816. Royall Tyler would forsake playwriting for the bench in Vermont. Other important cultural figures would not live into the nineteenth century. John Henry, having escaped the fate of five other actors who perished on the ship that brought them to America in 1767, would die aboard a ship in 1795. His wife, the popular Maria Storer, would die a year later in a house behind the Southwark Theatre, "miserably poor," by available accounts, and "a raving maniac." [3] Hallam, increasingly at odds with his actors and even coming to blows with Henry, would largely give over the management of the Company to William Dunlap, who would give up painting and become the country's first native theatrical entrepreneur, and a prolific playwright. After Hallam's death in 1808, his sons and their families would continue to perform, giving the Hallams a continuous history of nearly a century on the American stage.

William Billings, outliving Washington by a year, would die in 1800. "He died poor & neglected," William Bentley wrote, "& perhaps did too much neglect himself." Throughout the 1780's Billings was employed not only as a singing master but also as a sealer of leather, hog-reeve, coal inspector, and garbage collector. By 1790, he would be impoverished, the object of a charity concert given by William Selby. His music would come more and more into disfavor as a more sophisticated standard of "correct"

European music came to dominate the New England churches. Samuel Holyoke's 1791 *Harmonia Americana* would include only a few fuging-tunes because of "the trifling effect produced by that sort of music. . . ." By 1807, the *Massachusetts Collection of Sacred Harmony* would deplore "those wild fugues, and rapid and confused movements, which have so long been the disgrace of congregational psalmody." Five years later, one singing master would simply dismiss "Billings and other modern Pretenders." [4] Billings' music would, however, continue appealing to a small group of admirers in New England, and it would move west with the country. As the revival movements and camp meetings of the frontier would begin producing their own singing books, his tunes would appear again in collections like John Wyeth's *Repository of Sacred Music* (1813), to be sung as complements to "Amazing Grace" and "Wondrous Love."

Other major figures of the revolutionary period would live, work, and exert their influence well into the nineteenth century. Copley and West would contend for the presidency of the Royal Academy after the death of Reynolds in 1792, and feud for the next two decades, Copley passing his last days in fading reputation and senility, unable to paint; he died in 1815. West would stay productive as a teacher and painter until his death in 1820. Peale would live until the age of eighty-six, having made his natural history museum a nationally known institution, and leaving more than a thousand paintings and miniatures, as well as seventeen children, several of whom succeeded him as painters. Turning to actual profit some of the theories about commerce he had explored in his *Vision of Columbus*, Joel Barlow would become a wealthy and famous diplomat; in 1811 he would be sent to Moscow to negotiate a treaty, and would die the next year from the hardships he endured in the retreat of Napoleon's armies. The gloomy Freneau would last longest. In 1790 he would settle down in New York to edit the *Daily Advertiser*; trying to account for his unexpected move, he decided, " 'Twas chance, 'twas luck—I scarce can tell/ What genius play'd my cards so well!" [5] Freneau would become active in early national politics before setting out once more as a sea captain. Drinking heavily in old age, he would die of exposure during a snowstorm in 1832.

As the various artists who had matured during the Revolution continued their labors, went out of fashion, became uninterested, or died, many of their successors were growing up or beginning their own careers—painters like John Vanderlyn (b. 1775), Washington Allston (b. 1779), Thomas Sully (b. 1783), and John James Audubon (b. 1785), and writers like James Fenimore Cooper (b. 1789) and Washington Irving (b. 1783), who as a child in New York City witnessed his namesake's inauguration.

Bearing the certificate of Washington's election, Charles Thomson arrived at Mount Vernon at about noon on April 14. The election results were to have been announced on March 4, but the new Congress gathered tardily in New York and did not have a quorum until April 1. With Washington when the news arrived was his friend and aide David Humphreys, who had also been with him when he returned home on Christmas Eve six years earlier, after prolonged waiting for news of Peace. During Washington's retirement, Humphreys had often accompanied him to church and on foxhunts or plantation rounds at Mount Vernon, meanwhile translating into English a French tragedy, Antoine Le Mierre's *The Widow of Malabar.*[6]

Washington had prepared an acceptance speech to read to Thomson, for the results of the election came as no surprise. They had leaked out even before March 4, and for two years before that the importance of his becoming the first president had been urged on Washington by friends, newspapers, old war allies, and ordinary citizens. A popular engraving by Amos Doolittle in 1788, *Display of the United States of America*, showed him in civilian dress within a circle of linked rings, each containing a state seal. Versifiers acclaimed him as the one American capable of composing *Anarchia*:

> At his approach vile Faction stands aghast,
> And civil Discord breathes, in pangs, her last;
> Paper emissions too, at his command,
> With legal tenders, fly this happy land.

Or he was praised as the one American able to preserve the gains of the Revolution, and to be the architect of future glory:

> Methinks I see thee, Solon-like, design
> The future grandeur of confed'rate states
> High-tow'ring: or, for legislation met,
> Adjust in senate what thou sav'd'st in war.

The prominence of Washington's name and image turned the 1788 ratification parades into virtual plebiscites, the New York tallow chandlers, for instance, carrying a flag with Washington's picture and the words "may he be the first President of the United States."[7] On the dedication page of his *Seven Songs*, Hopkinson declared that a Washington presidency was the "universally avowed Wish of America."

Washington, however, did not share the wish. He told one correspondent after another, ever more wearily, of his "unfeigned reluctance to accept the office," that such a move would be "the greatest sacrifice of my personal feelings and wishes that ever I have been called upon to make," that if led "again on the Stage of public affairs, I certainly will decline. . . ."[8] His repugnance against the role came from several sources: wariness about taking on arduous and painful chores (particularly that of fending off hordes of office-seekers); a sense that he would be unacceptable to the anti-Federalists, many of whom believed that he had been used as a tool to propagate the Constitution; fear that a return to public life might seem inconsistent with his announced retirement, and would be taken for ambition.[9]

Nor were Washington's feelings unwarranted. Months before the election results became known, applicants began badgering him for jobs, even comrades and friends like Hopkinson. He had enemies, too. While the many hailed his future presidency as a "ZENITH OF GLORY," one engraver drew him riding a donkey led by David Humphreys, with some doggerel beneath:

> The glorious time has come to pass
> When David shall conduct an ass.

Washington had good reason, too, to fear that his behavior might be misconstrued, at least by those who could characterize him as did the author of *Saw ye my hero George*, in which Martha Washington flies Mount Vernon to join her husband at the Battle of Monmouth:

> O'er hills and high mountains, o'er rivers and fountains,
> Where the drums and trumpets sound alarms,
> Heav'n give the angels charge, to protect my Hero George,
> And return him safe back to my arms! [10]

Washington, to be sure, was a domestic creature and a man of feeling, but no figure of sentimental romance.

Yet, like other ideas, the idea of Washington was changing. Many, probably most, Americans continued to depict him as the powerful but benevolent Christian Hero, or as the patriotic farmer-soldier, or as "Columbia's Favourite Son,/ Her Father, Saviour, Friend and Guide!" But now these images did not always evoke chaste awe.[11] In *The Politician Out-Witted*, the slogan-mongering Federalist "Trueman" asserts that the Revolution "will immortalize the name of the renowned WASHING-TON,—more than that of Cincinnatus, Achilles, AEneas, Alexander the Great, Scipio, Gustavus Vassa, Mark Anthony, Kouli Khan, Caesar or Pompey." The bumpkin Humphry replies, "Caesar and Pompey! Why them is nigers names."

But for Washington, historicism was no crude or laughing matter. Perhaps his deepest reason for shunning the presidency was that he had already fulfilled his Cincinnatean ideal of public service. He had left the plow for the sword: having acted on the battlefield, it was now, he said, his "sole desire to live and die, in peace and retirement on my own farm." While contentedly preoccupied with his guests, his crops, his lands, he had found time to also keep up the part of an American Maecenas, celebrated as the "Parent of soothing airs and lofty strains." Here too, awareness of historical examples made him feel not only willing but obliged to support the arts in America. In May 1788 he wrote a long, informal letter to the marquis de Lafayette describing the artistic patronage of such military figures as Alexander the Great, Julius Caesar, and Augustus. He noted how national heroes and national poets had often created each other:

> Men of real talents in Arms have commonly approved themselves patrons of the liberal arts and friends to the poets, of their own as well as former times. In some instances by acting reciprocally, heroes have made poets, and poets heroes.

The current cultural scene in America, he told Lafayette, disproved the French naturalists' theory that America was a meteorological mistake: "Perhaps we shall be found at this moment, not inferior to the rest of the world in the performances of our poets and painters; notwithstanding many of the incitements are wanting which operate powerfully among older nations." [12]

Washington did not mention one incitement which American poets and painters did have—himself. He seems to have been painted from life only twice during his retirement (compared with eleven life portraits made before 1783), once at Mount Vernon by Robert Edge Pine and once by Peale when he emerged to preside over the Constitutional Convention.[13] Yet his face continued to be copied and engraved from other works, he continued to receive poems from admirers, and his name continued to be spread over the dedication pages and subscription lists of most of the important works of the period—most recently *The Conquest of Canäan, The Contrast,* and Hopkinson's *Seven Songs* (as well as Dr. John Leigh's 1788 *Experimental Inquiry into the Properties of Opium*). Washington's acknowledgments of these tributes were in character. He told Hopkinson that if the ancients were correct in thinking that the power of music could "charm the powers of Hell," then the "honor of my Country" obliged him to believe that Hopkinson's songs could "melt the Ice of the Delaware and Potomack." Yet if others disliked the volume, "what alas! can I do to support it? I can neither sing one of the songs, nor raise a single note on any instrument to convince the unbelieving." He recommended Joel Barlow to Lafayette by remarking that he was "considered by those who are good Judges to be a genius of the first magnitude." [14] Generous but frank, he invariably treated artistic homage with gratitude and encouragement without pretending to connoisseurship.

By the time Charles Thomson arrived at Mount Vernon, on April 14, Washington had done two things. He had prepared a statement to read to Thomson, in which he explained:

> I have been accustomed to pay so much respect to the opinion of my fellow-citizens, that the knowledge of their having given their unanimous suffrages in my favor, scarcely leaves me the alternative for an option. I can not, I believe, give a greater evidence of my sensibility of the honor which they have done me than by accepting the appointment.

Acquiescing to the argument that the good of the country was involved, he had come to accept as "a kind of inevitable necessity" the idea of being president.[15]

By the time Thomson arrived, Washington had also acquired a suit for his inauguration. Around January he had noticed a newspaper advertisement for some "superfine American Broad Cloths," manufactured in Hartford and available in New York. The item interested him in part because he bred sheep, but also because he thought no differently about native fabrics than about native culture. As he considered American poets and painters "not inferior to the rest of the world," he hoped that it would soon be "unfashionable for a gentleman to appear in any other dress." He wrote to Henry Knox, the acting secretary of war, in New York, asking him to obtain enough of the cloth to make a suit. The request cost Knox considerable effort and additional correspondence, in the course of which the idea spread. Jeremiah Wadsworth, a delegate from Connecticut, decided that he would come dressed in the same material on the opening session of Congress; the Hartford manufacturers presented enough cloth for a suit to John Adams as he passed through the town on his way to New York. Knox managed to obtain thirteen and a half yards for Washington, which seem to have arrived at Mount Vernon the beginning of March, followed next month by a set of gilt buttons engraved with the Seal of the United States. Washington wanted more of the buttons for trimming, but there was no time. He asked Knox to obtain and keep them in New York until he arrived.[16]

On April 16 Washington set out in a carriage for New York with Thomson and Humphreys, "accompanied," he said, "by feelings not unlike those of a culprit who is going to the place of his execution." He hoped to avoid fuss: "no reception," he wrote to Governor Clinton, "can be so congenial to my feelings as a quiet entry devoid of ceremony." [17]

After dinners, toasts, and speeches at Alexandria, Baltimore, and Wilmington, Washington and his party arrived on the morning of April 20 at Chester, Maryland, fifteen miles outside of Philadelphia. Here Washington was induced to alight from his carriage and mount a white horse so that he could be seen clearly as he entered the city. As he rode along the

Schuylkill, honor guards, war veterans, dignitaries came out to meet him at every intersection. When the swelling procession reached Gray's Ferry Bridge, Washington found a scene, said one newspaper, such as "even the pencil of a Raphael could not delineate." [18]

The bridge—little more than a carpet of logs stretching across the river to Philadelphia—had been turned by Charles Willson Peale into an allegorical avenue of triumph, lined with small shrubs, beginning and ending in twenty-foot-high Roman arches wreathed in laurel. From one railing flew flags of the eleven ratifying states; from the other, flags of Pennsylvania and of "The New Era." On one side of the river stood a twenty-five-foot liberty pole topped by a huge beehive-shaped pileus and the banner "DONT TREAD ON ME." Across the river an answering banner displayed the device of a sun, with the motto "BEHOLD THE RISING EMPIRE." [19]

As Washington passed beneath the entrance arch, Peale's daughter Angelica, robed in white, worked a machine that lowered a crown of laurel to his head. Crossing the bridge, he proceeded to Philadelphia, watched, from every fence and street, by some 20,000 spectators.

Resting the night in town after a banquet and fireworks, Washington set out again on the twenty-first, first by coach, then again on horseback, heading a company of infantry and a large procession of citizens. At the bridge leading to Trenton, a chorus of young girls dressed in white, decked in wreaths and chaplets, strewed flowers in his way from baskets, singing a "gratulatory ode" probably set to music for the occasion by Alexander Reinagle:

> WELCOME, mighty Chief! once more,
> Welcome to this grateful shore:
> Now no mercenary foe
> Aims again the fatal blow—
> *Aims at thee the fatal blow.*
>
> Virgins fair, and Matrons grave,
> Those thy conquering arms did save,
> Build for thee triumphal bowers.
> Strew, ye fair, his way with flowers—
> *Strew your Hero's way with flowers.*

At this bridge too, Washington passed under a laurel triumphal arch some twenty feet high, raised on thirteen pillars and inscribed in gilt:

THE DEFENDER OF THE MOTHERS
WILL BE THE PROTECTOR OF THE DAUGHTERS.

Above the inscription a cupola of flowers encircled the dates of the battles of Princeton and Trenton, and the image of a large sunflower facing the sun.[20]

Staying the night in Trenton after a public dinner and reception, Washington proceeded the next morning through Princeton and New Brunswick, piped in and out with music, speeches, salutes, cannonades, bells, and detachments of cavalry, infantry, and artillery, resting overnight again at Woodbridge.

At about nine o'clock on the morning of April 23, Washington arrived at Elizabethtown. Here he met a committee from Congress which had come to escort him across the Hudson. Surrounded by town officials and a large concourse of citizens, Washington, Humphreys, Thomson, and the congressional committee boarded a special barge that had been under construction for a month, using materials from the Federal Ship paraded down Broadway in 1788. Covered by an awning, festooned with red curtains, manned by New York harbor pilots and thirteen oarsmen in white smocks, it measured nearly fifty feet long.

Gaily dressed ships of all sizes joined in the wake of the barge, making a wide flotilla along the fifteen-mile waterborne trip to Manhattan. As the barge approached Bedloe's Island, a sloop in full sail drew alongside, from which about twenty men and women passengers sang Washington an "Ode" by Samuel Low, set to "God Save the King":

> Thrice welcome to this shore,
> Our Leader now no more,
>   But Ruler thou;
> Oh, truly good and great!
> Long live to glad our State,
> Where countless Honors wait
>   To deck thy Brow.

The performance, said the *Packet*, was "superior to the flutes that played with the stroke of the oars in Cleopatra's silken corded barge." [21] Washington and the others lifted their hats in return for the compliment. As the barge neared Staten Island, a second boat pulled up to its stern to sing still another ode, copies of which were handed across the water to the coxswain. Ships in New York harbor—which included the *Columbia*, piloted by Philip Freneau—broke out their flags.

As the barge approached the foot of Wall Street, at around two o'clock in the afternoon, thirteen guns thundered, church bells began ringing for half an hour, thousands of New Yorkers and others visiting the city huzzaed. Washington disembarked on carpeted steps and walked the half-mile to his new Cherry Street house, inching with Governor Clinton and his party for half an hour through dense crowds that strained to touch him, so that, one spectator wrote, he "was obliged to wipe his eyes several times." [22]

During the festivities of inauguration week Washington's name appeared everywhere—on the fronts of houses, on brass buttons stamped "GW," on polychrome papier-mâché tobacco boxes inscribed "God Save the President Washington" in a blaze of light. Transparencies illuminated on the night of the Inauguration, April 30, turned the city into a glowing lantern of Washington's face and name. In Broad Street appeared a portrait of "The Father of His Country"; the fort at the bottom of Broadway displayed emblems of Fortitude, Justice, and Wisdom, standing for Washington, the Senate, and the Representatives; in the harbor the ship *Carolina* exhibited a pyramid of stars; the Spanish minister displayed "MOVING PICTURES" at his house; on a transparency at the John Street Theatre, Fame descended from heaven to crown Washington with Immortality. Climaxed by two hours of fireworks with thirteen rockets and the discharge of thirteen cannon before and after, the display was judged equal to "anything of the kind ever before seen in America." [23]

Just after the Inauguration, two poems published in the *Gazette of the United States* tried to explain why these transparencies had been painted for Washington, why these arches and wreaths had been built for him, these odes sung to him. The first writer explained them not as idolatry but as self-reverence:

> Triumphal arches—gratulating song,
> And shouts of welcome from the mixed throng,
>   Thy laurels cannot raise.
> We praise ourselves; exalt our name,
> And in the scroll of time, we claim
>   An int'rest in thy bays.[24]

Americans gave their favorite father and son the adulation of a country that for decades had hungered for something of its own worthy of adulation. His greatest achievement was to satisfy their need for great achievements. Their tribute of love to him reflected glory on themselves.

The second writer expanded this interpretation, observing that at the Inauguration Adams and Washington had appeared in brown suits of native manufacture, the cloth so fine that many mistook it for European. Not only Washington and those who gloried in him, but also the means by which their love might be adequately declared had come into existence together, had helped to define and to create each other. Washington, the crowds, the theatres, the transparencies, the songs, marches, odes, the sprightly social comedies and fuging-tunes, the celebrated painters and epic poems, the museums and moving pictures and rising cities—were they not a single achievement, a single result, were they not all promises fulfilled, future promises to be fulfilled? *"From this bright Era,"* said the *Gazette,*

. . . see Columbia rise!
Her Empire prop'd by him who arch'd the Skies!
Freedom and Independence—ARTS, and Peace,
Shall crown the Scene till Time and Nature cease.

Documentation and Notes

Wherever convenient, I have given the titles, places of publication, and dates of primary printed material directly in the text. The following apparatus is intended to provide close and comprehensive documentation of the remaining sources.

Almost every footnote number encompasses several references, divided by semicolons in the order of their appearance within the paragraph. Some references are set off by commas instead of semicolons, indicating that the sources have been blended rather than used sequentially. The abbreviation "q." indicates primary material quoted secondhand, i.e., quoted from a quotation of the material in a secondary source. Because the considerable number and variety of the sources make conventional footnotes impractical, and highly susceptible to inconsistency and mechanical error, the references have been abbreviated. Dates of newspapers and correspondence appear as month/day/year. Locations of manuscripts are identified by a letter or letters, keyed to the list of repositories. Titles are identified by a letter and number, keyed to the list of sources. This list has some value as an independent bibliography, but is not meant as a bibliography. Titles on the list appear in the order in which they were consulted. Omitted numbers represent works that were consulted in the research for the book, but not drawn upon in the writing.

1. Repositories

The use of code letters below in no way diminishes my gratitude to the following institutions for allowing me to quote from manuscript and typescript material in their collections. I am equally obliged to the Archives of American Art, which does not appear on the list. Its extraordinary, ongoing collection of microfilm represents one of the most useful and farsighted projects ever undertaken in the study of American culture.

AAS: American Antiquarian Society
AP: Adams Papers (microfilm edition, by permission of the Massachusetts Historical Society)
APS: American Philosophical Society
BA: Boston Athenaeum
BPL: Boston Public Library
CHS: Connecticut Historical Society
CSL: Connecticut State Library
CW: Colonial Williamsburg Research Institute
F: Fordham University Library
FARL: Frick Art Reference Library (file folders on individual paintings)
H: Huntington Library
HA: Haverford College Library
HCL: Harvard College Library
HSP: Historical Society of Pennsylvania
LC: Library of Congress
M: Morristown National Historical Park
MdHS: Maryland Historical Society
MHS: Massachusetts Historical Society
MMA: Metropolitan Museum of Art Library
NHC: New Haven Colony Historical Society
NYHS: New-York Historical Society
NYPL: Manuscripts and Archives Division, New York Public Library (Astor, Lenox, and Tilden Foundations)
UVL: University of Virginia Library
WIN: Joseph Downs Manuscript Collection, Henry Francis du Pont Winterthur Museum
WM: Swem Library, College of William and Mary
YUL: Yale University Library

2. Sources

Art

A2 [Rita Susswein Gottesman.] *The Arts and Crafts in New York 1726-1776.* New York, 1938.

A3 Rita Susswein Gottesman. *The Arts and Crafts in New York 1777–1799*. New York, 1954.

A4 George Francis Dow. *The Arts & Crafts in New England 1704–1755*. Topsfield, Mass., 1927.

A5 Alfred Coxe Prime. *The Arts & Crafts in Philadelphia, Maryland and South Carolina 1721–1785*. N. pl., 1929.

A6 Alfred Coxe Prime. *The Arts & Crafts in Philadelphia Maryland and South Carolina 1786–1800*. N. pl., 1932.

A9 Jules David Prown. *American Painting From its Beginnings to the Armory Show*. Vol. I. Cleveland [1969].

A11 John W. McCoubrey. "Painting" section in *The Arts in America. The Colonial Period*. New York, 1966. Pp. 149–249.

A12 Waldron Phoenix Belknap, Jr. *American Colonial Painting. Materials for a History*. Cambridge, Mass., 1959.

A14 Oliver W. Larkin. *Art and Life in America*. Rev. ed. New York, 1960.

A15 Albert Ten Eyck Gardner and Stuart P. Feld. *American Paintings. A Catalogue of the Collection of the Metropolitan Museum of Art*. Vol. I. New York, 1965.

A16 Harry B. Wehle. *American Miniatures 1730–1850*. New York, 1927.

A17 Anna Wells Rutledge. *Artists in the Life of Charleston*. Philadelphia, 1949.

A19 Nina Fletcher Little. *American Decorative Wall Painting 1700–1850*. Sturbridge, 1952.

A20 Grose Evans. *Benjamin West and the Taste of his Times*. Carbondale, Ill., 1959.

A22 William Kelby. *Notes on American Artists 1754–1820*. New York, 1922.

A25 William and Susan Sawitzky. "Portraits by Reuben Moulthrop." *New-York Historical Society Quarterly*, XXXIX (Oct 1955), 385–404.

A26 Theodore Bolton. "John Hazlitt—Portrait Painter." *Essex Institute Historical Collections*, LVI (1920), 293–296.

A28 *American Landscape Painting*. New Haven, 1948.

A30 Mary Black and Jean Lipman. *American Folk Painting*. New York, 1966.

A31 Yvon Bizardel. *American Painters in Paris*. New York, 1960.

A34 Hans Huth. "Pierre Eugène Du Simitière and the Beginnings of the American Historical Museum." *Pennsylvania Magazine of History and Biography*, LXIX (Oct 1945), 315–325.

A38 Lawrence Park. "An Account of Joseph Badger, and a Descriptive List of his Work." *Proceedings of the Massachusetts Historical Society*, LI (1918), 158–201.

A39 William B. Stevens. "Samuel King of Newport." *Antiques*, XCVI (Nov 1969), 729–733.

A40 Wayne Craven. *Sculpture in America*. New York, 1968.

A41 E. P. Richardson. *Painting in America*. New York, 1956.

A42 Wendy J. Shadwell. "An Attribution for His Excellency and Lady Washington." *Antiques*, XCV (Feb 1969), 240–241.

A43 Ann C. Van Devanter. "A *Holy Family* attributed to Benjamin West." *Antiques*, XCVIII (Nov 1970), 774–775.

A44 D. R. Reilly. *Portrait Waxes*. London, 1953.

A45 Andrew Oliver. "Portraits of John and Abigail Adams: A quest for a likeness." *Antiques*, XCI (Apr 1967), 476–480.

A46 *This New Man. A Discourse in Portraits.* Ed. J. Benjamin Townsend. Washington, D.C., 1968.

A50 Paula D. Sampson. "Patience Wright and her 'new style of picturing'." *Antiques*, LXXXVII (May 1965), 586–589.

A51 Helen Comstock. "Spot news in American historical prints." *Antiques*, LXXX (Nov 1961), 446–449.

A55 David Sellin. "A Benbridge Conversation Piece." *Philadelphia Museum of Art Bulletin*, LV, no. 263/4.

A57 William H. Gerdts, Jr. "Philip de Loutherbourg." *Antiques*, LXVIII (Nov 1955), 464–467.

A60 David Irwin. *English Neoclassical Art.* Greenwich, Conn., 1966.

A62 Mabel M. Swan. "Simeon Skillin, Senior *The First American Sculptor.*" *Antiques*, XLVI (Jul 1944), 21.

A67 Hugh Honour. *Neo-classicism.* Harmondsworth, England, 1968.

A68 Rensselaer W. Lee. *"Ut Pictura Poesis:* The Humanistic Theory of Painting." *Art Bulletin*, XXII (Dec 1940), 197–269.

A69 Robert G. Stewart. "The rediscovery of Henry Benbridge." *Smithsonian*, II (Apr 1971), 48–53.

A70 Nina Fletcher Little. "Winthrop Chandler." *Art in America*, XXXV (Apr 1947), 75–168.

A71 Nina Fletcher Little. "Recently Discovered Paintings by Winthrop Chandler." *Art in America*, XXXVI (Apr 1948), 81–97.

A74 John Marshall Phillips. "Ralph Earl, Loyalist." *Art in America*, XXXVIII (Oct 1949), 187–189.

A78 Perry T. Rathbone. "Copley's Corkscrew." *Art in America* [no vol. no.] (Jun 1965), 48–51.

A79 Charles Henry Hart. "The Gordon Family: Painted by Henry Benbridge." *Art in America*, VI (Jun 1918), 191–200.

A82 James A. Porter. "Versatile Interests of the Early Negro Artist." *Art in America*, XXIV (Jan 1936), 16–27.

A83 Ellis Waterhouse. *Painting in Britain 1530 to 1790.* London, 1953.

A84 Frank H. Somer. "Emblem and Device: The Origin of the Great Seal of the United States." *Art Quarterly*, XXIV (Spring 1961), 57–76.

A85 G. L. M. Goodfellow. "Cosmo Alexander in America." *Art Quarterly*, XXVI (Autumn 1963), 309–322.

A86 Robert D. Crompton. "James Trenchard of the 'Columbian' and 'Columbianum'." *Art Quarterly*, XXIII (Winter 1960), 378–397.

A88 George C. Groce. "John Wollaston (Fl. 1736–1767): A Cosmopolitan Painter in the British Colonies." *Art Quarterly*, XV (Summer 1952), 132–149.

A89 Theodore Sizer. "The John Trumbulls and Mme. Vigée-Le Brun." *Art Quarterly*, XV (Summer 1952), 170–178.

A90 Frederick A. Sweet. "Mezzotint Sources of American Colonial Portraits." *Art Quarterly*, XIV (Summer 1951), 148–157.

A92 E. P. Richardson. "Watson and the Shark by John Singleton Copley." *Art Quarterly*, X (Summer 1947), 213–218.

A93 Robert Rosenblum. *Transformations in Late Eighteenth Century Art.* Princeton, 1967.

A94 Frank Weitenkampf. "Early American Landscape Prints." *Art Quarterly*, VIII (Winter 1945), 40–67.

A96 Theodore Bolton and George C. Groce, Jr. "John Hesselius." *Art Quarterly*, II (Winter 1939), 77–91.

A97 E. P. Richardson. "Charles Willson Peale's Engravings in the Year of National Crisis, 1787." *Winterthur Portfolio*, I (1964), 166–181.

A100 Ian M. G. Quimby. "The Doolittle Engravings of the Battle of Lexington and Concord." *Winterthur Portfolio*, IV (1968), 83–108.

A103 Monroe E. Deutsch. "E Pluribus Unum." *Classical Journal*, XVIII (Apr 1923), 387–407.

A104 Esther Singleton. *Social New York under the Georges 1714–1776.* New York, 1902.

A105 Richard K. Doud. "John Hesselius, Maryland Limner." *Winterthur Portfolio*, V (1969), 129–153.

A106 Ernest J. Moyne. "John Hazlitt, Miniaturist and Portrait Painter in America, 1783–1787." *Winterthur Portfolio*, V (1969), 33–40.

A107 David H. Dickason. "Benjamin West on William Williams. A Previously Unpublished Letter." *Winterthur Portfolio*, VI (1970), 127–133.

A108 Helen Burr Smith. "John Mare (1739–c. 1795) New York Artist." *New-York Historical Society Quarterly*, XXXV (Oct 1951), 355–399.

A109 A. J. Wall. "The Statues of King George III and the Honorable William Pitt Erected in New York City 1770." *New-York Historical Society Quarterly*, IV (Jul 1920), 36–57.

A111 Henry Wilder Foote. "Benjamin Blyth, of Salem: Eighteenth-Century Artist." *Proceedings of the Massachusetts Historical Society*, LXXI (1953–7), 64–107.

A112 [Gaillard Hunt]. *The History of the Seal of the United States.* Washington, D.C., 1909.

A113 B. J. Cigrand. *Story of the Great Seal of the United States.* Chicago, 1903.

A114 William Barrow Floyd. "The portraits and paintings at Mount Vernon from 1754 to 1799 Part I." *Antiques*, C (Nov 1971), 768–774.

A116 David Lloyd Dowd. *Pageant-Master of the Republic. Jacques-Louis David and the French Revolution.* Univ. of Nebraska Studies, no. 3. Lincoln, 1948.

A117 John Hill Morgan. *Two Early Portraits of George Washington Painted by Charles Willson Peale.* Princeton, 1927.

A118 John Hill Morgan and Mantle Fielding. *The Life Portraits of Washington and their Replicas.* Philadelphia [1931].

A119 Charles Henry Hart. *Catalogue of The Engraved Portraits of Washington.* New York, 1914.

A120 Charles Henry Hart and Edward Biddle. *Memoirs of the Life and Works of Jean Antoine Houdon.* Philadelphia, 1911.

A121 Gustavus A. Eisen. *Portraits of Washington.* 3 vols. New York, 1932.

A122 Fiske Kimball. "Joseph Wright and His Portraits of Washington: *Sculpture.*" *Antiques*, XVII (Jan 1930), 34–39.

A123 Fiske Kimball. "Joseph Wright and His Portraits of Washington, *Paintings and Engravings.*" *Antiques*, XV (May 1929), 376–382.

A124 M. Dorothy George. *English Political Caricature to 1792.* Vol. I. Oxford, 1959.

A125 Louisa Dresser. *Art in New England. Early American Printmakers.* Worcester, Mass. [1939].

A126 William Murrell. *A History of American Graphic Humor.* New York, 1933.

A127 Clarence S. Brigham. *Paul Revere's Engravings.* New York, 1969.

A128 Wendy J. Shadwell, *et al. American Printmaking. The First 150 Years.* New York, 1969.

A131 William A. Beardsley. *An Old New Haven Engraver and His Work: Amos Doolittle.* N. pl., n. d.

A132 Clarence S. Brigham, *et al.* "The John Carter Brown Exhibition of Early American Engravings." *The Walpole Society Note Book* (1945), 43–82.

A133 Lord Killanin. *Sir Godfrey Kneller and his Times, 1646–1723.* London, 1948.

A134 Henry Wilder Foote. *John Smibert Painter.* Cambridge, Mass., 1950.

A135 Frank Weitenkampf. "John Greenwood An American-born Artist in Eighteenth Century Europe." *Bulletin of the New York Public Library* (Aug 1927), 623–634.

A136 Charles Willson Peale to Rembrandt Peale, 28 October 1812, HSP. [An eight-page reminiscence by Peale concerning painters he knew in his lifetime.]

A137 Eleanore McSherry Fowble. "A Century of the Nude in American Art 1750–1850." M.A. Thesis. University of Delaware, 1967.

A140 William H. Gerdts. "JOHN WOLLASTON: *Family Group.*" *The Museum*, X (Winter 1958), 1–6.

A141 *The Papers of Sir William Johnson.* Ed. Alexander C. Flick. Vol. V. Albany, 1927.

A142 Margaret Simons Middleton. *Jeremiah Theus. Colonial Artist of Charles Town.* Columbia, S.C., 1953.

A144 Francis W. Bilodeau. *Art in South Carolina 1670–1970.* Charleston, 1970.

A145 David Howard Dickason. *William Williams. Novelist and Painter of Colonial America 1727–1791.* Bloomington, Ind., 1970.

A146 Albert Matthews. "The Snake Devices, 1754–1776, and the Constitutional Courant, 1765." *Publications of the Colonial Society of Massachusetts*, XI (1906–7), 409–452.

A147 Charles Henry Hart. "Autobiographical Notes of Matthew Pratt, Painter." *Pennsylvania Magazine of History and Biography*, XIX (1895), 460–467.

A149 Thomas E. French. "America's First Female International Spy." *Daughters of the American Revolution Magazine*, XCIX (Nov 1965), 910–913.

A150 Alan Burroughs. "A Brief Notice about a Face [by Matthew Pratt]." *Museum Notes*, XI (Fall 1953), 2–9.

A152 C. H. Hart. "Patience Wright, Modeller in Wax." *The Connoisseur*, XIX (Sept 1907), 18–22.

A154 Benjamin West. MS Autobiography. Charles Allen Munn Collection, F.

A155 Ellen Starr Brinton. "Benjamin West's Painting of Penn's Treaty with the Indians." *Bulletin of Friends' Historical Association*, XXX (Autumn 1941), 99–189.

A156 Lewis Einstein. *Divided Loyalties. Americans in England During the War of Independence.* 1933; rpt. New York, 1970.

A159 William Sawitzky. "The American Work of Benjamin West." *Pennsylvania Magazine of History and Biography* (Oct 1938), 433–462.

A161 John Galt. *The Life of Benjamin West.* 1820; rpt. Gainesville, Fla., 1960.

A162 David Irwin. "English Neo-Classicism and Some Patrons." *Apollo,* LXVIII (Nov 1963), 360–367.

A165 Charles Dufresnoy. *The Art of Painting.* Trans. John Dryden. London, 1716.

A166 William T. Whitley. *Artists and Their Friends in England 1700–1799.* 2 vols. London and Boston, 1928.

A168 Charles Mitchell. "Benjamin West's 'Death of General Wolfe' and the Popular History Piece." *Journal of the Warburg and Courtauld Institutes,* VII (1944), 20–33.

A169 James Thomas Flexner. *America's Old Masters.* Rev. ed. New York, 1967.

A170 " 'Revealed Religion' A Series of Paintings by Benjamin West." Pamphlet. Greenville, S.C., 1963.

A171 *Letters & Papers of John Singleton Copley and Henry Pelham 1739–1776.* Boston, 1914.

A175 Martha Babcock Amory. *The Domestic and Artistic Life of John Singleton Copley, R.A.* Boston, 1882.

A177 Barbara Neville Parker and Anne Bolling Wheeler. *John Singleton Copley. American Portraits in Oil, Pastel, and Miniature with Biographical Sketches.* Boston, 1938.

A178 Jules David Prown. *John Singleton Copley.* 2 vols. Cambridge, Mass., 1966.

A179 Sir Kenneth Clark. "Provincialism." Pamphlet. London, 1962.

A180 William Dunlap. *History of the Rise and Progress of the Arts of Design in the United States.* Vol. I. 1834; rpt. New York, 1969.

A181 Alfred Frankenstein. *The World of Copley 1738–1815.* New York, 1970.

A182 Charles Willson Peale. MS Letter Book. APS.

A183 Charles Willson Peale. MS Diaries. APS.

A184 Charles Willson Peale. MS Autobiography. APS.

A185 Rembrandt Peale. "Washington and His Portraits." MS Essay. Charles Roberts Autograph Letters Collection, HA.

A186 Charles Coleman Sellers. *Charles Willson Peale.* New York, 1969.

A189 Charles Coleman Sellers. *Portraits and Miniatures by Charles Willson Peale. Transactions of the American Philosophical Society,* XLII (1952).

A190 Charles Willson Peale. MS Diary (4 December 1776–20 January 1777). H (HM 974).

A191 *American Painting to 1776. A Reappraisal.* Ed. Ian M. G. Quimby. Charlottesville, 1971: (b) Samuel M. Green, "The English Origins of Seventeenth-Century Painting in New England," 15–69; (c) Wayne Craven, "Painting in New York City, 1750–1775," 251–297.

A192 Charles Coleman Sellers. "Charles Willson Peale with Patron and Populace." *Transactions of the American Philosophical Society,* LIX (1969).

A197 Ralph W. Thomas. "Reuben Moulthrop 1763–1814." *Connecticut Historical Society Bulletin,* XXI (Oct 1956), 97–111.

A198 Edward Orme. *An Essay on Transparent Prints and on Transparencies in General.* London, 1807.

A199 Samuel M. Green. "Uncovering the Connecticut School." *Art News,* LI (Jan 1953), 38–40, 57–8.

A201 James Thomas Flexner. "Winthrop Chandler: an Eighteenth-Century Artisan Painter." *Magazine of Art,* XL (Nov 1947), 274–278.

A202 Laurence B. Goodrich. *Ralph Earl. Recorder for an Era.* New York, 1967.

A203 William and Susan Sawitzky. "Two Letters from Ralph Earl with Notes on his English Period." *Worcester Art Museum Annual,* VIII (1960), 8–41.

A204 "Reuben Moulthrop, 1763–1814." *Connecticut Historical Society Bulletin,* XX (Apr 1955), 44–51.

A205 "William Johnston Portrait Painter, 1732–1772." *Connecticut Historical Society Bulletin,* XIX (Oct 1954), 97–9, 108; XX (Jan 1955), 25–32 [the continuation signed by Robert Vose].

A206 *Henry Benbridge (1743–1812): American Portrait Painter.* Washington, D.C., 1971.

A207 Helmut von Erffa. "Benjamin West at the Height of His Career." *American Art Journal,* I (Spring 1969), 19–33.

A208 Charles Coleman Sellers. "Charles Willson Peale as Sculptor." *American Art Journal,* II (Fall 1970), 5–12.

A209 William T. Whitley. *Gilbert Stuart.* Cambridge, Mass., 1932.

A210 George C. Mason. *The Life and Works of Gilbert Stuart.* New York, 1879.

A213 Barbara Novak O'Doherty. "Philosopher of the Face." *Art News,* LXVI (Summer 1967), 42–5, 80–81.

A215 John Hill Morgan. *Gilbert Stuart and His Pupils.* New York, 1939.

A216 Lawrence Park. *Gilbert Stuart. An Illustrated Descriptive List of His Works.* New York, 1926.

A217a. Jane Stuart. "The Youth of Gilbert Stuart." *Scribner's Monthly,* XIII (Mar 1877), 640–646.

A218 *The Autobiography of Colonel John Trumbull.* Ed. Theodore Sizer. New Haven, 1953.

A220 John Hill Morgan. *Paintings by John Trumbull at Yale University.* New Haven, 1926.

A221 *Autobiography, Reminiscences and Letters of John Trumbull from 1756 to 1841.* New York, 1841.

A222 Joan Dolmetsch. "European prints in eighteenth-century America," *Antiques,* CI (May 1972), 858–863.

A223 *Gilbert Stuart. Portraitist of the Young Republic 1755–1828.* Washington, D.C., 1967.

A225 Charles Henry Hart. [Untitled notes on Mather and Gawen Brown.] *Proceedings of the Massachusetts Historical Society,* XLVII (1913–14), 32–34, 289–293.

A226 Charles Henry Hart. " 'The Congress Voting Independence.' " *Pennsylvania Magazine of History and Biography,* XXIX (1905), 1–14.

A227 Charles Le Brun. *The Conference of Monsieur Le Brun . . . Upon Expression.* London, 1701.

A229 "Benjamin West's 'The Death of Wolfe.' " Pamphlet. Ann Arbor, 1928.

A230 E. H. Gombrich. *Meditations on a Hobby Horse.* Greenwich, Conn., 1963.

A231 Jonathan Richardson. *The Works of Jonathan Richardson.* London, 1792.

A232. Thompson H. Harlow. "Connecticut Engravers 1774–1820." *Connecticut Historical Society Bulletin,* XXXVI (Oct 1971), 97–136.

A233 William Henry Back. MS "Biographical Sketch of an old friend [Mather Brown]." MMA.

A234 Geraldine Pelles. *Art, Artists & Society . . . Painting in England and France, 1750–1850.* Englewood Cliffs, N.J., 1963.

A237 E. P. Richardson. "James Claypoole, Junior, Re-Discovered." *Art Quarterly,* XXXIII (Summer 1970), 159–175.

A238 Allan Cunningham. *The Lives of the Most Eminent British Painters.* 3 vols. London, 1879.

A239 Samuel Shoemaker. MS Diary. HSP (typed transcript at NYHS used in the text).

A241 H. W. Dickinson. *Robert Fulton. Engineer and Artist.* London, 1913.

A242 "Advertisements of Artists." *South-Carolina Historical and Genealogical Magazine,* XXI (1920), 88–91.

A244 Nina Fletcher Little. "The Blyths of Salem. Benjamin, Limner in Crayons and Oil, and Samuel, Painter and Cabinetmaker." *Essex Institute Historical Collections,* CVIII (Jan 1972), 49–57.

A245 E. P. Richardson. "Stamp Act Cartoons in the Colonies." *Pennsylvania Magazine of History and Biography,* XCVI (Jul 1972), 275–297.

A246 *Prints in and of America to 1850.* Ed. John D. Morse. Charlottesville, 1970: (a) Joan Dolmetsch, "Prints in Colonial America: Supply and Demand in the Mid-Eighteenth Century," 53–74; (b) Frank H. Sommer III, "Thomas Hollis and the Arts of Dissent," 111–159; (c) Charles B. Wood III, "Prints and Scientific Illustration in America," 161–187.

A248 "Statue of Lord Botetourt." Pamphlet. Williamsburg, 1971.

A250 Marie Kimball. "Jefferson, Patron of the Arts." *Antiques,* XLIII (Apr 1943), 164–167.

A251 *Houdon in America.* Ed. Gilbert Chinard. Baltimore, 1930.

A252 "A Sketch of the Character of Mrs. *Wright."* *London Magazine,* XLIV (Nov 1775), 555–556.

A253 "A Washington Miniature." *Antiques,* XCVI (Sept 1969), 318, 322, 344.

A254 "Extracts from Col. Paul Revere's Day-Book." *Proceedings of the Massachusetts Historical Society* (1869–70), 391.

A255 *Descriptive Catalogue of the Du Simitière Papers.* Philadelphia, 1940.

Drama

D1 Paul Leicester Ford. *Washington and the Theater.* 1899; rpt. New York, 1967.

D2 Eola Willis. *The Charleston Stage in the XVIII Century.* Columbia, S.C., 1924.

D3 J. Max Patrick. *Savannah's Pioneer Theater from its Origins to 1810.* Athens, Ga., 1953.

D4 Thomas Clark Pollock. *The Philadelphia Theatre in the Eighteenth Century.* Philadelphia, 1933.

D6   Julian Mates. *The American Musical Stage before 1800.* New Brunswick, N.J., 1962.

D7   Esther Cloudman Dunn. *Shakespeare in America.* New York, 1939.

D8   William Dunlap. *History of the American Theatre and Anecdotes of the Principal Actors.* 2d ed. [N. d.]; rpt. New York, 1963.

D9   George O. Seilhamer. *History of the American Theatre: Before the Revolution.* Philadelphia, 1888.

D10 George O. Seilhamer. *History of the American Theatre: During the Revolution and After.* Philadelphia, 1889.

D11 G. Thomas Tanselle. *Royall Tyler.* Cambridge, Mass., 1967.

D15 Kent G. Gallagher. *The Foreigner in Early American Drama.* The Hague, 1966.

D16 George O. Willard. *History of the Providence Stage 1762–1891.* Providence, 1891.

D18 Brooks McNamara. *The American Playhouse in the Eighteenth Century.* Cambridge, Mass., 1969.

D19 Alice Brown. *Mercy Warren.* New York, 1896.

D21 Frederic M. Litto. "Addison's *Cato* in the Colonies." *William and Mary Quarterly,* 3d Ser., XXIII (Jul 1966), 431–449.

D22 Hugh F. Rankin. *The Theater in Colonial America.* Chapel Hill, 1965.

D24 Marston Balch. "Jonathan the First." *Modern Language Notes,* XLVI (May 1931), 281–288.

D25 Hennig Cohen. "Shakespeare in Charleston on the Eve of the Revolution." *Shakespeare Quarterly,* IV (Jul 1953), 327–330.

D26 Rodney M. Baine. *Robert Munford. America's First Comic Dramatist.* Athens, Ga., 1967.

D27 Oral Sumner Coad. *William Dunlap.* New York, 1917.

D28 George C. D. Odell. *Annals of the New York Stage.* Vol. I. New York, 1927.

D29 Ota Thomas. "Student Dramatic Activities at Yale College During the Eighteenth Century." *Theatre Annual* (1944), 47–59.

D30 Ernest Bernbaum. *The Drama of Sensibility.* 1915; rpt. Gloucester, Mass., 1958.

D31 S. E. Morison. "Two 'Signers' on Salaries and the Stage, 1789." *Proceedings of the Massachusetts Historical Society,* LXII (1928–9), 55–63.

D32 S. E. Morison. "Henry Knox and the London Book-Store in Boston 1771–1774." *Proceedings of the Massachusetts Historical Society,* LXI (1927–8), 225–303.

D33 William S. Dye, Jr. "Pennsylvania *Versus* the Theatre." *Pennsylvania Magazine of History and Biography,* LV (1931), 333–372.

D34 Fred Lewis Pattee. "The British Theater in Philadelphia in 1778." *American Literature,* VI (1935), 381–388.

D35 Allardyce Nicoll. *A History of Late Eighteenth Century Drama, 1750–1800.* London, 1927.

D36 Philip Marsh. "Philip Freneau and the Theater." *Proceedings of the New Jersey Historical Society,* LXVI (Apr 1948), 96–105.

D37 S. Foster Damon. "Varnum's 'Ministerial Oppression,' A Revolutionary Drama." *Proceedings of the American Antiquarian Society,* LV (1945), 287–298.

D39 Charles Durang. *The Philadelphia Stage: from 1749 to 1821.* Series of articles from

Philadelphia *Sunday Dispatch*, beginning May 7, 1854, in bound scrapbook at University of Pennsylvania Library.

D40 Charles Hogan. "The New Wells, Goodman's Fields, 1739–1752." *Theatre Notebook*, III (Apr–Jun 1949), 67–72.

D41 Jonathan Curvin. "Realism in Early American Art and Theatre." *Quarterly Journal of Speech*, XXX (Dec 1944), 450–455.

D42 Robert Hamilton Ball. "Samuel Greville, First Player." *Princeton Alumni Weekly*, XXX (Oct 25, 1929), 117–124.

D43 Lewis P. Waldo. *The French Drama in America . . . 1701–1800*. Baltimore, 1942.

D45 S. Foster Damon. "Providence Theatricals in 1773." *Rhode Island History*, IV (Apr 1945), 55–58.

D47 Edward A. Wyatt. "Three Petersburg Theatres." *William and Mary Quarterly*, 2d Ser., XXI (Apr 1941), 83–110.

D49 "The Play-Bills of Baltimore Theatre for the Years 1782, and 1783. Wall, and Lindsay, Managers." Scrapbook. NYHS.

D50 Martin Staples Shockley. "The Richmond Theatre, 1780–1790." *Virginia Magazine of History and Biography*, LX (1952), 421–436.

D51 Van Carl Kussrow, Jr. "On with the Show: A Study of Public Arguments in Favor of Theatre in America during the Eighteenth Century." Ph.D. Dissertation. Indiana University, 1959.

D52 Ralph Borden Culp. "Drama-and-Theater as a Source of Colonial American Attitudes Toward Independence, 1758–1776." Ph.D. Dissertation. Cornell University, 1962.

D53 "Receipts of the Treasurer of the 'Theatre Royal,' John Street New York, A.D. 1779." MS Account Book. NYHS.

D57 Edward Robins. "David Garrick and 'Old Penn'." *Pennsylvania Magazine of History and Biography*, XXXIX (1915), 48–52.

D58 H. P. Phelps. *Players of a Century. A Record of the Albany Stage*. Albany, 1880.

D59 Sybil Rosenfeld. *Strolling Players & Drama in the Provinces 1660–1765*. Cambridge, England, 1939.

D62 Hugh Franklin Rankin. "The Colonial Theatre; its History and Operations." Ph.D. Dissertation. University of North Carolina, 1959.

D63 Susanne Ketchum Sherman. "Post-Revolutionary Theatre in Virginia, 1784–1801." M.A. Thesis. College of William and Mary, 1950.

D64 Susan Armstrong. "A Repertoire of the American Colonial Theatre." TS Notebook, CW, 1955.

D66 Brander Matthews and Laurence Hutton. *Actors and Actresses*. Vol. I, no. 8. [N. pl., n. d.; copy at Harvard Theatre Collection.]

D67 T. Allston Brown. *History of the American Stage*. New York, 1870.

D68 Roger Eliot Stoddard. "Notes on American Play-Publishing, 1765–1865." *Proceedings of the American Antiquarian Society*, LXXXI (Apr 1971), 161–190.

D70 Arthur W. Bloom. "The History of the Theatre in New Haven, Connecticut, before 1860." Ph.D. Dissertation. Yale University, 1966.

D73 Mary Julia Curtis. "The Early Charleston Stage: 1703–1798." Ph.D. Dissertation. Indiana University, 1968.

D74 Stanley T. Lewis. "The New York Theatre; its Background and Architectural Development: 1750–1853." Ph.D. Dissertation. Ohio State University, 1953.

D75 Gordon Eugene Beck. "British Military Theatricals in New York City During the Revolutionary War." Ph.D. Dissertation. University of Illinois, 1964.

D76 John W. Molnar. *Songs from the Williamsburg Theatre.* Williamsburg, 1972.

D77 Haller T. Laughlin. *"The Disappointment* and *The Wheel of Fortune:* Two Amateur Playwrights' Use of Local and National Events in Early American Plays." Ph.D. Dissertation. Southern Illinois University, 1970.

D78 *The Prose of Royall Tyler.* Ed. Marius B. Péladeau. Montpelier, Vt., 1972.

D79 Helen R. Yalof. "British Military Theatricals in Philadelphia during the Revolutionary War." Ph.D. Dissertation. New York University, 1972.

D80 Philip Highfil, Jr. "The British Background of the American Hallams." *Theatre Survey,* XI (May 1970), 1–35.

D81 Robert Fahrner. "David Garrick Presents *The Padlock:* An 18th-Century 'Hit'." *Theatre Survey,* XIII (May 1972), 52–69.

D82 Henry N. Paul. "Shakespeare in Philadelphia." *Proceedings of the American Philosophical Society,* LXXVI (1936), 719–729.

D83 "Letter from Hudson Muse. . . ." *William and Mary College Quarterly Historical Papers,* II (Apr 1894), 240–241.

D84 "F. H." *Virginia Magazine of History and Biography,* XXXV (Jul 1927), 295–296.

D85 Julian Mates. "The Dramatic Anchor: Research Opportunities in the American Stage Before 1800." *Early American Literature,* V (Winter 1971), 76–79.

General

G1 Bernard Bailyn. *The Ideological Origins of the American Revolution.* Cambridge, Mass., 1967.

G2 Philip Davidson. *Propaganda and the American Revolution 1763–1783.* Chapel Hill, 1941.

G3 *The Paxton Papers.* Ed. John R. Dunbar. The Hague, 1957.

G4 *Colonies to Nation: 1763–1789.* Ed. Jack P. Greene. New York, 1967.

G5 Bernard Bailyn. *The Battle of Bunker Hill.* Boston, 1968.

G8 *Dramas from the American Theatre 1762–1909.* Ed. Richard Moody. Boston, 1966.

G10 Willard M. Wallace. *Appeal to Arms. A Military History of the American Revolution.* 1951; rpt. Chicago, 1964.

G11 Peter Wells. *The American War of Independence.* 1967; rpt. [N. pl.], 1968.

G12 John Richard Alden. *The American Revolution 1775–1783.* 1954; rpt. New York, 1962.

G15 James Thomas Flexner. *George Washington and the New Nation (1783–1793).* Boston, 1969.

G16 Alexis de Tocqueville. *Democracy in America.* Trans. Henry Reeve. 2 vols. New York, 1961.

G17 Edmund S. Morgan and Helen M. Morgan. *The Stamp Act Crisis. Prologue to Revolution.* 1953; rpt. New York, 1963.

G19 J. P. Brissot de Warville. *New Travels in the United States of America 1788.* Trans. Mara Soceanu Vamos and Durand Echeverria. Cambridge, Mass., 1964.

G21 Arthur M. Schlesinger. *Prelude to Independence. The Newspaper War on Britain 1764–1776.* 1958; rpt. New York, 1965.

G22 Jackson Turner Main. *The Social Structure of Revolutionary America.* Princeton, 1965.

G23 Allan Kulikoff. "The Progress of Inequality in Revolutionary Boston." *William and Mary Quarterly,* 3d Ser., XXVIII (Jul 1971), 375–412.

G25 Alexander Graydon. *Memoirs of His Own Time With Reminiscences of the Men and Events of the Revolution.* 1846; rpt. New York, 1969.

G26 Gordon S. Wood. *The Creation of the American Republic 1776–1787.* Chapel Hill, 1969.

G27 Piers Mackesy. *The War for America 1775–1783.* Cambridge, Mass., 1965.

G28 Francois-Jean, Marquis de Chastellux. *Travels in North America in the Years 1780, 1781 and 1782.* Trans. Howard C. Rice, Jr. 2 vols. Chapel Hill, 1963.

G30 Henry Steele Commager and Elmo Giordanetti. *Was America a Mistake? An Eighteenth-Century Controversy.* New York, 1967.

G31 *Boston Under Military Rule 1768–1769 as revealed in A Journal of the Times.* Ed. Oliver M. Dickerson. 1936; rpt. New York, 1970.

G32 Frank Moore. *Diary of the American Revolution.* 2 vols. New York, 1860.

G33 E. McClung Fleming. "Symbols of the United States: From Indian Queen to Uncle Sam," in *Frontiers of American Culture.* Ed. Ray B. Browne, *et al.* [N. pl.; Purdue University Studies], 1968. Pp. 1–24.

G34 Robert Middlekauff. "The ritualization of the american revolution," in *The development of an american culture.* Ed. Stanley Coben and Lorman Ratner. Englewood Cliffs, N.J., 1970. Pp. 31–43.

G35 Charles Louis de Secondat, Baron de Montesquieu. *The Spirit of Laws.* 2 vols. New York, 1900.

G36 Catherine Snell Crary. "The Tory and the Spy: The Double Life of James Rivington." *William and Mary Quarterly,* 3d Ser., XVI (Jan 1959), 61–72.

G37 *Adams Family Correspondence.* Ed. L. H. Butterfield. 2 vols. Cambridge, Mass., 1963.

G39 *Letters of John Adams Addressed to his Wife.* Ed. Charles Francis Adams. 2 vols. Boston, 1841.

G40 *The Literary Diary of Ezra Stiles, D.D., LL.D.* Ed. Franklin Bowditch Dexter. 3 vols. New York, 1901.

G41 Simon Gratz. "Some Material for a Biography of Mrs. Elizabeth Fergusson, *née* Graeme." *Pennsylvania Magazine of History and Biography,* XXXIX (1915), 257–321.

G42 *Life and Correspondence of the Rev. William Smith, D.D.* Ed. Horace Wemyss Smith. 2 vols. Philadelphia, 1879.

G43 Jane Carson. *Colonial Virginians at Play.* Williamsburg, 1965.

G44 Whitfield J. Bell, Jr. "The Federal Processions of 1788." *New-York Historical Society Quarterly,* XLVI (Jan 1962), 5–39.

G45 Sarah H. J. Simpson. "The Federal Procession in the City of New York." *New-York Historical Society Quarterly Bulletin,* IX (Jul 1925), 39–57.

G46 *Letters from America 1776–1779 . . . of Brunswick, Hessian, and Waldeck Officers.* 1924; rpt. New York, 1964.

G47 *Quebec to Carolina in 1785–1786.* Ed. Louis B. Wright and Marion Tinling. San Marino, Calif., 1943.

G48 *Letters of Benjamin Rush.* Vol. I. Ed. L. H. Butterfield. Princeton, 1951.

G49 *Theatrum Majorum . . . The Diary of Dorothy Dudley.* Cambridge, Mass., 1876.

G50 *The Journal of John Harrower.* Ed. Edward Miles Riley. Williamsburg, 1963.

G51 *The Journal of Nicholas Cresswell 1774–1777.* New York, 1924.

G52 *The Diary of William Pynchon of Salem.* Ed. Fitch Edward Oliver. Boston, 1890.

G53 Philip Vickers Fithian. *Journal and Letters 1767–1774.* Ed. John Rogers Williams. 1900; rpt. Freeport, N.Y., 1969.

G54 James Thacher. *Military Journal of the American Revolution.* Hartford, 1862.

G56 *The Diaries of George Washington.* Ed. John C. Fitzpatrick. 4 vols. New York, 1925.

G57 *Letters of Noah Webster.* Ed. Harry R. Warfel. New York, 1953.

G58 *The Writings of George Washington.* Ed. Worthington Chauncey Ford. 14 vols. New York, 1889–93.

G59 William Eddis. *Letters from America.* Ed. Aubrey C. Land. Cambridge, Mass., 1969.

G62 Benjamin Woods Labaree. *The Boston Tea Party.* New York, 1964.

G64 *Men and Times of the Revolution; or, Memoirs of Elkanah Watson.* Ed. Winslow C. Watson. New York, 1857.

G65 *Seeing America and its Great Men. The Journal and Letters of Count Francesco dal Verme.* Trans. Elizabeth Cometti. Charlottesville, 1969.

G66 Anne Bezanson. *Prices and Inflation During the American Revolution. Pennsylvania, 1770–1790.* Philadelphia, 1951.

G67 Johann David Schoepf. *Travels in the Confederation (1783–1784).* Trans. Alfred J. Morrison. 2 vols. 1911; rpt. New York, 1968.

G68 *The New Democracy in America. Travels of Francisco de Miranda in the United States, 1783–84.* Trans. Judson P. Wood. Norman, Okla., 1963.

G69 *Our Revolutionary Forefathers. The Letters of François, Marquis de Barbé-Marbois.* Trans. Eugene Parker Chase. New York, 1929.

G70 *Reminiscences of an American Loyalist 1738–1789.* Ed. Jonathan Bouchier. Boston and New York, 1925.

G71 John Bernard. *Retrospections of America 1797–1811.* 1887; rpt. New York, 1969.

G72 Thomas Anburey. *Travels Through the Interior Parts of America.* 2 vols. Boston, 1923.

G73 Ewald Gustav Schaukirk. *Occupation of New York City by the British.* 1887; rpt. New York, 1969.

G74 *The American Journal of Ambrose Serle.* Ed. Edward H. Tatum, Jr. 1940; rpt. New York, 1969.

G75 *Letters and Diary of John Rowe Boston Merchant 1759–1762 1764–1779.* Ed. Anne Rowe Cunningham. 1903; rpt. New York, 1969.

G77 *Diary of Grace Growden Galloway.* 1931–4; rpt. New York, 1971.

G78 *The Washington Papers.* Ed. Saul K. Padover. 1955; rpt. New York, 1967.

G79 "Journal of a Tour to Connecticut—Autumn of 1789." *Proceedings of the Massachusetts Historical Society* (1869–70), 9–32.

G80 *Correspondence and Journals of Samuel Blachley Webb.* Ed. Worthington Chauncey Ford. 3 vols. New York, 1893.

G81e John P. Roche. "The Founding Fathers: A Reform Caucus in Action," in *Essays on the American Revolution.* Ed. David L. Jacobson. New York, 1970. Pp. 259–283.

G84 *Extracts from the Itineraries and other Miscellanies of Ezra Stiles.* Ed. Franklin B. Dexter. New Haven, 1916.

G86 Jane Carson. *James Innes and his brothers of the F.H.C.* Williamsburg, 1965.

G87 David Freeman Hawke. *Benjamin Rush. Revolutionary Gadfly.* Indianapolis, 1971.

G88 *The Selected Writings of Benjamin Rush.* Ed. Dagobert D. Runes. New York, 1947.

G89 Frank Luther Mott. *A History of American Magazines 1741–1850.* Cambridge, Mass., 1966.

G90 George Mifflin Dallas. *Life and Writings of Alexander James Dallas.* Philadelphia, 1871.

G91 Kenneth Wiggins Porter. *John Jacob Astor. Business Man.* Cambridge, Mass., 1931.

G92 *Belknap Papers. Collections of the Massachusetts Historical Society,* 5th Ser., II–III (1877); 6th Ser., IV (1891).

G93 David Hume. *Essays Moral, Political and Literary.* London, 1963.

G94 Albert Frank Gegenheimer. *William Smith. Educator and Churchman 1727–1803.* Philadelphia, 1943.

G95 Henri Petter. *The Early American Novel.* [N. pl., Ohio State University Press], 1971.

G97 *The Papers of Benjamin Franklin.* Ed. Leonard W. Labaree. New Haven, 1959– .

G98 Allen French. *General Gage's Informers.* Ann Arbor, 1932.

G99 Richard J. Hooker. "The American Revolution Seen Through a Wine Glass." *William and Mary Quarterly,* 3d Ser., XI (Jan 1954), 52–77.

G101 James William Johnson. *The Formation of English Neoclassical Thought.* Princeton, 1967.

G102 Richard W. Van Alstyne. *Empire and Independence. The International History of the American Revolution.* New York, 1965.

G103 J. H. Elliott. *The Old World and the New.* Cambridge, England, 1970.

G104 Robert J. Taylor. *Western Massachusetts in the Revolution.* Providence, 1954.

G107 *Letters & Papers of Ezra Stiles.* Ed. Isabel Calder. New Haven, 1933.

G108 Donald O. Schneider. "Education in Colonial American Colleges 1750–1770 and the Occupations and Political Offices of their Alumni." Ph.D. Dissertation. George Peabody College for Teachers, 1965.

G109 James Madison. *Notes of Debates in the Federal Convention of 1787.* New York, 1966.

G110 *The Montresor Journals.* Ed. G. D. Scull. *Collections of the New-York Historical Society,* 1881.

G111 Leroy Hewlett. "James Rivington, Loyalist Printer, Publisher, and Bookseller of the American Revolution, 1724–1802." Ph.D. Dissertation. University of Michigan, 1958.

G112 *Sources and Documents illustrating the American Revolution 1764–1788.* Ed. Samuel Eliot Morison. 2d ed., 1929; rpt. New York, 1967.

G113 Douglas Sloan. *The Scottish Enlightenment and the American College Ideal.* New York, 1971.

G115 *The Writings of John Dickinson.* Ed. Paul Leicester Ford. Vol. I. Philadelphia, 1895.

G116 John Witherspoon. *Works.* Vol. VII. Edinburgh, 1805.

G117 Albert Matthews. "The Book of America." *Proceedings of the Massachusetts Historical Society,* LXII (1928–9), 171–197.

G118 Arthur M. Schlesinger. "Liberty Tree: A Genealogy." *New England Quarterly,* XXV (Dec 1952), 435–458.

G119 Wayne C. Minnick. "The New England Execution Sermon, 1639–1800." *Speech Monographs,* XXXV (Mar 1968), 77–89.

G120 William Gribbin. "Rollin's Histories and American Republicanism." *William and Mary Quarterly,* 3d Ser., XXIX (Oct 1972), 611–622.

G121 Timothy Dwight. *Travels in New England and New York.* Ed. Barbara Miller Solomon. 4 vols. Cambridge, Mass., 1969.

G122 William B. Willcox. *Portrait of a General. Sir Henry Clinton in the War of Independence.* New York, 1964.

G123 Thomas Jefferson. *Notes on the State of Virginia.* Ed. H. A. Washington. 1861; rpt. New York, 1964.

G124 *The Siege of Charleston . . . Diaries and Letters of Hessian Officers.* Ed. Bernhard A. Uhlendorf. Ann Arbor, 1938.

G125 Lorenzo Sabine. *Biographical Sketches of Loyalists of the American Revolution.* 2 vols. 1864; rpt. New York, 1966.

G127 Robert L. Brunhouse. *The Counter-Revolution in Pennsylvania 1776–1790.* Harrisburg, Pa., 1942.

G128 James Austin Holden. "Influence of Death *[sic]* of Jane McCrea on Burgoyne Campaign." *Proceedings of the New York State Historical Association,* XII (1913), 249–310.

G130 Gladys Bryson. *Man and Society: The Scottish Inquiry of the Eighteenth Century.* Princeton, 1945.

G131 John Joseph Stoudt. *Ordeal at Valley Forge.* Philadelphia, 1963.

G132 George H. Haynes. *Historical Sketch First Congregational Church Sturbridge: Massachusetts [sic].* Worcester, Mass., 1910.

G134 Jay B. Hubbell. *The South in American Literature 1607–1900* [Durham, N.C.], 1954.

G135 Marvin Harris. *The Rise of Anthropological Theory.* New York, 1968.

G137 Frederick P. Bowes. *The Culture of Early Charleston.* Chapel Hill, 1942.

G138 Josiah Quincy. *The History of Harvard University.* Vol. II. Boston, 1860.

G139 Samuel Miller. *A Brief Retrospect of the Eighteenth Century.* 2 vols. 1803; rpt. New York, 1970.

G141 Peter Force. *American Archives.* 4th Ser. Washington, D.C., 1837–9.

G142 Alexander Hamilton, James Madison, and John Jay. *The Federalist Papers.* Ed. Clinton Rossiter. New York, 1961.

G143 *The Antifederalists.* Ed. Cecelia M. Kenyon. Indianapolis, 1966.

G146 *The Papers of Thomas Jefferson.* Ed. Julian P. Boyd. Princeton, 1950– .

G148 Marie Kimball. *Jefferson: The Scene of Europe 1784 to 1789.* New York, 1950.

G151 *The Works of John Adams.* Ed. Charles Francis Adams. Vols. VII–IX. Boston, 1852–4.

G152 Max Lavon Autrey. "The Shaftesbury-Mandeville Debate and its Influence in America." Ph.D. Dissertation. Wayne State University, 1965.

G153 Robert Francis Seybolt. *The Private Schools of Colonial Boston.* 1935; rpt. New York, 1969.

G155 *The English Libertarian Heritage.* Ed. David L. Jacobson. Indianapolis, 1965.

G156 *The Burd Papers.* Ed. Lewis Burd Walker. [N. pl.], 1897.

G157 A. R. Humphreys. *The Augustan World.* 1954; rpt. New York, 1963.

G158 Merrill Jensen. *The Founding of a Nation. A History of the American Revolution 1763–1776.* New York, 1968.

G159 Carl and Jessica Bridenbaugh. *Rebels and Gentlemen. Philadelphia in the Age of Franklin.* 1942; rpt. New York, 1962.

G160 *The Complete Works of Tacitus.* Trans. Alfred John Church and William Jackson Brodribb. New York, 1942.

G162 Mark Mayo Boatner III. *Encyclopedia of the American Revolution.* New York, 1966.

G163 *The Spirit of 'Seventy-Six.* Ed. Henry Steele Commager and Richard B. Morris. 2 vols. Indianapolis, 1958.

G165 John Richard Alden. *General Gage in America.* Baton Rouge, 1948.

G166 Curtis P. Nettels. "Washington on the Eve of the Revolution," in *George Washington. A Profile.* Ed. James Morton Smith. New York, 1969. Pp. 59–85.

G167 Oscar Theodore Barck. *New York City During the War for Independence.* New York, 1931.

G168a Milton C. Albrecht. "Art as an Institution," in *The Sociology of Art and Literature.* Ed. Milton C. Albrecht, *et al.* New York [1970]. Pp. 1–26.

G169 Carl Van Doren. *Secret History of the American Revolution.* New York, 1941.

G170 J. Thomas Scharf. *History of Maryland.* Vol. II. 1879; rpt. Hatboro, Pa., 1967.

G173 J. Thomas Scharf and Thompson Westcott. *History of Philadelphia 1609–1884.* Vol. I. Philadelphia, 1884.

G174 Douglas Southall Freeman. *George Washington. A Biography.* 6 vols. New York, 1948–54.

G175 Merrill Jensen. *The New Nation.* New York, 1965.

G176 *The Political Writings of John Adams.* Ed. George A. Peek, Jr. Indianapolis, 1954.

G177 *Diary and Autobiography of John Adams.* Ed. L. H. Butterfield. 4 vols. Cambridge, Mass., 1962.

G180 Thomas E. V. Smith. *The City of New York in the Year of Washington's Inauguration 1789.* New York, 1889.

G181 William David Andrews. "The *Translatio Studii* as a Theme in Eighteenth-

Century American Writing." Ph.D. Dissertation. University of Pennsylvania, 1971.

G182 René Wellek. *The Rise of English Literary History.* Chapel Hill, 1941.

G183 Georg Lukacs. *The Historical Novel.* New York, 1962.

G187 George Smith McCowen, Jr. *The British Occupation of Charleston, 1780–82.* Columbia, S.C., 1972.

G188 Kathryn Sullivan. *Maryland and France 1774–1789.* Philadelphia, 1936.

G189 *Correspondence of General Washington and Comte de Grasse.* Washington, D.C., 1931.

G190 *Itinerary of General Washington.* Ed. William S. Baker. 1892; rpt. Lambertville, N.J., 1970.

G192 *The Writings of George Washington.* Ed. John C. Fitzpatrick. 39 vols. Washington, D.C., 1931–44.

G193 Stephen Decatur, Jr. *Private Affairs of George Washington.* Boston, 1933.

G195 Burke Davis. *The Campaign that Won America.* New York, 1970.

G196 *The Diary of William Bentley, D.D.* 2 vols. Salem, Mass., 1907.

G197 *Statutes at Large of Pennsylvania.* Vols. XII–XIII (1785–1790). Harrisburg, Pa., 1906, 1908.

G198 *Pennsylvania Archives.* 1st Ser. Vols. X–XI. Philadelphia, 1854, 1855.

G199 *Life Journals and Correspondence of Rev. Manasseh Cutler, LL.D.* Ed. William Parker Cutler and Julia Perkins Cutler. 2 vols. Cincinnati, 1888.

G200 Samuel G. Drake. *The History and Antiquities of Boston.* Boston, 1856.

G202 William Smith. *History as Argument.* The Hague, 1966.

G203 *Worcester Town Records 1754–1783.* Worcester, Mass., 1882.

G204 "Josiah Smith's Diary, 1780–1781." *South-Carolina Historical and Genealogical Magazine,* XXXIII (1932), 24.

G205 "The French Fête in Philadelphia in Honor of the Dauphin's Birthday, 1782." *Pennsylvania Magazine of History,* XXI (1897), 257–262.

G206 John B. Reeves. "Extracts from the Letter-Books of Lieutenant Enos Reeves, of the Pennsylvania Line." *Pennsylvania Magazine of History,* XXI (1897), *passim.*

G207 Louis B. Wright. *The First Gentlemen of Virginia.* San Marino, Calif., 1940.

G208 Ivor Noël Hume. *Here Lies Virginia.* New York, 1963.

G209 *Peter Oliver's Origin & Progress of the American Rebellion.* Ed. Douglass Adair and John M. Schutz. San Marino, Calif., 1961.

G210 *Pennsylvania Historical Records Survey.* Philadelphia, 1940.

G211 *The Diary of Landon Carter.* Ed. Jack P. Greene. 2 vols. Charlottesville, 1965.

G212 Thomas Jones. *History of New York during the Revolutionary War.* 2 vols. New York, 1879.

G213 John K. Alexander. "The Fort Wilson Incident of 1779; A Case Study of the Revolutionary Crowd." *William and Mary Quarterly,* 3d Ser., XXXI (Oct 1974), 589–612.

G214 Hellmut Lehmann-Haupt. *The Book in America.* New York, 1939.

G215 *Publications of the Colonial Society of Massachusetts:* (a) "College Laws of 1655, 1692, and 1767," XXXI (1935), 323–384; (c) Albert Matthews. "The Sobriquet Favorite Son," XIII (1910–11), 99–109; (d) Charles K. Bolton. "Circulating

Libraries in Boston, 1765–1865," XI (1906–7), 196–207; (e) Albert Matthews. "Brother Jonathan," VII (1900–1902), 94–119.

Music

M1 Irving Lowens. *Music and Musicians in Early America.* New York, 1964.

M2 Oscar G. T. Sonneck. *Francis Hopkinson The First American Poet-Composer (1737–1791) and James Lyon Patriot, Preacher, Psalmodist (1735–1794).* 1905; rpt. New York, 1967.

M3 O. G. Sonneck *[sic].* *Early Concert-Life in America (1731–1800).* 1906; rpt. New York, 1949.

M4 William Arms Fisher. *Notes on Music in Old Boston.* Boston, 1918.

M6 John Tasker Howard. *The Music of George Washington's Time.* Washington, D. C., 1931.

M7 H. Wiley Hitchcock. *Music in the United States: A Historical Introduction.* Englewood Cliffs, N.J., 1969.

M8 Leonard Ellinwood. *The History of American Church Music.* Rev. ed. New York, 1970.

M9 Louis Pichierri. *Music in New Hampshire 1623–1800.* New York, 1960.

M10 Gilbert Chase. *America's music From the Pilgrims to the present.* New York, 1955.

M11 John Tasker Howard. *Our American Music. A Comprehensive History from 1620 to the Present.* 4th ed. New York, 1965.

M12 Robert Stevenson. *Protestant Church Music in America.* New York, 1970.

M13 Simon Vance Anderson. "American Music During the War for Independence, 1775–1783." Ph.D. Dissertation. University of Michigan, 1965.

M14 Carl Engel. "Introducing Mr. Braun." *Musical Quarterly,* XXX (Jan 1944), 63–83.

M15 Maurer Maurer. "The 'Professor of Musick' in Colonial America." *Musical Quarterly,* XXXVI (Oct 1950), 511–524.

M16 Carleton Sprague Smith. "The 1774 Psalm Book of the Reformed Protestant Dutch Church in New York City." *Musical Quarterly,* XXXIV (Jan 1948), 84–96.

M17 Maurer Maurer. "A Musical Family in Colonial Virginia." *Musical Quarterly,* XXXIV (Jul 1948), 358–364.

M18 H. Earle Johnson. "The Adams Family and Good Listening." *Journal of the American Musicological Society,* XI (Summer–Fall 1958), 165–176.

M20 M. D. Herter Norton. "Haydn in America (before 1820)." *Musical Quarterly,* XVIII (Apr 1932), 309–337.

M22 Frank J. Metcalf. *American Writers and Compilers of Sacred Music.* New York, 1925.

M24 O. G. Sonneck. *Early Opera in America.* 1915; rpt. New York, 1963.

M26 Carl E. Lindstrom. "William Billings and His Times." *Musical Quarterly,* XXV (Oct 1939), 479–497.

M27 Marian Hannah Winter. "American Theatrical Dancing from 1750 to 1800." *Musical Quarterly,* XXIV (Jan 1938), 58–73.

M28 Allen P. Britton. "The Singing School Movement in the United States."

Report of the Eighth Congress of the International Musicological Society. New York, 1961. Pp. 89–99.

M29 Henry Wilder Foote. *Three Centuries of American Hymnody.* Cambridge, Mass., 1940.

M30 Richard A. Crawford. *Andrew Law, American Psalmodist.* Evanston, Ill., 1968.

M32 Ralph T. Daniel. *The Anthem in New England before 1800.* Evanston, Ill., 1966.

M33 Joyce Ellen Mangler. "Music in the First Congregational Church, Providence, 1770–1850." *Rhode Island History,* XVII (Jan 1958), 1–14.

M34 George W. Williams. "Charleston Church Music 1562–1833." *Journal of the American Musicological Society,* VII (Spring 1954), 35–40.

M35 Alan C. Buechner. "The New England Harmony." Pamphlet in *The New England Harmony,* Folkways Records FA-32377.

M36 *The Memoir of John Durang American Actor 1785–1816.* Ed. Alan S. Downer. Pittsburgh, 1966.

M37 *Music in America. An Anthology from the Landing of the Pilgrims to the Close of the Civil War 1620–1865.* Ed. W. Thomas Marrocco and Harold Gleason. New York, 1964.

M39 Norman Arthur Benson. "The Itinerant Dancing and Music Masters of Eighteenth Century America." Ph.D. Dissertation. University of Minnesota, 1963.

M41 J. Murray Barbour. *The Church Music of William Billings.* East Lansing, 1960.

M42 Irving Lowens. "The American Harmony." Notes included in *The American Harmony . . . Used by Singing Schools . . . in the United States, 1779–1813,* Washington Records WR-418.

M43 Hans Engelke. "A Study of Ornaments in American Tunebooks, 1760–1800." Ph.D. Dissertation. University of Southern California, 1960.

M44 Wiley Hitchcock. "William Billings and the Yankee Tunesmiths." *Hi Fi/Stereo Review,* XVI (Feb 1966), 55–65.

M45 *Church Music and Musical Life in Pennsylvania in the Eighteenth Century.* 3 vols. Philadelphia, 1947.

M46 Byron Adams Wolverton. "Keyboard Music and Musicians in the Colonies and United States of America before 1830." Ph.D. Dissertation. University of Indiana, 1966.

M49 Howard R. Marraro. "Italian Music and Actors in America during the Eighteenth Century." *Italica,* XXIII (1946), 103–117.

M50 Jack W. Broucek. "Eighteenth Century Music in Savannah, Georgia." Ph.D. Dissertation. Florida State University, 1962.

M51 Cyclone Covey. "Of Music, and of America Singing," in Max Savelle, *Seeds of Liberty.* 1948; rpt. Seattle, 1965. Pp. 490–552.

M52 Alan Clark Buechner. "Yankee Singing Schools and the Golden Age of Choral Music in New England, 1760–1800." D.Ed. Dissertation. Harvard University, 1960.

M53 C. P. B. Jefferys. "Music and Singing at St. Peter's, 1761–1783." *Pennsylvania Magazine of History and Biography,* XLVIII (Apr 1924), 181–186.

M55 Marvin C. Genuchi. "The Life and Music of Jacob French (1754–1817),

Colonial American Composer." Ph.D. Dissertation. State University of Iowa, 1964.

M57 George W. Williams. "Eighteenth-Century Organists of St. Michael's, Charleston." *South-Carolina Historical and Genealogical Magazine*, LIII (Jul and Oct 1952), 146–154, 212–222.

M58 Frances Grace Smith. "The American Revolution Hits Church Music." *New England Quarterly*, IV (Oct 1931), 783–788.

M59 James M. Barriskill. "The Newburyport Theatre in the 18th Century." *Essex Institute Historical Collections*, XCI (Jul 1955), 211–245.

M60 S. Foster Damon. *Yankee Doodle.* [Providence], 1959.

M61 Allen Perdue Britton. "Theoretical Introductions in American Tune-Books to 1800." Ph.D. Dissertation. University of Michigan, 1949.

M62 Edmond McAdoo Gagey. *Ballad Opera.* New York, 1937.

M65 Albert L. Stoutamire. "A History of Music in Richmond, Virginia from 1742 to 1865." D.Ed. Dissertation. Florida State University, 1960.

M66 Nathaniel D. Gould. *Church Music in America.* Boston, 1853.

M67 Oscar Sonneck. *A Bibliography of Early Secular American Music (18th Century)* . . . *Revised and Enlarged by William Treat Upton.* Washington, D.C., 1945.

M69 Talmage Dean. "The Organ in Eighteenth Century English Colonial America." Ph.D. Dissertation. University of Southern California, 1960.

M70 O. G. Sonneck. *Suum Cuique. Essays in Music.* New York, 1916.

M71 David McKay. "William Selby, Musical Émigré in Colonial Boston." *Musical Quarterly*, LVII (Oct 1971), 609–627.

M72 John W. Molnar. "Art Music in Colonial Virginia," in *Art and Music in the South.* Ed. Francis B. Simkins. Farmville, Va., 1961. Pp. 63–108.

M73 Robert R. Drummond. *Early German Music in Philadelphia.* 1910; rpt. New York, 1970.

M75 Barbara Owen. "The Organs and Music of King's Chapel 1713–1964." Pamphlet. Boston, 1966.

M76 Arthur Loesser. *Men, Women and Pianos.* New York, 1954.

M77 S. Foster Damon. "The History of Square-Dancing." *Proceedings of the American Antiquarian Society*, LXII (1952), 63–98.

M79 [Letter from Benjamin Franklin to Francis Hopkinson, 8/15/65]. *Quarterly Journal of the Library of Congress*, XXVII (Jan 1970), 67–68.

M80 Raoul François Camus. "The Military Band in the United States Army Prior to 1834." Ph.D. Dissertation. New York University, 1969.

M83 Raymond Russell. *The Harpsichord and Clavichord.* London, 1959.

M84 Daniel Spillane. *History of the American Pianoforte.* 1890; rpt. New York, 1969.

M86 Hamilton C. Macdougall. *Early New England Psalmody.* 1940; rpt. New York, 1969.

M87 Charles Edward Lindsley. "Scoring and Placement of the 'Air' in Early American Tunebooks." *Musical Quarterly*, LVIII (Jul 1972), 365–382.

M88 Percy M. Young. *A History of British Music.* London, 1967.

M89 Lillian Moore. "John Durang The First American Dancer." *Dance Index*, I (Aug 1942), 120–139.

M90 David P. McKay and Richard Crawford. *William Billings of Boston. Eighteenth-Century Composer.* Princeton, 1975.

M91 M. E. Grenander. "Reflections on the String Quartet(s) Attributed to Franklin." *American Quarterly*, XXVII (Mar 1975), 73–87.

M92 Mary Goodwin. "Musical Instruments in Eighteenth-Century Virginia." TS Research Report, CW.

Newspapers and Magazines

N1   *The Virginia Gazette* [D = Dixon; DH = Dixon and Hunter; DN = Dixon and Nicolson; P = Purdie; PD = Purdie and Dixon; Pi = Pinkney; R = Rind]

N2   *The Pennsylvania Chronicle*

N4   *The United States Magazine*

N5   *The Massachusetts Spy*

N6   *The Boston Gazette*

N7   *The Massachusetts Centinel and the Republican Journal*

N9   *The Maryland Journal and Baltimore Advertiser*

N10 *The New-York Packet*

N11 *The New-York Gazette*

N12 *The Providence Gazette*

N13 *The Pennsylvania Gazette*

N14 *Rivington's New-York Gazetteer* [after 12/13/77, *The Royal Gazette*]

N15 *The Connecticut Journal*

N16 *The Virginia Journal and Alexandria Advertiser*

N17 *The Royal American Magazine*

N19 *The Gentleman and Lady's Town and Country Magazine*

N20 *The Censor*

N22 *The Worcester Magazine*

N23 *The Massachusetts Magazine*

N26 *The Pennsylvania Magazine*

N27 *The Boston Magazine*

N29 *The New-Haven Gazette, and the Connecticut Magazine*

N31 *The Columbian Magazine*

N32 Lyon N. Richardson. *A History of Early American Magazines 1741–1789.* New York, 1931.

N33 William J. Free. *The Columbian Magazine and American Literary Nationalism.* The Hague, 1968

N34 *The American Magazine*

N35 *The American Museum*

N36 Sister Mary Mauritia Redden. *The Gothic Fiction in the American Magazines, 1765–1800.* Washington, D.C., 1939.

N37 Mildred Davis Doyle. "Sentimentalism in American Periodicals 1741–1800." Ph.D. Dissertation. New York University, 1941.

N39 *The Royal Pennsylvania Gazette*

N40 *The Georgia Gazette*

N42 *The Newport Mercury*

N47 *The Independent Gazetteer; or, the Chronicle of Freedom*
N48 *The Daily Advertiser: Political, Historical, and Commercial*
N49 *The Constitutional Gazette*
N50 *The Freeman's Journal: or, the North-American Intelligencer*
N51 *The Connecticut Courant*
N52 *The Massachusetts Gazette and Boston News Letter*
N53 *The Columbian Herald*
N54 *The South-Carolina Gazette*
N55 *The New-York Journal; or, General Advertiser*
N56 *The Gazette of the United-States*
N57 *The Federal Gazette, And Philadelphia Evening Post*
N58 *The Pennsylvania Packet*
N59 *The City Gazette*
N60 *The Pennsylvania Mercury*
N61 *The Pennsylvania Journal, and Weekly Advertiser*
N62 *The Boston Evening-Post*
N63 *Courier de Boston*
N64 *The New England Chronicle*
N65 *The Continental Journal*

Poetry and Fiction

P2 Theodore Albert Zunder. *The Early Days of Joel Barlow A Connecticut Wit*. New Haven, 1934.

P3 Daniel Marder. *Hugh Henry Brackenridge*. New York, 1967.

P4 Lewis Leary. *That Rascal Freneau. A Study in Literary Failure*. 1941; rpt. New York, 1964.

P5 Philip Freneau. *The American Village . . . Reprinted in facsimile . . . with an introduction by Harry Lyman Koopman*. 1906; rpt. New York, 1968.

P10 *The Poems of Philip Freneau*. Ed. Fred Lewis Pattee. 3 vols. 1902; rpt. New York, 1963.

P12 J. A. Leo Lemay. "Robert Bolling and the Bailment of Colonel Chiswell." *Early American Literature*, VI (Fall 1971), 99–142.

P13 Patricia Meyer Spacks. *The Insistence of Horror. Aspects of the Supernatural in Eighteenth-Century Poetry*. Cambridge, Mass., 1962.

P15 Roy Harvey Pearce. *The Continuity of American Poetry*. Princeton, 1961.

P16 Philip Freneau. *The Miscellaneous Works of Mr. Philip Freneau*. Philadelphia, 1788.

P18 Philip Marsh. "The Freneau-Hopkinson Quarrel." *Proceedings of the New Jersey Historical Society*, LXXIV (Oct 1956), 304–314.

P19 Paul Fussell. *The Rhetorical World of Augustan Humanism*. 1965; rpt. New York, 1969.

P2ˀ James Woodress. *A Yankee's Odyssey. The Life of Joel Barlow*. Philadelphia, 1958.

P22 Charles Burr Todd. *Life and Letters of Joel Barlow, LL.D.* New York, 1886.

P23 Lewis Leary. "Thomas Day on American Poetry: 1786." *Modern Language Notes*, LXI (Nov 1946), 464–466.

P24 Theodore A. Zunder. "Six Letters of Joel Barlow to Oliver Wolcott." *New England Quarterly*, II (Jul 1929), 475–489.

P26 Emily Pendleton and Milton Ellis. *Philenia. The Life and Works of Sarah Wentworth Morton 1759–1846.* Orono, Me., 1931.

P27 William Williams. *Mr. Penrose. The Journal of Penrose, Seaman.* Ed. David Howard Dickason. Bloomington, Ind., 1969.

P28 Terry Weng Smith. "Exercises Presented During the Commencements of the College of Philadelphia and Other Colonial Colleges." Ph.D. Dissertation. University of Pennsylvania, 1962.

P29 Alan Dugald McKillop. *The Backgrounds of Thomson's "Liberty."* Rice Institute Pamphlet, XXXVIII, no. 2 (1951).

P32 Samuel Kliger. "Whig Aesthetics: A Phase of Eighteenth-Century Taste." *English Literary History*, XVI (Jun 1949), 135–150.

P34 Francis Hopkinson. *The Miscellaneous Essays and Occasional Writings.* 3 vols. Philadelphia, 1792.

P35 Phillis Wheatley. *The Poems of Phillis Wheatley.* Ed. Julian D. Mason, Jr. Chapel Hill, 1966.

P36 Nathaniel Evans. *Poems on Several Occasions.* Philadelphia, 1772.

P37 [Letters of Phillis Wheatley to Obour Tanner]. *Proceedings of the Massachusetts Historical Society* (1863–4), 267–278.

P39 George Everett Hastings. *The Life and Works of Francis Hopkinson.* Chicago, 1926.

P41 Mathew Carey. *Autobiography.* Brooklyn, 1942.

P43 David Humphreys, *et al. The Anarchiad: A New England Poem (1786–1787).* 1861 ed.; rpt. Gainesville, Fla., 1967.

P44 Lewis Leary. "Francis Hopkinson, Jonathan Odell, and 'The Temple of Cloacina': 1782." *American Literature*, XV (May 1943), 183–191.

P48 Ola Elizabeth Winslow. *American Broadside Verse.* New Haven, 1930.

P52 Lewis Winstock. *Songs & Music of the Redcoats.* London, 1970.

P53 *Revolutionary Memorials, Embracing Poems by the Rev. Wheeler Case.* Ed. Rev. Stephen Dodd. New York, 1852.

P54 *Songs and Ballads of the American Revolution.* Ed. Frank Moore. New York, 1856.

P57 *The Rhetoric of Blair, Campbell, and Whately.* Ed. James L. Golden and Edward P. J. Corbett. New York, 1968.

P59 Frank Moore. *Illustrated Ballad History of the American Revolution 1765–1783.* New York, 1876.

P61 Lewis Leary. "A Forgotten Charleston Poet: Joseph Brown Ladd, 1764–1786." *Americana*, XXXVI (Oct 1942), 571–588.

P62 *Miss McCrea (1784) A Novel of the American Revolution.* Ed. Lewis Leary. Gainesville, Fla., 1958.

P63 [Lucius Sargent]. *Dealings with the Dead.* Boston, 1856.

P65 *The Poetical Works of John Trumbull, LL.D.* Vol. II. Hartford, 1820.

P66 "One for Both." *William and Mary Quarterly*, 3d Ser., XXIX (Oct 1972), 636.

P67 Frank Landon Humphreys. *Life and Times of David Humphreys. Soldier-Statesman-Poet.* 2 vols. New York and London, 1917.

P68 *The Miscellaneous Works of Colonel Humphreys.* New York, 1790.

P69 Jack Bailey Moore. "Native Elements in American Magazine Short Fiction, 1741–1800." Ph.D. Dissertation. University of North Carolina, 1963.

P70 Roy Harvey Pearce. "Sterne and Sensibility in American Diaries." *Modern Language Notes*, LIX (Jun 1944), 403–407.

P74 Joseph Brown Ladd. *The Literary Remains of Joseph Brown Ladd, M.D.* New York, 1832.

P75 J. Hammond Trumbull. *The Origin of M'Fingal.* Morrisania, N.Y., 1868.

P77 *The Loyal Verses of Joseph Stansbury and Doctor Jonathan Odell.* Ed. Winthrop Sargent. Albany, 1860.

P78 *The Loyalist Poetry of the Revolution.* Ed. Winthrop Sargent. Philadelphia, 1857.

P80 Bruce Ingham Granger. *Political Satire in the American Revolution, 1763–1783.* Ithaca, 1960.

P81 Louis M. Miner. *Our Rude Forefathers. American Political Verse 1783–1788.* Cedar Rapids, 1937.

P83 Gordon E. Bigelow. *Rhetoric and American Poetry of the Early National Period.* Gainesville, Fla., 1960.

P84 Alexander Cowie. *John Trumbull. Connecticut Wit.* Chapel Hill, 1936.

P86 Dixon Wecter. "Francis Hopkinson and Benjamin Franklin." *American Literature*, XII (May 1940), 200–217.

P88 Charles Webster Wheelock. "Dr. Benjamin Young Prime (1733–1791): American Poet." Ph.D. Dissertation. Princeton University, 1967.

P90 Abe C. Ravitz. "The *Anarchiad* and the *Massachusetts Centinel.*" *Boston Public Library Quarterly*, IV (Apr 1952), 97–101.

P92 *Passages from the Correspondence and other Papers of Rufus W. Griswold.* Cambridge, Mass., 1898.

P93 Alexander Cowie. "John Trumbull Glances at Fiction." *American Literature*, XII (Mar 1940), 69–73.

P95 *Books in America's Past. Essays Honoring Rudolph H. Gjelsness.* Ed. David Kaser. Charlottesville, 1966: (a) Robert D. Harlan. "David Hall's Bookshop and Its British Sources of Supply." Pp. 2–23; (b) Benjamin M. Lewis. "Engravings in American Magazines, 1741–1810." Pp. 204–217.

P96 Charles E. Cuningham. *Timothy Dwight 1752–1817. A Biography.* New York, 1942.

P98 Carl Bridenbaugh. "The Earliest-Published Poem of Phillis Wheatley." *New England Quarterly*, XLII (Dec 1969), 583–584.

P99 George F. Sensabaugh. "Jefferson's Use of Milton in the Ecclesiastical Controversies of 1776." *American Literature*, XXVI (Jan 1955), 552–559.

P102 Rexmond C. Cochrane. "Bishop Berkeley and the Progress of Arts and Learning: Notes on a Literary Convention." *Huntington Library Quarterly*, XVII (May 1954), 229–249.

P103 Herbert Ross Brown. *The Sentimental Novel in America.* Durham, N.C., 1940.

P104 J. A. Leo Lemay. *A Calendar of American Poetry . . . Through 1765.* Worcester, Mass., 1972.

P105 Louis I. Bredvold. *The Natural History of Sensibility.* Detroit, 1962.

P106 Joseph L. Blau. "Joel Barlow, Enlightened Religionist." *Journal of the History of Ideas*, X (Jun 1949), 430–444.
P107 Kenneth Silverman. *Colonial American Poetry*. New York and London, 1968.

3. Notes

1. Commencement: 1763

[1] N11, 5/23/63; G102, 15. [2] Nathaniel Evans, *An Exercise, Containing a Dialogue and Ode on Peace* [Phil., 1763]. [3] G97, X, 232–3. [4] G151, IX, 600. [5] q. G181, 86. [6] q. G181, 118–19. [7] P107, 345.

2. The Art World

[1] See A104, 95 for a typical ad; A246a. Hogarth's *Harlot's Progress* was also advertised. [2] A4; q. P95a, 9; A222. [3] Mary R. M. Goodwin, "The Printing Office. Its Activities, Furnishings, and Articles for Sale," TS Research Report, CW. Royle sold the prints on commission. [4] A125; A2, 9; A5, 33; A132, 67. [5] To Nathaniel Scudder, 8/20/80, Du Simitière Letter Book, LC; A134, 123. [6] According to his son Titian, Charles Willson Peale as a young man in Annapolis loved the Van Dyck, and believed that the supposed Kneller was by Van Dyck also. (See Titian's MS "Portrait of Lord Baltimore," M.) Purdie's *Virginia Gazette* (1/21/73) printed an anecdote about Van Dyck to the effect that as a schoolboy he prevented a friend from being caned by painting a portrait on his posterior, which caused the schoolmaster to laugh forgivingly when he "drew up the Curtain." [7] N11, 12/24/64; A242, 88; A16 and A17. A collection of doubtful distinction was later amassed by Jefferson, catalogued in G148. [8] MS "Notes and Accounts," William Bentley Papers, AAS. [9] G22, 163; A105, 140; A141, 746. [10] N11, 9/3/64; q. A145, 30. [11] A184, 106; A28, 26. [12] Probably by John Hazlitt, a portrait painter and brother of the essayist. See A19, 53. [13] Here and throughout the book I have ignored limited, local traditions which had no contact with the larger provincial culture, in this case the interesting but relatively unknown paintings of the Moravian minister John Valentin Haidt (1700–1780). [14] A38 and A41. Some of Badger's later works, however, show the influence of the more worldly Kneller-Lely tradition, depicting latter-day Puritan gentlemen, hand on hip, in the finery of large cuffs and buttons, creating a sense of station, but without parade. Although painted continuously in New England since the mid-seventeenth century, it should be added, the limner style was neither indigenously American nor wholly confined to New England. The art historian Roy Strong traces its "bizarre neomedievalism" to a style which had been driven out of England by Van Dyck's influence, but which survived in the English provinces, including Scotland and Australia. See A191b. Traces of this international provincial style appear as well in the blackly outlined, rather unmodeled figures of the essentially New York painter John Durand, in whose richly clothed *Rapalje Children* (c. 1768) the style is adapted to a more urban clientele. The survival of the style in New York perhaps reflects the

shared Calvinist background of the Dutch and the New England Congregationalists, who both appreciated its starkness. [15] A105, A15, A96; A140; A142. [16] A12.
Belknap and his followers have emphasized the importance of imported prints in
transmitting Kneller's vision to the colonies. Kneller's works went into some 400
plates by some 40 different engravers. See A133, 57. [17] A41 and A142. The far
greater variety of costume in Theus reflects his European, as opposed to English,
training, and perhaps also the tastes of his occasionally German and Dutch sitters.
[18] A191c. Craven points out that several other English painters of the 1740's used
almond-shaped eyes; only Wollaston and Hesselius, however, seem to have used
the device in America. [19] A206. Belknap suggests that the borrowed poses may
have been requested by the patrons themselves. Patrons, it might be added, freely
advised on the paintings they commissioned. Peale was often asked to change or
retouch eyes or a sword, or to add a medal on a portrait done long before. Even
Copley, the most prestigious portraitist in the colonies, received explicit directions
from his sitters. One told him to show more drapery, another gave him elaborate
instructions on foreshortening the hand. See A183, 5/88; A171, 62 and 78. [20] A16,
11. [21] "On Miniature painting by Mrs. Stille" [c. mid-1760's], MS "Rhapsodies,"
LC. The miniature, she added, also could serve a didactic purpose, reviving with
"pleasing anguish" the lessons of a dead parent, and inhibiting the wearer from
"acting Sin or folly's Part/Thro', Love & Reverence to their Honour'd Shade."
[22] The entire account which follows is based upon A184, except for specially
footnoted items. [23] A186, 17. [24] A graphic expression of this bond is the engraving
The Sequel of Arts and Sciences, printed by James Rivington in New York in 1774,
probably by the Connecticut engraver Abel Buell. It consists of a group of vignettes
framing and illustrating such Franklinian mottoes as "Learning advances men of
mean degree." The vignettes—derived from an English magazine—include scenes
of printing, hat making, glass grinding, and other crafts, including portrait
painting. Drawing manuals of the period likewise stress the uses of painting, for
instance in architecture and engineering, far more than its esthetics. In several of
his letters Jefferson comments on the difficulty of absolutely distinguishing between
the fine and useful arts; the overlapping of categories proved troublesome to him in
classifying books for his splendid libraries. On Buell see A232. [25] A136. [26] A171, 26.
[27] A178, 38; A171, 35. [28] A178, 1–13 *passim.* [29] A134, 45. Finally it was presented as
a gift to Timothy Dwight for Yale. [30] A134, 14. The *Bentivoglio* especially influenced
Copley and, later, Trumbull, who did a copy of it. When Copley later sent his *Boy
with Squirrel* to be exhibited in London, Reynolds is said to have told West that the
painter had studied with Van Dyck, as West assured him he had not. See A134,
122. [31] A few nudes had appeared in America earlier. Some were made of Indians
by explorer-artists; Robert Feke had copied a European engraving of a nude in his
Judgment of Hercules (c. 1744); Gustavus Hesselius had done a *Bacchus and Ariadne*
and a *Bacchanale* in the 1720's. Copley later saw some of West's copies of European
nudes at the home of William Allen in Philadelphia. Several instruction books
with nude figures also appeared in America before the Revolution, such as *Anatomy
Improv'd and Illustrated* (London, 1723). See A137. [32] Blackburn seems to have
returned to England permanently around 1763. See A15 and A41. [33] A90, 157;

A254, 391; A237, 173. [34] A171, 31; A165, xix. [35] FARL; *New York Times*, 12/1/1974, Arts and Leisure section, 37. [36] q. A60, 41. [37] q. A60, 39. [38] A68 and A67, *passim*. [39] A231, 12–13. [40] A135. [41] A159; *Complete Writings*, Old Manse Edition, XII, 284. West's house is now part of Swarthmore College. [42] A154; A161; A107, 131. [43] G94, 105. [44] A161, pt. I, 44–5. [45] A159, 444. [46] A231, 18–19. By the mid-eighteenth century, many Quakers seem to have given up their historic contempt for painting. Several wealthy Quakers commissioned portraits: Theus painted the Ladsons, a prominent Quaker family; Hesselius painted the Maryland Quakeress Sophia Galloway. [47] A154. [48] G156, 47. Copley's half-brother went to Philadelphia to see the important collections owned by Allen, Governor Penn, and other local officials, men he regarded as "the first in America for fortune and Character, and highly distinguish'd for their love and Patronage of the Polite Arts and Artists. . . ." A171, 272. [49] A161, pt. I, 92–3 and 105. The thirty carriages seem plausible, since Americans were the rage among Europeans, to most of whom "American" meant Indian. The blind cardinal Alboni in Rome assumed that West himself was an Indian. Indeed, Americans abroad were usually vastly overpraised by their European hosts, receiving the sort of homage paid to mediocrity by those prepared to encounter inability. The Philadelphia poetess Elizabeth Fergusson, in London in 1764, was befriended by Sterne and granted a special audience with the king. [50] A161, pt. I, 146 and 158; q. A169, 42. [51] A154. [52] To Joseph Shippen, 5/11/62, #72×58, WIN; A43. *The Holy Family* is now in Old St. Joseph's Church, Philadelphia, where it seems to have arrived in exchange for letters of introduction in Rome, given to West by Father Farmer, a Philadelphia Jesuit. [53] To Shippen, above. [54] This is the date given by Dunlap. West in his later manuscript autobiography says that he arrived in August.

3. Musical Life

[1] *London Magazine*, 2/64. Robert Carter of Virginia owned several silver flutes and set down in his day-book instructions for making a twenty-inch "Common Concert Flute." See M92. [2] q. G43, 35. See also the poem by John Parke, "Addressed to my GERMAN FLUTE," in his *Lyric Works of Horace*. [3] Peale's *Rebecca Lewis* (1775), for instance, holds a reddish brown mandolin; his *Mary Rench* (1786) has a guitar and sheet music of "The Blush of Aurora." [4] G211, I, 336; N11, 4/16/64. [5] M15; M73, 39. The importance of dancing and music in training the young for adult life is suggested by the Reverend Hugh Jones's recommendation that the College of William and Mary include them in its curriculum. See G207, 83. I have not consistently traced the development of dance in the period, on which much more research is needed. Lillian Moore, "Studies in American Dance History," *Dancing Times* (Dec 1956), describes the activities of the important dancing master Thomas Pike, who in 1765 taught not only dancing but also dance notation or "ORCHESOGRAPHY." [6] q. M39, 73. Francis Hopkinson, recommending Stadler for a post as organist in Annapolis in 1763, called him "a very modest sober & well behaved Man who understands Music to great Perfection. . . ." To Samuel Galloway, 1/31/63, Miscellaneous Papers, NYPL. [7] M23;

M15; N11, 4/16/64. [8] N6, 7/21/66. [9] G97, XII, 401; A4, 300; A2, 373. The chamber organ consisted of "6 stops, 15 Mute Gilt Pipes in the Front, and a Set of Drawers at the Bottom." [10] M73, 43; G159, 153. Francis Hopkinson received a "forte-piano" from England whose strings arrived "spoiled." See Bremner to Hopkinson, c. 1785, Hopkinson Papers, HSP. In 1786, Thomas Jefferson ordered a mahogany harpsichord from Kirkman, asking him to keep the stops as simple as possible "as the instrument is to go to a country and to a situation where there will be no workman but myself to put it in order." Kirkman decided to use seasoned oak with a mahogany veneer instead of mahogany, since it was less sensitive to weather and climate. M83, 179. [11] To Joseph Shippen, 10/1/71, Joseph Shippen Papers, LC. [12] M83; A2, 367. [13] G208, 248. Robert Carter of Nomini employed Bucktrout to repair his instruments. [14] G97, X, 383; M70, 70; P36, 109. Francis Hopkinson later tried to apply a keyboard to the instrument, success in which Thomas Jefferson believed would be "the greatest present which has been made to the musical world this century, not excepting the pianoforte." M70, 70. [15] M11, 39; M39; G97, XII, 162; M10, 93ff.; M91. [16] M72, 69; M92, xx. An example of Jefferson's taste for richness is the bow made for him by the eighteenth-century craftsman François Tourte, who is to the bow what Stradivarius is to the violin. Decorated with thirteen stars and an American eagle, the bow is made of ivory and gold. See *New York Times*, 2/15/1971, 16. Later in Europe Jefferson and his family bought up music in large quantities and in every form, much of it now at UVL. [17] q. M10, 85; M17. [18] M80, 147. [19] q. M92, xxiv and xlix. See also M50, 79–80. Some northerners also sought domestics who could play instruments. The musical Governor Wentworth of New Hampshire tried to get servants from England on a five-year contract, hoping for "two that can play well on a French horn also if they can, or one of them play on a violin." q. M9, 56. [20] q. G50, 89; q. G43, 38; M13. [21] N62, 11/21/68; q. M3, 165; M50, 149. [22] M4, 15–16; G200, 641–2. [23] M3, 167. See also M11 and D28. [24] N11, 2/7/63; N13, 4/4/65; *The Plan of a Performance of Solemn Musick* (Phil., 1765). [25] M39, 34, 123 *et passim;* M3, 15 *et passim.* Collective patronage for concerts and plays, particularly in Charleston but throughout the colonies, came from local Masonic groups, branches of a movement which flourished worldwide in the eighteenth century. Music, as Mozart's *Magic Flute* suggests, accompanied many Masonic rituals. An "Anthem and Ode" by the Charleston organist Benjamin Yarnold, for instance, was performed at a local Masonic installation ceremony in 1762. Many actors and professional musicians (e.g. Alexander Reinagle) joined the fraternity in self-interest. At a Charleston performance by the American Company in 1766, the actor receiving the benefit for the night claimed to be a Mason. The Grand Master ordered lodge members to march in procession to the theatre, where the actor spoke the prologue in ritual dress. The Charleston bookseller Robert Wells was both Grand Master of Solomon's Lodge and treasurer for subscriptions to the Charleston theatre. Elsewhere in the colonies too, Masons patronized the theatre en bloc, occasionally buying out the pit; actors repaid them by singing Masonic songs from the stage, the Masons joining in the choruses. The installation of John Rowe as Grand Master of Masons for North America took place at the Boston Concert Hall; after the ceremony, the fraternity marched in procession accompanied by two brass bands. See M67; D22, 106; D2; M72, 78; G75, 180. American Masonic poetry in the period forms a sizable subject which I have not treated here. Masonic imagery (especially that of King Solomon's Temple) clearly influenced revolutionary and republican symbolism, perhaps contributing to the U.S. Seal the truncated pyramid and the glowing eye. [26] G97, X, 385. James Bremner had written a book of instructions and airs for the sticcado pastorale (a sort of xylophone) before arriving in America, and while in Philadelphia he seems also to have composed a march, a trumpet air, and some other short works, all unpublished. See M67, 209; M46, 103. [27] q. G157, 166. [28] *The Lawfulness, Excellency, and Advantage of Instrumental Musick in the Publick Worship of God*; East Apthorp, *Of Sacred Poetry and Music.* [29] On pre-1763 organs see M12, 50 and M75, 20. [30] M69, 43. The writer contends that Snetzler also sent an organ in 1762 to the Congregational Church in South Dennis, Massachusetts. This seems unlikely, and I have been unable to confirm it. [31] Goldsbrow Banyar to Richard Grubb, 8/17/61, and Richard Grubb to George Harison, *et al.*, 4/10/62, NYHS. [32] M69; M12, 50; M79, 180. As I have done in discussing the art world of 1763, I have omitted from the discussion of music what was in a sense the richest and most sophisticated religious and secular music of the period, that produced in Pennsylvania and the Carolinas by the Moravians, who began emigrating to Bethlehem and Winston-Salem in the 1730's. They developed an intense musical life replete with music libraries, brass ensembles, notable instrument makers, and composers of such outstanding gifts as John Antes (1741–1811). For all its esthetic value, the Moravian culture remained by choice cloistered, insular, so apart from the mainstream of life in the period, thus so European, as not to concern us here. [33] M46; M53. [34] M8; A244; M15; M2; M46. [35] M39, 136–9; M8, 51–2; TS "Extracts from the Letter of Dr. Carleton Sprague Smith April 25, 1938," CW. Pelham's minuet and some other works are among the Hubard Papers, Southern Historical Collection, University of North Carolina. A few pieces by the southern organists have been recorded. Yarnold's D Major March can be heard on *The Organ in America* (Columbia Records MS-6161); two pieces by Valton are included in *O Come Sweet Music* (Colonial Williamsburg Foundation); Pelham's minuet is played in *An Evening of Music at Carter's Grove Plantation* (Colonial Williamsburg Foundation). [36] Lyon was born in Newark, New Jersey, in 1735. An orphan, he was sent by his guardians to Princeton, where he took a B.A. in 1759. For his class commencement he wrote music and, the same year, published a poem on the taking of Louisburg for the *New American Magazine*. Ordained as a Presbyterian minister in 1764, he went to Nova Scotia until 1771, but, unable to support himself, moved to Machias, Maine, where he preached until his death in 1794. A precious glimpse of this early American composer is afforded by Fithian, who met Lyon in Virginia in April 1774, when he was feeling, Fithian said, "the hardy arm of want." Fithian applauded the "softness & accuracy" of his singing and found him "vastly fond of music & musical genius's." G53, 158. [37] *An Humble Attempt towards the Improvement of Psalmody* (Phil., 1763). [38] See M90; M32, 35; M43; M52. [39] "3d ed." (Boston, 1767). [40] Between 1764 and 1800 some 200 anthems were published in New England. See M12. The largest collection is John

Stickney's *The Gentleman and Lady's Musical Companion* (1774), containing 30 anthems. [41] When Fithian met him in 1774, Lyon was preparing to publish a new book of tunes, mostly by himself, the manuscript of which has become lost. G53, 158. [42] M29.

4. The Literary Scene

[1] Naturally such figures depend on definition of terms like "prose fiction" and "American." They and the later similar comparisons represent my tally of the items listed by Charles Evans, compared with items for the same year in Edward Kimber, ed., *The Monthly Catalogues from The London Magazine 1732–1766* (rpt. London, 1966). [2] P95a, 13; G137, 67; G215d, 198–200. Mein specialized in plays, which seem to have had a particularly large reading public in Boston, where theatre was banned. [3] Account based on G111. [4] P104. [5] P12; N1 (PD), 1/8/67. [6] *The Patriot Muse* (London, 1764); N42, 8/13/64. [7] G3, *passim.* [8] G3, 169; N11, 2/6/64; G3, 181. [9] For the large literature on the election see G97, XI, and Evans nos. 10014–10021; *The Counter-Medly* (Phil., 1765); *A Humble Attempt at Scurrility* (Phil., 1765). Several seemingly related poems deal with Philadelphia prostitutes, perhaps intended to represent friends of the political rivals. See *A New Song about Miss Ketty* (bds. Phil., 1765), and *Hilliad Magna. Being the Life and Adventures of Moll Placket-Hole* ([Phil.], 1765). [10] N52, 11/3/63 and 12/29/63. [11] G94, chs. 1–4 and p. 205. [12] G113, 84. [13] q. P28, 3 and 56; N13, 2/10/57. [14] 1/20–2/10/57. [15] P36, 120. [16] N40, 6/16/63; G42, I, 326; D57, 51. [17] G94, 105ff.; N13, 4/4/65. See also *The Plan of a Performance of Solemn Musick . . . April 10th, 1765* (Phil., 1765). [18] Thomas Godfrey, *Juvenile Poems on Various Subjects* (Phil., 1765). [19] P36, 106. [20] P39; M2; William Shippen to Joseph Shippen, 7/61, Joseph Shippen Papers, LC. Hopkinson probably also compiled a collection of psalm tunes for St. Peter's Church. See N13, 5/5/63. Benjamin Franklin sent one of Hopkinson's compositions abroad to his blind friend, the well-known composer John Stanley. G97, X, 233.

5. The Theatre

[1] D35, 3. [2] q. D80, 7. On the early career of the Hallams see also D59 and D40. [3] D84. [4] D18, 48–51; q. D74, 30; q. D73, 61. [5] D39, 24 *et passim;* q. G71, 269. [6] D8, 56; D6, 43–54. [7] N1 (P), 4/27/69. On the relative popularity of plays in London and the colonies, compare D62 and D64 (a significant and reliable study based on Rankin's voluminous research) with George Winchester Stone, Jr., *The London Stage 1747–1776* (Carbondale, Ill., 1968). Some other suggestive comparisons may be noted here. *The Beggar's Opera* was performed far less often in the colonies than in London, probably because its sixty-nine songs were too demanding for the actors in the American Company. For the entire colonial period, including the years before 1763, the most often performed play in America was Colley Cibber's version of *Richard III*, with thirty performances. (*Romeo and Juliet* was only slightly behind, with twenty-nine performances for the entire colonial period.) The most popular afterpieces in the colonial period were *The Padlock* and *Lethe*, with thirty-seven

recorded performances each. At Drury Lane, *The Padlock* was the second most popular afterpiece during roughly the same period, behind the commemorative *Jubilee*, which reached America only after the war. D25 compares the London and Charleston stages for the 1773–74 seasons alone and finds that 15 percent of all London productions were given to Shakespeare, against 27 percent of all Charleston performances, making Shakespeare even more popular in the colonies than at home. [8] q. D2, 125; q. D9, 323. [9] D6; M62. [10] q. D28, 281; N55, 5/26/88; q. G25, 87. [11] q. D66, 251. [12] N13, 1/22/67; q. D39, 23; q. D66, 251. [13] q. D62, 501; D80, 35; G25, 86–8. [14] q. D9, 275 and 321. [15] q. D33, 339; D51, 78. [16] q. D51, 1; q. D16, 5, 9, 6. [17] In 1768, a smaller troupe applied for a license in Rhode Island, offering testimony from North Carolina to their character, but they were not allowed to perform. Durang's memory must be erroneous when he asserts (D39, 19) that Douglass introduced a theatre in Rhode Island in 1760 which "flourished uninterruptedly till the advent of the revolution."

6. Stamp Act Protests

[1] Account based on G17. [2] q. G17, 43; *A New Collection of Verses* (New Haven, 1765); N62, 10/14/65. [3] q. G155, xxxvi. [4] P80, 75. Bute appeared in some 400 satirical, and often scurrilous, political cartoons. See A124, 121. [5] G1, ix. [6] The evidence is a copy of the cartoon in the Library Company of Philadelphia, discovered by Edgar P. Richardson, on which Du Simitière ascribed the work to Copley. Startling as the attribution seems, stylistic evidence supports it. The grouping of the central figures anticipates that in Copley's later *Brook Watson and the Shark*. Also, around 1765 Copley drew or painted several open-shirted or bare-armed figures—links to the naked Mercury and the exposed legs of the Liberty figure in the caricatura. Copley based his engraving on an English print attacking the Stamp Act, published in London in March. This print, it is worth noting, contains a prominent tree marked "To Liberty"—conceivably the inspiration of the Boston Liberty Tree, which was not so designated until the fall. See A245 and N6, 11/11/65. On November 4, Nathaniel Hurd advertised another "Caricatura, being a Representation of the Tree of Liberty, and the Distresses of the present Day." The work of Paul Revere, it shows a monster dragon, representing the Stamp Act, opposed by figures with drawn swords and guns, representing the colonies. See A127, 25. [7] A146. Franklin's device, in turn, derived from an accordion-pleated snake appearing in a seventeenth-century French compendium, with the motto *"Se rejoindre ou mourir."* See A84, 63. Many English prints, some of them gross, depicted events of the Stamp Act and were sold in colonial print and book shops. [8] q. G2, 184; A183, 8/65; G118, 438. [9] *Liberty, Property, and no Excise* (bds. Boston, 1765); N6, 8/19/65; G17, 162-4. [10] N62, 9/9/65; W. Almy to Elisha Story, 8/29/65, Miscellaneous Bound MSS, MHS. [11] N62, 9/9/65; D52, 110. [12] N6, 11/11/65. [13] N62 and N6, 11/11/65 [14] *Ibid.* [15] *Oppression* (rpt. Boston, 1765); N6, 11/25/65. [16] G97, XIII, 66–72, 189. See also A250. Franklin drew his idea from a 1749 image of a dismembered Britannia, whose limbs were labeled Cape Breton and Gibraltar. As he did with his Poor

Richard sayings, he simplified the print over the English original. He also made it less gory, and covered up Britannia's breasts, producing an allegorical manikin where the earlier engraver strove for anatomical realism.

7. Excursus: Whig Sentimentalism

[1] D68, 167; G101, 99. [2] Literally hundreds of examples might be given of Catonic language in the period. Several times during the Revolution Washington quoted Cato's " 'Tis not in mortals to command success." (q. D1, 1.) In the 1770's several newspapers used quotes from *Cato* on their mastheads, while "Cato" became a favorite pseudonym of political writers, and of both friends and foes to the theatre. The names "Juba" and "Marcia"—characters in *Cato*—became virtually synonymous with lovers. In 1758, while serving in the Seven Years' War, Washington wrote to Mrs. George Fairfax that instead of soldiering he wished he were "playing a part in Cato . . . doubly happy in being the Juba to such a Marcia, as you must make." (q. D21, 441.) One might illustrate the popularity of other Whiggish works by legions of examples as well. Harbottle Dorr, a Son of Liberty, began the second volume of his great collection of revolutionary newspapers with a quote from *Gustavus Vasa*; in 1770 a reward of £100 was offered for the identity of the person who posted on the Boston Town House a long, pointed quotation from Thomas Otway's *Venice Preserved* (N6, 12/17/70 and 12/24/70); the name "Jemmy," from *The Beggar's Opera*, was often pinned on English adversaries, notably the earl of Sandwich, who had turned on his former friend John Wilkes. [3] q. G17, 518. See for instance N1, 5/21/67, and G196. Indeed the number of professional performances has been exaggerated. *Cato* was performed professionally nineteen times in the colonies before 1775, the same number as the equally Whiggish *Douglas*. See D64. [4] D78, 149; G1, 44. [5] 12/30/65. [6] 1/1, probably by Robert Bolling. [7] N62, 9/9/65; G97, XII, 431, possibly by Franklin. [8] See Arthur Henkel and Albrecht Schöne, *Emblemata* (Stuttgart, 1967); A113, 90; A230. Interpretations of the emblems changed, however, in accord with emerging ideology. The author of "Origin and Properties of the Cap of Liberty" in the *Worcester Magazine* (8/87) interpreted the cap as a pyramid, according to the postwar emphasis on democratic solidarity. [9] A246b. [10] q. D51, 81. [11] Cf. Lewis Coser's theory that mass culture is a "safety valve institution" that offers means of releasing hostility while leaving social structures undisturbed. G168a. [12] G177, I, 282.

8. Benjamin West's American School

[1] A154; A166. [2] A147, 461; P39, 103. [3] A147, 462; Beekman Papers, NYHS. [4] A136; A206; A69.

9. Charles Willson Peale Flees

[1] A142; A184, 19. [2] A136; A183. In his letter to Rembrandt Peale, Peale,

mistakenly ascribes these events to 1768–69, when he was in England. He also mentions that during this visit he met Copley, although the meeting really took place after Peale returned to Boston from Newburyport. [3] A136. [4] A184.

10. Copley's *Boy with Squirrel*

[1] In an earlier sketch of Hurd (Memorial Art Gallery) Copley went even further, depicting him in a work doublet, parted over his bare chest and stomach, his thick arms bare to nearly the shoulder. Copley returned to this in the wholly open-shirted middle sailor of his *Brook Watson*. See section 37 and A178. [2] A171, 36 and 35.

11. Douglass' New Troupe

[1] G2, 176. [2] q. D73, 74 (see also G82, 207); D2; D76. [3] M62, 7; M24. [4] Mrs. Inchbald, ed., *The British Theatre*, XVII (London, 1808). Mrs. Inchbald, who edited several volumes of these plays not long after the French Revolution, apologized in her introduction, lest she be thought an encourager of social revolt. She noted that "the vast number of women elevated to high rank in this kingdom, since the French revolution took place, might almost draw upon their husbands the vulgar charge of jacobinism.—But love was among the passions let loose on that tremendous event. . . ." Tocqueville keenly commented later on the relationship between the theatre and revolutionary ideas: "When the revolution which subverts the social and political state of an aristocratic people begins to penetrate into literature, it generally first manifests itself in the drama, and it always remains conspicuous there. . . . If you would judge beforehand of the literature of a people which is lapsing into democracy, study its dramatic productions." G16, II, 96. [5] D6, 124–5; G25; D73; D76. A business card at CW announces, "Albany, Mr. Wall, Comedian, Engages to teach Ladies and Gentlemen to play on the Guitar." [6] N54, 11/4/65; D73, 76–7. Presumably to augment their incomes, Miss Wainwright and Sarah—not Nancy—Hallam gave a concert with Peter Valton, the church organist, on November 13, for which Valton composed special music, an early instance of joint performances by actors and church personnel in Charleston that lasted until the 1790's. [7] George Alexander Stevens, *Stevens's Celebrated New Lecture on Heads* (Boston, 1772). See D28; G43; N2, 9/7/67. An essay in Philip Freneau's 1788 volume is entitled "A Discourse on Beards." Occasionally not even the *Lecture* was safe. In Philadelphia in 1772, Douglass or some other actor issued a broadside saying he had received an anonymous warning to omit from the *Lecture* the "Tabernacle Harangue." He noted that Stevens, not he, wrote the piece, but offered to remove it to avoid offending anything sacred. *The Exhibitor of the Lecture on Heads* (bds. Phil., 1772).

12. Repeal of the Stamp Act

[1] q. G17, 335; G117; G4. [2] q. G17, 369. [3] N6, 5/26/66. [4] A198 contains some

actual transparencies made in 1806. [5] G158, 187; q. M9, 65; (bds. Phil., 1766); *Philadelphia den 19ten* (bds. Phil., 1766). [6] N11, 5/1/66. [7] N11, 5/8/66; G110, 364; typed transcription of contemporary newspaper account, W. Johnson Quinn Collection, NYHS. [8] G2, 186. The New York portrait of the king was perhaps commissioned from the very talented Hudson River limner John Mare, a brother-in-law of West's early mentor, William Williams. The same year, Mare did a forceful portrait of John Keteltas, a member of an old New York family, a lifelike fly resting darkly on his white linen cuff—one of the earliest American trompe-l'oeil paintings. See A108, A15, A41. [9] A40, 10; q. G158, 190; A144. The pillar for the Skillin bust seems to have been of stone, although it is unclear whether the head was of stone or wood. The earliest extant piece of American freestanding statuary is the "Little Admiral" (c. 1740) in the Old State House in Boston, some forty-two inches high, probably a shop sign that once held a beer mug or nautical instrument. It is possibly by Skillin, although Hawthorne ascribed it to Shem Drowne. See A62. [10] *A Grand Chorus, To be sung on the Fourth of June* (bds. Phil., 1766).

13. Hopkinson and Peale in London

[1] See for instance G97, XIV, 166; M79; M10. [2] P39, 132; A162; P39, 151. [3] A184. [4] A184, 31; A136. [5] A186, 55; A184, 33; A182, unaddressed and undated, c. 1767. [6] A203, 18; A171, 118; A186.

14. Success of *Boy with Squirrel*

[1] This paragraph and the next drawn from A171, 41ff. [2] Cf. Copley's *Thomas Aston Coffin* (c. 1758, Mrs. Constance Smith, Cambridge, Mass.), which depicts a young boy almost lost in doves, ribbons, fans, shuttlecocks, and paddles. [3] A171, 48–51. [4] A171, 64–6. [5] A171, 58 and 65.

15. Opening of the Southwark Theatre

[1] MS account of monthly meeting, Pemberton Papers, HSP; John Penn to Joseph Shippen, 7/11/66, Joseph Shippen Papers, LC. [2] D4, 85; D18, 55; D39, 22. [3] D76, 13. [4] D42; D22, 112. A physician named Samuel Greville later appeared in Charleston. [5] D39 suggests that the play may be by John Leacock, later a coroner in Philadelphia and the author of *The Fall of British Tyranny* (see section 31). [6] The other type of stage Negro has been called the "Plantation Darky." See D85. [7] Later in the year the play was published anonymously in New York, where in 1790 it also had its first production. The preceding quotations are from this New York edition. See D77. [8] *Juvenile Poems*, postscript. [9] Douglass also featured works by local playwrights in Jamaica. It may be, however, that his choice of native plays reflects only the fact that Americans had recently begun publishing them. A few months after publication of *The Prince of Parthia* there appeared another play by an American, the closet drama *Ponteach or the Savages of America*. Published anony-

mously in London, it was written by Major Robert Rogers of Methuen, Massachusetts, a hunter and trader who took part in suppressing Pontiac's Rebellion in 1763 and had met Pontiac himself. Rogers mixed realistic description of frontier warfare with a sentimental subplot and a romantic triangle, a formula successful through James Fenimore Cooper and John Ford. The play gives an unyieldingly condemnatory picture of white treatment of the Indians. In its Whiggish viewpoint, much influenced by *Cato*, Indian-English relationships closely resemble colonial-imperial ones, and even echo specific elements of the Stamp Act debate. Quite like the authors of *Oppression* or *The Times*, Pontiac tells his war council: "Oh! could our Fathers from their Country see/ Their antient Rights encroach'd upon and ravag'd,/ And we their Children slow, supine, and careless/ To keep the Liberty and Land they left us." A modern edition with copious notes is Allan Nevins, ed., *Ponteach or the Savages of America, A Tragedy* (Chicago, 1914). [10] Compare N2, 1/26/67, with 9/7/67; N13, 2/26/67; N61, 2/5/67. [11] N13, 1/29/67 and 2/5/67. [12] q. D9, 152; G97, XIV, 30. [13] N61, 2/12/67. [14] N13, 3/12/67; N2, 2/16/67; N13, 7/2/67. [15] N61, 3/12/67. [16] N2, 2/16/67. [17] N2, 3/2/67.

16. The Townshend Acts

[1] G102, 32. [2] G62, 27; N1 (PD), 12/24/67; G112, 47–8. [3] G158, 237–8, 253. [4] A127, 43–8; G158, 157; G11, 74. Robert Middlekauff suggests that the number symbolism had roots in "Protestant fascination with eschatological numerology." See G34, 36. It seems, however, that numbers fill the natural need of all revolutionary movements for symbols to simplify belief and consolidate support. The turmoil of the 1960's produced the Harlem Four and the Chicago Seven. One wit, I saw, wrote on a New York subway poster, "Free the Indianapolis 500." [5] G209, 41; G115, 421. [6] M67, 228; M4, 17. [7] N62, 8/22/68; G158, 260. [8] q. G31, 5; G177, I, 341. Adams' account leaves it unclear whether one or two songs were sung on the occasion. He also makes it seem that the verses were sung solo, the chorus ensemble: "We had also the Liberty Song—that by the Farmer, and that by Dr. Ch[urc]h, and the whole Company joined in the Chorus." [9] P54, 41 and 45; (bds. Boston, 1768). [10] See P29. The doctrine of Northern Liberty remained popular throughout the Revolution and after. The entire front page of the *Virginia Gazette* (DN) for January 22, 1780, was given to commentary about music and poetry among the Saxons, noting that they wrote their laws in verse and paid public homage to bards and druids. It seems probable to me that this commentary was in some part the work of Thomas Jefferson, then governor of Virginia, who was keenly interested in the subject. He later proposed the study of the Anglo-Saxon language at his University of Virginia, so that students could imbibe democratic and parliamentary principles at the source.

17. West's *Agrippina*, Peale's *Pitt*

[1] G160, 102. [2] A171, 57. On the moral quality of the style see A41 and A60. By

no accident, the other leading neoclassical history painter, Gavin Hamilton, was a Scotch Presbyterian. [3] G160, 104, 94, 98. [4] G183, 337. To speculate, it seems that historicism always accompanies the growth of revolutionary impulses. The appearance of *The Prince of Parthia* or of *Agrippina* could be matched by the spate of plays in the 1960's on Tom Paine and Jesus Christ, or of movies about Oliver Cromwell and Billy the Kid. The emergence of the forefathers legend could be matched by the street protestors who wore Civil War hats, Indian headbands, and World War II fatigue jackets. Perhaps the underlying intent of historicism is to show that the seditious motives operating at the moment have always existed, thus to work off the guilt that must accompany rebelliousness: They did it, why shouldn't I? [5] A180, 59ff.; A154. [6] A184, 33–4; A182, to Beale Bordley, c. 1768; A184, 34. [7] Facsimile in A186, 69. To reinforce this startling allusion, Peale may have dressed Pitt not simply as a Roman, but specifically as Brutus, the executioner of Caesar. The short-cut hair and bans in the engraving resemble those in the figure of Brutus which Thomas Hollis used on his liberty prints and library bindings. See A246b. [8] A186; N1(R), 4/21/69. [9] G87, 71; Benbridge to Thomas Gordon, 12/7/69, #Ph-32, WIN (courtesy of the owner, Mr. Gordon Saltar); A55; q. A79, 196.

18. Arrival of John Henry

[1] D22, 121ff.; D16. [2] D67, 171; D8, 52; D39, 23; D9, 274–5. [3] D9, 352; N1(R), 12/3/72 (here advertised; no copy of *The Storer* survives). [4] D18; D75, 99. [5] q. D28, 113; N55, 1/14, 21, 28/68 and 2/4/68. [6] q. G158, 284. [7] N55, 1/18/68 and 1/7/68; q. D28, 124; N55, 1/28/68. The complaint against playgoing by objects of charity casts doubt on Jackson Turner Main's contention (see G22) that the 'meaner sort' in the colonies did not attend the theatre. During later theatre controversies, too, proponents often argued that the theatre keeps the poor and unemployed off the streets, preventing crime, while opponents argued that it draws apprentices and servants from their work. See N48, 1/14/86. [8] D28. [9] D9, 219–20; D7, 75–6; M27, 59. [10] N55, 3/3/68. [11] Governor Tryon, applying to the bishop on the actor's behalf, told him that "If your Lordship grants Mr. Giffard his petition you will take off the best player on the American stage." D22, 141. It was Verling's Virginia Company, it might be added, which suggested to John Esten Cooke his novel *The Virginia Company of Comedians.* [12] G43, 229. Jefferson regularly attended Douglass' 1770 Williamsburg season; his October and November account book in that year record thirteen separate expenditures for tickets. [13] N1 (PD), 2/4/68; q. D22, 149; N1(PD), 6/30/68. [14] N1(PD), 8/11/68; M50. D3 incorrectly gives the date of the earliest dramatic performance in Savannah as 1781. [15] D22; M24. [16] D4, 100; D22, 130; D9, 246. [17] D28, 152ff.; D39. [18] Perhaps because of the appearance of Mungo, *The Padlock* was decidedly less popular in the South than in the North. There seem to have been only two performances of the work in Charleston before 1774, and one in Annapolis, as opposed to twenty-one in Philadelphia in the same time. See D64 and D81. [19] D6, 111; D8, 58. [20] D28, 147. [21] q. D73, 89–90.

19. British Troops in Boston

[1] Alexander Martin, *America* (see section 16); G31, 10/13/68. [2] G162, "Boston Garrison"; A127, 49ff. [3] G184, 753; N62, 1/30/69; G31, 38 and 33. The dances themselves became politicized. One dance book of the period contains directions for "The Humours of Boston," a choreographic representation of local Vicars of Bray: "The first couple change sides foot it & back again down in the middle & up again. . . ." MS dance book, c. 1770, BA. [4] G153, 60; M3; G31, 55. [5] M39, 360. Insulting, even blasphemous, as it seemed in Boston, the troops' effort to introduce plays had a recent precedent. In 1767, while Douglass was contending against the Philadelphia anti-theatre laws, an attempt had been made in Boston to repeal the 1750 prohibition. A representative named Joseph Tisdale, who acted in Boston something of the part of Governor Penn in Philadelphia, argued before the House that all civilized countries have countenanced plays, that clerical opposition stemmed from envy over the ability of the stage to promote virtue, and that it undermined the authority of the House to enact laws which the people would not obey. (A broadside printing of his speech is reproduced in D51, facing p. 140.) The debate in the House was augmented by the reprinting in Boston of two earlier English theatre tracts, John Chater's *Another High Road to Hell* and Sir Richard Hill's *Address to Persons of Fashion*. [6] [Proposal for printing *The Miser*] (bds. Boston, Dec 1768), copy at MHS; G75, 200; N6, 10/2/69 and 3/19/70; N6, 8/7/69. After leaving Boston, Douglass gave the *Lecture on Heads* and a lecture version of *Love a-la-Mode* in Portsmouth. [7] G31, 78; both poems were published in Boston in 1769. [8] N6, 7/3/69. [9] G31, 68; A40, 10; G31, 119. Another account of the June episode has survived. Several Bostonians wrote a letter of protest to Major Mackey saying that the captain of the regiment had ordered the fifes to play "what by them is Commonly Called ye Yankee Tune." They asked Mackey to omit music on such ceremonies, "as it is that, which draws great Numbers of persons to gather." Petition to Major G. Mackey, 6/17/69, Miscellaneous Bound MSS, MHS. The troops often interrupted the Sabbath with drum and fife music or by playing popular songs. See G31, 99. [10] q. M46, 56; M83, 89; M46, 57. [11] G215d, 198–200; *Description of the POPE, 1769* (bds. Boston, 1769); G158, 362. Revere's image has an older history. A seated Libertas holding a huge key and releasing a bird appears in an engraving by Jerome Wierix, *The Demolition of the Citadel of Antwerp* (copy at MMA). [12] M39, 372; M3, 263; M13, 178. [13] P48, 95. [14] P48, 45; (bds. Boston, 1770). [15] A171, 83. [16] A4, 2–3. Remick also advertised a view of the landing of the British troops.

20. Repeal of the Townshend Acts

[1] G2, 186; A144. The statue still stands in City Hall Park. For accounts of the raisings in New York and Charleston see N6, 9/10/70, and N2, 9/17/70.

21. Commencement: 1770

[1] *An Essay on the Use and Advantages of the Fine Arts* (New Haven, 1770).

22. The Art World

[1] Figures drawn from actual census and from the urban histories of Carl Bridenbaugh. [2] A242, 89; N14, 9/22/74; A242, 90; N14, 9/8/74; A5, 4. [3] A5, 20. [4] A5, 28 and 9–10; A17, 121. The Stevensons offered scholarships and free art supplies to gifted but poor boys. [5] A2, 1–2 and 15. [6] N1(P), 3/11/73; q. A15, 20. Pratt's 1773 *James McCulloch* is particularly interesting since it shows a robed Princeton graduate in a pose of oratory, a member of the literary Whig society founded by Freneau and Brackenridge. See *Antiques* (Nov 1967), 673, and A150. [7] To Hopkinson, 7/20/70, Miscellaneous Papers, NYPL (facsimile); A186; q. A69, 51. Although centered in Charleston, he painted in other places as well; he appears on ships' passenger lists with William Bartram and with Douglass of the American Company. See A17. [8] A182, possibly to Benjamin Franklin, c. 1771; to Peale, 6/21/70, Dreer Collection, HSP. [9] A182, to Jenings, 7/[10 or 18]/71; A182, unaddressed but almost certainly intended for Franklin, c. 1771; A182, to Bordley, 11/72. [10] A182, to Jenings, c. fall 1771. For some reason, Peale associated this trip with Copley's presence in New York. On August 15, he wrote to Bordley that since "Mr. Copeley (of Boston) I hear is now painting in New York, this is the time I ought to go to Philadelphia." Why Peale linked the two facts is unclear. Copley visited Philadelphia for two weeks later in the year. [11] A178, to Bordley, 12/27/71. [12] A186, 98; G56, II, 137. [13] A182, to Bordley, 7/29/72 and 11/72. [14] A182, to Benbridge, 5/1/73. [15] A182, to Bordley, 2/15/72, and to West, 4/20/7[1?]. [16] A182, to James Arbuckle, 1773, and to Thomas Allwood, 11/71. [17] A171, 101; A189. [18] Peale's essentially domestic bent shows through even in his later, well-known *Exhuming the Mastodon* (Peale Museum, Baltimore). A huge water-wheel dominates the painting, which records the technology of an archeological excavation. Yet Peale painted in several domestic vignettes amid the bystanders, including a mother dragging an unwilling child away from the busy scene. [19] A86, 105–7. [20] A182, to Allwood, 3/1/73 (see also the letter to West, 4/30/73, hinting that he would appreciate West's influence in getting his works shown), and to Bordley, c. 1770. [21] A186, 109. [22] A171, 95; Joseph Palmer to Joseph Cranch, 6/3/73, HCL; A171, 69. [23] A178, 66. [24] A171, 81. [25] A177, 18–19; A46, 73; A178, 84. At around this time Copley painted a trompe-l'oeil corkscrew on the front door of a friend's house, seemingly nailed into the wood, a token of his passion for delineating teapots, table looms, and engraving tools, and of his more general absorption in problems of still life. See A78. [26] A171, 94, 174, 127. [27] A171, 98. [28] A218, 11. [29] A171, 98, 69, 73; q. A180, 110. [30] A171, 194 and 191; Palmer, see note 22 above. [31] The painting must have been nearly finished and shown a year earlier, however. On June 21, 1770, West wrote to Peale that he had been ill and unable to paint for the last six months, but that his *Wolfe* had already "procured me great Honour." Dreer Collection, HSP. [32] A166; A154. [33] q. A14, 63; A181, 122. [34] A161, pt. II, 48–9. On decorum see A20, ch. 2. Despite his avowed documentary aim, West took liberties with the scene and also made some mistakes. He represented Wolfe as rather younger than he was at the time, and mistakenly painted the Indian barefooted. After Henry Laurens informed him that Indians never went barefoot into battle, he painted into the lower left corner of a replica a pair of moccasins.

See A229. Some license was allowed within the theory of history painting. Jonathan Richardson, a widely read theorist in the colonies, cited the made-up speeches in Thucydides to illustrate how the history painter can "improve" his story while "keeping within the bounds of probability." A231, 21. [35] A11, 227. On the Christian overtones see also A168, 21–30; A234, 101–3; A9, 40–43. [36] A166. [37] See A93. A207 interprets West's preoccupation with dying heroes psychologically, as evidence of Oedipal strife. [38] A155; A180, 43. [39] A154. [40] A252. John Trumbull in his *Progress of Dulness* describes how the adolescent Harriet Simper embroiders, weaves, and "shews in waxwork Goodman *Adam,/* And Serpent gay, gallanting Madam." [41] A44. [42] G97, XIV, 148 (the model was very probably by Patience Wright, although possibly by her sister Rachel Wells); N20, 5/2/71; A2, 289 and 391. [43] q. A50, 588; A252, 556; A31; q. A2, 393. [44] On Chandler see A70, A71, A201. His career initiates a distinct school of Connecticut country painters, culminating in the 1790's. Two other painters associated at this early date with the Connecticut school are John Durand of New York and William Johnson. Durand painted for a while in Connecticut, where his style, formed in a long tradition of Dutch limners, clearly appealed to the same patrons as Chandler's. Johnson (1732–1772), the son of the Boston painter and organ builder Thomas Johnson, worked in Hartford, New Haven, and New London, and knew Copley. He shares Chandler's liking for strong designs but his less-stark portraits suggest some acquaintance with works by Blackburn and Wollaston. See A15, 55–6, and A205. [45] *Ebenezer* is one of seven paintings by Chandler of the Devotion family. His companion portrait of Devotion's wife is also keenly observed. Her ear shows very faintly through the hair covering it; the baby sitting on her lap plants its shoes indecorously on her dress. (Mrs. Henry Bowers Collection, Scotland, Connecticut.) In an overmantel bookshelf which he painted for his brother-in-law, Chandler lovingly reproduced about fifty books in several scalloped compartments. He also made botanical drawings which have become lost. [46] A217a, 641; A180; A39; A82, 19. [47] A209, ch. 1 *passim;* q. A85, 315. [48] A213; q. A215, 87.

23. Musical Life

[1] q. Helen Bullock, "On Music in Colonial Williamsburg," TS Research Report, CW, 4; M39, 64; M72, 81; Oscar Sonneck autograph notes, LC Music Division. [2] G53, 83; G51, 19. [3] To Knox, 4/21/74, Henry Knox Papers, MHS (film); q. Bullock (see note 1), 3. [4] N6, 1/7/71; M76, 441; M84, 62 and xi. [5] N62, 2/1/73; G75, 239. [6] N6, 11/15/70; q. M9, 5–7; D51, 165. [7] M2; M3, 68 and 74; *To the Philharmonical Merchants* (bds. Phil., 1769); to John Penn, 10/17/71, Emmet 1586, NYPL. [8] M11, 32; D28, 175; N14, 5/6/73. [9] N14, 5/5/74 and 4/14/74; M49, 107; A2, 368. [10] *Rules of the St. Coecilia Society* (Charleston, 1774); N1(P), 9/19/71; q. M24, 51; M3. [11] M12, 55; M69, 43; G159. [12] M50; *This evening, the tenth of December. . . .* (bds. Providence, 1771); G40, I, 192. [13] M33, 3. Stiles later recorded a delightful dream in which he showed some ladies and gentlemen an organ with silver and gold pipes supposedly given to Yale by Bishop Berkeley. When he displayed the inside, "lifting up the Silk Covering & shoving upwards the

Whalebone Folds of the Bellows," the organ started playing and woke him. G40, I, 433. [14] q. M69, 120; M69 (a Tanneberger organ can be heard in performance by E. Power Biggs on *The Organ in America*, Columbia MS-6161); G72, 177. [15] M39, 163; M34. Hartley replaced a female organist, Ann Windsor, who began teaching harpsichord in the city and became perhaps America's first woman music teacher. See M57. [16] Oscar Sonneck autograph notes, LC Music Division; M46, 168. [17] M71; A2, 370. [18] M46; M67, 394; M72; D76, 193. [19] D76, 20. [20] D28 (the manuscript is reproduced in M15, facing 521); M71. [21] M67, 394; M8, 51–2. Valton's tunes have survived. See M57, 214–17. [22] Sonneck autograph notes. [23] 5/14. [24] William Bentley, MS "Miscellanies," William Bentley Papers, AAS. [25] M7; M52, 238. [26] M35, 3–4. [27] William Bentley, MS "Notes and Accounts," William Bentley Papers, AAS. [28] M52, 192–3.; M61, 117. [29] M52, 284; q. M1, 282. [30] 8/27/71. [31] M10, 123; N51, 9/25/69. [32] Samuel Dunlop to London Board of Indian Commissioners, 7/2/73, Miscellaneous Bound MSS, MHS; N62, 9/11/69. [33] M32, 17; M52, 270. To further enliven the singing, according to Nathaniel Gould, during the recess "ardent spirit was generously handed round among the singers in the gallery of the church, to cheer them on their course. . . ." M66, 102. [34] G177, II, 31; M35; M52, 278. [35] q. M9, 37–8; M66, 80; N6, 3/10/66. [36] M51, 507; M52, 279; M32, 17. [37] All the known information about Billings appears in M90, to which the following account is considerably indebted. [38] M66, 46; MS notes of Emily Cordelia Swan, AAS; G196, II, 351. [39] M66, 46. [40] M90, 40; M52, 158, and M61; M90, 226–7. The *New-England Psalm-Singer* was first advertised in the *Boston Gazette* on December 10, 1770, as a "Composition of Church Musick." It was sold in Boston at Edes and Gill's print shop and at Josiah Flagg's, and in Plymouth. Apparently the volume had been partly subscribed, for the ad calls for subscribers to pick up their now-available copies. The ad was repeated in February, March, and May the next year. [41] M52, 223. [42] M61; M43; M12; M32. [43] M42, liner notes. [44] A182, to Jenings, 7/[10?]/71; A171, 119. [45] A179, 6. [46] After an exhaustive analysis of tunebooks, Richard Crawford finds that of the 100 most popular psalm and hymn tunes in America before 1810, 59 were non-American, 38 were American, 3 were perhaps American (personally conveyed information). [47] Between 1764 and 1800, about 117 anthems by native Americans were published in New England, of which Billings wrote more than a third. M12, 71. [48] M1, 240. [49] M35. [50] q. M10, 142. [51] Hans Nathan identifies them as "Relikte aus der Renaissance" in a yet-unpublished supplement to F. Blume, *Musik in Geschichte und Gegenwart*, kindly supplied to me in a letter. J. Murray Barbour analyzes these modal features in M41. See also M61, M44, M86. [52] q. M12, 60. [53] Nathaniel Evans, *A Dialogue on Peace* (Phil., 1763). [54] P63, 367ff. [55] M28; q. M90, 70; M66, 77.

24. The Literary Scene

[1] A stodgy *American Magazine*, specializing in scientific articles, had a nine-month run in 1769, highlighted by the inclusion of perhaps the first American engraving of quality, *The manner of Fowling in Norway*, by the Philadelphia engraver James Smithers. P95b. Another important engraving of this period, perhaps by Henry

Dawkins, appeared in Morgan Edwards, *Materials Towards a History of the Baptists in Pennsylvania* (Phil., 1770), depicting immersion services in the Schuylkill River. [2] For the figures see section 4, note 1; D32, 290. [3] N6, 9/2/71; G159, 80. Garrick's play was so popular that John Henry sold copies of it on the side. A 1773 playbill for the Philadelphia theatre (HSP) mentions "Books of the Irish Widow to be had of Mr. Henry, and at the Offices where the Tickets are sold." [4] *A New Ballad, Upon a New Occasion* (bds. Phil., 1771); *A Monumental Inscription on the Fifth of March* (bds. Boston, 1772); N6, 3/11 and 18/71; James Allen, *The Poem which the Committee. . . .* (bds. Boston, 1772). The last poem was not read at the anniversary because a member of the March 5 committee believed, oversubtly, that it was "a bite," i.e. a disguised Tory satire on Whig ideas. The elaborate ceremonies ended in 1773, atlhough orations on that date continued throughout the war. [5] "Hodge Podge" appeared in *A Pennsylvania Sailor's Letters* (Phil., 1771). An instance of a home theatrical is "The modern Contest," a masque written around 1770, perhaps by the Norris family of Philadelphia. Based on the judgment of Paris, it requires Colin to choose among girls from Boston, New Jersey, and Philadelphia, and at one place gives the rather demanding stage direction "As a Symphony is playing, Cupid descends." MS, Loudon Collection, HSP. [6] G158; Warren Papers, MHS. [7] N6, 5/24/73 and 7/19/73; G202. [8] The text appears in G8. On Munford see D26. [9] D26 suggests that Ralpho represents not a black but a white servant. A stage direction in the play, however, has Woud'be breakfasting while *"several negroes go backwards and forwards, bringing in the breakfast."* [10] P98, 584. [11] P35, 67; Jane Dunlap, *Poems* (Boston, 1771). For other poems on Whitefield see Evans nos. 42085-6; Supplement to N6, 9/19/70; P48, 51. [12] G102, 72. [13] Part of a longer epitaph, Thomas Wallcut Papers, AAS; P35, 34. Several obscure black painters are also mentioned in print for the first, and seemingly the last, time in the early 1770's. Before leaving Charleston in 1773, a painter-gilder named John Allwood announced that he wished to "Dispose of His Negro Fellows, *Painters*, As to their Abilities, he thinks them evident, they having transacted the Whole of his Business [which was painting and gilding an altarpiece for St. Michael's Church], without any hired Assistance; and he had taken no little Pains in initiating them in the true Principles of their Profession. . . ." (A17, 121). The same year, the *Boston Gazette* advertised the availability of "a Negro man whose extraordinary Genius has been assisted by one of the best Masters in London. . . ." (A4, 6). Phillis Wheatley herself addressed verses to Scipio Moorhead, "A Young African Painter" in Boston whose works have not been identified. It seems likely that slaves and servants of painters were often trained as apprentices, much as southerners taught their slaves as musicians. It should be added that the discussion of inconsistencies in the Whig position called attention to other minorities as well, such as sectaries. The Baptist minister Elisha Rich, author of several broadside ballads on military engagements of the Revolution, asked in his 1776 broadside poem *On the late distress of the Town of Boston*: "Can Patriots for Liberty,/ Against a civil tyrant cry,/ And not give equal Liberty,/ To ev'ry diff'rent sectery *[sic]*." [14] P35, 106; P37, 303. The *Paradise Lost* is now at HCL. [15] q. P93, 288; q. P35, xxxvii; N62, 9/20/73; Hugh McConnel, MS commonplace book [catalogued as "Early American Songs and Poems"], Clifton

Waller Barrett Library, UVL. (McConnel thus identifies the author of her 1775 poem to Washington.) [16] G139, 375. [17] G108; G138, 275. [18] G113, 244; G116. [19] *Newport, September 11* (bds. 1769); G155, 186 and 189; q. G182, 58. [20] N62, 8/22/68; G176, 20. [21] G139, II, 375–6; G108; *Subscriptions of the Literary Society* (bds. NY, 1771), copy at NYHS. [22] D4 and G159, 142; P10. [23] Diary of Dwight Foster, 1772–1780, Foster Family Papers, AAS (typed transcript). [24] D29; q. D70, 54; D45, 56. [25] G215a, 358; N62, 9/9 and 30/71. The theatrical rage spread to lower schools as well. A New York newspaper advertised at Hull's Long Room a performance of *King Bassias* and the popular *Padlock*, by a "select party of little masters and misses" (N14, 1/6/74). Performances by children of *Cato* were particularly numerous in the 1770's. In whole or part, the play was performed at the Savannah, Georgia, orphan-house school in 1771, at Mr. Holt's school in Williamsburg in 1774, and at Joseph Rathell's school in Philadelphia in 1771, where it attracted an audience so large that it had to be removed to the Assembly Room, where admission of half a crown was charged. See G84, 602; Elizabeth Tucker to St. George Tucker, 3/16/75, Tucker-Coleman Collection, WM; G159, 143. Even the Puritans, it should be added, allowed for school theatricals. One of the first and most bitter Puritan attacks on the stage, John Northbrooke's *Treatise wherein Dicing Dauncing, Vain playes, or Enterludes . . . are reproved* (1577), allowed that plays devoid of lewdness might be used for didactic purposes in schools. The children who performed such works were not only future citizens likely to be molded by the ideology they declaimed, but also potential theatregoers not likely to become intolerant of the stage. [26] Accounts based on P84, P96, P75. [27] q. P84, 43; *An Elegy on the Death of Mr. Buckingham St. John* (bds. [New Haven, 1771?]); D70. [28] (New Haven, 1772); *Royal Melody Complete* (Boston, 1767). [29] To Silas Deane, 1/8/72, Miscellaneous MSS, LC (photostat); to Silas Deane, 3/28/72, HSP; P84, 115. [30] q. A17, 117. [31] P10, I, 26. Freneau's collegiate poems, it must be noted, imperfectly reveal his adolescent attitudes. They exist only in probably revised versions printed in later editions of his poetry, with the explanation "written in 1768" or "written in 1770." [32] P5, facsimile facing lx; P10, I, 85. [33] N1(P), 9/9/73; 1/74; q. P102, 245. [34] P83, 75–6; to Deane, LC (see note 29); q. P3, 17. Both the date and authorship of *America* have been disputed; for a discussion of the problem of attribution see my *Timothy Dwight* (New York, 1969). [35] G101, 226; G130. [36] These agents resemble the Faustian Columbus of Freneau's earlier "Discovery," but, typical of Freneau's ambivalent longings for both adventure and content, they are quite unlike the tranquil Farmers of Fancy who inhabit his later *American Village.* [37] A230, plates 67 and 69. The conjunction of Libertas and rayed glory may linger in the odd spiked crown of the French Statue of Liberty. [38] N17, 1/74; *An Oration . . . before . . . the American Philosophical Society* (Phil., 1773).

25. The Theatre

[1] Thomas Bradford Collection, HSP; N1 (PD), 4/9/72. [2] D4, 121; G56, II, 39. [3] q. D9, 293; q. D28, 170–1. [4] q. D30, 239; N1(P), 4/2/72; D64; N1(P), 9/27/70. [5] D22, 174. [6] G70, 71; M24. [7] q. D9, 287, which see for an account of the

subscriptions. [8] G59, 55; q. D9, 285. [9] M24, 45–6; q. D22, 167; N1(R), 10/22/72. [10] Account Book at CW; q. D22, 155; q. D9, 290; D83, 240–1. Nancy Hallam's success in part reflects a surge of interest in Shakespeare in the late 1760's. It was touched off by Garrick's Stratford Jubilee, produced at Drury Lane in 1769 and widely reported in colonial newspapers. The result was a number of colonial premieres of Shakespeare's works: *King John* and *Henry IV, Part One* (1768); *Julius Caesar*, *The Merry Wives of Windsor*, and *The Tempest* (1770). Other plays increased in popularity. Four American performances of *Hamlet* are recorded from 1750 to 1766, fourteen from 1767 to 1773. See D63. [11] q. D22, 158; A83. The position of Nancy Hallam's lifted sword reappears in Peale's later depiction of Washington at Yorktown. [12] "Williamsburg People," card file, CW. [13] q. D9, 315; q. D22, 176.

26. The Tea Act and the Boston Port Bill

[1] G62, 27; N1(P), 6/16/74; M3, 263. [2] A171, 201. [3] q. G163, 8. [4] N6, 12/6/73. [5] G62, 141; N62, 1/24/74. [6] G59, 59. See also the broadside *A New Song. Called the Gaspee*, in P48. [7] P59, 49–50; G11, 85. Another version of the Revolution-as-theatre metaphor appeared in the *Boston Gazette* on March 28, 1774, a skit on the ministry modeled on the popular *Lecture on Heads*. [8] This theatre is perhaps the best documented of all Douglass' theatres in the colonies, owing to the survival of a mesne conveyance from the bookseller Robert Wells and others to Douglass, made on August 28, 1773. It provides for yearly rental of the Church Street plot for £100 for fifteen years, payable the first of each year. Douglass also agreed to perform a yearly benefit for Wells and his partners "at any time that the same shall be ask'd for during the said Season," and as long as the play and farce were in his repertoire, on ten days' notice. The lease specified that the theatre must have a brick foundation at least ten feet above the surface of the ground, and upon it "a wooden frame of good and Substantial materials to be filled up with Bricks and also covered with brick on the outside with proper Necessary and convenient doors windows locks hinges bolts and other Materials. . . ." In Douglass' absence, Wells and his partners could use the building for their own profit, but could not without Douglass' permission let it to any other actors. In effect, Douglass agreed to build a theatre in exchange for a theatre monopoly in Charleston. "Record of Mesne Conveyance," Book C-5, Charleston County Court House. [9] N54, 8/25/73. [10] q. A17, 118; N54, 10/25/73; N54, 11/15/73. The "capital *Landscape-Painter*" may have been Thomas Leech, who arrived in October 1773 and took up subscription for printing a view of Charleston. [11] On the presentment see N54, 2/28/74. The mention of "frequent Robberies" in the presentment is one of several evidences of a crime wave in the colonies around 1773. The outbreak produced a small but grisly body of prison and gallows literature that blends luridness and benevolence, allowing the audience to indulge prurient interests in rape, bestiality, and murder and to assuage them by extending tears of pity, a situation roughly comparable to the idealized pain of *Wolfe*. See for instance *Verses . . . Composed in Albany Goal* (Boston, 1773), the verse broadside *Mr Occom's Address* (n. pl., 1773), and the verse skit *A Dialogue between Elizabeth Smith and John Sennet* ([Boston? 1773?]), in which a

male and female criminal on the gallows argue who has committed the worse crime. Elhanan Winchester's *EXECUTION HYMN* (Boston, 1773) provides a sidelight on the social function of the singing schools. Composed in Rehoboth, Massachusetts, for the burglar Levi Ames, the hymn was sung to him and to an audience assembled at the prison, and "at the Desire of the Prisoner, will be sung at the Place of Execution," presumably by members of the local singing school. [12] For general accounts see G21, G62, G158. [13] *An Address to New-England* (bds. Boston, 1774); G162, "Boston Garrison"; N62, 9/5/74; q. M59, 212. [14] q. G21, 196; N17, 10/74. [15] G21, 183; q. A126, 29; q. A146, 449. [16] N54, 7/4/74; N14, 9/2/74; N1, 8/14/74; G53, 96. [17] G141, I, 626. [18] *From the Virginia Gazette, August 25* (bds. n. pl., n. d.), facsimile at NYPL; N1(P), 9/29/74. [19] q. D19, 159–60.

27. Copley in Europe

[1] A171, 219. [2] To Sukey, 7/11/74, J. S. Copley Collection, LC. In editing Copley's letters to Sukey for her edition of the *Domestic Life*, Copley's daughter excised all of her father's many slighting references to Boston. [3] A171, 182 and 226. [4] To Sukey, 8/17/74, J. S. Copley Collection, LC. [5] A171, 245 and 255. [6] To Sukey, 10/8/74, J. S. Copley Collection, LC. [7] A238, II, 228–30. Cunningham, who reprints this material, says that Copley went to Rome in August 1774; actually the journey to Rome took place in October. [8] See note 6. [9] A171, 233; to Sukey, 10/25/74, J. S. Copley Collection, LC. [10] A175, 39, 41, 43. [11] To Sukey, 1/28/75, J. S. Copley Collection, LC; A175, 48. [12] A175, 51. [13] A175, 53; to Sukey, 6/9/75, J. S. Copley Collection, LC. [14] A171, 297–8. [15] A175, 56; A171, 291. [16] To Sukey (see note 11); A171, 301.

28. The First Continental Congress

[1] G163, I, 39. [2] N1(R), 9/1/74. [3] (New Haven, 1775). The poem first appeared in a Boston newspaper in September 1774. [4] P39, 164ff.; M16. [5] P34, I, 68ff. [6] G163, I, 53. [7] 2/10/75, Miscellaneous MSS, LC. [8] 3/10/75 and 4/6/75, HSP. [9] q. G2, 353. [10] A146, 447; N14, 1/19/75. [11] *A Dialogue, Between a Southern Delegate, and his Spouse* (NY, 1774); *Address of LIBERTY, to the BUCKSKINS of PENNSYLVANIA* (bds. Phil., 1775). [12] *The Poor Man's Advice to his Poor Neighbours* (NY, 1774); (NY, 1774). [13] G4, 248; D8. [14] M24; D73, 112; D76, 213. [15] *Gentleman's Magazine*, 8/88.

29. Lexington, Concord, Bunker's Hill

[1] Account based on G158 and G162. [2] A131; A100; A202. On the display of the engravings in American homes see G79, 13; A51, 448. [3] G158, 586; N26, 5/75. [4] G163, I, 65. Further evidence of its popularity as a march appears in the manuscript fife manual of Elisha Belknap of Framingham (HCL), which includes the tune along with "Baron Steuben's March," the "Boston March," and several quicksteps. For what may be the earliest copy of the tune by an American see Kate Van Winkle Keller, ed., *Giles Gibbs, Jr. His Book for the Fife* (Hartford, 1974). Here

the tune appears under the bewildering title "Thehos [the house? the horse?] Gendar." [5] G32, I, 45; G141, II, 438. A curious version survives at the Boston Public Library, entitled *Yankee Doodle. or The Negroes Farewell to America. The Words and Music by T. L.* Possibly printed around 1775, it recalls the fact that in *The Disappointment* the song is given to the black character Raccoon. Clearly the work of a conservative colonist or an Englishman, it presents a slave leaving America and enumerating its evils: "dangling & canting swearing & drinking/ Taring and Feath'ring for ser'ously thinking./ Yankee doodle &c./ Den Hey! for old Englan' where Liberty reigns/ Where Negroe no beaten or loaded with chains." Obviously this text cannot be sung to the "Yankee Doodle" tune, suggesting that the tune had lost its usefulness as a thorn in the radical side. [6] P52, 69 and 82; G92, III, 118; q. D24, 286. [7] G165, 263–4; (Hartford, 1775); N1(Pi), 7/20/75. [8] G5; M8; G162. [9] A70; G80, I, 111. [10] N1 (Pi), 7/20/75; G158, 616. [11] 7/13/75. The engraving of Adams was by Samuel Okey of Newport, who based his print on Copley's portrait of Adams. See A125. [12] BUNKER'S HILL (bds. [Boston? 1775?]); *A POEM, Upon the present Times* (bds. [Boston? 1775?]); (Chelmsford, 1775).

30. The Siege of Boston

[1] G166. [2] See for instance N26, 11/75, and G40, I, 662. James Lyon, whose *Urania* impelled the revival of singing, sent Washington plans for the conquest of Nova Scotia and asked permission to lead the conquering army. M2. [3] N1(DH), 2/24/76; *Present Situation of Affairs in North-America* (Phil., 1775). [4] P35, 90. [5] P35, 88. [6] G163, I, 145; P78, 71–2. [7] The play was recited at the Maryland academy where Brackenridge taught. Although hastily written, it is significant for treating contemporary events with which Americans were familiar in the solemn, elevated style in which they had been accustomed to think of other peoples' history. Another school-play on Bunker's Hill was written at this time, but not published: *Ministerial Oppression*, probably by James Varnum of Rhode Island College. See D37. [8] *The Poem which the Committee . . . had Voted Unanimously to be Published with the late Oration* (Boston, 1772); P10, I, 178; N64, 12/14/75. The title of the last-quoted work, "A REVERIE. By a SOLDIER," itself says much about contemporary views of the American army. [9] N1 (DH), 12/23/75; G32, I, 107; N64, 12/14/75. [10] G32, I, 105–6; P10, I, 150. In his unpublished play, "The Spy," Freneau listed the soldiers among his dramatis personae as "Peasants." [11] Governor Jonathan Trumbull to William Kneeland, 8/10/72, Governor Jonathan Trumbull Papers, CSL; A218, 11. [12] A218, 16. [13] To David Trumbull, 11/22/75, John Trumbull (artist) Papers, CHS. [14] *Ibid.* [15] E. *[sic]* Webster, MS "Memoir of Timothy Swan," Timothy Swan Papers, AAS; M55; P59, 136. Hewling's song, a version of the Scotch-plot theory, appears in N1 (DH), 7/29/75. [16] q. G32, I, 254. [17] (bds. Salem, 1775). [18] M60. See also "Yankee Doodle," folder, NYPL Rare Book Division. The "Yankee Doodle" tune continued to inspire sassy doggerel throughout the war. Verses were set to it on such occasions as the failure of the D'Estaing-Sullivan operation at Newport in 1778 (N14, 10/3/78), the elevation of Lord George Germaine to the peerage ("Poems of the American Revolution, Copies 1779–

1782," NYHS), and the siege of Yorktown (N51, 1/8/82)—the last being the cleverest of the wartime versions. For other versions see N14, 1/22/80 and 9/27/89. [19] A180 and A223; G10. [20] G162; q. D22, 93. [21] M75, 20; G10. [22] [Capt. James Wood?], MS Diary entitled "A Voyage to Boston," NYHS. The performance of *Zara*, an English version of a play by Voltaire, represents one of the early performances of a French play in the colonies, the first apparently being an English adaptation of Voltaire's *Orphan of China* in Charleston in 1764. Through these adaptations, French drama became quite widely known to the colonists, one of several lasting ways in which the British army influenced American taste. See D43, 116. [23] N1 (D), 1/13/76; q. D51, 156; G49, 53. [24] N1 (DH), 1/20/76. [25] q. G32, I, 200; G163, I, 166; D8; G49, 53. [26] G162, "Dorchester Heights"; G122, 95; G21, 256. [27] *Two favorite SONGS, made on the Evacuation of the Town of BOSTON* (bds. [Boston? 1776?]); G32, I, 216.

31. Outside Boston

[1] q. M76, 443. [2] N64, 3/14/76. In mid-1774, John Greenleaf took over Isaiah Thomas' *Royal American Magazine* and made it into an outstanding periodical. Steeped in imagery of Rising Glory, it featured some twenty engravings by Revere, as well as music, liberty songs, brief fiction, and verse by Phillis Wheatley. See N32. [3] A2, 366 and 373; M80, appendix B; q. P4, 53; N1 (DH), 8/19/75. [4] 2/10/75, Miscellaneous MSS, LC; 9/75; P34, I, 103. [5] G42, 501; D70, 8. [6] My tally of Evans; G21, 235. [7] *The Nature and Importance of the Duty of Singing Praise to GOD* (Hartford, 1775); N17, 6/74. [8] P65, 231-2. [9] G163, I, 158. [10] A171, 332; Greene to Copley, 5/10/75, J. S. Copley Collection, LC; A171, 316. [11] To Sukey, 7/2/75, J. S. Copley Collection, LC. [12] A171, 344-5. [13] A175, 61; to Sukey, 7/22/75, J. S. Copley Collection, LC. [14] A184, 40; A182, to John Dixon [early 1775?]. [15] A182, to Allwood, [8?]/30/75, and to West, 8/31/75. [16] A182, to West (see note 15) and to Jenings, 8/29/75. [17] A183; A186; A184, 39. [18] (NY, 1775); (NY, 1775); N49, 10/18/75. [19] P10, I, 196. See also "Mars and Hymen," of which this seems to be an earlier version. [20] q. P10, I, 142n. [21] P10, I, 206; q. P4, 65. [22] q. G32, I, 196; A183, 3/76. Contemporary historians are not alone in thinking the terms "Whig" and "Tory" treacherously vague. The confusion and injustice resulting from their use is dramatized in *The Patriots*, a play written around 1777 by the Virginia burgess Robert Munford. Those in the play who pass for Whigs are shown to be apolitical braggadocios motivated by fashion or the need to confirm their masculinity. Truly patriotic moderates are labeled Tories and hauled into court by accusers unable to define the term. The play appears in *William and Mary Quarterly*, 3d Ser., VI (Jul 1949). See also D26. [23] G125, I, 184, and P63, 367ff.; *To the Public, New-York*, November 16, *1774;* G111, 97, and G21, 225-7. On Rivington's activities at this time see his correspondence with Henry Knox, Knox Papers, MHS (film). [24] q. G98, 195. Church's duplicity casts backlight on the tepid political position reached at the end of the otherwise fiery *The Times*. [25] P78, 199-200; G162. The LC volume is entitled "Rhapsodies," although it has been discussed in print as "Loyalist Rhapsodies"—a title which gives the poems the

contrary of their actual meaning. [26] "Sung at a Venison Feast"; "Epigram," both in "Rhapsodies." [27] "American Liberty"; "Written on a Card . . . ," both in Robert Proud Papers, Box 8, HSP. [28] "Rhapsodies." [29] Proud Papers; "Song . . . At a fishing-party . . . ," in "Rhapsodies"; P77, 23; "Written on a Card . . . ," in Proud Papers. [30] D52. [31] N65, 9/26/76, italics reversed. [32] On New Year's Day, Dunmore directed the fleet to bombard Norfolk, destroying the largest town in Virginia. Leacock probably completed his play before that date, since he does not mention the event.

32. The Second Continental Congress Declares Independence

[1] "King Cong," MS "Rhapsodies," LC. [2] G162, "Montgomery, Richard" and "Canada Invasion"; N1(DH), 2/24/76 (see also 3/16/76); A40, 189. [3] Montgomery's is only one of several ghosts prominent in poems and plays of the 1770's, as in English poetry throughout the century. See P13. Aside from serving to dramatize the forefathers theme, the ghost illustrates again the current of luridity in the period. [4] Norman, an English architect and landscape engraver, appeared in Philadelphia in mid-1774 and opened a shop on Front Street. In addition to engraving, he taught a drawing school, did architectural plans, sold political cartoons and war maps, and, like Rivington in New York, occasionally displayed paintings by visiting artists, vended music, or served as middleman for patrons who wanted to sell off musical instruments. He later also sold coffins. A5, 22–6. [5] G42, I, 546. Stansbury's poem appears in P77, 29. [6] G163, I, 275–6. [7] (Phil., 1775); G177, II, 187; G39, I, 157. [8] A183, entries for May and June 1776. [9] G37, II, 103–4. Adams made the same description of the moribund delegate from Maryland, the odd-looking Caesar Rodney. [10] A182, 8/29/75. [11] A189, 221. On the sittings see A183, entries for May–December. Several articles and books have given what I believe is a faulty chronology for this portrait, stating that the commission came to Peale in June and that Washington sat on June 31. See for instance A121, II, 340. Evidence contradicting this chronology appears in Peale's unpublished diaries, which note that on May 19 "Mr Hancock bespoke Portraits of Genl Washington and Lady." The diaries mention sittings on the thirtieth and thirty-first of May, not June—when Washington, anyway, was in New York. Peale himself wrote an essay on his Washington portraits, unfortunately now lost. [12] G37, I, 96. [13] A84. [14] A113; "The History of Peru," in "Rhapsodies." [15] q. A112, 13. The "Rebellion to Tyrants" motto had been popular in the colonies. It derived from a fictitious epitaph supposedly placed over the body of John Bradshaw, president of the court which condemned Charles I to death. See A112. [16] G37, I, 97. [17] G210, 78–82; Du Simitière Memoranda Books, LC; A136. [18] G37, I, 96; A113. [19] Ultimately derived from Horace's *E Pluribus Una*, this motto appeared for many years on the title page of the London *Gentleman's Magazine*, an extremely popular magazine in the colonies. Here it meant simply that under one cover the reader would be offered a variety of literary treats. See A103. [20] N1, 8/24/76; G99. Words in praise of Franklin had been set to "God Save the King" and sung by a large company as he left for England in 1764: "Thy Knowledge Rich in Store,/ On Pennsylvania Pour"

etc. See *The Election* (Phil., 1764). [21] G32, I, 284 and 271. For other accounts of the toppling of the statue see A109. George Washington considered the act a riot. It was not the only one. The marble statue of Lord Botetourt in Williamsburg was pulled off its pedestal, the head and right arm broken off, the nose smashed. See A248. The statue has since been repaired and moved to the lobby of the Swem Library on the William and Mary campus.

33. New York, New Jersey, Pennsylvania

[1] "The Toriade," Col. John Peters Papers, NYHS. [2] *Conflagration. A Poem* (NY, 1780). [3] q. D10, 19; P77, 10. [4] q. G32, I, 386; Oscar Sonneck autograph notes, LC Music Division, quoting "New York Advertiser," 1/2/86. [5] G163, I, 504. [6] A186; A183 entries for August–December; A184. [7] A184, 42, 45, 43. [8] A184, 45; A185. [9] A190; A184. The American forces were barely leaving Princeton as Cornwallis' army entered it. Cornwallis' failure to take Washington at this point was later derided in a long anti-Scotch poem, "The Cornwalliad," published over several issues of the *United States Magazine* beginning in January 1779. [10] G163, I, 544–8. The parody is attributed to Livingston in a manuscript copy in the Feinstone Collection, APS. [11] G128. [12] G32, II, 296; P53; G28, 215. [13] *Song made on the Taking of General Burgoyne* (bds. n. pl., 1777). [14] G72, I, 31–2. Anburey seems to be referring here to Saratoga. [15] N9, 3/ 17/78; *A Song, On the Surrendry [sic] of General* Burgoyne (bds. [Boston? 1777?]). [16] A183, entries for June; A184; A186. [17] A184; A169, 199. According to a later account by Rembrandt Peale, the sitting took place on September 28 in a farmhouse at what is now Schwenksville, Pennsylvania, "in a room so small that, with his table near a low Window, the artist sitting on the only chair in the room, the General was obliged to sit on the side of his bed." While Peale was painting, Colonel Tench Tilghman arrived with news of Burgoyne's surrender. Washington exclaimed "Burgoyne is taken," handed the letter to Tilghman, and "continued sitting for the Miniature, with perfect composure, until it was finished." A185. Washington's unflappability became legendary, but otherwise Rembrandt's account of the episode must be suspected, since Burgoyne did not surrender for another three weeks. [18] A182, to West, 4/9/83; A184, 62. [19] P80, 95; N39 *passim*. [20] N39, 5/26/78, 5/1/78, and 4/7/78. [21] q. M3, 78. [22] D39, 22; q. D10, 31. [23] D34, 384. This prologue has been attributed to both André and Jonathan Odell; another manuscript version of it, entitled "Prologue to *no man's Enemy but his own*," appears in the Thomas Burke Papers, North Carolina Dept. of Archives and History. Locally written prologues to performances were often published in the occupation newspaper. [24] D79. Du Simitière, in Philadelphia during the occupation, kept a list of the plays acted. See his Memoranda Books, LC. [25] P77; G10, 181; P34. [26] D79. André published a lengthy account of the event in the *Gentleman's Magazine* in August 1778. See also M45. [27] Du Simitière Memoranda Books, LC; G32, II, 55. [28] MS account of *Mischianza*, Am. 30163, HSP; G74, 294; G162, "Philadelphia Campaign." However patriots dismissed the affair as an orgy of forgetting, they themselves did not quickly forget its galling opulence. In 1779, General Henry Knox tendered for Washington in West Jersey a

sort of *Anti-Mischianza*. One newspaper described it as "a festival given by men who had not enriched *themselves* by the war, the lights were cheap, and of their own manufacture; the seats the work of their own artisans; and for *knights of different orders*, there were hardy soldiers, happy in the thought of having some hand in bringing round what they were celebrating." G32, II, 133. [29] q. G131, 217. [30] P70, 406; q. M13, 104; G192, XI, 105–6. Parke included the poem in his later *Lyric Works of Horace*. See the discussion in Book Three. [31] A184, 65; A169; A186. [32] A189, 223; A208; Mrs. Titian Peale, "The Washington Portrait," M. The bust is perhaps the one shown in Peale's 1789 *Goldsborough Family*. [33] M13, 114; G131, 233 and 280; q. D4, 37.

34. Excursus: Music in the Army

[1] FARL; G212, I, 136; M13, 129. [2] G54, 77; G40, II, 366; G46, 151. [3] G46, 151. At camp the writing of poetry was essentially a diversion, although for a few soldiers such as Parke and Barlow a serious effort as well. Much of the camp verse shares with other pastimes a distinctive quality of contrived difficulty. A soldier named John Horn, for instance, wrote a long verse narrative, apparently from personal experience, of "The Engagement of Long Island." The middle portion forms a long acrostic, the initial letters of each line spelling out POLLY NANCY PATTY JENNY AND ELIZABETH CARVEL (Hollyday Papers, MdHS). Another form of camp verse was the double poem, written so that the lines give one meaning when read straight across, and an opposite meaning when read only up to the caesura. A poem by a Pennsylvania soldier describing a political Vicar of Bray begins: "I love with all my heart, The Tory party here,/ The Continental part, Most hatefull doth appear. . . ." (P66). In some camp poems, the pleasure in contrivance takes the form of a playful functionalism, serving to lighten the tedium of military regulation and dissipate fear into gallows humor, as in the doggerel pass dated Head Quarters, Boston, August 2, 1777, which begins: "Permit the Bearer, an Irish Lad,/ Nam'd Peter Hewson (as 'tis said,)/ To pass to Philadelphia—" (Miscellaneous Bound MSS, MHS). Like pieces of scrimshaw or whittling, such camp poems are objects made to kill time while preserving an illusion of purpose. By nature ephemeral, much of the versifying at camp has remained in manuscript, including all of the lines quoted above. The most remarkable of these surviving manuscripts is a commonplace book of over 400 large pages amassed by a soldier named Hugh McConnel, stationed at Fishkill, New York (Barrett Collection, UVL). McConnel transcribed from contemporary newspapers and magazines works by the leading American poets, and interspersed the collection with news items, gossip, many dirty jokes, and most important, his own attempts at verse. These are semiliterate and occasionally pornographic, but their coarse realism makes them more affecting than most other revolutionary poetry. [4] q. M80, 205. As this and the subsequent footnotes in this section suggest, the discussion of military music draws plentifully on the expert and unusually rich doctoral dissertation of Raoul Camus. [5] q. M13, 26; G10, 117. [6] q. M80, 205 and 186. [7] M13; MS "Inspection Return of the Music in the Army" [signed by John Hiwell], Gratz

Collection, HSP. [8] M13; N62, 3/21/63. Herbert Aptheker called attention to "the giant cooper, fifer, and drummer Barzillai Lew" who stayed with the army throughout the war. See M13, 55. [9] M80, 188. [10] q. M13, 62. Several of these brigade supply sheets are preserved at AAS. [11] M13, 27. The system of revolutionary calls has been reconstructed by George P. Carroll, drum major of the Colonial Williamsburg Fife and Drum Corps. Some can be heard, on instruments of the period, on *Colonial Williamsburg Presents The Fifes & Drums and The Band of Musick* (Colonial Williamsburg Foundation). [12] Colonel Peter Gansevoort, MS "Musick Book," NYPL. See also the MS Fife Book of John Greenwood, NYHS. [13] M80. [14] To Henry Knox, 1/27/82, and Lieutenant Colonel Fernald to Major General Heath [April 1782?], Heath Papers, MHS. [15] M80; M13; John Molnar, "Military Bands," TS Research Report, CW. [16] M80, 166ff. and 291. [17] q. M80, 201; q. G122, 101; P62, 27–8. [18] M13, 218; M80, 133. [19] q. M80, 368. Amid the more general feeling that pursuit of the arts was inappropriate to the time, some resented the bands. The huzzas at a celebration of the French alliance held in camp seemed to one soldier "a military music more agreeable . . . than the most finished pieces of your favorite Handel." G32, II, 51. [20] See M80, *passim*, for the information in this paragraph and the next. [21] G163, II, 706–7. [22] G69, 115; M13, 112; q. G159, 149; q. M80, 304. [23] M80. See also M13, 80–86. [24] q. M80, 315 and 202; G32, 375. [25] Oscar Sonneck autograph notes, LC Music Division.

35. Philadelphia and New York

[1] A183, June. [2] q. G32, II, 343; M8, 38. [3] To Jenings, 10/15/79, M; to Joseph Reed, 6/12/80, Emmet 13, 599, NYPL. [4] Du Simitière Memoranda Books and Letter Book, LC; A119; A183, October. [5] A186; A183, February; to Jenings, 10/15/79, M. On the engraving see A5, 6. St. George Tucker wrote from Virginia in 1780 asking Theodorick Bland in Philadelphia for two copies of the engraving, one rolled up and sent, the other neatly glazed and framed and brought back personally (Tucker Papers, WM). For discrepant versions of the Trenton portrait and its copies compare A121 and A189. Still a third version was offered by Mrs. Titian Peale. According to her, Peale based the portrait on a picture of Washington he took at Valley Forge. The background details, she said, were supplied by Washington in conversation with Peale. See her MS "The Washington Portrait," M. [6] P4, 73ff. [7] P3, 34. [8] q. D4, 38; to Samuel Savage, 10/17/78, Savage Papers, MHS. On Arnold's attendance see G169, 185. [9] q. M1, 93; q. D10, 52. [10] D4, 39 and 141. [11] M13, 116; G206; Bland to Francis Tucker, 3/30/81, Tucker-Coleman Collection, WM; G41, 309. [12] A112. [13] G66, 332–42; A186, 176; q. G87, 227. The inflation was widespread. A "Daughter of Liberty" in Marblehead complained: "It's hard and cruel times to live,/ Takes thirty dollars to buy a sieve" (*A New Touch on the Times*, bds. n. pl., 1779). A skit entitled *The Downfall of Justice* (Danvers, 1777) depicted a profiteering Connecticut farmer feasting on geese and cider, singing a heavily ironic Brechtian song on the benefits of poverty, and allowing his black servant—"you black Bastard"—to lick spilled gravy off the floor. [14] P77, 32. [15] Benjamin Rush Papers, HSP; Gratz Collection,

HSP. See also her letter to James Reed, 6/9/80, NYHS. [16] G77, 52. [17] q. A186, 182. [18] A186, 170ff. [19] G163, II, 810–13; G213. [20] A184, entries for June. [21] G167, 75–8. [22] G27, 213; G122, 61. [23] D78; A3, 370; "Sung at a Meeting of the Old Church & King Club, New York," MS "Rhapsodies," LC; *On this Day of Renown* (N.Y., 1779). [24] A16, 29, and A180, 226; N14, 5/5/79; A22, 14. [25] G32, II, 9; q. D28, 197. [26] N14, 3/6/79; A107, 133; A180. [27] q. G21, 292; G36. [28] A3, 24 and 372; Oscar Sonneck autograph notes, LC Music Division. [29] G111; P77; P78, 50. [30] N14, 1/3/78 and 1/13/79. [31] D53; D75, ch. 3. [32] D75, 20; D10, 37. [33] D75; G32, II, 123–5. See also Henrietta Hobart, MS Commonplace Book dated 1779, NYHS. [34] D53; D10, 34. [35] D75; D28; q. M84, 66–7. [36] D53; D8; D28. A commonplace book kept by a Miss Berkeley (related to the bishop), containing much information about the Theatre Royal, is transcribed as Appendix A of D75. [37] N14, 1/3/78; G32, II, 391. [38] D75, 126; D28.

36. The André Affair

[1] Account based on G169 and G162. [2] (Hartford, 1781). For identification of this work as Prime's see P88. [3] Martha Bland [to St. George Tucker?], 10/8/80, Tucker-Coleman Collection, WM; A184, 84–5; A126. [4] P54, 315; to Ruth Barlow, 10/2/80, HCL. [5] *Major Andre [sic]* (bds. [Boston? 1780?]). [6] G169, 440. The text of "The Spy" in P10 breaks off within Act III; a still unpublished fragment (V, i) survives at UVL, dramatizing André's military trial.

37. The American School

[1] q. G102, 108. [2] A238, II, 288n.; A152, 18. [3] *The American Jest Book* (Phil., 1789); A180, 134; A166, 56; A31, 17. [4] q. A149, 913; B. F. Stevens, ed., *Facsimiles of Manuscripts in European Archives* (rpt. Wilmington, Del., 1970), #138. [5] A184, 103; q. A166, I, 316; A169, 68. [6] A156, 313. [7] A161; A162; A170. [8] A180, 177; A210, 12. [9] A180, 174–5; A217a. [10] A216, 29 (facsimile). [11] A180, 181–2 and 190. [12] A218, 27; to Captain Varick, 7/29/76, Emmet 9257, NYPL. [13] 2/22/77, John Trumbull (artist) Papers, CHS; q. A218, 39. Many soldiers resigned their commissions, either envious of prospering civilians or feeling, after the entry of the French, that their services in the field were no longer required. Nevertheless, punctilio seems to have run in Trumbull's family. His brother Joseph was commissary general of the army, a key post. He, too, threatened Congress with resignation, and involved Washington's intercession on his behalf. Congress raised his pay, but he resigned the post anyway, perhaps influenced by his brother's earlier resignation. G58, IV, 129–30 and 186. [14] A218, 46 and 51; to David Trumbull, 10/9/78, John Trumbull (artist) Papers, CHS. [15] A218, 52ff. One exercise, according to Jane Stuart, called for "the faithful representation of some object or other, casually presented to the eye—such as a piece of drapery thrown carelessly over a chair." A210, 14. [16] A218, 53; MS "Memoirs of Captain Landolph," John Trumbull (artist) Papers, CHS. [17] To Jonathan Trumbull, 9/12/80, Governor Jonathan Trumbull Papers, CSL.

[18] A221, 326; to Jonathan Trumbull, 10/23/81, Governor Jonathan Trumbull Papers, CSL. [19] A218, 69. [20] 10/3/78, John Trumbull (artist) Papers, CHS (photostat). [21] 5/10/81, John Trumbull (artist) Papers, CHS. [22] To Jonathan Trumbull, 10/23/81, Governor Jonathan Trumbull Papers, CSL; A218, 70–71. [23] q. A218, 72; G107, 49. [24] A180, 178, 181, 179. [25] q. A209, 30 and 38. [26] A210, 15. [27] A74, 188. [28] A180, 224; A74, 188; A203, 9. [29] William Back, biographical sketch of Brown, MMA; to "Miss Byles," 6/19/81, Byles-Brown Letters, MHS. See also James H. Stark, *The Loyalists of Massachusetts* (Boston, 1910). [30] To "Miss Byles," 8/5/82 and 9/10/81, Byles-Brown Letters, MHS. [31] After the king formally recognized the United States, however, Copley invited Watson to his studio and with "a master's touch, and I believe an American heart, attached to the ship the *stars and stripes. . . . the first American flag hoisted in old England.*" G64, 203. [32] q. A178, 297. The painting survives in four different versions and several sketches. See A92. The remarks in the text concern the version at the Boston Museum of Fine Arts. [33] q. A178, 267.

38. Billings and Law

[1] M71, 620; Jolley Allen, MS Minute Book, Allen Family Collection, AAS. [2] *The Motley Assembly, A Farce* (Boston, 1779); M11; Abbé Robin, *New Travels Through North-America* (Phil., 1783). [3] P35 and P37. [4] q. M29, 161. [5] G203, 339. [6] To David Trumbull, 4/26/79, John Trumbull (artist) Papers, CHS; q. M90, 75; M66 and M26. [7] M66, 50; M90. [8] M52, 233. [9] M11, 52. [10] M58, 785. [11] M30, ch. 1; M61 and M43; G196, II, 246. [12] q. M1, 59. [13] A197, A199, A204, FARL. [14] A70 and A30; G12, 213, n. 1. [15] N15, 2/4/78; D29; G40, II, 230. [16] Oscar Sonneck autograph notes, LC Music Division; P24, 481. [17] P67, P2, P21. [18] P22, 18. [19] P68, 116. [20] G121, III, 305; P96. [21] MS plan for *The Vision of Columbus*, pMSAM 1448(51), HCL; to Ruth Barlow, 9/23/80, HCL; P67, I, 147. [22] P67, II, 429; to Webb, 7/8/76, David Humphreys Papers, NHC; "An Ode to His Excellency Gen'rl W," Miscellaneous MSS, LC.

39. Charleston and Yorktown

[1] q. P80, 188; P52 and G124, 293; A69. [2] q. G187, 117. [3] G163, II, 1073; G73, 12. [4] q. P67, I, 151; (bds, n. pl., 1780); P63, 368. [5] q. G10, 227. [6] G173. See also J. B. Bury, *The Idea of Progress* (N.Y., 1932). [7] G195, 77 and 176. After the armies passed through Philadelphia, vandals (presumably Loyalists) broke into the Philadelphia State House and defaced Peale's full-length Washington. N50, 9/12/81. [8] G188. For the handbills see Evans nos. 43924-40. Ironically and unfortunately, far more information about the workings of this distinctly third-rate company has survived than about the workings of Douglass' far better company. Wall kept playbills and newspaper clippings, and annotated them with many precious details concerning performers and performances. The bulk of this material is now at NYHS and MdHS. Wall and his actors also drew up what amount to the first American theatre contracts, providing fines for specific

infringements by either actors or management. If the infringements named in the articles of agreement were actually committed, Wall's players ignored or overslept rehearsals, showed up late for performances, wore their stage costumes home, used the theatre barber to powder their hair in civilian life, and deserted the company after reaping the profits of a personal benefit night. The contracts are at MdHS. [9] MS "Petition of Sundries in Baltimore," C. E. French Collection, MHS. The Society dates this lengthy petition "[1778?]" but the actual date is almost certainly 1781, just before Wall and Lindsay opened their theatre. [10] M27, 60. [11] G195, 223. [12] G189, 105; P52, 80–83; G195. For the fullest account of music at the surrender see M80, 344–9.

40. Philadelphia

[1] *A Poem, . . . by a Young Lady* (bds. Boston, 1782); G174, 398; G58, IX, 408. For other poems and celebrations following Yorktown see P34, I, 165; G42, I, 50; N50, 10/81; N51, 1/8/82. [2] P4. [3] N50, 12/19/81 and 2/27/82. [4] N14, 1/2 and 26/82; M20. [5] G167, 17; D75, 85; *New-York, Theatre, 1782* [published reckoning of receipts] (bds. N.Y., 1782, copy at NYPL). [6] To George Clinton, 6/6/83, Du Simitière Memoranda Books, LC; G173; N50, 1/2/82; G187, 63. [7] q. G190, 251; A186, 189. [8] q. P86, 204; *America Independent; An Oratorial Entertainment* (Phil., 1781), later republished as *The Temple of Minerva.* [9] G58, IX, 420; N14, 1/5/82. [10] N50, 1/9/82; q. G190, 254. See also D1, 13. [11] N50, 1/16/82. [12] Untitled poem enclosed in letter to Colonel [Jeremiah?] Wadsworth, 4/24/82, Jonathan Trumbull, Jr., Papers, CHS; q. G190, 255. To commemorate the moment when he returned the standards, Congress presented Humphreys with a sword, in whose grip was stamped a liberty cap. See P67, I, 239, and Miscellaneous MSS, LC. [13] The idea of using a warrior and a goddess to support the crest seems to have come from Francis Hopkinson. See the folder "US, Great Seal of," LC. [14] A113, A112, A84. [15] A112, 42n. Later interpretations of the seal differed, embroidering Thomson's intention. See for instance the long gloss in N7, 8/27/85, which notes that "white signifies purity and innocence; red, hardiness and valour; blue, the colour of the chief, signifies vigilance, perseverance, and justice." [16] A103; P19; A113. [17] N50, 5/22/82; G92, IV, 214; G28, 545. [18] Du Simitière Memoranda Books and Letter Book, LC; A34, 318; A25. The engravings ran into many other difficulties. To avoid a single, catastrophic loss, the sets were sent from Paris in batches. Many were seized in naval captures, lost in transit, or mistakenly delivered to other places. The Paris press advertised the engraving of Gouverneur Morris as "Le Gouverneur Morris." [19] While in Maryland, Henry also offered the *Lecture on Heads.* For some reason he advertised and perhaps gave it in Spanish. The playbill promised that "El Sr. Henrique de la Compañia Americana de Comediantes" would appear at "la Casa de Comedias" performing, among other things, an "Oracion funebre del famoso Comediante Ingles Garrick"—entrance "DOS PESOS." The playbill is at MdHS. [20] q. D10, 158f. [21] G58, X, 48. [22] G48, 278. [23] G48, 278–82; N50, 7/31/82; G205. [24] G58, X, 50 and 52. [25] M30, 37; P21, 77; P2, 159. [26] A182, to Benjamin Rush, 12/82, and to Joseph Brewer, 1/15/83. [27] A189, 17; to Edmund Jenings, 7/3/83, M. [28] N50, 6/19/82 and 7/3/82. [29] q. P44, 188; P18. [30] N50, 12/11/82.

41. 1783: Peace Returning

[1] q. G174, 438; G58, X, 197. [2] N50, 5/14/83; *Grand Exhibition* (bds. Phil., 1783); N47, 12/27/83. [3] A182, to General George Weedon, undated, and to William Mercer, 2/21/84. [4] N7, 6/9/84. This and the description that follows are based on accounts of the rebuilt arch, which presumably closely resembled the one destroyed by fire. See also N50, 5/12 and 19/84. [5] N5, 9/30/84; M32; P35, 94; (Phil., 1783). [6] *To Perpetuate the Memory of Peace* (Phil., 1784); *A Poem Composed July 4, 1783* (bds. n. pl., 1783); P48, 193; David Humphreys, *The Glory of America* (Phil., 1783); P34, II, 13. Perhaps the two most interesting treatments of the Peace are the Miltonic epic "America Delivered an Heroic Poem" and the five-act masque "Columbinus," by Nathaniel Tucker. I have omitted them from discussion because, although Tucker spent some time in America, he was born in Bermuda and living, at the time of writing, in Malton, England. Moreover, he published neither work and completed only one and a half books of the first. "America Delivered" is the most direct attempt by any poet to create the Revolution in Miltonic terms. Indeed Tucker undertook to rewrite *Paradise Lost* with American components. Parliament acts as Milton's infernal council, Satan arrives not at Eden but in Philadelphia, and the Archangel Michael explains Good, Evil, and Chaos not to Adam but to President Joseph Reed of Congress. The poem begins:

> FREEDOM triumphant, and her sacred cause
> With renovated might on western plains
> Asserted and assail'd, what time defeat
> At Saratoga of the British host
> Beleaguer'd, from the parent state at last
> Had call'd forth terms of peace, then in her strength
> Scorn'd by America as deem'd insidious,
> Not honorable or safe, till the discomfiture
> And final overthrow of proud Cornwallis
> With all his veteran legions, victor once
> Now vanquish'd, had the throne of heaven-born liberty
> Immoveable establish'd in the west
> Sing heavenly Muse. . . .

In "Columbinus," Tucker used not Milton but the whole Shakespearean world as a vehicle for tracing the course of the Revolution. With its blank verse and many echoes of Shakespeare's major tragedies, the technique resembles West's use of Roman history and Dwight's later use of the Old Testament. Tucker succeeded, too, in keeping the complex political significations clear while writing a not-unaffecting domestic tragedy, a drama of loyalty and betrayal concerning old Albion's estrangement from his son Columbinus. "Columbinus" has recently been edited by Lewis Leary and published in *The Complete Published Poems of Nathaniel Tucker.* [7] M80, 370; G58, X, 285; G127. [8] G58, X, 302; P34, III, 167; to Peale, 6/15/83, M. [9] A111, A42, A119. [10] A121, III, 892; A189, 223. [11] *A Poem, . . . by a Young Lady* (bds. Boston, 1782); G215c; N50, 9/5/81; N50, 5/19/84. The first recorded use of the phrase "Father of his Country" seems to be in a letter to

Washington from Henry Knox on 3/19/87. [12] Enlightenment monarchs such as Charles III of Spain also came to be depicted as rustic hunters or farmers, praised not for mettle but for kindness and family feelings. See Michael Levy, *Painting at Court* (N.Y., 1971). The emphasis on Washington's paternal role reflects contemporary theories of the affections, which postulated hierarchies of love whereby marriage leads to patriotism, and patriotism to love for all mankind, so that "extreme humanity" is but an expanded version of domestic contentment. See N37, 148–9, and N4, 1/79 (p. 19). Only Loyalist poets said anything about Washington's less fatherly side. Burgoyne, for example, deplored disciplinary flogging; Washington urged Congress to increase the biblical maximum of thirty-nine strokes to five hundred strokes. Congress refused. In being assimilated to Whig neoclassical ideals, too, some of Washington's deficiencies were transformed. His occasional procrastination drew much criticism in military circles; but historicists turned it to account by imagining him as Fabius, the shrewdly dawdling general who lets the enemy wear itself out: "By slow degrees to make their forces less,/ And by delaying gain the wish'd success" (N50, 7/9/83). [13] G192, XXX, 5. [14] G58, X, 324 and 316. [15] A186, 201; N50, 11/26/83. [16] A123, 378. See also A31, A40, A122. Wright also made a numismatic bas-relief profile of Washington with Roman features and a laurel wreath, now at the Winterthur Museum. [17] This and the next paragraph drawn from A180, 150ff., A118, and D27, ch. 1. [18] G190, 310. [19] D10, D49, D28. [20] *Order of Exhibition* (bds. N.Y., 1783); N11, 12/3/83; N50, 12/31/83 and 1/7/84. [21] N50, 12/10/83. For other details of Washington's homeward trek see G170, 498ff., and G15, 13.

42. Commencement: 1783

[1] William Smith, *An Account of Washington College* (Phil., 1784), 29 and 40.

43. The Art World

[1] To Abraham Beekman, 3/10/83, Beekman Papers, Box 17, NYHS. [2] A22, 19–20. [3] D63; M65. [4] A6, 46; A3, 47. [5] P95a; A94; A86; A246c. [6] A3, 47 and 4; A5, 14; A17. [7] A106; A26, 295. [8] q. A226, 5; A186, 222; A83, 196; A180, 318. [9] A184. [10] To Washington, 4/19/85, Emmet 775, NYPL; G58, X, 451; G56, II, 370; to Washington, 10/10/86, British Literary Misc., HSP. Washington himself liked the portrait enough to commission Pine to paint Martha Washington's four grandchildren. See A114. [11] q. A67, 83; A120. [12] A182, to Benjamin Harrison, [7?]/84; q. A120, 187; A251, 6–7; to Washington, 7/17/85, HCL. [13] A120, 200. [14] The account that follows based on G56, II, 419ff. [15] G58, XI, 51. [16] A120, 205; G146, VIII, 671. [17] A117. Peale found more harmonious companions for this rather raffish Washington in the near-copy of the Princeton portrait commissioned by the state of Maryland in 1784–5 (Annapolis State House), where he replaced the dying Mercer with Lafayette and Tilghman on an elevation observing the Yorktown entrenchments. [18] A182, to Chase, 11/23/84; to Dr. David Ramsay, 2/2[2?]/87; to Thomas Mifflin, 3/29/84; to Carmichael, 9/23/86, M. [19] A189, 8; A182, 2/21/86;

Alonzo J. May Collection, MdHS, which cites an annotation on a 1784 playbill.
[20] A182, to Weedon, 3/7/86; A57, D39, and A184, 79. [21] N47, 1/4/87; *A Descriptive CATALOGUE of MR. PEALE'S Exhibition* (bds. Phil., [1786?]); A184, 83. [22] A182, to Bordley, 7/13/85. [23] A3, 11; D51, 188. [24] A182, to Weedon, 7/13/85; MS Account Book, APS. [25] While many painters advertised having studied with West or Copley, only one—Charles Peale Polk—seems to have advertised studying with "the celebrated Mr. Peale of Philadelphia." N16, 7/14/85. [26] N7, 12/14/85; N47, 4/24/87. [27] N9, 5/23/86; N35, 3/87; N31, 11/87. [28] G64, 137; A180, 136. [29] N9, 5/23/86; A3, 385; N9, 5/23/86. [30] G177, III, 150; G39, II, 104. [31] A178; A45; A83, 203. [32] N7, 9/8/84; A180, 117. [33] A239, 242; 6/15/83, M; G80, III, 20–21, which almost certainly refers to West. [34] A182, 8/25/83 and 12/10/83. [35] N5, 9/23/84; A178; A166, 48. [36] A250; Jacob Duché to unnamed sister, 6/5/83, Hopkinson Papers, HSP; A239, 481; A209, 44. [37] Warren Papers, MHS; q. A225, 292. [38] To his aunts, 7/86, Byles Family Papers, MHS. [39] A233; A225; to his aunts, 6/6/83 and 7/28/84, Byles-Brown Letters, MHS; A22, 26. [40] To Benjamin Franklin, 11/9/84, APS. William Franklin goes on to explain that he understood West to mean not only that Stuart's likenesses were perfect but also that "his colouring did not change; a fault common to some of the first Painters in this Country—& particularly to Sr Joshua." [41] A215, 83; A180, 185. [42] A209, 48. [43] A210, 19; A209, 65. [44] 2/5/84, HSP; A209, 66. [45] A180, 67. [46] A180, 70 and 261. [47] A241, 13. [48] A218, 82. Discouragement also came from Edmund Burke, who had helped secure Trumbull's release from prison. Burke advised him to study architecture, since the new republic would have more need of public buildings than of paintings. Trumbull later felt that he should have taken Burke's advice. *Ibid.* [49] 10/13/83, B. F. Stevens, ed., *Facsimiles of Manuscripts in European Archives* (rpt. Wilmington, Del., 1970), #2107. [50] To Governor Jonathan Trumbull, 3/10/84, John Trumbull (artist) Papers, CHS. [51] A239; A218; to Jonathan Trumbull, Jr., 6/6/84, John Trumbull (artist) Papers, CHS. [52] 11/23/84, John Trumbull (artist) Papers, CHS. [53] G84, 578; see note 52. [54] A218; to David Trumbull, 4/17/84, John Trumbull (artist) Papers, CHS. [55] To Jonathan Trumbull, Jr., 12/14/85, John Trumbull Papers, YUL. [56] To Andrew Elliott, 3/4/86, Andrews-Eliot Papers, MHS; A218, 90–91; to David Trumbull, 1/31/86, John Trumbull (artist) Papers, CHS. Sizer lists the *Bunker's Hill* as having been completed in March 1786; but Trumbull's letter to his brother David (1/31/86, above) notes that "my first picture of the Death of Warren at Bunker's Hill is finish'd." [57] A221. [58] A178, 309. [59] A220, 29. [60] To Andrew Elliott, 3/4/86, Andrews-Eliot Papers, MHS; to Jonathan Trumbull, Jr., 12/14/85, John Trumbull Papers, YUL. [61] A89; A218, 92; q. A31, 40. [62] G146, X, 250. [63] A218, 146; P67, I, 235. [64] To Jonathan Trumbull, Jr., 2/27/87, John Trumbull Papers, YUL.

44. Musical Life

[1] G67, I, 90. [2] G67, II, 168; q. M9, 112; M80, 402, and M50. Phile later composed the best of the several marches dedicated to Washington. [3] M72; N16, 11/4/84. [4] G175, 123; q. D2, 92; N16, 10/7/84. [5] N7, 9/17/85; A3, 368; M46, 79;

A3, 363; M46, 79–81. [6] G91, 21–2, 31. [7] M11; M3, 130; M14 and M46; q. M3, 79. A trifling but heated quarrel between Brown and Bentley perhaps explains why the concerts were soon held on alternate weeks, first as "The Bentley Concert," then as "The German Concert," and then abandoned altogether until the arrival of Reinagle. Francis Hopkinson satirized the struggle: "The parties are enraged— *Tweedledum* [Bentley] seizes the diapason pipe of an organ—*Tweedledee* [Brown] defends himself with a silver mounted flute. . . ." P34, II, 144. [8] M10 and M11; M88, 352; q. M73, 74. [9] D28; M3, 79ff. For programs of the concerts see N47 for 1787, esp. 1/10 and 24, 2/21, and 3/8. The desire to hear sophisticated European music seems not to have been matched by a desire to buy it. In 1785 Hopkinson returned to London a batch of music that had been sent for sale in Philadelphia, observing that it contained "too great a proportion of expensive Concert Music and unknown Authors." The dealer, Robert Bremner, told Hopkinson that such works "ought to be seen in your new world." See Bremner to Hopkinson, 2/5/85, Redwood Transcripts (MS 1530.1), MdHS. [10] M46, 58; "W. Jackson" to Otho Williams, 7/20/84, Williams Papers (MS 908), MdHS. Mrs. Robert Morris considered buying the instrument. [11] N22, 10/87; N50, 7/9/83. As late as 1792, the New York firm of Dodds & Claus boasted how their instruments could "stand the effect of our climate, which imported instruments never do." M84. [12] Most of the earlier Episcopal organists continued to play in the postwar period. The distinguished Charleston organist Benjamin Yarnold stayed abroad during the war but returned to St. Michael's Church in 1784. Peter Valton also continued to play in Charleston. Copley's stepbrother Peter Pelham served as keeper of the Williamsburg jail during the war and was charged with supervising British prisoners, some of whom escaped; Pelham moved to Richmond when it became the state capital. The Williamsburg instrument maker Benjamin Bucktrout, it might be added, joined the British army during the war. See M39, 136–9; M72; "The Public Gaol," TS Looseleaf Notebook, CW. [13] G40, III, 162; q. M71, 616; G92, 6th Ser., IV, 291. [14] M90, 132; M3; M71, 620. [15] M32; M71, 614–15; *Musica Spiritualis* (Boston, 1782). [16] N5, 7/9/85; N7, 8/20/85 and 10/8/85; N7, 11/30/85. [17] N1, 9/8/84; M88, 352; q. M18, 168–9. [18] The programs appear in N6, 1/9/86 and 1/15/87. For the 1787 performance the committee voted to exclude from the charity persons "reduced to poverty by Idleness, or other vicious habits," those already supported in the Alms House, and those "who have always been poor." Benjamin Stillman to "Rev. Parker," 1/18/87, MS letters catalogued as "Boston Musical Society. 1787," LC Music Division. [19] N48, 1/23/86; q. M3, 279. [20] Noah Webster, MS Diary, NYPL; N47, 4/10/87. [21] *Plan of Mr. Adgate's Institution* (bds. Phil., 1785); N60, 4/3/88. [22] M12, 88; M30. [23] G88, 92; N10, 10/27/85; D28, 247. [24] N29, 3/16/86. The ode was published in Read's *American Musical Magazine*. [25] M52, 302; G52, 244. [26] q. G87, 334; G40, III, 102. [27] M45, M43, M22. [28] M1, 178–93. [29] Notes by Lucy Swan in George Hood, MS Scrapbook, BPL Music Division; M67, 405; MS "Memoir of Timothy Swan," Timothy Swan Papers, AAS. No evidence seems to exist for attributing to Swan, as Evans does, a 1785 collection entitled *The Federal Harmony*. Although Swan's 1801 *New England Harmony* went through eight editions, his daughter felt that his tunebooks never became popular, because the music was too difficult and her father was of a too-retiring nature, "while others were publishing their own books, and going about with them, and introducing them into their own schools"—a sidelight on the necessarily aggressive personalities of successful tunesmiths like Billings. [30] M35; M44, 60. See also the MS notes on Read by his son in Hood's scrapbook, above, and Read's handstitched MS Music Book, dated 1777, at NHC. [31] q. M52, 142. [32] q. M11, 66. Selby also hoped to publish his major works in a series of volumes entitled *Apollo and the Muses*. The project floundered in 1791 after two issues, which contained part of his interesting 'Christmas Cantata,' *Matchless is Thy Form*. This work has recently been edited and published by David P. McKay (St. Louis, 1973). Selby's organ voluntary is printed in M37. [33] N29, 5/17/87; Jocelin to Swan, 6/9 and 27/86, Timothy Swan Papers, AAS. [34] N7, 1/26/85; Alex Ely to Swan, 7/86, Timothy Swan Papers, AAS. Five or six earlier collections used movable type, several of them in German. Thomas was the first to use movable type for a collection of mainstream polyphonic psalmody, however. [35] N31, 4/88. [36] *Institutes*, Bk. III, ch. 20. [37] G68, 110. [38] q. M87, 373.

45. The Literary Scene

[1] N7, 1/12/85. [2] *Tom Bolin* (bds. Boston, 1786). The translator of the unpublished *Electra* was the former Loyalist Robert Proud; see Proud Papers, HSP. A description of an American attempt to translate Young's *Night Thoughts* into Latin appears in Thomas Cushing to William Bentley, 5/8/86, MS Correspondence of Rev. William Bentley, AAS. [3] G214, 99. By 1798 the number had quintupled. [4] P61, 582. [5] *Bell's Address to Every Free-Man* (bds. Phil., 1784). [6] G92, 6th Ser., IV, 268. See also N32, 218. [7] P41; G192, XXX, 8. [8] N31, 9/86. [9] G19, 259. [10] M90, 228. [11] q. P2, 164 and 166. On the copyright see also P75; G53, 2 and 9; M30; M90. [12] 2/88; P92, 9; N33, 38. [13] 3/31/86, AP, reel 367. [14] G57, 37; G78, 390. [15] N50, 2/84 *passim*; q. Henry Hatfield, *Goethe* (N.Y., 1963), p. 37; G47, 253. [16] q. P61, 578. [17] N19, 7/84; N7, 4/28/84; to Timothy Dwight, 4/4/86, AP, reel 113. [18] *A Poem, on the Prospects of America* (bds. [Providence?], 1787). [19] 4/4/86, AP, reel 113; P43, 25. [20] N53, 1/16/86; *The Columbian Magazine. Plan and Conditions* (bds. Phil., 1786). [21] P92, 9; Barlow to Governor William Livingston, 7/21/85, MHS. [22] *Lyric Works of Horace; Poem, on the Happiness of America; Poems of Arouet.* [23] G36; N7, 12/17/85. [24] G116, 239; G32, I, 268; P34, 55; P74, 183; G113, 205. [25] P57, 31. [26] N31, 10/86; N27, 4/20/86. [27] N31, 10/86. [28] G146, I, 76; G25, 94-5. [29] N27, 7/85. [30] N31, beginning 6/87. [31] P69, 147, n. 48. It was serialized in N31, beginning 10/87. [32] G95; the *History* was serialized in the *New-York Magazine*, beginning 9/90. [33] q. P27, 22. [34] *An Essay on the Beauties and Excellencies of Painting, Music, and Poetry* (Hartford, 1774); to John Trumbull, 4/27/85, AP, reel 107. [35] G40, III, 274. [36] The discussion of the poem which follows is a revised and abbreviated version of the discussion in my *Timothy Dwight* (N.Y., 1969). I am obliged to Twayne Publishers, Inc., for allowing me to reprint some of this material. [37] G92, 6th Ser., IV, 249. [38] G32, I, 223; *The Grand Exploits Of one of his Majesty's Generals* (bds. n. pl., 1777). [39] P23, 466; G84, 407; to John Quincy Adams, 3/19/86, AP, reel 367. [40] G23, 383;

G68, 162; N42, 3/6/84. [41] G4, 424-5. [42] 9/28/86; q. G26, 418; G35, xxxv. [43] G26, 68. Indeed the virtue of the postwar period became in some persons more puritan than the Puritans themselves. In 1788 Ebenezer Hazard discussed with Jeremy Belknap the possibility of publishing John Winthrop's *Journal*. He noted that the Latin phrase *"An contactus et fricatio"*—apparently relating to cases of sodomy and bestiality that had come to light in the Plymouth colony—would have to be suppressed as too indecent for the public eye. G92, III, 87. [44] G120; N1(P), 5/1/78; to Governor John Trumbull, 4/17/84, John Trumbull (artist) Papers, CHS. [45] G92, II, 129; N48, 4/17/87. [46] A few pages of what seem to be a Worcester edition turned up in the marbled endpapers, ironically, of an 1807 *Essay on the Life of . . . George Washington*. *Fanny Hill* was advertised by several American booksellers. See Robert Vail, TS "Facetiae Americana," NYPL Rare Book Room. [47] To Andrew Elliott, 10/16/84, Andrews-Eliot Papers, MHS; "Epistle from Dr. Dwight. . . ," P68. [48] G123, 83; *Advertisement* (bds. [N.Y.? mid-1780's?]), copy at NYPL; q. P81, 61-2. [49] q. G22, 238; N31, 4/88; N50, 4/14/84; *The Power of Sympathy* (Boston, 1789). [50] P26; q. G26, 422; G92, 6th Ser., IV, 286. [51] Warville noted in 1788 a great deal of card playing in Boston and considered it a natural diversion "for a people who have no theaters" although "very unfortunate in a republican state." G19, 90. [52] G152; G93; G120, 619. [53] N31, 1/87; *New-England Mercury*, 10/31/85; q. D41, 450; q. M27, 62; N47, 1/8 and 9/87. [54] "W. Jackson" to Otho Williams, 2/27/84, Williams Papers (MS 908), MdHS. [55] N7, 7/16/85 and 9/10/85. Eaton seems to have managed several performances before the Pantheon closed in September 1785. [56] G88, 333; N27, 7/85; G4, 507. This and the following account of Shays' Rebellion are based largely on G104, 103ff. [57] P67, I, 380. See also P90. [58] P67, I, 341. [59] G30, 82 *et passim*. [60] N53, 1/12/86. [61] (bds. n. pl., 1787); G40, III, 214; N29, 10/5/86. [62] G28, II, 543; N48, 1/23/86; N42, 8/7/84. [63] N27, 4/84. [64] P67, I, 341. On Humphreys' manner of addressing Washington see for instance his letter of 5/19/84, David Humphreys Papers, NHC. [65] Adams to Barlow, 4/4/86, AP, reel 113; q. P2, 206. [66] G146, II, 473. [67] G30, G103. [68] The way of thinking in these poems developed in the nineteenth century into the social sciences. See G135, especially 9-44. [69] Webster's copy at NYPL; q. M10, 42-3. [70] P15, P106.

46. The Theatre

[1] N12, 4/26/83. [2] D22, 195-6 and 187; compare N7, 8/17/85, and N16, 8/25/85. [3] D10, 183. Reluctantly again, I have quoted Henry's important speech from Seilhamer, to my knowledge the only extant source. [4] Hallam to Thomas Bradford, 11/15/[85?], Thomas Bradford Collection, HSP; N48, 3/29/87; D22, 196; D39. [5] Williams to Knox, 6/28/86, Williams Papers (MS 908), MdHS; D15, 83. [6] Hallam to Thomas Bradford, 8/31/[86?], Thomas Bradford Collection, HSP; indenture signed by Douglass and Hallam, 4/85, *ibid.* [7] q. D68, 168; G80, III, 54-5. So popular was the play that Robert Bell, the Philadelphia bookseller, passed through Virginia using copies of it as currency, asking "Who would not prefer Sheridan's *Sterling*, to the counterfeit creations of Congress. . . ." G28, I, 337, n. 7.

[8] q. D28, 244; John Henry to Thomas Bradford, 12/11/85, Thomas Bradford Collection, HSP. [9] q. D28, 258; N48, 4/23/87. [10] M36, 11 and 17–18; M89. [11] D22, D8, D39. St. George Tucker saw *The Poor Soldier* performed during the 1786 New York season and wrote: "I never saw a better presentation. The characters were all well filled and well supported—Mrs. Morris shone in Kathleen, Mr. Wignell top'd the part of Darby. There was a beautiful Scene in which a fall of Water was most admirably represented. Your Mama & Mrs Peachy declared they were quite sick at the sight, it was so perfectly natural." MS journal of 1786 trip to New York, Tucker-Coleman Collection, WM. See also N48, 4/12/87. The national types represented in *The Poor Soldier* and in similar postwar plays became sensitive issues, however, in a nation experiencing a large, and to some a threatening, wave of immigration. Mathew Carey published an attack on *The Poor Soldier* for representing "an Irish coward." P41, 17. New York newspapers disputed for several weeks whether the play insulted the French allies in its treatment of the French barber Bagatelle, forcing Hallam and Henry to revise the part, and, when they did so, bringing denunciations of their "servile compliance." See N48, 3/24, 26, 30/87; 4/6 and 7/87. [12] M51; D10, 168; q. D28, 233. [13] M24, 60; M67, 267; (Phil., 1784). [14] N7, 8/10/85; A3, 25–6. [15] D2, 110; N48, 4/29/88, 6/2/87, 4/4/87. [16] D63, 9–12. The company's itinerary can be followed in N9, N7, and N16. [17] Mrs. Ryan's ad is quoted in Alonzo J. May Collection, MdHS. The society also owns a copy of the *Pennsylvania Magazine* for 1775 in which is pasted an invitation to Dennis Ryan's funeral on March 9, 1786. [18] D18; N53, 7/6 and 13/86. [19] D28, 263; N10, 9/19/85. [20] D10; D58; N16, 9/13/87. [21] Noah Webster MS Diary, NYPL; D63. [22] N10, 2/2/86; N47, 1/25/87; D45, 56; D51, 175. [23] N22, 8/87; G52, 142. [24] Richard Randolph to his mother, 4/19/85, Tucker-Coleman Papers, WM; N12, 6/16/87. [25] D18; D63, 36ff.; D50, 429; G86, 48. [26] N10, 10/20/85; q. D51, 208; N10, 1/23/86. [27] N50, 3/10/84 and 2/18/84. [28] N48, 6/2/87 and 5/25/87; D28, 259; N48, 2/25/86. [29] q. D51, 208; q. M24, 70; q. D2, 95; N10, 10/10/85. [30] N7, 8/10/85 and 10/15/85; N48, 4/6/87. [31] N48, 1/12/86; N55, 1/12/86; N48, 2/25/86. [32] q. D8, 111; N48, 1/11/86; q. D2, 91. [33] N55, 1/26/86; q. D58, 24; P74, 227. [34] q. G89, 55; N48, 1/12/86. [35] q. G120, 619; N47, 2/21/84. [36] N50, 2/25/84 and 2/11/84; N10, 1/23/86. [37] N50, 2/25/84; N10, 3/2/86. [38] N10, 1/16/86; N50, 2/25/84. [39] N48, 1/12/86. [40] N50, 3/17/84; N12, 6/23/87. [41] N50, 2/18/84. [42] N47, 1/31/87; q. D51, 190; N47, 2/14/84. [43] N50, 2/18/84 and 3/24/84; N47, 2/14/84; N48, 4/18/87. [44] N48, 1/14/86; N50, 3/24/84; D51, 218. [45] N10, 2/16/86. [46] D58, 26; q. M50, 121; N10, 4/6/86. [47] G67, 380. On the politics of the debate see G127. [48] N10, 2/86 *passim*. A summary of the debates appears in D8, 105–9. See also D33, 362ff. [49] Hallam enlisted the aid of Judge Alexander James Dallas (later an important political figure in Philadelphia), whom he had persuaded to come to America from Jamaica. A literary man, Dallas wrote prologues and epilogues for actor-friends in the Company, and in 1787 took over the editorship of the *Columbian Magazine*. Apparently several months before the legislative debate, he drew up for Hallam a memorial to send to the Assembly, proposing that the Company pay the state £1,000 a year for the use of a theatre within Philadelphia, and that it perform under "proper regulations" such as "may

tend to the cultivation of morality, and good manners." In exchange for a license, Hallam thus offered to fatten the purse of government and to submit to censorship—an earlier version of Wayne's bill. See N33, 50; G90, 12–14; *Minutes of the Second Session of the Ninth General Assembly* (Phil., 1785). [50] G197, XII (1785–87), 320–321. [51] D73, 140; D47, 87; D50; D73; M39, 360. [52] D4, 42; M14, 74; N47, 1/25/87. The army surgeon Johann Schoepf went to hear a 'concert' by Ryan's company in Philadelphia in 1783, before Hallam's return but while the earlier anti-theatre laws were in force. The 'concert' turned out to be a performance of *Douglas*: "The music was as customary," he found, "and the actors and actresses came on with a bit of paper in their hands which they did not look at and finally threw away, but for the rest played their rôles as formerly." G67, 382. [53] N7, 8/17/85; Henry to Thomas Bradford, 12/11/86, Thomas Bradford Collection, HSP. [54] D50, 423; D8, 111. [55] D11, 1–26 *passim*. The quotes from *The Contrast* which follow are from the Dunlap Society edition (N.Y., 1887). [56] The Jonathan character appears as early as Peter Folger's *Looking Glass for the Times* (1676), where he represents the New England husbandman; during the war, 'Jonathan' was a popular Loyalist nickname for patriots or for continental troops. See G215e, G33, D24. [57] N16, 11/15/87; N22, 5/87; q. D11, 55; D10, 233. [58] N9, 5/23/86. [59] q. D10, 233; M36, 12. [60] M11, 106; G65, 35; G47, 133; G28, I, 324. [61] P16, 197 and 42; N53, 7/10/86; N50, 3/9/85; N50, 4/11/87; P16, 53 and 42. [62] N35, 1/88. [63] N63, 6/4/89. [64] Among Du Simitière's last plans was a multimedia depiction of American history using medals, seals, coins, devices, statues, monuments, and badges, and including Peale's triumphal arch. His effects, sold by lottery at his house on Arch Street, included books on drawing by Dürer, Leonardo, and others; a large collection of broadsides, newspapers, and pamphlets from which he intended to compile a history of the Revolution; coins and curiosities; a portfolio of drawings and maps; and more than a thousand prints—clues to what the presence of Du Simitière and of other immigrant Europeans meant to the country's Rising Glory. See his LC Memoranda Books and the broadside catalogue for the lottery, *For Sale at Public Vendue on . . . the 10th Day of March* (Phil., 1784). [65] N16, 7/15/84; q. M12, 93; G89, 121; P41, 23.

47. The Constitution

[1] q. G15, 159. [2] M30; P67; M3, 131. [3] N31, 7/87; M24, 74; D33, 363. [4] N47, 9/7/87; D1, 30 and n. During the Convention the *Columbian Magazine* used for its frontispiece a portrait of Shakespeare, the first engraved in America. In Philadelphia in 1788 also appeared the first volume of Shakespeare criticism published in America, William Richardson's *A Philosophical Analysis . . . of some of Shakespeare's Remarkable Characters*. See D82. [5] A182, 2/22/87 and 5/12/87; q. A97, 181. [6] N47, 1/9/87. [7] A182, 8/86 to 2/87 *passim* and N48, 3/12/87. [8] A186, 219; A182, to Bordley, 12/5/86. [9] A182, to Washington, 9/27/87. [10] G199, I, 26off. [11] A182, to Washington, 5/26/87; A119; A6, 21. [12] G109, 438 and 632. [13] G4, 515; G109, 477 and 620. In May 1790 a broader federal statute was passed, immediately copyrighting *The Contrast*, Mercy Warren's *Poems*, and David Hum-

phreys' *Miscellaneous Works.* See D68. [14] G109, 659. [15] G143, 77 and 403; G142, nos. 6 and 15. See also G81e. [16] A147, 467 (see also A180, 102); q. D28, 266; P34, II, 283 and 320. [17] q. P81, 221; *Four Excellent NEW SONGS* (N.Y., 1788). [18] G44; Hopkinson Papers, HSP. [19] q. P34, 417. [20] G48, 470. [21] G40, III, 321-2. [22] q. A116, 66, which see for a discussion of the French revolutionaries' use of festivals, and possible American influence upon them. [23] *Four . . . SONGS* (see note 17). [24] A184, 126. Peale lamented, however, that two guineas was "all that they were able to pay me for my trouble in having the transparent scenes exhibited at Baltimore." A183. [25] G44, 14; P81, 243. [26] q. A192, 9; A17, 123; N35, 10/89. [27] q. M9, 68; P81, 251; N29, 7/10/88; N51, 7/14/88. [28] A183, June 30ff., and A184, July 2. Peale watched the procession from his house, together with his brother James, the engraver Trenchard, and the painter Matthew Pratt. See A183. [29] M80, 404. The account in the next six paragraphs is based largely on P34 and G44. See also *Order of Procession* (bds. Phil., 1788). [30] The costume was wrought by Benjamin Franklin's daughter, who fitted Durang in her father's presence. M36, 9. [31] *Order of Procession* (bds. N.Y., 1788); *Ode for the Federal Procession* (bds. N.Y., 1788); N10, 8/5/88. Webster said that he found the parade "Very brilliant, but fatiguing." MS Diary, NYPL. [32] q. G45, 46. [33] G44, 33ff.

48. Late Developments

[1] q. M2, 113. More grandly and less accurately, Hopkinson in his printed dedicatory letter to Washington took credit for being "the first Native of the United States who has produced a Musical Composition." His meaning can only be guessed. Perhaps he did not regard Billings and the psalmodists as musicians; or perhaps he meant that his was the first music published by a native "of the United States," i.e., the first published by a native American since the adoption of the Constitution. In what follows I have unfortunately not been able to consult Irving Lowens' *Bibliography of Songsters Printed in America before 1821,* which appeared just as this history went to press. [2] N16, 11/13/88; M3. [3] M77; M67, which see for a listing of other magazine essays on music. [4] P103, 15. [5] 11/89; (Litchfield, Conn., 1789); N31, 11/89. [6] Margaret Hutchinson, unaddressed letter of 4/25/89, Mascarene Family Papers, MHS (film). [7] Apparently some other Boston families also tried to suppress the novel, believing themselves to be defamed in it. A satire on their efforts is the anonymous *Occurrences of the Times* (Boston, 1789), whose main character threatens to blow out the brains of the author of *"The Trumpets of Nature."* [8] The "Young Ladies" listened, too. Students at Bennington, Vermont, turned the novel into a verse play, *The Fatal Effects of Seduction,* and performed it at quarter-day exercises in 1789. [9] A3, 5; A203, 35. [10] N48, 4/6/87. [11] D4, 45; G198, XI, 342-3; D33, 363. [12] D10, II, 252. Unable to locate the original of this recommendation, I have, reluctantly, copied the text in Seilhamer. [13] N57, 2/9 and 10/89. [14] N57, 2/17/89. [15] N57, 2/19/89. [16] D33, 368. [17] q. D33, 366; N57, 2/21/89. [18] N58, 2/4, 10, 16/89. [19] N57, 2/18, 28, 14, 19/89. [20] MS Petition, Gallatin 1789 #3, NYHS. [21] q. D33, 368-9. [22] D51, 237. [23] D31, 60; Adams to Gerry, 7/29/89, BPL. It seems likely that the Company had planned to drive a wedge into New England even

before returning to America, for the first newspaper reports of Hallam's return mention that he had been invited to open a theatre in Boston. As early as January 1788, Henry had enlisted Rufus King of Newburyport—a delegate to the Constitutional Convention and a friend of Madison's—to help him open a theatre in Portsmouth, certain that "one of the most liberal minds of the Western World" would be pleased to serve "a harmless set of people. . . ." See Henry to King, 1/23/88, NYHS. [24] "W. Casons" to William Bentley, 10/3/89, Correspondence of Rev. William Bentley, William Bentley Papers, AAS. [25] G146, XII, 499.

49. The Inauguration of Washington

[1] N23, 6/89. [2] N56, 4/22/89; N6, 5/11/89; to Oliver Wolcott, Jr., 12/9/89, CHS. [3] D39, 24; D67, 171. [4] G196, II, 351; M90; q. M12, 74 and 75; q. M52, 133. [5] N59, 11/30/89. [6] G174, VI, 163; P67, II, 424. [7] A128; N35, 2/89; N35, 3/89; G174, VI, 147. [8] G192, XXX, 97, 119, 169. [9] G174, VI, 149; G143. [10] A126, 34; (bds. [Boston? 1789?]). The engraving is known only from written accounts. [11] N23, 10/89. The 1788–89 poems on Washington seem to contain the first instances of the phrase "favorite son" as an American political slogan. See G215c. [12] G192, XXX, 67; M6, 47; G58, XI, 265-6. [13] A180 and A121. [14] N9, 5/13/88; G192, XXX, 197; G58, XI, 265. [15] G192, XXX, 285 and 143. [16] G192, XXX, 151–87 passim; G193, 8–12. [17] G192, XXX, 268; G58, XI, 375. [18] N56, 4/29/89. [19] N31, 5/89. [20] N56, 4/29/89. Oscar Sonneck believed that the music played to the chorus was not Reinagle's, but Handel's "See the conquering hero comes" or Philip Phile's "President's March," later "Hail Columbia." M67, 63-4. [21] Ode to be sung on the arrival of the President (bds. N.Y., 1789); q. G180, 219. [22] G15, 180; see also G174, VI. [23] N56, 5/2/89. On the tobacco boxes see Antiques (Sept 1967), 314. [24] 5/13/89; the final quotation is from the issue of 5/6/89.

Index

Index

Some names are followed by a brief statement of occupation in parentheses, to distinguish persons known to have been active in the arts in America during the Revolution.

A Cultural History
OF THE
American Revolution
KENNETH SILVERMAN
53 illustrations

Amid a host of Bicentennial books, this one stands out as unique: It is the first comprehensive cultural history of the revolutionary period, from 1763, when peace returned to the colonies with the ending of the French and Indian War, to 1789, when the newly united States inaugurated George Washington as their first president.

It has not been recognized before that this was a quarter-century of surprising cultural progress as well as political revolution. In this short span, America produced its first novel, first epic poems, first composer, first professionally acted play, first actor and dancer, its first important painters, sculptor, musical-instrument makers, magazines, engravers, museums—most of the elements, indeed, that define modern metropolitan cultural life.

Tracing the growth of American painting, music, literature, and the theatre against and around the more familiar contours of political and military history, Kenneth Silverman has produced a text immensely rich in ideas and information. He vividly conveys the exuberance of the era, integrating such well-known historical events as the Stamp Act, the Boston Massacre, the Battle of Bunker's Hill, the Siege of Yorktown, and the struggle to draft and ratify the Constitution with such unfamiliar cultural events as the destruction of the New York theatre by the Sons of Liberty, the first American performance of Handel's *Messiah*, the production of plays at Valley Forge and other army camps, the mounting